Fractional Differential Equations: Computation and Modelling with Applications

Fractional Differential Equations: Computation and Modelling with Applications

Guest Editors

Rajarama Mohan Jena
Snehashish Chakraverty

MDPI

Basel • Beijing • Wuhan • Barcelona • Belgrade • Novi Sad • Cluj • Manchester

Guest Editors

Rajarama Mohan Jena
Department of Mathematics
C.V. Raman Global University
Bhubaneswar
India

Snehashish Chakraverty
Department of Mathematics
National Institute of
Technology Rourkela
Rourkela
India

Editorial Office
MDPI AG
Grosspeteranlage 5
4052 Basel, Switzerland

This is a reprint of the Special Issue, published open access by the journal *Fractal and Fractional* (ISSN 2504-3110), freely accessible at: https://www.mdpi.com/journal/fractalfract/special_issues/6H09E1PSTB?listby=date&view=default.

For citation purposes, cite each article independently as indicated on the article page online and as indicated below:

Lastname, A.A.; Lastname, B.B. Article Title. *Journal Name* **Year**, *Volume Number*, Page Range.

ISBN 978-3-7258-4741-9 (Hbk)
ISBN 978-3-7258-4742-6 (PDF)
https://doi.org/10.3390/books978-3-7258-4742-6

Contents

fractal and fractional

MDPI

Article

Dynamic of Some Relapse in a Giving Up Smoking Model Described by Fractional Derivative

Fawaz K. Alalhareth [1], Ahmed Boudaoui [2,*], Yacine El hadj Moussa [3], Noura Laksaci [2] and Mohammed H. Alharbi [4]

1 Department of Mathematics, College of Arts & Sciences, Najran University, Najran 61441, Saudi Arabia; fkalalhareth@nu.edu.sa
2 Laboratory of Mathematics Modeling and Applications, University of Adrar, National Road No. 06, Adrar 01000, Algeria; nor.laksaci@univ-adrar.edu.dz
3 Department of Probability and Statistics, University of Djillali Liabes, Sidi Bel Abbes 22000, Algeria; elhadjmoussa@univ-ghardaia.dz
4 Department of Mathematics, Faculty of Science, University of Jeddah, P.O. Box 80327, Jeddah 21589, Saudi Arabia; mhhalharbi1@uj.edu.sa
* Correspondence: ahmedboudaoui@univ-adrar.edu.dz

Abstract: Smoking is associated with various detrimental health conditions, including cancer, heart disease, stroke, lung illnesses, diabetes, and fatal diseases. Motivated by the application of fractional calculus in epidemiological modeling and the exploration of memory and nonlocal effects, this paper introduces a mathematical model that captures the dynamics of relapse in a smoking cessation context and presents the dynamic behavior of the proposed model utilizing Caputo fractional derivatives. The model incorporates four compartments representing potential, persistent (heavy), temporally recovered, and permanently recovered smokers. The basic reproduction number R_0 is computed, and the local and global dynamic behaviors of the free equilibrium smoking point ($\mathscr{Y}_0$) and the smoking-present equilibrium point ($\mathscr{Y}^*$) are analyzed. It is demonstrated that the free equilibrium smoking point ($\mathscr{Y}_0$) exhibits global asymptotic stability when $R_0 \leq 1$, while the smoking-present equilibrium point ($\mathscr{Y}^*$) is globally asymptotically stable when $R_0 > 1$. Additionally, analytical results are validated through a numerical simulation using the predictor–corrector PECE method for fractional differential equations in Matlab software.

Keywords: smoking model; Caputo fractional derivatives; existence and uniqueness; smoking-free equilibrium; basic reproduction number; numerical simulation

MSC: 34A08; 37C75; 37N25; 65L07

1. Introduction

Smoking addiction is a major global cause of respiratory and cancer diseases, leading to premature deaths. It is estimated that over five million people die each year due to tobacco consumption. According to statistics from the World Health Organization, this number could exceed eight million by 2030 if effective control systems are not established [1]. Smokers face a 70% higher risk of heart attack than nonsmokers, and their life expectancy is typically 10–13 years shorter [2]. The harmful effects of smoking extend beyond the smokers themselves. Secondhand smoke, which comprises both exhaled smoke and the smoke directly emitted from burning tobacco, contains harmful substances. Nonsmokers frequently exposed to secondhand tobacco smoke are at increased risk of developing similar diseases as smokers, including lung cancer and cardiovascular disease [3]. Carcinogens are the primary agents responsible for causing cancer, and studies have identified over 60 different carcinogens present in tobacco smoke [4].

Researchers, physicians, and mathematicians desire to reduce cigarette use to extend human life expectancy. Mathematicians have developed various models to depict the smoking phenomenon accurately, and several researchers have contributed to these smoking models. Castillo-Garsow et al. [5] presented an initial smoking model that focused on studying smoking dynamics in society, particularly the behavior of individuals trying to quit smoking. Zaman et al. [6] concentrated on smoking control by identifying optimal control factors. Recognizing that some smokers experience relapses while others continue smoking due to constant interactions, Rahman et al. [7] developed a smoking model that included terms for quit smoker relapse. Huo and Zhu [8] derived and analyzed a model taking into account light smokers compartment, recovery compartment, and two relapses in the giving up smoking model based on ordinary differential equations. Since smoking can have harmful effects after some time, many mathematical models of evolutionary systems with a memory effect on dynamics have used fractional calculus (see [9] and references therein). There have been many mathematical models for the smoking epidemic using fractional derivatives. Erturk et al. [10] investigated a model for smoking cessation linked to the Caputo fractional derivative. Zaman explored the optimal campaign in a smoking dynamical system [6]. Numerous researchers have also examined the effects of smoking. Lubin and Caporaso [11] discussed the association between cigarettes and lung cancer. Garsow et al. analyzed the mathematical description of tobacco use, cessation, and relapse in [5]. Alkhudhari et al. [12] studied the global dynamics of mathematical equations describing smoking. Khalid et al. [13] explained a fractional mathematical model for smoking cessation. Singh et al. [14] analyzed a fractional smoking cessation model in relation to a new fractional derivative with a nonsingular kernel. Ahmad et al. [15] created and studied a smoking epidemic model using Atangana–Baleanu (AB) with the Mittag–Leffler kernel and Atangana–Toufik method (ATM) fractional derivative. Addai et al. [16] presented a nonlinear fractional mathematical model for the smoke epidemic that includes two age groups using the Atangana–Baleanu–Caputo fractional derivative. More recently, Addai et al. [17] studied the dynamics of the age-structure smoking model under fractal-fractional (F-F) derivatives with government intervention coverage in the Caputo–Fabrizio framework. Zeb et al. [18] presented a four-class mathematical model—S (potential smokers), C (chain smokers), R (temporary quitters that can be movable to the relapse habit), and Q (permanent quitters of smoking)—in the form of fractional order. However, they did not assume that a fraction of the heavy smokers can enrich the permanently recovered smokers class and that temporally recovered smokers can relapse into the heavy smokers class. Therefore, we construct a new mathematical model that incorporates this phenomenon. Moreover, motivated by applying fractional calculus in the epidemiology model and examining the memory and the nonlocal you effect, the considering model's dynamic is presented in terms of Caputo fractional derivatives of order $\alpha \in (0, 1]$.

The control strategy is implemented by considering tobacco as an epidemic that causes several deaths. Its spread is mainly linked to the human factor, including factors such as the living environment, curiosity, and contact between people (smokers), which facilitate tobacco use. Mathematical models, described by differential equations, are utilized to interpret the spread of an infectious agent (smokers) within a population. The numbers of healthy and sick individuals evolve over time based on the contacts during which this agent passes from an infected individual to a healthy, immunized individual, subsequently infecting them in turn. The dynamics of the propagation in the population are determined through the resolution of these equations. Hence, we study the dynamics of the smoking epidemic problem. The model is based on four compartment classes: potential, persistent or heavy, temporally recovered, and permanently recovered smokers.

The paper's organization is as follows: Section 2 provides the essential introductory concepts required throughout the article. Section 3 describes the construction and development of our model. The mathematical analysis of the model is presented in Section 4. In Section 5, numerical simulations of the proposed model are provided. Ultimately, the conclusions are shown in the final section.

2. Preliminary

In this section, important definitions and preliminaries for fractional calculus are given, and for more details, see [19].

- The Riemann–Liouville fractional integral of order α is defined by

$$I_{0,t}^{\alpha}f(t) = \frac{1}{\Gamma(\alpha)}\int_0^t (t-\varsigma)^{\alpha-1}f(\varsigma)d\varsigma, \tag{1}$$

where $\alpha \in \mathbb{R}_+$ is the order of integration, and $\Gamma(\alpha) = \int_0^{+\infty} e^{-t}t^{\alpha-1}dt$ is the gamma function.

- The Caputo fractional derivatives of order $\alpha \in \mathbb{R}_+$ are defined as

$$^{C}\mathcal{D}_{0,t}^{\alpha}f(t) = \frac{1}{\Gamma(n-\alpha)}\int_0^t (t-\varsigma)^{n-\alpha-1}f^{(n)}(\varsigma)d\varsigma, \tag{2}$$

where $n = [\alpha] + 1$, with $[\alpha]$ being the integer part of $\alpha \in \mathbb{R}_+$.

- The Caputo derivative and the Riemann–Liouville integral satisfy the following properties:
  (a) $^{C}\mathcal{D}_{0,t}^{\alpha}(I_{0,t}^{\alpha}f(t)) = f(t)$.
  (b) $^{C}\mathcal{D}_{0,t}^{\alpha}(C) = 0$, where $C \in \mathbb{R}$.
  (c) $I_{0,t}^{\alpha}(^{C}\mathcal{D}_{0,t}^{\alpha}f(t)) = f(t) - \sum_{k=0}^{n-1}\frac{f^{(k)}(0)}{k!}t^k$.
  (d) If α is such that $0 < \alpha < 1$, then $I_{0,t}^{\alpha}(^{C}\mathcal{D}_{0,t}^{\alpha}f(t)) = f(t) - f(0)$.

3. Mathematical Modeling of a Giving Up Smoking Model

In this section, we develop a mathematical model of the dynamic of some relapse in a giving up smoking described by fractional derivatives. The model is based on four compartments: potential, persistent or heavy, temporally recovered, and permanently recovered smokers. As shown in Figure 1 (the flow diagram), the total host population $N(t)$ is partitioned into four classes, namely, the potential smokers $P(t)$, persistent smokers $S(t)$, temporally recovered smokers $X(t)$, and permanently recovered smokers $Q(t)$. The number of recruits per unit of time is denoted by ω. The smoking-related death rates are denoted by ϖ_i, $i = 1,2,3,4$. We assume that $\varpi_1 < \varpi_4 < \varpi_3 < \varpi_2$, which is biologically relevant since the death rate is higher if the smokers do not quit smoking.

A person joins the potential smoker's compartment, denoted as $P(t)$, at a constant recruitment rate ω. It is assumed that the potential smokers start smoking as a result of contact with the persistent smokers class, denoted as $S(t)$, at a rate $\wp_1 P(t)S(t)$, where $\wp_1$ represents the contact rate between potential smokers and the persistent smokers class (see Table 1). Upon leaving the persistent smokers class $S(t)$, a fraction $(1-\theta)$ enters the temporary quit smokers class, while the remaining fraction θ enters the permanently quit smokers class $Q(t)$, both at a rate ϑ. Temporary quit smokers have the possibility of relapsing into the persistent smokers class at the rate $\wp_2 X(t)S(t)$, where $\wp_2$ represents the contact rate between temporary quit smokers and the persistent smokers class. Finally, individuals in each compartment will vacate the compartment at a constant natural death $\mho$ and the smoking-related death rate ϖ_i, $i = 1,\ldots,4$.

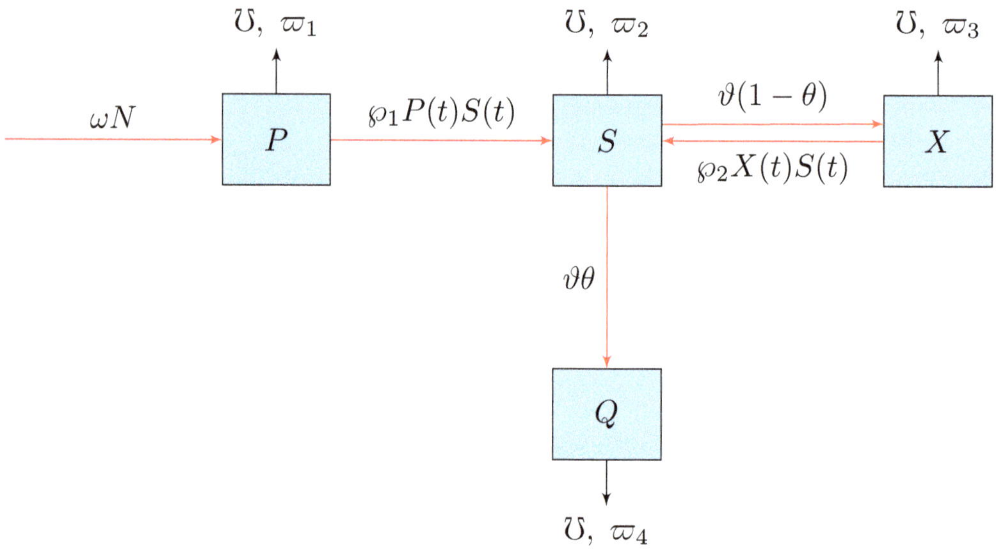

Figure 1. Diagram of the smoking model.

Table 1. Model parameter description (3).

Parameter	Description
ω	The overall recruits number into the considered homogeneously mixed population.
$\wp_1$	The rate of spread from potential to persistent smokers.
$\wp_2$	The relapse rate of temporally recovered smokers who contact persistent smokers.
$\vartheta(1-\theta)$, $0<\theta<1$	The rate of smokers who temporarily stop.
$\vartheta\theta$	The rate of people who have successfully stopped smoking.
$\mho$	The natural rate of mortality.
ϖ_i, $i=1,\dots,4$	The mortality rate from smoking.

In view of the transfer diagram shown in Figure 1, we can derive the following system of ordinary differential equations:

$$\begin{cases} \frac{dP(t)}{dt} = \omega - \wp_1 P(t)S(t) - (\varpi_1 + \mho)P(t), \\ \frac{dS(t)}{dt} = \wp_1 P(t)S(t) + \wp_2 X(t)S(t) - (\vartheta + \varpi_2 + \mho)S(t), \\ \frac{dX(t)}{dt} = \vartheta(1-\theta)S(t) - \wp_2 X(t)S(t) - (\varpi_3 + \mho)X(t), \\ \frac{dQ(t)}{dt} = \vartheta\theta S(t) - (\varpi_4 + \mho)Q(t). \end{cases} \tag{3}$$

where $N(t) = P(t) + S(t) + X(t) + Q(t)$.

Remark 1. *Adding up the equations given in System* (3), *we have*

$$\begin{aligned} \frac{dN(t)}{dt} &= \omega - (\varpi_1 + \mho)P(t) - (\varpi_2 + \mho)S(t) - (\varpi_3 + \mho)X(t) - (\varpi_4 + \mho)Q(t) \\ &= \omega - \mho N(t) - (\varpi_1 P(t) + \varpi_2 S(t) + \varpi_3 X(t) + \varpi_4 Q(t)) \\ &\leq \omega - \mho N(t). \end{aligned}$$

If, in addition, we know the size of the total population $N(0)$, *it follows that*

$$0 \leq N(t) \leq \frac{\omega}{\mho} + N(0)e^{-\mho t}.$$

Thus, $0 \leq N(t) \leq \frac{\omega}{\mho}$ *as* $t \to +\infty$.

Lemma 1. *Thesolutions of System* (3) *remain bounded and enter the region*

$$\Gamma = \{(P, S, X, Q) \in \mathbb{R}^4_+,\ P + S + X + Q \leq \frac{\omega}{\mho}\}.$$

We wish to investigate System (3) for fractional orders. Fractional order differential equations have been widely utilized in the literature to model real-life phenomena, as they provide a more accurate representation compared with classical order differential equations. It is important to note that fractional order differential equations generalize the classical order counterparts. Fractional calculus is recognized for its various advantages in diverse applications, allowing for the modeling of complex phenomena beyond the limitations of classical derivatives. These advantages include capturing the memory effect by incorporating past information, enabling long-term (nonlocal) dynamics without focusing on local aspects of derivation, and facilitating the study of stability through control of the derivation order. Moreover, fractional calculus is commonly employed in epidemiological modeling, and as smoking is regarded as an epidemic, we have incorporated fractional calculus into our model.

In our study, we specifically focus on the Caputo fractional derivative ${}^{C}\mathcal{D}^{\alpha}_{0,t}$ with an order of α, where $0 < \alpha < 1$. Subsequently, we analyze the following system:

$$\begin{cases} {}^{C}\mathcal{D}^{\alpha}_{0,t}(P(t)) = \omega - \wp_1 P(t)S(t) - (\varpi_1 + \mho)P(t), \\ {}^{C}\mathcal{D}^{\alpha}_{0,t}(S(t)) = \wp_1 P(t)S(t) + \wp_2 X(t)S(t) - (\vartheta + \varpi_2 + \mho)S(t), \\ {}^{C}\mathcal{D}^{\alpha}_{0,t}(X(t)) = \vartheta(1-\theta)S(t) - \wp_2 X(t)S(t) - (\varpi_3 + \mho)X(t), \\ {}^{C}\mathcal{D}^{\alpha}_{0,t}(Q(t)) = \vartheta\theta S(t) - (\varpi_4 + \mho)Q(t), \end{cases} \tag{4}$$

with initial conditions

$$P(0) = P_0,\ S(0) = S_0,\ X(0) = X_0,\ Q(0) = Q_0. \tag{5}$$

Remark 2. *Adding up equations given in System* (4)*, taking into account the linearity of the Caputo fractional derivative operator, we have*

$${}^{C}\mathcal{D}^{\alpha}_{0,t}(N(t)) = \omega - \mho N(t) - (\varpi_1 P(t) + \varpi_2 S(t) + \varpi_3 X(t) + \varpi_4 Q(t)).$$

4. Mathematical Analysis

In this section, System (4) is found to have a unique solution that is positive whenever the initial condition is positive. Moreover, System (4) is found to have two equilibria, the smoking-free equilibrium and the smoking-present equilibrium. Finally, the equilibria's local and global stability results are also obtained.

4.1. Existence and Uniqueness

For the existence and uniqueness of the solution to System (4), we proceed in several steps. Applying the fractional integral (1), taking into count the property (d), we obtain another version of System (4) in the following manner:

$$\begin{cases} P(t) - P_0 = I^{\alpha}_{0,t}(\omega - \wp_1 P(t)S(t) - (\varpi_1 + \mho)P(t)), \\ S(t) - S_0 = I^{\alpha}_{0,t}(\wp_1 P(t)S(t) + \wp_2 X(t)S(t) - (\vartheta + \varpi_2 + \mho)S(t)), \\ X(t) - X_0 = I^{\alpha}_{0,t}(\vartheta(1-\theta)S(t) - \wp_2 X(t)S(t) - (\varpi_3 + \mho)X(t)), \\ Q(t) - Q_0 = I^{\alpha}_{0,t}(\vartheta\theta S(t) - (\varpi_4 + \mho)Q(t)), \end{cases} \tag{6}$$

or

$$\begin{cases} P(t) - P_0 = \frac{1}{\Gamma(\alpha)} \int_0^t (t-\varsigma)^{\alpha-1}((\omega - \wp_1 P(\varsigma)S(\varsigma) - (\varpi_1 + \mho)P(\varsigma))d\varsigma, \\ S(t) - S_0 = \frac{1}{\Gamma(\alpha)} \int_0^t (t-\varsigma)^{\alpha-1}(\wp_1 P(\varsigma)S(\varsigma) + \wp_2 X(\varsigma)S(\varsigma) - (\vartheta + \varpi_2 + \mho)S(\varsigma))d\varsigma, \\ X(t) - X_0 = \frac{1}{\Gamma(\alpha)} \int_0^t (t-\varsigma)^{\alpha-1}(\vartheta(1-\theta)S(\varsigma) - \wp_2 X(\varsigma)S(\varsigma) - (\varpi_3 + \mho)X(\varsigma))d\varsigma, \\ Q(t) - Q_0 = \frac{1}{\Gamma(\alpha)} \int_0^t (t-\varsigma)^{\alpha-1}(\vartheta\theta S(\varsigma) - (\varpi_4 + \mho)Q(\varsigma))d\varsigma. \end{cases} \tag{7}$$

Definition 1. *The space of continuous valued functions f on an interval I with the norm $\| f \| = \sup_{t \in I} |f(t)|$ is denoted by $C^0(I)$.*

Remark 3. *We define the following kernels:*

$$K_1(t, P) = \omega - \wp_1 P(t)S(t) - (\varpi_1 + \mho)P(t), \tag{8}$$
$$K_2(t, S) = \wp_1 P(t)S(t) + \wp_2 X(t)S(t) - (\vartheta + \varpi_2 + \mho)S(t), \tag{9}$$
$$K_3(t, X) = \vartheta(1-\theta)S(t) - \wp_2 X(t)S(t) - (\varpi_3 + \mho)X(t), \tag{10}$$
$$K_4(t, Q) = \vartheta\theta S(t) - (\varpi_4 + \mho)Q(t). \tag{11}$$

Proposition 1. *If $P(t)$, $S(t)$, $X(t)$, and $Q(t)$ are bounded functions in $C^0(I)$, and let*

$$\lambda = \max\{\wp_1 M_2 + \varpi_1 + \mho,\ \wp_1 M_1 + \wp_2 M_3 + \vartheta + \varpi_2 + \mho,\ (\vartheta(1-\theta) + \wp_2)M_2 + \varpi_3 + \mho,\ \vartheta\theta M_2 + \varpi_4 + \mho\},$$

where $M_1 = \sup_{t \in I} |P(t)|$, $M_2 = \sup_{t \in I} |S(t)|$, $M_3 = \sup_{t \in I} |X(t)|$, $M_4 = \sup_{t \in I} |Q(t)|$, then the kernels $K_1(t, P)$, $K_2(t, S)$, $K_3(t, X)$, $K_4(t, Q)$ satisfy the Lipschitz condition and contraction if $0 \le \lambda < 1$.

Proof. We proof the proposition for $K_1(t, P)$; the statement for $K_2(t, S)$, $K_3(t, X)$, $K_4(t, Q)$ can be proved using similar arguments. Let P_1 and P_2 be two functions, so we have

$$\begin{aligned} \| K_1(t, P_1) - K_1(t, P_2) \| &= \| \omega - \wp_1 P_1(t)S(t) - (\varpi_1 + \mho)P_1(t) - \omega + \wp_1 P_2(t)S(t) + (\varpi_1 + \mho)P_2(t) \| \\ &= \| -(\wp_1 S(t))(P_1(t) - P_2(t)) - ((\varpi_1 + \mho)(P_1(t) - P_2(t)) \| \\ &\le (\wp_1 M_2 + \varpi_1 + \mho) \| P_1(t) - P_2(t) \| . \end{aligned}$$

Hence, the Lipschitz condition is satisfied for K_1, and since $\lambda < 1$, K_1 is also a contraction. □

In the following, we adopt the approach in [20]. First, we define

$$\begin{aligned} \zeta_1 &= \wp_1 M_2 + \varpi_1 + \mho, \\ \zeta_2 &= \wp_1 M_1 + \wp_2 M_3 + \vartheta + \varpi_2 + \mho, \\ \zeta_3 &= (\vartheta(1-\theta) + \wp_2)M_2 + \varpi_3 + \mho, \\ \zeta_4 &= \vartheta\theta M_2 + \varpi_4 + \mho. \end{aligned}$$

Using the definition of kernels in (8), then the equations in (7) become

$$\begin{cases} P(t) = P(0) + \frac{1}{\Gamma(\alpha)} \int_0^t (t-\varsigma)^{\alpha-1} K_1(\varsigma, P)d\varsigma, \\ S(t) = S(0) + \frac{1}{\Gamma(\alpha)} \int_0^t (t-\varsigma)^{\alpha-1} K_2(\varsigma, S)d\varsigma, \\ X(t) = X(0) + \frac{1}{\Gamma(\alpha)} \int_0^t (t-\varsigma)^{\alpha-1} K_3(\varsigma, X)d\varsigma, \\ Q(t) = Q(0) + \frac{1}{\Gamma(\alpha)} \int_0^t (t-\varsigma)^{\alpha-1} K_4(\varsigma, Q)d\varsigma. \end{cases} \tag{12}$$

Additionally, we give the following recursive formula:

$$\begin{cases} P_n(t) = \frac{1}{\Gamma(\alpha)} \int_0^t (t-\varsigma)^{\alpha-1} K_1(\varsigma, P_{n-1}) d\varsigma, \\ S_n(t) = \frac{1}{\Gamma(\alpha)} \int_0^t (t-\varsigma)^{\alpha-1} K_2(\varsigma, S_{n-1}) d\varsigma, \\ X_n(t) = \frac{1}{\Gamma(\alpha)} \int_0^t (t-\varsigma)^{\alpha-1} K_3(\varsigma, X_{n-1}) d\varsigma, \\ Q_n(t) = \frac{1}{\Gamma(\alpha)} \int_0^t (t-\varsigma)^{\alpha-1} K_4(\varsigma, Q_{n-1}) d\varsigma. \end{cases} \tag{13}$$

where the initial conditions are defined by

$$\begin{aligned} P_0(t) &= P(0), \\ S_0(t) &= S(0), \\ X_0(t) &= X(0), \\ Q_0(t) &= Q(0). \end{aligned}$$

Definition 2. *We define the difference between successive terms by*

$$\Upsilon_n(t) = P_n(t) - P_{n-1}(t) = \frac{1}{\Gamma(\alpha)} \int_0^t (t-\varsigma)^{\alpha-1} (K_1(\varsigma, P_{n-1}) - K_1(\varsigma, P_{n-2})) d\varsigma, \tag{14}$$

$$\Phi_n(t) = S_n(t) - S_{n-1}(t) = \frac{1}{\Gamma(\alpha)} \int_0^t (t-\varsigma)^{\alpha-1} (K_2(\varsigma, S_{n-1}) - K_2(\varsigma, S_{n-2})) d\varsigma, \tag{15}$$

$$\Psi_n(t) = X_n(t) - X_{n-1}(t) = \frac{1}{\Gamma(\alpha)} \int_0^t (t-\varsigma)^{\alpha-1} (K_3(\varsigma, X_{n-1}) - K_3(\varsigma, X_{n-2})) d\varsigma, \tag{16}$$

$$\Omega_n(t) = Q_n(t) - Q_{n-1}(t) = \frac{1}{\Gamma(\alpha)} \int_0^t (t-\varsigma)^{\alpha-1} (K_4(\varsigma, Q_{n-1}) - K_4(\varsigma, Q_{n-2})) d\varsigma. \tag{17}$$

Proposition 2. *With the notations in Definition 2, we have*

$$\begin{aligned} P_n(t) &= \sum_{k=0}^{n} \Upsilon_k(t), \\ S_n(t) &= \sum_{k=0}^{n} \Phi_k(t), \\ X_n(t) &= \sum_{k=0}^{n} \Psi_k(t), \\ Q_n(t) &= \sum_{k=0}^{n} \Omega_k(t), \end{aligned}$$

and

$$\begin{aligned} \| \Upsilon_n(t) \| &\leq \frac{\zeta_1}{\Gamma(\alpha)} \int_0^t (t-\varsigma)^{\alpha-1} \| \Upsilon_{n-1}(t) \| d\varsigma, \\ \| \Phi_n(t) \| &\leq \frac{\zeta_2}{\Gamma(\alpha)} \int_0^t (t-\varsigma)^{\alpha-1} \| \Phi_{n-1}(t) \| d\varsigma, \\ \| \Psi_n(t) \| &\leq \frac{\zeta_3}{\Gamma(\alpha)} \int_0^t (t-\varsigma)^{\alpha-1} \| \Psi_{n-1}(t) \| d\varsigma, \\ \| \Omega_n(t) \| &\leq \frac{\zeta_4}{\Gamma(\alpha)} \int_0^t (t-\varsigma)^{\alpha-1} \| \Omega_{n-1}(t) \| d\varsigma. \end{aligned}$$

Proof. The first statement is the telescoping sums. Performing the norm to both sides of Equation (14), we obtain

$$\begin{aligned} \parallel \Upsilon_n(t) \parallel = \parallel P_n(t) - P_{n-1}(t) \parallel &= \parallel \frac{1}{\Gamma(\alpha)} \int_0^t (t-\varsigma)^{\alpha-1}(K_1(\varsigma, P_{n-1}) - K_1(\varsigma, P_{n-2}))d\varsigma \parallel \\ &\leq \frac{1}{\Gamma(\alpha)} \int_0^t (t-\varsigma)^{\alpha-1} \parallel (K_1(\varsigma, P_{n-1}) - K_1(\varsigma, P_{n-2})) \parallel d\varsigma. \end{aligned}$$

Since the kernel K_1 satisfies the Lipschitz condition (Proposition 1), we find

$$\parallel \Upsilon_n(t) \parallel \leq \frac{\zeta_1}{\Gamma(\alpha)} \int_0^t (t-\varsigma)^{\alpha-1} \parallel \Upsilon_{n-1}(t) \parallel d\varsigma.$$

Similarly, one can obtained the results for $\Phi_n(t),\ \Psi_n(t),\ \Omega_n(t)$. □

Proposition 3. *If $P(t),\ S(t),\ X(t)$, and $Q(t)$ are bounded functions in $C^0(I)$, then we have*

$$\begin{aligned} \parallel \Upsilon_n(t) \parallel &\leq \parallel P_0(t) \parallel \left(\frac{\zeta_1\, t^\alpha}{\alpha\, \Gamma(\alpha)}\right)^n, \\ \parallel \Phi_n(t) \parallel &\leq \parallel S_0(t) \parallel \left(\frac{\zeta_2\, t^\alpha}{\alpha\, \Gamma(\alpha)}\right)^n, \\ \parallel \Psi_n(t) \parallel &\leq \parallel X_0(t) \parallel \left(\frac{\zeta_3\, t^\alpha}{\alpha\, \Gamma(\alpha)}\right)^n, \\ \parallel \Omega_n(t) \parallel &\leq \parallel Q_0(t) \parallel \left(\frac{\zeta_4\, t^\alpha}{\alpha\, \Gamma(\alpha)}\right)^n. \end{aligned}$$

Proof. For the proof, we use Proposition 2, the Lipschitz condition, and employ the recursive method. □

Theorem 1. *Let $t_0 = \min(t_1, t_2, t_3, t_4)$, where*

$$\begin{aligned} t_1 &< \sqrt[\alpha]{\frac{\alpha\, \Gamma(\alpha)}{\zeta_1}}, \\ t_2 &< \sqrt[\alpha]{\frac{\alpha\, \Gamma(\alpha)}{\zeta_2}}, \\ t_3 &< \sqrt[\alpha]{\frac{\alpha\, \Gamma(\alpha)}{\zeta_3}}, \\ t_4 &< \sqrt[\alpha]{\frac{\alpha\, \Gamma(\alpha)}{\zeta_4}}. \end{aligned}$$

Then $P_n(t),\ S_n(t),\ X_n(t)$, and $Q_n(t)$ defined by Proposition 2 exist and are smooth.

Proof. For $t_0 = \min(t_1, t_2, t_3, t_4)$, $\frac{\zeta_1\, t_0^\alpha}{\alpha\, \Gamma(\alpha)} < 1$; then the series $\sum_{k=0}^{n} \Upsilon_k(t)$ converges and $P_n(t)$ exists. □

We can write

$$\begin{aligned}P(t)-P(0)=&P_n(t)-\Theta_n^P(t),\\S(t)-S(0)=&S_n(t)-\Theta_n^S(t),\\X(t)-X(0)=&X_n(t)-\Theta_n^X(t),\\Q(t)-Q(0)=&Q_n(t)-\Theta_n^Q(t),\end{aligned}$$

where

$$\begin{aligned}\Theta_n^P(t)=&\frac{1}{\Gamma(\alpha)}\int_0^t(t-\varsigma)^{\alpha-1}(K_1(\varsigma,P_{n-1})-K_1(\varsigma,P))d\varsigma,\\\Theta_n^S(t)=&\frac{1}{\Gamma(\alpha)}\int_0^t(t-\varsigma)^{\alpha-1}(K_1(\varsigma,S_{n-1})-K_1(\varsigma,S))d\varsigma,\\\Theta_n^X(t)=&\frac{1}{\Gamma(\alpha)}\int_0^t(t-\varsigma)^{\alpha-1}(K_1(\varsigma,X_{n-1})-K_1(\varsigma,X))d\varsigma,\\\Theta_n^Q(t)=&\frac{1}{\Gamma(\alpha)}\int_0^t(t-\varsigma)^{\alpha-1}(K_1(\varsigma,Q_{n-1})-K_1(\varsigma,Q))d\varsigma.\end{aligned}$$

For $\Theta_n^P(t)$, we have

$$\begin{aligned}\parallel\Theta_n^P(t)\parallel=&\parallel\frac{1}{\Gamma(\alpha)}\int_0^t(t-\varsigma)^{\alpha-1}(K_1(\varsigma,P_{n-1})-K_1(\varsigma,P))d\varsigma\parallel\\\leq&\frac{1}{\Gamma(\alpha)}\int_0^t(t-\varsigma)^{\alpha-1}\parallel K_1(\varsigma,P_{n-1})-K_1(\varsigma,P)\parallel d\varsigma\\\leq&\frac{t^\alpha}{\alpha\,\Gamma(\alpha)}\zeta_1\parallel P-P_{n-1}\parallel.\end{aligned}$$

On the other hand, we have

$$\begin{aligned}\parallel P-P_{n-1}\parallel=&\parallel\frac{1}{\Gamma(\alpha)}\int_0^t(t-\varsigma)^{\alpha-1}(K_1(\varsigma,P_{n-2})-K_1(\varsigma,P))d\varsigma\parallel\\\leq&\frac{1}{\Gamma(\alpha)}\int_0^t(t-\varsigma)^{\alpha-1}\parallel K_1(\varsigma,P_{n-2})-K_1(\varsigma,P)\parallel d\varsigma\\\leq&\frac{t^\alpha}{\alpha\,\Gamma(\alpha)}\zeta_1\parallel P-P_{n-2}\parallel.\end{aligned}$$

Therefore, repeating this process recursively, we obtain

$$\begin{aligned}\parallel\Theta_n^P(t)\parallel\leq&\left(\frac{t^\alpha\zeta_1}{\alpha\,\Gamma(\alpha)}\right)^{n+1}\parallel P_0\parallel\\\leq&\left(\frac{t^\alpha\zeta_1}{\alpha\,\Gamma(\alpha)}\right)^{n+1}M_1.\end{aligned}$$

Thus, we also have

$$\begin{aligned}\parallel\Theta_n^S(t)\parallel\leq&\left(\frac{t^\alpha\zeta_2}{\alpha\,\Gamma(\alpha)}\right)^{n+1}M_2,\\\parallel\Theta_n^X(t)\parallel\leq&\left(\frac{t^\alpha\zeta_3}{\alpha\,\Gamma(\alpha)}\right)^{n+1}M_3,\\\parallel\Theta_n^Q(t)\parallel\leq&\left(\frac{t^\alpha\zeta_4}{\alpha\,\Gamma(\alpha)}\right)^{n+1}M_4.\end{aligned}$$

Lemma 2. *For $t_0 = \min(t_1, t_2, t_3, t_4)$, we have*

$$\begin{aligned}
\lim_{n\to+\infty} \parallel \Theta_n^P(t) \parallel &= 0, \\
\lim_{n\to+\infty} \parallel \Theta_n^S(t) \parallel &= 0, \\
\lim_{n\to+\infty} \parallel \Theta_n^X(t) \parallel &= 0, \\
\lim_{n\to+\infty} \parallel \Theta_n^Q(t) \parallel &= 0.
\end{aligned}$$

Proof. For $t_0 = \min(t_1, t_2, t_3, t_4)$, we have $\frac{t^\alpha \zeta_i}{\alpha\,\Gamma(\alpha)} < 1$ for all $i = 1, 2, 3, 4$. □

Combining the above results, we have established the following theorem, which ensures that System (4) has a solution.

Theorem 2 (Existence). *For $t_0 = \min(t_1, t_2, t_3, t_4)$, the giving up smoking model* (4) *has a solution defined by*

$$P(t) = P(0) + \lim_{n\to+\infty} P_n(t). \tag{18}$$

The following theorem ensures that Model (4) has a unique solution, which is an important condition for Model (4) to be well posed.

Theorem 3 (Uniqueness). *For $t_0 = \min(t_1, t_2, t_3, t_4)$, the giving up smoking model* (4) *has a unique solution.*

Proof. For the uniqueness of the solution of System (4), let $P_1(t)$, $S_1(t)$, $X_1(t)$, $Q_1(t)$ be another solution to System (4). We have

$$P(t) - P_1(t) = \frac{1}{\Gamma(\alpha)} \int_0^t (t-\varsigma)^{\alpha-1} (K_1(\varsigma, P) - K_1(\varsigma, P_1)) d\varsigma,$$

and

$$\begin{aligned}
\parallel P(t) - P_1(t) \parallel &\le \frac{1}{\Gamma(\alpha)} \int_0^t (t-\varsigma)^{\alpha-1} \parallel (K_1(\varsigma, P) - K_1(\varsigma, P_1)) \parallel d\varsigma \\
&\le \frac{t^\alpha}{\alpha\,\Gamma(\alpha)} \zeta_1 \parallel P(t) - P_1(t) \parallel .
\end{aligned}$$

Then, we have

$$\left(1 - \frac{t^\alpha}{\alpha\,\Gamma(\alpha)} \zeta_1\right) \parallel P(t) - P_1(t) \parallel \le 0.$$

Therefore, also

$$\begin{aligned}
\left(1 - \frac{t^\alpha}{\alpha\,\Gamma(\alpha)} \zeta_2\right) \parallel S(t) - S_1(t) \parallel &\le 0, \\
\left(1 - \frac{t^\alpha}{\alpha\,\Gamma(\alpha)} \zeta_3\right) \parallel X(t) - X_1(t) \parallel &\le 0, \\
\left(1 - \frac{t^\alpha}{\alpha\,\Gamma(\alpha)} \zeta_4\right) \parallel Q(t) - Q_1(t) \parallel &\le 0.
\end{aligned}$$

For $t_0 = \min(t_1, t_2, t_3, t_4)$, we have

$$\left(1 - \frac{t_0^\alpha}{\alpha\,\Gamma(\alpha)} \zeta_2\right) > 0,$$

and

$$\left(1-\frac{t^{\alpha}}{\alpha\,\Gamma(\alpha)}\zeta_1\right)\parallel P(t)-P_1(t)\parallel\leq 0,$$

so

$$\parallel P(t)-P_1(t)\parallel=0\,;\text{ then } P(t)=P_1(t).$$

The statement for $S(t),\ X(t),\ Q(t)$ can be shown in a similar way. □

4.2. Non-Negative Solutions

Let $\mathbb{R}^4_+=\{Y\in\mathbb{R}^4,\ Y\geq 0\}$ and $Y(t)=(P(t),S(t),X(t),Q(t))^T$; we investigate the non-negative solution of System (4). To proceed, we need the following lemmas:

Lemma 3. *[21] Let $f(x)\in C([a,b])$ and ${}^{C}\mathcal{D}^{\alpha}_{a,t}f(x)\in C((a,b])$ for $0<\alpha\leq 1$; then we have*

$$f(x)=f(a)+\frac{1}{\Gamma(\alpha)}\,{}^{C}\mathcal{D}^{\alpha}_{a,t}f(x)(x-\xi)^{\alpha},$$

with $a\leq\xi\leq x,\ \forall x\in(a,b]$.

Remark 4. *Notice, for $a=0$ in Lemma 3, we have*

$$f(x)=f(0)+\frac{1}{\Gamma(\alpha)}\,{}^{C}\mathcal{D}^{\alpha}_{0,t}f(x)(x)^{\alpha}.$$

Then,

1. *If ${}^{C}\mathcal{D}^{\alpha}_{0,t}f(x)\geq 0$, then the function f is nondecreasing for all $x\in(0,b]$.*
2. *If ${}^{C}\mathcal{D}^{\alpha}_{0,t}f(x)\leq 0$, then the function f is nonincreasing for all $x\in(0,b]$.*

Lemma 4. *[22] Let $0<\alpha\leq 1$ and consider the two fractional differential equations*

$${}^{C}\mathcal{D}^{\alpha}_{0,t}(S(t))=F(t,S)+\frac{1}{k}\quad\text{and}\quad{}^{C}\mathcal{D}^{\alpha}_{0,t}(S(t))=F(t,S),\tag{19}$$

with the same initial condition $S(0)=S_0$, where $k\in\mathbb{N}^*$ and $F:[0,b]\times\mathbb{R}\to\mathbb{R}$ are a continuous function and Lipschitz with respect to the second component; that is, there exists a constant L such that

$$|F(t,S_1)-F(t,S_2)|\leq L\|S_1-S_2\|.$$

If S^*_k and S^* are the solution of (19), respectively, then

$$S^*_k\xrightarrow[k\to+\infty]{}S^*,$$

for all $t\in[0,b]$.

Theorem 4. *The solution to the initial value problem given by (4) and (5), if it exists, belongs to*

$$\mathbb{R}^4_+=\{Y=(P(t),S(t),X(t),Q(t))^T\in\mathbb{R}^4,\ Y\geq 0\}.$$

Proof. First, we prove that $S(t)>0$. In view of Lemma 19, we consider the following alternative equation of the fractional differential equation:

$${}^{C}\mathcal{D}^{\alpha}_{0,t}(S^*_k(t))=\underbrace{\wp_1P(t)S(t)+\wp_2X(t)S(t)-(\vartheta+\varpi_2+\mho)S(t)+\frac{1}{k}}_{=F(t,S)}.$$

Obviously, $F(t,S)$ is Lipschitz with respect to the second variable with a Lipschitz constant $L = \frac{\omega}{\mho}(\wp_1 + \wp_2) + (\vartheta + \varpi_2 + \mho)$. We use the contradiction argument. Let us assume that there exists t_0 such that $(S_k^*(t_0)) = 0$. Since

$$
\begin{aligned}
{}^{C}\mathcal{D}_{0,t}^{\alpha}(S_k^*(t_0)) &= \wp_1 P(t_0)S(t_0) + \wp_2 X(t_0)S(t_0) - (\vartheta + \varpi_2 + \mho)S(t_0) + \frac{1}{k} \\
&= \frac{1}{k} > 0.
\end{aligned}
$$

By Lemma 3, we obtain that $(S_k^*(t_0)) > 0$ since t_0 is arbitrary, so $S_k^* > 0$, obtaining a contradiction. By Lemma 4, as $k \to +\infty$, we obtain that $S^* > 0$.
On the other hand, since

$$
\begin{aligned}
&{}^{C}\mathcal{D}_{0,t}^{\alpha}(P(t))|_{P=0} = \omega > 0, \\
&{}^{C}\mathcal{D}_{0,t}^{\alpha}(X(t))|_{X=0} = \vartheta(1-\theta)S(t) > 0, \\
&{}^{C}\mathcal{D}_{0,t}^{\alpha}(Q(t))|_{X=0} = \vartheta\theta S(t) > 0,
\end{aligned}
$$

we conclude by Lemma 3 that $P(t) > 0,\ X(t) > 0,\ Q(t) > 0$; that is, the domain $\mathbb{R}_+^4$ is positively invariant with respect to System (4). □

4.3. Equilibrium and Smokers Generation Number

In this subsection, we analyze the existence of the smoking-free equilibrium (SFE) point of Model (4). In view of [23], the smoker compartment is S, which gives $m = 1$, and using the next-generation matrix method as formulated in [23], with $Y = (S, X, Q, P)^T$, Model (4) can be written as

$$
{}^{C}\mathcal{D}_{0,t}^{\alpha}(Y(t)) = \mathcal{F}(Y) - \mathcal{V}(Y),
$$

where

$$
\mathcal{F}(Y) = \begin{pmatrix} \wp_1 PS \\ 0 \\ 0 \\ 0 \end{pmatrix}, \tag{20}
$$

and

$$
\mathcal{V}(Y) = \begin{pmatrix} (\vartheta + \varpi_2 + \mho)S(t) - \wp_2 XS \\ \wp_2 X(t)S(t) + (\varpi_3 + \mho)X(t) - \vartheta(1-\theta)S(t) \\ (\varpi_4 + \mho)Q(t) - \vartheta\theta S(t) \\ \wp_1 P(t)S(t) + (\varpi_1 + \mho)P(t) - \omega \end{pmatrix}. \tag{21}
$$

Proposition 4. *For the giving up smoking model* (4), *there exists the smoking-free equilibrium* $\mathscr{Y}_0 = (\frac{\omega}{\varpi_1 + \mho}, 0, 0, 0)$.

Proof. Thanks to (20) and (21), an equilibrium solution with $S = 0$ has the form $\mathscr{Y}_0 = (\frac{\omega}{\varpi_1 + \mho}, 0, 0, 0)$. □

Proposition 5. *The basic reproduction number, denoted by* R_0, *is given by*

$$
R_0 = \rho(FV^{-1}) = \frac{\wp_1 b}{(\varpi_1 + \mho)(\vartheta + \varpi_2 + \mho)},
$$

where the matrix F and V are such that

$$DF(\mathscr{Y}_0)=\left(\begin{array}{ccc:c} & F_{3\times 3} & & \begin{matrix}0\\0\\0\end{matrix}\\ \hdashline 0 & 0 & 0 & 0\end{array}\right),\quad D\mathcal{V}(\mathscr{Y}_0)=\left(\begin{array}{c:c} V_{3\times 3} & \begin{matrix}0\\0\\0\end{matrix}\\ \hdashline J_{1\times 3} & c\end{array}\right),$$

where $D\mathcal{F}(\mathscr{Y}_0)$ and $D\mathcal{V}(\mathscr{Y}_0)$ are the Jacobian matrix of $\mathcal{F}(Y)$ and $\mathcal{V}(Y)$ at the smoking-free equilibrium $\mathscr{Y}_0$, respectively.

Proof. The definitions of $D\mathcal{F}(\mathscr{Y}_0)$ *and* $D\mathcal{V}(\mathscr{Y}_0)$ are given in [23]. Furthermore, a simple calculation gives

$$D\mathcal{F}(\mathscr{Y}_0)=\left(\begin{array}{ccc:c}\frac{\wp_1 b}{\varpi_1+\mho} & 0 & 0 & 0\\ 0 & 0 & 0 & 0\\ 0 & 0 & 0 & 0\\ \hdashline 0 & 0 & 0 & 0\end{array}\right),\quad D\mathcal{V}(\mathscr{Y}_0)=\left(\begin{array}{ccc:c}\vartheta+\varpi_2+\mho & 0 & 0 & 0\\ -\vartheta(1-\theta) & \varpi_3+\mho & 0 & 0\\ -\vartheta\theta & 0 & \varpi_4+\mho & 0\\ \hdashline \frac{\wp_1 b}{\varpi_1+\mho} & 0 & 0 & \varpi_1+\mho\end{array}\right).$$

Thus,

$$F=\begin{pmatrix}\frac{\wp_1 b}{\varpi_1+\mho} & 0 & 0\\ 0 & 0 & 0\\ 0 & 0 & 0\end{pmatrix},\quad V=\begin{pmatrix}\vartheta+\varpi_2+\mho & 0 & 0\\ -\vartheta(1-\theta) & \varpi_3+\mho & 0\\ -\vartheta\theta & 0 & \varpi_4+\mho\end{pmatrix}.$$

Next, we have

$$V^{-1}=\begin{pmatrix}\frac{1}{\vartheta+\varpi_2+\mho} & 0 & 0\\ \frac{\vartheta(1-\theta)}{(\vartheta+\varpi_2+\mho)(\varpi_3+\mho)} & \frac{1}{(\varpi_3+\mho)} & 0\\ \frac{\vartheta\theta}{(\vartheta+\varpi_2+\mho)(\varpi_4+\mho)} & 0 & \frac{1}{d4+\mho}\end{pmatrix},$$

and

$$FV^{-1}=\begin{pmatrix}\frac{\wp_1 b}{(\varpi_1+\mho)(\vartheta+\varpi_2+\mho)} & 0 & 0\\ 0 & 0 & 0\\ 0 & 0 & 0\end{pmatrix}.$$

Therefore,

$$\rho(FV^{-1})=\frac{\wp_1 b}{(\varpi_1+\mho)(\vartheta+\varpi_2+\mho)}.$$

□

Proposition 6. *For the giving up smoking model* (4)*, there exists the smoking-present equilibrium $\mathscr{Y}^*=(P^*,S^*,X^*,Q^*)$, where*

$$\begin{aligned}P^*&=\frac{\omega}{\wp_1 S^*+(\varpi_1+\mho)},\\ X^*&=\frac{\vartheta(1-\theta)S^*}{\wp_2 S^*+(\varpi_3+\mho)},\\ Q^*&=\frac{\vartheta\theta S^*}{\varpi_4+\mho},\end{aligned}$$

and S^* satisfies the equation

$$S^{*2}+AS^*+B=0,$$

where

$$A = \frac{\wp_1(\mho + \varpi_3)(\vartheta + \mho + \varpi_2) + \wp_2(\mho + \varpi_1)(\vartheta\theta + \mho + \varpi_2) - \wp_1\wp_2 b}{\wp_1\wp_2(\vartheta\theta + \mho + \varpi_2)},$$
$$B = \frac{(\vartheta + \mho + \varpi_2)(\mho + \varpi_1)(\mho + \varpi_3) - \wp_1\omega(\mho + \varpi_3)}{\wp_1\wp_2(\vartheta\theta + \mho + \varpi_2)}.$$

Proof. To evaluate the existence of the positive smoking-present equilibrium $\mathscr{Y}^*$ of System (4), let $S^* > 0$ and

$$\begin{aligned} {}^{C}\mathcal{D}^{\alpha}_{0,t}(P^*) &= 0,\\ {}^{C}\mathcal{D}^{\alpha}_{0,t}(S^*) &= 0,\\ {}^{C}\mathcal{D}^{\alpha}_{0,t}(X^*) &= 0,\\ {}^{C}\mathcal{D}^{\alpha}_{0,t}(Q^*) &= 0. \end{aligned}$$

This gives

$$\omega - \wp_1 P^* S^* - (\varpi_1 + \mho)P^* = 0, \tag{22}$$
$$\wp_1 P^* S^* + \wp_2 X^* S^* - (\vartheta + \varpi_2 + \mho)S^* = 0, \tag{23}$$
$$\vartheta(1-\theta)S^* - \wp_2 X^* S^* - (\varpi_3 + \mho)X^* = 0, \tag{24}$$
$$\vartheta\theta S^* - (\varpi_4 + \mho)Q^* = 0. \tag{25}$$

From Equation (25), we obtain

$$Q^* = \frac{\vartheta\theta S^*}{\varpi_4 + \mho}. \tag{26}$$

From Equation (24), we have

$$X^* = \frac{\vartheta(1-\theta)S^*}{\wp_2 S^* + (\varpi_3 + \mho)}. \tag{27}$$

Then it follows from Equation (22)

$$P^* = \frac{\omega}{\wp_1 S^* + (\varpi_1 + \mho)}. \tag{28}$$

Finally, (23) gives

$$S^*(\wp_1 P^* + \wp_2 X^* - (\vartheta + \varpi_2 + \mho)) = 0.$$

Since $S^* \neq 0$, we obtain

$$\wp_1 P^* + \wp_2 X^* - (\vartheta + \varpi_2 + \mho) = 0. \tag{29}$$

Substituting (28) and (27) in Equation (29), we obtain

$$S^{*2} + AS^* + B = 0, \tag{30}$$

with

$$A = \frac{\wp_1(\mho + \varpi_3)(\vartheta + \mho + \varpi_2) + \wp_2(\mho + \varpi_1)(\vartheta\theta + \mho + \varpi_2) - \wp_1\wp_2 b}{\wp_1\wp_2(\vartheta\theta + \mho + \varpi_2)},$$
$$B = \frac{(\vartheta + \mho + \varpi_2)(\mho + \varpi_1)(\mho + \varpi_3) - \wp_1\omega(\mho + \varpi_3)}{\wp_1\wp_2(\vartheta\theta + \mho + \varpi_2)}.$$

□

Theorem 5. *For the existence of a smoking-present equilibrium point $\mathscr{Y}^* = (P^*, S^*, X^*, Q^*)$, we have*

(i) *If $R_0 = 1$, there is no positive present equilibrium point $\mathscr{Y}^*$.*

(ii) *If $R_0 < 1$, and $\frac{\mho}{\wp_1} > \frac{\omega}{\mho}$, then there is no positive present equilibrium point $\mathscr{Y}^*$.*

(iii) *If $R_0 > 1$, there exists one positive present equilibrium point $\mathscr{Y}^*$ given by* (26), (27), (28), *and* (30).

Proof. Using the quadratic formula, notice that Equation (30) can be solved as follows:

$$S_1^* = -\frac{A}{2} + \frac{1}{2}\sqrt{A^2 - 4B},$$
$$S_2^* = -\frac{A}{2} - \frac{1}{2}\sqrt{A^2 - 4B},$$

with

$$A = \frac{\wp_1(\mho + \varpi_3)(\vartheta + \mho + \varpi_2) + \wp_2(\mho + \varpi_1)(\vartheta\theta + \mho + \varpi_2) - \wp_1\wp_2 b}{\wp_1\wp_2(\vartheta\theta + \mho + \varpi_2)},$$
$$B = \frac{(\vartheta + \mho + \varpi_2)(\mho + \varpi_1)(\mho + \varpi_3) - \wp_1\omega(\mho + \varpi_3)}{\wp_1\wp_2(\vartheta\theta + \mho + \varpi_2)}$$
$$= \frac{(\vartheta + \mho + \varpi_2)(\mho + \varpi_1)(\mho + \varpi_3)(1 - R_0)}{\wp_1\wp_2(\vartheta\theta + \mho + \varpi_2)}.$$

Then, we have

1. If $R_0 = 1$, then $B = 0$, which gives $S_1^* = 0$ and $S_2^* = -A < 0$; then there is no positive solution.
2. If $R_0 > 1$, then $B < 0$. Consequently, $\sqrt{A^2 - 4B} > A$, so we obtain one positive solution

$$S^* = -\frac{A}{2} + \frac{1}{2}\sqrt{A^2 - 4B}.$$

3. If $R_0 < 1$, then $B > 0$; if, in addition, $A > 0$, then there is no positive solution. However, we can write A as

$$A = \frac{\mho(\wp_1(\vartheta + \mho + \varpi_2 + \varpi_3) + \wp_2(\vartheta\theta + \varpi_2) + \wp_2(\mho - \wp_1\frac{\omega}{\mho})) + \wp_1\varpi_3(\vartheta + \varpi_2) + \wp_2\varpi_1(\vartheta\theta + \mho + \varpi_2)}{\wp_1\wp_2(\vartheta\theta + \mho + \varpi_2)}.$$

Then, to ensure that A remains positive, we take $\mho > \wp_1\frac{\omega}{\mho}$; that is, $\frac{\mho}{\wp_1} > \frac{\omega}{\mho}$.

□

4.4. Local Stability for the Free Smoker Equilibrium Point

We use the result proven in [24,25]. The local stability of the equilibrium point $\mathscr{Y}_0 = (\frac{\omega}{\varpi_1 + \mho}, 0, 0, 0)$ is studied in the following theorem.

Theorem 6. *The smoking-free equilibrium point $\mathscr{Y}_0 = (\frac{\omega}{\varpi_1 + \mho}, 0, 0, 0)$ is locally asymptotically stable if $R_0 < 1$, locally stable if $R_0 = 1$, and unstable if $R_0 > 1$.*

Proof. By using the Jacobian matrix of System (4) evaluated at $\mathscr{Y}_0 = (\frac{\omega}{\varpi_1+\mho}, 0, 0, 0)$, we obtain

$$J(\mathscr{Y}_0) = \begin{pmatrix} -(\varpi_1+\mho) & -\frac{\wp_1 b}{(\varpi_1+\mho)} & 0 & 0 \\ 0 & \frac{\wp_1\omega-(\vartheta+\varpi_2+\mho)}{(\varpi_1+\mho)} & 0 & 0 \\ 0 & \vartheta(1-\theta) & -(\varpi_3+\mho) & 0 \\ 0 & \vartheta\theta & 0 & -(\varpi_4+\mho) \end{pmatrix}$$
$$= \begin{pmatrix} -(\varpi_1+\mho) & (\vartheta+\varpi_2+\mho)R_0 & 0 & 0 \\ 0 & -(\vartheta+\varpi_2+\mho)(1-R_0) & 0 & 0 \\ 0 & \vartheta(1-\theta) & -(\varpi_3+\mho) & 0 \\ 0 & \vartheta\theta & 0 & -(\varpi_4+\mho) \end{pmatrix}.$$

Thus, the characteristic polynomial is given by

$$P(\lambda) = (\lambda + (\varpi_1 + u))(\lambda + (\varpi_3 + \mho))(\lambda + (\varpi_4 + \mho))(\lambda + (\varpi_2 + \mho + \vartheta)(1 - R_0)).$$

Therefore, the eigenvalues of $J(\mathscr{Y}_0)$ are

$$\lambda_1 = -(\varpi_1 + u),\ \lambda_2 = -(\varpi_3 + u),\ \lambda_3 = -(\varpi_4 + u),\ \lambda_4 = -(\varpi_2 + \mho + \vartheta)(1 - R_0)).$$

Clearly, we have $\lambda_4 < 0$ if $R_0 < 1$, so all eigenvalues of $J(\mathscr{Y}_0)$ are negative and verify the condition $|arg(\lambda_i)| > \alpha\frac{\pi}{2}$, $i = 1, \ldots, 4$; then $\mathscr{Y}_0$ is locally asymptotically stable (refer to [24,25]). On the other hand, when $R_0 = 1$, then $\lambda_4 = 0$, then $\mathscr{Y}_0$ is locally stable, and when $R_0 > 1$, then $\lambda_4 > 0$ and $|arg(\lambda_4)| = 0 < \alpha\frac{\pi}{2}$. Then, $\mathscr{Y}_0$ is unstable.

4.5. Local Stability for the Present Equilibrium Point

Here, we investigate the local stability of the present equilibrium point. By using the Jacobian matrix of System (4) evaluated at $\mathscr{Y}^* = (P^*, S^*, X^*, Q^*)$, we obtain

$$J(\mathscr{Y}^*) = \begin{pmatrix} -(\wp_1 S^* + (\varpi_1+\mho)) & -\wp_1 P^* & 0 & 0 \\ \wp_1 S^* & \wp_1 P^* + \wp_2 X^* - (\vartheta+\varpi_2+\mho) & \wp_2 S^* & 0 \\ 0 & \vartheta(1-\theta) - \wp_2 X^* & -(\wp_2 S^* + (\varpi_3+\mho)) & 0 \\ 0 & \vartheta\theta & 0 & -(\varpi_4+\mho) \end{pmatrix}$$
$$= \begin{pmatrix} -\frac{P^*}{\omega} & -\wp_1 P^* & 0 & 0 \\ \wp_1 S^* & 0 & \wp_2 S^* & 0 \\ 0 & \vartheta(1-\theta) - \wp_2 X^* & -\frac{X^*}{\vartheta(1-\theta)S^*} & 0 \\ 0 & \vartheta\theta & 0 & -(\varpi_4+\mho) \end{pmatrix}.$$

Thus, the characteristic polynomial is given by

$$(\lambda + (\varpi_4 + \mho))(\lambda^3 + A_1\lambda^2 + A_2\lambda + A_3),$$

where

$$A_1 = \frac{\vartheta(1-\theta)P^*S^* + \omega X^*}{\omega\vartheta(1-\theta)S^*}, \tag{31}$$

$$A_2 = \frac{P^*X^* + v\vartheta(1-\theta)S^{*2}(\wp_1^2 P^* + \wp_2 X^*) - \omega\wp_2\vartheta^2(1-\theta)^2 S^{*2}}{\omega\vartheta(1-\theta)S^*}, \tag{32}$$

$$A_3 = \frac{P^*S^*X^*(\omega\wp_1^2 + \vartheta(1-\theta)\wp_2^2 S^*) - \wp_2\vartheta^2(1-\theta)^2 P^* S^{*2}}{\omega\vartheta(1-\theta)S^*}. \tag{33}$$

The eigenvalues of the characteristic polynomial are $\lambda_1 = -(\varpi_4 + \mho)$ and the solutions of the cubic equation

$$\lambda^3 + A_1\lambda^2 + A_2\lambda + A_3 = 0. \tag{34}$$

Using the Routh–Hurwitz criterion [26], all the eigenvalue of the characteristic Equation (34) has a negative real part if and only if

$$A_1 > 0,\ A_2 > 0,\ A_3 > 0,\ A_1A_2 > A_3;$$

then we have the following result. □

Theorem 7. *Let A_1, A_2, and A_3 be given by* (31), (32), *and* (33), *respectively; then the present equilibrium point of System* (3) *is locally asymptotically stable if*

$$A_1 > 0,\ A_2 > 0,\ A_3 > 0,\ A_1A_2 > A_3.$$

4.6. Global Stability

In this section, we establish results on global stability for the free smoker equilibrium and the present equilibrium. To do so, we introduce the following lemma:

Lemma 5. *[27,28] Suppose $\phi(t) \in \mathbb{R}_+$ is a continuous and differentiable function. Then, for any $t \geq 0$, we have the following inequalities:*

$${}^{C}\mathcal{D}^{\alpha}_{0,t}(\phi(t) - \phi^* - \phi^* \ln \frac{\phi(t)}{\phi^*}) \leq (1 - \frac{\phi^*}{\phi(t)})\, {}^{C}\mathcal{D}^{\alpha}_{0,t}(\phi(t)),$$

and

$$\frac{1}{2}\, {}^{C}\mathcal{D}^{\alpha}_{0,t}(\phi^2(t)) \leq \phi(t)\, {}^{C}\mathcal{D}^{\alpha}_{0,t}(\phi(t)).$$

The following theorem presents the global stability result for the free smoker equilibrium.

Theorem 8. *The smoker free equilibrium point $\mathscr{Y}_0 = (\frac{\omega}{\varpi_1 + \mho}, 0, 0, 0)$ of System* (4) *is globally asymptotically stable when $R_0 \leq 1$.*

Proof. Let $L(t)$ be the Lyapunov candidate function, such that

$$L(t) = (P(t) - P_0 - P_0 \ln \frac{P(t)}{P_0}) + S(t) + X(t) + Q(t), \tag{35}$$

$L(t)$ is defined, continuous and positive for all $t \leq 0$. For this function, we have

$${}^{C}\mathcal{D}^{\alpha}_{0,t}(L(t)) = {}^{C}\mathcal{D}^{\alpha}_{0,t}((P(t) - P_0 - P_0 \ln \frac{P(t)}{P_0}) + S(t) + X(t) + Q(t)).$$

Using the linearity propriety of the Caputo derivative and Lemma 5, we obtain

$$\begin{aligned}
{}^{C}\mathcal{D}^{\alpha}_{0,t}(L(t)) &= {}^{C}\mathcal{D}^{\alpha}_{0,t}((P(t) - P_0 - P_0 \ln \frac{P(t)}{P_0}) + S(t) + X(t) + Q(t)) \\
&= {}^{C}\mathcal{D}^{\alpha}_{0,t}((P(t) - P_0 - P_0 \ln \frac{P(t)}{P_0})) + {}^{C}\mathcal{D}^{\alpha}_{0,t}(S(t)) + {}^{C}\mathcal{D}^{\alpha}_{0,t}(X(t)) + {}^{C}\mathcal{D}^{\alpha}_{0,t}(Q(t)) \\
&\leq (1 - \frac{P_0}{P(t)})\, {}^{C}\mathcal{D}^{\alpha}_{0,t}(P(t)) + {}^{C}\mathcal{D}^{\alpha}_{0,t}(S(t)) + {}^{C}\mathcal{D}^{\alpha}_{0,t}(X(t)) + {}^{C}\mathcal{D}^{\alpha}_{0,t}(Q(t)).
\end{aligned}$$

From System (4), and with direct calculation, we obtain

$$\begin{aligned}{}^{C}\mathcal{D}^{\alpha}_{0,t}(L(t)) &\leq (1-\frac{P_0}{P(t)})(\omega-\wp_1 P(t)S(t)-(\varpi_1+\mho)P(t))+(\wp_1 P(t)S(t)+\wp_2 X(t)S(t)-(\vartheta+\varpi_2+\mho)S(t))\\ &\quad+(\vartheta(1-\theta)S(t)-\wp_2 X(t)S(t)-(\varpi_3+\mho)X(t))+(\vartheta\theta S(t)-(\varpi_4+\mho)Q(t))\\ &\leq \omega(2-\frac{P(t)}{P_0}-\frac{P_0}{P(t)})+(\wp_1 P_0-(\varpi_2+\mho))S(t)-(\varpi_3+\mho)X(t)-(\varpi_4+\mho)Q(t)\\ &\leq \omega(2-\frac{P(t)}{P_0}-\frac{P_0}{P(t)})+\frac{1}{\varpi_1+\mho}(\wp_1\omega-(\varpi_1+\mho)(\varpi_2+\mho))S(t)-(\varpi_3+\mho)X(t)-(\varpi_4+\mho)Q(t).\end{aligned}$$

We know by the arithmetic–geometric means that

$$(2-\frac{P(t)}{P_0}-\frac{P_0}{P(t)})\leq 0.$$

Then, if we have $(\wp_1\omega-(\varpi_1+\mho)(\varpi_2+\mho))\leq 0$, we obtain ${}^{C}\mathcal{D}^{\alpha}_{0,t}(L(t))\leq 0$. In addition, we have ${}^{C}\mathcal{D}^{\alpha}_{0,t}(L(t)) = 0$ if and only if $(P(t),S(t),X(t),Q(t)) = \mathscr{Y}_0$; then the maximum invariant set for

$$\{(P(t),S(t),X(t),Q(t))\in\mathbb{R}^4_+,\ {}^{C}\mathcal{D}^{\alpha}_{0,t}(L(t))=0\}$$

is the set $\{\mathscr{Y}_0\}$, and according to LaSalle's invariance principle, the free equilibrium point $\mathscr{Y}_0$ is globally asymptotically stable. □

The following theorem presents the global stability result for the present equilibrium.

Theorem 9. *Let $R_0 > 1$ and suppose we have*

$$(\frac{Q^*}{Q}>\frac{X^*}{X}>1 \text{ and } \frac{S^*}{S}<1); \qquad or \qquad (\frac{Q}{Q^*}>\frac{X}{X^*}>1 \text{ and } \frac{S^*}{S}>1).$$

Then, the present smoker equilibrium $\mathscr{Y}^*$ given in Proposition 6 is globally asymptotically stable.

Proof. Let $L^*(t)$ be the Lyapunov function defined by

$$\begin{aligned}L^*(t) &= (P(t)-P^*-P^*\ln\frac{P(t)}{P^*})+(S(t)-S^*-S^*\ln\frac{S(t)}{S^*})+(X(t)-X^*-X^*\ln\frac{X(t)}{X^*})\\ &\quad+(Q(t)-Q^*-Q^*\ln\frac{Q(t)}{Q^*}).\end{aligned}$$

The function $L^*(t)$ is defined as positive and continuous for all $t\geq 0$. Now using the linearity propriety of the Caputo derivative and Lemma 5, we obtain

$$\begin{aligned}{}^{C}\mathcal{D}^{\alpha}_{0,t}(L^*(t)) &\leq (1-\frac{P^*}{P(t)})\,{}^{C}\mathcal{D}^{\alpha}_{0,t}(P(t))+(1-\frac{S^*}{S(t)})\,{}^{C}\mathcal{D}^{\alpha}_{0,t}(S(t))+(1-\frac{X^*}{X(t)})\,{}^{C}\mathcal{D}^{\alpha}_{0,t}(X(t))\\ &\quad+(1-\frac{Q^*}{Q(t)})\,{}^{C}\mathcal{D}^{\alpha}_{0,t}(Q(t)).\end{aligned}$$

From System (4), we have

$$(1-\frac{P^*}{P(t)})\ {}^C\mathcal{D}^{\alpha}_{0,t}(P(t)) = (1-\frac{P^*}{P(t)})(\omega - \wp_1 P(t)S(t) - (\varpi_1 + \mho)P(t)), \quad (36)$$
$$(1-\frac{S^*}{S(t)})\ {}^C\mathcal{D}^{\alpha}_{0,t}(S(t)) = (1-\frac{S^*}{S(t)})(\wp_1 P(t)S(t) + \wp_2 X(t)S(t) - (\vartheta + \varpi_2 + \mho)S(t)), \quad (37)$$
$$(1-\frac{X^*}{X(t)})\ {}^C\mathcal{D}^{\alpha}_{0,t}(X(t)) = (1-\frac{X^*}{X(t)})(\vartheta(1-\theta)S(t) - \wp_2 X(t)S(t) - (\varpi_3 + \mho)X(t)), \quad (38)$$
$$(1-\frac{Q^*}{Q(t)})\ {}^C\mathcal{D}^{\alpha}_{0,t}(Q(t)) = (1-\frac{Q^*}{Q(t)})(\vartheta\theta S(t) - (\varpi_4 + \mho)Q(t)). \quad (39)$$

On the other hand, Equations (22) to (25) give

$$(\varpi_1 + \mho) = \frac{\omega}{P^*} - \wp_1 S^*, \quad (40)$$
$$(\vartheta + \varpi_2 + \mho) = \wp_1 P^* + \wp_2 X^*, \quad (41)$$
$$(\varpi_3 + \mho) = \vartheta(1-\theta)\frac{S^*}{X^*} - \wp_2 S^*, \quad (42)$$
$$(\varpi_4 + \mho) = \vartheta\theta\frac{S^*}{Q^*}. \quad (43)$$

Substituting Equations (40) to (43) in Equations (36) to (39), we obtain

$$(1-\frac{P^*}{P(t)})\ {}^C\mathcal{D}^{\alpha}_{0,t}(P(t)) = (1-\frac{P^*}{P(t)})(\omega - \wp_1 P(t)S(t) - (\frac{\omega}{P^*} - \wp_1 S^*)P(t)), \quad (44)$$
$$(1-\frac{S^*}{S(t)})\ {}^C\mathcal{D}^{\alpha}_{0,t}(S(t)) = (1-\frac{S^*}{S(t)})(\wp_1 P(t)S(t) + \wp_2 X(t)S(t) - (\wp_1 P^* + \wp_2 X^*)S(t)), \quad (45)$$
$$(1-\frac{X^*}{X(t)})\ {}^C\mathcal{D}^{\alpha}_{0,t}(X(t)) = (1-\frac{X^*}{X(t)})(\vartheta(1-\theta)S(t) - \wp_2 X(t)S(t) - (\vartheta(1-\theta)\frac{S^*}{X^*} - \wp_2 S^*)X(t)), \quad (46)$$
$$(1-\frac{Q^*}{Q(t)})\ {}^C\mathcal{D}^{\alpha}_{0,t}(Q(t)) = (1-\frac{Q^*}{Q(t)})(\vartheta\theta S(t) - (\vartheta\theta\frac{S^*}{Q^*})Q(t)). \quad (47)$$

Direct calculation gives

$$\begin{aligned}
(1-\frac{P^*}{P(t)})\ {}^C\mathcal{D}^{\alpha}_{0,t}(P(t)) &= \omega(2 - \frac{P^*}{P} - \frac{P}{P^*}) - \wp_1(PS + P^*S^* - PS^* - P^*S),\\
(1-\frac{S^*}{S(t)})\ {}^C\mathcal{D}^{\alpha}_{0,t}(S(t)) &= \wp_1(PS + P^*S^* - PS^* - P^*S) + \wp_2(XS + X^*S^* - X^*S - XS^*),\\
(1-\frac{X^*}{X(t)})\ {}^C\mathcal{D}^{\alpha}_{0,t}(X(t)) &= \vartheta S(1-\frac{X^*}{X}) + \vartheta S^*(1-\frac{X}{X^*}) + \vartheta\theta S^*\frac{X}{X^*} + \vartheta\theta S\frac{X^*}{X} - \vartheta\theta(S+S^*)\\
&\quad - \wp_2(XS + X^*S^* - X^*S - XS^*),\\
(1-\frac{Q^*}{Q(t)})\ {}^C\mathcal{D}^{\alpha}_{0,t}(Q(t)) &= \vartheta\theta(S+S^*) - \vartheta\theta S^*\frac{Q}{Q^*} - \vartheta\theta S\frac{Q^*}{Q}.
\end{aligned}$$

Finally, we obtain

$$\begin{aligned}
{}^C\mathcal{D}^{\alpha}_{0,t}(L^*(t)) &\le (1-\frac{P^*}{P(t)})\ {}^C\mathcal{D}^{\alpha}_{0,t}(P(t)) + (1-\frac{S^*}{S(t)})\ {}^C\mathcal{D}^{\alpha}_{0,t}(S(t)) + (1-\frac{X^*}{X(t)})\ {}^C\mathcal{D}^{\alpha}_{0,t}(X(t))\\
&\quad + (1-\frac{Q^*}{Q(t)})\ {}^C\mathcal{D}^{\alpha}_{0,t}(Q(t))\\
&= \omega(2 - \frac{P^*}{P} - \frac{P}{P^*}) + \vartheta S(1-\frac{X^*}{X}) + \vartheta S^*(1-\frac{X}{X^*}) + \vartheta\theta S(\frac{X^*}{X} - \frac{Q^*}{Q(t)}) + \vartheta\theta S^*(\frac{X}{X^*} - \frac{Q}{Q^*}).
\end{aligned}$$

We know that

$$(2 - \frac{P^*}{P} - \frac{P}{P^*}) \le 0,$$

and if

$$(\frac{Q^*}{Q} > \frac{X^*}{X} > 1 \text{ and } \frac{S^*}{S} < 1), \quad \text{or} \quad (\frac{Q}{Q^*} > \frac{X}{X^*} > 1 \text{ and } \frac{S^*}{S} > 1).$$

We obtain

$$^C\mathcal{D}^{\alpha}_{0,t}(L^*(t)) \leq 0.$$

In addition, we have $^C\mathcal{D}^{\alpha}_{0,t}(L^*(t)) = 0$ if and only if $(P(t), S(t), X(t), Q(t)) = \mathscr{Y}^*$; then the maximum invariant set for $\{(P(t), S(t), X(t), Q(t)) \in \mathbb{R}_+, {}^C\mathcal{D}^{\alpha}_{0,t}(L^*(t)) = 0\}$ is the set $\{\mathscr{Y}^*\}$, and according to LaSalle's invariance principle, the present smoker equilibrium point $\mathscr{Y}^*$ is globally asymptotically stable. □

5. Numerical Simulations and Discussions

We present here some numerical implementation of System (4); the data are taken from [8] and are presented in Table 2 for $R_0 < 1$ and Table 3 for $R_0 > 1$.

Additionally, we use the following initial condition:

$$(P(0), S(0), X(0), Q(0)) = (0.75,\ 0.15,\ 0.1,\ 0),$$

such that $P + S + X + Q = 1$. For the data from Table 2, we obtain $R_0 = \frac{\wp_1 b}{(\varpi_1+\mho)(\vartheta+\varpi_2+\mho)} = 0.59 < 1$, so the smoking-free equilibrium $\mathscr{Y}_0$ of System (4) is (3.63, 0, 0, 0), while for the data from Table 3, we obtain $R_0 = 2.5123 > 1$. According to the data in Tables 2 and 3 and with the help of the Matlab program for fractional differential equations, we obtain the following graphical representation for the smoking dynamic progression of System (4).

Table 2. The parameter values for $R_0 < 1$.

Parameter	Estimation	Source
ω	0.2	[8]
$\wp_1$	0.009	Estimated
$\wp_2$	0.003	Estimated
ϑ	0.0013	Estimated
θ	0.35	Estimated
$\mho$	0.05	Estimated
ϖ_1	0.005	Estimated
ϖ_2	0.0021	[8]
ϖ_3	0.0037	[8]
ϖ_4	0.0012	[8]

Table 3. The parameter values for $R_0 > 1$.

Parameter	Estimation	Source
ω	0.2	[8]
$\wp_1$	0.038	[8]
$\wp_2$	0.0411	[8]
ϑ	0.0013	Estimated
θ	0.35	Estimated
$\mho$	0.05	Estimated
ϖ_1	0.005	Estimated
ϖ_2	0.0021	[8]
ϖ_3	0.0037	[8]
ϖ_4	0.0012	[8]

Discussions

Figure 2 demonstrates that each compartment class converges to its free equilibrium point $\mathscr{Y}_0$ as time progresses. The simulation confirms the asymptotic stability of the smoking-free equilibrium point, consistent with the expected theoretical result when $R_0 < 1$.

Additionally, we observe the influence of the fractional derivative order on the numerical solutions for values close to $\alpha = 1$, such as $\alpha = 0.9$ and $\alpha = 0.8$, and notice that the graphs of the numerical solutions approach the solutions obtained from ordinary derivatives at $\alpha = 1$. On the other hand, Figure 3 represents the scenario where $R_0 = 2.5123 > 1$. We observe the existence and stability of the smoking-present equilibrium $\mathscr{Y}^*$ as predicted by the theoretical result.

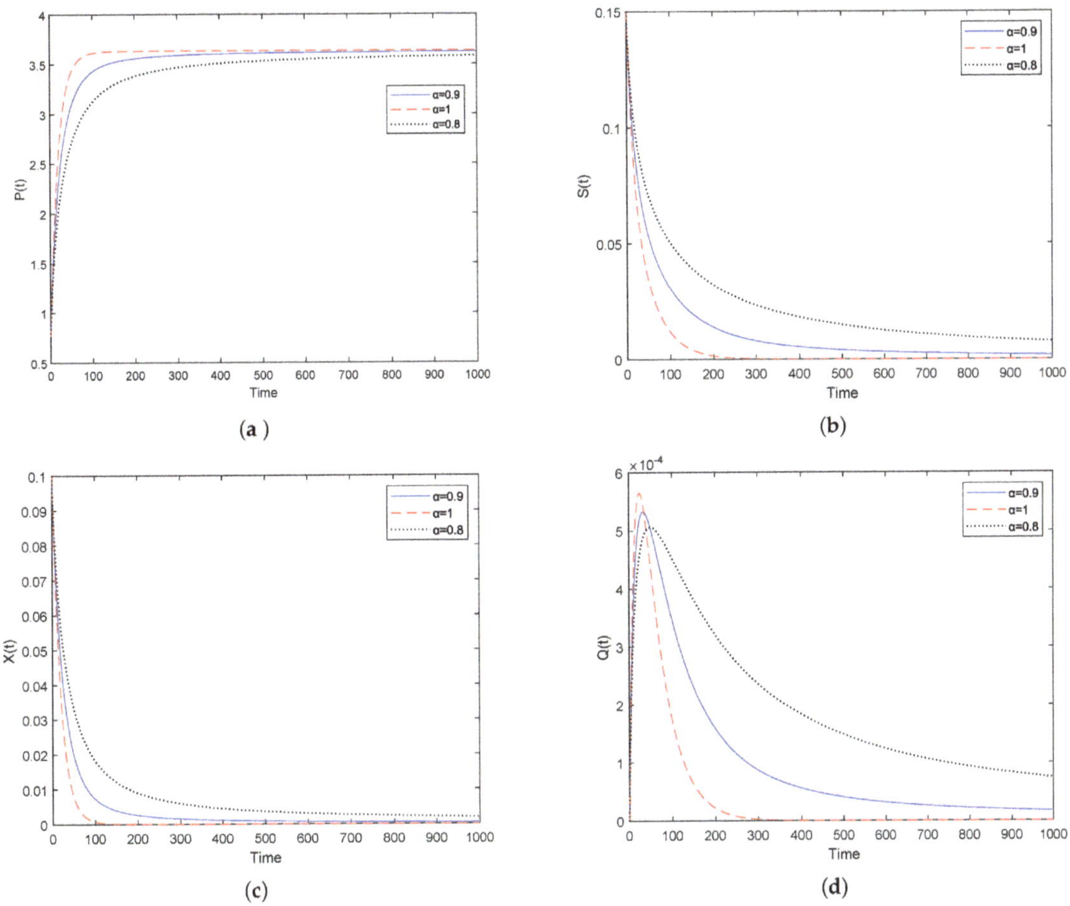

Figure 2. Time series plots of potential, persistent, temporally recovered, and permanently recovered smokers for $R_0 = 0.5950 < 1$. (**a**) Potential smokers with a different value of α. (**b**) Persistent smokers with a different value of α. (**c**) Temporally recovered smokers with a different value of α. (**d**) Permanently recovered smokers with a different value of α.

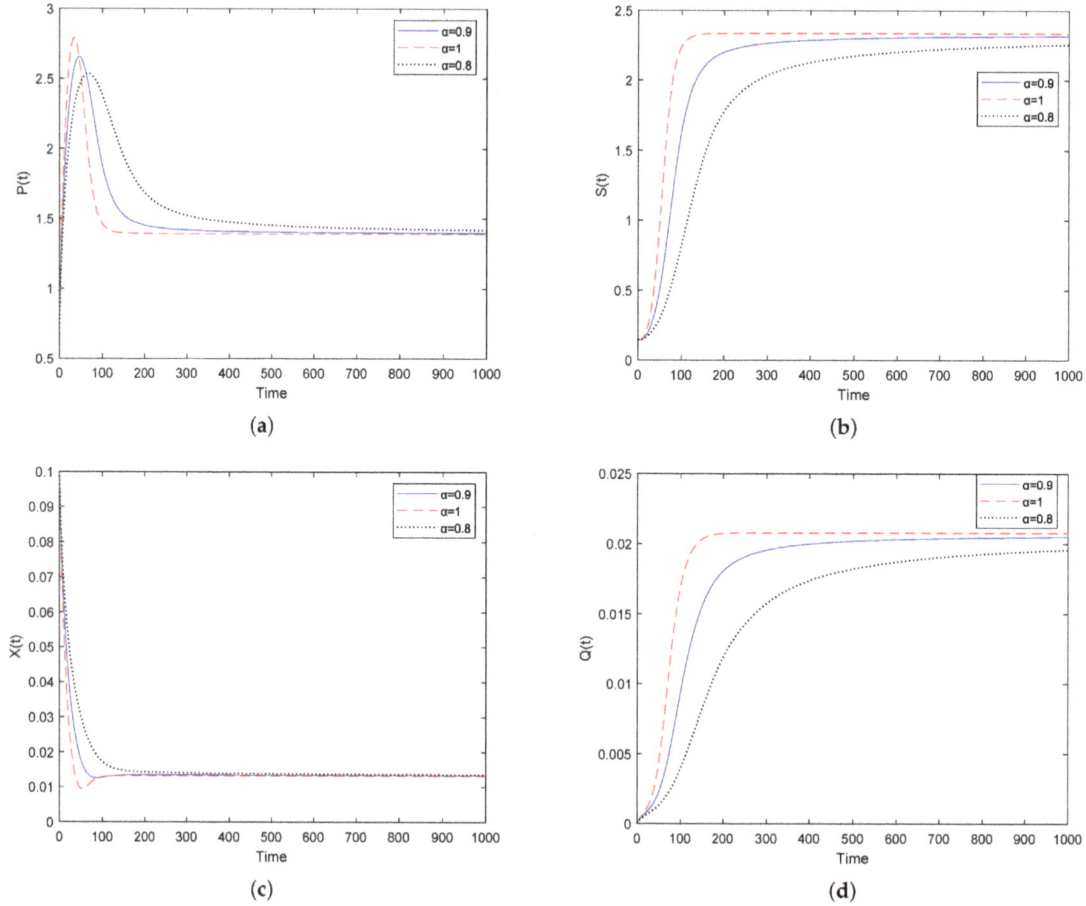

Figure 3. Timeseries plots of potential, persistent, temporally recovered, and permanently recovered smokers for $R_0 = 2.5123 > 1$. (**a**) Potential smokers with a different value of α. (**b**) Persistent smokers with a different value of α. (**c**) Temporally recovered smokers with a different value of α. (**d**) Permanently recovered smokers with a different value of α.

6. Conclusions

In this study, we introduced a mathematical model that describes the dynamics of relapse in the context of smoking cessation and presents the dynamic behavior of the proposed model using Caputo fractional derivatives (see Figure 1). The model considers four categories of individuals: potential smokers, persistent smokers, temporarily recovered smokers, and permanently recovered smokers. Each class was described by a Caputo fractional differential equation of order α. Although specific parameters were introduced and estimated in this work [8], the model could accurately represent the dynamics of a smoking epidemic in real life if the actual parameter values were obtained. The model exhibited a smoking-free equilibrium point, representing a state without smoking, and a present smoking equilibrium point. We derived the reproduction number R_0 by employing the next-generation matrix method. The analysis revealed that if $R_0 < 1$, the smoking-free equilibrium point is asymptotically stable. Conversely, if $R_0 > 1$, the present smoking equilibrium point is asymptotically stable. We performed numerical simulations using the predictor–corrector PECE method for fractional differential equations to validate our findings. The simulation results confirmed the conclusions drawn from the analytical investigation.

Author Contributions: Conceptualization, Y.E.h.M.; Methodology, F.K.A., A.B., N.L. and M.H.A.; Software, Y.E.h.M.; Formal analysis, F.K.A., Y.E.h.M., N.L. and M.H.A.; Investigation, M.H.A.; Writing—original draft, Y.E.h.M.; Writing—review & editing, F.K.A., A.B., N.L. and M.H.A.; Supervision, A.B. All authors have read and agreed to the published version of the manuscript.

Funding: This research was funded by the General Research Funding Program, grant code (NU/DRP/SERC/12/6).

Institutional Review Board Statement: Not applicable.

Informed Consent Statement: Not applicable.

Data Availability Statement: Not applicable.

Acknowledgments: The authors are thankful to the Deanship of Scientific Research (DSR) at Najran University for funding this work under the General Research Funding Program grant code (NU/DRP/SERC/12/6).

Conflicts of Interest: The authors declare no conflict of interest.

References

1. World Health Organization. *WHO Report on the Global Tobacco Epidemic, 2008: The MPOWER Package*; World Health Organization: Geneva, Switzerland, 2008.
2. Anjam, Y.N.; Shafqat, R.; Sarris, I.E.; Rahman, M.U.; Touseef, S.; Arshad, M. A fractional order investigation of smoking model using caputo-fabrizio differential operator. *Fractal Fract.* **2022**, *6*, 623. [CrossRef]
3. Rezapour, S.; Etemad, S.; Sinan, M.; Alzabut, J.; Vinodkumar, A. A mathematical analysis on the new fractal-fractional model of second-hand smokers via the power law type kernel: Numerical solutions, equilibrium points, and sensitivity analysis. *J. Funct. Spaces* **2022**, *2022*, 3553021. [CrossRef]
4. Hecht, S.S. Cigarette smoking: Cancer risks, carcinogens, and mechanisms. *Langenbeck's Arch. Surg.* **2006**, *391*, 603–613. [CrossRef]
5. Castillo-Garsow, C.; Jordan-Salivia, G.; Rodriguez-Herrera, A. Mathematical Models for the Dynamics of Tobacco Use, Recovery and Relapse. 1997. Available online: https://www.semanticscholar.org/paper/Mathematical-Models-for-the-Dynamics-of-Tobacco-and-Castillo-Garsow-Jordan-Salivia/d29de75a1ea86e9b7649e65070431c4dd78a96c0 (accessed on 11 June 2023).
6. Zaman, G. Optimal campaign in the smoking dynamics. *Comput. Math. Methods Med.* **2011**, *2011*, 163834. [CrossRef] [PubMed]
7. Rahman, G.u.; Agarwal, R.P.; Din, Q. Mathematical analysis of giving up smoking model via harmonic mean type incidence rate. *Appl. Math. Comput.* **2019**, *354*, 128–148. [CrossRef]
8. Huo, H.; Zhu, C. Influence of relapse in a giving up smoking model. *Abstr. Appl. Anal.* **2013**, *2013*, 525461. [CrossRef]
9. de Barros, L.C.; Lopes, M.M.; Pedro, F.S.; Esmi, E.a.; Santos, J.P.C.d.; Sánchez, D.E. The memory effect on fractional calculus: An application in the spread of COVID-19. *Comput. Appl. Math.* **2021**, *40*, 72. [CrossRef]
10. Ertürk, V.S.; Zaman, G.; Momani, S. A numeric–analytic method for approximating a giving up smoking model containing fractional derivatives. *Comput. Math. Appl.* **2012**, *64*, 3065–3074. [CrossRef]
11. Lubin, J.H.; Caporaso, N.E. Cigarette smoking and lung cancer: Modeling total exposure and intensity. *Cancer Epidemiol. Biomarkers Prev.* **2006**, *15*, 517–523. [CrossRef]
12. Alkhudhari, Z.; Al-Sheikh, S.; Al-Tuwairqi, S. Global dynamics of a mathematical model on smoking. *Int. Sch. Res. Not.* **2014**, *2014*, 847075. [CrossRef]
13. Khalid, M.; Khan, F.S.; Iqbal, A. Perturbation-iteration algorithm to solve fractional giving up smoking mathematical model. *Int. J. Comput. Appl.* **2016**, *142*, 975-8887. [CrossRef]
14. Singh, J.; Kumar, D.; Qurashi, M.A.; Baleanu, D. A new fractional model for giving up smoking dynamics. *Adv. Differ. Equ.* **2017**, *2017*, 88. [CrossRef]
15. Ahmad, A.; Farman, M.; Ghafar, A.; Inc, M.; Ahmad, M.O.; Sene, N. Analysis and simulation of fractional order smoking epidemic model. *Comput. Math. Methods Med.* **2022**, *2022*, 9683187. [CrossRef] [PubMed]
16. Addai, E.; Zhang, L.; Asamoah, J.K.K.; Essel, J.F. A fractional order age-specific smoke epidemic model. *Appl. Math. Model.* **2023**, *119*, 99–118. [CrossRef]
17. Addai, E.; Adeniji, A.; Peter, O.J.; Agbaje, J.O.; Oshinubi, K. Dynamics of age-structure smoking models with government intervention coverage under fractal-fractional order derivatives. *Fractal Fract.* **2023**, *7*, 370. [CrossRef]
18. Zeb, A.; Kumar, S.; Saeed, T. A robust computational dynamics of fractional-order smoking model with relapse habit. *Fractals* **2022**, *30*, 2240034. [CrossRef]
19. Podlubny, I. An introduction to fractional derivatives, fractional differential equations, to methods of their solution and some of their applications. *Math. Sci. Eng.* **1999**, *198*, 340.

20. Sumeyr, U.; Esmehan, U.; Necati, O.; Zakia, H. Mathematical analysis and numerical simulation for smoking model with atangana-baleanu derivative. *Chaos Solitons Fractals* **2019**, *118*, 300–306.
21. Odibat, Z.M.; Shawagfeh, N.T. Generalized taylor's formula. *Appl. Math. Comput.* **2007**, *186*, 286–293. [CrossRef]
22. Almeida, R.; Artur, M.C.; Natalia, M.; Teresa, M. An epidemiological mseir model desribed by the caputo fractional derivative. *Int. J. Dyn. Control.* **2019**, *7*, 776–784. [CrossRef]
23. Van den Driessche, P.; Watmough, J. Reproduction numbers and sub-threshold endemic equilibria for compartmental models of disease transmission. *Math. Biosiences* **2002**, *180*, 29–48. [CrossRef] [PubMed]
24. Matignon, D. Stability results for fractional differential equations with applications to control processing. *Comput. Eng. Syst. Appl.* **1996**, *2*, 963.
25. Li, Ho.; Muhammadhaji, A.; Zhang1, L.; Teng1, Z. Stability analysis of a fractional-order predator–prey model incorporating a constant prey refuge and feedback control. *Adv. Differ. Equ.* **2018**, *2018*, 325. [CrossRef]
26. David, R.M. *Introduction to the Theory of Stability*; Springer: Berlin/Heidelberg, Germany, 1997.
27. Vargas de León, C. Volterra-type lyapunov functions for fractional-order epidemic systems. *Commun. Nonlinear Sci. Numer. Simul.* **2015**, *24*, 75–85. [CrossRef]
28. Aguila-Camacho, N.; Duate-Mermoud, M.A.; Gallegos, J.A. Lyapunov functions for fractional order systems. *Commun. Nonlinear Sci. Numer Simul.* **2014**, *19*, 2951–2957. [CrossRef]

fractal and fractional

Article

Exploring Families of Solitary Wave Solutions for the Fractional Coupled Higgs System Using Modified Extended Direct Algebraic Method

Muhammad Bilal [1], Javed Iqbal [1,*], Rashid Ali [2,*], Fuad A. Awwad [3] and Emad A. A. Ismail [3]

[1] Department of Mathematics, Abdul Wali Khan University, Mardan 23200, Pakistan; muhammadbilaluop45@gmail.com
[2] School of Mathematics and Statistics, Central South University, Changsha 410083, China
[3] Department of Quantitative Analysis, College of Business Administration, King Saud University, P.O. Box 71115, Riyadh 11587, Saudi Arabia; fawwad@ksu.edu.sa (F.A.A.); emadali@ksu.edu.sa (E.A.A.I.)
* Correspondence: javedmath@awkum.edu.pk (J.I.); rashidali@csu.edu.cn (R.A.)

Abstract: In this paper, we suggest the modified Extended Direct Algebraic Method (mEDAM) to examine the existence and dynamics of solitary wave solutions in the context of the fractional coupled Higgs system, with Caputo's fractional derivatives. The method begins with the formulation of nonlinear differential equations using a fractional complex transformation, followed by the derivation of solitary wave solutions. Two-dimensional, Three-dimensional and contour graphs are used to investigate the behavior of traveling wave solutions. The research reveals many families of solitary wave solutions as well as their deep interrelationships and dynamics. These discoveries add to a better understanding of the dynamics of the fractionally coupled Higgs system and have potential applications in areas that use nonlinear Fractional Partial Differential Equations (FPDEs).

Keywords: FPDEs; mEDAM; variable transformation; NODE; kink waves; lump waves

1. Introduction

FPDEs are essential mathematical tools for correctly simulating systems with non-local behavior [1], anomalous diffusion [2], and long-range interactions [3]. They are also widely used in the fields of data analysis [4], image and signal processing [5] and materials research [6]. FPDEs are therefore receiving a lot of attention as a result of their capacity to give more accurate modelling of systems.

Because of their intrinsic non-local and non-linear properties, both Partial Differential Equations (PDEs) and FPDEs can pose major obstacles in their solutions. Though they are often employed, numerical approaches, such as finite difference method [7], finite element method [8] and many more [9–17], can be computationally costly for complicated FPDEs. When feasible, analytical approaches are chosen since they produce precise results. These techniques employ mathematical approaches to reduce the complexity of the FPDE such that it may be resolved analytically. Analytical techniques are useful because they shed light on the system's behavior and connections between its variables. They also make it possible to examine unusual circumstances and spot singularities that numerical approaches could overlook. In general, analytical approaches are suggested for solving FPDEs due to their precision, effectiveness, and capacity to offer insightful information about the system under study.

Therefore, the Laplace transform method [18], Fourier transform method [19], Adomian decomposition method [20], direct algebraic method [21], homotopy perturbation method [22], variational iteration method [23] and other analytical techniques have all been employed by researchers to solve FPDEs. Each approach has benefits and drawbacks, and the selection of approach relies on the particular topic being investigated. However, where possible, analytical approaches are preferable over numerical methods because they offer precise solutions and insightful information about how the system behaves.

To construct solitary wave solutions for PDEs and FPDEs, one of the novel analytical methods is mEDAM . The technique entails transforming the FPDE into a nonlinear ODE using the appropriate transformation, which is then resolved using a series form solution. The nonlinear ODE that results from this solution is then utilized to create a set of algebraic equations, which are then solved to get the solitary wave solutions for the FPDE. A soliton, commonly referred to as a solitary wave, is a self-sustaining wave-like solution to certain nonlinear PDEs and FPDEs that retains its shape and speed while traveling with no alteration to its form. Among the different analytical approaches for developing soliton solutions, the mEDAM stands out as the most successful, producing a wider range of soliton solution families. For instance, Sayed et al., have employed mEDAM to construct a number of families of soliton solutions for the three different types of Tzitzeica type PDEs arising in nonlinear optics [24]. Similarly, Yasmin et al., have investigated 32 different families of symmetric soliton solutions for the fractional coupled Konno–Onno system in [25] and 33 families of 131 optical soliton solutions for a fractional perturbed Radhakrishnan-Kundu–Lakshmanan model in [26], respectively, using mEDAM.

The mEDAM is employed in this work to examine solitary wave solutions for the fractional coupled Higgs system. In a relativistic quantum field theory, the fractional coupled Higgs system is a mathematical model that describes the dynamics of two scalar fields. In this system, the interaction of the two scalar fields results in intricate behavior. We considered this system in fractional form to characterize anomalous diffusion and non-local behavior, which are known to occur in many physical systems. By accounting for non-local influences on the system, fractional derivatives allow for more detailed models of solitons' behavior. The mathematical form of this system is given as follows [27]:

$$\begin{cases} D_t^{\gamma}(D_t^{\gamma}u) - D_x^{\delta}(D_x^{\delta}u) + |u|^2u - 2uv = 0, \\ D_t^{\gamma}(D_t^{\gamma}v) + D_x^{\delta}(D_x^{\delta}v) - D_x^{\delta}(D_x^{\delta}|u|^2) = 0. \end{cases} \tag{1}$$

where $0 < \gamma, \delta \leq 1$ and $u = u(x,t)$, and $v = v(x,t)$. It should be noted that the proposed model in [27] is time-fractional; however, we have generalized the model by replacing the space derivative by Caputo's fractional derivative. The system is composed of two equations: the first represents how the amplitude and phase of the soliton have changed over time, and the second defines how the background field has changed over time. The system shows a wide range of events, including solitons production, scattering, and formation. The fractional Higgs system is especially important in particle physics since it controls particle interactions and behavior, including how particles are assigned mass. As a result of the system's symmetry breakdown, topological solitons, and nontrivial scattering amplitudes, much theoretical and experimental study has been conducted.

Several researchers have already used various analytical methods to investigate the coupled Higgs system in integer and fractional orders. The Sin–Gorden method was utilized by Rezazadeh et al. in [27] to solve the coupled Higgs system in time-fractional form. Jabbari et al., obtained precise solutions to the coupled Higgs system (in integer order) and the Maccari system using He's semi-inverse technique and a simple $(\frac{G'}{G})$-expansion method [28]. Similar to this, Atas et al. [29] identified invariant optical soltons as coupled-Higgs equation solutions. The exp-expansion method was utilized by Seadway et al. [30] to get traveling wave solutions for the given system. Mu and Qin provided Rogue Waves for the Coupled Schrödinger–Boussinesq Equation and the Coupled Higgs Equation using the Hirota technique [31].

The fractional derivatives present in (1) are defined using Caputo's derivative operator. This operator with some of its properties is defined as follows [32]:

$$^{C}D_t^{\alpha} f(t) = \frac{1}{\Gamma(n-\alpha)} \int_0^t \frac{\frac{\partial^n f(s)}{\partial s^n}}{(t-s)^{\alpha-n+1}}\, ds, \tag{2}$$

$$D_y^{\alpha} y^p = \frac{\Gamma(1+p)}{\Gamma(1+p-\alpha)} y^{p-\alpha}, \tag{3}$$

$$D_y^{\alpha} g[h(y)] = g_h'(h(y)) D_y^{\alpha} h(y) = D_h^{\alpha} g(h(y)) [h'(y)]^{\alpha} \quad 0 < \alpha \leq 1, \tag{4}$$

where α is the order of the derivative, $g(t)$ and $h(t)$ are the functions to be differentiated, n is the smallest integer greater than or equal to α, and $\Gamma(\cdot)$ is the Gamma function.

2. Methodology of mEDAM

This section outlines the modified EDAM technique. Consider the FPDE of the form [25,26]:

$$P(w, \partial_t^{\alpha} w, \partial_{y_1}^{\beta} w, \partial_{y_2}^{\gamma} w, w^2, \ldots) = 0, \ \ 0 < \alpha, \beta, \gamma \leq 1, \tag{5}$$

where w is a function of $y_1, y_2, y_3, \ldots, y_r$ and t.

The below steps are used to solve Equation (5):

1. We start by transforming the variables $w(y_1, y_2, y_3, ldots, y_r)$ into $W(xi)$, where ξ is specified in a variety of ways. Equation (5) is changed by this transformation into a nonlinear ODE of the following form:

$$Q(W, W'W, W', \ldots) = 0, \tag{6}$$

   where W in (6) has derivatives with respect to ξ. Equation (6) may be integrated once or more times to obtain the constant(s) of integration.
2. Next, we assume that (6) has the following solution:

$$W(\xi) = \sum_{l=-m}^{m} d_l (Z(\xi))^l, \tag{7}$$

   where $d_l (l = -m, \ldots, 0, 1, 2, \ldots, m)$ are constants to be determined, and $Z(\xi)$ is the general solution of the following ODE:

$$Z'(\xi) = ln(A)(a + bZ(\xi) + c(Z(\xi))^2), \tag{8}$$

   where a, b and c are constants and $A \neq 0, 1$.
3. Establishing the homogeneous balance between the greatest nonlinear term and the highest-order derivative in (6) yields the positive integer m given in (7). More precisely the balance number can be estimated by using the given two formulas [33]:

$$D\left(\frac{d^k W}{d\xi^k}\right) = m + k \ \text{ and } \ D\left(W^j \left(\frac{d^k W}{d\xi^k}\right)^l\right) = mj + l(k+m),$$

   where D stands for degree of $W(\xi)$ as $D[W(\xi)] = m$ and j, k and l are positive integers.
4. Then, we put (7) into (6) or the equation that comes from integrating (6), and arrange all of the terms of $Z(\xi)$ in the same order. The subsequent polynomial's coefficients are then all set to zero, resulting in a system of algebraic equations for $d_l (l = -m, ..., 0, 1, 2, ..., m)$ and additional parameters.
5. To solve this set of algebraic equations, we use MAPLE.
6. The analytical solutions to (5) are then obtained by determining the unknown values and inserting them into (7) together with the $Z(\xi)$(solution of Equation (8)). Using the general solution of (8), we may produce the following families of solutions.

Family 1. *For $M < 0$ and $c \neq 0$,*

$$Z_1(\xi) = -\frac{b}{2c} + \frac{\sqrt{-M} \tan_A \left(1/2 \sqrt{-M} \xi\right)}{2c},$$

$$Z_2(\xi) = -\frac{b}{2c} - \frac{\sqrt{-M}\cot_A(1/2\sqrt{-M}\xi)}{2c},$$

$$Z_3(\xi) = -\frac{b}{2c} + \frac{\sqrt{-M}(\tan_A(\sqrt{-M}\xi) \pm (\sqrt{pq}\sec_A(\sqrt{-M}\xi)))}{2c},$$

$$Z_4(\xi) = -\frac{b}{2c} - \frac{\sqrt{-M}(\cot_A(\sqrt{-M}\xi) \pm (\sqrt{pq}\csc_A(\sqrt{-M}\xi)))}{2c},$$

and

$$Z_5(\xi) = -\frac{b}{2c} + \frac{\sqrt{-M}(\tan_A(1/4\sqrt{-M}\xi) - \cot_A(1/4\sqrt{-M}\xi))}{4c}.$$

Family 2. *For $M > 0$ and $c \neq 0$,*

$$Z_6(\xi) = -\frac{b}{2c} - \frac{\sqrt{M}\tanh_A\left(1/2\sqrt{M}\xi\right)}{2c},$$

$$Z_7(\xi) = -\frac{b}{2c} - \frac{\sqrt{M}\coth_A\left(1/2\sqrt{M}\xi\right)}{2c},$$

$$Z_8(\xi) = -\frac{b}{2c} - \frac{\sqrt{Z}\left(\tanh_A\left(\sqrt{M}\xi\right) \pm \left(\sqrt{pq}sech_A\left(\sqrt{M}\xi\right)\right)\right)}{2c},$$

$$Z_9(\xi) = -\frac{b}{2c} - \frac{\sqrt{M}\left(\coth_A\left(\sqrt{M}\xi\right) \pm \left(\sqrt{pq}csch_A\left(\sqrt{M}\xi\right)\right)\right)}{2c},$$

and

$$Z_{10}(\xi) = -\frac{b}{2c} - \frac{\sqrt{M}\left(\tanh_A\left(1/4\sqrt{M}\xi\right) - \coth_A\left(1/4\sqrt{M}\xi\right)\right)}{4c}.$$

Family 3. *For $ac > 0$ and $b = 0$,*

$$Z_{11}(\xi) = \sqrt{\frac{a}{c}}\tan_A(\sqrt{ac}\xi),$$

$$Z_{12}(\xi) = -\sqrt{\frac{a}{c}}\cot_A(\sqrt{ac}\xi),$$

$$Z_{13}(\xi) = \sqrt{\frac{a}{c}}(\tan_A(2\sqrt{ac}\xi) \pm (\sqrt{pq}\sec_A(2\sqrt{ac}\xi))),$$

$$Z_{14}(\xi) = -\sqrt{\frac{a}{c}}(\cot_A(2\sqrt{ac}\xi) \pm (\sqrt{pq}\csc_A(2\sqrt{ac}\xi))),$$

and

$$Z_{15}(\xi) = \frac{1}{2}\sqrt{\frac{a}{c}}(\tan_A(1/2\sqrt{ac}\xi) - \cot_A(1/2\sqrt{ac}\xi)).$$

Family 4. *For $ac < 0$ and $b = 0$, then*

$$Z_{16}(\xi) = -\sqrt{-\frac{a}{c}}\tanh_A\left(\sqrt{-ac}\xi\right),$$

$$Z_{17}(\xi) = -\sqrt{-\frac{a}{c}}\coth_A\left(\sqrt{-ac}\xi\right)$$

$$Z_{18}(\xi) = -\sqrt{-\frac{a}{c}}\left(\tanh_A\left(2\sqrt{-ac}\xi\right) \pm \left(i\sqrt{pq}sech_A\left(2\sqrt{-ac}\xi\right)\right)\right),$$

$$Z_{19}(\xi) = -\sqrt{-\frac{a}{c}}\left(\coth_A\left(2\sqrt{-ac}\xi\right) \pm \left(\sqrt{pq}csch_A\left(2\sqrt{-ac}\xi\right)\right)\right),$$

and

$$Z_{20}(\xi) = -\frac{1}{2}\sqrt{-\frac{a}{c}}\left(\tanh_A\left(1/2\sqrt{-ac}\xi\right) + \coth_A\left(1/2\sqrt{-ac}\xi\right)\right).$$

Family 5. *For $c = a$ and $b = 0$,*

$$Z_{21}(\xi) = \tan_A(a\xi),$$
$$Z_{22}(\xi) = -\cot_A(a\xi),$$
$$Z_{23}(\xi) = \tan_A(2a\xi) \pm (\sqrt{pq}\sec_A(2a\xi)),$$
$$Z_{24}(\xi) = -\cot_A(2a\xi) \pm (\sqrt{pq}\csc_A(2a\xi)),$$

and

$$Z_{25}(\xi) = \frac{1}{2}\tan_A(1/2\,a\xi) - 1/2\,\cot_A(1/2\,a\xi).$$

Family 6. *For $c = -a$ and $b = 0$,*

$$Z_{26}(\xi) = -\tanh_A(a\xi),$$
$$Z_{27}(\xi) = -\coth_A(a\xi),$$
$$Z_{28}(\xi) = -\tanh_A(2a\xi) \pm (i\sqrt{pq}sech_A(2a\xi)),$$
$$Z_{29}(\xi) = -\coth_A(2a\xi) \pm (\sqrt{pq}csch_A(2a\xi)),$$

and

$$Z_{30}(\xi) = -\frac{1}{2}\tanh_A(1/2\,a\xi) - 1/2\,\coth_A(1/2\,a\xi).$$

Family 7. *For $M = 0$,*

$$Z_{31}(\xi) = -2\,\frac{a(b\xi\ln(A)+2)}{b^2\xi\ln(A)}.$$

Family 8. *For $b = \lambda$, $a = n\lambda (n \neq 0)$ and $c = 0$,*

$$Z_{32}(\xi) = A^{\lambda\,\xi} - n.$$

Family 9. *For $b = c = 0$,*

$$Z_{33}(\xi) = a\xi\ln(A).$$

Family 10. *For $b = a = 0$,*

$$Z_{34}(\xi) = -\frac{1}{c\xi\ln(A)}.$$

Family 11. *For $a = 0$, $b \neq 0$ and $c \neq 0$,*

$$Z_{35}(\xi) = -\frac{pb}{c(\cosh_A(b\xi) - \sinh_A(b\xi) + p)},$$

and

$$Z_{36}(\xi) = -\frac{b(\cosh_A(b\xi) + \sinh_A(b\xi))}{c(\cosh_A(b\xi) + \sinh_A(b\xi) + q)}.$$

Family 12. *For $b = \lambda$, $c = n\lambda (n \neq 0)$ and $a = 0$,*

$$Z_{37}(\xi) = \frac{pA^{\lambda\,\xi}}{p - nqA^{\lambda\,\xi}}.$$

where $M = b^2 - 4ac$ and $p, q > 0$ and are referred to as deformation parameters. The generalized trigonometric and hyperbolic functions are described as follows:

$$\cos_A(\xi) = \frac{pA^{i\xi} + qA^{-i\xi}}{2}, \quad \sin_A(\xi) = \frac{pA^{i\xi} - qA^{-i\xi}}{2i},$$
$$\cot_A(\xi) = \frac{\cos_A(\xi)}{\sin_A(\xi)}, \quad \tan_A(\xi) = \frac{\sin_A(\xi)}{\cos_A(\xi)},$$
$$\csc_A(\xi) = \frac{1}{\sin_A(\xi)}, \quad \sec_A(\xi) = \frac{1}{\cos_A(\xi)}.$$

Similarly,

$$\cosh_A(\xi) = \frac{pA^{\xi} + qA^{-\xi}}{2}, \quad \sinh_A(\xi) = \frac{pA^{\xi} - qA^{-\xi}}{2},$$
$$\coth_A(\xi) = \frac{\cosh_A(\xi)}{\sinh_A(\xi)}, \quad \tanh_A(\xi) = \frac{\sinh_A(\xi)}{\cosh_A(\xi)},$$
$$\operatorname{csch}_A(\xi) = \frac{1}{\sinh_A(\xi)}, \quad \operatorname{sech}_A(\xi) = \frac{1}{\cosh_A(\xi)}.$$

3. Execution of the Approach

In the present section, we use the suggested method for solving the fractional coupled Higgs system (1). We offer a transformation so that this approach may be expanded to solve (1):

$$u(x,t) = U(\xi)e^{i\theta}, \quad v(x,t) = V(\xi),$$
$$\text{where} \quad \xi = \frac{x^{\delta}}{\Gamma(1+\delta)} + \frac{kt^{\gamma}}{\Gamma(1+\gamma)}, \quad \theta = \frac{a_1 x^{\delta}}{\Gamma(1+\delta)} + \frac{b_1 t^{\gamma}}{\Gamma(1+\gamma)}, \tag{9}$$

in (9), the soliton's phase component is denoted by $\theta(x,t)$, its wavenumber is denoted by b_1, and its velocity is denoted by a_1. When (9) is substituted into (1), we have

$$\begin{aligned} &(k^2-1)U'' + (a_1^2 - b_1^2)U - 2UV + U^3 = 0, \\ &(k^2+1)V'' - 2(U')^2 - 2UU'' = 0. \end{aligned} \tag{10}$$

Ignoring the integration constant and integrating the second equation in (10), we get

$$V(1+k^2) = U^2. \tag{11}$$

Putting (11) into the first equation of (10) and integrating gives us

$$(k^4-1)U'' + (a_1^2 - b_1^2)(k^2+1)U + (k^2-1)U^3 = 0, \tag{12}$$

where prime represents differentiation with respect to ξ. $m = 1$ is obtained by balancing the terms of U'' and U^3 in (12).

Implementation of mEDAM to the Problem

To solve the NODE in (12) generated from the fractional coupled Higgs system using mEDAM, put $m = 1$ in (7). Thus, we have

$$U(\xi) = \sum_{i=-1}^{1} d_i (Z(\xi))^i = d_{-1}(Z(\xi))^{-1} + d_0 + d_1 (Z(\xi))^1, \tag{13}$$

where d_{-1}, d_0 and d_1 are coefficients that will be determined.

With the help of (8), we insert (13) into (12), which creates a polynomial in $Z(\xi)$ by collecting the terms with the same power of $Z(\xi)$. By equating the coefficients of the polynomial to zero, we get a system of nonlinear algebraic equations. We use Maple to solve the system, leading to the identification of the following two distinct cases of solutions:

Case 1:

$$d_1 = 2\sqrt{\frac{-M(\ln(A))^2 - \Omega}{M}}c, d_{-1} = 0, d_0 = \sqrt{\frac{-M(\ln(A))^2 - \Omega}{M}}b, k = \sqrt{\frac{M(\ln(A))^2 + 2\Omega}{M(\ln(A))^2}}. \tag{14}$$

Case 2:

$$d_1 = 0, d_{-1} = 2\sqrt{\frac{-M(\ln(A))^2 - \Omega}{M}}a, d_0 = \sqrt{\frac{-M(\ln(A))^2 - \Omega}{M}}b, k = \sqrt{\frac{M(\ln(A))^2 + 2\Omega}{M(\ln(A))^2}}, \tag{15}$$

where $\Omega = a_1^2 - b_1^2$ and $M = b^2 - 4ac$.

Assuming Case 1, we get the following families of solutions:

Family 13. *When $M < 0$ and $a, b, c \neq 0$, then the following set of equations presents the corresponding family of solitary wave solutions:*

$$U_1(x,t) = \sqrt{-\frac{Z(\ln(A))^2 + \Omega}{Z}}\sqrt{-Z}\tan_A\left(1/2\sqrt{-Z}\xi\right). \tag{16}$$

Using (9) and (11), the subsequent solitary wave solutions are obtained for (1) as

$$u_1(x,t) = e^{i\theta}\left(\sqrt{-\frac{Z(\ln(A))^2 + \Omega}{Z}}\sqrt{-Z}\tan_A\left(1/2\sqrt{-Z}\xi\right)\right), \tag{17}$$

and

$$v_1(x,t) = \frac{1}{1+k^2}\left(\sqrt{-\frac{Z(\ln(A))^2 + \Omega}{Z}}\sqrt{-Z}\tan_A\left(1/2\sqrt{-Z}\xi\right)\right)^2, \tag{18}$$

$$U_2(x,t) = -\sqrt{-\frac{M(\ln(A))^2 + \Omega}{M}}\sqrt{-M}\cot_A\left(1/2\sqrt{-M}\xi\right). \tag{19}$$

Utilizing (9) and (11), the subsequent solitary wave solutions are obtained for (1) as

$$u_2(x,t) = e^{i\theta}\left(-\sqrt{-\frac{M(\ln(A))^2 + \Omega}{M}}\sqrt{-M}\cot_A\left(1/2\sqrt{-M}\xi\right)\right), \tag{20}$$

and

$$v_2(x,t) = \frac{1}{1+k^2}\left(-\sqrt{-\frac{M(\ln(A))^2 + \Omega}{M}}\sqrt{-M}\cot_A\left(1/2\sqrt{-M}\xi\right)\right)^2, \tag{21}$$

$$U_3(x,t) = \frac{\sqrt{M(\ln(A))^2 + \Omega}(\sin_A(\sqrt{-M}\xi) + \sqrt{pq})}{\cos_A(\sqrt{-M}\xi)}. \tag{22}$$

Using (9) and (11), the subsequent solitary wave solutions are obtained for (1) as

$$u_3(x,t) = e^{i\theta}\left(\frac{\sqrt{M(\ln(A))^2+\Omega}\left(\sin_A\left(\sqrt{-M}\xi\right)+\sqrt{pq}\right)}{\cos_A\left(\sqrt{-M}\xi\right)}\right), \tag{23}$$

and

$$v_3(x,t) = \frac{1}{1+k^2}\left(\frac{\sqrt{M(\ln(A))^2+\Omega}\left(\sin_A\left(\sqrt{-M}\xi\right)+\sqrt{pq}\right)}{\cos_A\left(\sqrt{-M}\xi\right)}\right)^2, \tag{24}$$

$$U_4(x,t) = -\frac{\sqrt{M(\ln(A))^2+\Omega}\left(\cos_A\left(\sqrt{-M}\xi\right)+\sqrt{pq}\right)}{\sin_A\left(\sqrt{-M}\xi\right)}. \tag{25}$$

Using (9) and (11), the subsequent solitary wave solutions are obtained for (1) as

$$u_4(x,t) = e^{i\theta}\left(-\frac{\sqrt{M(\ln(A))^2+\Omega}\left(\cos_A\left(\sqrt{-M}\xi\right)+\sqrt{pq}\right)}{\sin_A\left(\sqrt{-M}\xi\right)}\right), \tag{26}$$

and

$$v_4(x,t) = \frac{1}{1+k^2}\left(-\frac{\sqrt{M(\ln(A))^2+\Omega}\left(\cos_A\left(\sqrt{-M}\xi\right)+\sqrt{pq}\right)}{\sin_A\left(\sqrt{-M}\xi\right)}\right)^2, \tag{27}$$

and

$$U_5(x,t) = -1/2\,\frac{\sqrt{M(\ln(A))^2+\Omega}\left(-1+2\left(\cos_A\left(1/4\sqrt{-M}\xi\right)\right)^2\right)}{\cos_A\left(1/4\sqrt{-M}\xi\right)\sin_A\left(1/4\sqrt{-M}\xi\right)}. \tag{28}$$

Using (9) and (11), the subsequent solitary wave solutions are obtained for (1) as

$$u_5(x,t) = e^{i\theta}\left(-1/2\,\frac{\sqrt{M(\ln(A))^2+\Omega}\left(-1+2\left(\cos_A\left(1/4\sqrt{-M}\xi\right)\right)^2\right)}{\cos_A\left(1/4\sqrt{-M}\xi\right)\sin_A\left(1/4\sqrt{-M}\xi\right)}\right), \tag{29}$$

and

$$v_5(x,t) = \frac{1}{1+k^2}\left(-1/2\,\frac{\sqrt{M(\ln(A))^2+\Omega}\left(-1+2\left(\cos_A\left(1/4\sqrt{-M}\xi\right)\right)^2\right)}{\cos_A\left(1/4\sqrt{-M}\xi\right)\sin_A\left(1/4\sqrt{-M}\xi\right)}\right)^2. \tag{30}$$

Family 14. *For $M > 0$ and $a, b, c \neq 0$, then the following set of equations presents the corresponding family of solitary wave solutions:*

$$U_6(x,t) = -\sqrt{M(\ln(A))^2+\Omega}\tanh_A\left(1/2\sqrt{M}\xi\right). \tag{31}$$

Utilizing (9) and (11), the subsequent solitary wave solutions are obtained for (1) as

$$u_6(x,t) = e^{i\theta}\left(-\sqrt{M(\ln(A))^2+\Omega}\tanh_A\left(1/2\sqrt{M}\xi\right)\right), \tag{32}$$

and

$$v_6(x,t) = \frac{1}{1+k^2}\left(-\sqrt{M(\ln(A))^2+\Omega}\tanh_A\left(1/2\sqrt{M}\xi\right)\right)^2, \tag{33}$$

$$U_7(x,t) = -\sqrt{M(\ln(A))^2+\Omega}\coth_A\left(1/2\sqrt{M}\xi\right). \tag{34}$$

Utilizing (9) and (11), the subsequent solitary wave solutions are obtained for (1) as

$$u_7(x,t) = e^{i\theta}\left(-\sqrt{M(\ln(A))^2+\Omega}\coth_A\left(1/2\sqrt{M}\xi\right)\right), \tag{35}$$

and

$$v_7(x,t) = \frac{1}{1+k^2}\left(-\sqrt{M(\ln(A))^2+\Omega}\coth_A\left(1/2\sqrt{M}\xi\right)\right)^2, \tag{36}$$

$$U_8(x,t) = -\frac{\sqrt{M(\ln(A))^2+\Omega}\left(\sinh_A\left(\sqrt{M}\xi\right)+\sqrt{pq}\right)}{\cosh_A\left(\sqrt{M}\xi\right)}. \tag{37}$$

Utilizing (9) and (11), the subsequent solitary wave solutions are obtained for (1) as

$$u_8(x,t) = e^{i\theta}\left(-\frac{\sqrt{M(\ln(A))^2+\Omega}\left(\sinh_A\left(\sqrt{M}\xi\right)+\sqrt{pq}\right)}{\cosh_A\left(\sqrt{M}\xi\right)}\right), \tag{38}$$

and

$$v_8(x,t) = \frac{1}{1+k^2}\left(-\frac{\sqrt{M(\ln(A))^2+\Omega}\left(\sinh_A\left(\sqrt{M}\xi\right)+\sqrt{pq}\right)}{\cosh_A\left(\sqrt{M}\xi\right)}\right)^2, \tag{39}$$

$$U_9(x,t) = -\frac{\sqrt{M(\ln(A))^2+\Omega}\left(\cosh_A\left(\sqrt{M}\xi\right)+\sqrt{pq}\right)}{\sinh_A\left(\sqrt{M}\xi\right)}. \tag{40}$$

Utilizing (9) and (11), the subsequent solitary wave solutions are obtained for (1) as

$$u_9(x,t) = e^{i\theta}\left(-\frac{\sqrt{M(\ln(A))^2+\Omega}\left(\cosh_A\left(\sqrt{M}\xi\right)+\sqrt{pq}\right)}{\sinh_A\left(\sqrt{M}\xi\right)}\right), \tag{41}$$

and

$$v_9(x,t) = \frac{1}{1+k^2}\left(-\frac{\sqrt{M(\ln(A))^2+\Omega}\left(\cosh_A\left(\sqrt{M}\xi\right)+\sqrt{pq}\right)}{\sinh_A\left(\sqrt{M}\xi\right)}\right)^2, \tag{42}$$

and

$$U_{10}(x,t) = 1/2\,\frac{\sqrt{M(\ln(A))^2+\Omega}}{\cosh_A\left(1/4\sqrt{M}\xi\right)\sinh_A\left(1/4\sqrt{M}\xi\right)}. \tag{43}$$

Utilizing (9) and (11), the subsequent solitary wave solutions are obtained for (1) as

$$u_{10}(x,t) = e^{i\theta}\left(1/2\,\frac{\sqrt{M(\ln(A))^2+\Omega}}{\cosh_A\left(1/4\sqrt{M}\xi\right)\sinh_A\left(1/4\sqrt{M}\xi\right)}\right), \tag{44}$$

and

$$v_{10}(x,t) = \frac{1}{1+k^2}\left(1/2\,\frac{\sqrt{M(\ln(A))^2+\Omega}}{\cosh_A\left(1/4\sqrt{M}\xi\right)\sinh_A\left(1/4\sqrt{M}\xi\right)}\right)^2. \tag{45}$$

Family 15. *For $ca > 0$ and $b = 0$, the following set of equations presents the corresponding family of solitary wave solutions:*

$$U_{11}(x,t) = \sqrt{-(4\,(\ln(A))^2ca - \Omega)}\,\tan_A(\sqrt{ca}\xi). \tag{46}$$

Utilizing (9) and (11), the subsequent solitary wave solutions are obtained for (1) as

$$u_{11}(x,t) = e^{i\theta}(\sqrt{-(4\,(\ln(A))^2ca - \Omega)}\,\tan_A(\sqrt{ca}\xi)), \tag{47}$$

and

$$v_{11}(x,t) = \frac{1}{1+k^2}(\sqrt{-(4\,(\ln(A))^2ca - \Omega)}\,\tan_A(\sqrt{ca}\xi))^2, \tag{48}$$

$$U_{12}(x,t) = -\sqrt{-(4\,(\ln(A))^2ca - \Omega)}\,\cot_A(\sqrt{ca}\xi). \tag{49}$$

Utilizing (9) and (11), the subsequent solitary wave solutions are obtained for (1) as

$$u_{12}(x,t) = e^{i\theta}(-\sqrt{-(4\,(\ln(A))^2ca - \Omega)}\,\cot_A(\sqrt{ca}\xi)), \tag{50}$$

and

$$v_{12}(x,t) = \frac{1}{1+k^2}(-\sqrt{-(4\,(\ln(A))^2ca - \Omega)}\,\cot_A(\sqrt{ca}\xi))^2, \tag{51}$$

$$\begin{aligned} U_{13}(x,t) = {} & \sqrt{-(4\,(\ln(A))^2ca - \Omega)}\times \\ & (\tan_A(2\sqrt{ca}\xi) \pm (\sqrt{pq}\sec_A(2\sqrt{ca}\xi))). \end{aligned} \tag{52}$$

Utilizing (9) and (11), the subsequent solitary wave solutions are obtained for (1) as

$$\begin{aligned} u_{13}(x,t) = e^{i\theta}\Big(& \sqrt{-(4\,(\ln(A))^2ca - \Omega)}\times \\ & (\tan_A(2\sqrt{ca}\xi) \pm (\sqrt{pq}\sec_A(2\sqrt{ca}\xi)))\Big), \end{aligned} \tag{53}$$

and

$$\begin{aligned} v_{13}(x,t) = \frac{1}{1+k^2}\Big(& \sqrt{-(4\,(\ln(A))^2ca - \Omega)}\times \\ & (\tan_A(2\sqrt{ca}\xi) \pm (\sqrt{pq}\sec_A(2\sqrt{ca}\xi)))\Big)^2, \end{aligned} \tag{54}$$

$$U_{14}(x,t) = -\sqrt{-(4\,(\ln(A))^2 ca - \Omega)}\times \\ \left(\cot_A(2\sqrt{ca}\xi) \pm (\sqrt{pq}\csc_A(2\sqrt{ca}\xi))\right). \tag{55}$$

Utilizing (9) and (11), the subsequent solitary wave solutions are obtained for (1) as

$$u_{14}(x,t) = e^{i\theta}\Bigg(-\sqrt{-(4\,(\ln(A))^2 ca - \Omega)}\times \\ \left(\cot_A(2\sqrt{ca}\xi) \pm (\sqrt{pq}\csc_A(2\sqrt{ca}\xi))\right)\Bigg), \tag{56}$$

and

$$v_{14}(x,t) = \frac{1}{1+k^2}\Bigg(-\sqrt{-(4\,(\ln(A))^2 ca - \Omega)}\times \\ \left(\cot_A(2\sqrt{ca}\xi) \pm (\sqrt{pq}\csc_A(2\sqrt{ca}\xi))\right)\Bigg)^2, \tag{57}$$

and

$$U_{15}(x,t) = \frac{\sqrt{-(4\,(\ln(A))^2 ca - \Omega)}}{2}\times \\ \left(\tan_A\left(\frac{\sqrt{ca}\xi}{2}\right) - \cot_A\left(\frac{\sqrt{ca}\xi}{2}\right)\right). \tag{58}$$

Utilizing (9) and (11), the subsequent solitary wave solutions are obtained for (1) as

$$u_{15}(x,t) = e^{i\theta}\Bigg(\frac{\sqrt{-(4\,(\ln(A))^2 ca - \Omega)}}{2}\times \\ \left(\tan_A\left(\frac{\sqrt{ca}\xi}{2}\right) - \cot_A\left(\frac{\sqrt{ca}\xi}{2}\right)\right)\Bigg), \tag{59}$$

and

$$v_{15}(x,t) = \frac{1}{1+k^2}\Bigg(\frac{\sqrt{-(4\,(\ln(A))^2 ca - \Omega)}}{2}\times \\ \left(\tan_A\left(\frac{\sqrt{ca}\xi}{2}\right) - \cot_A\left(\frac{\sqrt{ca}\xi}{2}\right)\right)\Bigg)^2. \tag{60}$$

Family 16. *For $ca < 0$ and $b = 0$, the following set of equations presents the corresponding family of solitary wave solutions:*

$$U_{16}(x,t) = -\sqrt{4\,(\ln(A))^2 ca - \Omega}\tanh_A\left(\sqrt{-ca}\xi\right). \tag{61}$$

As a result of utilizing (9) and (11), the subsequent solitary wave solutions are obtained for (1):

$$u_{16}(x,t) = e^{i\theta}\left(-\sqrt{4\,(\ln(A))^2 ca - \Omega}\tanh_A\left(\sqrt{-ca}\xi\right)\right), \tag{62}$$

and

$$v_{16}(x,t) = \frac{1}{1+k^2}\left(-\sqrt{4\,(\ln(A))^2 ca - \Omega}\tanh_A\left(\sqrt{-ca}\xi\right)\right)^2, \tag{63}$$

$$U_{17}(x,t) = -\sqrt{4\,(\ln(A))^2 ca - \Omega}\coth_A\left(\sqrt{-ca}\xi\right). \tag{64}$$

As a result of utilizing (9) and (11), the subsequent solitary wave solutions are obtained for (1):

$$u_{17}(x,t) = e^{i\theta}\left(- \sqrt{4\,(\ln(A))^2 ca - \Omega}\coth_A\left(\sqrt{-ca}\xi\right)\right), \tag{65}$$

and

$$v_{17}(x,t) = \frac{1}{1+k^2}\left(- \sqrt{4\,(\ln(A))^2 ca - \Omega}\coth_A\left(\sqrt{-ca}\xi\right)\right)^2, \tag{66}$$

$$\begin{aligned} U_{18}(x,t) = -\sqrt{4\,(\ln(A))^2 ca - \Omega}\times \\ \left(\tanh_A\left(2\sqrt{-ca}\xi\right) \pm \left(i\sqrt{pq}sech_A\left(2\sqrt{-ca}\xi\right)\right)\right). \end{aligned} \tag{67}$$

As a result of utilizing (9) and (11), the subsequent solitary wave solutions are obtained for (1):

$$\begin{aligned} u_{18}(x,t) = e^{i\theta}\bigg(- \sqrt{4\,(\ln(A))^2 ca - \Omega}\times \\ \left(\tanh_A\left(2\sqrt{-ca}\xi\right) \pm \left(i\sqrt{pq}sech_A\left(2\sqrt{-ca}\xi\right)\right)\right)\bigg), \end{aligned} \tag{68}$$

and

$$\begin{aligned} v_{18}(x,t) = \frac{1}{1+k^2}\bigg(- \sqrt{4\,(\ln(A))^2 ca - \Omega}\times \\ \left(\tanh_A\left(2\sqrt{-ca}\xi\right) \pm \left(i\sqrt{pq}sech_A\left(2\sqrt{-ca}\xi\right)\right)\right)\bigg)^2, \end{aligned} \tag{69}$$

$$\begin{aligned} U_{19}(x,t) = -\sqrt{4\,(\ln(A))^2 ca - \Omega}\times \\ \left(\coth_A\left(2\sqrt{-ca}\xi\right) \pm \left(\sqrt{pq}csch_A\left(2\sqrt{-ca}\xi\right)\right)\right). \end{aligned} \tag{70}$$

As a result of utilizing (9) and (11), the subsequent solitary wave solutions are obtained for (1):

$$\begin{aligned} u_{19}(x,t) = e^{i\theta}\bigg(- \sqrt{4\,(\ln(A))^2 ca - \Omega}\times \\ \left(\coth_A\left(2\sqrt{-ca}\xi\right) \pm \left(\sqrt{pq}csch_A\left(2\sqrt{-ca}\xi\right)\right)\right)\bigg), \end{aligned} \tag{71}$$

and

$$\begin{aligned} v_{19}(x,t) = \frac{1}{1+k^2}\bigg(- \sqrt{4\,(\ln(A))^2 ca - \Omega}\times \\ \left(\coth_A\left(2\sqrt{-ca}\xi\right) \pm \left(\sqrt{pq}csch_A\left(2\sqrt{-ca}\xi\right)\right)\right)\bigg)^2, \end{aligned} \tag{72}$$

and

$$U_{20}(x,t) = -\sqrt{4\,(\ln(A))^2 ca - \Omega}\left(\tanh_A\left(\sqrt{-ca}\xi\right) + \coth_A\left(\sqrt{-ca}\xi\right)\right). \tag{73}$$

As a result of utilizing (9) and (11), the subsequent solitary wave solutions are obtained for (1):

$$u_{20}(x,t) = e^{i\theta}\Big(-\sqrt{4\,(\ln(A))^2 ca - \Omega}\times \Big(\tanh_A\big(\sqrt{-ca}\xi\big) + \coth_A\big(\sqrt{-ca}\xi\big)\Big)\Big), \tag{74}$$

and

$$v_{20}(x,t) = \frac{1}{1+k^2}\Big(-\sqrt{4\,(\ln(A))^2 ca - \Omega}\times \Big(\tanh_A\big(\sqrt{-ca}\xi\big) + \coth_A\big(\sqrt{-ca}\xi\big)\Big)\Big)^2. \tag{75}$$

Family 17. *For $c = a$ and $b = 0$, the following set of equations presents the corresponding family of solitary wave solutions:*

$$U_{21}(x,t) = \sqrt{-(4\,(\ln(A))^2 c^2 - \Omega)}\tan_A(c\xi). \tag{76}$$

As a result of utilizing (9) and (11), the subsequent solitary wave solutions are obtained for (1):

$$u_{21}(x,t) = e^{i\theta}(\sqrt{-(4\,(\ln(A))^2 c^2 - \Omega)}\tan_A(c\xi)), \tag{77}$$

and

$$v_{21}(x,t) = \frac{1}{1+k^2}(\sqrt{-(4\,(\ln(A))^2 c^2 - \Omega)}\tan_A(c\xi))^2, \tag{78}$$

$$U_{22}(x,t) = -\sqrt{-(4\,(\ln(A))^2 c^2 - \Omega)}\cot_A(c\xi). \tag{79}$$

As a result of utilizing (9) and (11), the subsequent solitary wave solutions are obtained for (1):

$$u_{22}(x,t) = e^{i\theta}(-\sqrt{-(4\,(\ln(A))^2 c^2 - \Omega)}\cot_A(c\xi)), \tag{80}$$

and

$$v_{22}(x,t) = \frac{1}{1+k^2}(-\sqrt{-(4\,(\ln(A))^2 c^2 - \Omega)}\cot_A(c\xi))^2, \tag{81}$$

$$U_{23}(x,t) = \sqrt{-(4\,(\ln(A))^2 c^2 - \Omega)}(\tan_A(2\,c\xi) \pm (\sqrt{pq}\sec_A(2\,c\xi))). \tag{82}$$

As a result of utilizing (9) and (11), the subsequent solitary wave solutions are obtained for (1):

$$u_{23}(x,t) = e^{i\theta}\Big(\sqrt{-(4\,(\ln(A))^2 c^2 - \Omega)}\times (\tan_A(2\,c\xi) \pm (\sqrt{pq}\sec_A(2\,c\xi)))\Big), \tag{83}$$

and

$$v_{23}(x,t) = \frac{1}{1+k^2}\Big(\sqrt{-(4\,(\ln(A))^2c^2 - \Omega)}\times \\ (\tan_A(2\,c\xi) \pm (\sqrt{pq}\sec_A(2\,c\xi)))\Big)^2, \tag{84}$$

$$U_{24}(x,t) = \sqrt{-(4\,(\ln(A))^2c^2 - \Omega)}\times \\ (-\cot_A(2\,c\xi) \mp (\sqrt{pq}\csc_A(2\,c\xi))). \tag{85}$$

Utilizing (9) and (11), the subsequent solitary wave solutions are obtained for (1) as

$$u_{24}(x,t) = e^{i\theta}\Big(\sqrt{-(4\,(\ln(A))^2c^2 - \Omega)}\times \\ (-\cot_A(2\,c\xi) \mp (\sqrt{pq}\csc_A(2\,c\xi)))\Big), \tag{86}$$

and

$$v_{24}(x,t) = \frac{1}{1+k^2}\Big(\sqrt{-(4\,(\ln(A))^2c^2 - \Omega)}\times \\ (-\cot_A(2\,c\xi) \mp (\sqrt{pq}\csc_A(2\,c\xi)))\Big)^2, \tag{87}$$

and

$$U_{25}(x,t) = \sqrt{-\left(4\,(\ln(A))^2c^2 - \Omega\right)}\left(\frac{1}{2}\left(\tan_A\left(\frac{c\xi}{2}\right) - \cot_A\left(\frac{c\xi}{2}\right)\right)\right). \tag{88}$$

As a result of utilizing (9) and (11), the subsequent solitary wave solutions are obtained for (1):

$$u_{25}(x,t) = e^{i\theta}\Big(\sqrt{-(4\,(\ln(A))^2c^2 - \Omega)}\times \\ \left(\frac{1}{2}(\tan_A\left(\frac{c\xi}{2}\right) - \cot_A\left(\frac{c\xi}{2}\right))\right)\Big), \tag{89}$$

and

$$v_{25}(x,t) = \frac{1}{1+k^2}\Big(\sqrt{-(4\,(\ln(A))^2c^2 - \Omega)}\times \\ \left(\frac{1}{2}(\tan_A\left(\frac{c\xi}{2}\right) - \cot_A\left(\frac{c\xi}{2}\right))\right)\Big)^2. \tag{90}$$

Family 18. *For $c = -a$ and $b = 0$, the following set of equations presents the corresponding family of solitary wave solutions:*

$$U_{26}(x,t) = -\sqrt{-4\,(\ln(A))^2c^2 - \Omega}\,\tanh_A(c\xi). \tag{91}$$

As a result of utilizing (9) and (11), the subsequent solitary wave solutions are obtained for (1):

$$u_{26}(x,t) = e^{i\theta}(-\sqrt{-4\,(\ln(A))^2c^2 - \Omega}\,\tanh_A(c\xi)), \tag{92}$$

and

$$v_{26}(x,t) = \frac{1}{1+k^2}(-\sqrt{-4\,(\ln(A))^2c^2 - \Omega}\tanh_A(c\xi))^2, \tag{93}$$

$$U_{27}(x,t) = -\sqrt{-4\,(\ln(A))^2c^2 - \Omega}\coth_A(c\xi). \tag{94}$$

As a result of utilizing (9) and (11), the subsequent solitary wave solutions are obtained for (1):

$$u_{27}(x,t) = e^{i\theta}\Big(-\sqrt{-4\,(\ln(A))^2c^2 - \Omega}\coth_A(c\xi)\Big), \tag{95}$$

and

$$v_{27}(x,t) = \frac{1}{1+k^2}\Big(-\sqrt{-4\,(\ln(A))^2c^2 - \Omega}\coth_A(c\xi)\Big)^2, \tag{96}$$

$$U_{28}(x,t) = \sqrt{-(2c\ln(A))^2 - \Omega}(-\tanh_A(2\,c\xi) \mp (i\sqrt{pq}sech_A(2\,c\xi))). \tag{97}$$

As a result of utilizing (9) and (11), the subsequent solitary wave solutions are obtained for (1):

$$u_{28}(x,t) = e^{i\theta}\Big(\sqrt{-(2c\ln(A))^2 - \Omega} \\ (-\tanh_A(2\,c\xi) \mp (i\sqrt{pq}sech_A(2\,c\xi)))\Big), \tag{98}$$

and

$$v_{28}(x,t) = \frac{1}{1+k^2}\Big(\sqrt{-(2c\ln(A))^2 - \Omega}\times \\ (-\tanh_A(2\,c\xi) \mp (i\sqrt{pq}sech_A(2\,c\xi)))\Big)^2, \tag{99}$$

$$U_{29}(x,t) = \sqrt{-(2c\ln(A))^2 - \Omega}(-\coth_A(2\,c\xi) \mp (\sqrt{pq}csch_A(2\,c\xi))). \tag{100}$$

As a result of utilizing (9) and (11), the subsequent solitary wave solutions are obtained for (1):

$$u_{29}(x,t) = e^{i\theta}\Big(\sqrt{-(2c\ln(A))^2 - \Omega}\times \\ (-\coth_A(2\,c\xi) \mp (\sqrt{pq}csch_A(2\,c\xi)))\Big), \tag{101}$$

and

$$v_{29}(x,t) = \frac{1}{1+k^2}\Big(\sqrt{-(2c\ln(A))^2 - \Omega}\times \\ (-\coth_A(2\,c\xi) \mp (\sqrt{pq}csch_A(2\,c\xi)))\Big)^2, \tag{102}$$

and

$$U_{30}(x,t) = \sqrt{-(2c\ln(A))^2 - \Omega}\left(-\frac{1}{2}\left(\tanh_A\left(\frac{c\xi}{2}\right) + \coth_A\left(\frac{c\xi}{2}\right)\right)\right). \tag{103}$$

As a result of utilizing (9) and (11), the subsequent solitary wave solutions are obtained for (1):

$$\begin{aligned} u_{30}(x,t) = e^{i\theta}\Bigg(&\sqrt{-(2c\ln(A))^2 - \Omega}\times \\ &\left(-\frac{1}{2}(\tanh_A\left(\frac{c\xi}{2}\right) + \coth_A\left(\frac{c\xi}{2}\right))\right)\Bigg), \end{aligned} \tag{104}$$

and

$$\begin{aligned} v_{30}(x,t) = \frac{1}{1+k^2}\Bigg(&\sqrt{-(2c\ln(A))^2 - \Omega}\times \\ &\left(-\frac{1}{2}(\tanh_A\left(\frac{c\xi}{2}\right) + \coth_A\left(\frac{c\xi}{2}\right))\right)\Bigg)^2. \end{aligned} \tag{105}$$

Family 19. *For $a = 0$, $b \neq 0$ and $c \neq 0$, the following set of equations presents the corresponding family of solitary wave solutions:*

$$\begin{aligned} U_{31}(x,t) = &\sqrt{-(\ln(A))^2b^2 - \Omega} \\ &- 2\sqrt{-(\ln(A))^2b^2 - \Omega}p(\cosh_A(b\xi) - \sinh_A(b\xi) + p)^{-1}. \end{aligned} \tag{106}$$

As a result of utilizing (9) and (11), the subsequent solitary wave solutions are obtained for (1):

$$\begin{aligned} u_{31}(x,t) = e^{i\theta}\Bigg(&\sqrt{-(\ln(A))^2b^2 - \Omega} \\ &- 2\sqrt{-(\ln(A))^2b^2 - \Omega}p(\cosh_A(b\xi) - \sinh_A(b\xi) + p)^{-1}\Bigg), \end{aligned} \tag{107}$$

and

$$\begin{aligned} v_{31}(x,t) = \frac{1}{1+k^2}\Bigg(&\sqrt{-(\ln(A))^2b^2 - \Omega} \\ &- 2\sqrt{-(\ln(A))^2b^2 - \Omega}p(\cosh_A(b\xi) - \sinh_A(b\xi) + p)^{-1}\Bigg)^2, \end{aligned} \tag{108}$$

and

$$\begin{aligned} U_{32}(x,t) = &\sqrt{-(\ln(A))^2b^2 - \Omega} \\ &- 2\sqrt{-(\ln(A))^2b^2 - \Omega}\frac{(\cosh_A(b\xi) + \sinh_A(b\xi))}{(\cosh_A(b\xi) + \sinh_A(b\xi) + q)}. \end{aligned} \tag{109}$$

As a result of utilizing (9) and (11), the subsequent solitary wave solutions are obtained for (1):

$$\begin{aligned} u_{32}(x,t) = e^{i\theta}\Bigg(&\sqrt{-(\ln(A))^2b^2 - \Omega} \\ &- 2\sqrt{-(\ln(A))^2b^2 - \Omega}\frac{(\cosh_A(b\xi) + \sinh_A(b\xi))}{(\cosh_A(b\xi) + \sinh_A(b\xi) + q)}\Bigg), \end{aligned} \tag{110}$$

and

$$v_{32}(x,t) = \frac{1}{1+k^2}\left(\sqrt{-(\ln(A))^2 b^2 - \Omega} - 2\sqrt{-(\ln(A))^2 b^2 - \Omega}\frac{(\cosh_A(b\xi) + \sinh_A(b\xi))}{(\cosh_A(b\xi) + \sinh_A(b\xi) + q)}\right)^2. \tag{111}$$

Family 20. *For $b = \lambda$, $c = n\lambda (n \neq 0)$ and $a = 0$, the following set of equations presents the corresponding family of solitary wave solutions:*

$$U_{33}(x,t) = \sqrt{-(\ln(A))^2\lambda^2 - \Omega} + 2\sqrt{-(\ln(A))^2\lambda^2 - \Omega}npA^{\lambda\xi}\left(p - nqA^{\lambda\xi}\right)^{-1}. \tag{112}$$

As a result of utilizing (9) and (11), the subsequent solitary wave solutions are obtained for (1):

$$u_{33}(x,t) = e^{i\theta}\left(\sqrt{-(\ln(A))^2\lambda^2 - \Omega} + 2\sqrt{-(\ln(A))^2\lambda^2 - \Omega}npA^{\lambda\xi}\left(p - nqA^{\lambda\xi}\right)^{-1}\right), \tag{113}$$

and

$$v_{33}(x,t) = \frac{1}{1+k^2}\left(\sqrt{-(\ln(A))^2\lambda^2 - \Omega} + 2\sqrt{-(\ln(A))^2\lambda^2 - \Omega}npA^{\lambda\xi}\left(p - nqA^{\lambda\xi}\right)^{-1}\right)^2, \tag{114}$$

where $\xi = \frac{x^\delta}{\Gamma(1+\delta)} + \sqrt{\frac{b^2(\ln(A))^2 + 2{a_1}^2 - 4c(\ln(A))^2 a - 2{b_1}^2}{(b^2 - 4ac)(\ln(A))^2}}\frac{t^\gamma}{\Gamma(1+\gamma)}$ *and* $\theta = \frac{a_1 x^\delta}{\Gamma(1+\delta)} + \frac{b_1 t^\gamma}{\Gamma(1+\gamma)}$.

Now, assuming Case 2, we get the following families of solitary wave solutions.

Family 21. *When $M < 0$ and $a, b, c \neq 0$, then the following set of equations presents the corresponding family of solitary wave solutions:*

$$U_{34}(x,t) = \frac{\sqrt{M(\ln(A))^2 + \Omega}(\sqrt{-M} + b\tan_A(1/2\sqrt{-M}\xi))}{-b + \sqrt{-M}\tan_A(1/2\sqrt{-M}\xi)} \tag{115}$$

As a result of utilizing (9) and (11), the subsequent solitary wave solutions are obtained for (1):

$$u_{34}(x,t) = e^{i\theta}\left(\frac{\sqrt{M(\ln(A))^2 + \Omega}(\sqrt{-M} + b\tan_A(1/2\sqrt{-M}\xi))}{-b + \sqrt{-M}\tan_A(1/2\sqrt{-M}\xi)}\right), \tag{116}$$

and

$$v_{34}(x,t) = \frac{1}{1+k^2}\left(\frac{\sqrt{M(\ln(A))^2 + \Omega}(\sqrt{-M} + b\tan_A(1/2\sqrt{-M}\xi))}{-b + \sqrt{-M}\tan_A(1/2\sqrt{-M}\xi)}\right)^2, \tag{117}$$

$$U_{35}(x,t) = \frac{\sqrt{M(\ln(A))^2 + \Omega}(\sqrt{-M} + b\cot_A(1/2\sqrt{-M}\xi))}{-b + \sqrt{-M}\cot_A(1/2\sqrt{-M}\xi)}, \tag{118}$$

As a result of utilizing (9) and (11), the subsequent solitary wave solutions are obtained for (1):

$$u_{35}(x,t) = e^{i\theta}\left(\frac{\sqrt{M(\ln(A))^2+\Omega}\left(\sqrt{-M}+b\cot_A(1/2\sqrt{-M}\xi)\right)}{-b+\sqrt{-M}\cot_A(1/2\sqrt{-M}\xi)}\right), \tag{119}$$

and

$$v_{35}(x,t) = \frac{1}{1+k^2}\left(\frac{\sqrt{M(\ln(A))^2+\Omega}\left(\sqrt{-M}+b\cot_A(1/2\sqrt{-M}\xi)\right)}{-b+\sqrt{-M}\cot_A(1/2\sqrt{-M}\xi)}\right)^2, \tag{120}$$

$$U_{36}(x,t) = \frac{\sqrt{M(\ln(A))^2+\Omega}\left(\sqrt{-M}\cos_A(\sqrt{-M}\xi)+b\sin_A(\sqrt{-M}\xi)+b\sqrt{pq}\right)}{-b\cos_A(\sqrt{-M}\xi)+\sqrt{-M}\sin_A(\sqrt{-M}\xi)+\sqrt{-M}\sqrt{pq}}, \tag{121}$$

As a result of utilizing (9) and (11), the subsequent solitary wave solutions are obtained for (1):

$$u_{36}(x,t) = e^{i\theta}\left(\frac{\sqrt{M(\ln(A))^2+\Omega}\left(\sqrt{-M}\cos_A(\sqrt{-M}\xi)+b\sin_A(\sqrt{-M}\xi)+b\sqrt{pq}\right)}{-b\cos_A(\sqrt{-M}\xi)+\sqrt{-M}\sin_A(\sqrt{-M}\xi)+\sqrt{-M}\sqrt{pq}}\right), \tag{122}$$

and

$$v_{36}(x,t) = \frac{1}{1+k^2}\left(\frac{\sqrt{M(\ln(A))^2+\Omega}\left(\sqrt{-M}\cos_A(\sqrt{-M}\xi)+b\sin_A(\sqrt{-M}\xi)+b\sqrt{pq}\right)}{-b\cos_A(\sqrt{-M}\xi)+\sqrt{-M}\sin_A(\sqrt{-M}\xi)+\sqrt{-M}\sqrt{pq}}\right)^2, \tag{123}$$

$$U_{37}(x,t) = \frac{\sqrt{M(\ln(A))^2+\Omega}\left(\sqrt{-M}\sin_A(\sqrt{-M}\xi)+b\cos_A(\sqrt{-M}\xi)+b\sqrt{pq}\right)}{b\sin_A(\sqrt{-M}\xi)+\sqrt{-M}\cos_A(\sqrt{-M}\xi)+\sqrt{-M}\sqrt{pq}}, \tag{124}$$

As a result of utilizing (9) and (11), the subsequent solitary wave solutions are obtained for (1):

$$u_{37}(x,t) = e^{i\theta}\left(\frac{\sqrt{M(\ln(A))^2+\Omega}\left(\sqrt{-M}\sin_A(\sqrt{-M}\xi)+b\cos_A(\sqrt{-M}\xi)+b\sqrt{pq}\right)}{b\sin_A(\sqrt{-M}\xi)+\sqrt{-M}\cos_A(\sqrt{-M}\xi)+\sqrt{-M}\sqrt{pq}}\right), \tag{125}$$

and

$$v_{37}(x,t) = \frac{1}{1+k^2}\left(\frac{\sqrt{M(\ln(A))^2+\Omega}\left(\sqrt{-M}\sin_A(\sqrt{-M}\xi)+b\cos_A(\sqrt{-M}\xi)+b\sqrt{pq}\right)}{b\sin_A(\sqrt{-M}\xi)+\sqrt{-M}\cos_A(\sqrt{-M}\xi)+\sqrt{-M}\sqrt{pq}}\right)^2, \tag{126}$$

and

$$U_{38}(x,t) = -\frac{\sqrt{M(\ln(A))^2+\Omega}\left(2R+b-2b\left(\cos_A(1/4\sqrt{-M}\xi)\right)^2\right)}{2R-\sqrt{-M}+2\sqrt{-M}\left(\cos_A(1/4\sqrt{-M}\xi)\right)^2}, \tag{127}$$

As a result of utilizing (9) and (11), the subsequent solitary wave solutions are obtained for (1):

$$u_{38}(x,t) = e^{i\theta}\left(-\frac{\sqrt{M(\ln(A))^2+\Omega}\left(2R+b-2b\left(\cos_A(1/4\sqrt{-M}\xi)\right)^2\right)}{2bR-\sqrt{-M}+2\sqrt{-M}\left(\cos_A(1/4\sqrt{-M}\xi)\right)^2}\right), \tag{128}$$

and

$$v_{38}(x,t) = \frac{1}{1+k^2}\left(-\frac{\sqrt{M(\ln(A))^2+\Omega}\left(2\,R+b-2\,b(\cos_A(1/4\,\sqrt{-M}\xi))^2\right)}{2\,R-\sqrt{-M}+2\,\sqrt{-M}(\cos_A(1/4\,\sqrt{-M}\xi))^2}\right)^2, \quad (129)$$

where $R = \sqrt{-M}\cos_A(1/4\,\sqrt{-M}\xi)\sin_A(1/4\,\sqrt{-M}\xi)$.

Family 22. *For $M > 0$ and $a, b, c \neq 0$, the following set of equations presents the corresponding family of solitary wave solutions:*

$$U_{39}(x,t) = \frac{\sqrt{-M(\ln(A))^2-\Omega}\left(\sqrt{M}+b\tanh_A\left(1/2\,\sqrt{M}\xi\right)\right)}{b+\sqrt{M}\tanh_A\left(1/2\,\sqrt{M}\xi\right)}, \quad (130)$$

As a result of utilizing (9) and (11), the subsequent solitary wave solutions are obtained for (1):

$$u_{39}(x,t) = e^{i\theta}\left(\frac{\sqrt{-M(\ln(A))^2-\Omega}\left(\sqrt{M}+b\tanh_A\left(1/2\,\sqrt{M}\xi\right)\right)}{b+\sqrt{M}\tanh_A\left(1/2\,\sqrt{M}\xi\right)}\right), \quad (131)$$

and

$$v_{39}(x,t) = \frac{1}{1+k^2}\left(\frac{\sqrt{-M(\ln(A))^2-\Omega}\left(\sqrt{M}+b\tanh_A\left(1/2\,\sqrt{M}\xi\right)\right)}{b+\sqrt{M}\tanh_A\left(1/2\,\sqrt{M}\xi\right)}\right)^2, \quad (132)$$

$$U_{40}(x,t) = \frac{\sqrt{-M(\ln(A))^2-\Omega}\left(\sqrt{M}+b\coth_A\left(1/2\,\sqrt{M}\xi\right)\right)}{b+\sqrt{M}\coth_A\left(1/2\,\sqrt{M}\xi\right)}, \quad (133)$$

As a result of utilizing (9) and (11), the subsequent solitary wave solutions are obtained for (1):

$$u_{40}(x,t) = e^{i\theta}\left(\frac{\sqrt{-M(\ln(A))^2-\Omega}\left(\sqrt{M}+b\coth_A\left(1/2\,\sqrt{M}\xi\right)\right)}{b+\sqrt{M}\coth_A\left(1/2\,\sqrt{M}\xi\right)}\right), \quad (134)$$

and

$$v_{40}(x,t) = \frac{1}{1+k^2}\left(\frac{\sqrt{-M(\ln(A))^2-\Omega}\left(\sqrt{M}+b\coth_A\left(1/2\,\sqrt{M}\xi\right)\right)}{b+\sqrt{M}\coth_A\left(1/2\,\sqrt{M}\xi\right)}\right)^2, \quad (135)$$

$$U_{41}(x,t) = \frac{\sqrt{-M(\ln(A))^2-\Omega}\left(\sqrt{M}\cosh_A\left(\sqrt{M}\xi\right)+b\sinh_A\left(\sqrt{M}\xi\right)+b\sqrt{pq}\right)}{b\cosh_A\left(\sqrt{M}\xi\right)+\sqrt{M}\sinh_A\left(\sqrt{M}\xi\right)+\sqrt{M}\sqrt{pq}}, \quad (136)$$

As a result of utilizing (9) and (11), the subsequent solitary wave solutions are obtained for (1):

$$u_{41}(x,t) = e^{i\theta}\left(\frac{\sqrt{-M(\ln(A))^2-\Omega}\left(\sqrt{M}\cosh_A\left(\sqrt{M}\xi\right)+b\sinh_A\left(\sqrt{M}\xi\right)+b\sqrt{pq}\right)}{b\cosh_A\left(\sqrt{M}\xi\right)+\sqrt{M}\sinh_A\left(\sqrt{M}\xi\right)+\sqrt{M}\sqrt{pq}}\right), \quad (137)$$

and

$$v_{41}(x,t) = \frac{1}{1+k^2}\left(\frac{\sqrt{-M(\ln(A))^2 - \Omega}\left(\sqrt{M}\cosh_A\left(\sqrt{M}\xi\right) + b\sinh_A\left(\sqrt{M}\xi\right) + b\sqrt{pq}\right)}{b\cosh_A\left(\sqrt{M}\xi\right) + \sqrt{M}\sinh_A\left(\sqrt{M}\xi\right) + \sqrt{M}\sqrt{pq}}\right)^2, \quad (138)$$

$$U_{42}(x,t) = \frac{\sqrt{-M(\ln(A))^2 - \Omega}\left(\sqrt{M}\sinh_A\left(\sqrt{M}\xi\right) + b\cosh_A\left(\sqrt{M}\xi\right) + b\sqrt{pq}\right)}{b\sinh_A\left(\sqrt{M}\xi\right) + \sqrt{M}\cosh_A\left(\sqrt{M}\xi\right) + \sqrt{M}\sqrt{pq}}. \quad (139)$$

Utilizing (9) and (11), the subsequent solitary wave solutions are obtained for (1) as

$$u_{42}(x,t) = e^{i\theta}\left(\frac{\sqrt{-M(\ln(A))^2 - \Omega}\left(\sqrt{M}\sinh_A\left(\sqrt{M}\xi\right) + b\cosh_A\left(\sqrt{M}\xi\right) + b\sqrt{pq}\right)}{b\sinh_A\left(\sqrt{M}\xi\right) + \sqrt{M}\cosh_A\left(\sqrt{M}\xi\right) + \sqrt{M}\sqrt{pq}}\right), \quad (140)$$

and

$$v_{42}(x,t) = \frac{1}{1+k^2}\left(\frac{\sqrt{-M(\ln(A))^2 - \Omega}\left(\sqrt{M}\sinh_A\left(\sqrt{M}\xi\right) + b\cosh_A\left(\sqrt{M}\xi\right) + b\sqrt{pq}\right)}{b\sinh_A\left(\sqrt{M}\xi\right) + \sqrt{M}\cosh_A\left(\sqrt{M}\xi\right) + \sqrt{M}\sqrt{pq}}\right)^2, \quad (141)$$

and

$$U_{43}(x,t) = \frac{\sqrt{M(\ln(A))^2 + \Omega}\left(2\sqrt{-M}\cosh_A\left(1/4\sqrt{M}\xi\right)\sinh_A\left(1/4\sqrt{M}\xi\right) + b\right)}{-2b\cosh_A\left(1/4\sqrt{M}\xi\right)\sinh_A\left(1/4\sqrt{M}\xi\right) + \sqrt{M}}. \quad (142)$$

Utilizing (9) and (11), the subsequent solitary wave solutions are obtained for (1) as

$$u_{43}(x,t) = e^{i\theta}\left(\frac{\sqrt{M(\ln(A))^2 + \Omega}\left(2\sqrt{-M}\cosh_A\left(1/4\sqrt{M}\xi\right)\sinh_A\left(1/4\sqrt{M}\xi\right) + b\right)}{-2b\cosh_A\left(1/4\sqrt{M}\xi\right)\sinh_A\left(1/4\sqrt{M}\xi\right) + \sqrt{M}}\right), \quad (143)$$

and

$$v_{43}(x,t) = \frac{1}{1+k^2}\left(\frac{\sqrt{M(\ln(A))^2 + \Omega}\left(2\sqrt{-M}\cosh_A\left(1/4\sqrt{M}\xi\right)\sinh_A\left(1/4\sqrt{M}\xi\right) + b\right)}{-2b\cosh_A\left(1/4\sqrt{M}\xi\right)\sinh_A\left(1/4\sqrt{M}\xi\right) + \sqrt{M}}\right)^2. \quad (144)$$

Family 23. *For $ac > 0$ and $b = 0$, the following set of equations presents the corresponding family of solitary wave solutions:*

$$U_{44}(x,t) = \sqrt{-(4c(\ln(A))^2 a - \Omega)}\left(\tan_A\left(\sqrt{ac}\xi\right)\right)^{-1}. \quad (145)$$

As a result of utilizing (9) and (11), the subsequent solitary wave solutions are obtained for (1):

$$u_{44}(x,t) = e^{i\theta}\left(\sqrt{-(4c(\ln(A))^2 a - \Omega)}\left(\tan_A\left(\sqrt{ac}\xi\right)\right)^{-1}\right), \quad (146)$$

and

$$v_{44}(x,t) = \frac{1}{1+k^2}\left(\sqrt{-(4c(\ln(A))^2 a - \Omega)}\left(\tan_A\left(\sqrt{ac}\xi\right)\right)^{-1}\right)^2, \quad (147)$$

$$U_{45}(x,t) = -\sqrt{-(4\,c(\ln(A))^2 a - \Omega)}\left(\cot_A\left(\sqrt{ac}\xi\right)\right)^{-1}. \tag{148}$$

As a result of utilizing (9) and (11), the subsequent solitary wave solutions are obtained for (1):

$$u_{45}(x,t) = e^{i\theta}\left(- \sqrt{-(4\,c(\ln(A))^2 a - \Omega)}\left(\cot_A\left(\sqrt{ac}\xi\right)\right)^{-1}\right), \tag{149}$$

and

$$v_{45}(x,t) = \frac{1}{1+k^2}\left(- \sqrt{-(4\,c(\ln(A))^2 a - \Omega)}\left(\cot_A\left(\sqrt{ac}\xi\right)\right)^{-1}\right)^2, \tag{150}$$

$$\begin{aligned} U_{46}(x,t) = {} & \sqrt{-(4\,c(\ln(A))^2 a - \Omega)} \times \\ & \left(\tan_A(2\sqrt{ac}\xi) \pm \left(\sqrt{pq}\sec(2\sqrt{ac}\xi)\right)\right)^{-1}. \end{aligned} \tag{151}$$

As a result of utilizing (9) and (11), the subsequent solitary wave solutions are obtained for (1):

$$\begin{aligned} u_{46}(x,t) = e^{i\theta}\Bigg(& \sqrt{-(4\,c(\ln(A))^2 a - \Omega)} \times \\ & \left(\tan_A(2\sqrt{ac}\xi) \pm \left(\sqrt{pq}\sec_A(2\sqrt{ac}\xi)\right)\right)^{-1}\Bigg), \end{aligned} \tag{152}$$

and

$$\begin{aligned} v_{46}(x,t) = \frac{1}{1+k^2}\Bigg(& \sqrt{-(4\,c(\ln(A))^2 a - \Omega)} \times \\ & \left(\tan_A(2\sqrt{ac}\xi) \pm \left(\sqrt{pq}\sec_A(2\sqrt{ac}\xi)\right)\right)^{-1}\Bigg)^2, \end{aligned} \tag{153}$$

$$\begin{aligned} U_{47}(x,t) = {} & -\sqrt{-(4\,c(\ln(A))^2 a - \Omega)} \times \\ & \left(\cot_A(2\sqrt{ac}\xi) \pm \left(\sqrt{pq}\csc_A(2\sqrt{ac}\xi)\right)\right)^{-1}. \end{aligned} \tag{154}$$

As a result of utilizing (9) and (11), the subsequent solitary wave solutions are obtained for (1):

$$\begin{aligned} u_{47}(x,t) = e^{i\theta}\Bigg(& -\sqrt{-(4\,c(\ln(A))^2 a - \Omega)} \times \\ & \left(\cot_A(2\sqrt{ac}\xi) \pm \left(\sqrt{pq}\csc_A(2\sqrt{ac}\xi)\right)\right)^{-1}\Bigg), \end{aligned} \tag{155}$$

and

$$\begin{aligned} v_{47}(x,t) = \frac{1}{1+k^2}\Bigg(& -\sqrt{-(4\,c(\ln(A))^2 a - \Omega)} \times \\ & \left(\cot_A(2\sqrt{ac}\xi) \pm \left(\sqrt{pq}\csc_A(2\sqrt{ac}\xi)\right)\right)^{-1}\Bigg)^2, \end{aligned} \tag{156}$$

and

$$U_{48}(x,t) = 2\sqrt{-(4c(\ln(A))^2a - \Omega)}\times \left(\tan_A\left(\frac{\sqrt{ac}\xi}{2}\right) - \cot_A\left(\frac{\sqrt{ac}\xi}{2}\right)\right)^{-1}. \tag{157}$$

As a result of utilizing (9) and (11), the subsequent solitary wave solutions are obtained for (1):

$$u_{48}(x,t) = e^{i\theta}\left(2\sqrt{-(4c(\ln(A))^2a - \Omega)}\times \left(\tan_A\left(\frac{\sqrt{ac}\xi}{2}\right) - \cot_A\left(\frac{\sqrt{ac}\xi}{2}\right)\right)^{-1}\right), \tag{158}$$

and

$$v_{48}(x,t) = \frac{1}{1+k^2}\left(2\sqrt{-(4c(\ln(A))^2a - \Omega)}\times \left(\tan_A\left(\frac{\sqrt{ac}\xi}{2}\right) - \cot_A\left(\frac{\sqrt{ac}\xi}{2}\right)\right)^{-1}\right)^2. \tag{159}$$

Family 24. *For $ac < 0$ and $b = 0$, then the following set of equations presents the corresponding family of solitary wave solutions:*

$$U_{49}(x,t) = -\sqrt{4c(\ln(A))^2a - \Omega}\left(\tanh_A\left(\sqrt{-ac}\xi\right)\right)^{-1}. \tag{160}$$

As a result of utilizing (9) and (11), the subsequent solitary wave solutions are obtained for (1):

$$u_{49}(x,t) = e^{i\theta}\left(-\sqrt{4c(\ln(A))^2a - \Omega}\left(\tanh_A\left(\sqrt{-ac}\xi\right)\right)^{-1}\right), \tag{161}$$

and

$$v_{49}(x,t) = \frac{1}{1+k^2}\left(-\sqrt{4c(\ln(A))^2a - \Omega}\left(\tanh_A\left(\sqrt{-ac}\xi\right)\right)^{-1}\right)^2, \tag{162}$$

$$U_{50}(x,t) = -\sqrt{4c(\ln(A))^2a - \Omega}\left(\coth_A\left(\sqrt{-ac}\xi\right)\right)^{-1}. \tag{163}$$

As a result of utilizing (9) and (11), the subsequent solitary wave solutions are obtained for (1):

$$u_{50}(x,t) = e^{i\theta}\left(-\sqrt{4c(\ln(A))^2a - \Omega}\left(\coth_A\left(\sqrt{-ac}\xi\right)\right)^{-1}\right), \tag{164}$$

and

$$v_{50}(x,t) = \frac{1}{1+k^2}\left(-\sqrt{4c(\ln(A))^2a - \Omega}\left(\coth_A\left(\sqrt{-ac}\xi\right)\right)^{-1}\right)^2, \tag{165}$$

$$U_{51}(x,t) = -\sqrt{4c(\ln(A))^2a - \Omega}\times \left(\tanh_A\left(2\sqrt{-ac}\xi\right) \pm \left(i\sqrt{pq}\,\mathrm{sech}_A\left(2\sqrt{-ac}\xi\right)\right)\right)^{-1}. \tag{166}$$

As a result of utilizing (9) and (11), the subsequent solitary wave solutions are obtained for (1):

$$u_{51}(x,t) = e^{i\theta}\bigg(-\sqrt{4c(\ln(A))^2 a - \Omega}\times \\ \Big(\tanh_A\big(2\sqrt{-ac}\xi\big) \pm \big(i\sqrt{pq}sech_A\big(2\sqrt{-ac}\xi\big)\big)\Big)^{-1}\bigg), \tag{167}$$

and

$$v_{51}(x,t) = \frac{1}{1+k^2}\bigg(-\sqrt{4c(\ln(A))^2 a - \Omega}\times \\ \Big(\tanh_A\big(2\sqrt{-ac}\xi\big) \pm \big(i\sqrt{pq}sech_A\big(2\sqrt{-ac}\xi\big)\big)\Big)^{-1}\bigg)^2, \tag{168}$$

$$U_{52}(x,t) = -\sqrt{4c(\ln(A))^2 a - \Omega}\times \\ \Big(\coth_A\big(2\sqrt{-ac}\xi\big) \pm \big(\sqrt{pq}csch_A\big(2\sqrt{-ac}\xi\big)\big)\Big)^{-1}. \tag{169}$$

As a result of utilizing (9) and (11), the subsequent solitary wave solutions are obtained for (1):

$$u_{52}(x,t) = e^{i\theta}\bigg(-\sqrt{4c(\ln(A))^2 a - \Omega}\times \\ \Big(\coth_A\big(2\sqrt{-ac}\xi\big) \pm \big(\sqrt{pq}csch_A\big(2\sqrt{-ac}\xi\big)\big)\Big)^{-1}\bigg), \tag{170}$$

and

$$v_{52}(x,t) = \frac{1}{1+k^2}\bigg(-\sqrt{4c(\ln(A))^2 a - \Omega}\times \\ \Big(\coth_A\big(2\sqrt{-ac}\xi\big) \pm \big(\sqrt{pq}csch_A\big(2\sqrt{-ac}\xi\big)\big)\Big)^{-1}\bigg)^2, \tag{171}$$

and

$$U_{53}(x,t) = -\sqrt{4c(\ln(A))^2 a - \Omega}\times \\ \left(\tanh_A\left(\frac{\sqrt{-ac}\xi}{2}\right) + \coth_A\left(\frac{\sqrt{-ac}\xi}{2}\right)\right)^{-1}. \tag{172}$$

As a result of utilizing (9) and (11), the subsequent solitary wave solutions are obtained for (1):

$$u_{53}(x,t) = e^{i\theta}\left(-\sqrt{4c(\ln(A))^2 a - \Omega}\times \\ \left(\tanh_A\left(\frac{\sqrt{-ac}\xi}{2}\right) + \coth_A\left(\frac{\sqrt{-ac}\xi}{2}\right)\right)^{-1}\right), \tag{173}$$

and

$$v_{53}(x,t) = \frac{1}{1+k^2}\left(-\sqrt{4c(\ln(A))^2 a - \Omega}\times \\ \left(\tanh_A\left(\frac{\sqrt{-ac}\xi}{2}\right) + \coth_A\left(\frac{\sqrt{-ac}\xi}{2}\right)\right)^{-1}\right)^2. \tag{174}$$

Family 25. *For $c = a$ and $b = 0$, the following set of equations presents the corresponding family of solitary wave solutions:*

$$U_{54}(x,t) = \sqrt{-(4\,(\ln(A))^2 a^2 - \Omega)}(\tan_A(a\xi))^{-1}, \tag{175}$$

As a result of utilizing (9) and (11), the subsequent solitary wave solutions are obtained for (1):

$$u_{54}(x,t) = e^{i\theta}(\sqrt{-(4\,(\ln(A))^2 a^2 - \Omega)}(\tan_A(a\xi))^{-1}), \tag{176}$$

and

$$v_{54}(x,t) = \frac{1}{1+k^2}(\sqrt{-(4\,(\ln(A))^2 a^2 - \Omega)}(\tan_A(a\xi))^{-1})^2, \tag{177}$$

$$U_{55}(x,t) = -\sqrt{-(4\,(\ln(A))^2 a^2 - \Omega)}(\cot_A(a\xi))^{-1}. \tag{178}$$

As a result of utilizing (9) and (11), the subsequent solitary wave solutions are obtained for (1):

$$u_{55}(x,t) = e^{i\theta}(-\sqrt{-(4\,(\ln(A))^2 a^2 - \Omega)}(\cot_A(a\xi))^{-1}), \tag{179}$$

and

$$v_{55}(x,t) = \frac{1}{1+k^2}(-\sqrt{-(4\,(\ln(A))^2 a^2 - \Omega)}(\cot_A(a\xi))^{-1})^2, \tag{180}$$

$$U_{56}(x,t) = \sqrt{-(4\,(\ln(A))^2 a^2 - \Omega)}(\tan_A(2\,a\xi) \pm (\sqrt{pq}\sec_A(2\,a\xi)))^{-1}. \tag{181}$$

As a result of utilizing (9) and (11), the subsequent solitary wave solutions are obtained for (1):

$$u_{56}(x,t) = e^{i\theta}\Big(\sqrt{-(4\,(\ln(A))^2 a^2 - \Omega)}\times (\tan_A(2\,a\xi) \pm (\sqrt{pq}\sec_A(2\,a\xi)))^{-1}\Big), \tag{182}$$

and

$$v_{56}(x,t) = \frac{1}{1+k^2}\Big(\sqrt{-(4\,(\ln(A))^2 a^2 - \Omega)}\times (\tan_A(2\,a\xi) \pm (\sqrt{pq}\sec_A(2\,a\xi)))^{-1}\Big)^2, \tag{183}$$

$$U_{57}(x,t) = \sqrt{-(4\,(\ln(A))^2 a^2 - \Omega)}\times (-\cot_A(2\,a\xi) \mp (\sqrt{pq}\csc_A(2\,a\xi)))^{-1}. \tag{184}$$

As a result of utilizing (9) and (11), the subsequent solitary wave solutions are obtained for (1):

$$u_{57}(x,t) = e^{i\theta}\Big(\sqrt{-(4\,(\ln(A))^2 a^2 - \Omega)}\times (-\cot_A(2\,a\xi) \mp (\sqrt{pq}\csc_A(2\,a\xi)))^{-1}\Big), \tag{185}$$

and

$$v_{57}(x,t) = \frac{1}{1+k^2}\Bigg(\sqrt{-(4\,(\ln(A))^2a^2 - \Omega)}\times \\ (-\cot_A(2\,a\xi) \mp (\sqrt{pq}\csc_A(2\,a\xi)))^{-1}\Bigg)^2, \tag{186}$$

and

$$U_{58}(x,t) = \sqrt{-(4\,(\ln(A))^2a^2 - \Omega)}\times \\ \left(\frac{1}{2}(\tan_A\left(\frac{a\xi}{2}\right) - \cot_A\left(\frac{a\xi}{2}\right))\right)^{-1}. \tag{187}$$

As a result of utilizing (9) and (11), the subsequent solitary wave solutions are obtained for (1):

$$u_{58}(x,t) = e^{i\theta}\Bigg(\sqrt{-(4\,(\ln(A))^2a^2 - \Omega)}\times \\ \left(\frac{1}{2}(\tan_A\left(\frac{a\xi}{2}\right) - \cot_A\left(\frac{a\xi}{2}\right))\right)^{-1}\Bigg), \tag{188}$$

and

$$v_{58}(x,t) = \frac{1}{1+k^2}\Bigg(\sqrt{-(4\,(\ln(A))^2a^2 - \Omega)}\times \\ \left(\frac{1}{2}(\tan_A\left(\frac{a\xi}{2}\right) - \cot_A\left(\frac{a\xi}{2}\right))\right)^{-1}\Bigg)^2. \tag{189}$$

Family 26. *For $c = -a$ and $b = 0$, the following set of equations presents the corresponding family of solitary wave solutions:*

$$U_{59}(x,t) = -\sqrt{-4\,(\ln(A))^2a^2 - \Omega}(\tanh_A(a\xi))^{-1}. \tag{190}$$

As a result of utilizing (9) and (11), the subsequent solitary wave solutions are obtained for (1):

$$u_{59}(x,t) = e^{i\theta}(-\sqrt{-4\,(\ln(A))^2a^2 - \Omega}(\tanh_A(a\xi))^{-1}), \tag{191}$$

and

$$v_{59}(x,t) = \frac{1}{1+k^2}(-\sqrt{-4\,(\ln(A))^2a^2 - \Omega}(\tanh_A(a\xi))^{-1})^2, \tag{192}$$

$$U_{60}(x,t) = -\sqrt{-4\,(\ln(A))^2a^2 - \Omega}(\coth_A(a\xi))^{-1}. \tag{193}$$

As a result of utilizing (9) and (11), the subsequent solitary wave solutions are obtained for (1):

$$u_{60}(x,t) = e^{i\theta}(-\sqrt{-4\,(\ln(A))^2a^2 - \Omega}(\coth_A(a\xi))^{-1}), \tag{194}$$

and

$$v_{60}(x,t) = \frac{1}{1+k^2}(-\sqrt{-4\,(\ln(A))^2a^2 - \Omega}(\coth_A(a\xi))^{-1})^2, \tag{195}$$

$$U_{61}(x,t) = \sqrt{-4\,(\ln(A))^2a^2 - \Omega}\times \\ (-\tanh_A(2\,a\xi) \mp (i\sqrt{pq}sech_A(2\,a\xi)))^{-1}. \tag{196}$$

As a result of utilizing (9) and (11), the subsequent solitary wave solutions are obtained for (1):

$$u_{61}(x,t) = e^{i\theta}\Bigg(\sqrt{-4\,(\ln(A))^2a^2 - \Omega}\times \\ (-\tanh_A(2\,a\xi) \mp (i\sqrt{pq}sech_A(2\,a\xi)))^{-1}\Bigg), \tag{197}$$

and

$$v_{61}(x,t) = \frac{1}{1+k^2}\Bigg(\sqrt{-4\,(\ln(A))^2a^2 - \Omega}\times \\ (-\tanh_A(2\,a\xi) \mp (i\sqrt{pq}sech_A(2\,a\xi)))^{-1}\Bigg)^2, \tag{198}$$

$$U_{62}(x,t) = \sqrt{-4\,(\ln(A))^2a^2 - \Omega}\times \\ (-\coth_A(2\,a\xi) \mp (\sqrt{pq}csch_A(2\,a\xi)))^{-1}. \tag{199}$$

As a result of utilizing (9) and (11), the subsequent solitary wave solutions are obtained for (1):

$$u_{62}(x,t) = e^{i\theta}\Bigg(\sqrt{-4\,(\ln(A))^2a^2 - \Omega}\times \\ (-\coth_A(2\,a\xi) \mp (\sqrt{pq}csch_A(2\,a\xi)))^{-1}\Bigg), \tag{200}$$

and

$$v_{62}(x,t) = \frac{1}{1+k^2}(\sqrt{-4\,(\ln(A))^2a^2 - \Omega}\times \\ (-\coth_A(2\,a\xi) \mp (\sqrt{pq}csch_A(2\,a\xi)))^{-1})^2, \tag{201}$$

and

$$U_{63}(x,t) = \sqrt{-4\,(\ln(A))^2a^2 - \Omega}\times \\ \left(\frac{-1}{2}(\tanh_A\left(\frac{a\xi}{2}\right) + \coth_A\left(\frac{a\xi}{2}\right))\right)^{-1}. \tag{202}$$

As a result of utilizing (9) and (11), the subsequent solitary wave solutions are obtained for (1):

$$u_{63}(x,t) = e^{i\theta}\Bigg(\sqrt{-4\,(\ln(A))^2a^2 - \Omega}\times \\ \left(\frac{-1}{2}(\tanh_A\left(\frac{a\xi}{2}\right) + \coth_A\left(\frac{a\xi}{2}\right))\right)^{-1}\Bigg), \tag{203}$$

and

$$v_{63}(x,t) = \frac{1}{1+k^2}\left(\sqrt{-4\,(\ln(A))^2 a^2 - \Omega}\times\right.$$
$$\left.\left(\frac{-1}{2}\left(\tanh_A\left(\frac{a\xi}{2}\right) + \coth_A\left(\frac{a\xi}{2}\right)\right)\right)^{-1}\right)^2. \tag{204}$$

Family 27. *For $b = \lambda$, $a = n\lambda (n \neq 0)$ and $c = 0$, the following set of equations presents the corresponding family of solitary wave solutions:*

$$U_{64}(x,t) = 2\sqrt{-b^2(\ln(A))^2 - \Omega}n\left(A^{\lambda\xi} - n\right)^{-1} +$$
$$\sqrt{-b^2(\ln(A))^2 - \Omega}. \tag{205}$$

As a result of utilizing (9) and (11), the subsequent solitary wave solutions are obtained for (1):

$$u_{64}(x,t) = e^{i\theta}\left(2\sqrt{-b^2(\ln(A))^2 - \Omega}n\left(A^{\lambda\xi} - n\right)^{-1} +\right.$$
$$\left.\sqrt{-b^2(\ln(A))^2 - \Omega}\right), \tag{206}$$

and

$$v_{64}(x,t) = \frac{1}{1+k^2}\left(2\sqrt{-b^2(\ln(A))^2 - \Omega}n\left(A^{\lambda\xi} - n\right)^{-1} +\right.$$
$$\left.\sqrt{-b^2(\ln(A))^2 - \Omega}\right)^2, \tag{207}$$

where $\xi = \frac{x^\delta}{\Gamma(1+\delta)} + \sqrt{\frac{b^2(\ln(A))^2 + 2a_1{}^2 - 4c(\ln(A))^2 a - 2b_1{}^2}{(b^2-4ac)(\ln(A))^2}}\frac{t^\gamma}{\Gamma(1+\gamma)}$ *and* $\theta = \frac{a_1 x^\delta}{\Gamma(1+\delta)} + \frac{b_1 t^\gamma}{\Gamma(1+\gamma)}$.

4. Discussion and Graphs

The findings of this work provide significant light on how the fractional coupled Higgs system behaves. By analyzing the graphs and traveling wave solutions, we were able to identify a number of crucial system characteristics. In the solutions, we discovered solitary waves, kink waves, rogue waves, periodic and hyperbolic solitary waves, all of which are crucial to the physical fields that the fractional coupled Higgs system represents.

Confined disturbances known as solitary waves maintain their shape and amplitude as they pass through a medium. These waves are typically seen in nonlinear systems, where the interaction between dispersive and nonlinear effects balances out to determine how they behave. Solitary waves suggest that the fractional coupled Higgs system may behave in a nonlinear and dispersive manner.

On the other hand, kink waves are disturbances that move over the boundary between two different media with different physical properties. These waves typically occur in systems with phase transitions and are characterized by their sudden change from one medium to another. Kink waves in the solutions demonstrate that the fractional Higgs system may undergo phase transitions under certain circumstances.

Strong and sporadic phenomena known as rogue waves appear unpredictably in otherwise well-behaved systems. These waves have the power to completely destroy physical systems, including fiber-optic communications and sea waves. The existence of rogue waves in the fractional Higgs system demonstrates that the system is vulnerable to catastrophic and unexpected phenomena, which might have important ramifications for comprehending the system's behavior.

In the fractional coupled Higgs system, we mostly found periodic and hyperbolic solitary wave solutions. These responses are crucial because they provide a more thorough understanding of the system's conduct in diverse circumstances.

This study demonstrates that mEDAM offers a reliable and flexible method for solving challenging mathematical models. The idea has been used to study a number of physical systems, and it seems to be a workable method for figuring out how nonlinear and dispersive systems behave. Investigating the solutions obtained with this method can provide us with information on the behavior of the fractional Higgs system and related phenomena, which may have significant ramifications for our knowledge of fundamental physics. Furthermore, our analytical methodology has the benefit of allowing us to derive solutions produced by other analytical methods such as the tan-method, (G'/G)-expansion method, subequation method, and many others. The three families of solitary solutions produced by the (G'/G)-expansion approach, for example, may be derived from our results. Similarly, by substituting generalized trigonometric and hyperbolic functions with ordinary trigonometric and hyperbolic functions, we may recover all families of solutions found using the tan-method. This adaptability in acquiring multiple answers broadens our understanding of the problem from numerous angles and broadens the usefulness of our discoveries in varied contexts.

Remark 1. *Overall, Figure 1 shows the solitary kink wave profile, which is a special and distinctive wave form distinguished by a steep bend or abrupt change in direction.*

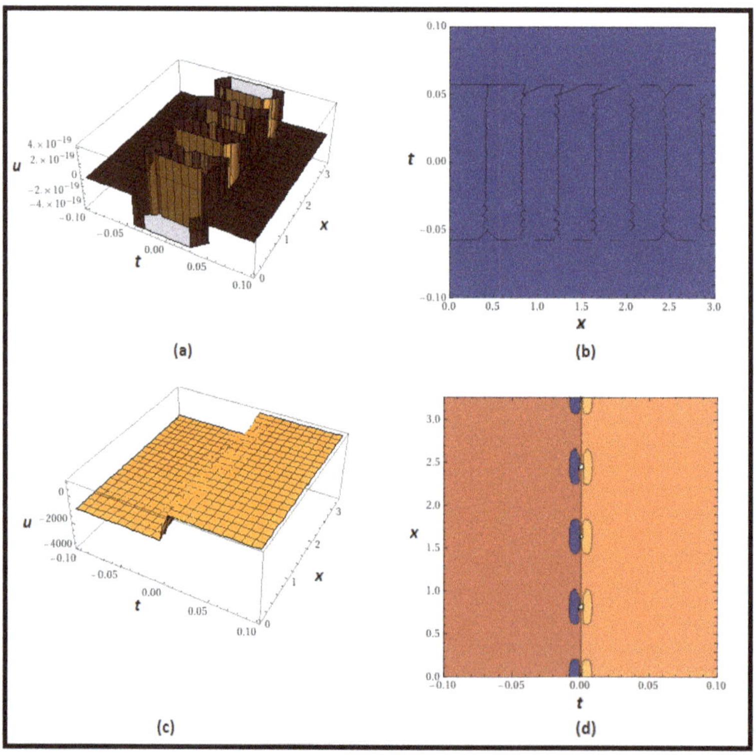

Figure 1. Graph of (28) in which (**a**,**b**) present 3D and contour plots of real part respectively while (**c**,**d**) present 3D and contour plots of imaginary part respectively for $a = 3$, $b = 1$, $c = 5$, $A = e$, $a_1 = 1000$, $b_1 = 0$, $\gamma = \delta = 1$.

Remark 2. *Overall, Figure 2 shows a lump wave, which is a little bulge or disturbance in a waveform that exhibits a quick rise in amplitude followed by a steady fall to its initial level.*

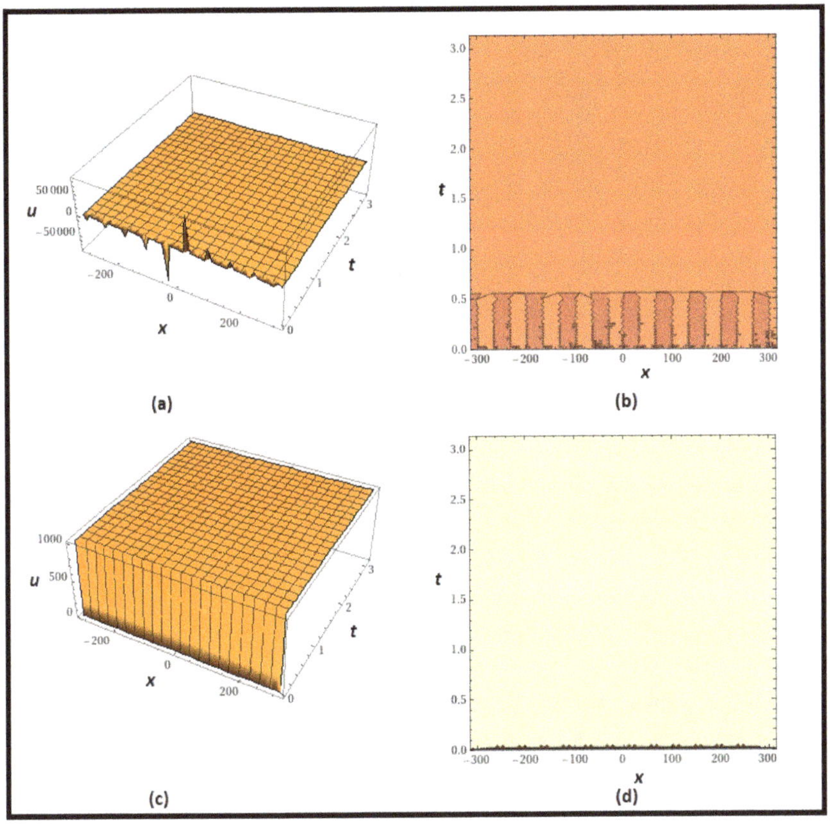

Figure 2. Graph of (46) in which (**a**,**b**) present 3D and contour plots of real part respectively while (**c**,**d**) and present 3D and contour plots of imaginary part respectively for $a = 3$, $b = 0$, $c = 5$, $A = e$, $a_1 = 1000$, $b_1 = 0$, $\gamma = \delta = 1$.

Remark 3. *Figure 3 shows the periodic kink wave profile, which is a special and distinctive wave form distinguished by a steep bend or abrupt change in direction.*

Remark 4. *Overall, lone rogue wave, a rare and extreme oceanic occurrence in physics, is depicted in Figure 4. With a noticeably larger amplitude and steeper profile than the other waves, it stands out for its size and unpredictability.*

Remark 5. *Overall, a singular kink wave is depicted in Figure 5. Singular kink waves are nonlinear wave system amplitude or phase variations that occur in a variety of scientific environments, including particle physics. They are especially important in theories including scalar fields, such as the Higgs field in the Standard Model, which influences particle mass. To solve unexplained events, extensions such as the "Fractional Coupled Higgs System" include more scalar fields. The mEDAM's analysis of these waves provides insights into the interaction of new scalar fields with the Higgs field. This research extends particle physics beyond the Standard Model by improving scalar field comprehension in the Higgs region.*

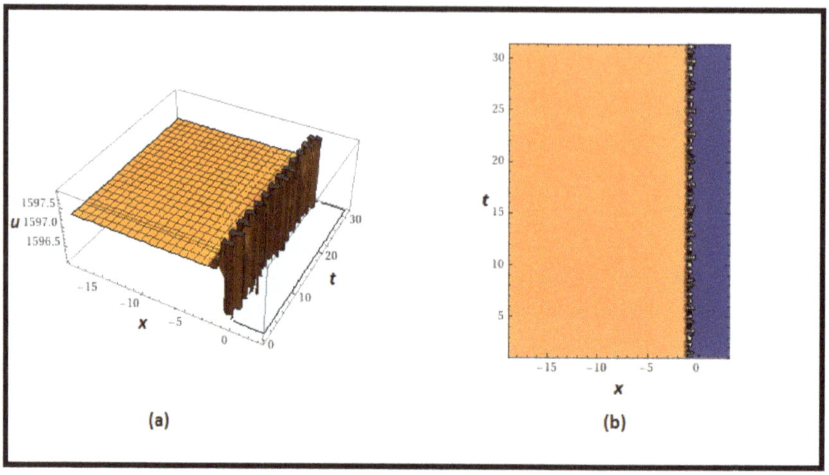

Figure 3. Graph of the real part of (136) in which (**a**,**b**) present 3D and contour plots of real part respectively for $a = 3, b = 10, c = 5, A = 2, a_1 = 1000, b_1 = 0, \gamma = \delta = 1$.

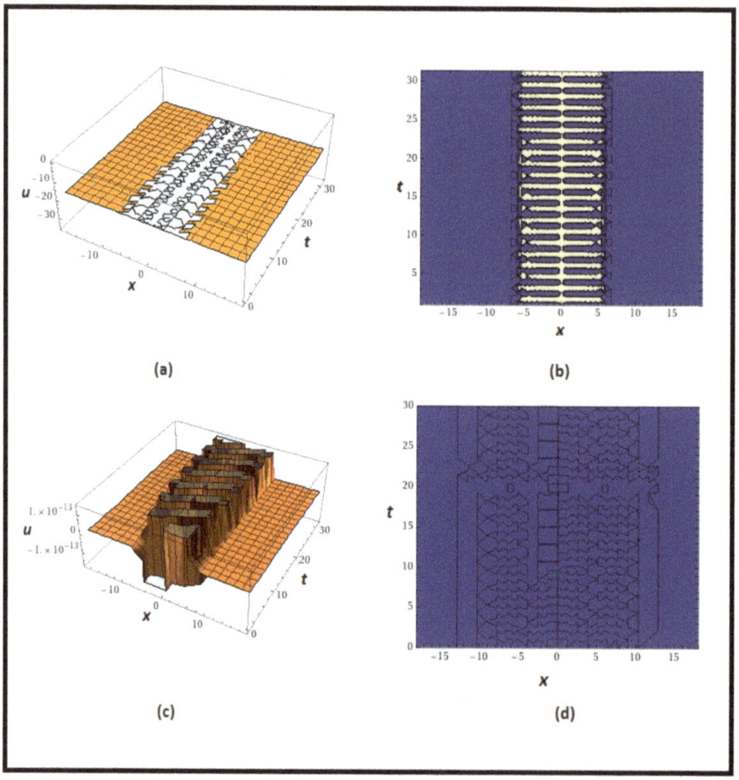

Figure 4. Graph of (204) in which (**a**,**b**) present 3D and contour plots of real part respectively while (**c**,**d**) present 3D and contour plots of imaginary part respectively for $a = 3, b = 0, c = -3, A = e$, $a_1 = 1000, b_1 = 10{,}000, \gamma = \delta = 1$.

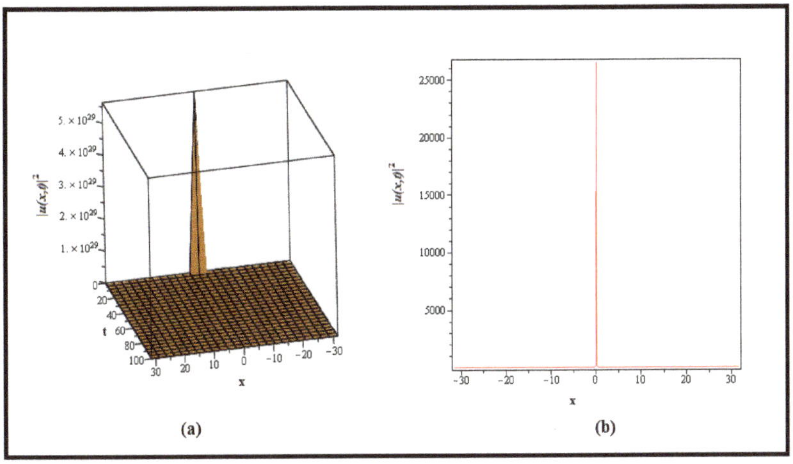

Figure 5. Depicts graph of the squared norm of (44). The 3D graph in (**a**) is plotted for $a = 3$, $b = 10, c = 1, A = e, a_1 = b_1 = 25, \gamma = \delta = 1$ while the 2D graph in (**b**) is drawn for $t = 0$ and the similar values of involved parameters.

Remark 6. *Overall, a lump wave is depicted in Figure 6. A lump wave, also known as a compacton, is a specialized localized solution in nonlinear systems that, unlike other waves, retains a fixed spatial extent while propagating. Nonlinear and dispersive effects cause this behavior. The study of lump waves is relevant in the context of the "Fractional Coupled Higgs System", an extension of the Standard Model of particle physics. The study of lump waves within this system, which includes various scalar fields in addition to the Higgs field, provides insights on scalar field behavior and interactions. Exploring lump waves contributes to a better understanding of scalar field dynamics and their influence on system behavior, which contributes to the larger objective of grasping extended particle physics models and hypothetical phenomena beyond the standard model.*

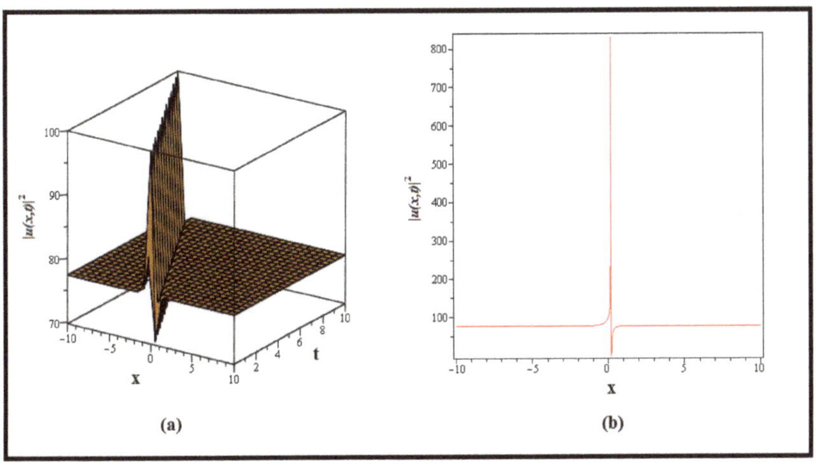

Figure 6. Depicts graph of the squared norm of (62). The 3D graph in (**a**) is plotted for $a = 2$, $b = 0, c = -1, A = e, a_1 = 0, b_1 = 0, \gamma = \delta = 1$ while the 2D graph in (**b**) is drawn for $t = 0$ and the similar values of involved parameters.

5. Conclusions

We used mEDAM's power to construct insightful solitary wave solutions for the fractional coupled Higgs system, adding critical generalized functions to describe its intricate physical processes. We investigated the dynamic behavior of adjustable free parameters and built practical linkages by incorporating them. This study expands our understanding of the system's features and dynamic patterns, proving mEDAM's resilience in decoding complicated mathematical models. The relevance of these results extends beyond engineering and scientific areas, promising useful paths for future research into the complicated dynamics of the fractional coupled Higgs system and its associated phenomena.

Author Contributions: The ideas of the present paper come from J.I. and M.B.; J.I., F.A.A. and R.A. wrote and completed the calculations; M.B., E.A.A.I. and R.A. checked all the results. All authors have read and agreed to the published version of the manuscript.

Funding: This project is funded by King Saud University, Riyadh, Saudi Arabia.

Data Availability Statement: The data used to support the findings of this study are available from the corresponding author upon request.

Acknowledgments: Researchers supporting project number (RSPD2023R576), King Saud University, Riyadh, Saudi Arabia.

Conflicts of Interest: The authors declare no conflict of interest.

References

1. Abro, K.A.; Atangana, A. Dual fractional modeling of rate type fluid through non-local differentiation. *Numer. Methods Partial Differ. Equ.* **2020**, *38*, 390–405. [CrossRef]
2. Metzler, R.; Glöckle, W.G.; Nonnenmacher, T.F. Fractional model equation for anomalous diffusion. *Phys. Stat. Mech. Its Appl.* **1994**, *211*, 13–24. [CrossRef]
3. Tarasov, V.E.; Zaslavsky, G.M. Fractional dynamics of systems with long-range interaction. *Commun. Nonlinear Sci. Numer. Simul.* **2006**, *11*, 885–898. [CrossRef]
4. Su, N. Random fractional partial differential equations and solutions for water movement in soils: Theory and applications. *Hydrol. Process.* **2023**, *37*, e14844. [CrossRef]
5. Che, J.; Guan, Q.; Wang, X. Image denoising based on adaptive fractional partial differential equations. In Proceedings of the 2013 6th International Congress on Image and Signal Processing (CISP), Hangzhou, China, 16–18 December 2013; Volume 1, pp. 288–292.
6. Kachhia, K.B.; Prajapati, J.C. Solution of fractional partial differential equation aries in study of heat transfer through diathermanous materials. *J. Interdiscip. Math.* **2015**, *18*, 125–132. [CrossRef]
7. Zhang, Y. A finite difference method for fractional partial differential equation. *Appl. Math. Comput.* **2009**, *215*, 524–529. [CrossRef]
8. Ford, N.J.; Xiao, J.; Yan, Y. A finite element method for time fractional partial differential equations. *Fract. Calc. Appl. Anal.* **2011**, *14*, 454–474. [CrossRef]
9. Lyu, W.; Wang, Z.A. Global classical solutions for a class of reaction-diffusion system with density-suppressed motility. *arXiv* **2021**, arXiv:2102.08042.
10. Li, C.; Chen, A. Numerical methods for fractional partial differential equations. *Int. J. Comput. Math.* **2018**, *95*, 1048–1099. [CrossRef]
11. Yang, Q.; Liu, F.; Turner, I. Numerical methods for fractional partial differential equations with Riesz space fractional derivatives. *Appl. Math. Model.* **2010**, *34*, 200–218. [CrossRef]
12. Lin, X.; Liu, Y.; Yu, J.; Yu, R.; Zhang, J.; Wen, H. Stability analysis of three-phase grid-connected inverter under the weak grids with asymmetrical grid impedance by LTP theory in time domain. *Int. J. Electr. Power Energy Syst.* **2022**, *142*, 108244. [CrossRef]
13. Naeem, M.; Azhar, O.F.; Zidan, A.M.; Nonlaopon, K.; Shah, R. Numerical analysis of fractional-order parabolic equations via Elzaki transform. *J. Funct. Spaces* **2021**, *2021*, 3484482. [CrossRef]
14. Liu, X.; Shi, T.; Zhou, G.; Liu, M.; Yin, Z.; Yin, L.; Zheng, W. Emotion classification for short texts: An improved multi-label method. *Humanit. Soc. Sci. Commun.* **2023**, *10*, 306. [CrossRef]
15. Al-Sawalha, M.M.; Ababneh, O.Y.; Shah, R.; Nonlaopon, K. Numerical analysis of fractional-order Whitham-Broer-Kaup equations with non-singular kernel operators. *Aims Math.* **2023**, *8*, 2308–2336. [CrossRef]
16. Liu, X.; Zhou, G.; Kong, M.; Yin, Z.; Li, X.; Yin, L.; Zheng, W. Developing Multi-Labelled Corpus of Twitter Short Texts: A Semi-Automatic Method. *Systems* **2023**, *11*, 390. [CrossRef]
17. Chen, D.; Wang, Q.; Li, Y.; Li, Y.; Zhou, H.; Fan, Y. A general linear free energy relationship for predicting partition coefficients of neutral organic compounds. *Chemosphere* **2020**, *247*, 125869. [CrossRef]

18. Elagan, S.K.; Sayed, M.; Higazy, M. An analytical study on fractional partial differential equations by Laplace transform operator method. *Int. J. Appl. Eng. Res.* **2018**, *13*, 545–549.
19. Mahor, T.C.; Mishra, R.; Jain, R. Analytical solutions of linear fractional partial differential equations using fractional Fourier transform. *J. Comput. Appl. Math.* **2021**, *385*, 113202. [CrossRef]
20. Thabet, H.; Kendre, S. New modification of Adomian decomposition method for solving a system of nonlinear fractional partial differential equations. *Int. J. Adv. Appl. Math. Mech.* **2019**, *6*, 1–13.
21. Duran, S. Exact solutions for time-fractional Ramani and Jimbo—Miwa equations by direct algebraic method. *Adv. Sci. Eng. Med.* **2020**, *12*, 982–988. [CrossRef]
22. Momani, S.; Odibat, Z. Homotopy perturbation method for nonlinear partial differential equations of fractional order. *Phys. Lett. A* **2007**, *365*, 345–350. [CrossRef]
23. Odibat, Z.; Momani, S. The variational iteration method: An efficient scheme for handling fractional partial differential equations in fluid mechanics. *Comput. Math. Appl.* **2009**, *58*, 2199–2208. [CrossRef]
24. Mirhosseini-Alizamini, S.M.; Rezazadeh, H.; Eslami, M.; Mirzazadeh, M.; Korkmaz, A. New extended direct algebraic method for the Tzitzica type evolution equations arising in nonlinear optics. *Comput. Methods Differ. Equ.* **2020**, *8*, 28–53.
25. Yasmin, H.; Aljahdaly, N.H.; Saeed, A.M.; Shah, R. Investigating Symmetric Soliton Solutions for the Fractional Coupled Konno–Onno System Using Improved Versions of a Novel Analytical Technique. *Mathematics* **2023**, *11*, 2686. [CrossRef]
26. Yasmin, H.; Aljahdaly, N.H.; Saeed, A.M.; Shah, R. Probing Families of Optical Soliton Solutions in Fractional Perturbed Radhakrishnan–Kundu–Lakshmanan Model with Improved Versions of Extended Direct Algebraic Method. *Fractal Fract.* **2023**, *7*, 512. [CrossRef]
27. Rezazadeh, H.; Mirhosseini-Alizamini, S.M.; Neirameh, A.; Souleymanou, A.; Korkmaz, A.; Bekir, A. Fractional Sine–Gordon equation approach to the coupled higgs system defined in time-fractional form. *Iran. J. Sci. Technol. Trans. A Sci.* **2019**, *43*, 2965–2973. [CrossRef]
28. Jabbari, A.; Kheiri, H.; Bekir, A. Exact solutions of the coupled Higgs equation and the Maccari system using He's semi-inverse method and (G′/G)-expansion method. *Comput. Math. Appl.* **2011**, *62*, 2177–2186. [CrossRef]
29. Atas, S.S.; Ali, K.K.; Sulaiman, T.A.; Bulut, H. Invariant optical soliton solutions to the Coupled-Higgs equation. *Opt. Quantum Electron.* **2022**, *54*, 754. [CrossRef]
30. Seadawy, A.R.; Lu, D.; Khater, M.M. Bifurcations of traveling wave solutions for Dodd–Bullough–Mikhailov equation and coupled Higgs equation and their applications. *Chin. J. Phys.* **2017**, *55*, 1310–1318. [CrossRef]
31. Mu, G.; Qin, Z. Rogue waves for the coupled Schrödinger–Boussinesq equation and the coupled Higgs equation. *J. Phys. Soc. Jpn.* **2012**, *81*, 084001. [CrossRef]
32. Sikora, B. Remarks on the Caputo fractional derivative. *MINUT* **2023**, *5*, 76–84
33. Khan, H.; Barak, S.; Kumam, P.; Arif, M. Analytical Solutions of Fractional Klein-Gordon and Gas Dynamics Equations, via the (G'/G)-Expansion Method. *Symmetry* **2019**, *11*, 566. [CrossRef]

fractal and fractional

Article

Modeling and Dynamical Analysis of a Fractional-Order Predator–Prey System with Anti-Predator Behavior and a Holling Type IV Functional Response

Baiming Wang and Xianyi Li *

Department of Big Data Science, School of Science, Zhejiang University of Science and Technology, Hangzhou 310023, China; 222109252018@zust.edu.cn
* Correspondence: mathxyli@zust.edu.cn

Abstract: We here investigate the dynamic behavior of continuous and discrete versions of a fractional-order predator–prey system with anti-predator behavior and a Holling type IV functional response. First, we establish the non-negativity, existence, uniqueness and boundedness of solutions to the system from a mathematical analysis perspective. Then, we analyze the stability of its equilibrium points and the possibility of bifurcations using stability analysis methods and bifurcation theory, demonstrating that, under specific parameter conditions, the continuous system exhibits a Hopf bifurcation, while the discrete version exhibits a Neimark–Sacker bifurcation and a period-doubling bifurcation. After providing numerical simulations to illustrate the theoretically derived conclusions and by summarizing the various analytical results obtained, we finally present four interesting conclusions that can contribute to better management and preservation of ecological systems.

Keywords: Caputo fractional derivative; memory effect; supercritical Hopf bifurcation; Neimark–Sacker bifurcation; period-doubling bifurcation

MSC: 39A28; 39A30

1. Introduction

The study of predator–prey systems can be traced back to the 18th century. However, the establishment of predator–prey systems in the modern sense is primarily attributed to the work of Alfred J. Lotka and Vito Volterra in the early 20th century. They independently proposed models for predator–prey systems and conducted in-depth research on their dynamical behavior. Their research laid an important theoretical foundation for the dynamics of predator–prey systems. Lotka–Volterra systems describe the interactions between predator and prey, and quickly became a hot topic in dynamical research. Even today, studying the dynamical relationship between predator and prey remains an important subject. To comprehend the intricate dynamical properties presented in predator–prey systems, numerous researchers have dedicated themselves to studying predator–prey models in depth. During the course of their research, they have found multitudes of fascinating dynamical properties among various systems. Berryman [1] pointed out that the original Lotka–Volterra predator–prey equations were built around the principle of mass action, and equations derived in this way lead to the paradoxes of enrichment and biological control. Wang and Chen [2] established the condition for the permanence of populations and sufficient conditions under which positive equilibrium of the model is globally stable. References [3,4] investigated the complex dynamical behavior of discrete predator–prey systems. Qi and Meng [5] found that in a predator–prey system with prey refuge and the fear effect, the survival rate of prey can be improved by increasing the strength of the refuge, decreasing the cost of fear or reducing the intensity of white noise. Blasius, Rudolf, et al. [6] found through experiments that a long-term cyclic persistence exists in a simple predator–prey model. Mukherjee [7] and Qiu and Guo [8] investigated the complex dynamics of a predator–prey system with the fear effect and a predator–prey system with prey taxis, respectively. Although we may subconsciously assume that prey are inherently disadvantaged in a predator–prey system, there are many instances where prey can resist predation and cause harm to predators, even leading to the death of the predator. The existence of such scenarios underscores the significance of determining which entities hold the advantage of prey in a predator–prey system [9].

The anti-predator behavior of prey is widely observed in the natural world. Many scholars have conducted research on the anti-predator behavior of prey and have identified two main ways in which prey exhibit such behaviors: (1) through morphological or behavioral changes [10,11], or (2) by actively attacking the predator [12–14].

In 1987, Ives and Dobson [15] proposed the following system to simulate anti-predator behavior (1):

$$\begin{cases} \frac{dx}{dt} = \alpha x\left(1 - \frac{x}{k}\right) - \beta - \frac{e^{-\gamma\beta}qxy}{1+ax}, \\ \frac{dy}{dt} = \frac{be^{-\gamma\beta}qxy}{1+ax} - dy, \end{cases} \tag{1.1}$$

where the meanings of all parameters are presented in Table 1.

Table 1. Biological meanings of all parameters in system (1.1).

Parameter	Meaning
x	Prey population density
y	Predator population density
$\alpha > 0$	Natality of prey population
$k > 0$	Carrying capacity of the environment to prey
$\beta > 0$	Cost incurred by the prey as a result of anti-predator behavior
$\gamma > 0$	Effects resulting from the anti-predator behavior of prey
$\frac{qx}{1+ax}, q > 0, a > 0$	Holling II functional response function
$b > 0$	Conversion rate of prey consumed by predator
$d > 0$	Death rate of predator population

The prey requirements in anti-predator behavior (2) are higher, as they not only demand that adult prey can resist predation by predators but also require adult prey to have the ability to kill the juveniles of the predator. However, there have been few studies on anti-predator behavior (2). In 2015, Tang and Xiao [16] proposed a system to simulate anti-predator behavior (2), and considered the following Holling type IV functional response function system:

$$\begin{cases} \frac{du}{dt} = au\left(1 - \frac{u}{k}\right) - \frac{buv}{h+u^2}, \\ \frac{dv}{dt} = \frac{cbuv}{h+u^2} - dv - guv, \end{cases} \tag{1.2}$$

where the meanings of all parameters are given in Table 2. It is worth noting that the Holling type IV functional response function used in this paper was originally proposed by W. Sokol [17] and has been widely applied in predator–prey systems for several decades. It primarily describes a nonlinear interaction between a predator and its prey. The predation rate of the predator adjusts to changes in the population density of prey, exhibiting a saturation tendency.

Table 2. Biological meanings of parameters in systems (1.2) and (1.3).

Parameter	Meaning
u	Prey population density
v	Predator population density
$a > 0$	Natality of prey population
$k > 0$	Carrying capacity of the environment to prey
$b > 0$	Predator's capture rate
$c > 0$	Conversion rate of prey into predator
$\frac{bu}{h+u^2}, h > 0$	Holling type IV functional response function
$d > 0$	Death rate of predator
$g > 0$	Mortality rate of predator due to the anti-predator effects of prey
$0 < \alpha \leq 1$	Order of fractional-order derivative

The concept of fractional derivatives can be traced back to the 18th century, and the mathematician who first proposed fractional derivatives was Liouville [18]. In the 20th century, the mathematician Riesz made the initial reference to the concept of fractional derivatives and conducted research on their properties in reference [19], combining the studies of Liouville and Riesz to establish the Riesz–Liouville definition of fractional derivatives that is used today. Subsequently, the mathematician Caputo introduced the Caputo definition of fractional derivatives in reference [20].

Definition 1. *Denote*

$${}_0^C D_t^\alpha f(t) = J^{l-\alpha} f^{(l)}(t),\ \alpha > 0,$$

where $f^{(l)}$ denotes the derivative of f with order l, l is the nearest integer value of α, and J^q is the operator of the Riemann–Liouville integral of q order:

$$J^q h(t) = \frac{\int_0^t (t-\tau_e)^{q-1} h(\tau_e) d\tau_e}{\Gamma(q)},$$

where $\Gamma(q)$ is Euler's Gamma function. The alpha-order Caputo differential operator is the term used to describe the operator ${}_0^C D_t^\alpha$.

From a biological perspective, considering a fractional-order predator–prey system makes logical sense; for most organisms in the natural world, their current behaviors are influenced by historical context. In fractional calculus, the rate of change at any given moment, i.e., the fractional-order derivative, depends on the population density over a certain period of time. Therefore, fractional-order predator–prey systems have unique advantages in describing memory effects within populations. Over the past two decades, owing to the advantages of fractional derivatives in studying various ecological systems' memory effects, numerous mathematicians have turned their attention to investigating fractional-order ecological systems, finding many interesting dynamical properties presented in them [21–28]. At present, a relatively comprehensive research framework has been established for mathematical models of integer-order ecosystems, while the study of fractional-order ecosystems is still in its early stages. Hence, the authors of this paper intend to introduce the Caputo fractional derivation to system (1.2) and extend it to a fractional-order ecosystem. We intend to employ the Caputo definition of fractional derivatives to analyze how anti-predator behavior and the Holling type IV functional response function in a fractional-order ecosystem will impact the dynamics of the system. As a result, we introduce the following fractional-order predator–prey system with a Holling type IV functional response and anti-predator behaviors:

$$\begin{cases} {}_0^C D_t^{\alpha} u(t) = au\left(1 - \frac{u}{k}\right) - \frac{buv}{h+u^2}, \\ {}_0^C D_t^{\alpha} v(t) = \frac{cbuv}{h+u^2} - dv - guv, \end{cases} \tag{1.3}$$

where the meanings of all parameters are presented in Table 2. For the method of introducing the Caputo fractional differential equation into an ecosystem model, reference [29] may be consulted.

There is a current lack of comprehensive dynamic analysis methods for continuous fractional-order predator–prey systems. For example, in the literature [30], the analysis of fractional-order systems has mainly focused on Hopf bifurcations, while more extensive research has been dedicated to analyzing integer-order cases.

In references [31,32], the authors, respectively, conducted dynamical analyses of different discretized predator–prey models and found that discrete predator–prey models, in comparison to their continuous counterparts, exhibit a greater variety of dynamical behaviors and hold advantages in numerical simulations. In reference [33], the authors employed the piecewise constant approximation (PCA) method to discretize a continuous fractional-order predator–prey system and analyzed the dynamical properties of and discussed the types of bifurcations present in this system. Their work motivates us to consider the discrete counterpart of system (1.3). In recent years, many researchers have studied the dynamical behavior of discrete fractional-order predator–prey systems and have discovered numerous intriguing dynamical properties within these systems [34–36].

Hence, in order to better understand the properties of system (1.3), we here also consider discretizing system (1.3) for further dynamical analyses and comparing its properties with the continuous model (1.3), finding that there are many differences in dynamical properties between system (1.3) and its discrete version (1.6). This sufficiently shows that it is very helpful to consider the same problems from different angles.

We use the PCA method to discretize model (1.3), and the specific steps are as follows:

Assume that the initial conditions of system (1.3) are $u(0) = u_0$ and $v(0) = v_0$. The discretized version of model (1.3) is given as

$$\begin{cases} {}_0^C D_t^{\alpha} u(t) = au([\tfrac{t}{\rho}])\left(1 - \frac{u([\frac{t}{\rho}])}{k}\right) - \frac{bu([\frac{t}{\rho}])v([\frac{t}{\rho}])}{h+u([\frac{t}{\rho}])^2}, \\ {}_0^C D_t^{\alpha} v(t) = \frac{cbu([\frac{t}{\rho}])v([\frac{t}{\rho}])}{h+u([\frac{t}{\rho}])^2} - dv([\tfrac{t}{\rho}]) - gu([\tfrac{t}{\rho}])v([\tfrac{t}{\rho}]). \end{cases}$$

First, let $t \in [0, \rho)$, then $\frac{t}{\rho} \in [0, 1)$. Thus, we obtain

$$\begin{cases} {}_0^C D_t^{\alpha} u(t) = au_0\left(1 - \frac{u_0}{k}\right) - \frac{bu_0v_0}{h+u_0^2}, \\ {}_0^C D_t^{\alpha} v(t) = \frac{cbu_0v_0}{h+u_0^2} - dv_0 - gu_0v_0. \end{cases} \tag{1.4}$$

The answer to (1.4) is simplified to

$$\begin{aligned} u_1(t) &= u_0 + J^{\alpha}\left(au_0\left(1 - \frac{u_0}{k}\right) - \frac{bu_0v_0}{h+u_0^2}\right) \\ &= u_0 + \frac{t^{\alpha}}{\alpha\Gamma(\alpha)}\left(au_0\left(1 - \frac{u_0}{k}\right) - \frac{bu_0v_0}{h+u_0^2}\right), \\ v_1(t) &= v_0 + J^{\alpha}\left(\frac{cbu_0v_0}{h+u_0^2} - dv_0 - gu_0v_0\right) \\ &= v_0 + \frac{t^{\alpha}}{\alpha\Gamma(\alpha)}\left(\frac{cbu_0v_0}{h+u_0^2} - dv_0 - gu_0v_0\right). \end{aligned}$$

Second, let $t \in [\rho, 2\rho)$, so $\frac{t}{\rho} \in [1, 2)$. Then,

$$\begin{cases} {}_{0}^{C}D_{t}^{\alpha}u(t) = au_1(1-\frac{u_1}{k}) - \frac{bu_1v_1}{h+u_1^2}, \\ {}_{0}^{C}D_{t}^{\alpha}v(t) = \frac{cbu_1v_1}{h+u_1^2} - dv_1 - gu_1v_1. \end{cases} \tag{1.5}$$

After simplifying (1.5), we can obtain the following solution

$$\begin{aligned} u_1(t) &= u_1(\rho) + J_{\rho}^{\alpha}(au_1(1-\frac{u_1}{k}) - \frac{bu_1v_1}{h+u_1^2}) \\ &= u_1(\rho) + \frac{(t-\rho)^{\alpha}}{\alpha\Gamma(\alpha)}(au_1(1-\frac{u_1}{k}) - \frac{bu_1v_1}{h+u_1^2}), \\ v_1(t) &= v_1(\rho) + J_{\rho}^{\alpha}(\frac{cbu_1v_1}{h+u_1^2} - dv_1 - gu_1v_1) \\ &= v_1(\rho) + \frac{(t-\rho)^{\alpha}}{\alpha\Gamma(\alpha)}(\frac{cbu_1v_1}{h+u_1^2} - dv_1 - gu_1v_1), \end{aligned}$$

where $J_{\rho}^{\alpha} = \frac{1}{\Gamma(\alpha)}\int_{\rho}^{t}(t-\tau_e)^{\alpha-1}d\tau_e$, $0 < \alpha < 1$. After n repetitions, we obtain

$$\begin{aligned} u_{n+1}(t) &= u_n(n\rho) + \frac{(t-n\rho)^{\alpha}}{\alpha\Gamma(\alpha)}(au_n(n\rho)(1-\frac{u_n(n\rho)}{k}) - \frac{bu_n(n\rho)v_n(n\rho)}{h+u_n(n\rho)^2}), \\ v_{n+1}(t) &= v_n(n\rho) + \frac{(t-n\rho)^{\alpha}}{\alpha\Gamma(\alpha)}(\frac{cbu_n(n\rho)v_n(n\rho)}{h+u_n(n\rho)^2} - dv_n(n\rho) - gu_n(n\rho)v_n(n\rho)), \end{aligned}$$

where $t \in [n\rho, (n+1)\rho)$. For $t \to (n+1)\rho$, the system above becomes

$$\begin{cases} u_{n+1} = u_n + \frac{(\rho)^{\alpha}}{\Gamma(\alpha+1)}(au_n(1-\frac{u_n}{k}) - \frac{bu_nv_n}{h+u_n^2}), \\ v_{n+1} = v_n + \frac{(\rho)^{\alpha}}{\Gamma(\alpha+1)}(\frac{cbu_nv_n}{h+u_n^2} - dv_n - gu_nv_n). \end{cases} \tag{1.6}$$

The overall structure of this paper is described as follows: In Section 2, some preliminaries are provided for some definitions, lemmas and theorems that will be used to analyze the dynamical properties of systems (1.3) and (1.6). In Section 3, the well-posedness of system (1.3) is analyzed. In Section 4, the existence and stability of the equilibrium points of systems (1.3) and (1.6) are investigated, respectively. In Section 5, we demonstrate that, under certain parameter conditions, system (1.3) exhibits a Hopf bifurcation, while system (1.6) exhibits a Neimark–Sacker bifurcation and a period-doubling bifurcation. In Section 6, numerical simulations are performed to validate the results of our theoretical analysis. In Section 7, interesting conclusions are drawn based on some findings in the previous sections.

2. Preliminaries

In this section, we primarily introduce the definition and some conclusions of Caputo fractional derivatives that are necessary for our subsequent research.

Definition 2 ([37]). *Under the definition of Caputo fractional derivatives, the fractional derivative of function $f(\xi) \in AC^n([0,+\infty],\mathbb{R})$ is given as*

$${}_{0}^{C}D_{\xi}^{\alpha}f(\xi) = \int_0^{\xi}\frac{f^{(n)}(\vartheta)}{\Gamma(n-\alpha)(\xi-\vartheta)^{\alpha-n+1}}d\vartheta,$$

where α represents the order of the fractional derivative.

When $n = 1$, the fractional derivative ${}_{0}^{C}D_{\xi}^{\alpha}f(\xi)$ takes the form of

$${}_{0}^{C}D_{\xi}^{\alpha}f(\xi) = \int_0^{\xi}\frac{f(\vartheta)}{\Gamma(1-\alpha)(\xi-\vartheta)^{\alpha}}d\vartheta.$$

Definition 3 ([37]). *The Mittag–Leffler function M_i, when the order i of M_i is positive, is defined as*

$$M_i(\zeta) = \sum_{j=0}^{\infty} \frac{\zeta_j}{\Gamma(ji+1)}, \; \zeta_j \in \mathbb{C},$$

as the sequence converges.

Definition 4 ([38]). *Let $Q(u,v)$ be a fixed piont of system (1.6) with multipliers λ_1 and λ_2.*
(i) If $|\lambda_1| < 1$ and $|\lambda_2| < 1$, the fixed point $Q(u,v)$ is called a sink, and the sink is locally asymptotically stable.
(ii) If $|\lambda_1| > 1$ and $|\lambda_2| > 1$, the fixed point $Q(u,v)$ is called a source, and the source is locally asymptotically unstable.
(iii) If $|\lambda_1| < 1$ and $|\lambda_2| > 1$ (or $|\lambda_1| > 1$ and $|\lambda_2| < 1$), the fixed point $Q(u,v)$ is called a saddle.
(iv) If either $|\lambda_1| = 1$ or $|\lambda_2| = 1$, the fixed point $Q(u,v)$ is called non-hyperbolic.

Lemma 1 ([39]). *For ${}_0^C D_\xi^\alpha f(\xi) \in AC([0,\Xi],\mathbb{R})$, if $f(\xi_1) = 0$ and $f(\xi_0) > 0$ (all $\xi_0 \in [0,\xi_1)$), then ${}_0^C D_\xi^\alpha f(\xi_1) < 0$.*

Lemma 2 ([40]). *For the fractional-order system*

$${}_0^C D_\xi^\alpha Y(\xi) = Z(\xi, Y), \; \xi \geq 0,$$

with initial condition $Y(0) = (u(0), v(0))$, where $0 < \alpha \leq 1$, $Z : [0,+\infty) \times \tau \to \mathbb{R}^n$, $\tau \subseteq \mathbb{R}$, if $Z(\xi, Y)$ fulfills the local Lipschitz condition for $Z \in \mathbb{R}_n$,

$$\|Z(\xi,Y) - Z(\xi,\tilde{Y})\| \leq \Delta \cdot \|Y - \tilde{Y}\|,$$

then the system has a unique solution on $[0,+\infty) \times \tau$, and

$$\|Y(y_1,y_2,y_3,\ldots,y_n) - Y(\tilde{y_1},\tilde{y_2},\tilde{y_3},\ldots,\tilde{y_n})\| \leq \sum_{i=1}^{n} |y_i - \tilde{y_i}|,$$

for $i = 1,2,3,\ldots,n, y_i, \tilde{y_i} \in \mathbb{R}$.

Lemma 3 ([41]). *Let $F(\lambda) = \lambda^2 + B\lambda + C$, where B and C are two real constants. Suppose λ_1 and λ_2 are two roots of $F(\lambda) = 0$. Then, the following statements hold.*
(i) If $F(1) > 0$, then
(i.1) $|\lambda_1| < 1$ and $|\lambda_2| < 1$ if and only if $F(-1) > 0$ and $C < 1$;
(i.2) $\lambda_1 = -1$ and $\lambda_2 \neq -1$ if and only if $F(-1) = 0$ and $B \neq 2$;
(i.3) $|\lambda_1| < 1$ and $|\lambda_2| > 1$ if and only if $F(-1) < 0$;
(i.4) $|\lambda_1| > 1$ and $|\lambda_2| > 1$ if and only if $F(-1) > 0$ and $C > 1$;
(i.5) λ_1 and λ_2 are a pair of conjugate complex roots and $|\lambda_1| = |\lambda_2| = 1$ if and only if $-2 < B < 2$ and $C = 1$;
(i.6) $\lambda_1 = \lambda_2 = -1$ if and only if $F(-1) = 0$ and $B = 2$.
(ii) If $F(1) = 0$, namely, 1 is a root of $F(\lambda) = 0$, then the another root λ satisfies $|\lambda| = (<,>)1$ if and only if $|C| = (<,>)1$.
(iii) If $F(1) < 0$, then $F(\lambda) = 0$ has one root lying in $(1,\infty)$. Moreover,
(iii.1) The other root λ satisfies $\lambda < (=) -1$ if and only if $F(-1) < (=)0$;
(iii.2) The other root $-1 < \lambda < 1$ if and only if $F(-1) > 0$.

Theorem 1 ([42]). *The Laplace transform of ${}_0^C D_\xi^\alpha f(\xi)$ is*

$$\mathscr{L}\left[{}_0^C D_\xi^\alpha f(\xi)\right] = \vartheta^\alpha F(\vartheta) - \sum_{j=0}^{n-1} \vartheta^{\alpha-j-1} f^j(0),$$

where $F(\vartheta) = \mathscr{L}[f(\xi)]$, $\alpha \in (n-1,n), n \in \mathbb{Z}_+$.

Theorem 2 ([43]). *Assume* $\alpha > 0$, $\beta > 0$ *and* $K \in \mathbb{C}^{n\times n}$, *then*

$$\mathscr{L}[\xi^{\beta-1}E_{\alpha,\beta}(K\xi^{\alpha})] = \frac{\vartheta^{\alpha-\beta}}{\vartheta^{\alpha}-K},$$

for $Re(\vartheta) > \|K\|^{\frac{1}{\alpha}}$, *where* $Re(\vartheta)$ *is the real part of complex number* ϑ *and* $E_{\alpha,\beta}$ *is the Mittag–Leffler function.*

Theorem 3 ([44]). *For the following fractional-order system*

$${}_0^C D_{\xi}^{\alpha} f(\xi) = g(f(\xi)), f(0) = f_0 \in \mathbb{R}^N, \alpha \in (0,1),$$

where $f(\xi) = (f_1(\xi), f_2(\xi), f_3(\xi), \ldots, f_n(\xi))^T \in \mathbb{R}^n$ *and* $g = (g_1, g_2, g_3, \ldots, g_n)^T : \mathbb{R}^n \to \mathbb{R}^n$. *If* $g(f^*) = 0$, *then* f^* *is an equilibrium point. Set* $J(f^*)$ *as the Jacobian matrix* $J = \frac{\partial g}{\partial f} = \frac{\partial(g_1,g_2,g_3,\ldots,g_n)}{\partial(f_1,f_2,f_3,\ldots,f_n)}$ *for* $f = f^*$. *If the characteristic values* $\lambda_i (i = 1,2,3,\ldots,n)$ *of* $J(f^*)$ *meet* $|arg(\lambda_i)| > \frac{\alpha\pi}{2} (i = 1,2,3,\ldots,n)$, *then* f^* *is locally asymptotically stable.*

Theorem 4 ([45]). *We say that a fractional-order system undergoes a fractional Hopf bifurcation if there exists a critical value* $\beta = \beta_c$ *such that the following conditions are satisfied:*

1. $\lambda_1(\beta_c)$ *and* $\lambda_2(\beta_c)$ *satisfy* $|arg(\lambda_i(\beta_c))| = \frac{\pi\alpha}{2}, (i = 1,2)$;
2. $|arg(\lambda_i(\beta_c))| \neq \frac{\pi\alpha}{2}, (i = 3,4,5,\ldots,n)$;
3. $\frac{d}{d\beta}|arg(\lambda_i(\beta))||_{\beta=\beta_c} \neq 0, (i = 1,2)$,

where λ *represents the eigenvalues of the Jacobian matrix of the system.*

3. Analysis of the Well-Posedness of System (1.3)

In this section, we consider the uniqueness, non-negativity and boundedness of the solutions of system (1.3).

Theorem 5. *For the initial condition* $(u(0), v(0)) \in A$, *system (1.3) has a unique solution* $U(t) = (u(t), v(t)) \in A$ *for all* $t \geq 0$, *where* $A = \{(u,v) \in \mathbb{R}^2 : max\{|u|, |vs.|\} < \gamma_1, min\{|u|, |vs.|\} > \gamma_2\}$.

Proof. Consider the time interval $[0, t_1], t_1 < +\infty$. Construct a mapping $G(U) = (G_1(U), G_2(U))^T$, where $U = (u,v)^T$ and

$$\begin{cases} G_1(U) = au(1-\frac{u}{k}) - \frac{buv}{h+u^2}, \\ G_2(U) = \frac{cbuv}{h+u^2} - dv - guv. \end{cases}$$

For $U, \tilde{U} \in A$, we have

$$\begin{aligned} &\|G(U) - G(\tilde{U})\| \\ &= |G_1(U) - G_1(\tilde{U})| + |G_2(U) - G_2(\tilde{U})| \\ &= |au(1-\frac{u}{k}) - \frac{buv}{h+u^2} - a\tilde{u}(1-\frac{\tilde{u}}{k}) + \frac{b\tilde{u}\tilde{v}}{h+\tilde{u}^2}| \end{aligned}$$

$$
\begin{aligned}
&+|\frac{cbuv}{h+u^2}-dv-guv-\frac{cb\tilde{u}\tilde{v}}{h+\tilde{u}^2}-d\tilde{v}-g\tilde{u}\tilde{v}| \\
&\le a|u-\tilde{u}|+\frac{a}{k}|u+\tilde{u}||u-\tilde{u}|+|\frac{buv(h+\tilde{u}^2)-b\tilde{u}\tilde{v}(h+u^2)}{(h+u^2)(h+\tilde{u}^2)}| \\
&+|\frac{cbuv(h+\tilde{u}^2)-cb\tilde{u}\tilde{v}(h+u^2)}{(h+u^2)(h+\tilde{u}^2)}|+d|v-\tilde{v}|+g|uv-\tilde{u}\tilde{v}| \\
&= a|u-\tilde{u}|+\frac{a}{k}|u+\tilde{u}||u-\tilde{u}| \\
&+(1+c)|\frac{bhu(v-\tilde{v})+bh\tilde{v}(u-\tilde{u})}{(h+u^2)(h+\tilde{u}^2)}+\frac{bu^2\tilde{u}(v-\tilde{v})-bu\tilde{u}v(u-\tilde{u})}{(h+u^2)(h+\tilde{u}^2)}| \\
&+d|v-\tilde{v}|+g|u(v-\tilde{v})+\tilde{v}(u-\tilde{u})| \\
&\le (a+g\gamma_1+\frac{2a\gamma_1}{k}+\frac{b(1+c)(h\gamma_2+\gamma_2^3)}{(h+\gamma_2^2)^2})|u-\tilde{u}| \\
&+(d+g\gamma_1+\frac{b(1+c)(h\gamma_2+\gamma_2^3)}{(h+\gamma_2^2)^2})|v-\tilde{v}| \\
&= L_1|u-\tilde{u}|+L_2|v-\tilde{v}|\le L\|U-\tilde{U}\|,
\end{aligned}
$$

where $L = max\{L_1, L_2\}$ with $L_1 = a + g\gamma_1 + \frac{2a\gamma_1}{k} + \frac{b(1+c)(h\gamma_2+\gamma_2^3)}{(h+\gamma_2^2)^2}$ and $L_2 = d + g\gamma_1 + \frac{b(1+c)(h\gamma_2+\gamma_2^3)}{(h+\gamma_2^2)^2}$. □

Hence, $G(U)$ conforms to the local Lipschitz condition, and system (1.3) has a unique solution by Lemma 2.

Theorem 6. *All solutions of system (1.3) initiating from $(u(0), v(0)) \in \mathbb{R}^+$ are non-negative and bounded in the region W, where*

$$
W = \left\{(u(t), v(t) \in \mathbb{R}_+^2)\|0 \le u(t) + \frac{v(t)}{c} \le \frac{k(a+d)^2}{4ad}\right\}.
$$

Proof. First, let us prove the non-negativity of the solution. Assume that there exists a constant $\mu(>0)$ that satisfies

$$
\begin{cases}
u(t) > 0, t \in [0, \mu), \\
u(\mu) = 0, \\
u(\mu^+) < 0.
\end{cases}
$$

We can easily find that ${}_0^C D_t^\alpha u(t)|_\mu = 0$, and derive $u(\mu^+) = 0$ from Lemma 1, which obviously contradicts $u(\mu^+) < 0$. Thus, $u(t) > 0$ for any $t \in [0, +\infty)$. Similarly, we can prove $v(t) > 0$ for $\forall t \in [0, +\infty)$.

Now, construct a function $X(t) = u(t) + \frac{v(t)}{c}$, which will help us prove the boundedness of the solution. The Caputo fractional derivative of $X(t)$ with order α is

$$
\begin{aligned}
{}_0^C D_t^\alpha X(t) &= au(t) - \frac{au(t)^2}{k} - \frac{dv(t)}{c} - \frac{guv}{c} \\
&= au(t)(1 - \frac{u(t)}{k}) - \frac{gu(t)v(t)}{c} - d(X(t) - u(t)).
\end{aligned}
$$

Then,

$$
\begin{aligned}
{}_{0}^{C}D_{t}^{\alpha}X(t)+dX(t) &= au(t)(1-\frac{u(t)}{k})-\frac{gu(t)v(t)}{c}+du(t)\\
&\leq \frac{k(a+d)^2}{4a}-(u(t)\sqrt{\frac{a}{k}}-\frac{(a+d)}{2}\sqrt{\frac{k}{a}})^2\\
&\leq \frac{k(a+d)^2}{4a},
\end{aligned}
$$

i.e.,

$$
{}_{0}^{C}D_{t}^{\alpha}X(t)+dX(t)\leq \frac{k(a+d)^2}{4a}.
$$

Applying Theorem 1 and taking the Laplace transform on both sides of the above inequality at the same time, one has

$$
\mathscr{L}[{}_{0}^{C}D_{t}^{\alpha}X(t)+dX(t)]\leq \mathscr{L}[\frac{k(a+d)^2}{4a}].
$$

This leads to

$$
\vartheta^{\alpha}F(\vartheta)-\vartheta^{\alpha-1}X(0)+dF(\vartheta)\leq \frac{1}{\vartheta}\frac{k(a+d)^2}{4a},
$$

where $F(\vartheta)=\mathscr{L}[X(t)]$. Hence,

$$
F(\vartheta)\leq \frac{k(a+d)^2}{4\vartheta a(\vartheta^{\alpha}+d)}+\frac{\vartheta^{\alpha-1}}{\vartheta^{\alpha}+d}X(0).
$$

By using the inverse Laplace transform on both sides of the above inequality, we may derive

$$
\begin{aligned}
\mathscr{L}^{-1}[F(\vartheta)] &\leq T\mathscr{L}^{-1}[\frac{1}{\vartheta(\vartheta^{\alpha}+d)}]+X(0)\mathscr{L}^{-1}[\frac{\vartheta^{\alpha-1}}{\vartheta^{\alpha}+d}]\\
\Rightarrow X(t) &\leq T\mathscr{L}^{-1}[\frac{\vartheta^{-1}}{\vartheta^{\alpha}+d}]+X(0)\mathscr{L}^{-1}[\frac{\vartheta^{\alpha-1}}{\vartheta^{\alpha}+d}],
\end{aligned}
$$

where $T=\frac{k(a+d)^2}{4a}$. From Theorem 2, one obtains

$$
X(t)\leq Tt^{\alpha}E_{\alpha,\alpha+1}(-dt^{\alpha})+X(0)E_{\alpha,1}(-dt^{\alpha}).
$$

According to the properties of the Mittag–Leffer function, we get

$$
E_{\alpha,1}(-dt^{\alpha})=-dt^{\alpha}E_{\alpha,\alpha+1}(-dt^{\alpha})+\frac{1}{\Gamma(1)},
$$

i.e.,

$$
-\frac{1}{d}[E_{\alpha,1}(-dt^{\alpha})-1]=t^{\alpha}E_{\alpha,\alpha+1}(-dt^{\alpha}),
$$

which displays

$$
X(t)\leq (X(0)-\frac{T}{d})E_{\alpha,1}(-dt^{\alpha})+\frac{T}{d}.
$$

Note that $E_{\alpha,1}\to 0$ when $t\to\infty$. Thus, we have $X(t)\leq\frac{T}{d}$ for large t, i.e., $X(t)\leq\frac{k(a+d)^2}{4ad}$ for large t. Accordingly, all solutions of system (1.3) are bounded in the region

$$W = \left\{ (u(t), v(t)) \in \mathbb{R}_+^2 \| 0 \le u(t) + \frac{v(t)}{c} \le \frac{k(a+d)^2}{4ad} \right\}.$$

The proof is over. □

4. Local Stability of Systems (1.3) and (1.6)

In this section, we first identify the equilibrium points of systems (1.3) and (1.6), which are the same, then analyze their local stability.

4.1. Existence of an Equilibrium Point

We first can easily observe that the two points $Q_0(0,0)$ and $Q_k(k,0)$ always are equilibrium points of systems (1.3) and (1.6).

Next, we consider the positive equilibrium points of systems (1.3) and (1.6). It is evident that the positive equilibrium solutions of systems (1.3) and (1.6) satisfy the following equations:

$$\begin{cases} a(1-\frac{u}{k}) - \frac{bv}{h+u^2} = 0, \\ \frac{cbu}{h+u^2} - d - gu = 0. \end{cases} \tag{4.1}$$

By performing a transformation on the second equation, we find that the component u of positive equilibrium point (u,v) meets the following equation

$$p(u) = gu^3 + du^2 + (gh - cb)u + dh = 0, \tag{4.2}$$

while the positive component $v = \frac{a}{b}(1-\frac{u}{k})(h+u^2)$. Therefore, the problem of finding positive equilibrium points of systems (1.3) and (1.6) is transferred to that of solving the positive solutions of Equation (4.2). It is easy to derive

$$p^{'}(u) = 3gu^2 + 2du + gh - cb, p^{''}(u) = 6gu + 2d. \tag{4.3}$$

Obviously, $p^{''}(u) > 0$ always holds for $u > 0$. This implies $p^{'}(u)$ is monotonically increasing for $u > 0$. Now, consider the solutions of $p(u) = 0$ according to the following two cases.

Case 1: $gh - cb \ge 0$. Then, $p^{'}(u) > 0$, indicating that $p(u)$ is monotonically increasing. Again, $p(0) = dh > 0$. Therefore, there are no positive solutions of $p(u) = 0$ for $gh - cb \ge 0$, which then implies that system (1.3) has no positive equilibrium points.

Case 2: $gh - cb < 0$. Then, $p^{'}(u) = 0$ has a unique positive solution, denoted by u_*, where $u_* = \frac{-d+\sqrt{d^2-3g(gh-cb)}}{3g}$. Furthermore, since $p^{'}(u)$ is monotonically increasing, we can conclude that $p(u)$ is monotonically decreasing in the interval $(0, u_*)$, whereas it is monotonically increasing in the interval $(u_*, +\infty)$. Thus, the function $p(u)$ has a minimum at $u = u_*$ for $u \in (0,\infty)$. Substituting u_* into (4.2), we obtain

$$\begin{aligned} p(u_*) =& \frac{1}{27g^2}[R^3 + 3(3hg^2 - 3bcg - d^2)R + 3(d^2 + 3bcdg + 6dhg^2)] \\ =& \frac{1}{27g^2}\big[-2R^3 + 3(d^2 + 3bcdg + 6dhg^2)\big] = \frac{2}{27g^2}(R_0^3 - R^3), \end{aligned}$$

where $R = \sqrt{d^2 - 3g(gh-cb)}$ and $R_0 = \sqrt[3]{\frac{3}{2}(d^2 + 3bcdg + 6dhg^2)}$. Then, we can discuss the positive solution of $p(u) = 0$ in view of the following three subcases:

Subcase 1. $p(u_*) > 0 \iff R < R_0$. This means that the equation $p(u) = 0$ has no positive roots.

Subcase 2. $p(u_*) = 0 \iff R = R_0$. This indicates that there is only one positive solution u_* of the equation $p(u) = 0$.

Subcase 3. $p(u_*) < 0 \Longleftrightarrow R > R_0$. This means that there are two positive roots of the equation $p(u) = 0$, denoted by u_1 and u_2. Namely,

$$u_1 = \frac{-d + \sqrt{R}(cos(\frac{o}{3}) - \sqrt{3}sin(\frac{o}{3}))}{3g},$$
$$u_2 = \frac{-d + \sqrt{R}(cos(\frac{o}{3}) + \sqrt{3}sin(\frac{o}{3}))}{3g},$$

where $o = arccot(J)$, $J = \frac{2dR^2 - 3gT}{2R^3}(J \in (-1,1))$ and $T = d(gh - cb) - 9ghd$. Evidently, $0 < u_1 < u_* < u_2$.

Denote the two positive equilibria as $Q_i(u_i, v_i)$ if $u_i < k, i = 1,2$. Summarizing the above analysis, we can obtain the following result.

Theorem 7. *Let R, R_0, u_*, u_1, u_2 be, respectively, defined in Case 2 and Case 3. For the existence of an equilibrium point of systems (1.3) and (1.6), the following statements hold.*

1. *Regardless of the value of the parameters, systems (1.3) and (1.6) always have a trivial equilibrium point $Q_0(0,0)$ and a boundary equilibrium point $Q_k(k,0)$.*
2. *When $gh - cb \geq 0$, systems (1.3) and (1.6) do not have positive equilibrium points.*
3. *When $gh - cb < 0$, we further have the following conclusions.*
   (a) *If $R_0 > R$, then systems (1.3) and (1.6) do not have positive equilibrium points.*
   (b) *If $R_0 = R$, then, for $0 < k \leq u_*$, systems (1.3) and (1.6) do not have positive equilibrium points; for $u_* < k$, systems (1.3) and (1.6) have one positive equilibrium point $Q_*(u_*, v_*)$.*
   (c) *If $R_0 < R$, then, for $0 < k \leq u_1$, systems (1.3) and (1.6) do not have positive equilibrium points; for $u_1 < k \leq u_2$, systems (1.3) and (1.6) have only one positive equilibrium point $Q_1(u_1, v_1)$; for $u_2 < k$, systems (1.3) and (1.6) have two positive equilibrium points $Q_1(u_1, v_1)$ and $Q_2(u_2, v_2)$.*

Next, we analyze the stability of these equilibrium points of systems (1.3) and (1.6).

4.2. *Stability Analysis of Equilibrium Points of System (1.3)*

The Jacobian matrix of system (1.3) at any equilibrium $Q(u,v)$ is as follows

$$J_c(u,v) = \begin{pmatrix} a(1 - \frac{2u}{k}) - \frac{bv}{h+u^2} + \frac{2bu^2v}{(h+u^2)^2} & -\frac{bu}{h+u^2} \\ \frac{bcv(h-u^2)}{(h+u^2)^2} - gv & \frac{bcu}{h+u^2} - d - gu \end{pmatrix}.$$

4.2.1. The Stability of the Trivial Equilibrium Point $Q_0(0,0)$

Theorem 8. *The trivial equilibrium point $Q_0(0,0)$ is a saddle.*

Proof. Substituting the trivial equilibrium point $Q_0(0,0)$ into the Jacobian matrix $J_c(u,v)$, we obtain

$$J_c(Q_0) = \begin{pmatrix} a & 0 \\ 0 & -d \end{pmatrix},$$

and it is easy to see that the Jacobian matrix $J_c(Q_0)$ has two eigenvalues: $\lambda_1 = a > 0$ and $\lambda_2 = -d < 0$. Since $|arg(\lambda_1)| = 0 < \frac{\alpha\pi}{2}$ and $|arg(\lambda_2)| = \pi > \frac{\alpha\pi}{2}$, the trivial equilibrium point Q_0 is a saddle. □

4.2.2. The Stability of Boundary Equilibrium Point $Q_k(k,0)$

Theorem 9. *The boundary equilibrium point $Q_k(k,0)$ is a stable node for $d > \frac{cbk}{h+k^2} - gk$, while it is a saddle for $d < \frac{cbk}{h+k^2} - gk$.*

Proof. Substituting boundary equilibrium point $Q_k(k,0)$ into the Jacobian matrix $J_c(u,v)$, we have

$$J_c(Q_k) = \begin{pmatrix} -a & \frac{-bk}{h+k^2} \\ 0 & \frac{cbk}{h+k^2} - d - gk \end{pmatrix}.$$

Now, consider the following two cases:

Case 1: $d < \frac{cbk}{h+k^2} - gk$. Then, we obtain the two eigenvalues of the Jacobian matrix $J_c(Q_k)$: $\lambda_1 = -a < 0$ and $\lambda_2 = \frac{cbk}{h+k^2} - gk - d > 0$. Therefore, $|arg(\lambda_1)| = \pi > \frac{\alpha\pi}{2}$ and $|arg(\lambda_2)| = 0 < \frac{\alpha\pi}{2}$. Thus, the boundary equilibrium point Q_k is a saddle.
Case 2: $d > \frac{cbk}{h+k^2} - gk$. Then, the two eigenvalues of the Jacobian matrix $J_c(Q_k)$ are $\lambda_1 = -a < 0$ and $\lambda_2 = \frac{cbk}{h+k^2} - d - gk < 0$. As a result of $|arg(\lambda_1)| = \pi > \frac{\alpha\pi}{2}$ and $|arg(\lambda_2)| = \pi > \frac{\alpha\pi}{2}$, the boundary equilibrium point Q_k is a stable node.
□

4.2.3. The Stability of Positive Equilibrium Points $Q_i(u_i, v_i)$ $(i = 1,2)$

Theorem 10. *The positive equilibrium point $Q_1(u_1, v_1)$ is stable for $k > \frac{h+3u_1^2}{2u_1}$ and unstable for $k < \frac{h+3u_1^2}{2u_1}$; the postive equilibrium point $Q_2(u_2, v_2)$ is always a saddle point.*

Proof. For a better comprehension, let us begin to analyze the stability of the positive equilibrium point $Q_2(u_2, v_2)$.

Substituting the equilibrium point $Q_2(u_2, v_2)$ into the Jacobian matrix $J_c(u,v)$, one obtains

$$J_c(Q_2) = \begin{pmatrix} -a\frac{u_2}{k} + \frac{2bu_2^2v_2}{(h+u_2^2)^2} & -\frac{bu_2}{h+u_2^2} \\ \frac{bcv_2(h-u_2^2)}{(h+u_2^2)^2} - gv_2 & 0 \end{pmatrix},$$

from which we can easily derive the following result:

$$|J_c(Q_2)| = \frac{bu_2v_2}{h+u_2^2}\left(\frac{bc(h-u_2^2)}{(h+u_2^2)^2} - g\right). \tag{4.4}$$

From (4.2), we can deduce

$$h = \frac{bcu_2}{gu_2+d} - u_2^2. \tag{4.5}$$

Substituting (4.5) into (4.4) obtains

$$|J_c(Q_2)| = \frac{(gu_2+d)v_2}{bc^2u_2}(bcd - 2g^2u_2^3 - 4gdu_2^2 - 2d^2u_2). \tag{4.6}$$

Let $q(u_2) = bcd - 2g^2u_2^3 - 4gdu_2^2 - 2d^2u_2$. Since $p'(u_*) = 0$, $p(u_*) < 0$ and $q(u_2)$ is monotonically decreasing for $u_2 > 0$, we can obtain

$$
\begin{aligned}
q(u_2) < q(u_*) &= bcd - 2g^2{u_*}^3 - 4gd{u_*}^2 - 2d^2u_* \\
&= g(dh - 2g{u_*}^3 - d{u_*}^2) \\
&< g(-2g{u_*}^3 - d{u_*}^2 - g{u_*}^3 - d{u_*}^2 - (gh - cb)u_*) \\
&= gu_*(-3g{u_*}^2 - 2du_* - gh + cb) = 0.
\end{aligned}
\tag{4.7}
$$

This verifies that $|J_c(Q_2)| < 0$ holds if Q_2 exists, which reads $\lambda_1\lambda_2 < 0$. Accordingly, $\lambda_1 > (<)0 \Rightarrow |arg(\lambda_1)| < (>)\frac{\alpha\pi}{2}$ and $\lambda_2 < (>)0 \Rightarrow |arg(\lambda_1)| > (<)\frac{\alpha\pi}{2}$. Thus, the postive equilibrium point $Q_2(u_2, v_2)$ is always a saddle.

Similarly, for the postive equilibrium point $Q_1(u_1, v_1)$, we have

$$
\begin{aligned}
q(u_1) &= bcd - 2g^2u_1^3 - 4gdu_1^2 - 2d^2u_1 \\
&> g(dh - 2g{u_*}^3 - d{u_*}^2) \\
&> gu_*(-3g{u_*}^2 - 2du_* - gh + cb) = 0.
\end{aligned}
\tag{4.8}
$$

Thus, $|J_c(Q_1)| > 0$, which reads $\lambda_1\lambda_2 > 0$. In order to determine the signs of λ_1 and λ_2, we need to further consider the sign of the trace of matrix $J_c(Q_1)$. Note that the trace of $J_c(Q_1)$ is $tr(J_c(u_1, v_1)) = -a\frac{u_1}{k} + \frac{2bu_1^2v_1}{(h+u_1)^2}$. Note that $\frac{cbu_1v_1}{h+u_1^2} - dv_1 - gu_1v_1 = 0$ and $v_1 = \frac{a}{b}(1 - \frac{u_1}{k})(h + u_1^2)$. So,

$$
tr(J_c(u_1, v_1)) = \frac{2au_1^2}{k(h+u_1^2)}(k - \frac{h+3u_1^2}{2u_1}) > (=,<)\ 0 \Leftrightarrow k > (=,<)\ \frac{h+3u_1^2}{2u_1}.
$$

Therefore, we can conclude that if $k < \frac{h+3u_1^2}{2u_1}$, then $\lambda_1 < 0 (\Rightarrow |arg(\lambda_1)| > \frac{\alpha\pi}{2})$ and $\lambda_2 < 0 (\Rightarrow |arg(\lambda_2)| > \frac{\alpha\pi}{2})$; thus, system (1.3) is stable at $Q_1(u_1, v_1)$. If $k > \frac{h+3u_1^2}{2u_1}$, then $\lambda_1 > 0 (\Rightarrow |arg(\lambda_1)| = 0 < \frac{\alpha\pi}{2})$ and $\lambda_2 > 0 (\Rightarrow |arg(\lambda_2)| = 0 < \frac{\alpha\pi}{2})$; hence, system (1.3) is unstable at $Q_1(u_1, v_1)$. □

For readers' convenience, we summarize the stability of the equilibrium points of system (1.3) in Table 3.

Table 3. The stability of the equilibrium points of system (1.3).

Point	Conditions	Properties
$Q_0(0,0)$		saddle
$Q_k(k,0)$	$d > \frac{bck}{h+k^2} - gk$	stable
	$d < \frac{bck}{h+k^2} - gk$	saddle
$Q_1(u_1, v_1)$	$k < \frac{h+3u_1^2}{2u_1}$	unstable
	$k > \frac{h+3u_1^2}{2u_1}$	stable
$Q_2(u_2, v_2)$		saddle

4.3. Stability Analysis of the Equilibrium Points of System (1.6)

The Jacobian matrix of system (1.6) at any equilibrium point $Q(u, v)$ is as follows:

$$
J_d(u,v) = \begin{pmatrix} 1 + \frac{\rho^\alpha}{\Gamma(\alpha+1)}\left(a(1 - \frac{2u}{k}) - \frac{bv}{h+u^2} + \frac{2bu^2v}{(h+u^2)^2}\right) & \frac{\rho^\alpha}{\Gamma(\alpha+1)}\left(-\frac{bu}{h+u^2}\right) \\ \frac{\rho^\alpha}{\Gamma(\alpha+1)}\left(\frac{bcv(h-u^2)}{(h+u^2)^2} - gv\right) & 1 + \frac{\rho^\alpha}{\Gamma(\alpha+1)}\left(\frac{bcu}{h+u^2} - d - gu\right) \end{pmatrix}.
$$

The characteristic polynomial of the Jacobian matrix $J(Q)$ reads

$$F(\lambda) = \lambda^2 - \hat{P}\lambda + \hat{Q},$$

where

$$\hat{P} = 2 + \frac{\rho^\alpha}{\Gamma(\alpha+1)}\left(-\frac{au}{k} + \frac{2bu^2v^2}{(h+u^2)^2}\right),$$
$$\hat{Q} = 1 + \frac{\rho^\alpha}{\Gamma(\alpha+1)}\left(-\frac{au}{k} + \frac{2bu^2v^2}{(h+u^2)^2}\right) + \frac{\rho^{2\alpha}buv}{(\Gamma(\alpha+1))^2 h + u^2}\left(\frac{bc(h-u^2)}{(h+u^2)^2} - g\right).$$

Denote $\Delta = \frac{\rho^\alpha}{\Gamma(\alpha+1)}$, $\Omega_1 = \frac{buv}{h+u^2}\left(\frac{bc(h-u^2)}{(h+u^2)^2} - g\right)$, and $\Omega_2 = -\frac{au}{k} + \frac{2bu^2v^2}{(h+u^2)^2}$.

4.3.1. The Stability of Trivial Equilibrium Point $Q_0(0,0)$

Theorem 11. *The following statements about the trivial equilibrium point $Q_0(0,0)$ of system (1.6) are true.*

1. *If $d < \frac{2}{\Delta}$, then $Q_0(0,0)$ is a saddle.*
2. *If $d = \frac{2}{\Delta}$, then $Q_0(0,0)$ is non-hyperbolic.*
3. *If $d > \frac{2}{\Delta}$, then $Q_0(0,0)$ is a stable node.*

Proof. Substituting the trivial equilibrium point $Q_0(0,0)$ into the Jacobian matrix $J_d(u,v)$, we obtain

$$J_d(Q_0) = \begin{pmatrix} 1+\Delta a & 0 \\ 0 & 1-\Delta d \end{pmatrix},$$

and it is easy to see that the Jacobian matrix $J_d(Q_0)$ has two eigenvalues: $\lambda_1 = 1 + \Delta a > 1$ and $|\lambda_2| = |1 - \Delta d| < (=,>)1$ for $d < (=,>)\frac{2}{\Delta}$. By using Definition 4, we can derive Theorem 14. □

4.3.2. The Stability of Boundary Equilibrium Point $Q_k(k,0)$

Theorem 12. *The following conclusions for the fixed point $Q_k(k,0)$ of system (1.6) are true.*

1. *If $a < \frac{2}{\Delta}$, then,*
   (a) *For $d < \frac{cbk}{h+k^2} - gk$ or $d > \frac{2}{\Delta} + \frac{cbk}{h+k^2} - gk$, $Q_k(k,0)$ is is a saddle;*
   (b) *For $d = \frac{cbk}{h+k^2} - gk$ or $d = \frac{2}{\Delta} + \frac{cbk}{h+k^2} - gk$, $Q_k(k,0)$ is non-hyperbolic;*
   (c) *For $\frac{cbk}{h+k^2} - gk < d < \frac{2}{\Delta} + \frac{cbk}{h+k^2} - gk$, $Q_k(k,0)$ is a stable node, i.e., a sink.*
2. *If $a = \frac{2}{\Delta}$, then $Q_k(k,0)$ is non-hyperbolic.*
3. *If $a > \frac{2}{\Delta}$, then,*
   (a) *For $d < \frac{cbk}{h+k^2} - gk$ or $d > \frac{2}{\Delta} + \frac{cbk}{h+k^2} - gk$, $Q_k(k,0)$ is an unstable node, i.e., a source;*
   (b) *For $d = \frac{cbk}{h+k^2} - gk$ or $d = \frac{2}{\Delta} + \frac{cbk}{h+k^2} - gk$, $Q_k(k,0)$ is non-hyperbolic;*
   (c) *For $\frac{cbk}{h+k^2} - gk < d < \frac{2}{\Delta} + \frac{cbk}{h+k^2} - gk$, $Q_k(k,0)$ is a saddle.*

Proof. Substituting boundary equilibrium point $Q_k(k,0)$ into the Jacobian matrix $J_d(u,v)$, we have

$$J_d(Q_k) = \begin{pmatrix} 1-\Delta a & -\Delta\frac{bk}{h+k^2} \\ 0 & 1+\Delta\left(\frac{cbk}{h+k^2} - d - gk\right) \end{pmatrix}.$$

Now, consider the following three cases.

Case 1: $a < \frac{2}{\Delta}$. Then, the two eigenvalues of the Jacobian matrix $J_c(Q_k)$ satisfy $|\lambda_1| = |1 - \Delta a| < 1$ and $|\lambda_2| = |1 + \Delta(\frac{cbk}{h+k^2} - d - gk)| > 1$ for $d < \frac{cbk}{h+k^2} - gk$ or $d > \frac{2}{\Delta} + \frac{cbk}{h+k^2} - gk$,

so $Q_k(k,0)$ is a saddle; $|\lambda_2| = 1$ for $d = \frac{cbk}{h+k^2} - gk$ or $d = \frac{2}{\Delta} + \frac{cbk}{h+k^2} - gk$, then $Q_k(k,0)$ is non-hyperbolic; and $|\lambda_2| < 1$ for $\frac{cbk}{h+k^2} - gk < d < \frac{2}{\Delta} + \frac{cbk}{h+k^2} - gk$, thus $Q_k(k,0)$ is a stable node, i.e., a sink.
Case 2: $a = \frac{2}{\Delta}$. Then, one eigenvalue of the Jacobian matrix $J_c(Q_k)$ meets $|\lambda_1| = |1 - \Delta a| = 1$. Thus, $Q_k(k,0)$ is non-hyperbolic.
Case 3: $a > \frac{2}{\Delta}$. Then, the two eigenvalues of the Jacobian matrix $J_c(Q_k)$ meet $|\lambda_1| = |1 - \Delta a| > 1$ and $|\lambda_2| = |1 + \Delta(\frac{cbk}{h+k^2} - d - gk)| > 1$ for $d < \frac{cbk}{h+k^2} - gk$ or $d > \frac{2}{\Delta} + \frac{cbk}{h+k^2} - gk$, then $Q_k(k,0)$ is an unstable node, i.e., a source; $|\lambda_2| = 1$ for $d = \frac{cbk}{h+k^2} - gk$ or $d = \frac{2}{\Delta} + \frac{cbk}{h+k^2} - gk$, then $Q_k(k,0)$ is non-hyperbolic; and $|\lambda_2| < 1$ for $\frac{cbk}{h+k^2} - gk < d < \frac{2}{\Delta} + \frac{cbk}{h+k^2} - gk$, then at this time, $Q_k(k,0)$ is a saddle.
The proof is over. □

4.3.3. The Stability of Positive Equilibrium Points $Q_i(u_i,v_i)$ $(i = 1,2)$

Theorem 13. *When the positive equilibrium $Q_i(u_i,v_i)$ $(i = 1,2)$ exists, let $\Omega_1(i) = \frac{bu_iv_i}{h+u_i^2}(\frac{bc(h-u_i^2)}{(h+u_i^2)^2} - g)$, $\Omega_2(i) = -\frac{au_i}{k} + \frac{2bu_i^2v_i^2}{(h+u_i^2)^2}(i = 1,2)$. Then, the results for the positive fixed points $Q_i(u_i,v_i)$ $(i = 1,2)$ of system (1.6) summarized in Tables 4 and 5 are true.*

Proof. Substituting the positive equilibrium points $Q_i(u_i,v_i)(i = 1,2)$ into the Jacobian matrix $J_d(u,v)$, one can see

$$J_d(Q_i) = \begin{pmatrix} 1 + \Delta(a(1 - \frac{2u_i}{k}) - \frac{bv_i}{h+u_i^2} + \frac{2bu_i^2v_i}{(h+u_i^2)^2}) & \Delta(-\frac{bu_i}{h+u_i^2}) \\ \Delta(\frac{bcv_i(h-u_i^2)}{(h+u_i^2)^2} - gv_i) & 1 + \Delta(\frac{bcu_i}{h+u_i^2} - d - gu_i) \end{pmatrix}.$$

We first analyze the stability of the positive equilibrium point $Q_2(u_2,v_2)$. By computing $J_d(Q_2)$, we can obtain its characteristic polynomial

$$F_2(\lambda) = \lambda^2 - \hat{P}_2\lambda + \hat{Q}_2,$$

where

$$\hat{P}_2 = 2 + \Delta(-\frac{au_2}{k} + \frac{2bu_2^2v_2^2}{(h+u_2^2)^2}),$$
$$\hat{Q}_2 = 1 + \Delta(-\frac{au_2}{k} + \frac{2bu_2^2v_2^2}{(h+u_2^2)^2}) + \Delta^2\frac{bu_2v_2}{h+u_2^2}(\frac{bc(h-u_2^2)}{(h+u_2^2)^2} - g).$$

Denote $\Omega_1(2) = \frac{bu_2v_2}{h+u_2^2}(\frac{bc(h-u_2^2)}{(h+u_2^2)^2} - g)$ and $\Omega_2(2) = -\frac{au_2}{k} + \frac{2bu_2^2v_2^2}{(h+u_2^2)^2}$. Then,

$$F_2(1) = \Delta^2\Omega_1(2), \quad F_2(-1) = \Omega_1(2)\Delta^2 + 2\Omega_2(2)\Delta + 4.$$

From (4.7), we know that $\Omega_1(2) < 0$; hence, $F_2(1) < 0$, which shows that $F_2(\lambda) = 0$ has one root lying in $(1,\infty)$. For the value of $F_2(-1)$, we consider the following three cases for discussion:

Case 1: $0 < \Delta < \frac{-\Omega_2(2)-\sqrt{\Omega_2^2(2)-4\Omega_1(2)}}{\Omega_1(2)}$. Then, $F_2(-1) > 0$. Lemma 3 reads that $|\lambda_1| > 1$ and $|\lambda_2| < 1$, which shows that Q_2 is a saddle.
Case 2: $\Delta = \frac{-\Omega_2(2)-\sqrt{\Omega_2^2(2)-4\Omega_1(2)}}{\Omega_1(2)}$. Then, $F_2(-1) = 0$. This shows that Q_2 is non-hyperbolic.
Case 3: $\Delta > \frac{-\Omega_2(2)-\sqrt{\Omega_2^2(2)-4\Omega_1(2)}}{\Omega_1(2)}$. Then, $F_2(-1) < 0$. Lemma 3 tells us that $|\lambda_1| > 1$ and $|\lambda_2| > 1$, so Q_2 is an unstable node.

Next, we discuss the stability of the positive equilibrium point $Q_1(u_1, v_1)$. Similarly, after calculating $J_d(Q_1)$, we obtain its characteristic polynomial

$$F_1(\lambda) = \lambda^2 - \hat{P}_1\lambda + \hat{Q}_1,$$

where

$$\begin{aligned}\hat{P}_1 &= 2 + \Delta\Big(-\frac{au_1}{k} + \frac{2bu_1^2v_1^2}{(h+u_1^2)^2}\Big),\\ \hat{Q}_1 &= 1 + \Delta\Big(-\frac{au_1}{k} + \frac{2bu_1^2v_1^2}{(h+u_1^2)^2}\Big) + \Delta^2\frac{bu_1v_1}{h+u_1^2}\Big(\frac{bc(h-u_1^2)}{(h+u_1^2)^2} - g\Big).\end{aligned}$$

Let $\Omega_1(1) = \frac{bu_1v_1}{h+u_1^2}\big(\frac{bc(h-u_1^2)}{(h+u_1^2)^2} - g\big)$ and $\Omega_2(1) = -\frac{au_1}{k} + \frac{2bu_1^2v_1^2}{(h+u_1^2)^2}$. Then,

$$F_1(1) = \Delta^2\Omega_1(1), F_1(-1) = \Omega_1(1)\Delta^2 + 2\Omega_2(1)\Delta + 4.$$

From (4.8), we know that $\Omega_1(1) > 0$, so $F_1(1) > 0$. Note also that $\hat{Q}_1 > (=,<)1 \iff \Delta > (=,<) -\frac{\Omega_2(1)}{\Omega_1(1)}$. Now, consider the following three cases for discussion.

Case 1: $\Omega_2^2(1) - 4\Omega_1(1) < 0$. This implies that $F_1(-1) > 0$. Thus, we consider the following three subcases for discussion:

Subcase 1. $\Delta < -\frac{\Omega_2(1)}{\Omega_1(1)}$. Then, $\hat{Q}_1 < 1$. Lemma 3 reads $|\lambda_1| < 1$ and $|\lambda_2| < 1$. Thus, Q_1 is a stable node, i.e., a sink.

Subcase 2. $\Delta = -\frac{\Omega_2(1)}{\Omega_1(1)}$. Then, $\hat{Q}_1 = 1$.

Subcase 3. $\Delta > -\frac{\Omega_2(1)}{\Omega_1(1)}$. Then, $\hat{Q}_1 > 1$. Thus, $|\lambda_1| > 1$, $|\lambda_2| > 1$, and hence Q_1 is an unstable node, i.e., a source.

Case 2: $\Omega_2^2(1) - 4\Omega_1(1) = 0$. Consider the following three subcases:

Subcase 1. $\Delta < -\frac{\Omega_2(1)}{\Omega_1(1)}$. Then, $F_1(-1) > 0, \hat{Q}_1 < 1$. Hence, $|\lambda_1| < 1, |\lambda_2| < 1$, and so Q_1 is a stable node, i.e., a sink.

Subcase 2. $\Delta = -\frac{\Omega_2(1)}{\Omega_1(1)}$. Then, $F_1(-1) = 0$. Thus, Q_1 is non-hyperbolic.

Subcase 3. $\Delta > -\frac{\Omega_2(1)}{\Omega_1(1)}$. Then, $F_1(-1) > 0$ and $\hat{Q}_1 > 1$. It follows from Lemma 3 that $|\lambda_1| > 1$ and $|\lambda_2| > 1$. Thus, Q_1 is an unstable node, i.e., a source.

Case 3: $\Omega_2^2(1) - 4\Omega_1(1) > 0$. Then, $\Omega_2(1) > 2\sqrt{\Omega_1(1)}$ or $\Omega_2(1) < -2\sqrt{\Omega_1(1)}$. Consider the following two subcases:

Subcase 1. $\Omega_2(1) > 2\sqrt{\Omega_1(1)}$. Then, $\Delta > 0 > \frac{-\Omega_2(1)+\sqrt{\Omega_2^2(1)-4\Omega_1(1)}}{\Omega_1(1)}$. So, $F_1(-1) > 0, \hat{Q}_1 > 1$, which, in view of Lemma 3, implies $|\lambda_1| > 1$ and $|\lambda_2| > 1$. Thus, Q_1 is an unstable node, i.e., a source.

Subcase 2. $\Omega_2(1) < -2\sqrt{\Omega_1(1)}$. We further consider the following five subsubcases.

Subsubcase 1. $0 < \Delta < \frac{-\Omega_2(1)-\sqrt{\Omega_2^2(1)-4\Omega_1(1)}}{\Omega_1(1)} < -\frac{\Omega_2(1)}{\Omega_1(1)}$. Then, $F_1(-1) > 0, \hat{Q}_1 < 1$, indicating $|\lambda_1| < 1, |\lambda_2| < 1$. Hence, Q_1 is a stable node, i.e., a sink.

Subsubcase 2. $\Delta = \frac{-\Omega_2(1)-\sqrt{\Omega_2^2(1)-4\Omega_1(1)}}{\Omega_1(1)}$. Then, $F_1(-1) = 0$ and so Q_1 is non-hyperbolic.

Subsubcase 3. $\frac{-\Omega_2(1)-\sqrt{\Omega_2^2(1)-4\Omega_1(1)}}{\Omega_1(1)} < \Delta < \frac{-\Omega_2(1)+\sqrt{\Omega_2^2(1)-4\Omega_1(1)}}{\Omega_1(1)}$. Then, $F_1(-1) < 0$. In light of Lemma 3, $|\lambda_1| > (<)1, |\lambda_2| < (>)1$. Thus, Q_1 is a saddle.

Subsubcase 4. $\Delta = \frac{-\Omega_2(1)+\sqrt{\Omega_2^2(1)-4\Omega_1(1)}}{\Omega_1(1)}$. Then, $F_1(-1) = 0$ and so Q_1 is non-hyperbolic.

Subsubcase 5. $\Delta > \frac{-\Omega_2(1)+\sqrt{\Omega_2^2(1)-4\Omega_1(1)}}{\Omega_1(1)} > -\frac{\Omega_2(1)}{\Omega_1(1)}$. Then, $F_1(-1) > 0, \hat{Q}_1 > 1$ and so $|\lambda_1| > 1, |\lambda_2| > 1$. Therefore, Q_1 is an unstable node, i.e., a source.

The proof is finished. □

Table 4. Properties of the fixed point $Q_1(u_1, v_1)$ of system (1.6).

Conditions			Eigenvalues	Properties
$\Omega_2^2(1) - 4\Omega_1(1) < 0$		$\Delta < -\frac{\Omega_2(1)}{\Omega_1(1)}$	$\lvert\lambda_1\rvert < 1, \lvert\lambda_2\rvert < 1$	sink
		$\Delta = -\frac{\Omega_2(1)}{\Omega_1(1)}$	$\lvert\lambda_1\rvert = 1$ or $\lvert\lambda_2\rvert = 1$	non-hyperbolic
		$\Delta > -\frac{\Omega_2(1)}{\Omega_1(1)}$	$\lvert\lambda_1\rvert > 1, \lvert\lambda_2\rvert > 1$	source
$\Omega_2^2(1) - 4\Omega_1(1) = 0$		$\Delta < -\frac{\Omega_2(1)}{\Omega_1(1)}$	$\lvert\lambda_1\rvert < 1, \lvert\lambda_2\rvert < 1$	sink
		$\Delta = -\frac{\Omega_2(1)}{\Omega_1(1)}$	$\lvert\lambda_1\rvert = 1$ or $\lvert\lambda_2\rvert = 1$	non-hyperbolic
		$\Delta > -\frac{\Omega_2(1)}{\Omega_1(1)}$	$\lvert\lambda_1\rvert > 1, \lvert\lambda_2\rvert > 1$	source
$\Omega_2^2(1) - 4\Omega_1(1) > 0$	$\Omega_2(1) > 2\sqrt{\Omega_1(1)}$		$\lvert\lambda_1\rvert > 1, \lvert\lambda_2\rvert > 1$	source
	$\Omega_2(1) < -2\sqrt{\Omega_1(1)}$	$\Delta < \frac{-\Omega_2(1)-\sqrt{\Omega_2^2(1)-4\Omega_1(1)}}{\Omega_1(1)}$	$\lvert\lambda_1\rvert < 1, \lvert\lambda_2\rvert < 1$	sink
		$\Delta = \frac{-\Omega_2(1)-\sqrt{\Omega_2^2(1)-4\Omega_1(1)}}{\Omega_1(1)}$	$\lvert\lambda_1\rvert = (\neq)1, \lvert\lambda_2\rvert \neq (=)1$	non-hyperbolic
		$\frac{-\Omega_2(1)-\sqrt{\Omega_2^2(1)-4\Omega_1(1)}}{\Omega_1(1)} < \Delta < \frac{-\Omega_2(1)+\sqrt{\Omega_2^2(1)-4\Omega_1(1)}}{\Omega_1(1)}$,	$\lvert\lambda_1\rvert < (>)1, \lvert\lambda_2\rvert > (<)1$	saddle
		$\Delta = \frac{-\Omega_2(1)+\sqrt{\Omega_2^2(1)-4\Omega_1(1)}}{\Omega_1(1)}$	$\lvert\lambda_1\rvert \neq (=)1, \lvert\lambda_2\rvert = (\neq)1$	non-hyperbolic
		$\Delta > \frac{-\Omega_2(1)-\sqrt{\Omega_2^2(1)-4\Omega_1(1)}}{\Omega_1(1)}$	$\lvert\lambda_1\rvert > 1, \lvert\lambda_2\rvert > 1$	source

Table 5. Properties of the fixed point $Q_2(u_2, v_2)$ of system (1.6).

Conditions	Eigenvalues	Properties
$\Delta < \frac{-\Omega_2(2)-\sqrt{\Omega_2^2(2)-4\Omega_1(2)}}{\Omega_1(2)}$	$\lvert\lambda_1\rvert > 1, \lvert\lambda_2\rvert < 1$	saddle
$\Delta = \frac{-\Omega_2(2)-\sqrt{\Omega_2^2(2)-4\Omega_1(2)}}{\Omega_1(2)}$	$\lvert\lambda_1\rvert > 1, \lvert\lambda_2\rvert = 1$	non-hyperbolic
$\Delta > \frac{-\Omega_2(2)-\sqrt{\Omega_2^2(2)-4\Omega_1(2)}}{\Omega_1(2)}$	$\lvert\lambda_1\rvert > 1, \lvert\lambda_2\rvert > 1$	source

5. Bifurcation Analysis

In this section, we, respectively, analyze the existence of bifurcations in the positive equilibrium point $Q_1(u_1, v_1)$ of systems (1.3) and (1.6).

5.1. Bifurcation Analysis of the Positive Equilibrium Point $Q_1(u_1, v_1)$ in System (1.3)

In Section 3, we see that the Jacobian matrix of system (1.3) at the positive equilibrium point $Q_1(u_1, v_1)$ is as follows:

$$J(Q_1) = \begin{pmatrix} -a\frac{u_1}{k} + \frac{2bu_1^2 v_1}{(h+u_1^2)^2} & -\frac{bu_1}{h+u_1^2} \\ \frac{cbv_1(h-u_1^2)}{(h+u_1^2)^2} - gv_1 & 0 \end{pmatrix}.$$

The characteristic equation of the Jacobian matrix $J(Q_1)$ is given by

$$\lambda^2 - \Big(-a\frac{u_1}{k} + \frac{2bu_1^2 v_1}{(h+u_1^2)^2}\Big)\lambda + \frac{bu_1}{h+u_1^2}\Big(\frac{cbv_1(h-u_1^2)}{(h+u_1^2)^2} - gv_1\Big) = 0. \quad (5.1)$$

Substituting $v_1 = \frac{a}{b}(1 - \frac{u_1}{k})(h + u_1^2)$ into Equation (5.1), we have

$$\lambda^2 - au_1(\frac{2ku_1 - 3u_1^2 - h}{k(h + u_1^2)})\lambda + au_1(1 - \frac{u_1}{k})(\frac{cb(h - u_1^2)}{(h + u_1^2)^2} - g) = 0. \tag{5.2}$$

Take k as the bifurcation parameter of system (1.3). If k takes a critical value, $k_0 > 0$, such that the corresponding eigenvalues are $\lambda_{k_0} = re^{i\gamma}$, where $\gamma = \pm\frac{\alpha\pi}{2}$, then a bifurcation occurs. Now, we look for k_0 such that λ_{k_0} satisfies Equation (5.2).

Substituting λ_{k_0} into (5.2), we can obtain the following equation:

$$r^2 e^{2i\gamma} - au_1(\frac{2k_0u_1 - 3u_1^2 - h}{k_0(h + u_1^2)})re^{i\gamma} + au_1(1 - \frac{u_1}{k_0})(\frac{cb(h - u_1^2)}{(h + u_1^2)^2} - g) = 0.$$

Namely,

$$r^2(cos(2\gamma) + isin(2\gamma)) - au_1(\frac{2k_0u_1 - 3u_1^2 - h}{k_0(h + u_1^2)})r(cos\gamma + isin\gamma)$$
$$+ au_1(1 - \frac{u_1}{k_0})(\frac{cb(h - u_1^2)}{(h + u_1^2)^2} - g) = 0.$$

Hence,

$$\begin{cases} r^2cos(2\gamma) - au_1(\frac{2k_0u_1 - 3u_1^2 - h}{k_0(h+u_1^2)})rcos\gamma + au_1(1 - \frac{u_1}{k_0})(\frac{cb(h-u_1^2)}{(h+u_1^2)^2} - g) = 0, \\ r^2sin(2\gamma) - au_1(\frac{2k_0u_1 - 3u_1^2 - h}{k_0(h+u_1^2)})rsin\gamma = 0. \end{cases} \tag{5.3}$$

Since we are interested in non-zero solutions for r in (5.3), from the second equation of (5.3) we can derive $r = au_1(\frac{2k_0u_1 - 3u_1 - h}{2cos\gamma k_0(h+u_1^2)})$. After substitution into the first equation of (5.3), one has

$$(\frac{2k_0u_1 - 3u_1^2 - h}{k_0(h + u_1^2)})^2\frac{-a^2u_1^2}{4cos^2\gamma} + au_1(1 - \frac{u_1}{k_0})(\frac{cb(h - u_1^2)}{(h + u_1^2)^2} - g) = 0.$$

So,

$$au_1(\frac{2k_0u_1 - 3u_1^2 - h}{k_0(h + u_1^2)})^2 = 4cos^2\gamma(1 - \frac{u_1}{k_0})(\frac{cb(h - u_1^2)}{(h + u_1^2)^2} - g),$$

namely,

$$\omega_1 k_0^2 - \omega_2 k_0 + \omega_3 = 0, \tag{5.4}$$

where

$$\omega_1 = 4au_1^3 - 4cos^2\gamma(cb(h - u_1^2) - g(h + u_1^2)^2),$$
$$\omega_2 = 4au_1^2(3u_1^2 + h) - 4cos^2\gamma\, u_1(cb(h - u_1^2) - g(h + u_1^2)^2),$$
$$\omega_3 = au_1(3u_1^2 + h)^2 > 0.$$

$|J(Q_1)| > 0$ implies $cb(h - u_1^2) - g(h + u_1^2)^2 > 0$. Let $\gamma_0 = \frac{au_1{}^3}{cb(h-u_1^2)-g(h+u_1^2)^2}$. Then, $\gamma_0 > 0$. After a lengthy and tedious calculation, we can classify the following three cases for further discussion:

Case 1: $cos^2\gamma > \gamma_0$. Then, we have $\omega_1 < 0$. Due to $k_0 > 0$, we can obtain $k_0 = \frac{\omega_2 - \sqrt{\omega_2^2 - 4\omega_1\omega_3}}{2\omega_1}$.

Case 2: $cos^2\gamma = \gamma_0$. Then, $\omega_1 = 0$. Noticing $k_0 > 0$, we can obtain $k_0 = \frac{\omega_3}{\omega_2}$.

Case 3: $cos^2\gamma < \gamma_0$. Then, we have $\omega_1 > 0$ and $\omega_2 > 0$. Calculate $\omega_2^2 - 4\omega_1\omega_3$ to obtain $\omega_2^2 - 4\omega_1\omega_3 = 16u_1cos^2\gamma[u_1cos\gamma^2(cb(h-u_1^2) - g(h+u_1^2)) + a(3u_1^2+h)(u_1^2+h)] > 0$. Then, we can derive that k_0 has two values: $\frac{\omega_2 \pm \sqrt{\omega_2^2 - 4\omega_1\omega_3}}{2\omega_1}$.

In any case, the critical value k_0 always exists. Next, we prove that system (1.3) satisfies the conditions of Theorem 4 at the positive equilibrium point $Q_1(u_1, v_1)$.

From the existence of k_0, we see that $|arg(\lambda_i(k_0))| = \frac{\alpha\pi}{2}(i = 1,2)$; hence, the first condition in Theorem 4 holds true. The Jacobian matrix of system (1.3) has only two eigenvalues; thus, we do not need to consider the second condition in Theorem 4. Next, we focus on proving that system (1.3) satisfies the third condition of Theorem 4. Take the derivative of Equation (5.2) with respect to k to obtain

$$\begin{aligned} &2\lambda\frac{d\lambda}{dk} - au_1(\frac{2u_1}{h+u_1^2} - \frac{3u_1^2+h}{k(h+u_1^2)})\frac{d\lambda}{dk} - au_1\frac{3u_1^2+h}{k^2(h+u_1^2)}\lambda + \\ &\frac{au_1^2}{k^2}(\frac{cb(h-u_1^2)}{(h+u_1^2)^2} - g) = 0. \end{aligned} \tag{5.5}$$

Thus,

$$\frac{d\lambda}{dk} = \frac{\frac{au_1(3u_1^2+h)}{k^2(h+u_1^2)}\lambda - \frac{au_1^2}{k^2}(\frac{cb(h-u_1^2)}{(h+u_1^2)^2} - g)}{2\lambda + \frac{3au_1^3+au_1h-2aku_1^2}{k(h+u_1^2)}}. \tag{5.6}$$

It suffices for us to verify $\lambda_{1,k_0} = re^{i\frac{\alpha\pi}{2}}$. Substituting $k = k_0$ and $\lambda_{1,k_0} = re^{i\frac{\alpha\pi}{2}}$ into the right-hand side of (5.6) obtains

$$\begin{aligned} \frac{d\lambda}{dk}\Big|_{k=k_0} &= \frac{\frac{au_1(3u_1^2+h)}{k_0^2(h+u_1^2)}re^{i\gamma} - \frac{au_1^2}{k_0^2}(\frac{cb(h-u_1^2)}{(h+u_1^2)^2} - g)}{2re^{i\gamma} + \frac{3au_1^3+au_1h-2ak_0u_1^2}{k_0(h+u_1^2)}} \\ &= \frac{\frac{au_1(3u_1^2+h)}{k_0^2(h+u_1^2)}r(cos\gamma + isin\gamma) - \frac{au_1^2}{k_0^2}(\frac{cb(h-u_1^2)}{(h+u_1^2)^2} - g)}{2r(cos\gamma + isin\gamma) + \frac{3au_1^3+au_1h-2ak_0u_1^2}{k_0(h+u_1^2)}} \\ &= \frac{\psi_1 + \psi_2 i}{\psi_3^2 + \psi_4^2}, \end{aligned} \tag{5.7}$$

where

$$\begin{aligned} \psi_1 =& (\frac{au_1(3u_1^2+h)}{k_0^2(h+u_1^2)}rcos\gamma - \frac{au_1^2}{k_0}(\frac{cb(h-u_1^2)}{(h+u_1^2)^2} - g)) \\ &\times (2rcos\gamma + \frac{3au_1^3+au_1h-2ak_0u_1^2}{k_0(h+u_1^2)}) + \frac{au_1(3u_1^2+h)}{k_0^2(h+u_1^2)}2r^2sin^2\gamma, \\ \psi_2 =& (\frac{a(3u_1^2+h)(3u_1^2+h-2k_0u_1)}{k_0^3(h+u_1^2)^2} + \frac{2}{k_0}(\frac{cb(h-u_1^2)}{(h+u_1^2)^2} - g))au_1^2rsin\gamma, \\ \psi_3 =& 2rcos\gamma + \frac{3au_1^3+au_1h-2ak_0u_1^2}{k_0(h+u_1^2)}, \psi_4 = 2rsin\gamma. \end{aligned}$$

Denote $\lambda(k) = m(k) + i\ n(k)$, then $arg(\lambda(k)) = arctan(\frac{n}{m})$. By differentiating $arg(\lambda(k))$ with respect to k, we get

$$\frac{d}{dk}arg(\lambda(k)) = \frac{mn' - nm'}{m^2+n^2} = \frac{W(m,n)}{|\lambda(k)|^2} \tag{5.8}$$

where $W(m,n) = \begin{vmatrix} m & n \\ m' & n' \end{vmatrix}$.

Therefore,

$$\begin{aligned}\frac{d}{dk}arg(\lambda(k))\Big|_{k=k_0} &= \frac{W(m(k_0),n(k_0))}{|\lambda(k_0)|^2} \\ &= \frac{1}{|\lambda(k_0)|^2}\begin{vmatrix} m(k_0) & n(k_0) \\ m'(k_0) & n'(k_0) \end{vmatrix} \\ &= \frac{1}{|\lambda(k_0)|^2}\begin{vmatrix} rcos\gamma & rsin\gamma \\ \frac{\psi_1}{\psi_3^2+\psi_4^2} & \frac{\psi_2}{\psi_3^2+\psi_4^2} \end{vmatrix}.\end{aligned} \tag{5.9}$$

We can easily deduce that when k_0 exists, $|\lambda(k_0)|^2 \neq \infty$ holds true.

Next, we prove the conditions under which $W(m,n)(k_0) \neq 0$ holds true.

In fact,

$$\begin{aligned} & W(m,n)(k_0) = \begin{vmatrix} rcos\gamma & rsin\gamma \\ \frac{\psi_1}{\psi_3^2+\psi_4^2} & \frac{\psi_2}{\psi_3^2+\psi_4^2} \end{vmatrix} \neq 0 \\ \Longleftrightarrow & \frac{1}{\psi_3^2+\psi_4^2}(rcos\gamma\psi_2 - rsin\gamma\psi_1) \neq 0 \\ \Longleftrightarrow & cos\gamma\psi_2 - sin\gamma\psi_1 \neq 0 \\ \Longleftrightarrow & 4u_1rcos\gamma(\frac{cb(h-u_1^2)}{(h+u_1^2)^2} - g) + \\ & u_1(\frac{cb(h-u_1^2)}{(h+u_1^2)^2} - g)(\frac{3au_1^3 + au_1h - 2ak_0u_1^2}{k_0(h+u_1^2)}) - 2r^2\frac{3u_1^2+h}{k_0(h+u_1^2)} \neq 0 \\ \Longleftrightarrow & k_0 \neq k_h, \end{aligned} \tag{5.10}$$

where

$$k_h = \frac{2r^2(3u_1^2+h)(h+u_1^2)^2 - u_1(cb(h-u_1^2) - g(h+u_1^2))(3au_1^3+au_1h)}{u_1(cb(h-u_1^2) - g(h+u_1^2))(4rcos\gamma(h+u_1^2) - 2au_1^2)}. \tag{5.11}$$

This is true by adding the assumption $k_0 \neq k_h$. So, summarizing the above analysis, one has the following results.

Theorem 14. *Suppose that all parameters in system (1.3) are positive. Let R_0, R, k_0, k_h be defined as above. If $gh - cb < 0$, $R_0 < R$, $u_1 < k$, $k_0 \neq k_h$, then system (1.3) undergoes a fractional Hopf bifurcation at the positive equilibrium point $Q_1(u_1,v_1)$.*

5.2. *Bifurcation Analysis of the Positive Equilibrium Point $Q_1(u_1,v_1)$ in System (1.6)*

In this subsection, we study the bifurcation problems of system (1.6) at the positive equilibrium point $Q_1(u_1,v_1)$ by using the center manifold theorem and local bifurcation theory.

5.2.1. Neimark–Sacker Bifurcation at the Fixed Point $Q_1(u_1,v_1)$

From Case 1 in the proof of Theorem 13 for the stability of the positive equilibrium point $Q_1(u_1,v_1)$, we see that the dimension numbers for the stable manifold and unstable manifold of system (1.6) at the positive equilibrium point $Q_1(u_1,v_1)$ change when Δ varies in the vicinity of Δ_0 (correspondingly, ρ varies in the vicinity of ρ_0) for $\Delta < -\frac{4}{\Omega_2(1)}$ and $\Omega_2^2(1) - 4\Omega_1(1) < 0$, where

$$\Delta_0 == -\frac{\Omega_2(1)}{\Omega_1(1)}, \quad \rho_0 = (\Gamma(1+\alpha)\Delta_0)^{\frac{1}{\alpha}}. \tag{5.12}$$

Thus, a bifurcation, to be shown to be Neimark–Sacker, may occur. Let

$$\widehat{NS}_{Q_1} = \left\{(a,b,c,d,g,h,k,\alpha,\rho) \in R_+^7 | \Delta < -\frac{4}{\Omega_2(1)}, \Omega_2^2(1) - 4\Omega_1(1) < 0\right\}.$$

To analyze the Neimark–Sacker bifurcation, we perform the following.

Let $x_n = u_n - u_1$, $y_n = v_n - v_1$, which transforms the fixed point $Q_1(u_1, v_1)$ to the origin $O(0,0)$. Assume that ρ^* is a small perturbation of ρ with $|\rho^*| \ll 1$. After shifting and perturbation, system (1.6) takes the following form:

$$\begin{cases} x_{n+1} &= x_n + \frac{(\rho+\rho^*)^\alpha}{\Gamma(\alpha+1)}\left(a(x_n+u_1)(1-\frac{(x_n+u_1)}{k}) - \frac{b(x_n+u_1)(y_n+v_1)}{h+(x_n+u_1)^2}\right), \\ y_{n+1} &= y_n + \frac{(\rho+\rho^*)^\alpha}{\Gamma(\alpha+1)}\left(\frac{cb(x_n+u_1)(y_n+v_1)}{h+(x_n+u_1)^2} - d(y_n+v_1) - g(x_n+u_1)(y_n+v_1)\right). \end{cases} \tag{5.13}$$

Using the Taylor series expansion of system (5.13) at $O(0,0)$ to the third order results in the following system:

$$\begin{cases} x_{n+1} = & \epsilon_{10}x_n + \epsilon_{01}y_n + \epsilon_{20}x_n^2 + \epsilon_{11}x_ny_n + \epsilon_{02}y_n^2 \\ & +\epsilon_{30}x_n^3 + \epsilon_{21}x_n^2y_n + \epsilon_{12}x_ny_n^2 + \epsilon_{03}y_n^3 + o(\rho_1^3), \\ y_{n+1} = & \zeta_{10}x_n + \zeta_{01}y_n + \zeta_{20}x_n^2 + \zeta_{11}x_ny_n + \zeta_{02}y_n^2 \\ & +\zeta_{30}x_n^3 + \zeta_{21}x_n^2y_n + \zeta_{12}x_ny_n^2 + \zeta_{03}y_n^3 + o(\rho_1^3), \end{cases} \tag{5.14}$$

where $\rho_1 = \sqrt{x_n^2 + y_n^2}$,

$$\begin{aligned}
\epsilon_{10} =& 1 + \frac{\rho^\alpha}{\Gamma(\alpha+1)}(a(1-\frac{2u_1}{k}) - bv_1(\frac{h-u_1^2}{(u_1^2+h)^2})), \epsilon_{01} = -\frac{\rho^\alpha bu_1}{\Gamma(\alpha+1)(u_1^2+h)}, \\
\epsilon_{20} =& \frac{\rho^\alpha}{\Gamma(\alpha+1)}((3h-u_1^2)\frac{bu_1v_1}{(u_1^2+h)^3} - \frac{a}{k}), \epsilon_{02} = 0, \epsilon_{11} = \frac{\rho^\alpha b}{\Gamma(\alpha+1)}(\frac{u_1^2-h}{(u_1^2+h)^2}), \\
\epsilon_{30} =& \frac{\rho^\alpha bv_1}{\Gamma(\alpha+1)(u_1^2+h)^3}(h + \frac{2u_1^2(3u_1^2-h)}{u_1^2+h} - 5u_1^2), \epsilon_{03} = 0, \\
\epsilon_{21} =& \frac{\rho^\alpha bu_1}{\Gamma(\alpha+1)(u_1^2+h)^2}(2 - \frac{3(u_1^2-h)}{u_1^2+h}), \epsilon_{12} = 0, \\
\zeta_{10} =& \frac{\rho^\alpha v_1}{\Gamma(\alpha+1)}(\frac{bc}{u_1^2+h}(1-\frac{2u_1^2}{u_1^2+h}) - g), \zeta_{01} = 1 - \frac{\rho^\alpha}{\Gamma(\alpha+1)}(d + gu_1 - \frac{bcu_1}{u_1^2+h}), \\
\zeta_{20} =& \frac{\rho^\alpha bcu_1v_1}{\Gamma(\alpha+1)(u_1^2+h)^2}, \zeta_{02} = 0, \zeta_{11} = \frac{\rho^\alpha}{\Gamma(\alpha+1)}(\frac{bc}{u_1^2+h}(1-\frac{2u_1^2}{u_1^2+h}) - g), \\
\zeta_{30} =& \frac{\rho^\alpha bcv_1}{\Gamma(\alpha+1)(u_1^2+h)^2}(\frac{4u_1^2}{u_1^2+h} + 4u_1^2(1-2u_1^2) - 1), \zeta_{03} = 0 \\
\zeta_{21} =& \frac{\rho^\alpha bcu_1}{\Gamma(\alpha+1)(u_1^2+h)^2}(\frac{4u_1^2}{u_1^2+h} - 3), \zeta_{12} = 0.
\end{aligned}$$

The characteristic equation of the linearized equation of system (5.14) is

$$\lambda^2 + \hat{P}_1(\rho^*)\lambda + \hat{Q}_1(\rho^*) = 0,$$

where $\hat{P}_1(\rho^*) = 2 + \Delta(\rho^*)\Omega_2(1)$, $\hat{Q}_1(\rho^*) = 1 + \Delta(\rho^*)\Omega_2(1) + \Delta^2(\rho^*)\Omega_1(1)$, $\Delta(\rho^*) = \frac{(\rho+\rho^*)^\alpha}{\Gamma(\alpha+1)}$. Noting that $\Delta(0) = \Delta_0$ and $\hat{P}_1^2(0) - 4\hat{Q}_1(0) = \Delta_0^2(\Omega_2^2(1) - 4\Omega_1(1)) < 0$, the two roots of the characteristic equation are

$$\lambda_{1,2}(\rho^*) = \frac{-\hat{P}_1(\rho^*) \pm i\sqrt{4\hat{Q}_1(\rho^*) - \hat{P}_1^2(\rho^*)}}{2}.$$

Moreover,

$$(|\lambda_{1,2}(\rho^*)|)\big|_{\rho^*=0} = \sqrt{\hat{Q}_1(\rho^*)}\big|_{\rho^*=0} = 1,$$
$$\left(\frac{d|\lambda_{1,2}(\rho^*)|}{d\rho^*}\right)\bigg|_{\rho^*=0} = -\frac{\rho^{\alpha-1}\Omega_2(1)}{2\Gamma(\alpha)} \neq 0.$$

It is obvious that $\lambda_{1,2}^i(0) \neq 1$, for $i = 1,2,3,4$. Thus, the transversal and nondegenerate conditions hold for a Neimark–Sacker bifurcation to occur.

In order to derive the normal form of system (5.14), let

$$T = \begin{pmatrix} 0 & \epsilon_{01} \\ \mu & 1-\omega \end{pmatrix},$$

where $\omega = -\frac{\hat{P}_1(\rho^*)}{2}, \mu = \frac{\sqrt{4\hat{Q}_1(\rho^*)-\hat{P}_1^2(\rho^*)}}{2}$. Then, we have

$$T^{-1} = \begin{pmatrix} \frac{\omega-1}{\mu\epsilon_{01}} & \frac{1}{\mu} \\ \frac{1}{\epsilon_{01}} & 0 \end{pmatrix}.$$

Change the variables to

$$(x,y)^T = T(U,V)^T,$$

then, system (5.14) changes to the following form:

$$\begin{pmatrix} U \\ V \end{pmatrix} \to \begin{pmatrix} \omega & -\mu \\ \mu & \omega \end{pmatrix} \begin{pmatrix} U \\ V \end{pmatrix} + \begin{pmatrix} F(U,V) + o(\rho_2^3) \\ G(U,V) + o(\rho_2^3) \end{pmatrix},$$

where $\rho_1 = \sqrt{x_n^2 + y_n^2}$

$$F(U,V) = \eta_{20}x^2 + \eta_{11}xy + \eta_{02}y^2 + \eta_{30}x^3 + \eta_{21}x^2y + \eta_{12}xy^2 + \eta_{03}y^3,$$
$$G(U,V) = \theta_{20}x^2 + \theta_{11}xy + \theta_{02}y^2 + \theta_{30}x^3 + \theta_{21}x^2y + \theta_{12}xy^2 + \theta_{03}y^3,$$
$$x = \epsilon_{01}V, y = \mu U + (1-\omega)V,$$
$$\eta_{20} = \frac{\epsilon_{20}(\omega-1)}{\mu\epsilon_{01}} + \frac{\zeta_{20}}{\mu}, \eta_{02} = \frac{\epsilon_{02}(\omega-1)}{\mu\epsilon_{01}} + \frac{\zeta_{02}}{\mu}, \eta_{11} = \frac{\epsilon_{11}(\omega-1)}{\mu\epsilon_{01}} + \frac{\epsilon_{11}}{\mu},$$
$$\eta_{30} = \frac{\epsilon_{30}(\omega-1)}{\mu\epsilon_{01}} + \frac{\zeta_{30}}{\mu}, \eta_{03} = \frac{\epsilon_{03}(\omega-1)}{\mu\epsilon_{01}} + \frac{\zeta_{03}}{\mu}, \eta_{21} = \frac{\epsilon_{21}(\omega-1)}{\mu\epsilon_{01}} + \frac{\zeta_{21}}{\mu},$$
$$\eta_{12} = \frac{\epsilon_{12}(\omega-1)}{\mu\epsilon_{01}} + \frac{\zeta_{12}}{\mu},$$
$$\theta_{20} = \frac{\epsilon_{20}}{\epsilon_{01}}, \theta_{02} = \frac{\epsilon_{11}}{\epsilon_{01}}, \theta_{11} = \frac{\epsilon_{02}}{\epsilon_{01}}, \theta_{30} = \frac{\epsilon_{30}}{\epsilon_{01}}, \theta_{03} = \frac{\epsilon_{03}}{\epsilon_{01}}, \theta_{21} = \frac{\epsilon_{21}}{\epsilon_{01}}, \theta_{12} = \frac{\epsilon_{12}}{\epsilon_{01}}.$$

Furthermore,

$$F_{uu}|_{(0,0)} = 2\eta_{02}\mu^3, F_{uv}|_{(0,0)} = \eta_{11}\epsilon_{01}\mu + 2\eta_{02}\mu(1-\omega),$$
$$F_{vv}|_{(0,0)} = 2\eta_{02}\epsilon_{01}^2 + 2\eta_{11}\epsilon_{01}(1-\omega), F_{uuu}|_{(0,0)} = 6\eta_{03}\mu^3,$$
$$F_{uuv}|_{(0,0)} = 2\eta_{21}\epsilon_{01}\mu^2 + 6\eta_{03}\mu^2(1-\omega),$$
$$F_{uvv}|_{(0,0)} = 2\eta_{21}\epsilon_{01}^2\mu + 4\eta_{12}\epsilon_{01}\mu(1-\omega) + 6\eta_{03}\mu(1-\omega)^2,$$
$$F_{vvv}|_{(0,0)} = 4(1-\omega)^3 + 6\eta_{30}\epsilon_{01}^3 + 4\eta_{21}\epsilon_{01}^2(1-\omega) + 6\eta_{12}\epsilon_{01}(1-\omega)^2,$$
$$G_{uu}|_{(0,0)} = 2\theta_{02}\mu^3, G_{uv}|_{(0,0)} = \theta_{11}\epsilon_{01}\mu + 2\theta_{02}\mu(1-\omega),$$
$$G_{vv}|_{(0,0)} = 2\theta_{02}\epsilon_{01}^2 + 2\theta_{11}\epsilon_{01}(1-\omega), G_{uuu}|_{(0,0)} = 6\theta_{03}\mu^3,$$

$$G_{uuv}|_{(0,0)} = 2\theta_{21}\epsilon_{01}\mu^2 + 6\theta_{03}\mu^2(1-\omega),$$
$$G_{uvv}|_{(0,0)} = 2\theta_{21}\epsilon_{01}^2\mu + 4\theta_{12}\epsilon_{01}\mu(1-\omega) + 6\theta_{03}\mu(1-\omega)^2,$$
$$G_{vvv}|_{(0,0)} = 4(1-\omega)^3 + 6\theta_{30}\epsilon_{01}^3 + 4\theta_{21}\epsilon_{01}^2(1-\omega) + 6\theta_{12}\epsilon_{01}(1-\omega)^2.$$

To determine the stability and direction of the bifurcated closed orbit of system (1.4), the following discriminating quantity L should be calculated and not to be zero, where

$$L = -Re\Big(\frac{(1-2\lambda_1)\lambda_2^2}{1-\lambda_1}\tau_{20}\tau_{11}\Big) - \frac{1}{2}|\tau_{11}|^2 - |\tau_{02}|^2 + Re(\lambda_2\tau_{21}), \tag{5.15}$$

$$\tau_{20} = \frac{1}{8}[F_{XX} - F_{YY} + 2G_{XY} + i(G_{XX} - G_{YY} - 2F_{XY})]|_{(0,0)},$$

$$\tau_{11} = \frac{1}{4}[F_{XX} + F_{YY} + i(G_{XX} + G_{YY})]|_{(0,0)},$$

$$\tau_{02} = \frac{1}{8}[F_{XX} - F_{YY} - 2G_{XY} + i(G_{XX} - G_{YY} + 2F_{XY})]|_{(0,0)},$$

$$\tau_{21} = \frac{1}{16}[F_{XXX} + F_{XYY} + G_{XXY} + G_{YYY} + i(G_{XXX} + G_{XYY} - F_{XXY} - F_{YYY})]|_{(0,0)}.$$

We now come to the following conclusion as a result of the analysis derived above.

Theorem 15. *Suppose that the positive equilibrium point $Q_1(u_1, v_1)$ of system (1.6) exists. Let the parameters $(a, b, c, d, g, h, k, \alpha, \rho) \in \widehat{NS}_{Q_1}$ and Δ_0 and ρ_0 be defined as in (5.12). If the parameter ρ varies in a vicinity of ρ_0 (correspondingly, Δ varies around Δ_0) and $L \neq 0$, then system (1.6) undergoes a Neimark–Sacker bifurcation at the equilibrium point $Q_1(u_1, v_1)$. Moreover, if $L < (>)0$, a stable (an unstable) smooth closed invariant curve can be bifurcated out and the bifurcation is supercritical (subcritical).*

5.2.2. Period-Doubling Bifurcation at the Fixed Point $Q_1(u_1, v_1)$

From Case 3 in the proof of Theorem 13 for the stability of the positive equilibrium point $Q_1(u_1, v_1)$, one can see that the dimension numbers for the stable manifold and unstable manifold of system (1.6) at the equilibrium point $Q_1(u_1, v_1)$ change when Δ varies in the vicinity of Δ_0 (correspondingly, ρ varies in the vicinity of ρ_0) for $\Omega_2(1) < -2\sqrt{\Omega_1(1)}$, where

$$\Delta_0 = \frac{-\Omega_2(1) \pm \sqrt{\Omega_2^2(1) - 4\Omega_1(1)}}{\Omega_1(1)}, \quad \rho_0 = (\Gamma(1+\alpha)\Delta_0)^{\frac{1}{\alpha}}. \tag{5.16}$$

Hence, a bifurcation may occur. Noting that $\lambda_1 = -1$ and $|\lambda_2| \neq 1$ for $\Delta = \Delta_0$, we show that this bifurcation is a period-doubling one. Let

$$\widehat{PD}_{Q_1} = \left\{(a,b,c,d,g,h,k,\alpha,\rho) \in R_+^7 | \Omega_2(1) < -2\sqrt{\Omega_1(1)}\right\}.$$

To analyze the period-doubling bifurcation of system (1.6) at the fixed point $Q_1(u_1,v_1)$, it suffices for us to consider $\Delta_0 = \frac{-\Omega_2(1)+\sqrt{\Omega_2^2(1)-4\Omega_1(1)}}{\Omega_1(1)}$. The proof for the case $\Delta_0 = \frac{-\Omega_2(1)-\sqrt{\Omega_2^2(1)-4\Omega_1(1)}}{\Omega_1(1)}$ is completely similar and will be omitted here. Now, proceed in the following way.

Let $x_n = u_n - u_1$, $y_n = v_n - v_1$, which transforms the fixed point $Q_1(u_1,v_1)$ to the origin $O(0,0)$. Consider ρ^* as a small perturbation of ρ, i.e., $\rho^* = \rho - \rho_0$, with $|\rho^*| \ll 1$. After the perturbation, system (1.6) takes the following form:

$$\begin{cases} x_{n+1} = x_n + \frac{(\rho+\rho^*)^\alpha}{\Gamma(\alpha+1)}\left(a(x_n+u_1)(1-\frac{(x_n+u_1)}{k}) - \frac{b(x_n+u_1)(y_n+v_1)}{h+(x_n+u_1)^2}\right), \\ y_{n+1} = y_n + \frac{(\rho+\rho^*)^\alpha}{\Gamma(\alpha+1)}\left(\frac{cb(x_n+u_1)(y_n+v_1)}{h+(x_n+u_1)^2} - d(y_n+v_1) - g(x_n+u_1)(y_n+v_1)\right). \end{cases} \tag{5.17}$$

Set $\rho^*_{n+1} = \rho^*_n = \rho^*$, then (5.17) can be seen as

$$\begin{cases} x_{n+1} &= x_n + \frac{(\rho+\rho^*)^\alpha}{\Gamma(\alpha+1)}\left(a(x_n+u_1)(1-\frac{(x_n+u_1)}{k}) - \frac{b(x_n+u_1)(y_n+v_1)}{h+(x_n+u_1)^2}\right), \\ y_{n+1} &= y_n + \frac{(\rho+\rho^*)^\alpha}{\Gamma(\alpha+1)}\left(\frac{cb(x_n+u_1)(y_n+v_1)}{h+(x_n+u_1)^2} - d(y_n+v_1) - g(x_n+u_1)(y_n+v_1)\right) \\ \rho^*_{n+1} &= \rho^*_n, \end{cases} \tag{5.18}$$

Taylor expanding system (5.18) at $(x_n, v_n, \rho^*_n) = (0,0,0)$ results in

$$\begin{pmatrix} x_n \\ y_n \\ \rho^*_n \end{pmatrix} \to \begin{pmatrix} \epsilon_{100} & \epsilon_{010} & 0 \\ \zeta_{100} & \zeta_{010} & 0 \\ 0 & 0 & 1 \end{pmatrix} \begin{pmatrix} x_n \\ y_n \\ \rho^* \end{pmatrix} + \begin{pmatrix} M(x_n,y_n,\rho^*_n) + o(\rho_3^3) \\ N(x_n,y_n,\rho^*_n) + o(\rho_3^3) \\ 0 \end{pmatrix}, \tag{5.19}$$

where $\rho_3 = \sqrt{x_n^2 + y_n^2 + \rho_n^{*2}}$,

$$\begin{aligned} M(x_n,y_n,\rho^*_n) =& \epsilon_{200}x_n^2 + \epsilon_{020}y_n^2 + \epsilon_{002}\rho_n^{*2} + \epsilon_{110}x_ny_n + \epsilon_{101}x_n\rho^* + \epsilon_{011}y_n\rho^*_n \\ &+ \epsilon_{300}x_n^3 + \epsilon_{030}y_n^3 + \epsilon_{003}\rho_n^{*3} + \epsilon_{210}x_n^2y_n + \epsilon_{120}x_ny_n^2 \\ &+ \epsilon_{021}y_n^2\rho^*_n + \epsilon_{012}y_n\rho_n^{*2} + \epsilon_{201}x_n^2\rho^*_n + \epsilon_{102}x_n\rho_n^{*2} + \epsilon_{111}x_ny_n\rho^*_n, \\ N(x_n,y_n,\rho^*_n) =& \zeta_{200}x_n^2 + \zeta_{020}y_n^2 + \zeta_{002}\rho_n^{*2} + \zeta_{110}x_ny_n + \zeta_{101}x_n\rho^* + \zeta_{011}y_n\rho^*_n \\ &+ \zeta_{300}x_n^3 + \zeta_{030}y_n^3 + \zeta_{003}\rho_n^{*3} + \zeta_{210}x_n^2y_n + \zeta_{120}x_ny_n^2 \\ &+ \zeta_{021}y_n^2\rho^*_n + \zeta_{012}y_n\rho_n^{*2} + \zeta_{201}x_n^2\rho^*_n + \zeta_{102}x_n\rho_n^{*2} + \zeta_{111}x_ny_n\rho^*_n, \end{aligned}$$

$$\epsilon_{100} = 1 + \frac{\rho^\alpha}{\Gamma(\alpha+1)}\left(a(1-\frac{2u_1}{k}) - bv_1(\frac{h-u_1^2}{(u_1^2+h)^2})\right),\ \epsilon_{010} = -\frac{\rho^\alpha b u_1}{\Gamma(\alpha+1)(u_1^2+h)},$$

$$\epsilon_{200} = \frac{\rho^\alpha}{\Gamma(\alpha+1)}\left((3h-u_1^2)\frac{bu_1v_1}{(u_1^2+h)^3} - \frac{a}{k}\right),\ \epsilon_{020} = 0,$$

$$\epsilon_{002} = \frac{\alpha(1-\alpha\rho^{\alpha-2}u_1)}{2\Gamma(\alpha+1)}\left(a(\frac{u_1}{k}-1) + \frac{bv_1}{u_1^2+h}\right),\ \epsilon_{110} = \frac{\rho^\alpha b}{\Gamma(\alpha+1)}\left(\frac{u_1^2-h}{(u_1^2+h)^2}\right),$$

$$\epsilon_{101} = \frac{\alpha\rho^{\alpha-1}}{\Gamma(\alpha+1)}(\frac{bv_1}{u_1^2+h}(\frac{2u_1^2 v_1}{u_1^2}-1)+a(1-\frac{2u_1}{k})),\ \epsilon_{011} = -\frac{\alpha\rho^{\alpha-1}bu_1}{\Gamma(\alpha+1)(u_1^2+h)},$$

$$\epsilon_{300} = \frac{\rho^{\alpha}bv_1}{\Gamma(\alpha+1)(u_1^2+h)^3}(h+\frac{2u_1^2(3u_1^2-h)}{u_1^2+h}-5u_1^2), \epsilon_{030} = 0,$$

$$\epsilon_{003} = \frac{\alpha(3\alpha-\alpha^2-2)\rho^{\alpha-3}}{6\Gamma(\alpha+1)}(au_1(\frac{u_1}{k}-1)+\frac{bu_1v_1}{u_1^2+h}),$$

$$\epsilon_{210} = \frac{\rho^{\alpha}bu_1}{\Gamma(\alpha+1)(u_1^2+h)^2}(2-\frac{3(u_1^2-h)}{u_1^2+h}), \epsilon_{120} = 0,\ \epsilon_{021} = 0,$$

$$\epsilon_{012} = \frac{\alpha(1-\alpha)\rho^{\alpha-2}bu_1}{2\Gamma(\alpha+1)(u_1^2+h)},\ \epsilon_{201} = \frac{\alpha\rho^{\alpha-1}}{\Gamma(\alpha+1)}((3h-u_1^2)\frac{bu_1v_1}{(u_1^2+h)^3}-\frac{a}{k}),$$

$$\epsilon_{102} = \frac{\alpha(1-\alpha)\rho^{\alpha-2}bu_1}{2\Gamma(\alpha+1)(u_1^2+h)},\ \epsilon_{111} = \frac{\alpha\rho^{\alpha-1}b(u_1^2-h)}{\Gamma(\alpha+1)(u_1^2+h)^2},$$

$$\zeta_{100} = \frac{\rho^{\alpha}v_1}{\Gamma(\alpha+1)}(\frac{bc}{u_1^2+h}(1-\frac{2u_1^2}{u_1^2+h})-g),\ \zeta_{010} = 1-\frac{\rho^{\alpha}}{\Gamma(\alpha+1)}(d+gu_1-\frac{bcu_1}{u_1^2+h}),$$

$$\zeta_{200} = \frac{\rho^{\alpha}bcu_1v_1}{\Gamma(\alpha+1)(u_1^2+h)^2},\ \zeta_{020} = 0,\ \zeta_{002} = \frac{\alpha(1-\alpha)\rho^{\alpha-2}v1}{2\Gamma(\alpha+1)}(d-gu_1-\frac{bcu_1}{u_1^2+h}),$$

$$\zeta_{110} = \frac{\rho^{\alpha}}{\Gamma(\alpha+1)}(\frac{bc}{u_1^2+h}(1-\frac{2u_1^2}{u_1^2+h})-g), \zeta_{101} = \frac{\alpha\rho^{\alpha-1}v_1}{\Gamma(\alpha+1)}(\frac{bc}{u_1^2+h}(1-\frac{2u_1}{u_1^2+h})-g),$$

$$\zeta_{011} = \frac{\alpha\rho^{\alpha-1}}{\Gamma(\alpha+1)}(\frac{bcu_1}{u_1^2+h}-d-gu_1),\ \zeta_{300} = \frac{\rho^{\alpha}bcv_1}{\Gamma(\alpha+1)(u_1^2+h)^2}(\frac{4u_1^2}{u_1^2+h}+4u_1^2(1-2u_1^2)-1),$$

$$\zeta_{030} = 0,\ \zeta_{003} = \frac{\alpha(3\alpha-\alpha^2-2)\rho^{\alpha-3}}{6\Gamma(\alpha+1)}(d+gu_1-\frac{bcu_1}{u_1^2+h}),$$

$$\zeta_{210} = \frac{\rho^{\alpha}bcu_1}{\Gamma(\alpha+1)(u_1^2+h)^2}(\frac{4u_1^2}{u_1^2+h}-3), \zeta_{120} = 0, \zeta_{021} = 0,$$

$$\zeta_{012} = \frac{\alpha(1-\alpha\rho^{\alpha-2})}{2\Gamma(\alpha+1)}(d+gu_1-\frac{bcu_1}{u_1^2+h}), \zeta_{201} = \frac{\alpha\rho^{\alpha-1}bcu_1v_1}{\Gamma(\alpha+1)}(\frac{4u_1^2}{u_1^2+h}-1),$$

$$\zeta_{102} = \frac{\alpha(1-\alpha)\rho^{\alpha-2}v_1}{2\Gamma(\alpha+1)}(g-\frac{bc}{u_1^2+h}(1-\frac{2u_1}{u_1^2+h})),$$

$$\zeta_{111} = \frac{\alpha\rho^{\alpha-1}}{\Gamma(\alpha+1)}(\frac{bc}{u_1^2+h}(1-\frac{2u_1^2}{u_1^2+h}-g)).$$

Take

$$T = \begin{pmatrix} \epsilon_{010} & \epsilon_{010} \\ -1-\epsilon_{100} & \lambda_2-\epsilon_{100} \end{pmatrix},$$

which is invertible. Now, using the transformation

$$\begin{pmatrix} x_n \\ y_n \end{pmatrix} = T \begin{pmatrix} \bar{u} \\ \bar{v} \end{pmatrix},$$

system (5.19) becomes

$$\begin{cases} \bar{u}_{n+1} = -\bar{u}_n + M(x_n, y_n, \rho_n^*), \\ \bar{v}_{n+1} = \lambda_2\bar{v}_n + N(x_n, y_n, \rho_n^*). \end{cases} \tag{5.20}$$

System (5.20) has a center manifold $W^c(0,0,0)$ at $(0,0)$ in the neighborhood of $\rho^* = 0$, which can be deduced using the center manifold theorem and is essentially expressed as follows:

$$W^c(0,0,0) = \left\{ (\bar{u}_n, \bar{v}_n, \rho^*) \in R^3 : \bar{v}_n = \eta_1 \bar{u}_n^2 + \eta_2 \bar{u}_n \rho^* + o((|\bar{u}_n| + |\rho^*|)^2) \right\}$$

where

$$\eta_1 = \frac{\epsilon_{010}((1+\epsilon_{100})\epsilon_{200} + \epsilon_{010}\zeta_{200}) + \zeta_{020}(1+\epsilon_{100})^2 - (1+\epsilon_{100})(\epsilon_{110}(1+\epsilon_{100}) + \epsilon_{010}\zeta_{110})}{1-\lambda_2^2},$$

$$\eta_2 = \frac{(1+\epsilon_{100})(\epsilon_{011}(1+\epsilon_{100}) + \epsilon_{010}\zeta_{011})}{\epsilon_{010}(1+\lambda_2)^2} - \frac{(1+\epsilon_{100})(\epsilon_{101} + \epsilon_{010}\zeta_{101})}{(1+\lambda_2)^2}.$$

So, system (5.20) restrained on the center manifold $W^c(0,0,0)$ has the following form:

$$\bar{u}_{n+1} = -\bar{u}_n + \theta_1 \bar{u}_n^2 + \theta_2 \bar{u}_n \rho^* + \theta_3 \bar{u}_n^2 \rho^* + \theta_4 \bar{u}_n \rho^{*2} + \theta_5 \bar{u}_n^3 + o((|\bar{u}_n| + |\rho^*|)^3) \equiv Z(\bar{u}_n, \rho^*),$$

where

$$\begin{aligned}
\theta_1 =& \frac{\eta_2((\lambda_2-\eta_1)\epsilon_{200} - \eta_2\zeta_{200})}{1+\lambda_2} - \frac{\zeta_{020}(1+\eta_1)^2}{1+\lambda_2} - \frac{(1+\eta_1)((\lambda_2-\eta_1)\epsilon_{110} - \eta_2\zeta_{110})}{1+\lambda_2}, \\
\theta_2 =& \frac{(\lambda_2-\eta_1)\epsilon_{101} - \eta_2\zeta_{101}}{1+\lambda_2} - \frac{(1+\eta_1)(\lambda_2-\eta_1)\epsilon_{011} - \eta_2\zeta_{011}}{\eta_2(1+\lambda_2)}, \\
\theta_3 =& \frac{(\lambda_2-\epsilon_{100})\eta_1\epsilon_{101} - \epsilon_{010}\zeta_{101}}{1+\lambda_2} + \frac{((\lambda_2-\epsilon_{100})\epsilon_{011} - \eta_2\zeta_{011})(\lambda_2-\epsilon_{100})\eta_1}{\epsilon_{010}(1+\lambda_2)} \\
&- \frac{(1-\epsilon_{100})((\lambda_2-\epsilon_{100})\epsilon_{111} - \epsilon_{010}\zeta_{111})}{1+\lambda_2} + \frac{\epsilon_{010}((\lambda_2-\epsilon_{100})\epsilon_{201} - \epsilon_{010}\zeta_{201})}{1+\lambda_2} \\
&- \frac{\zeta_{021}(1-\epsilon_{100})^2}{1+\lambda_2} + \frac{2\epsilon_{100}\eta_2((\lambda_2-\epsilon_{100})\epsilon_{200} - \epsilon_{010}\zeta_{200})}{1+\lambda_2} \\
&- \frac{2\zeta_{020}\eta_2(1+\epsilon_{100})(\lambda_2-\epsilon_{100})}{1+\lambda_2} + \frac{\eta_2((\lambda_2-\epsilon_{100})\epsilon_{110} - \epsilon_{010}\zeta_{110})(\lambda_2-1-2\epsilon_{100})}{1+\lambda_2}, \\
\theta_4 =& \frac{\eta_2((\lambda_2-\epsilon_{100})\epsilon_{101} - \epsilon_{010}\zeta_{101})}{1+\lambda_2} + \frac{((\lambda_2-\epsilon_{100})\epsilon_{011} - \epsilon_{010}\zeta_{011})(\lambda_2-\epsilon_{100})\eta_2}{\epsilon_{010}(1+\lambda_2)} \\
&+ \frac{2\epsilon_{010}\eta_2((\lambda_2-\epsilon_{100})\epsilon_{200} - \epsilon_{010}\zeta_{200})}{1+\lambda_2} + \frac{2\zeta_{020}\eta_2(1+\epsilon_{100})(\lambda_2-\epsilon_{100})}{1+\lambda_2} \\
&+ \frac{\eta_2(\lambda_2-1-2\epsilon_{100})((\lambda_2-\epsilon_{100})\epsilon_{110} - \epsilon_{010}\zeta_{110})}{1+\lambda_2}, \\
\theta_5 =& \frac{2\epsilon_{010}\eta_1((\lambda_2-\epsilon_{100})\epsilon_{200} - \epsilon_{010}\zeta_{200})}{1+\lambda_2} + \frac{\eta_1(\lambda_2-1-2\epsilon_{100})((\lambda_2-\epsilon_{100})\epsilon_{200} - \epsilon_{010}\zeta_{200})}{2+\lambda_2} \\
&+ \frac{2\zeta_{020}\eta_1(\lambda_2-\epsilon_{100})(1+\epsilon_{100})}{1+\lambda_2} + \frac{\eta_2^2((\lambda_2-\epsilon_{100})\epsilon_{300} - \epsilon_{010}\zeta_{300})}{1+\lambda_2} \\
&- \frac{\eta_2(1+\epsilon_{100})((\lambda_2-\epsilon_{100})\epsilon_{210} - \epsilon_{010}\zeta_{210})}{1+\lambda_2}.
\end{aligned}$$

In order for the period-doubling bifurcation to occur, the two determinating quantities ξ_1 and ξ_2 must both be nonzero, where

$$\xi_1 = \left(\frac{\partial^2 Z}{\partial \bar{u} \partial \rho^*} + \frac{1}{2} \frac{\partial Z}{\partial \rho^*} \frac{\partial^2 Z}{\partial \bar{u}^2} \right)|_{(0,0)}, \quad \xi_2 = \left(\frac{1}{6} \frac{\partial^3 Z}{\partial \bar{u}^3} + \left(\frac{1}{2} \frac{\partial^2 Z}{\partial \bar{u}^2}\right)^2 \right)|_{(0,0)}.$$

Finally, the outcome of the analysis above is as follows.

Theorem 16. *Suppose that the positive equilibrium point $Q_1(u_1, v_1)$ of system (1.6) exists. Let the parameters $(a,b,c,d,g,h,k,\alpha,\rho) \in \widehat{PD}_{Q_1}$ and Δ_0 and ρ_0 be defined as in (5.16). If the parameter*

ρ varies in a neighbourhood of ρ_0 (correspondingly, Δ varies around Δ_0) and $\xi_1\xi_2 \neq 0$, then system (1.6) undergoes a period-doubling bifurcation at the equilibrium point $Q_1(u_1, v_1)$. Furthermore, for $\xi_2 > (<)\ 0$, the period-two orbit that bifurcates from $Q_1(u_1, v_1)$ is stable (unstable).

6. Numerical Simulation

In this section, we perform numerical simulations of the dynamical behavior of systems (1.3) and (1.6) using Matlab, aiming to provide readers with a more intuitive understanding to the dynamics of systems (1.3) and (1.6) .

In Figure 1, the parameter values in system (1.3) are $c = 0.015$, $k = 0.3$, $a = 0.1$, $b = 0.9$, $d = 0.3$, $h = 0.2$, $g = 0.1$ and $\alpha = 0.98$. Figure 1a displays the trajectories of system (1.3) starting from different points. Although it can be observed that system (1.3) exhibits a saddle at the origin, it is not entirely clear. To provide a more clear representation of the behavior of system (1.3) at the origin, we constructed streamline plots, depicted in Figure 1b. From Figure 1b, it is evident that system (1.3) possesses a saddle at the origin.

In Figure 2a,b, the parameter values of system (1.3) are $c = 0.9$, $k = 10$, $b = 0.2$, $a = 3$, $h = 0.9$, $d = 0.2$, $g = 0.2$ and $\alpha = 0.98$, which satisfy $d > \frac{cbk}{h+k^2} - gk$. Figure 2a shows that the behavior of system (1.3), regardless of whether it starts from the point $(30, 10)$, $(30, 12)$ or $(30, 14)$, will eventually converge to the point $(10, 0)$. Figure 2b demonstrates how the populations of prey and predator change over time when starting from the point $(30, 10)$. We can observe that as time increases, the population of prey tends to 10, while the predator becomes extinct. In Figure 2c, the parameter values of system (1.3) are $c = 0.6$, $k = 1$, $b = 0.5$, $a = 0.1$, $h = 0.6$, $d = 0.1$, $g = 0.1$ and $\alpha = 0.98$, which satisfy $d < \frac{cbk}{h+k^2} - gk$. We can clearly see that system (1.3) exhibits a saddle at the boundary equilibrium point $(1,0)$.

For the positive equilibrium point of system (1.3), we are interested in its bifurcation behavior. In Figure 3, the parameter values of system (1.3) are $c = 0.6$, $b = 0.5$, $a = 0.1$, $h = 0.6$, $d = 0.1$, $g = 0.1$ and $\alpha = 0.98$. Figure 3a,b shows that the positive equilibrium point $Q_1(u_1, v_1)$ is stable and unstable when $k = 1$ and $k = 10$, respectively. Furthermore, we can see from Figure 3b that when k crosses the critical value, a stable limit cycle emerges, indicating the occurrence of a supercritical Hopf bifurcation in system (1.3).

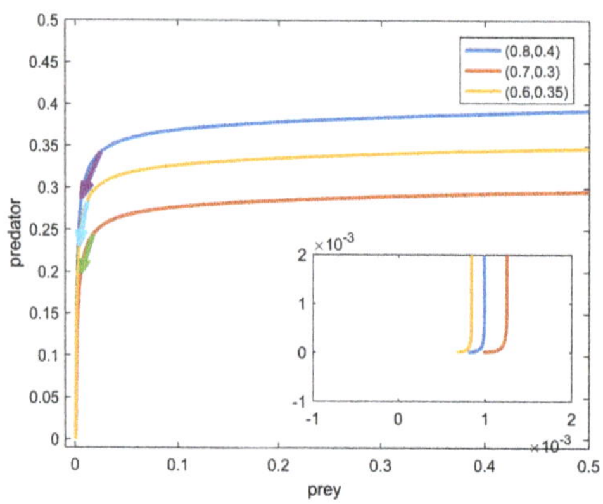

(a)

Figure 1. *Cont.*

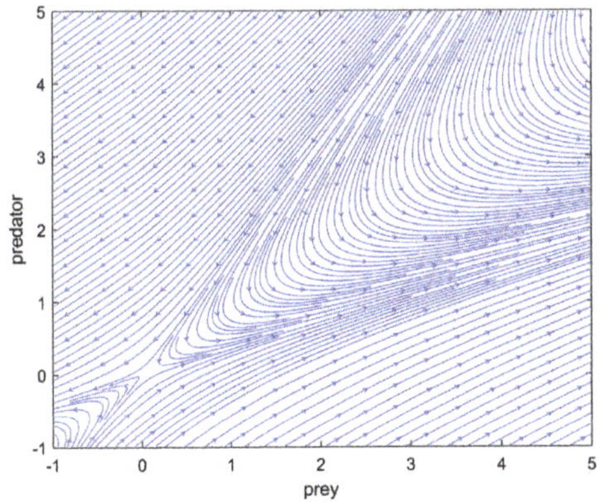

(**b**)

Figure 1. (**a**) shows the trajectories of system (1.3) starting from points $(0.8, 0.4)$, $(0.7, 0.3)$ and $(0.6, 0.35)$, respectively; (**b**) represents the streamline plots of system (1.3) at the origin.

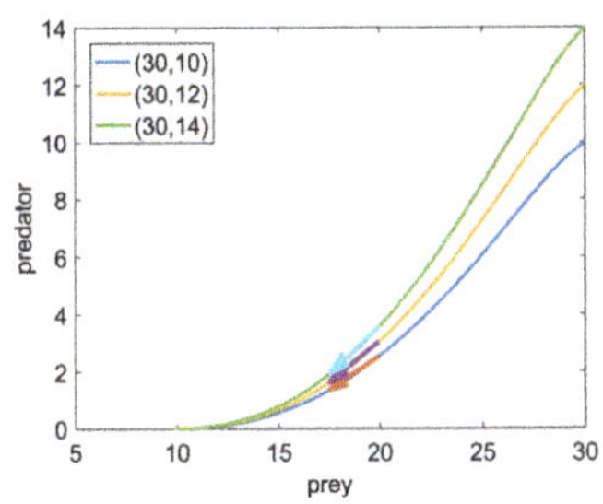

(**a**)

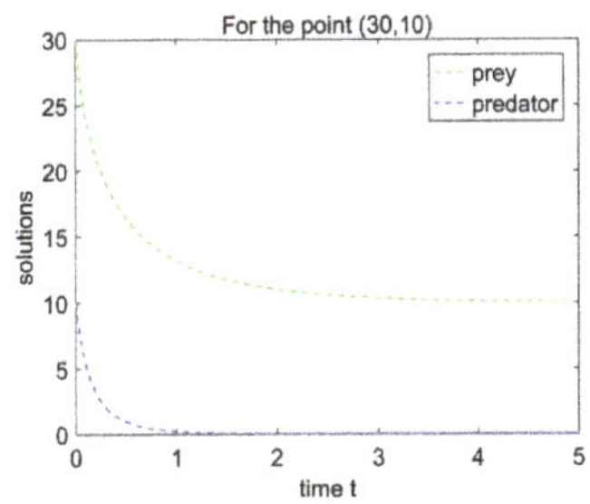

(**b**)

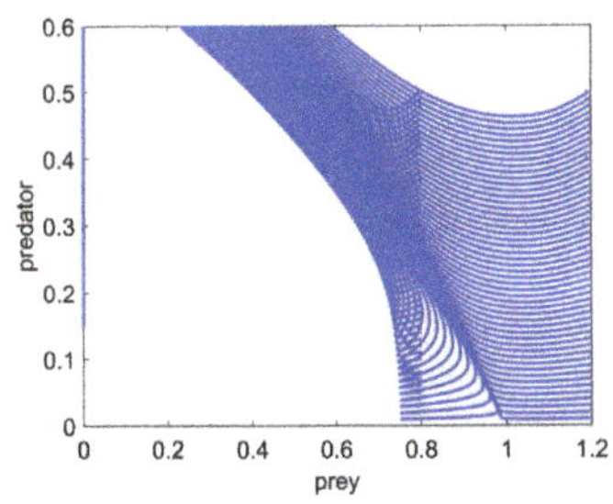

(**c**)

Figure 2. (**a**) The properties of system (1.3) at the boundary equilibrium point (10,0) for $d > \frac{cbk}{h+k^2} - gk$; (**b**) the quantities of prey and predators starting from the point $(30, 10)$ over time; (**c**) the properties of system (1.3) at the boundary equilibrium point (1,0) for $d < \frac{cbk}{h+k^2} - gk$.

With values of $\alpha = 0.75, b = 0.9, a = 0.2, k = 3, h = 5, c = 0.7, d = 0.2$ and $g = 0.1$, Figure 4 is the bifurcation diagram of system (1.6) starting from the point $(u_0, v_0) = (0.6, 0.1)$, and we can clearly observe that system (1.6) undergoes a period-doubling bifurcation at the critical value. With values of $\alpha = 0.75, b = 0.9, a = 0.2, k = 3$, $h = 5, c = 1, d = 0.2, g = 0.1$, Figure 5 is the bifurcation diagram of system (1.6) starting from the point $(u_0, v_0) = (0.5, 0.1)$, and it is clear that system (1.6) undergoes a Neimark–Sacker bifurcation at the critical value.

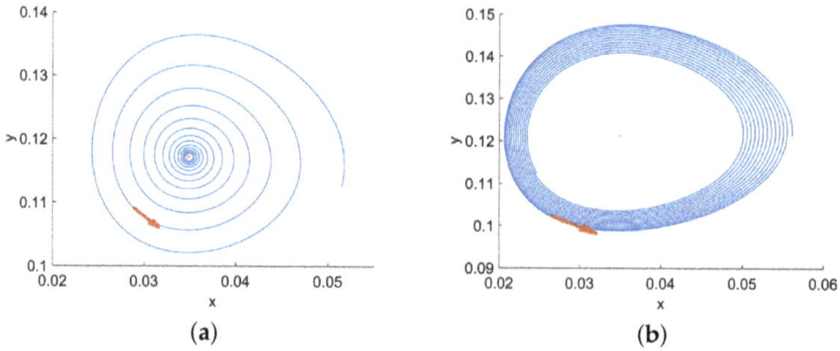

Figure 3. The existence of a supercritical Hopf bifurcation of system (1.3) with the parameter values $c = 0.6, b = 0.5, a = 0.1, h = 0.6, d = 0.1, g = 0.1$ and $\alpha = 0.98$ for $k = 1$ (**a**) and $k = 10$ (**b**).

Figure 6 depicts the phase diagram of system (1.6) starting from the point $(u_0, v_0) = (0.5888, 4.324)$ with parameters $\alpha = 0.75, b = 0.9, a = 0.2, k = 3, h = 5, c = 1,$ $d = 0.2, g = 0.1$. We can observe that as ρ increases, the equilibrium point gradually transitions from a stable focus to an unstable focus, and a stable limit cycle emerges.

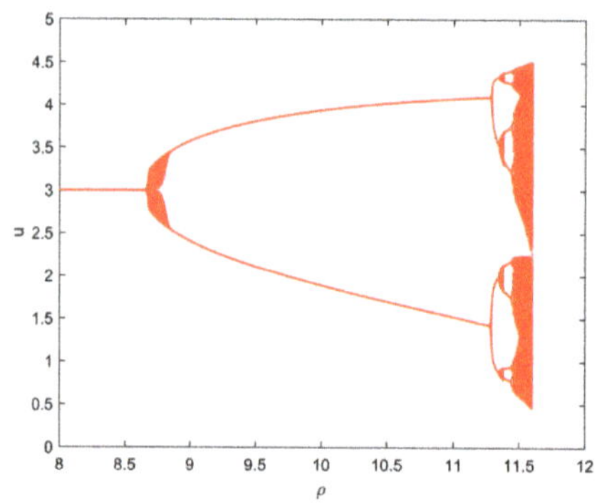

Figure 4. The existence of a period-doubling bifurcation of system (1.6) with the k taking values from 8 to 11.6.

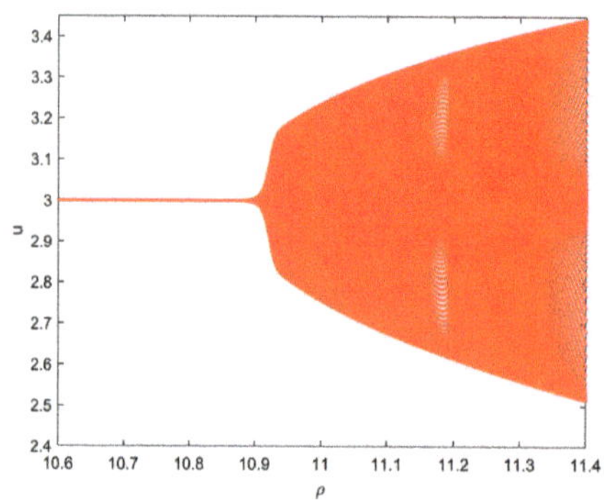

Figure 5. The existence of a Neimark–Sacker bifurcation of system (1.6) with the k taking values from 10.6 to 11.4.

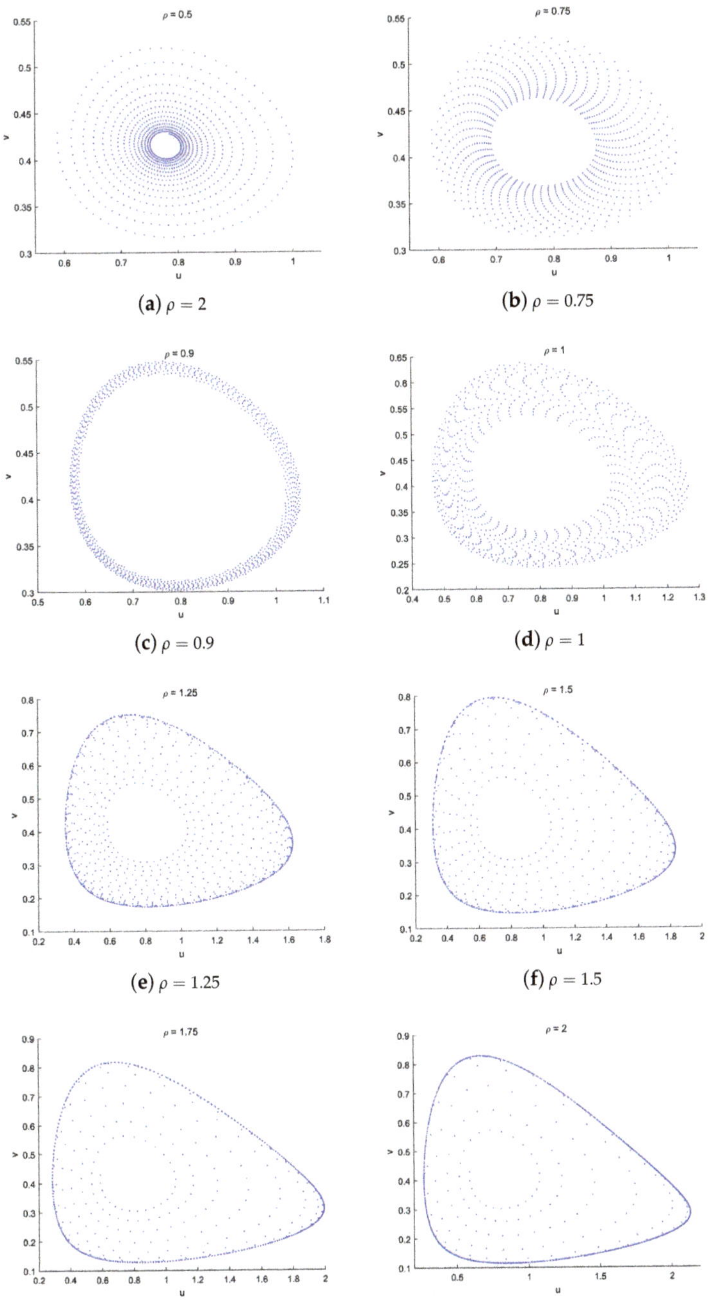

(a) $\rho = 2$ **(b)** $\rho = 0.75$

(c) $\rho = 0.9$ **(d)** $\rho = 1$

(e) $\rho = 1.25$ **(f)** $\rho = 1.5$

(g) $\rho = 1.75$ **(h)** $\rho = 2$

Figure 6. Phase portraits of system (1.6) with $\alpha = 0.75, b = 0.9, a = 0.2, k = 3, h = 5, c = 1, d = 0.2,$ $g = 0.1$ and different ρ when the initial value $(x_0, y_0) = (0.5888, 0.4324)$.

7. Conclusions

In this paper, we propose a fractional-order predator–prey model with a Holling type IV functional response and anti-predator behavior. According to the discrete and continuous versions, from two different perspectives we analyzed their dynamical behavior in detail, including the feasibility, existence and stability of equilibrium points and the possibility of local bifurcations. Our main aim is to provide readers with a better understanding of the dynamics of the system. As there is currently a lack of effective ways and methods to study the dynamics of fractional-order differential systems, in this paper, we propose an effective way to consider this problem from different angles—both continuous and discrete. This is the novelty of this paper. Indeed, we find that there exist some differences in the dynamics of the system between the continuous version and the discrete version. Numerical simulations also illustrate corresponding theoretical results. By analyzing the dynamical behavior of systems (1.3) and (1.6), respectively, we can deduce the following conclusions:

(1) By analyzing the stability of the equilibrium point $Q_0(0,0)$ and conducting numerical simulations, we can determine that the equilibrium point $Q_0(0,0)$ is a saddle point. This implies that under any conditions existing in nature, the simultaneous extinction of predator and prey does not occur.

(2) Through the study of the dynamical behavior of the boundary equilibrium point $Q_k(k,0)$ and numerical simulations, we have found that when d is large, it leads to the extinction of predator. In this case, the prey population tends towards a stable density. On the other hand, when d is small, the extinction of the predator does not occur, and the prey population tends to a stable state. This indicates that when a detrimental condition for the survival of predator and prey arises in nature, the predator may tend towards extinction, while the prey population, although it may decrease, does not tend towards extinction. Instead, it stabilizes at a certain level.

(3) Based on the analysis and numerical simulations of the positive equilibrium point $Q_1(u_1,v_1)$, we can draw the following conclusions: When the parameter k exceeds a critical value, the system exhibits a stable limit cycle. This implies that the interaction between predator and prey leads to periodic oscillations. The presence of this limit cycle indicates that the system exhibits rich dynamic behavior, and under specific conditions, the populations of predator and prey undergo periodic fluctuations. Therefore, we can achieve a steady coexistence state and eliminate the limit cycle by reducing the environmental carrying capacity to the prey.

(4) Through the bifurcation analysis used in this paper, we find that the analysis methods for bifurcation problems are applicable to other types of fractional differential systems. It is well known that the current analysis methods for bifurcation problems in fractional-order dynamic systems are not well developed. Thus, in order to better understand the dynamics of this system, we discretize the fractional-order system to study its dynamics from a different angle. A richer set of dynamical properties is obtained, indicating that investigations after discretizing this system are indeed more valuable and helpful to understanding the properties of this system.

Author Contributions: Methodology, X.L.; Software, B.W.; Formal analysis, B.W.; Resources, B.W.; Data curation, B.W.; Writing—original draft, B.W.; Writing—review & editing, X.L.; Supervision, X.L.; Project administration, X.L.; Funding acquisition, X.L. All authors contributed equally and significantly to writing this paper. All authors have read and agreed to the final manuscript.

Funding: This work was partly supported by the National Natural Science Foundation of China (61473340), the Distinguished Professor Foundation of Qianjiang Scholar in Zhejiang Province (F703108L02), and the Natural Science Foundation of Zhejiang University of Science and Technology (F701108G14).

Data Availability Statement: There are no applicable data associated with this manuscript.

Conflicts of Interest: The authors declare no conflict of interest.

References

1. Berryman, A.A. The orgins and evolution of predator-prey theory. *Ecology* **1992**, *73*, 1530–1535. [CrossRef]
2. Wang, W.; Chen, L. A Predator-Prey System with Stage-Structure for Predator. *Comput. Math. Appl.* **1997**, *33*, 83–91. [CrossRef]
3. Ba, Z.; Li, X. Period-doubling bifurcation and Neimark-Sacker bifurcation of a discrete predator-prey model with Allee effect and cannibalism. *Electron. Res. Arch.* **2023**, *31*, 1405–1438. [CrossRef]
4. Liu, Y.; Li, X. Dynamics of a discrete predator-prey model with Holling-II functional response. *Int. J. Biomath.* **2021**, *14*, 2150068. [CrossRef]
5. Qi, H.; Meng, X. Threshold behavior of a stochastic predator–prey system with prey refuge and fear effect. *Appl. Math. Lett.* **2021**, *113*, 106846. [CrossRef]
6. Blasius, B.; Rudolf, L.; Weithoff, G.; Gaedke, U.; Fussmann, G.F. Long-term cyclic persistence in an experimental predator–prey system. *Nature* **2020**, *577*, 226–230. [CrossRef]
7. Mukherjee, D. Role of fear in predator–prey system with intraspecific competition. *Math. Comput. Simul.* **2020**, *177*, 263–275. [CrossRef]
8. Qiu, H.; Guo, S.; Li, S. Stability and Bifurcation in a Predator–Prey System with Prey-Taxis. *Int. J. Bifurc. Chaos* **2020**, *30*, 2050022. [CrossRef]
9. Perc, M.; Grigolini, P. Collective behavior and evolutionary games–An introduction. *Chaos Solitons Fractals* **2013**, *56*, 1–5. [CrossRef]
10. Lima, S.L. Stress and Decision Making under the Risk of Predation: Recent Developments from Behavioral, Reproductive, and Ecological Perspectives. *Adv. Study Behav.* **1998**, *27*, 215–290.
11. Tollrian, R. Predator-Induced Morphological Defenses: Costs, Life History Shifts, and Maternal Effects in Daphnia Pulex. *Ecology* **1995**, *76*, 1691–1705. [CrossRef]
12. Choh, Y.; Lgnacio, M.; Sabelis, M.W.; Janssen, A. Predator-prey role reversals, juvenile experience and adult antipredator behavior. *Lab. Appl. Entomol.* **2012**, *2*, 728.
13. Janssen, A.; Faraji, F.; Hammen, T.V.D.; Magalhaes, S.; Sabelis, M.W. Interspecific infanticide deters predators. *Ecol. Lett.* **2002**, *5*, 490–494. [CrossRef]
14. Saito, Y. Prey kills predator: Counter-attack success of a spider mite against its specific phytoseiid predator. *Exp. Appl. Acarol.* **1986**, *2*, 47–62. [CrossRef]
15. Ives, A.; Dobson, A. Antipredator behavior and the population dynamics of simple predator-prey systems. *Am. Nat.* **1987**, *130*, 431–447. [CrossRef]
16. Tang, B.; Xiao, Y. Bifurcation analysis of a predator–prey model with anti-predator behavior. *Chaos Solitons Fractals* **2015**, *70*, 58–68. [CrossRef]
17. Sokol, W. Oxidation of an Inhibitory Substrate by Washed Celts (Oxidation of Phenol by *Pseudornonas putida*). *Biotechnol. Bioeng.* **1987**, *30*, 921–927. [CrossRef]
18. Liouville, J. Troisième mémoire sur le développement des fonctions ou parties de fonctions en séries dont les divers termes sont assujettis à satisfaire à une même équation différentielle du second ordre, contenant un paramètre variable. *J. Math. Pures Appl.* **1837**, *2*, 418–436.
19. Riesz, M. L'intégrale de Riemann–Liouville et le problème de Cauchy pour l'équation des ondes. *Bull. Soc. Math. Fr.* **1939**, *67*, 153–170. [CrossRef]
20. Caputo, M. Linear Models of Dissipation whose Q is almost Frequency Independent-II. *Geophys. J. R. Astron. Soc.* **1976**, *13*, 529–539. [CrossRef]
21. Debnath, S.; Majumdar, P.; Sarkar, S.; Ghosh, U. Memory effect on prey–predator dynamics: Exploring the role of fear effect, additional food and anti-predator behaviour of prey. *J. Comput. Sci.* **2023**, *66*, 101929. [CrossRef]
22. Singh, A.; Sharma, V.S. Bifurcations and chaos control in a discrete-time prey–predator model with Holling type-II functional response and prey refuge. *J. Comput. Appl. Math.* **2023**, *418*, 114666. [CrossRef]
23. Kumar, S.; Kumar, R.; Cattani, C.; Samet, B. Chaotic behaviour of fractional predator-prey dynamical system. *Chaos Solitons Fractals* **2020**, *135*, 109811. [CrossRef]
24. Das, M.; Samanta, G. A delayed fractional order food chain model with fear effect and prey refuge. *Math. Comput. Simul.* **2020**, *178*, 218–245. [CrossRef]
25. Barman, D.; Roy, J.; Alrabaiah, H.; Panja, P.; Mondal, S.P.; Alam, S. Impact of predator incited fear and prey refuge in a fractional order prey predator model. *Chaos Solitons Fractals* **2021**, *142*, 110420. [CrossRef]
26. Das, M.; Samanta, G. A prey-predator fractional order model with fear effect and group defense. *Int. J. Dyn. Control* **2021**, *9*, 334–349. [CrossRef]
27. Yousef, F.; Yousef, A.; Maji, C. Effects of fear in a fractional-order predator-prey system with predator density-dependent prey mortality. *Chaos Solitons Fractals* **2021**, *145*, 110711. [CrossRef]
28. Zhang, N.; Kao, Y.; Xie, B. Impact of fear effect and prey refuge on a fractional order prey–predator system with Beddington–DeAngelis functional response. *Chaos* **2022**, *32*, 043125. [CrossRef]
29. Majumdar, P.; Mondal, B.; Debnath, S.; Ghosh, U. Controlling of periodicity and chaos in a three dimensional prey predator model introducing the memory effect. *Chaos Solitons Fractals* **2022**, *164*, 112585. [CrossRef]
30. Xie, B.; Zhang, Z. Impact of Allee and fear effects in a fractional order prey–predator system incorporating prey refuge. *Chaos* **2023**, *33*, 013131. [CrossRef]

31. Salmana, S.M.; Yousef, A.M.; Elsadanyc, A.A. Stability, bifurcation analysis and chaos control of a discrete predator-prey system with square root functional response. *Chaos Solitons Fractals* **2016**, *93*, 20–31. [CrossRef]
32. Yousef, A.M.; Rida, S.Z.; Ali, H.M.; Zaki, A.S. Stability, co-dimension two bifurcations and chaos control of a host-parasitoid model with mutual interference. *Chaos Solitons Fractals* **2023**, *166*, 112923. [CrossRef]
33. Yousef, A.M.; Rida, S.Z.; Gouda, Y.G.; Zaki, A.S. Dynamical Behaviors of a Fractional-Order Predator–Prey Model with Holling Type IV Functional Response and Its Discretization. *Int. J. Nonlinear Sci. Numer. Simul.* **2019**, *20*, 125–136. [CrossRef]
34. Singh, A.; Elsadany, A.A.; Elsonbaty, A. Complex dynamics of a discrete fractional-order Leslie-Gower predator-prey model. *Math. Methods Appl. Sci.* **2019**, *42*, 3992–4007. [CrossRef]
35. Elsonbaty, A.; Elsadany, A.A. On discrete fractional order Lotka Volterra model based on the Caputo diference discrete operator. *Math. Sci.* **2023**, *17*, 67–79. [CrossRef]
36. Uddin, M.J.; Rana, S.M.S.; Işık, S.; Kangalgil, F. On the qualitative study of a discrete fractional order prey–predator model with the effects of harvesting on predator population. *Chaos Solitons Fractals* **2023**, *175*, 113932. [CrossRef]
37. Kai, D. *The Analysis of Fractional Differential Equations (An Application-Oriented Exposition Using Differential Operators of Caputo Type)*; Springer Scienc & Business Media: Berlin/Heidelberg, Germany, 2010; Volume 2004, pp. 237–244.
38. Li, W.; Li, X.Y. Neimark–Sacker bifurcation of a semi-discrete hematopoiesis model. *J. Appl. Anal. Comput.* **2018**, *8*, 1679–1693.
39. Cieck, M.; Yakar, C.; Oğur, B. Stability, Boundedness, and Lagrange Stability of Fractional Differential Equations with Initial Time Difference. *Sci. World J.* **2014**, *2014*, 939027.
40. Odibat, Z.; Shawagfeh, N. Generalized Taylor's formula. *Appl. Math. Comput.* **2007**, *186*, 286–293. [CrossRef]
41. Wang, C.; Li, X.Y. Stability and Neimark–Sacker bifurcation of a semi-discrete population model. *J. Appl. Anal. Comput.* **2014**, *4*, 419–435.
42. Liang, S.; Wu, R.; Chen, L. Laplace transform of fractional order differential equations. *Electron. J. Differ. Equ.* **2015**, *2015*, 1–15.
43. Kexue, L.; Jigen, P. Laplace transform and fractional differential equations. *Appl. Math. Lett.* **2011**, *24*, 2019–2023. [CrossRef]
44. Petráš, I. *Fractional-Order Nonlinear Systems: Modeling, Analysis and Simulation*; Springer: Berlin/Heidelberg, Germany, 2011.
45. Deshpande, A.; Daftardar-Gejji, V.; Sukale, Y.V. On Hopf bifurcation in fractional dynamical systems. *Chaos Solitons Fractals* **2017**, *98*, 189–198. [CrossRef]

fractal and fractional

MDPI

Article

The Müntz–Legendre Wavelet Collocation Method for Solving Weakly Singular Integro-Differential Equations with Fractional Derivatives

Haifa Bin Jebreen

Department of Mathematics, College of Science, King Saud University, P.O. Box 2455, Riyadh 11451, Saudi Arabia; hjebreen@ksu.edu.sa

Abstract: We offer a wavelet collocation method for solving the weakly singular integro-differential equations with fractional derivatives (WSIDE). Our approach is based on the reduction of the desired equation to the corresponding Volterra integral equation. The Müntz–Legendre (ML) wavelet is introduced, and a fractional integration operational matrix is constructed for it. The obtained integral equation is reduced to a system of nonlinear algebraic equations using the collocation method and the operational matrix of fractional integration. The presented method's error bound is investigated, and some numerical simulations demonstrate the efficiency and accuracy of the method. According to the obtained results, the presented method solves this type of equation well and gives significant results.

Keywords: Müntz–Legendre wavelets; wavelet collocation method; weakly singular integral equation; fractional differential equation

1. Introduction

The wavelet collocation approach is employed in this study to solve WSIDE [1]

$$ {}^{C}\mathcal{D}_0^{\beta_1}u(x) = \int_0^x (x-t)^{\beta_2-1}u(t)dt + g(x)u(x) + f(x), \quad \beta_1, \beta_2 \in \mathbb{R}^+, \quad x \in [0,1], \tag{1} $$

with initial condition

$$ u^{(\kappa)}(0) = \eta_\kappa, \quad \kappa = 0, 1, \dots, n_1 - 1, \tag{2} $$

where ${}^{c}\mathcal{D}_0^{\beta_1}$ specifies the Caputo fractional derivative (CFD) defined by

$$ {}^{c}D_0^{\beta_1}(u)(x) := \frac{1}{\Gamma(n_1-\beta_1)} \int_0^x \frac{u^{(n)}(t)dt}{(x-t)^{\beta_1-n_1+1}}, \tag{3} $$

and $n_i = \beta_i$ for $\beta_i \in \mathbb{N}$, and $[\beta_i] + 1 := n_i \in \mathbb{N}$, for $\beta_i \notin \mathbb{N}$ $(i = 1, 2)$. The functions f and g are considered to be sufficiently smooth functions on the interval $[0, 1]$.

Various physical phenomena can be modeled using fractional integro-differential equations (FIDEs), such as the epidemic process [2], viscoelasticity [3] and glass-forming process [4]. Some papers have explored numerical methods for solving equations of this type, and we mention a few of them. In [5], FIDEs are solved using a fractional differential transform scheme. In [6], the authors employed the Adomian decomposition scheme to solve FIDEs. Then, Momani et al. [7] applied this method for solving systems of FIDEs. To solve Equation (1), Zhao et al. [1] used a collocation approach based on a piecewise polynomial. Rawashdeh [8] applied the collocation method using Spline functions to solve the problem (1) and (2).

In recent years, fractional derivatives instead of positive integer derivatives have been used to modeling of physical phenomena. These types of equations have gained a special place for themselves, and many researchers are looking into how to model phenomena with these types of derivatives, as well as how to solve them. Meanwhile, some applications of these equations can be mentioned such as dynamics of interfaces between substrates and nanoparticles [9], colored noise [10], bioengineering [11], fluid-dynamic traffic model [12], solid mechanics [13], earthquakes [14], anomalous transport [15], continua and statistical mechanics [16], economics [17]. There are some analytical methods to solve these types of equations [18–20]. But, when the equations become more complicated, these methods no longer work. So, numerical approaches can address this shortage. Here, we mention some of these methods, including the finite difference method [21], collocation method [22–25], Galerkin method [26–28], finite element method [29], integral transform method [30], etc.

In recent years, among the existing bases, wavelets have played an essential role in solving various equations and representing differential and integral operators [31]. In the numerical solution of equations, two forms of wavelets are utilized, which are scalar wavelets and multi-wavelets. Multi-wavelets, including the Müntz–Legendre wavelets, use multi-generators instead of a single-generator in the multiresolution analysis [32]. For this reason, they do not have some of the disadvantages of scalar wavelets. One of the most famous multi-wavelets are Alpert multi-wavelets, which have many applications in numerical solution and image processing [31,33–35]. The Müntz wavelets are another instance of multi-wavelets that have recently been used in some numerical work, such as solving fractional optimal control problems [36], multi-order fractional differential equations [37], and pantograph equations with fractional derivatives [38].

As we are aware, the singularity and existing fractional derivatives in equations are two very important challenges in solving these types of equations. Another challenge is the existence of a non-smooth solution for these equations near the boundaries, which many numerical methods fail to overcome. In this study, we apply the Müntz–Legendre wavelets collocation method with various choices of collocation points, including Chebyshev and Legendre nodes, as well as uniform grids to overcome such challenges. Because of the concentration of Chebyshev nodes in the boundaries (this is a common choice for solving the singular integrals, too) and the properties of the Müntz–Legendre wavelets, we expect our presented method to work well. Example 4 shows that the present method can solve problems where the exact solution is non-smooth near the origin.

The structure of this paper is as follows: We introduce the Müntz–Legendre wavelets and their properties in Section 2. The wavelet collocation method is implemented to solve WSIDE in Section 3. An error-bound investigation is also surveyed in this section. Section 4 is about some numerical experiments that show how accurate and useful the method is.

2. Müntz–Legendre Wavelets

Assume that $S_l(\mathcal{L}) := span\{x^{\eta_0}, x^{\eta_1}, \ldots, x^{\eta_l}\}$ for each l where $\mathcal{L} = \{0 = \eta_0 < \eta_1 < \ldots\}$ is an increasing sequence. Motivated by [39], we introduce the space $S(\mathcal{L})$, which is spanned by $\{x^{\eta_l}\}_{l=0}^{\infty}$ as

$$S(\mathcal{L}) := \bigcup_{l=0}^{\infty} S_n(\mathcal{L}) = span\{x^{\eta_l}, l = 0, 1, \ldots\}, \quad x \in (0,1). \tag{4}$$

This space is dense in $C[0,1]$. S. N. Bernstein, a Russian mathematician, demonstrated explicitly that the sufficient and necessary criteria for having $\overline{S(\mathcal{L})} = C[0,1]$ are

$$\sum_{\eta_k > 0} \frac{1 + \log \eta_k}{\eta_k} = \infty, \tag{5}$$

and

$$\lim_{k\to\infty} \frac{\eta_k}{k\log k} = 0, \tag{6}$$

respectively. He also proposed that

$$\sum_{k=1}^{\infty} \frac{1}{\eta_k} = \infty, \tag{7}$$

is a necessary and sufficient condition for $\mathcal{L} = \{0 = \eta_0 < \eta_1 < \ldots\}$ to exist.

Müntz, however, verified this conjecture two years later [40]. It may be demonstrated that the same holds true for $L^2(0,1)$ [41]. It should be noted that the functions $\{x^{\eta_l}\}_{l=0}^{\infty}$ are not appropriate as bases. Thus, in the subsequent part, the Müntz–Legendre (ML) functions will be described in a way that makes them straightforward to evaluate and orthogonal.

The ML polynomials are specified as follows [41,42]:

$$L_l(x;\mathcal{L}) := \frac{1}{2\pi i}\int_{\chi}\prod_{k=1}^{l-1}\frac{t+\eta_k+1}{t-\eta_k}\frac{x^t}{t-\eta_l}dt, \tag{8}$$

where χ is a simple contour that encircles all zeros in the integrand's denominator. Here is another representation for these functions. Given $\eta_n := \{n\nu : \nu \in \mathbb{R}, n = 0,\ldots l\}$, let the coefficient $c_{n,l}$ be calculated by

$$c_{n,l} := \frac{\prod_{i=0}^{l-1}(\eta_n+\eta_i+1)}{\prod_{i=0,i\neq n}^{l}(\eta_n-\eta_i)}. \tag{9}$$

Using these coefficients, we can state the ML polynomials as follows.

$$L_l(x;\mathcal{L}) = \sum_{n=0}^{l} c_{n,l}x^{\eta_n}, \quad x \in [0,1]. \tag{10}$$

It is possible to demonstrate that the ML polynomials constitute an orthogonal function system in the sense of $C[0,1]$ and $L^2(0,1)$. In the following, for simplicity, we put $L_l(x) := L_l(x;\mathcal{L})$.

Given $s \in \mathbb{N}_0$ and $r \in \mathbb{N}$, we consider a subspace of $L^2([0,1])$ as follows

$$A_s = span\{\phi^l_{s,b} : \quad b \in \mathcal{B},\ l \in \mathcal{R}\}, \tag{11}$$

where $\mathcal{B} := \{0,1,\ldots,2^s-1\}$, $\mathcal{R} := \{0,1,\ldots,r-1\}$, and the dilatation and translation of ϕ^l result in $\phi^l_{s,b}$. In addition, the parameters r and s are referred to as the multiplicity and refinement level, respectively.

The ML wavelets are introduced in [37], and are determined by

$$\phi^n_{s,b} = \begin{cases} 2^{s/2}\sqrt{2\eta_n+1}L_n(2^s x-b), & \frac{b}{2^s} \le x \le \frac{b+1}{2^s}, \\ 0, & otherwise. \end{cases} \tag{12}$$

To map a function $u \in L^2[0,1]$ onto A_s, we provide the following projection operator $\mathcal{P}_s$, i.e.,

$$u(x) \approx \mathcal{P}_s(u)(x) = \sum_{b=0}^{2^s-1}\sum_{l=0}^{r-1} u_{b,l}\phi^l_{s,b}(x) = U^T\Phi(x) \in A_s, \tag{13}$$

where the $(br+l+1)$-th element of $N = 2^s r$ dimensional vector function $\Phi(x)$ is $\phi^l_{s,b}(x)$.

To assess the coefficients $u_{b,l}$, one has

$$u_{b,l} = \langle u, \phi^l_{s,b} \rangle = \int_0^1 u(x)\phi^l_{s,b}(x)dx. \tag{14}$$

The approximation (13), can be bounded [36].

Lemma 1 ([36]). *Given $r > m$, assume that $u \in H^m[0,1]$, then we have*

$$\|u - \mathcal{P}_s(u)\|_2 \leq c(r-1)^{-m}(2^{s-1})^{-m}\|u^{(m)}\|_2, \tag{15}$$

and when $J \geq 1$, we obtain

$$\|u - \mathcal{P}_s(u)\|_{H^J([0,1])} \leq c(2^{s-1})^{J-m}(r-1)^{2J-\frac{1}{2}-m}\|u^{(m)}\|_2, \tag{16}$$

where $H^m([0,1])$ indicates the Sobolev space and its associated norm is specified by

$$\|u\|_{H^m([0,1])} = \left(\sum_{j=0}^{m} \|u^{(j)}\|_2^2\right)^{1/2}. \tag{17}$$

Operational Matrix of Fractional Integration

We begin this section with the definition of Riemann–Liouville (RL) fractional integration (FI). From here on, we use β for both β_1 and β_2 unless specifically noted.

Definition 1. *Given $\beta \in \mathbb{R}^+$, the RL-FI operator $\mathcal{I}_0^\beta$ of order β is specified by*

$$\mathcal{I}_0^\beta(u)(x) := \frac{1}{\Gamma(\beta)}\int_0^x (x-z)^{\beta-1}u(z)dz, \quad x \in [a,b], \tag{18}$$

in which $\Gamma(\beta)$ indicates the Gamma function.

To give rise to a matrix representation for the FI of ML wavelets, it is straightforward to approximate the effect of the operator $\mathcal{I}_0^\beta$ on the vector function $\Phi(x)$ via the projection $\mathcal{P}_s$ as

$$\mathcal{P}_s(\mathcal{I}_0^\beta)(\Phi(x)) \approx I_\beta\Phi(x), \tag{19}$$

in which I_β is called the RL-FI operational matrix. Before obtaining the elements of the matrix I_β for ML wavelets, the piecewise fractional-order Taylor functions must be introduced. These functions are determined by

$$v^l_{s,b} = \begin{cases} x^{\eta_l}, & \frac{b}{2^s} \leq x \leq \frac{b+1}{2^s}, \\ 0, & otherwise, \end{cases} \quad b \in \mathcal{B}, l \in \mathcal{R}, s \in \mathbb{N}_0. \tag{20}$$

Owing to this introduction of function $v^l_{s,b}$ and vector function $\Phi(x)$, one can find a closed relationship between these functions, viz.

$$\Phi(x) = V^{-1}\Upsilon(x), \tag{21}$$

where $v^l_{s,b}$ is $(br+l+1)$-th element of the vector function $\Upsilon(x)$, and V is an square matrix of order N with elements

$$V_{i,j} = \langle \Phi_i(x), \Upsilon_j(x) \rangle = \int_0^1 \Upsilon_j(x)\Phi_i(x)dx, \quad i,j = 1,\ldots,N. \tag{22}$$

Now, setting the r-dimension vector W with the i-th element x^{η_i}, it is simple in order to demonstrate that

$$\Upsilon(x) = [W, \ldots, W]^T. \tag{23}$$

Due to Definition 1, it is easy to verify that

$$\mathcal{I}_0^{\beta}(x^{\gamma}) = \frac{\Gamma(\gamma+1)}{\Gamma(\gamma+\beta+1)} x^{\gamma+\beta}. \tag{24}$$

Thus, one can verify that

$$\mathcal{I}_0^{\beta}(\Upsilon_i)(x) = \frac{\Gamma(\eta_i+1)}{\Gamma(\eta_i+\beta+1)} x^{\eta_i+\beta}, \quad i = 1, 2, \ldots, N. \tag{25}$$

It follows from (25) that there exists a matrix $I_{\Upsilon,\beta}(x)$ that satisfies

$$\mathcal{I}_0^{\beta}(\Upsilon)(x) = I_{\Upsilon,\beta}(x)\Upsilon(x). \tag{26}$$

Setting $E_{\beta}(x) := x^{\beta} B$ ($\mathcal{I}_0^{\beta}(W)(x) = E_{\beta}(x)W(x)$), where B is a diagonal matrix whose elements are

$$(B)_{i,i} = (\Gamma(\eta_i+1))(\Gamma(\eta_i+\beta+1))^{-1}, \tag{27}$$

the matrix $I_{\Upsilon,\beta}(x)$ can be obtained as

$$I_{\Upsilon,\beta}(x) = diag\big[E_{\beta}(x), \ldots, E_{\beta}(x)\big]. \tag{28}$$

We can now derive the FI operational matrix for ML wavelets.

$$\begin{aligned} \mathcal{P}_s(\mathcal{I}_0^{\beta})(\Phi(x)) &= \mathcal{P}_s(\mathcal{I}_0^{\beta})(V^{-1}\Upsilon(x)) \\ &= V^{-1} I_{\Upsilon,\beta}(x)\Upsilon(x) \\ &= V^{-1} I_{\Upsilon,\beta}(x) V \Phi(x). \end{aligned} \tag{29}$$

Thus, we obtain

$$I_{\beta}(x) := V^{-1} I_{\Upsilon,\beta}(x) V. \tag{30}$$

3. Wavelet Collocation Method

This section is dedicated to developing an algorithm based on the collocation method using the well-known ML wavelets for solving the WSIDE (1). To implement the collocation method, using the operator $\mathcal{P}_s$, we can expand the unknown solution $u(x)$ based on ML wavelets, viz.,

$$u(x) \approx \mathcal{P}_s(u)(x) = U^T\Phi(x) := u_N(x). \tag{31}$$

where the N-dimensional vector U contains the unknowns, which should be specified. It is straightforward enough to prove that the function $u(x)$ is a WSIDE (1) solution if and only if it satisfies the integral equation

$$u(x) - u_0(x) = \mathcal{I}_0^{\beta_1}(gu)(x) + \Gamma(\beta_2)\mathcal{I}_0^{\beta_1+\beta_2}(u)(x) + \mathcal{I}_0^{\beta_1}(f)(x), \tag{32}$$

where

$$u_0(x) = \sum_{\kappa=0}^{n_1-1} \frac{u^{(\kappa)}(0)}{\kappa!} x^{\kappa}.$$

Inserting $u_N(x)$ into Equation (32), we obtain

$$u_N(x) - u_0(x) = \mathcal{I}_0^{\beta_1}(gu_N)(x) + \Gamma(\beta_2)\mathcal{I}_0^{\beta_1+\beta_2}(u_N)(x) + \mathcal{I}_0^{\beta_1}(f)(x). \tag{33}$$

By approximating the functions $u_0(x)$, $gu_N(x)$ and $f(x)$ using the projection operator $\mathcal{P}_s$, we have

$$\begin{aligned} u_0(x) &\approx \mathcal{P}_s(u_0)(x) = U_0^T\Phi(x), \\ gu_N(x) &\approx \mathcal{P}_s(gu_N)(x) = U^T G\Phi(x), \\ f(x) &\approx \mathcal{P}_s(f)(x) = F^T\Phi(x). \end{aligned} \tag{34}$$

Using (31) and the matrix I_β, we can write

$$\begin{aligned} \mathcal{I}_0^{\beta_1}(gu_N)(x) &\approx \mathcal{P}_s(\mathcal{I}_0^{\beta_1}(\mathcal{P}_S)(gu_N))(x) = U^T G I_{\beta_1}\Phi(x), \\ \mathcal{I}_0^{\beta_1+\beta_2}(u)(x) &\approx \mathcal{P}_S(\mathcal{I}_0^{\beta_1+\beta_2}(u))(x) = U^T I_{\beta_1+\beta_2}\Phi(x), \\ \mathcal{I}_0^{\beta_1}(f)(x) &\approx \mathcal{P}_S(\mathcal{I}_0^{\beta_1}(\mathcal{P}_S)(f))(x) = F^T I_{\beta_1}\Phi(x). \end{aligned} \tag{35}$$

Inserting Equations (35) into (33), one can introduce the residual as

$$R(x) = \Big(U^T(I - GI_{\beta_1} - I_{\beta_1+\beta_2}) - U_0^T - F^T I_{\beta_1}\Big)\Phi(x). \tag{36}$$

Our goal is to minimize the residual function $R(x)$ to zero. We generate a system of nonlinear algebraic equations by selecting the collocation points $\{x_i\}_{i=1}^N \in [0,1]$ that satisfy $R(x_i) = 0$. We can determine the unknown coefficients U after solving this system. The collocation points in our study are uniformly spaced meshes or the roots of shifted Chebyshev and Legendre polynomials. To solve the aforementioned nonlinear system, we use the Newton method. It is worth noting that Newton's method is implemented with starting point $U = O$ (null vector) and the termination criterion is selected to be absolute residual which is less than the given tolerance 10^{-16}.

In a more abstract form, there is a projection operator Q_N such that it maps $C([0,1])$ onto A_J. On the other hand, given $u \in C([0,1])$, the projection $Q_N(u)$ is an element of A_J that interpolates u at the points $\{x_i\}_{i=1}^N \in [0,1]$. Note that $Q_N R = 0$ if and only if $R(x_i) = 0$ for $\{x_i\}_{i=1}^N \in [0,1]$. Considering this preface, the condition $R(x_i) = 0$ can be written as

$$Q_N R = 0. \tag{37}$$

Equivalently, we have

$$Q_N\Big(\big(U^T(I - GI_{\beta_1} - I_{\beta_1+\beta_2})\big)\Phi(x)\Big) = Q_N\Big(U_0^T + F^T I_{\beta_1}\Big)\Phi(x). \tag{38}$$

Error Analysis

It is possible to demonstrate that $\mathcal{I}_0^\beta$ is bounded. The following lemma can be helpful in obtaining this bound.

Lemma 2 ([43])**.** *There is an estimation of the bound of the FI operator $\mathcal{I}_0^\beta$ in $L_q([0,1])$, viz.*

$$\|\mathcal{I}_0^\beta(u)\|_q \le \frac{1}{\Gamma(\beta+1)}\|u\|_q, \quad 1 \le q \le \infty. \tag{39}$$

Theorem 1. *Let $\beta_i \in \mathbb{R}^+$ and $\mathbb{N} \ni n_i = -[-\beta]$ for $i = 1,2$. Furthermore, assume that the functions u_0, g, and f are sufficiently smooth functions on $[0,1]$ in Equation (1). Thus, the error bound for desired equation based on the ML wavelets collocation method is obtained by*

$$\|u - u_N\| \leq CM(r-1)^{-m}(2^{J-1})^{-m} + \frac{1}{(N+1)!}\|R^{(N+1)}\|, \tag{40}$$

where u_N is the approximate solution and C and M are constants.

Proof. Subtracting (38) from (32), we obtain

$$\begin{aligned} u(x) - Q_N(u_N)(x) &= u_0(x) - Q_N(\mathcal{P}_s(u_0))(x) + \mathcal{I}_0^{\beta_1}(gu)(x) - Q_N(\mathcal{P}_s(\mathcal{I}_0^{\beta_1}(\mathcal{P}_s(gu))))(x) \\ &+ \Gamma(\beta_2)\mathcal{I}_0^{\beta_1+\beta_2}(u)(x) - \Gamma(\beta_2)Q_N(\mathcal{P}_s(\mathcal{I}_0^{\beta_1+\beta_2}(u_N))(x)) \\ &+ \mathcal{I}_0^{\beta_1}(f)(x) - Q_N(\mathcal{I}_0^{\beta_1}(\mathcal{P}_s(f)))(x), \end{aligned} \tag{41}$$

Given $e_N = u - u_N$, by adding and subtracting several terms and simplifying by considering $\mathcal{E}_s := I - \mathcal{P}_s$ for the pair of terms in Equation (41), we have

1.

$$\begin{aligned} u(x) - Q_N(u_N)(x) &= u(x) - u_N(x) + u_N(x) - Q_N(u_N)(x) \\ &= e_N(x) + (I - Q_N)(u_N)(x), \end{aligned} \tag{42}$$

2.

$$\begin{aligned} u_0(x) - Q_N(\mathcal{P}_s(u_0))(x) &= u_0(x) - \mathcal{P}_s(u_0)(x) + \mathcal{P}_s(u_0)(x) - Q_N(\mathcal{P}_s(u_0)(x)) \\ &= \mathcal{E}_s(u_0)(x) + (I - Q_N)(\mathcal{P}_s(u_0))(x), \end{aligned} \tag{43}$$

3.

$$\begin{aligned} \mathcal{I}_0^{\beta_1}(gu)(x) - Q_N(\mathcal{P}_s(\mathcal{I}_0^{\beta_1}(\mathcal{P}_s(gu))))(x) &= \mathcal{I}_0^{\beta_1}(gu)(x) - \mathcal{I}_0^{\beta_1}(gu_N)(x) \\ &+ \mathcal{I}_0^{\beta_1}(gu_N)(x) - \mathcal{I}_0^{\beta_1}(\mathcal{P}_s(gu_N))(x) + \mathcal{I}_0^{\beta_1}(\mathcal{P}_s(gu_N))(x) \\ &- \mathcal{P}_s(\mathcal{I}_0^{\beta_1}(\mathcal{P}_s(gu_N)))(x) + (I - Q_N)\mathcal{P}_s(\mathcal{I}_0^{\beta_1}(\mathcal{P}_s(gu_N)))(x) \\ &= \mathcal{I}_0^{\beta_1}(ge_N)(x) + \mathcal{I}_0^{\beta_1}(\mathcal{E}_s(gu_N))(x) \\ &+ \mathcal{E}_s(\mathcal{I}_0^{\beta_1}(\mathcal{P}_s(gu_N)))(x) + (I - Q_N)\mathcal{P}_s(\mathcal{I}_0^{\beta_1}(\mathcal{P}_s(gu_N)))(x), \end{aligned} \tag{44}$$

4.

$$\begin{aligned} \mathcal{I}_0^{\beta_1+\beta_2}(u)(x) - Q_N(\mathcal{P}_s(\mathcal{I}_0^{\beta_1+\beta_2}(u_N))(x)) &= \mathcal{I}_0^{\beta_1+\beta_2}(u)(x) - \mathcal{I}_0^{\beta_1+\beta_2}(u_N)(x) \\ &+ \mathcal{I}_0^{\beta_1+\beta_2}(u_N)(x) - \mathcal{P}_s(\mathcal{I}_0^{\beta_1+\beta_2}(u_N))(x) + (I - Q_N)(\mathcal{P}_s(\mathcal{I}_0^{\beta_1+\beta_2}(u_N)))(x) \\ &= \mathcal{I}_0^{\beta_1+\beta_2}(e_N)(x) + \mathcal{E}_s(\mathcal{I}_0^{\beta_1+\beta_2}(u_N))(x) \\ &+ (I - Q_N)(\mathcal{P}_s(\mathcal{I}_0^{\beta_1+\beta_2}(u_N)))(x), \end{aligned} \tag{45}$$

5.

$$\begin{aligned} \mathcal{I}_0^{\beta_1}(f)(x) - Q_N(\mathcal{I}_0^{\beta_1}(\mathcal{P}_s(f)))(x) &= \mathcal{I}_0^{\beta_1}(f - \mathcal{P}_s(f))(x) + \mathcal{I}_0^{\beta_1}(\mathcal{P}_s(f))(x) \\ &- \mathcal{P}_s(\mathcal{I}_0^{\beta_1}(\mathcal{P}_s(f)))(x) + (I - Q_N)(\mathcal{P}_s(\mathcal{I}_0^{\beta_1}(\mathcal{P}_s(f))))(x) \\ &= \mathcal{I}_0^{\beta_1}(\mathcal{E}_s(f))(x) + \mathcal{E}_s(\mathcal{I}_0^{\beta_1}(\mathcal{P}_s(f)))(x) \\ &+ (I - Q_N)(\mathcal{P}_s(\mathcal{I}_0^{\beta_1}(\mathcal{P}_s(f))))(x). \end{aligned} \tag{46}$$

Now, referring to Equation (41) and using Equations (42)–(46), we have

$$\begin{aligned} e_N(x) + (I - Q_N)(u_N)(x) &= \mathcal{E}_s(u_0)(x) + (I - Q_N)(\mathcal{P}_s(u_0))(x) \\ &+ \mathcal{I}_0^{\beta_1}(ge_N)(x) + \mathcal{I}_0^{\beta_1}(\mathcal{E}_s(gu_N))(x) \\ &+ \mathcal{E}_s(\mathcal{I}_0^{\beta_1}(\mathcal{P}_s(gu_N)))(x) + (I - Q_N)\mathcal{P}_s(\mathcal{I}_0^{\beta_1}(\mathcal{P}_s(gu_N)))(x) \\ &+ \mathcal{I}_0^{\beta_1+\beta_2}(e_N)(x) + \mathcal{E}_s(\mathcal{I}_0^{\beta_1+\beta_2}(u_N))(x) \\ &+ (I - Q_N)(\mathcal{P}_s(\mathcal{I}_0^{\beta_1+\beta_2}(u_N)))(x) \\ &\mathcal{I}_0^{\beta_1}(\mathcal{E}_s(f))(x) + \mathcal{E}_s(\mathcal{I}_0^{\beta_1}(\mathcal{P}_s(f)))(x) \\ &+ (I - Q_N)(\mathcal{P}_s(\mathcal{I}_0^{\beta_1}(\mathcal{P}_s(f))))(x). \end{aligned}$$

Given

$$\begin{aligned} R(x) = u_N(x) - \mathcal{P}_s(u_0)(x) - \mathcal{P}_s(\mathcal{I}_0^{\beta_1}(\mathcal{P}_s(gu_N)))(x) - \mathcal{P}_s(\mathcal{I}_0^{\beta_1+\beta_2}(u_N))(x) \\ - \mathcal{P}_s(\mathcal{I}_0^{\beta_1}(\mathcal{P}_s(f)))(x), \end{aligned} \tag{47}$$

some simplification gives rise to obtain

$$\begin{aligned} e_N(x) = \mathcal{E}_s(u_0)(x) + \mathcal{I}_0^{\beta_1}(ge_N)(x) + \mathcal{I}_0^{\beta_1}(\mathcal{E}_s(gu_N))(x) \\ + \mathcal{E}_s(\mathcal{I}_0^{\beta_1}(\mathcal{P}_s(gu_N)))(x) + \Gamma(\beta_2)\mathcal{I}_0^{\beta_1+\beta_2}(e_N)(x) + \Gamma(\beta_2)\mathcal{E}_s(\mathcal{I}_0^{\beta_1+\beta_2}(u_N))(x) \\ + \mathcal{I}_0^{\beta_1}(\mathcal{E}_s(f))(x) + \mathcal{E}_s(\mathcal{I}_0^{\beta_1}(\mathcal{P}_s(f)))(x) + (I - Q_N)(R)(x). \end{aligned} \tag{48}$$

Taking the norm from both sides of (49), we obtain

$$\begin{aligned} \|e_N(x)\| \leq \|\mathcal{E}_s(u_0)(x)\| + \|\mathcal{I}_0^{\beta_1}(ge_N)(x)\| + \|\mathcal{I}_0^{\beta_1}(\mathcal{E}_s(gu_N))(x)\| \\ + \|\mathcal{E}_s(\mathcal{I}_0^{\beta_1}(\mathcal{P}_s(gu_N)))(x)\| + \Gamma(\beta_2)\|\mathcal{I}_0^{\beta_1+\beta_2}(e_N)(x)\| \\ + \Gamma(\beta_2)\|\mathcal{E}_s(\mathcal{I}_0^{\beta_1+\beta_2}(u_N))(x)\| + \|\mathcal{I}_0^{\beta_1}(\mathcal{E}_s(f))(x)\| \\ + \|\mathcal{E}_s(\mathcal{I}_0^{\beta_1}(\mathcal{P}_s(f)))(x)\| + \|(I - Q_N)(R)(x)\|, \end{aligned} \tag{49}$$

where the triangle inequality is used. Considering each norm in (49) and using Lemmas 1 and 2, the following inequalities can be obtained:

$$\begin{aligned} \|\mathcal{E}_s(u_0)(x)\| &\leq c(r-1)^{-m}(2^{s-1})^{-m}\|u_0^{(m)}\|, \\ \|\mathcal{I}_0^{\beta_1}(ge_N)(x)\| &\leq \frac{1}{\Gamma(\beta_1+1)}\|ge_N\| \leq \frac{M_1}{\Gamma(\beta_1+1)}\|e_N\|, \quad (M_1 = \max_{x\in[0,1]}|g(x)|), \\ \|\mathcal{I}_0^{\beta_1}(\mathcal{E}_s(gu_N))(x)\| &\leq \frac{1}{\Gamma(\beta_1+1)}\|\mathcal{E}_s(gu_N)(x)\| \\ &\leq \frac{c}{\beta_1+1}(r-1)^{-m}(2^{s-1})^{-m}\|(gu_N)^{(m)}\| \end{aligned}$$

$$
\begin{aligned}
\|\mathcal{E}_s(\mathcal{I}_0^{\beta_1}(\mathcal{P}_s(gu_N)))(x)\| &\leq c(r-1)^{-m}(2^{s-1})^{-m}\|\mathcal{D}^m\mathcal{I}_0^{\beta_1}(\mathcal{P}_s(gu_N))\|, \\
\|\mathcal{I}_0^{\beta_1+\beta_2}(e_N)(x)\| &\leq \frac{\Gamma(\beta_2)}{\Gamma(\beta_1+\beta_2+1)}\|e_N\|, \\
\|\mathcal{E}_s(\mathcal{I}_0^{\beta_1+\beta_2}(u_N))(x)\| &\leq c\Gamma(\beta_2)(r-1)^{-m}(2^{s-1})^{-m}\|\mathcal{D}^m\mathcal{I}_0^{\beta_1+\beta_2}(u_N)\|, \\
\|\mathcal{I}_0^{\beta_1}(\mathcal{E}_s(f))(x)\| &\leq \frac{1}{\Gamma(\beta_1+1)}\|\mathcal{E}_s(f)\| \\
&\leq \frac{c}{\Gamma(\beta_1+1)}(r-1)^{-m}(2^{s-1})^{-m}\|f^{(m)}\|, \\
\|\mathcal{E}_s(\mathcal{I}_0^{\beta_1}(\mathcal{P}_s(f)))(x)\| &\leq c(r-1)^{-m}(2^{s-1})^{-m}\|\mathcal{D}^m\mathcal{I}_0^{\beta_1}(\mathcal{P}_s(f))\|, \\
\|(I-Q_N)(R)(x)\| &\leq \frac{1}{(N+1)!}\|R^{(N+1)}\|. \qquad (50)
\end{aligned}
$$

As a result, it makes sense to demonstrate that

$$
\|e_N(x)\| \leq CM(r-1)^{-m}(2^{s-1})^{-m} + \frac{1}{(N+1)!}\|R^{(N+1)}\|, \qquad (51)
$$

where $M = M_{\max}M_2^{-1}$ with $M_2^{-1} := \left(1 - \frac{M_1}{\Gamma(\beta_1+1)} - \frac{\Gamma(\beta_2)}{\Gamma(\beta_1+\beta_2+1)}\right)$ and

$$
\begin{aligned}
M_{\max} = \max\Big\{&\|u_0^{(m)}\|, \|(gu_N)^{(m)}\|, \|\mathcal{D}^m\mathcal{I}_0^{\beta_1}(\mathcal{P}_s(gu_N))\|, \|\mathcal{D}^m\mathcal{I}_0^{\beta_1+\beta_2}(u_N)\| \\
&, \|f^{(m)}\|, \|\mathcal{D}^m\mathcal{I}_0^{\beta_1}(\mathcal{P}_s(f))\|\Big\}. \qquad (52)
\end{aligned}
$$

It is worth mentioning that $M_{\max}$ exists because $u_0(x), g(x), f(x)$ are sufficiently smooth functions and $gu_N \in A_s, \mathcal{P}_s(gu_N) \in A_s, \mathcal{P}_s(f) \in A_s$. □

4. Numerical Simulations and Results

To demonstrate the performance of the present method, some examples are provided in this section. To illustrate the results and make a global view of the present method and its efficiency, sometimes, the absolute errors

$$
e_N = |u(x) - u_N(x)|,
$$

and L_2 error

$$
L^2 - error = \left(\int_0^1 |u(x) - u_N(x)|^2\right)^{1/2},
$$

are reported in Tables or plotted in Figures.

All examples are carried out with the combined use of Maple and Matlab software (version 2022) with an Intel(R) Core(TM) i7-7700k CPU 4.20 GHz (RAM 32 GB).

Example 1. *To contrast the suggested approach with the one described in [1], we consider the following WSIDE:*

$$
{}^C\mathcal{D}_0^{1/3}u(x) = -\frac{32}{35}x^{1/2}u(x) + \int_0^x (x-t)^{-1/2}u(t)dt + f(x), \quad x \in [0,1],
$$

with $u(0) = 0$, *and*

$$
f(x) = \frac{6x^{8/3}}{\Gamma(11/3)} + \left(32/35 - \frac{\Gamma(1/2)\Gamma(7/3)}{\Gamma(17/6)}\right)x^{11/6} + \Gamma(7/3)x.
$$

It is worth mentioning that $u(x) = x^3 + x^{4/3}$ is the exact solution for this example.

To demonstrate the effect of choosing the collocation points, we report Table 1. In Table 2, we compare the proposed method using Legendre nodes and the trapezoidal collocation method (TCM) [1]. We demonstrate the effect of increasing parameter r with different collocation points in Figure 1. According to the results, reported in the tables and in Figure 1, using the Legendre nodes gives better accuracy for this example. Also, compared to the trapezoidal collocation method, the presented method has better results.

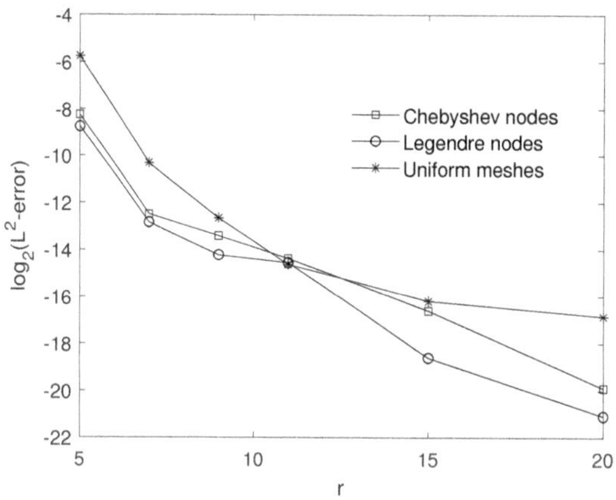

Figure 1. The influence of the multiplicity parameter r on L^2-errors for Example 1.

Table 1. The absolute error at different points, taking $\nu = 2/3$, for Example 1.

	$r\backslash x$	0.1	0.3	0.5	0.7	0.9	CPU Time
Chebyshev nodes	5	8.26×10^{-4}	1.30×10^{-3}	4.40×10^{-3}	4.56×10^{-3}	3.33×10^{-3}	0.438
	9	3.72×10^{-5}	5.33×10^{-6}	1.41×10^{-4}	1.18×10^{-4}	8.99×10^{-5}	1.125
Legendre nodes	5	9.00×10^{-4}	7.99×10^{-4}	3.29×10^{-3}	3.09×10^{-3}	2.15×10^{-3}	0.485
	9	1.88×10^{-5}	1.07×10^{-5}	8.10×10^{-5}	6.76×10^{-5}	4.52×10^{-5}	1.125
Uniform meshes	5	2.07×10^{-2}	1.91×10^{-2}	1.58×10^{-2}	1.55×10^{-2}	2.15×10^{-2}	0.094
	9	1.76×10^{-4}	1.25×10^{-4}	1.25×10^{-4}	1.43×10^{-4}	1.58×10^{-4}	0.531

Table 2. A comparison between the presented method and TCM [1] for Example 1.

	Proposed Method		TCM [1]	
	$r = 5$	$r = 9$	$h = 1/5$	$h = 1/10$
Error	3.51×10^{-3}	8.76×10^{-5}	2.08×10^{-2}	5.18×10^{-3}

Example 2. *The following example focuses on the equation*

$$^{C}\mathcal{D}_0^{\beta} u(x) = \frac{1}{2}\int_0^x (x-t)^{-1/2} u(t)dt + f(x), \quad x \in [0,1],$$

with $u(0) = 0$, and

$$f(x) = 2x + 3x^2 - \frac{1/2x^{5/2}\Gamma(3)}{\Gamma(7/2)} - \frac{1/2x^{7/2}\Gamma(4)}{\Gamma(9/2)}.$$

Note that $u(x) = x^3 + x^2$ is the exact solution of this equation for $\beta = 1$.

Considering that by choosing all three types of collocation points, the exact solution is obtained by choosing $r = 4$, so the results are reported only by choosing Chebyshev nodes.

Recall that CFD of a function u tends to integer derivative as $\beta \to n$, viz.

$$\lim_{\beta \to n} {}^{c}D^{\beta}u(x) = u^{(n)}(x),$$

$$\lim_{\beta \to n-1} {}^{c}D^{\beta}u(x) = u^{(n-1)}(x) - u^{(n-1)}(0).$$

To demonstrate this effect, our results illustrated in Figure 2, obviously, demonstrate it. We can see that when $\beta \to n$, the approximate solution with increasing β tends to the results for n. To show the efficiency and accuracy of the method, we reported the absolute value error in Figure 3 for $\beta = 1$, taking $r = 4$, $J = 1$ and $\nu = 1$.

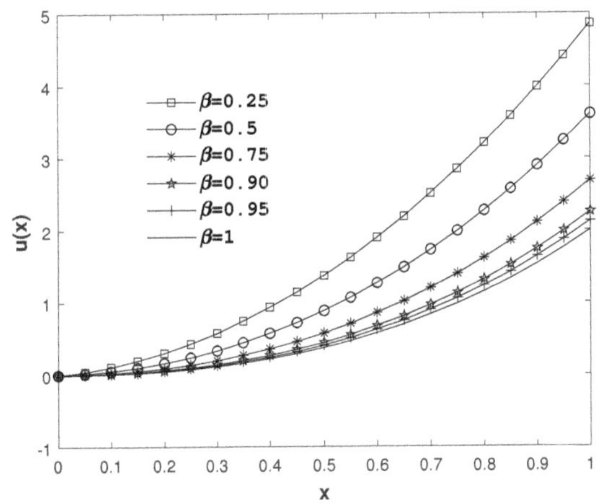

Figure 2. Approximate solutions associated with different values of β, when $\nu = 1$, $r = 4$ and $J = 1$, for Example 2.

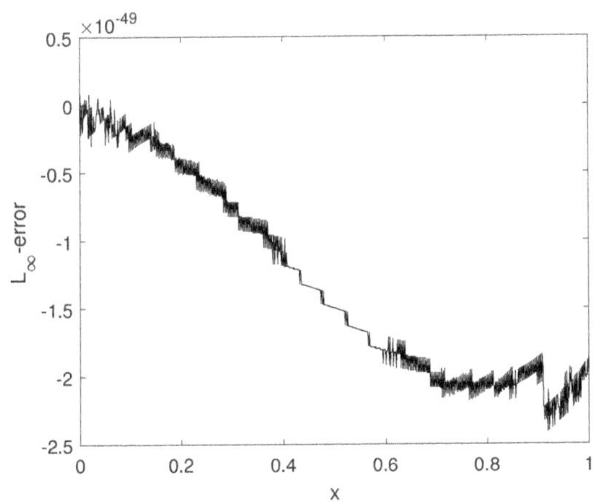

Figure 3. Plot of absolute error for Example 2.

Example 3. *For the third one, we consider the equation*

$$^{C}\mathcal{D}_0^{1/2}u(x) = e^x u(x) + \int_0^x (x-t)^{-1/2} u(t)dt + f(x), \quad x \in [0,1],$$

with $u(0) = 0$*, and*

$$f(x) = \sqrt{2}\,(\cos(x) - \sin(x))\mathrm{C}\left(\frac{\sqrt{2x}}{\sqrt{\pi}}\right) + \sqrt{2}\,(\sin(x) + \cos(x))\mathrm{S}\left(\frac{\sqrt{2x}}{\sqrt{\pi}}\right) - e^x \sin(x),$$

in which $S(x)$ *and* $C(x)$ *are the Fresnel integrals. The exact solution is considered for this example to be* $u(x) = \sin(x)$*.*

Table 3 is tabulated to demonstrate the effect of picking the collocation points. We illustrate the effect of increasing parameter r with different collocation points in Figure 4. We have also presented Figure 5 to show the accuracy of the method with different choices of collocation points.

Table 3. The absolute error at different points, taking $\nu = 1$, for Example 3.

	$r\backslash x$	0.1	0.3	0.5	0.7	0.9	CPU Time
Chebyshev nodes	5	4.44×10^{-6}	8.12×10^{-7}	2.82×10^{-5}	4.34×10^{-5}	2.10×10^{-4}	0.360
	9	2.80×10^{-12}	3.68×10^{-11}	2.80×10^{-10}	9.56×10^{-10}	3.91×10^{-9}	0.937
Legendre nodes	5	2.08×10^{-6}	3.41×10^{-6}	2.37×10^{-5}	4.94×10^{-5}	2.37×10^{-4}	0.359
	9	2.59×10^{-12}	2.83×10^{-11}	2.14×10^{-10}	7.24×10^{-10}	2.97×10^{-9}	0.406
Uniform meshes	5	1.39×10^{-5}	1.58×10^{-5}	3.99×10^{-5}	1.18×10^{-4}	5.00×10^{-4}	0.406
	9	4.35×10^{-10}	6.30×10^{-10}	1.44×10^{-9}	4.37×10^{-9}	1.88×10^{-8}	0.500

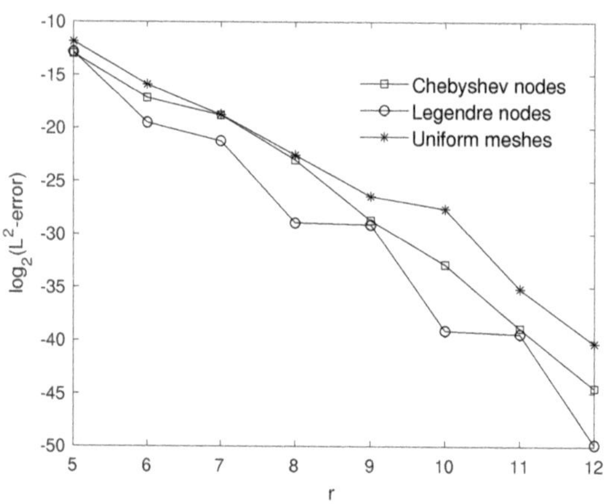

Figure 4. The effect of multiplicity parameter r on L^2-errors for Example 3.

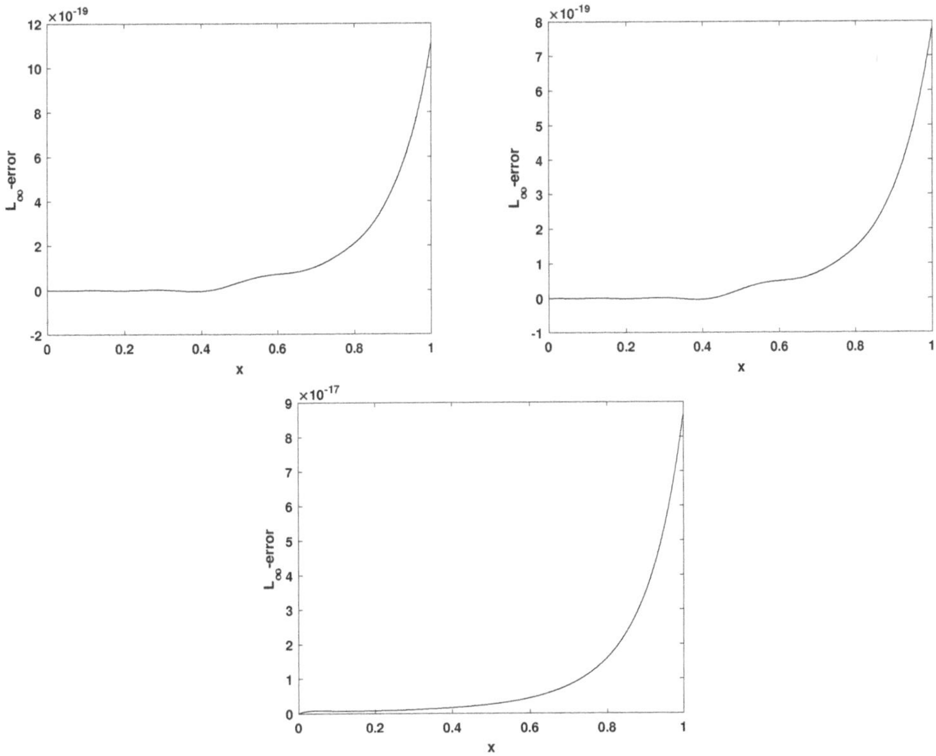

Figure 5. The absolute errors using Chebyshev nodes (**top left**), Legendre nodes (**top right**) and Uniform meshes for Example 3, taking $r = 15$ and $\nu = 1$.

Example 4. *Consider the following WSIDE*

$$^{C}\mathcal{D}_0^{1/2}u(x) = \frac{1}{2}u(x) + \int_0^x (x-t)^{-1/2}u(t)dt + f(x), \quad x \in [0,1],$$

with $u(0) = 0$, *and*

$$f(x) = \frac{\sqrt{\pi}}{2} - \frac{\pi x}{2} - \frac{\sqrt{x}}{2}.$$

The exact solution is considered for this example to be $u(x) = \sqrt{x}$.

To illustrate the efficiency of the presented method for a non-smooth solution near the origin, the absolute error of approximation is plotted in Figure 6. As we observe, the accuracy of the approximate solution near the origin is also good. To demonstrate the effect of choosing the collocation points, we report Table 4.

Table 4. The absolute error at different points, taking $\nu = 1/8$, for Example 4.

	$r\backslash x$	**0.1**	**0.3**	**0.5**	**0.7**	**0.9**	**CPU Time**
Chebyshev nodes	12	1.67×10^{-4}	2.34×10^{-4}	3.67×10^{-4}	5.94×10^{-4}	1.00×10^{-3}	8.046
	20	2.87×10^{-5}	3.81×10^{-5}	6.06×10^{-5}	9.98×10^{-5}	1.66×10^{-4}	75.250
Legendre nodes	12	2.20×10^{-4}	3.02×10^{-4}	4.77×10^{-4}	7.74×10^{-4}	1.30×10^{-3}	8.203
	20	3.22×10^{-5}	4.28×10^{-5}	6.81×10^{-5}	1.12×10^{-4}	1.86×10^{-4}	75.265
Uniform meshes	12	2.04×10^{-4}	2.81×10^{-4}	4.44×10^{-4}	7.20×10^{-4}	1.21×10^{-3}	8.172
	20	4.79×10^{-5}	6.36×10^{-5}	1.01×10^{-4}	1.67×10^{-4}	2.77×10^{-4}	83.828

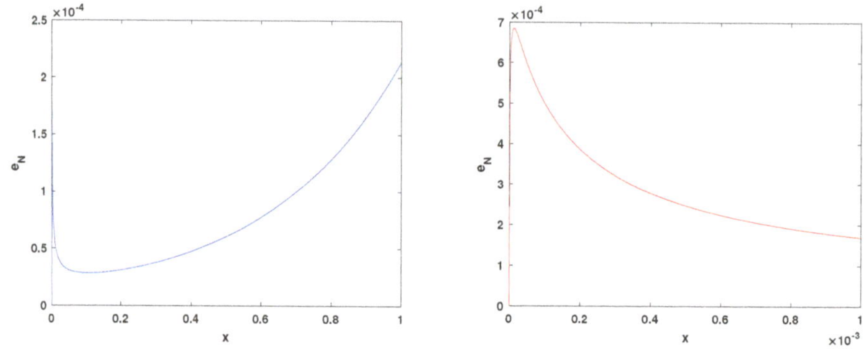

Figure 6. The absolute error using the Chebyshev nodes, taking $\nu = 1/8, r = 20$, for Example 4.

5. Conclusions

The main objective of this work is to solve the WSIDE using the collocation method and Müntz–Legendre wavelet. We use the collocation approach to solve the problem after reducing the desired equation to a weakly singular Volterra integral equation. To accomplish this, the Volterra equation is reduced to a system of nonlinear algebraic equations using the fractional integration operational matrix. We can determine the unknown coefficients U after solving this system. The collocation points in this study are uniformly spaced meshes or the roots of shifted Legendre and Chebyshev polynomials. The numerical simulations illustrate the method's effectiveness and correctness. The proposed method offers superior outcomes compared to some existing methods. The error bound for the desired equation based on the presented method is investigated.

In the future, we plan to extend our numerical approaches for solving generalized fractional models, including the generalized time-space fractional diffusion equations with variable coefficients [44] and time-fractional diffusion equations with a time-invariant type variable order [45], etc.

Funding: This project was supported by Researchers Supporting Project number (RSP2023R210), King Saud University, Riyadh, Saudi Arabia.

Data Availability Statement: The author does not have permission to share the data.

Conflicts of Interest: The author declares that they have no conflict of interest.

Abbreviations

The following abbreviations/nomenclatures are used in this manuscript:

Abbreviations	
WSIDE	Weakly singular integro-differential equations with fractional derivatives
ML	Müntz–Legendre
RL	Riemann–Liouville
FI	Fractional integration
Nomenclatures	
$S(\mathcal{L})$	Space of Müntz–Legendre polynomials
$C[0,1]$	Space of continuous functions on $[0,1]$
$L_l(x)$	Müntz–Legendre polynomials
A_s	Space of Müntz–Legendre wavelets
s	Refinement level
r	Multiplicity
$\mathcal{P}_s$	Projection operator
$\mathcal{I}_0^{\beta}$	Riemann–Liouville fractional integration
$\phi_{s,b}^{n}$	Müntz–Legendre wavelets
$R(x)$	Residual function

References

1. Zhao, J.; Xiao, J.; Ford, N.J. Collocation methods for fractional integro-differential equations with weakly singular kernels. *Numer. Algorithms* **2014**, *65*, 723–743. [CrossRef]
2. Angstmann, C.N.; Henry, B.I.; McGann, A.V. A fractional order recovery SIR model from a stochastic process. *Bull. Math. Biol.* **2016**, *78*, 468–499. [CrossRef] [PubMed]
3. Eslahchi, M.R.; Dehghan, M.; Parvizi, M. Application of the collocation method for solving nonlinear fractional integro-differential equations. *J. Comput. Appl. Math.* **2014**, *257*, 105–128. [CrossRef]
4. Aminikhah, H. A new analytical method for solving systems of linear integro-differential equations. *J. King Saud Univ. Sci.* **2011**, *23*, 349–353. [CrossRef]
5. Arikoglu, A.; Ozkol, I. Solution of fractional integro-differential equations by using fractional differential transform method. *Chaos Solitons Fractals* **2009**, *40*, 521–529. [CrossRef]
6. Momani, S.; Noor, M.A. Numerical methods for fourth order fractional integro-differential equations. *Appl. Math. Comput.* **2006**, *182*, 754–760. [CrossRef]
7. Momani, S.; Qaralleh, A. An Efficient Method for Solving Systems of Fractional Integro-Differential Equations. *Comput. Math. Appl.* **2006**, *52*, 459–470. [CrossRef]
8. Rawashdeh, E.A. Numerical solution of fractional integro-differential equations by collocation method. *Appl. Math. Comput.* **2006**, *176*, 1–6. [CrossRef]
9. Chow, T.S. Fractional dynamics of interfaces between soft-nanoparticles and rough substrates. *Phys. Lett. A* **2005**, *342*, 148–155. [CrossRef]
10. Mandelbrot, B. Some noises with $1/f$ spectrum, a bridge between direct current and white noise. *IEEE Trans. Inform. Theory* **1967**, *13*, 289–298. [CrossRef]
11. Magin, R.L. *Fractional Calculus in Bioengineering*, Illustrated ed.; Begell House: Danbury, CT, USA, 2006.
12. He, J.H. Some applications of nonlinear fractional differential equations and their approximations. *Bull. Sci. Technol.* **1999**, *15*, 86–90.
13. Rossikhin, Y.A.; Shitikova, M.V. Applications of fractional calculus to dynamic problems of linear and nonlinear hereditary mechanics of solids. *Appl. Mech. Rev.* **1997**, *50*, 15–67. [CrossRef]
14. He, J.H. Nonlinear oscillation with fractional derivative and its applications. In Proceedings of the International Conference on Vibrating Engineering'98, Dalian, China, 25–28 May 1998; pp. 288–291.
15. Metzler, R.; Klafter, J. The restaurant at the end of the random walk: Recent developments in the description of anomalous transport by fractional dynamics. *J. Phys. A* **2004**, *37*, 161–208. [CrossRef]
16. Mainardi, F. Fractional calculus: Some basic problems in continuum and statistical mechanics. In *Fractals and Fractional Calculus in Continuum Mechanics*; Carpinteri, A., Mainardi, F., Eds.; Springer: New York, NY, USA, 1997.
17. Baillie, R.T. Long memory processes and fractional integration in econometrics. *J. Econom.* **1996**, *73*, 5–59. [CrossRef]
18. Alquran, M.; Jaradat, H.M.; Syam, M.I. Analytical solution of the time-fractional Phi-4 equation by using modified residual power series method. *Nonlinear Dynam.* **2017**, *90*, 2525–2529. [CrossRef]
19. El-Ajou, A.; Arqub, O.A.; Al Zhour, Z.; Momani, S. New results on fractional power series: Theories and applications. *Entropy* **2013**, *15*, 5305–5323. [CrossRef]
20. Qazza, A.; Saadeh, R.; Salah, E. Solving fractional partial differential equations via a new scheme. *AIMS Math.* **2022**, *8*, 5318–5337. [CrossRef]
21. Zhang, Y. A finite difference method for fractional partial differential equation. *Appl. Math. Comput.* **2009**, *215*, 524–529. [CrossRef]
22. Bonyadi, S.; Mahmoudi, Y.; Lakestani, M.; Jahangiri rad, M. Numerical solution of space-time fractional PDEs with variable coefficients using shifted Jacobi collocation method. *Comput. Methods Differ. Equ.* **2023**, *11*, 81–94.
23. Shahriari, M.; Saray, B.N.; Mohammadalipour, B.; Saeidian, S. Pseudospectral method for solving the fractional one-dimensional Dirac operator using Chebyshev cardinal functions. *Phys. Scr.* **2023**, *98*, 055205. [CrossRef]
24. Yang, X.; Wu, L.; Zhang, H. A space-time spectral order sinc-collocation method for the fourth-order nonlocal heat model arising in viscoelasticity. *Appl. Math. Comput.* **2023**, *457*, 128192. [CrossRef]
25. Zhang, H.; Yang, X.; Tang, Q.; Xu, D. A robust error analysis of the OSC method for a multi-term fourth-order sub-diffusion equation. *Comput. Math. Appl.* **2022**, *109*, 180–190. [CrossRef]
26. Asadzadeh, M.; Saray, B.N. On a multiwavelet spectral element method for integral equation of a generalized Cauchy problem. *BIT* **2022**, *62*, 383–1416. [CrossRef]
27. Li, C.; Li, Z.; Wang, Z. Mathematical analysis and the local discontinuous Galerkin method for Caputo–Hadamard fractional partial differential equation. *J. Sci. Comput.* **2020**, *85*, 41. [CrossRef]
28. Mao, Z.; Shen, J. Efficient spectral–Galerkin methods for fractional partial differential equations with variable coefficients. *J. Comput. Phys.* **2016**, *307*, 243–261. [CrossRef]
29. Ford, N.J.; Xiao, J.; Yan, Y. A finite element method for time fractional partial differential equations. *Fract. Calc. Appl. Anal.* **2011**, *14*, 454–474. [CrossRef]
30. Shah, N.A.; El-Zahar, E.R.; Akgül, A.; Khan, A.; Kafle, J. Analysis of Fractional-Order Regularized Long-Wave Models via a Novel Transform. *J. Funct. Spaces* **2022**, *2022*, 2754507. [CrossRef]

31. Alpert , B.; Beylkin, G.; Coifman, R.R.; Rokhlin, V. Wavelet-like bases for the fast solution of second-kind integral equations. *SIAM J. Sci. Stat. Comput.* **1993**, *14*, 159–184. [CrossRef]
32. Heller, V.; Strang, G.; Topiwala, P.N.; Heil, C. The application of multiwavelet filterbanks to image processing. *IEEE Trans. Image Process.* **1999**, *8*, 548–563.
33. Saray, B.N. Abel's integral operator: Sparse representation based on multiwavelets. *BIT Numer. Math.* **2021**, *61*, 587–606. [CrossRef]
34. Saray, B.N. An effcient algorithm for solving Volterra integro-differential equations based on Alpert's multi-wavelets Galerkin method. *J. Comput. Appl. Math.* **2019**, *348*, 453–465. [CrossRef]
35. Saray, B.N. Sparse multiscale representation of Galerkin method for solving linear-mixed Volterra-Fredholm integral equations. *Math. Method Appl. Sci.* **2020**, *43*, 2601–2614. [CrossRef]
36. Rahimkhani, P.; Ordokhani, Y.; Babolian, E. Müntz-Legendre wavelet operational matrix of fractional-order integration and its applications for solving the fractional pantograph differential equations. *Numer. Algorithms* **2018**, *77*, 1283–1305. [CrossRef]
37. Jebreen, H.B.; Tchier, F. A New Scheme for Solving Multiorder Fractional Differential Equations Based on Müntz–Legendre Wavelets. *Complexity* **2021**, *2021*, 9915551. [CrossRef]
38. Rahimkhani, P.; Ordokhani, Y. Numerical solution a class of 2D fractional optimal control problems by using 2D Müntz-Legendre wavelets. *Optim. Contr. Appl. Met.* **2018**, *39*, 1916–1934. [CrossRef]
39. Almira, J.M. Müntz type theorems. *I Surv. Approx. Theory* **2007**, *3*, 152–194.
40. Müntz, C.H . Über den Approximationssatz von Weierstrass. In *Mathematische Abhandlungen Hermann Amandus Schwarz*; Springer: Berlin/Heidelberg, Germany, 1914; pp. 303–312.
41. Shen , J.; Wang, Y. Müntz-Galerkin methods and applicationa to mixed dirichlet-neumann boundary value problems. *Siam J. Sci. Comput.* **2016**, *38*, 2357–2381. [CrossRef]
42. Borwein , P.; Erdélyi, T.; Zhang, J. Müntz systems and orthogonal Müntz–Legendre polynomials. *Trans. Am. Math. Soc.* **1994**, *342*, 523–542.
43. Kilbas, A.; Srivastava, H.M.; Trujillo, J.J. *Theory and Applications of Fractional Differential Equations, 24*; Elsevier B.V.: Amsterdam, The Netherlands, 2006.
44. Gu, X.M.; Huang, T.Z.; Zhao, Y.L.; Lyu, P.; Carpentieri, B. A fast implicit difference scheme for solving the generalized time–space fractional diffusion equations with variable coefficients. *Numer. Methods Partial Differ. Equ.* **2021**, *37*, 1136–1162. [CrossRef]
45. Gu, X.M.; Sun, H.W.; Zhao, Y.L.; Zheng, X. An implicit difference scheme for time-fractional diffusion equations with a time-invariant type variable order. *Appl. Math. Lett.* **2021**, *120*, 107270. [CrossRef]

fractal and fractional

Article

Qualitative Analysis of RLC Circuit Described by Hilfer Derivative with Numerical Treatment Using the Lagrange Polynomial Method

Naveen S. [1], Parthiban V. [1] and Mohamed I. Abbas [2,*]

[1] School of Advanced Sciences, Vellore Institute of Technology, Chennai Campus, Chennai 600127, India; naveen.2020a@vitstudent.ac.in (N.S.); parthiban.v@vit.ac.in (P.V.)

[2] Department of Mathematics and Computer Science, Faculty of Science, Alexandria University, Alexandria 21511, Egypt

* Correspondence: miabbas@alexu.edu.eg

Abstract: This paper delves into an examination of the existence, uniqueness, and stability properties of a non-local integro-differential equation featuring the Hilfer fractional derivative with order $\omega \in (1,2)$ for the RLC model. Based on Schaefer's fixed point theorem and Banach's contraction principle, the existence and uniqueness results are established. Furthermore, Ulam–Hyers and Ulam–Hyers–Rassias stability results for the boundary value problem of the RLC model are discussed. To showcase the practicality and efficacy of our theoretical findings, a two-step Lagrange polynomial interpolation method is applied to solve some numerical examples.

Keywords: fixed point theorem; fractional order integro-differential RLC circuit; Hilfer fractional derivative; non-local boundary conditions

1. Introduction

Numerous studies in science and engineering have shown the importance of mathematical modeling and numerical simulations. Fractional-order modeling is one of the well-researched areas which has provided scientists with a useful technique for the generalization of classical results. The development of fractional order operators includes both local and non-local kernels, and singular and non-singular kernels are of great interest as well in the community of researchers. There have been some fascinating new studies examining these factors; see [1–5].

Hilfer [3] proposed an extended form of Riemann–Liouville (R-L) and Caputo fractional derivatives, called the "Hilfer fractional derivative", which allows one to interpolate with another; see [6–14].

Fractional derivatives offer numerous advantages when compared to their conventional counterparts. To begin with, they encompass memory, a fundamental characteristic in non-integer type differential equations. This quality renders fractional derivatives more effective in precisely characterizing physical systems in contrast to classical derivatives [15–18]. Furthermore, fractional derivatives play a pivotal role in enabling the exploration of various diffusion phenomena, encompassing superdiffusion, hyperdiffusion, and ballistic diffusion. This presents a fertile area of research for those intrigued by these phenomena [19].

The introduction of fractional derivatives resulted in the development of several types of novel mathematical models, particularly in the discipline of electrical circuits, which can be found in [20–22]. Some results have emerged for the investigation of fractional modeling of RL and RC circuits; hence, we refer the reader to [23–27]. The fractional LC circuit, first introduced in [25], extends to the repertory of available models. The exploration of both numerical and analytical solutions that provide the foundation of these investigations are essential to the investigation of fractional electrical circuits [26,27].

In [25], the AB derivative is employed to explore the numerical solutions for fractional RL and RC circuits. In [19], Aguilar et al. proposed the solutions for non-integer order electrical RC, LC, and RL circuits using the Mittag–Leffler fractional derivative. In [26], Rawdan et al. discussed fractional-order RL and LC circuits, suggesting a comparative analysis with conventional electrical circuits. Additionally, in [28], Aguilar et al. introduced fractional electrical circuits characterized by a non-integer derivative with a regular Kernel.

Integer order integro-differential equations find applications in various domains of science and engineering, including circuit analysis. According to Kirchhoff's second law, the total voltage drop across a closed loop is equal to the applied voltage, denoted as $\mathbb{E}(t)$. This principle essentially stems from the law of energy conservation. Consequently, an RLC circuit equation has the form

$$\mathbb{L}\frac{d}{dt}\mathbb{I}(t) + \mathbb{R}\mathbb{I}(t) + \frac{1}{\mathbb{C}}\int_0^t \mathbb{I}(s)ds = \mathbb{E}(t).$$

The RLC circuit serves as a fundamental component in the assembly of more intricate electrical circuits and networks. Illustrated in Figure 1, it comprises a resistor with a resistance of $\mathbb{R}$ ohms, an inductor with an inductance of $\mathbb{L}$ henries, and a capacitor with a capacitance of $\mathbb{C}$ farads, all arranged in series with an electromotive force source (like a battery or a generator) providing a voltage of $\mathbb{E}(t)$ volts at time t.

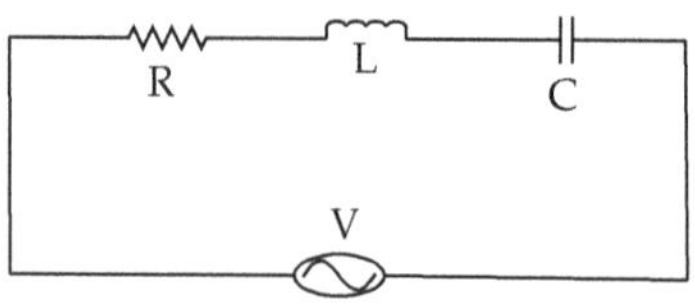

Figure 1. Diagram of a series RLC circuit.

In [29] U. Arshad et al. investigated the fractional order RLC derivative using three numerical methodologies of the system:

$$\begin{aligned} D^{2\alpha}\mathbb{I}(t) + \frac{1}{\mathbb{L}\mathbb{C}}\mathbb{I}(t) &= \frac{\mathbb{E}(t)}{\mathbb{L}} \\ D^{\alpha}\mathbb{V}(t) + \frac{1}{\mathbb{C}\mathbb{R}}\mathbb{V}(t) &= \frac{\mathbb{E}(t)}{\mathbb{R}} \\ D^{\alpha}\mathbb{I}(t) + \frac{\mathbb{R}}{\mathbb{L}}\mathbb{I}(t) &= \frac{\mathbb{E}(t)}{\mathbb{L}}. \end{aligned} \tag{1}$$

In [30], Malarvizhi et al. discussed the transient analysis of an RLC circuit in the RK4 order method. In [24], Gomez-Aguilar et al. studied the electrical circuits RC and RL for the Atangana–Beleanu–Caputo (ABC) fractional bi-order system:

$$^{ABC}D^{\beta}\mathbb{V}(t) = \delta\mathbb{E}(t) - \delta\mathbb{V}. \tag{2}$$

Inspired by the above mentioned work, we are interested in studying the existence and uniqueness of solutions and the Ulam stability analysis for the following Hilfer fractional differential equation for the RLC circuit model with non-local boundary conditions:

$$\begin{cases} D^{\omega,\tau}\mathbb{I}(t) = \frac{\mathbb{E}(t)}{\mathbb{L}} - \frac{\mathbb{R}}{\mathbb{L}}\mathbb{I}(t) - \frac{1}{\mathbb{C}\mathbb{L}}\int_0^t \mathbb{I}(s)ds, & t \in J = [a,b], \\ y(a) = 0, \quad y(b) = \sum_{j=1}^{k} \varrho_j I^{\nu_j} y(\zeta_j), & \nu_j > 0, \varrho_j \in \mathbb{R}, \zeta_j \in J. \end{cases} \tag{3}$$

The primary contribution of this endeavor can be outlined as follows:

1. The existence, uniqueness, and stability of the solution of the Hilfer fractional integro-differential equation for the RLC circuit model has been investigated via the fixed point approach.
2. We apply a novel hypothesis to verify the existence, uniqueness, and Ulam–Hyers stability of the solution to the RLC circuit Equation (3). Additionally, we illustrate numerical results using the two step Lagrangian polynomial approach, in order to validate the theoretical outcomes.

The paper is structured as follows. In Section 2, we introduce various definitions and preliminaries. The existence and uniqueness results for the Hilfer fractional boundary value problem for the RLC model are discussed in Section 3. The Ulam-type stability results are studied in Section 4. Some numerical examples are listed in Section 5. We end with Section 6 containing the conclusions.

2. Auxiliary Results

In this section, we recall some important preliminaries that are related to our analysis.

Let $Y = C[J,\mathbb{R}]$ be the space of all continuous function form J into $\mathbb{R}$ with norm $||v|| = \max\{|v(t)|,\ t \in J\}$. Obviously, Y is a Banach space under this norm, and hence, the product is also a Banach space with norm $||(v,w)|| = ||v|| + ||w||$.

Definition 1 ([10] Caputo fractional derivative). *The Caputo derivative of order q for the function $g : J \to \mathbb{R}$ is defined as:*

$$^{c}D^{\omega}g(x) = \frac{1}{\Gamma(p-\omega)}\int_a^x \frac{g^{(p)}(s)}{(x-s)^{\omega+1-p}}\,ds = I^{p-\omega}g^{(p)}(x), \quad x > 0,\ p-1 < \omega < p.$$

Definition 2 ([10] Riemann–Liouville fractional integral). *The R-L fractional integral of order $\omega > 0$ of the function g is defined as:*

$$I_a^{\omega}g(x) = \frac{1}{\Gamma(p-\omega)}\int_a^x \frac{g(s)}{(x-s)^{p-\omega-1}}\,ds, \quad p-1 < \omega < p.$$

Definition 3 ([10] Riemann–Liouville fractional derivative). *The R-L fractional derivative of order $\omega > 0$ of a continuous function g is defined as:*

$$\begin{aligned} ^{RL}D^{\omega}g(t) &= D^{p}I^{p-\omega}g(t) \\ &= \frac{1}{\Gamma(p-\omega)}\left(\frac{d^p}{dt^p}\right)\int_a^t \frac{g(s)}{(t-s)^{p-\omega-1}}\,ds, \quad p-1 < \omega < p. \end{aligned}$$

By a new theory of the fractional derivative which had been proposed by Hilfer [3], the generalized R-L fractional derivative of a continuous function g is defined as:

Definition 4 ([10] Hilfer fractional derivative). *The generalized R-L fractional derivative of order ω and parameter τ of a function g is described as:*

$$^{H}D^{\omega,\tau}g(x) = I^{\tau(p-\omega)}D^{p}I^{(1-\tau)(p-\omega)}g(x),$$

where $\omega \in (p-1,p)$, $\tau \in [0,1]$, $x > a, D = \frac{d}{dx}$.

Remark 1 ([10]). *From Definition 4, we observe that:*

1. *The operator $^{H}D^{\omega,\tau}$ can be written as*

$$^{H}D^{\omega,\tau} = I^{\tau(1-\omega)}DI^{(1-\gamma)} = I^{\tau(1-\omega)}D^{\gamma}, \qquad \gamma = \omega + \tau - \tau\omega.$$

2. *The Hilfer fractional derivative can be interpolated between the R-L fractional derivative* $(\tau = 0)$ *and the Caputo fractional derivative* $(\tau = 1)$ *as:*

$$^{H}D^{\omega,\tau} = \begin{cases} DI^{(1-\omega)} = D^{\omega}, & \text{if } \tau = 0; \\ I^{(1-\omega)}D = {}^{C}D^{\omega}, & \text{if } \tau = 1. \end{cases}$$

Lemma 1 ([10]). *If* $1 < \omega \leq 2$*, then,*

$$I^{\omega}(D^{\omega}g)(t) = g(t) - \frac{(I^{1-\omega}g)(a)}{\Gamma(\omega)}(t-a)^{\omega-1} - \frac{(I^{2-\omega}g)(a)}{\Gamma(\omega-1)}(t-a)^{\omega-2}. \tag{4}$$

3. Main Results

Here, we introduce some assumptions for the following sequels.

$(A1)$ The function $g : J \times Y \times Y \to Y$ is completely continuous and there exists a function $\mu \in L^1(J, \mathbb{R})$ such that:

$$|g(t,x,y)| \leq \mu(t), \quad \forall t \in J,\ x,y \in Y.$$

$(A2)$ The function g is continuous and there exist constants $\mathbb{L}_1, \mathbb{L}_2 > 0$ such that:

$$|g(t,x_1,y_1) - g(t,x_2,y_2)| \leq \mathbb{L}_1|x_1 - x_2| + \mathbb{L}_2|y_1 - y_2|, \quad \forall t \in J,\ x_i, y_i \in Y,\ i = 1,2.$$

$(A3)$ The function f is continuous and there exists a constant $\mathtt{M} > 0$ such that:

$$|f(t,s,x_1) - f(t,s,x_2)| \leq \mathtt{M}|x_1 - x_2|, \quad \forall t \in J,\ x_i \in Y,\ i = 1,2.$$

Problem Formulation

Let us consider the general structure of the Hilfer fractional order RLC circuit integro-differential equation with nonlocal boundary conditions:

$$^{H}D^{\omega,\tau}y(t) = g(t, y(t), H(y(s))), \quad t \in J, \tag{5}$$

$$y(a) = 0, \quad y(b) = \sum_{j=1}^{k} \varrho_j I^{\nu_j} y(\zeta_j), \quad \nu_j > 0, \varrho_j \in \mathbb{R}, \zeta_j \in J, \tag{6}$$

where $^{H}D^{\omega,\tau}$ is the Hilfer fractional derivative of order $\omega \in (1,2)$, and parameter $\tau \in [0,1]$, I^{ν_j} is the R-L fractional integral of order $\nu_j > 0, \zeta_j \in [a,b], a \geq 0$, $\varrho_j \in \mathbb{R}$, $j = 1,\ldots,k$, $g(t, y(t), \int_a^t f(t,s,y(s)ds) = \frac{\mathbb{E}(t)}{\mathbb{L}} - \frac{\mathbb{R}}{\mathbb{L}}\mathbb{I}(t) - \frac{1}{\mathbb{CL}}\int_0^t \mathbb{I}(s)ds$, and $H(y(s)) = \int_a^t f(t,s,y(s))ds$. Using some fixed point theorems, the existence and uniqueness results are established. For (5) and (6), we employ Banach's fixed point theorem and Schaefer's fixed point theorem for uniqueness and existence results.

Lemma 2. *For* $g \in C(J, \mathbb{R})$*, it is a solution of the boundary value problem,*

$$^{H}D^{\omega,\tau}y(t) = g(t, y(t), Hy(s)), \quad t \in J,$$

$$y(a) = 0, \quad y(b) = \sum_{j=1}^{k} \varrho_j I^{\nu_j} y(\zeta_j), \quad \nu_j > 0, \varrho_j \in \mathbb{R}, \zeta_j \in J,$$

which satisfies the following equation:

$$y(t) = \frac{(t-a)^{\sigma-1}}{\Phi\Gamma(\sigma)}\left(I^{\omega}g(s,y(s),Hy(s))(b) - \sum_{j=1}^{k}\varrho_j I^{\omega+\nu_j}g(s,y(s),Hy(s))(\zeta_j)\right)$$
$$+ I^{\omega}g(s,y(s),Hy(s))(t), \tag{7}$$

where

$$\Phi = \sum_{j=1}^{k}\frac{\varrho_j(\zeta_j-a)^{\sigma-\nu_j-1}}{\Gamma(\sigma+\nu_j)} - \frac{(b-a)^{\sigma-1}}{\Gamma(\sigma)} \neq 0, \tag{8}$$

where $j = 1,2,3,...,k,\ 1 < \omega < 2,\ \sigma = \omega + \tau - \omega\tau.$

Proof. Equation (7) can be written as:

$$I^{\tau(2-\omega)}D^2 I^{(1-\tau)(2-\tau)}y(t) = g(t). \tag{9}$$

As a result of determining the ω order integral of the related inequality, we obtain

$$I^{\omega}I^{\tau(2-\omega)}D^2 I^{(1-\tau)(2-\tau)}y(t) = I^{\omega}g(t).$$

Indeed,

$$I^{\omega}I^{\tau(2-\omega)}D^2 I^{(1-\tau)(2-\tau)}y(t) = I^{\sigma}D^2 I^{2-\sigma}y(t) = I^{\sigma}\left({}^{RL}D^{\sigma}y\right)(t),$$

and therefore,

$$I^{\sigma}\left({}^{RL}D^{\sigma}y\right)(t) = I^{\omega}g(t).$$

By using Equation (4) and setting $\left[I^{2-\omega}g\right](a) = c_1,\ \left[I^{1-\omega}g\right](a) = c_2$, one has

$$y(t) = \frac{c_2}{\Gamma(\sigma)}(t-a)^{\sigma-1} + \frac{c_1}{\Gamma(\sigma-1)}(t-a)^{\sigma-2} + I^{\omega}g(t,y(t),Hy(t)). \tag{10}$$

By the condition $y(a) = 0$, we obtain $c_1 = 0$. Then, we obtain

$$y(t) = \frac{c_2}{\Gamma(\sigma)}(t-a)^{\sigma-1} + I^{\omega}g(t,y(t),Hy(t)), \tag{11}$$

and

$$\sum_{j=1}^{k}\varrho_j I^{\nu_j}y(\zeta_j) = c_2\sum_{j=1}^{k}\frac{\varrho_j(\zeta_j-a)^{\sigma+\nu_j-1}}{\Gamma(\sigma+\nu_j)} + \sum_{j=1}^{k}\varrho_j I^{\omega+\nu_j}g(s,y(s),Hy(s))(\zeta_j). \tag{12}$$

From our condition, by using (12), one has

$$c_2\left(\sum_{j=1}^{k}\frac{\varrho_j(\zeta_j-a)^{\sigma+\nu_j-1}}{\Gamma(\sigma+\nu_j)} - \frac{(t-a)^{\sigma-1}}{\Gamma(\sigma)}\right) = I^{\omega}g(s,y(s),Hy(s))(b)$$
$$- \sum_{j=1}^{k}\varrho_j I^{\omega+\nu_j}g(s,y(s),Hy(s))(\zeta_j), \tag{13}$$

from which we obtain

$$c_2 = \frac{1}{\Phi}\left(I^{\omega}g(s,y(s),Hy(s))(b) - \sum_{j=1}^{k}\varrho_j I^{\omega+\nu_j}g(s,y(s),Hy(s))(\zeta_j)\right). \tag{14}$$

Substituting the value of c_1 and c_2 in (10), we obtain the solution (7). This completes the proof. □

Theorem 1. *Assume that $(A1)$ is verified. Then (5) and (6) admit at least one solution on J.*

Proof. Let $C = C_{1-\sigma}[J, Y]$ and define the operator $P : C \to C$ by,

$$\begin{aligned}(Py)(t) =& \frac{(t-a)^{\sigma-1}}{\Phi\Gamma(\sigma)} I^{\omega} g(s, y(s), Hy(s))(b) \\ &- \frac{(t-a)^{\sigma-1}}{\Phi\Gamma(\sigma)} \sum_{j=1}^{k} \varrho_j I^{\omega+v_j} g(s, y(s), Hy(s))(\zeta) + I^{\omega} g(s, y(s), Hy(s))(t).\end{aligned}$$

For $q > 0$, let

$$B_q = \{y |\, y \in C : \|y\| \leq q\}.$$

Step 1: P is continuous.

Let y_n be a sequence such that $y_n \to y$ in C. For each $t \in J$, one has

$$\begin{aligned}&|(t-a)^{1-\sigma}((Py_n)(t) - (Py)(t))| \\ &= |\frac{1}{\Phi\Gamma(\sigma)}\Big[\frac{1}{\Gamma(\omega)}\int_a^t (b-s)^{\omega-1}(g(s, y_n(s), Hy_n(s)) - g(s, y(s), Hy(s)))ds \\ &- \sum_{j=1}^{k} \varrho_j \frac{1}{\Gamma(\omega+\zeta_j)}\int_a^t (\zeta_j - s)^{\omega+\zeta_j-1}(g(s, y_n(s), Hy_n(s)) - g(s, y(s), Hy(s)))ds\Big] \\ &+ \frac{(t-a)^{1-\sigma}}{\Gamma(\omega)}\int_a^t (t-s)^{\omega-1}(g(s, y_n(s), Hy_n(s)) - g(s, y(s), Hy(s)))ds| \\ &\leq \frac{1}{|\Phi|\Gamma(\sigma)}\Big[\frac{1}{\Gamma(\omega)}\int_a^t (b-s)^{\omega-1}|(g(s, y_n(s), Hy_n(s)) - g(s, y(s), Hy(s)))|ds \\ &- \sum_{j=1}^{k} |\varrho_j| \frac{1}{\Gamma(\omega+\zeta_j)}\int_a^t (\zeta_j - s)^{\omega+\zeta_j-1}|(g(s, y_n(s), Hy_n(s)) - g(s, y(s), Hy(s)))|ds\Big] \\ &+ \frac{(t-a)^{1-\sigma}}{\Gamma(\omega)}\int_a^t (t-s)^{\omega-1}|(g(s, y_n(s), Hy_n(s)) - g(s, y(s), Hy(s)))|ds, \\ &\leq \frac{1}{\|\Phi\|\Gamma(\sigma)}\Big[\frac{(b-s)^{\omega}}{\Gamma(\omega+1)}\|(g(s, y_n(s), Hy_n(s)) - g(s, y(s), Hy(s)))\|_C \\ &- \sum_{j=1}^{k} \|\varrho_j\| \frac{(\zeta_j - s)^{\omega+\zeta_j}}{\Gamma(\omega+\zeta_j+1)}\|(g(s, y_n(s), Hy_n(s)) - g(s, y(s), Hy(s)))\|_C\Big] \\ &+ \frac{(t-s)^{\omega}(t-a)^{\sigma-1}}{\Gamma(\omega+1)}\|g(s, y_n(s), Hy_n(s)) - g(s, y(s), Hy(s))\|_C.\end{aligned}$$

Since the function g is continuous, then we obtain

$$\begin{aligned}&\|(t-a)^{1-\sigma}((Py_n)(t) - (Py)(t))\| \\ &\leq \frac{1}{\|\Phi\|\Gamma(\sigma)}\Big[\frac{(b-s)^{\omega}}{\Gamma(\omega+1)}\|(g(., y_n(.), Hy_n(.)) - g(., y(.), Hy(.)))\|_C \\ &- \sum_{j=1}^{k} \|\varrho_j\| \frac{(\zeta_j - s)^{\omega+\zeta_j}}{\Gamma(\omega+\zeta_j+1)}\|(g(., y_n(.), Hy_n(.)) - g(., y(.), Hy(.)))\|_C\Big] \\ &+ \frac{(t-s)^{\omega}(t-a)^{\sigma-1}}{\Gamma(\omega+1)}\|g(., y_n(.), Hy_n(.)) - g(., y(.), Hy(.))\|_C \to 0, \quad \text{as } n \to \infty.\end{aligned}$$

Therefore, the operator P is continuous.
Step 2: $P(B_q)$ is bounded.
For each $t \in J$ and $y \in B_q$, we obtain that:

$$
\begin{aligned}
|(t-a)^{1-\sigma}(Py)(t)| \leq & \frac{1}{|\Phi|\Gamma(\sigma)}\left[\frac{1}{\Gamma(\omega)}\int_a^t (b-s)^{\omega-1}|g(s,y(s),Hy(s))|ds\right. \\
& \left. -\sum_{j=1}^{k}|\varrho_j|\frac{1}{\Gamma(\omega+\zeta_j)}\int_a^t (\zeta_j-s)^{\omega+\zeta_j-1}|g(s,y(s),Hy(s))|ds\right] \\
& +\frac{(t-a)^{1-\sigma}}{\Gamma(\omega)}\int_a^t (t-s)^{\omega-1}|g(s,y(s),Hy(s))|ds, \\
& \leq \frac{1}{|\Phi|\Gamma(\sigma)}\left[\frac{1}{\Gamma(\omega)}\int_a^t (b-s)^{\omega-1}|\mu(s)|ds - \sum_{j=1}^{k}|\varrho_j|\frac{1}{\Gamma(\omega+\zeta_j)}\right. \\
& \left. \times\int_a^t (\omega\zeta_j-s)^{\omega+\zeta_j-1}|\mu(s)|ds\right] + \frac{(t-a)^{1-\sigma}}{\Gamma(\omega)}\int_a^t (t-s)^{\omega-1}|\mu(s)|ds \\
& \leq \frac{\|\mu(s)\|_C}{|\Phi|\Gamma(\sigma)}\left[\frac{(b-s)^{\omega}}{\Gamma(\omega+1)} - \sum_{j=1}^{k}|\varrho_j|\frac{(\zeta_j-s)^{\omega+\zeta_j}}{\Gamma(\omega+\zeta_j+1)}\right] + \frac{(t-s)^{\omega}(t-a)^{1-\sigma}}{\Gamma(\omega+1)} := \ell.
\end{aligned}
$$

Thus, $\|P(y)\| \leq \ell$.
Step 3: $P(B_q)$ is equicontinuous.
For $a \leq t_1 < t_2 \leq b$, and $y \in B_q$, we obtain
$|(t_2-a)^{1-\sigma}(Py)(t_2) - (t_1-a)^{1-\sigma}(Py)(t_1)|$

$$
\begin{aligned}
& \leq \frac{1}{|\Phi|\Gamma(\sigma)}\left[\frac{1}{\Gamma(\omega)}\int_a^{t_2} (b-s)^{\omega-1}|g(s,y(s),Hy(s))|ds\right. \\
& \left. -\sum_{j=1}^{k}\frac{|\varrho_j|}{\Gamma(\omega+\zeta_j)}\int_a^{t_2} (\zeta_j-s)^{\omega+\zeta_j}|g(s,y(s),Hy(s))|ds\right] \\
& +\frac{(t_2-a)^{\sigma-1}}{\Gamma(\omega)}\int_a^{t_2} (t_2-s)^{\omega-1}|g(s,y(s),Hy(s))|ds \\
& -\frac{1}{|\Phi|\Gamma(\sigma)}\left[\frac{1}{\Gamma(\omega)}\int_a^{t_1} (b-s)^{\omega-1}|g(s,y(s),Hy(s))|ds\right. \\
& \left. +\sum_{j=1}^{k}\frac{|\varrho_j|}{\Gamma(\omega+\zeta_j)}\int_a^{t_1} (\zeta_j-s)^{\omega+\zeta_j}|g(s,y(s),Hy(s))|ds\right] \\
& -\frac{(t_1-a)^{\sigma-1}}{\Gamma(\omega)}\int_a^{t_1} (t_1-s)^{\omega-1}|g(s,y(s),Hy(s))|ds \\
& \leq \frac{|g(s,y(s),Hy(s))|}{|\Phi|\Gamma(\sigma)\Gamma(\omega)}\left[\int_a^{t_2} (b-s)^{\omega-1}ds - \int_a^{t_1} (b-s)^{\omega-1}ds\right]
\end{aligned}
$$

$$
\begin{aligned}
&-\sum_{j=1}^{k}\frac{|\varrho_j||g(s,y(s),Hy(s))|}{|\Phi|\Gamma(\sigma)\Gamma(\omega+\zeta_j)}\left[\int_a^{t_2}(\zeta_j-s)^{\omega+\zeta_j-1}ds-\int_a^{t_1}(\zeta_j-s)^{\omega-1}ds\right]\\
&+\frac{|g(s,y(s),Hy(s))|(t_2-a)^{\sigma-1}}{\Gamma(\omega)}\int_{t_1}^{t_2}(t_2-t_1)^{\omega-1}ds\\
&\leq\frac{\|\mu\|_C}{|\Phi|\Gamma(\sigma)\Gamma(\omega)}\left[\int_a^{t_2}(b-s)^{\omega-1}ds-\int_a^{t_1}(b-s)^{\omega-1}ds\right]\\
&-\sum_{j=1}^{k}\frac{|\varrho_j|\|\mu\|_C}{|\Phi|\Gamma(\sigma)\Gamma(\omega+\zeta_j)}\left[\int_a^{t_2}(\zeta_j-s)^{\omega+\zeta_j-1}ds-\int_a^{t_1}(\zeta_j-s)^{\omega-1}ds\right]\\
&+\frac{\|\mu\|_C(t_2-a)^{\sigma-1}}{\Gamma(\omega)}\int_{t_1}^{t_2}(t_2-t_1)^{\omega-1}ds.
\end{aligned}
$$

As $t_2\to t_1$, the R.H.S. of the above inequality $\to 0$. Consequently, we deduce that P is completely continuous.

Step 4: The priori bounds.

We need to show that the set $\Lambda=\{y\in C: y=\varrho(P(y));\ \varrho\in(0,1)\}$ is bounded.

For this, let $y\in\Lambda$, $y=\varrho(P(y))$ for some $\varrho\in(0,1)$. Thus, for each $t\in J$, one has

$$
\begin{aligned}
y(t)=\varrho\Big[&\frac{(t-a)^{\sigma-1}}{\Phi\Gamma(\sigma)}I^{\omega}g(s,y(s),Hy(s))(b)\\
&+\frac{(t-a)^{\sigma-1}}{\Phi\Gamma(\sigma)}\sum_{j=1}^{k}\varrho_j I^{\omega+v_j}g(s,y(s),Hy(s))(\zeta)+I^{\omega}g(s,y(s),Hy(s))(t)\Big].
\end{aligned}
$$

This implies, by $(A2)$, that:

$$
\begin{aligned}
|y(t)(t-a)^{1-\sigma}|&\leq|(t-a)^{1-\sigma}(Py)(t)|\\
&\leq\frac{1}{|\Phi|\Gamma(\sigma)}\left[\frac{1}{\Gamma(\omega)}\int_a^{t}(b-s)^{\omega-1}|g(s,y(s),Hy(s))|ds\right.\\
&\left.-\sum_{j=1}^{k}|\varrho_j|\frac{1}{\Gamma(\omega+\zeta_j)}\int_a^{t}(\zeta_j-s)^{\omega+\zeta_j-1}|g(s,y(s),Hy(s))|ds\right]\\
&+\frac{(t-a)^{1-\sigma}}{\Gamma(\omega)}\int_a^{t}(t-s)^{\omega-1}|g(s,y(s),Hy(s))|ds\\
&\leq\frac{1}{|\Phi|\Gamma(\sigma)}\left[\frac{1}{\Gamma(\omega)}\int_a^{t}(b-s)^{\omega-1}|\mu(s)|ds\right.\\
&\left.-\sum_{j=1}^{k}|\varrho_j|\frac{1}{\Gamma(\omega+\zeta_j)}\int_a^{t}(\zeta_j-s)^{\omega+\zeta_j-1}|\mu(s)|ds\right]\\
&+\frac{(t-a)^{1-\sigma}}{\Gamma(\omega)}\int_a^{t}(t-s)^{\omega-1}|\mu(s)|ds\\
&\leq\frac{1}{|\Phi|\Gamma(\sigma)}\left[\frac{(b-s)^{\omega}}{\Gamma(\omega+1)}\|\mu(s)\|_C-\sum_{j=1}^{k}|\varrho_j|\frac{(\zeta_j-s)^{\omega}}{\Gamma(\omega+\zeta_j+1)}\|\mu(s)\|_C\right]\\
&+\frac{(t-a)^{1-\sigma}(t-s)^{\omega}}{\Gamma(\omega+1)}\|\mu(s)\|_C:=\Re.
\end{aligned}
$$

Thus, $\|\mu(s)\|_C \leq \Re$.

Therefore, the set Λ is bounded. Hence, we deduce that P has a fixed point that is a solution of the presumed problems (5) and (6) as an outcome of Schaefer's Fixed point theorem. □

The next theorem contains the second main result in this paper that is the uniqueness of the solution to the presumed problems (5) and (6).

Theorem 2. *Suppose that the conditions $(A2)$ and $(A3)$ are satisfied such that:*

$$(L_1+L_2M)\left[\frac{(b-a)^{\omega+\sigma-1}}{|\Phi|\Gamma(\sigma)\Gamma(\omega+1)}+\frac{(b-a)^{\omega+\sigma-1}}{|\Phi|\Gamma(\sigma)}\sum_{i=0}^{m}\frac{|\varrho_j|(\zeta_j-a)^{\omega+\zeta_j}}{\Gamma(\omega+\nu_j+1)}+\frac{(b-a)^{\omega}}{\Gamma(\omega+1)}\right]<1. \tag{15}$$

Then, the presumed problem (5) and (6) has a unique solution on J.

Proof. We consider the operator $P : C \to C$ defined as

$$(Py)(t)=\frac{(t-a)^{\sigma-1}}{\Phi\Gamma(\sigma)}I^{\omega}g(s,y(s),Hy(s))(b)+\frac{(t-a)^{\sigma-1}}{\Phi\Gamma(\sigma)}\sum_{j=1}^{k}\varrho_j I^{\omega+\nu_j}g(s,y(s),Hy(s))(\zeta)$$
$$+I^{\omega}g(s,y(s),Hy(s))(t).$$

We shall show that P is a contraction map. Let $x,y \in C$, then one has for each $t \in J$

$$\begin{aligned}|(Py)(t)-(Px)(t)| \leq{}& \frac{(b-a)^{\sigma-1}}{\Phi\Gamma(\sigma)}I^{\omega}|g(s,y(s),Hy(s))-g(s,x(s),Hx(s))|(b)\\ &+\frac{(b-a)^{\sigma-1}}{\Phi\Gamma(\sigma)}\sum_{j=1}^{k}\varrho_j I^{\omega+\nu_j}|g(s,y(s),Hy(s))-g(s,x(s),Hx(s))|(\zeta)\\ &+I^{\omega}|g(s,y(s),Hy(s))-g(s,x(s),Hx(s))|(t)\\ &\leq (\mathrm{L}_1+\mathrm{L}_2\mathrm{M})|y(s)-x(s)|\left[\frac{(b-a)^{\omega+\sigma-1}}{|\Phi|\Gamma(\sigma)\Gamma(\omega+1)}\right.\\ &\left.+\frac{(b-a)^{\omega+\sigma-1}}{|\Phi|\Gamma(\sigma)}\sum_{i=0}^{m}\frac{|\varrho_j|(\zeta_j-a)^{\omega+\zeta_j}}{\Gamma(\omega+\nu_j+1)}+\frac{(t-a)^{\omega}}{\Gamma(\omega+1)}\right].\end{aligned}$$

Therefore, we obtain

$$\begin{aligned}\|(Py)(t)-(Px)(t)\| \leq{}&(\mathrm{L}_1+\mathrm{L}_2\mathrm{M})\left[\frac{(b-a)^{\omega+\sigma-1}}{|\Phi|\Gamma(\sigma)\Gamma(\omega+1)}\right.\\ &\left.+\frac{(b-a)^{\omega+\sigma-1}}{|\Phi|\Gamma(\sigma)}\sum_{i=0}^{m}\frac{|\varrho_j|(\zeta_j-a)^{\omega+\zeta_j}}{\Gamma(\omega+\nu_j+1)}+\frac{(b-a)^{\omega}}{\Gamma(\omega+1)}\right]\|y-x\|.\end{aligned}$$

Hence, in view of the condition (15) and the Banach contraction principle, P has a unique fixed point. Thus, the existence of the unique solution of the presumed problems (5) and (6). □

4. Ulam Stability Results

An important part of the qualitative theory of linear and nonlinear differential equations is the stability of Ulam–Hyers (UH), originally formulated by Hyers and Ulam in 1940. Also, the study of stability analysis of Hyers–Ulam (HU) and the Ulam–Hyers–Rassias (UHS) for non-linear fractional differential equations is a hot topic of research and the study of this area has grown to be one of the most important subjects in the mathematical analysis, see [31–35]. A general view of the development of the Ulam–Hyers (UH) and the Ulam—Hyers–Rassias (UHS) stability theory for fractional differential equations can be found in [36–39].

Definition 5 ([11]). *Equations (5) and (6) are UH stable if there exists a real number $C_g > 0$ such that for each $\epsilon > 0$ and for each $z \in C^{\sigma}_{1-\sigma}[J]$ solution of the inequality:*

$$|D^{\omega,\tau}_{0^+} z(t) - g(t, z(t), Hz(t))| \leq \epsilon, \quad t \in J, \tag{16}$$

there exists a solution $y \in C^{\sigma}_{1-\sigma}(J)$ of Equations (5) and (6) such that:

$$| z(t) - y(t) | \leq C_g \epsilon, \quad t \in J.$$

Definition 6 ([11]). *Equations (5) and (6) are generalized UH stable if there exists $\psi_g \in C(\mathbb{R}_+, \mathbb{R}_+)$ with $\psi_g(0) = 0$, such that for a solution $z \in C^{\sigma}_{1-\sigma}(J)$ of the inequality:*

$$|D^{\omega,\tau}_{0^+} z(t) - g(t, z(t), Hz(t))| \leq \epsilon, \quad t \in J, \tag{17}$$

there exists a solution $y \in C^{\sigma}_{1-\sigma}(J)$ of Equations (5) and (6) such that:

$$| z(t) - y(t) | \leq \psi_g(\epsilon), \quad t \in J.$$

Definition 7 ([11]). *Equations (5) and (6) are UHS stable with respect to $v \in C(J, \mathbb{R}_+)$ if there exists a real number $c_{g,v} > 0$ such that for each $\epsilon > 0$ and for each $z \in C^{\sigma}_{1-\sigma}(J)$ solution of the inequality:*

$$|D^{\omega,\tau}_{0^+} z(t) - g(t, z(t), Hz(t))| \leq \epsilon v(t), \quad t \in J, \tag{18}$$

there exists a solution $y \in C^{\sigma}_{1-\sigma}(J)$ of Equations (5) and (6) such that:

$$| z(t) - y(t) | \leq c_{g,v} \epsilon v(t), \quad t \in J.$$

Definition 8 ([11]). *Equations (5) and (6) is generalized UHS stable with respect to $v \in C(J, \mathbb{R}_+)$ if there exist $C_{g,v} > 0$ such that for each $z \in C^{\sigma}_{1-\sigma}(J)$ solution of the inequality:*

$$|D^{\omega,\tau}_{0^+} z(t) - g(t, z(t), Hz(t))| \leq v(t), \quad t \in J, \tag{19}$$

there exists $y \in C^{\sigma}_{1-\sigma}(J)$ solution of Equations (5) and (6) such that:

$$| z(t) - y(t) | \leq c_{g,v} v(t), \quad t \in J.$$

Remark 2 ([11]). *A function $z \in C^{\sigma}_{1-\sigma}(J)$ is a solution of the inequality:*

$$|D^{\omega,\tau}_{0^+} z(t) - g(t, z(t), Hz(t))| \leq \epsilon, \quad t \in J,$$

if there exists a function $w \in C^{\sigma}_{1-\sigma}(J)$ such that:

1. $| w(t) | \leq \epsilon, \quad t \in J,$
2. $D^{\omega,\tau}_{0^+} z(t) = g(t, z(t), Hz(t)) + w(t), \quad t \in J.$

Remark 3 ([11]). *It is clear that:*

1. *Definition* (5) $\Rightarrow$ *Definition* (6).
2. *Definition* (7) $\Rightarrow$ *Definition* (8).

Theorem 3. *Assume that $(A1)$ and (15) are satisfied, then the presumed problems (5) and (6) is UH stable.*

Proof. Let $z \in C^{\sigma}_{1-\sigma}(J)$ be a solution of the inequality (16) and let $y \in C^{\sigma}_{1-\sigma}[a, b]$ be a unique solution of the given system:

$$
\begin{aligned}
&{}^{H}D^{\omega,\tau}y(t) = g(t, y(t), \int_{a}^{t} g(t,s,y(s))ds), \quad t \in J, 1 < \omega < 2, 0 \le \tau \le 1,\\
&y(a) = 0, \quad y(b) = \sum_{j=1}^{k} \varrho_j I^{\nu_j} x(\zeta_j), \quad \nu_j > 0, \varrho_j \in \mathbb{R}, \zeta_j \in J,
\end{aligned}
$$

where $1 < \omega < 2$ and parameter $0 \le \tau \le 1$.

In view of Remark 2, we have

$$
\begin{aligned}
|z(t) - \frac{(b-a)^{\sigma-1}}{\Phi\Gamma(\sigma)} I^{\omega} g(s, z(s), Hz(s))(b) + \frac{(b-a)^{\sigma-1}}{\Phi\Gamma(\sigma)} \sum_{j=1}^{k} \varrho_j I^{\omega+\nu_j} g(s, z(s), Hz(s))(\zeta)\\
- I^{\omega} g(s, z(s), Hz(s))(t)| \le \frac{\epsilon t^{\omega}}{\Gamma(\omega+1)} \le \frac{\epsilon b^{\omega}}{\Gamma(\omega+1)}.
\end{aligned}
$$

Then for each $t \in J$, we obtain

$$
\begin{aligned}
|z(t) - y(t)| \le & |z(t) - \frac{(b-a)^{\sigma-1}}{\Phi\Gamma(\sigma)} I^{\omega} g(s, y(s), Hy(s))(b)\\
& + \frac{(b-a)^{\sigma-1}}{\Phi\Gamma(\sigma)} \sum_{j=1}^{k} \varrho_j I^{\omega+\nu_j} g(s, y(s), Hy(s))(\zeta) - I^{\omega} g(s, y(s), Hy(s))(t)|\\
\le & |z(t) - \frac{(b-a)^{\sigma-1}}{\Phi\Gamma(\sigma)} I^{\omega} g(s, z(s), Hz(s))(b)\\
& + \frac{(b-a)^{\sigma-1}}{\Phi\Gamma(\sigma)} \sum_{j=1}^{k} \varrho_j I^{\omega+\nu_j} g(s, z(s), Hz(s))(\zeta) - I^{\omega} g(s, z(s), Hz(s))(t)|\\
& + |\frac{(b-a)^{\sigma-1}}{\Phi\Gamma(\sigma)} I^{\omega} \{g(s, z(s), Hz(s)) - g(s, y(s), Hy(s))\}(b)\\
& - \frac{(b-a)^{\sigma-1}}{\Phi\Gamma(\sigma)} \sum_{j=1}^{k} \varrho_j I^{\omega+\nu_j} \{g(s, z(s), Hz(s)) - g(s, y(s), Hy(s))\}(\zeta)\\
& + I^{\omega} \{g(s, z(s), Hz(s)) - g(s, y(s), Hy(s))\}(t)|\\
\le & \frac{\epsilon b^{\omega}}{\Gamma(\omega+1)} + (\mathtt{L}_1 + \mathtt{L}_2\mathtt{M}) \Bigg(\frac{(b-a)^{\omega+\sigma-1}}{|\Phi|\Gamma(\sigma)\Gamma(\omega+1)}\\
& + \frac{(b-a)^{\omega+\sigma-1}}{|\Phi|\Gamma(\sigma)} \sum_{i=0}^{m} \frac{|\varrho_j|(\zeta_j - a)^{\omega+\zeta_j}}{\Gamma(\omega+\nu_j+1)} + \frac{(b-a)^{\omega}}{\Gamma(\omega+1)} \Bigg) |z(t) - y(t)|,\\
\le & \frac{\epsilon b^{\omega}}{\Gamma(\omega+1)} + \mathtt{K}|z(t) - y(t)|\\
\le & \frac{\epsilon b^{\omega}}{(1-\mathtt{K})\Gamma(\omega+1)}.
\end{aligned}
$$

Therefore,

$$
|z(t) - y(t)| \le c_g \epsilon,
$$

where,

$$\mathrm{K} =: (\mathrm{L}_1 + \mathrm{L}_2\mathrm{M})\left(\frac{(b-a)^{\omega+\sigma-1}}{\mid \Phi \mid \Gamma(\sigma)\Gamma(\omega+1)} + \frac{(b-a)^{\omega+\sigma-1}}{\mid \Phi \mid \Gamma(\sigma)}\sum_{i=0}^{m}\frac{\mid \varrho_j \mid (\zeta_j - a)^{\omega+\zeta_j}}{\Gamma(\omega+v_j+1)} + \frac{(b-a)^{\omega}}{\Gamma(\omega+1)}\right).$$

This shows that (5) and (6) is UH stable. □

Theorem 4. *Assume that* $(A1)$*–*$(A3)$ *and (15) hold. Then, there exists an increasing function* $v \in C_{1-\sigma}[J]$ *and a real number* $\varsigma_v > 0$ *such that:*

$$|z(t) - y(t)| \le \varsigma_v \varphi(t), \quad t \in J.$$

Then (5) and (6) are UHR stable.

Proof. Let $z \in C^{\sigma}_{1-\sigma}[a,b]$ be a solution of the inequality (18) and let $x \in C^{\sigma}_{1-\sigma}(J)$ be the unique solution of the given system:

$$^{H}D^{\omega,\tau}y(t) = g(t, y(t), \int_a^t g(t,s,y(s))ds), \quad t,$$

$$y(a) = 0, \quad y(b) = \sum_{j=1}^{k}\varrho_j I^{v_j}x(\zeta_j), \quad v_j > 0, \varrho_j \in \mathbb{R}, \zeta_j,$$

where $1 < \omega < 2$ and parameter $0 \le \tau \le 1$.

By Remark 2, we have

$$\begin{aligned}|z(t) - \frac{(b-a)^{\sigma-1}}{\Phi\Gamma(\sigma)}I^{\omega}g(s,z(s),Hz(s))(b) + \frac{(b-a)^{\sigma-1}}{\Phi\Gamma(\sigma)}\sum_{j=1}^{k}\varrho_j I^{\omega+v_j}g(s,z(s),Hz(s))(\zeta)\\ - I^{\omega}g(s,z(s),Hz(s))(t)| \le \epsilon\varsigma_v\varphi(t).\end{aligned}$$

Then, for any $t \in J$, we obtain

$$\begin{aligned}|z(t) - y(t)| \le& \Bigg|z(t) - \frac{(b-a)^{\sigma-1}}{\Phi\Gamma(\sigma)}I^{\omega}g(s,y(s),Hy(s))(b)\\ &+ \frac{(b-a)^{\sigma-1}}{\Phi\Gamma(\sigma)}\sum_{j=1}^{k}\varrho_j I^{\omega+v_j}g(s,y(s),Hy(s))(\zeta) - I^{\omega}g(s,y(s),Hy(s))(t)\Bigg|\\ \le& \Bigg|z(t) - \frac{(b-a)^{\sigma-1}}{\Phi\Gamma(\sigma)}I^{\omega}g(s,z(s),Hz(s))(b)\\ &+ \frac{(b-a)^{\sigma-1}}{\Phi\Gamma(\sigma)}\sum_{j=1}^{k}\varrho_j I^{\omega+v_j}g(s,z(s),Hz(s))(\zeta) - I^{\omega}g(s,z(s),Hz(s))(t)\Bigg|\\ &+ \Bigg|\frac{(b-a)^{\sigma-1}}{\Phi\Gamma(\sigma)}I^{\omega}\{g(s,z(s),Hz(s)) - g(s,y(s),Hy(s))\}(b)\\ &- \frac{(b-a)^{\sigma-1}}{\Phi\Gamma(\sigma)}\sum_{j=1}^{k}\varrho_j I^{\omega+v_j}\{g(s,z(s),Hz(s)) - g(s,y(s),Hy(s))\}(\zeta)\\ &+ I^{\omega}\{g(s,z(s),Hz(s)) - g(s,y(s),Hy(s))\}(t)\Bigg|\end{aligned}$$

$$
\begin{aligned}
&\leq \epsilon \varsigma_{\nu} \varphi(t) + (\mathrm{L}_1 + \mathrm{L}_2 \mathrm{M}) \left(\frac{(b-a)^{\omega+\sigma-1}}{|\Phi| \Gamma(\sigma)\Gamma(\omega+1)} \right. \\
&\left. + \frac{(b-a)^{\omega+\sigma-1}}{|\Phi| \Gamma(\sigma)} \sum_{i=0}^{m} \frac{|\varrho_j| (\zeta_j - a)^{\omega+\zeta_j}}{\Gamma(\omega+\nu_j+1)} + \frac{(b-a)^{\omega}}{\Gamma(\omega+1)} \right) |z(t) - y(t) \\
&\leq \epsilon \varsigma_{\nu} \varphi(t) + \mathrm{K}|z(t) - y(t)| \\
&\leq \frac{\epsilon \varsigma_{\nu} \varphi(t)}{(1-\mathrm{K})\Gamma(\omega)}.
\end{aligned}
$$

Therefore, we obtain that:

$$|z(t) - y(t)| \leq c_{g,\nu} \epsilon \nu(t).$$

Hence, (5) and (6) are UHR stable. □

5. Examples

Example 1. *Consider the nonlocal BVP's by using Hilfer FIDE's of the form.*

$$
\begin{cases}
{}^{H}D^{\omega,\tau} y(t) = \frac{\cos^2 t}{(e^{-t+2})^2 |y(t)|} + \frac{1}{2} \int\limits_{0}^{t} e^{-1/2} y(s) ds, & t \in [\frac{3}{10}, \frac{13}{10}], \\
y(\frac{3}{10}) = 0, \quad y(\frac{13}{10}) = \frac{17}{50} I^{\frac{13}{15}} y(\frac{23}{50}) + \frac{21}{50} I^{\frac{37}{100}} y(\frac{91}{100}) + \frac{3}{25} I^{\frac{41}{100}} y(\frac{4}{5}). &
\end{cases}
\tag{20}
$$

where $\omega = \frac{6}{5}, \tau = \frac{1}{5}, \sigma = \frac{7}{4}, a = \frac{3}{10}, b = \frac{13}{10}, \varrho_1 = \frac{17}{50}, \varrho_2 = \frac{21}{50}, \varrho_3 = \frac{3}{25}, \nu_1 = \frac{13}{15}, \nu_2 = \frac{37}{100}, \nu_3 = \frac{41}{100}, \zeta_1 = \frac{23}{50}, \zeta_2 = \frac{91}{100}, \zeta_3 = \frac{4}{5}, L_1 = L_2 = \frac{1}{9}, M = \frac{1}{8}$.

Hence, the assumptions $(A2)$ *and* $(A3)$ *hold.*

We check the condition,

$$
(L_1 + L_2 M) \left[\frac{(b-a)^{\omega+\sigma-1}}{|\Phi| \Gamma(\sigma)\Gamma(\omega+1)} + \frac{(b-a)^{\omega+\sigma-1}}{|\Phi| \Gamma(\sigma)} \sum_{i=0}^{m} \frac{|\varrho_j| (\zeta_j - a)^{\omega+\zeta_j}}{\Gamma(\omega+\nu_j+1)} + \frac{(b-a)^{\omega}}{\Gamma(\omega+1)} \right] < 1 \approx 0.7347.
$$

Hence, the problem (20) *has a unique solution on* $[\frac{3}{10}, \frac{13}{10}]$.

Example 2. *Examine the RLC circuit equation of the Hilfer fractional differential equation of the form.*

$$
\begin{cases}
{}^{H}D^{\omega,\tau} \mathbb{I}(t) = \frac{\mathbb{E}_0}{\mathbb{L}} - \frac{\mathbb{R}}{\mathbb{L}} \mathbb{I}(t) - \frac{1}{\mathbb{CL}} \int\limits_{0}^{t} \mathbb{I}(s) ds, \quad t \in [0,1], \\
y(0) = 0, \quad y(1) = 0.34 I^{0.87} y(0.46) + 0.42 I^{0.37} y(0.91) + 0.12 I^{0.41} y(0.8).
\end{cases}
\tag{21}
$$

RLC circuits are commonly used in filter design, where they can be configured as low-pass, high-pass, band-pass, or band-stop filters. These filters are crucial in signal processing, telecommunications, and audio electronics. It is used in tuned circuits, which are employed in radio receivers to select a particular frequency from a mixture of signals. This is essential for tuning in to specific radio stations. It can be used in control systems for tasks such as damping oscillations and stabilizing feedback loops.

In Figure 2a, various fractional orders fix the parameter value at 0.5 for the RLC circuit equation. Figure 2b represents the three-dimensional view of RLC with the circuit elements, $\mathbb{R} = 4$, $\mathbb{I} = 2$, $\mathbb{C} = 5$, and $\mathbb{E}_0 = 10$.

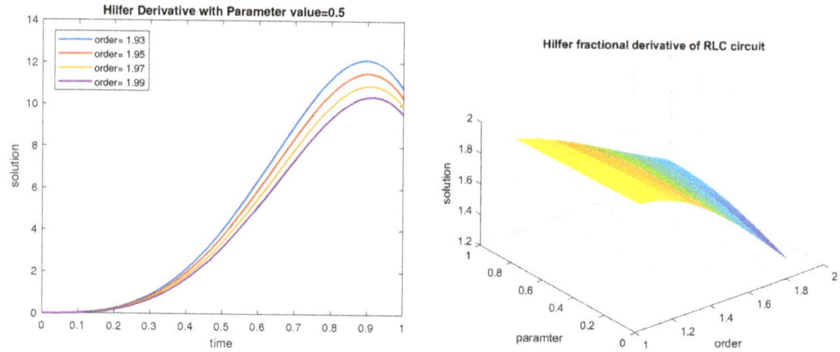

(a) (b)

Figure 2. RLC circuit equation with Hilfer fractional derivative of parameters $\mathbb{R} = 4$, $\mathbb{I} = 2$, $\mathbb{C} = 5$, and $\mathbb{E}_0 = 10$. (**a**) Hilfer Fractional Derivative of RLC circuit; (**b**) 3D-view of RLC circuit.

Example 3. *Consider the following integro-differential equation of the Hilfer fractional differential equation of the form.*

$$\begin{cases} {}^{H}D^{\omega,\tau}y(t) = \frac{\cos^2(t)}{(e^{-t+2})^2} + \frac{1}{2}e^{-1/2}\int_0^t y(s)ds, \qquad t \in [0,5], \\ y(0) = 0, \quad y(5) = 0.34I^{0.87}y(0.46) + 0.42I^{0.37}y(0.91) + 0.12I^{0.41}y(0.8). \end{cases} \tag{22}$$

In these figures, the significance of fractional order derivatives is clearly revealed. In order to show the significance of the fractional order derivative, the output responses of the considered systems with respect to the Riemann-Liouville, Caputo, and Hilfer derivative are graphically represented in Figures 3–5.

Notably, in Figure 3a, for the distinct values of order ω, $(\omega = 1.2, 1.4, 1.6, 1.8)$ with the parameter $\tau = 0$ is plotted. Similarly, for $\tau = 1$, it is plotted in Figure 3b. Figure 4a pictures $\tau = 0.9$. In Figure 4b, it should be noted that the Hilfer fractional order derivative is defined for different values of τ, which lies between 0 and 1.

In addition to this, a 3D plot with respect to the order ω, parameter τ and $y(t)$ is given in Figure 5. This figure clearly pictures the the impact of order ω and parameter τ for obtaining the solution of the considered systems. Overall, from the simulation result, the robustness of the developed methodology is validated.

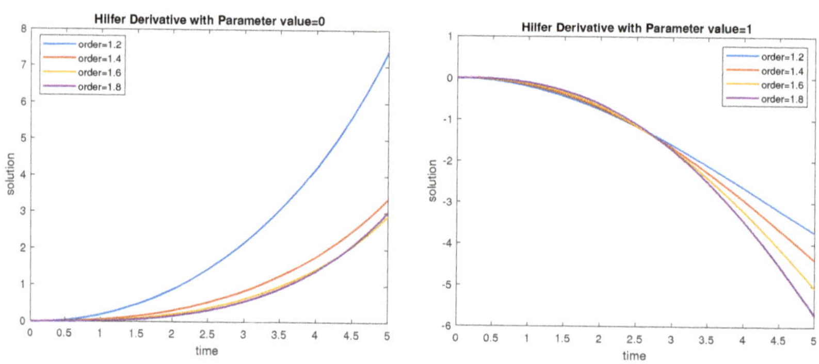

(a) (b)

Figure 3. Different Fractional order of R-L and Caputo Derivative. (**a**) Riemann-Liouville Fractional Derivative, (**b**) Caputo Fractional Derivative.

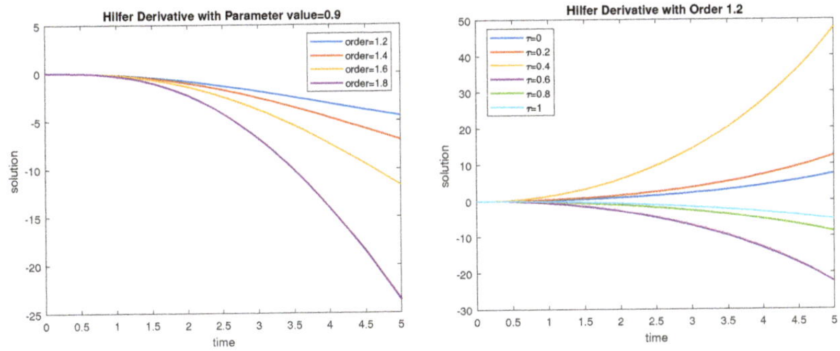

(a) (b)

Figure 4. Hilfer Fractional Derivative. (**a**) Different Fractional Order, (**b**) Different Parameter Values.

The solution representation is modified when we change the order and parameter. One of the main benefits of our problem of non-local integro differential boundary value problems is that, while this changes the small size of the order and parameter values, it can have a major effect when applied to a real-world problem.

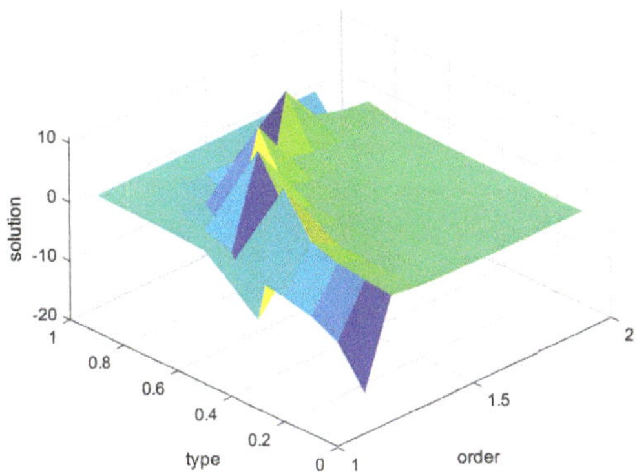

Figure 5. 3D-View of Hilfer Derivative of Different Orders and Parameter at $t = 2.5$.

Example 4. *Consider the following non-local boundary value problem with the integro-differential equation of the Hilfer fractional differential equation of the form.*

$$\begin{cases} {}^{H}D^{\omega,\tau}y(t) = \frac{4}{4t+7}\left(\frac{y^2(t)}{1+|y(t)|} + \frac{2}{3}\right) + \frac{1}{2}e^{-1/2}\int\limits_0^t y(s)ds, & t \in [0,3], \\ y(0) = 0, \quad y(3) = 0.8I^{0.75}y(0.5) + 0.5I^{0.85}y(0.75) + 0.48I^{0.54}y(0.25). \end{cases} \tag{23}$$

In Figure 6a, the solution is plotted for different values of $\omega = 1.2,\ 1.4,\ 1.6,\ 1.8$ with parameter $\tau = 0$, which is the Riemann-Liouville derivative. In Figure 6b, the solution is plotted for distinct values of the order $\omega = 1.2,\ 1.4,\ 1.6,\ 1.8$ with parameter $\tau = 1$, which is the Caputo derivative.

In Figure 7a, the solution is plotted for different fractional orders and the Hilfer derivative with parameter $\tau = 0.6$. In Figure 7b, the solution is plotted for fractional order $\omega = 1.2$ with different parameter values. In Figure 6, the solution is plotted for the parameter values $\tau = 1$ and $\tau = 0$, then it is referred to as the Caputo derivative and the R-L derivative, respectively. In Figure 7, the solution is plotted for the Hilfer derivative of various parameter values.

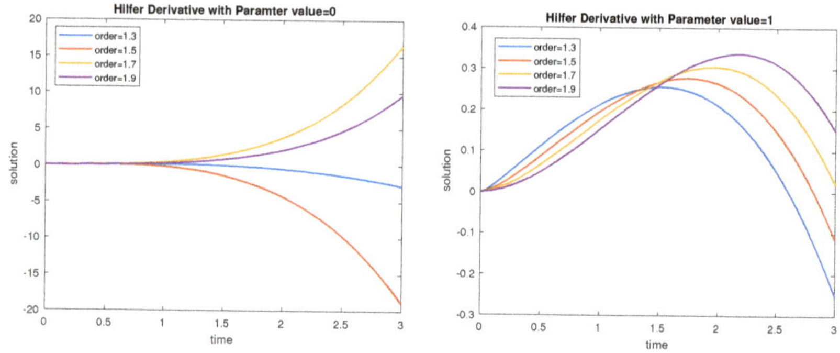

(a) (b)

Figure 6. Various Fractional order of R-L and Caputo Derivative. (**a**) Riemann–Liouville Fractional Derivative, (**b**) Caputo Fractional Derivative.

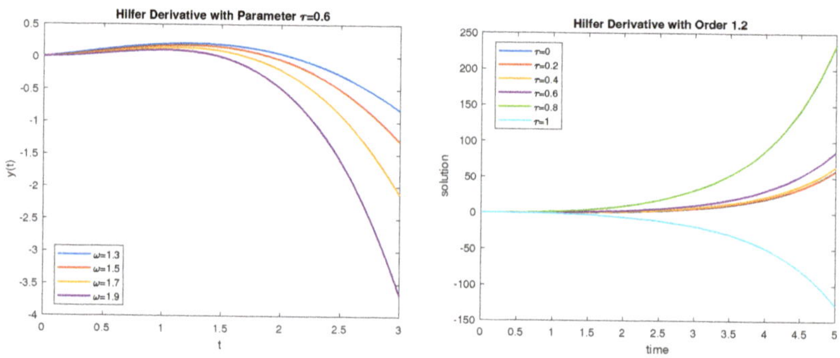

(a) (b)

Figure 7. Hilfer Fractional Derivative. (**a**) Different Fractional Order, (**b**) Differential Parameter Values.

6. Conclusions

In this paper, the existence and uniqueness results of the RLC circuit equation are investigated utilizing Schaefer's fixed point theorem and Banach's contractions principle. The Ulam-type stability results for the Hilfer fractional integro-differential equations with non-local boundary conditions are studied for the RLC model. Finally, some numerical examples are provided for illustrating the theoretical results. A similar generalized system involving (k, ψ)-Hilfer fractional derivatives with particular multi-point boundary conditions, and various constant and distributed delays will be further studied in future works.

Author Contributions: Conceptualization, N.S.; Methodology, N.S. and P.V.; Writing—original draft, N.S.; Software, N.S. and P.V.; Investigation, P.V.; Visualization, P.V.; Validation, P.V. and M.I.A.; Supervision, P.V.; Writing—review & editing, P.V. and M.I.A.; Funding acquisition, M.I.A. All authors have read and agreed to the published version of the manuscript.

Funding: This research received no external funding.

Data Availability Statement: Authors have no data and materials.

Conflicts of Interest: The authors declare no conflict of interest.

Notations

The following abbreviations are used in this manuscript:

$\mathbb{I}(t)$	Current
$\mathbb{V}(t)$	charge at t
$\mathbb{E}(t)$	Supplied source (volt)
$\mathbb{C}$	Capacitance (farad)
$\mathbb{R}$	Resistance (ohms)
t	time

References

1. Diethelm, K.; Ford, N.J. Analysis of fractional differential equations. *J. Math. Anal. Appl.* **2002**, *265*, 229–248. [CrossRef]
2. Gupta, V.; Dabas, J.; Fečkan, M. Existence results of solutions for impulsive fractional differential equations. *Nonautonomous Dyn. Syst.* **2018**, *5*, 35–51. [CrossRef]
3. Hilfer, R. *Applications of Fractional Calculus in Physics*; World Scientific: Singapore, 2000.
4. Podlubny, I. Fractional differential equations. In *Mathematics in Science and Engineering*; Elsevier: Amsterdam, The Netherlands, 1999.
5. Zhou, Y. *Basic Theory of Fractional Differential Equations*; World Scientific Publishing Co., Pte. Ltd.: Hackensack, NJ, USA, 2014.
6. Ahmad, B.; Nieto, J.J. Riemann-Liouville fractional integro-differential equations with fractional nonlocal integral boundary conditions. *Bound. Value Probl.* **2011**, *2011*, 36. [CrossRef]
7. Borisut, P.; Kumam, P.; Ahmed, I.; Jirakitpuwapat, W. Existence and uniqueness for ψ-Hilfer fractional differential equation with nonlocal multi-point condition. *Math. Methods Appl. Sci.* **2021**, *44*, 2506–2520. [CrossRef]
8. Furati, K.M.; Kassim, M.D. Existence and uniqueness for a problem involving Hilfer fractional derivative. *Comput. Math. Appl.* **2012**, *64*, 1616–1626. [CrossRef]
9. Gu, H.; Trujillo, J.J. Existence of mild solution for evolution equation with Hilfer fractional derivative. *Appl. Math. Comput.* **2015**, *257*, 344–354. [CrossRef]
10. Asawasamrit, S.; Kijjathanakorn, A.; Ntouyas, S.K.; Tariboon, J. Nonlocal boundary value problems for Hilfer fractional differential equations. *Bull. Korean Math. Soc.* **2018**, *55*, 1639–1657.
11. Vivek, D.; M Elsayed, E.; Kanagarajan, K. Nonlocal Initial Value Problems for Nonlinear Neutral Pantograph Equations with Hilfer-Hadamard Fractional Derivative. *Inf. Sci. Lett.* **2021**, *10*, 111–119.
12. Wang, J.; Zhang, Y. Nonlocal initial value problems for differential equations with Hilfer fractional derivative. *Appl. Math. Comput.* **2015**, *266*, 850–859. [CrossRef]
13. Gholami, Y. Existence and uniqueness criteria for the higher-order Hilfer fractional boundary value problems at resonance. *Adv. Differ. Equ.* **2020**, *2020*, 482. [CrossRef]
14. Naveen, S.; Srilekha, R.; Suganya, S.; Parthiban, V. Controllability of damped dynamical systems modelled by Hilfer fractional derivatives. *J. Taibah Univ. Sci.* **2022**, *16*, 1254–1263. [CrossRef]
15. Owolabi, K.M. Numerical Analysis and Pattern Formation Process for Space-Fractional Superdiffusive Systems. *Discret. Contin. Dyn. Syst.-Ser.* **2019**, *12*, 543–566. [CrossRef]
16. Gómez-Aguilar, J. Fundamental solutions to electrical circuits of non-integer order via fractional derivatives with and without singular kernels. *Eur. Phys. J. Plus* **2018**, *133*, 197. [CrossRef]
17. Sabir, Z.; Saoud, S.; Raja, M.A.Z.; Wahab, H.A.; Arbi, A. Heuristic computing technique for numerical solutions of nonlinear fourth order Emden-Fowler equation. *Math. Comput. Simul.* **2020**, *178*, 534–548. [CrossRef]
18. Sabir, Z.; Raja, M.A.Z.; Arbi, A.; Altamirano, G.C.; Cao, J. Neuro-swarms intelligent computing using Gudermannian kernel for solving a class of second order Lane-Emden singular nonlinear model. *AIMS Math* **2021**, *6*, 2468–2485. [CrossRef]
19. Gómez-Aguilar, J.; Atangana, A. New insight in fractional differentiation: Power, exponential decay and Mittag-Leffler laws and applications. *Eur. Phys. J. Plus* **2017**, *132*, 13. [CrossRef]
20. Sene, N.; Abdelmalek, K. Analysis of the fractional diffusion equations described by Atangana-Baleanu-Caputo fractional derivative. *Chaos Solitons Fractals* **2019**, *127*, 158–164. [CrossRef]
21. Aguilar, J.F.G. Behavior characteristics of a cap-resistor, memcapacitor, and a memristor from the response obtained of RC and RL electrical circuits described by fractional differential equations. *Turk. J. Electr. Eng. Comput. Sci.* **2016**, *24*, 1421–1433. [CrossRef]
22. Morales-Delgado, V.F.; Gómez-Aguilar, J.F.; Taneco-Hernández, M.A.; Escobar-Jiménez, R.F. Fractional operator without singular kernel: Applications to linear electrical circuits. *Int. J. Circuit Theory Appl.* **2018**, *46*, 2394–2419. [CrossRef]
23. Morales-Delgado, V.; Gómez-Aguilar, J.; Taneco-Hernandez, M. Analytical solutions of electrical circuits described by fractional conformable derivatives in Liouville-Caputo sense. *AEU Int. J. Electron. Commun.* **2018**, *85*, 108–117. [CrossRef]
24. Gómez-Aguilar, J.; Escobar-Jiménez, R.; Olivares-Peregrino, V.; Taneco-Hernandez, M.; Guerrero-Ramírez, G. Electrical circuits RC and RL involving fractional operators with bi-order. *Adv. Mech. Eng.* **2017**, *9*, 1687814017707132. [CrossRef]
25. Gómez-Aguilar, J.F.; Atangana, A.; Morales-Delgado, V.F. Electrical circuits RC, LC, and RL described by Atangana-Baleanu fractional derivatives. *Int. J. Circuit Theory Appl.* **2017**, *45*, 1514–1533. [CrossRef]
26. Radwan, A.G.; Salama, K.N. Fractional-order RC and RL circuits. *Circuits Syst. Signal Process.* **2012**, *31*, 1901–1915. [CrossRef]

27. Sene, N.; Gómez-Aguilar, J. Analytical solutions of electrical circuits considering certain generalized fractional derivatives. *Eur. Phys. J. Plus* **2019**, *134*, 260. [CrossRef]
28. Gómez-Aguilar, J.; Córdova-Fraga, T.; Escalante-Martínez, J.; Calderón-Ramón, C.; Escobar-Jiménez, R. Electrical circuits described by a fractional derivative with regular kernel. *Rev. Mex. De Física* **2016**, *62*, 144–154.
29. Arshad, U.; Sultana, M.; Ali, A.H.; Bazighifan, O.; Al-Moneef, A.A.; Nonlaopon, K. Numerical solutions of fractional-order electrical rlc circuit equations via three numerical techniques. *Mathematics* **2022**, *10*, 3071. [CrossRef]
30. Malarvizhi, M.; Karunanithi, S.; Gajalakshmi, N. Numerical Analysis Using RK-4 In Transient Analysis Of RLC Circuit. *Adv. Math. Sci. J.* **2020**, *9*, 6115–6124. [CrossRef]
31. Abbas, S.; Benchohra, M.; Sivasundaram, S. Dynamics and Ulam stability for Hilfer type fractional differential equations. *Nonlinear Stud.* **2016**, *23*, 627–637.
32. András, S.; Kolumbán, J.J. On the Ulam-Hyers stability of first order differential systems with nonlocal initial conditions. *Nonlinear Anal. Theory Methods Appl.* **2013**, *82*, 1–11. [CrossRef]
33. Harikrishnan, S.; Kanagarajan, K.; Vivek, D. Some Existence and Stability Results for Integro-Differential Equation by Hilfer-Katugampola Fractional Derivative. *Palest. J. Math.* **2020**, *9*, 254–262.
34. Sudsutad, W.; Thaiprayoon, C.; Ntouyas, S.K. Existence and stability results for ψ-Hilfer fractional integro-differential equation with mixed nonlocal boundary conditions. *AIMS Math* **2021**, *6*, 4119–4141. [CrossRef]
35. Wang, J.; Zhou, Y.; Medved, M. Existence and stability of fractional differential equations with Hadamard derivative. *Topol. Methods Nonlinear Anal.* **2013**, *41*, 113–133.
36. Ibrahim, R.W. Generalized Ulam-Hyers stability for fractional differential equations. *Int. J. Math.* **2012**, *23*, 1250056. [CrossRef]
37. Pachpatte, D.B. Existence and stability of some nonlinear ψ-Hilfer partial fractional differential equation. *Partial Differ. Equ. Appl. Math.* **2021**, *3*, 100032. [CrossRef]
38. Rus, I.A. Ulam stabilities of ordinary differential equations in a Banach space. *Carpathian J. Math.* **2010**, *26*, 103–107.
39. Wang, J.; Lv, L.; Zhou, Y. New concepts and results in stability of fractional differential equations. *Commun. Nonlinear Sci. Numer. Simul.* **2012**, *17*, 2530–2538. [CrossRef]

fractal and fractional

MDPI

Article

Computational Analysis of Fractional-Order KdV Systems in the Sense of the Caputo Operator via a Novel Transform

Mashael M. AlBaidani [1], Abdul Hamid Ganie [2] and Adnan Khan [3,*]

[1] Department of Mathematics, College of Science and Humanities, Prince Sattam bin Abdulaziz University, Al Kharj 11942, Saudi Arabia; m.albaidani@psau.edu.sa
[2] Basic Science Department, College of Science and Theoretical Studies, Saudi Electronic University, Riyadh 11673, Saudi Arabia; a.ganie@seu.edu.sa
[3] Department of Mathematics, Abdul Wali Khan University Mardan, Mardan 23200, Pakistan
* Correspondence: adnanmummand@gmail.com

Abstract: The main features of scientific efforts in physics and engineering are the development of models for various physical issues and the development of solutions. In order to solve the time-fractional coupled Korteweg–De Vries (KdV) equation, we combine the novel Yang transform, the homotopy perturbation approach, and the Adomian decomposition method in the present investigation. KdV models are crucial because they can accurately represent a variety of physical problems, including thin-film flows and waves on shallow water surfaces. The fractional derivative is regarded in the Caputo meaning. These approaches apply straightforward steps through symbolic computation to provide a convergent series solution. Different nonlinear time-fractional KdV systems are used to test the effectiveness of the suggested techniques. The symmetry pattern is a fundamental feature of the KdV equations and the symmetrical aspect of the solution can be seen from the graphical representations. The numerical outcomes demonstrate that only a small number of terms are required to arrive at an approximation that is exact, efficient, and trustworthy. Additionally, the system's approximative solution is illustrated graphically. The results show that these techniques are extremely effective, practically applicable for usage in such issues, and adaptable to other nonlinear issues.

Keywords: Adomian decomposition method; homotopy perturbation method; Yang transform; time-fractional coupled KdV equation; Caputo operator

1. Introduction

Fractional calculus (FC) theory offers a foundation for the extension of differentiation to non-integer orders. The fractional derivative operators [1] provide a concise explanation of modelling issues involving the concepts of non-locality and memory effects that are not adequately explained by integer-order operators. The discussion of a variety of issues, including viscoelastic systems and electrode–electrolyte polarisation, which are modelled by fractional equations, is made possible by the use of fractional calculus [2]. FC more precisely and aggressively defines physical phenomena than classical calculus. Fractional-order nonlinear models are widely used in many areas and are also important in nonlinear wave phenomena [3,4]. Fractional derivatives have been defined in several ways, including the Riemann–Liouville, Caputo, and Grunwald–Letnikov operators, the most well known of which are the Caputo and Riemann–Liouville fractional derivatives, which have often been employed in recent research. Many scientific domains have successfully used the idea of fractional derivatives to represent a variety of real-world occurrences in recent years [5]. The evolution of a physical phenomenon from its original state to its current state is included in fractional-order operators. Thus, model systems that explain the impact of memory effects are often evaluated through the application of fractional-order operators [6].

Differential equations that involve unknown multivariable functions and their fractional or fractional-integer partial derivatives with respect to those variables are known as fractional partial differential equations (PDEs). These kinds of equations are used to formulate, and afterwards aid in the solution of, problems involving functions of numerous variables, such as sound or heat propagation, electrostatics, electrodynamics, fluid flow, elasticity, and many more [7–12]. These two physically different occurrences can be formulated similarly using fractional PDEs. Fractional-order partial differential equations (FPDEs) have been suggested and studied during the past few decades in a variety of scientific areas, including biology, plasma physics, finance, chemistry, fluid mechanics, and mechanics of materials. In order to better express physical and control systems, systems of fractional partial differential equations have become more and more popular [13–17]. Approximative or numerical techniques are typically used because some fractional-order partial differential equations do not have accurate analytic solutions. In the literature, there are numerous analytical and numerical techniques for handling FPDEs, such as the multiple exp-function algorithm for solving the nonlinear fractional Sharma–Tasso–Olver equation [18] and the fractional-order Hirota–Satsuma coupled KdV [19]; the homotopy perturbation transform method for solving time-fractional Belousov–Zhabotinsky reactions [20] and diffusion equations of fractional-order in a plasma and fluids [21]; the fractional complex transformation for fractional nonlinear partial differential equations in mathematical physics [22] and the time-fractional heat conduction equation [23]; the variational iteration transform method for the investigation of the Newell–Whitehead–Segel equations having fractional order [24]; the homotopy analysis method for solving fractional Lorenz systems [25] and time-fractional Schrödinger equations [26]; the finite element method for parabolic equations of fractional order [27] and the time-fractional Fokker–Planck equation [28]; the fractional sub-equation method for generalised fractional KdV–Zakharov–Kuznetsov equations [29]; and so on.

A dimensionless form of the equation known as the KdV equation was derived by "Korteweg" and "de Vries" for the study of dispersive wave events in plasma physics and quantum mechanics. Korteweg and de Vries developed the traditional KdV equation in 1895 as a nonlinear partial differential equation to simulate waves on shallow water surfaces. Numerous research papers have been written regarding this specific solvable model. Numerous researchers have recently proposed novel uses for the classical KdV equation, including its usage to represent long internal waves in a density-stratified ocean, ion-acoustic waves in a plasma, and acoustic waves on a crystal lattice. In this study, we determine approximations to the nonlinear coupled time-fractional KdV equations that are given by

$$\begin{aligned} D_t^{\varsigma}\mathbf{J}(x,t) &= \mathbf{a}\mathbf{J}_{xxx}(x,t) + \mathbf{b}\mathbf{J}(x,t)\mathbf{J}_x(x,t) + \mathbf{c}\mathbf{K}(x,t)\mathbf{K}_x(x,t) \\ D_t^{\beta}\mathbf{K}(x,t) &= \mathbf{d}\mathbf{J}_{xxx}(x,t) - \mathbf{e}\mathbf{K}(x,t)\mathbf{K}_x(x,t), \quad 0 < \varsigma, \beta \leq 1, \end{aligned} \tag{1}$$

subjected to the initial sources

$$\mathbf{J}(x,0) = h_1(x), \quad \mathbf{K}(x,0) = h_2(x), \tag{2}$$

where $\mathbf{a}, \mathbf{d} < 0$; $\mathbf{b}, \mathbf{c}$, and $\mathbf{e}$ are constant parameters. The KdV equation has been the subject of a considerable number of studies because it has applications in the analysis of shallow-water waves and many other physical phenomena. It is possible that the precise solution to the KdV equation does not exist. For its numerical solution, many analytical techniques have been employed [30]. The numerical solutions of the third- and fifth-order terms, which serve as the primary dispersive terms in the KdV equation, were examined in [31]. However, plasma physics is described by the fifth-order KdV equation [32]. Nonlinear KdV reductive perturbation theories were investigated in [33]. The higher-order nonlinear KdV equation was investigated in [34] using a variational iteration method. A compact-type interpolation of constrained profiles was used in [35] to obtain numerical solutions for the KdV–Burgers equation. In [30], the approach of converting homotopy perturbation is used to analyse the numerical results of fifth-order KdV equations. Two computational techniques were applied to the third- and fifth-order KdV equations in [31].

The main objective of this study is to apply the homotopy perturbation transform method (HPTM) and the Yang transform decomposition method (YTDM) to the time-fractional coupled KdV equations in the frame of the Caputo derivative. To create the YTDM, the decomposition method and the Yang transform are merged. The Yang transform was introduced by Xiao-Jun Yang and can be used to solve a variety of differential equations with constant coefficients [36]. George Adomian introduced the Adomian decomposition method [37,38]. An extensive class of linear and nonlinear equations that are helpful for numerous research projects have been subjected to the Adomian decomposition approach. This method's ability to correctly and accurately solve these equations is its key characteristic. The time-fractional Fisher's equation [39], time-fractional Lax's Korteweg–De Vries equation [40], time-fractional Phi-four equation [41], and many other differential equations have been solved using the YTDM in the literature. A key role is played by the homotopy perturbation approach, which was first presented by J.H. He in 1998. This is because it solves the issue at hand without the need for any kind of transformation, linearisation, or discrimination. Analytical findings for the suggested strategy show how computationally advantageous and simple to use the method is.

The introduction and purpose of the article are presented in Section 1 of the paper. The fundamental principles of fractional calculus are covered in Section 2. We outline the notion of the suggested methods in Section 3. In Section 4, a few numerical examples are used to illustrate how effective the suggested solutions are. The manuscript's conclusion is presented in Section 5.

2. Basic Concept

Some fractional calculus definitions and notation needed in the course of this work are discussed in this section.

Definition 1. *The fractional Caputo derivative is stated as [42]*

$$D_t^{\varsigma}\mathbf{J}(x,t)=\frac{1}{\Gamma(k-\varsigma)}\int_0^t(t-\tau)^{k-\varsigma-1}\mathbf{J}^{(k)}(x,\tau)d\tau,\quad k-1<\varsigma\leq k,\quad k\in N. \tag{3}$$

Definition 2. *The Yang transform (YT) of the function is [43]*

$$Y\{\mathbf{J}(t)\}=M(u)=\int_0^{\infty}e^{\frac{-t}{u}}\mathbf{J}(t)dt,\ \ t>0, \tag{4}$$

with u illustrating the transform variable.

Some basic properties of the YT are the following:

$$\begin{aligned}Y[1]&=u,\\ Y[t]&=u^2,\\ Y[t^q]&=\Gamma(q+1)u^{q+1}.\end{aligned} \tag{5}$$

and the inverse YT is

$$Y^{-1}\{M(u)\}=\mathbf{J}(t). \tag{6}$$

Definition 3. *The YT of a function of nth order is [43]*

$$Y\{\mathbf{J}^n(t)\}=\frac{M(u)}{u^n}-\sum_{k=0}^{n-1}\frac{\mathbf{J}^k(0)}{u^{n-k-1}},\ \forall\ n=1,2,3,\cdots \tag{7}$$

Definition 4. *The YT of a function of fractional order is [43]*

$$Y\{\mathbf{J}^{\varsigma}(t)\}=\frac{M(u)}{u^{\varsigma}}-\sum_{k=0}^{n-1}\frac{\mathbf{J}^k(0)}{u^{\varsigma-(k+1)}},\ \ n-1<\varsigma\leq n. \tag{8}$$

3. Algorithm of the HPTM

The algorithm of the HPTM on a general nonlinear fractional model is illustrated in the following section.

$$D_t^{\varsigma}\mathbf{J}(x,t) = \mathcal{L}[x]\mathbf{J}(x,t) + \mathcal{M}[x]\mathbf{J}(x,t), \ \ 0 < \varsigma \leq 1, \tag{9}$$

with the initial condition

$$\mathbf{J}(x,0) = \vartheta(x).$$

Here, $D_t^{\varsigma} = \frac{\partial^{\varsigma}}{\partial t^{\varsigma}}$ denotes the fractional Caputo operator, $\mathcal{L}[x]$ is the linear, and $\mathcal{M}[x]$ is the nonlinear operator.

Computing the YT, we obtain

$$Y[D_t^{\varsigma}\mathbf{J}(x,t)] = Y[\mathcal{L}[x]\mathbf{J}(x,t) + \mathcal{M}[x]\mathbf{J}(x,t)], \tag{10}$$

$$\frac{1}{u^{\varsigma}}\{M(u) - u\mathbf{J}(0)\} = Y[\mathcal{L}[x]\mathbf{J}(x,t) + \mathcal{M}[x]\mathbf{J}(x,t)]. \tag{11}$$

After that, we have

$$M(\mathbf{J}) = u\mathbf{J}(0) + u^{\varsigma}Y[\mathcal{L}[x]\mathbf{J}(x,t) + \mathcal{M}[x]\mathbf{J}(x,t)]. \tag{12}$$

Operating the inverse YT, we have

$$\mathbf{J}(x,t) = \mathbf{J}(0) + Y^{-1}[u^{\varsigma}Y[\mathcal{L}[x]\mathbf{J}(x,t) + \mathcal{M}[x]\mathbf{J}(x,t)]]. \tag{13}$$

By means of homotopy perturbation method [44], we have

$$\mathbf{J}(x,t) = \mathbf{J}(0) + \epsilon[Y^{-1}[u^{\varsigma}Y[\mathcal{L}[x]\mathbf{J}(x,t) + \mathcal{M}[x]\mathbf{J}(x,t)]]], \tag{14}$$

with parameter $\epsilon \in [0,1]$.

The solution is expanded in series form as

$$\mathbf{J}(x,t) = \sum_{k=0}^{\infty} \epsilon^k \mathbf{J}_k(x,t), \tag{15}$$

with

$$\mathcal{M}[x]\mathbf{J}(x,t) = \sum_{k=0}^{\infty} \epsilon^k H_n(\mathbf{J}). \tag{16}$$

The following strategy can be operated to acquire He's polynomials [45] as

$$H_n(\mathbf{J}_0, \mathbf{J}_1, \ldots, \mathbf{J}_n) = \frac{1}{\Gamma(n+1)} D_{\epsilon}^k \left(\mathcal{M}\left(\sum_{k=0}^{\infty} \epsilon^i \mathbf{J}_i \right) \right) \Bigg|_{\epsilon=0}, \tag{17}$$

where $D_{\epsilon}^k = \frac{\partial^k}{\partial \epsilon^k}$.

Now, we substitute (15) and (16) into (14) to obtain

$$\sum_{k=0}^{\infty} \epsilon^k \mathbf{J}_k(x,t) = \mathbf{J}(0) + \epsilon \times \left(Y^{-1} \left[u^{\varsigma} Y\{\mathcal{L} \sum_{k=0}^{\infty} \epsilon^k \mathbf{J}_k(x,t) + \sum_{k=0}^{\infty} \epsilon^k H_k(\mathbf{J})\} \right] \right). \tag{18}$$

Equating the similar components of ϵ, we obtain

$$\begin{aligned}
&\epsilon^0 : \mathbf{J}_0(x,\mathtt{t}) = \mathbf{J}(0), \\
&\epsilon^1 : \mathbf{J}_1(x,\mathtt{t}) = Y^{-1}[u^{\varsigma}Y(\mathcal{L}[x]\mathbf{J}_0(x,\mathtt{t}) + H_0(\mathbf{J}))], \\
&\epsilon^2 : \mathbf{J}_2(x,\mathtt{t}) = Y^{-1}[u^{\varsigma}Y(\mathcal{L}[x]\mathbf{J}_1(x,\mathtt{t}) + H_1(\mathbf{J}))], \\
&\dots \\
&\epsilon^k : \mathbf{J}_k(x,\mathtt{t}) = Y^{-1}[u^{\varsigma}Y(\mathcal{L}[x]\mathbf{J}_{k-1}(x,\mathtt{t}) + H_{k-1}(\mathbf{J}))],
\end{aligned} \tag{19}$$

$k > 0, k \in N$.

Lastly, the analytical solution is stated as

$$\mathbf{J}(x,\mathtt{t}) = \lim_{\epsilon \to 1} \sum_{k=0}^{\infty} \epsilon^k \mathbf{J}_k(x,\mathtt{t}). \tag{20}$$

4. Algorithm of the YTDM

The algorithm of the YTDM on a general nonlinear fractional model is illustrated in the following section.

$$D_{\mathtt{t}}^{\varsigma}\mathbf{J}(x,\mathtt{t}) = \mathcal{L}(x,\mathtt{t}) + \mathcal{M}(x,\mathtt{t}), \ \ 0 < \varsigma \leq 1, \tag{21}$$

with the initial condition

$$\mathbf{J}(x,0) = \vartheta(x).$$

Here, $D_{\mathtt{t}}^{\varsigma} = \frac{\partial^{\varsigma}}{\partial \mathtt{t}^{\varsigma}}$ denotes the fractional Caputo operator, $\mathcal{L}$ is the linear, and $\mathcal{M}$ is the nonlinear operator.

Computing the YT, we obtain

$$\begin{aligned}
&Y[D_{\mathtt{t}}^{\varsigma}\mathbf{J}(x,\mathtt{t})] = Y[\mathcal{L}(x,\mathtt{t}) + \mathcal{M}(x,\mathtt{t})], \\
&\frac{1}{u^{\varsigma}}\{M(u) - u\mathbf{J}(0)\} = Y[\mathcal{L}(x,\mathtt{t}) + \mathcal{M}(x,\mathtt{t})].
\end{aligned} \tag{22}$$

After that, we have

$$M(\mathbf{J}) = u\mathbf{J}(0) + u^{\varsigma}Y[\mathcal{L}(x,\mathtt{t}) + \mathcal{M}(x,\mathtt{t})], \tag{23}$$

Operating the inverse YT, we have

$$\mathbf{J}(x,\mathtt{t}) = \mathbf{J}(0) + Y^{-1}[u^{\varsigma}Y[\mathcal{L}(x,\mathtt{t}) + \mathcal{M}(x,\mathtt{t})]. \tag{24}$$

The unknown function $\mathbf{J}(x,\mathtt{t})$ in terms of infinite series [37] is stated as

$$\mathbf{J}(x,\mathtt{t}) = \sum_{m=0}^{\infty} \mathbf{J}_m(x,\mathtt{t}). \tag{25}$$

Here, we illustrate the nonlinear term as

$$\mathcal{M}(x,\mathtt{t}) = \sum_{m=0}^{\infty} \mathcal{A}_m, \tag{26}$$

with

$$\mathcal{A}_m = \frac{1}{m!}\left[\frac{\partial^m}{\partial \ell^m}\left\{\mathcal{M}\left(\sum_{k=0}^{\infty} \ell^k x_k, \sum_{k=0}^{\infty} \ell^k \mathtt{t}_k\right)\right\}\right]_{\ell=0}. \tag{27}$$

Now, we substitute (25) and (26) into (24) to obtain

$$\sum_{m=0}^{\infty} \mathbf{J}_m(x,t) = \mathbf{J}(0) + Y^{-1}u^{\varsigma}\left[Y\left\{\mathcal{L}(\sum_{m=0}^{\infty} x_m, \sum_{m=0}^{\infty} t_m) + \sum_{m=0}^{\infty} \mathcal{A}_m\right\}\right]. \tag{28}$$

So, we obtain

$$\mathbf{J}_0(x,t) = \mathbf{J}(0), \tag{29}$$
$$\mathbf{J}_1(x,t) = Y^{-1}[u^{\varsigma}Y\{\mathcal{L}(x_0, t_0) + \mathcal{A}_0\}].$$

Finally, in general for $m \geq 1$, we have

$$\mathbf{J}_{m+1}(x,t) = Y^{-1}[u^{\varsigma}Y\{\mathcal{L}(x_m, t_m) + \mathcal{A}_m\}].$$

5. Application

Example 1. *Let us assume a fractional coupled KdV Equation (1) with* $\boldsymbol{a} = -\kappa, \boldsymbol{b} = -6\kappa$, $\boldsymbol{c} = 2\nu, \boldsymbol{d} = -\mu$, *and* $\boldsymbol{e} = 3\mu$, *having initial condition*

$$\mathbf{J}(x,0) = \frac{\zeta}{\kappa}\left(\operatorname{sech}\left(\frac{1}{2}\sqrt{\frac{\zeta}{\kappa}}x\right)\right)^2, \mathbf{K}(x,0) = \frac{\zeta}{\sqrt{2\kappa}}\left(\operatorname{sech}\left(\frac{1}{2}\sqrt{\frac{\zeta}{\kappa}}x\right)\right)^2.$$

Case I: Solution by HPTM

Computing the YT, we obtain

$$Y\left[\frac{\partial^{\varsigma}\mathbf{J}}{\partial t^{\varsigma}}\right] = Y\left[-\kappa\mathbf{J}_{xxx}(x,t) - 6\kappa\mathbf{J}(x,t)\mathbf{J}_x(x,t) + 2\nu\mathbf{K}(x,t)\mathbf{K}_x(x,t)\right],$$
$$Y\left[\frac{\partial^{\beta}\mathbf{K}}{\partial t^{\beta}}\right] = Y\left[-\mu\mathbf{J}_{xxx}(x,t) - 3\mu\mathbf{J}(x,t)\mathbf{K}_x(x,t)\right]. \tag{30}$$

After that, we have

$$\frac{1}{u^{\varsigma}}\{M(u) - u\mathbf{J}(0)\} = Y\left[-\kappa\mathbf{J}_{xxx}(x,t) - 6\kappa\mathbf{J}(x,t)\mathbf{J}_x(x,t) + 2\nu\mathbf{K}(x,t)\mathbf{K}_x(x,t)\right],$$
$$\frac{1}{u^{\beta}}\{M(u) - u\mathbf{K}(0)\} = Y\left[-\mu\mathbf{J}_{xxx}(x,t) - 3\mu\mathbf{J}(x,t)\mathbf{K}_x(x,t)\right], \tag{31}$$

$$M(u) = u\mathbf{J}(0) + u^{\varsigma}\left[-\kappa\mathbf{J}_{xxx}(x,t) - 6\kappa\mathbf{J}(x,t)\mathbf{J}_x(x,t) + 2\nu\mathbf{K}(x,t)\mathbf{K}_x(x,t)\right],$$
$$M(u) = u\mathbf{K}(0) + u^{\beta}\left[-\mu\mathbf{J}_{xxx}(x,t) - 3\mu\mathbf{J}(x,t)\mathbf{K}_x(x,t)\right]. \tag{32}$$

Operating the inverse YT, we have

$$\begin{aligned}
\mathbf{J}(x,t) &= \mathbf{J}(0) + \Upsilon^{-1}\left[u^{\varsigma}\left\{\Upsilon\left(-\kappa\mathbf{J}_{xxx}(x,t) - 6\kappa\mathbf{J}(x,t)\mathbf{J}_x(x,t) + 2\nu\mathbf{K}(x,t)\mathbf{K}_x(x,t)\right)\right\}\right],\\
\mathbf{K}(x,t) &= \mathbf{K}(0) + \Upsilon^{-1}\left[u^{\beta}\left\{\Upsilon\left(-\mu\mathbf{J}_{xxx}(x,t) - 3\mu\mathbf{J}(x,t)\mathbf{K}_x(x,t)\right)\right\}\right],\\
\mathbf{J}(x,t) &= \frac{\zeta}{\kappa}\left(\operatorname{sech}\left(\frac{1}{2}\sqrt{\frac{\zeta}{\kappa}}x\right)\right)^2 + \Upsilon^{-1}\left[u^{\varsigma}\left\{\Upsilon\left(-\kappa\mathbf{J}_{xxx}(x,t) - 6\kappa\mathbf{J}(x,t)\mathbf{J}_x(x,t) + 2\nu\mathbf{K}(x,t)\mathbf{K}_x(x,t)\right)\right\}\right],\\
\mathbf{K}(x,t) &= \frac{\zeta}{\sqrt{2\kappa}}\left(\operatorname{sech}\left(\frac{1}{2}\sqrt{\frac{\zeta}{\kappa}}x\right)\right)^2 + \Upsilon^{-1}\left[u^{\beta}\left\{\Upsilon\left(-\mu\mathbf{J}_{xxx}(x,t) - 3\mu\mathbf{J}(x,t)\mathbf{K}_x(x,t)\right)\right\}\right].
\end{aligned} \tag{33}$$

By means of the homotopy perturbation method, we have

$$\begin{aligned}
\sum_{k=0}^{\infty}\epsilon^k\mathbf{J}_k(x,t) &= \frac{\zeta}{\kappa}\left(\operatorname{sech}\left(\frac{1}{2}\sqrt{\frac{\zeta}{\kappa}}x\right)\right)^2 + \epsilon\left(\Upsilon^{-1}\left[u^{\varsigma}\Upsilon\left[-\kappa\left(\sum_{k=0}^{\infty}\epsilon^k\mathbf{J}_k(x,t)\right)_{xxx} - 6\kappa\left(\sum_{k=0}^{\infty}\epsilon^k H_k(x,t)\right) + \right.\right.\right.\\
&\left.\left.\left. 2\nu\left(\sum_{k=0}^{\infty}\epsilon^k H_k(x,t)\right)\right]\right]\right),\\
\sum_{k=0}^{\infty}\epsilon^k\mathbf{K}_k(x,t) &= \frac{\zeta}{\sqrt{2\kappa}}\left(\operatorname{sech}\left(\frac{1}{2}\sqrt{\frac{\zeta}{\kappa}}x\right)\right)^2 + \epsilon\left(\Upsilon^{-1}\left[u^{\beta}\Upsilon\left[-\mu\left(\sum_{k=0}^{\infty}\epsilon^k\mathbf{J}_k(x,t)\right)_{xxx} - 3\mu\left(\sum_{k=0}^{\infty}\epsilon^k H_k(x,t)\right)\right]\right]\right).
\end{aligned} \tag{34}$$

Equating the similar components of ϵ, we obtain

$$\begin{aligned}
\epsilon^0 &: \mathbf{J}_0(x,t) = \frac{\zeta}{\kappa}\left(\operatorname{sech}\left(\frac{1}{2}\sqrt{\frac{\zeta}{\kappa}}x\right)\right)^2,\\
\epsilon^0 &: \mathbf{K}_0(x,t) = \frac{\zeta}{\sqrt{2\kappa}}\left(\operatorname{sech}\left(\frac{1}{2}\sqrt{\frac{\zeta}{\kappa}}x\right)\right)^2,\\
\epsilon^1 &: \mathbf{J}_1(x,t) = \left(\frac{1}{2}\varsigma\left(\frac{\zeta}{\kappa}\right)^{\frac{3}{2}}\left(7 - 2\nu + \cosh\left(\sqrt{\frac{\zeta}{\kappa}}x\right)\right)\operatorname{sech}^4\left(\frac{1}{2}\sqrt{\frac{\zeta}{\kappa}}x\right)\tanh\left(\frac{1}{2}\sqrt{\frac{\zeta}{\kappa}}x\right)\right)\frac{t^{\varsigma}}{\Gamma(\varsigma+1)},\\
\epsilon^1 &: \mathbf{K}_1(x,t) = \left(4\sqrt{2}\sqrt{\kappa}\mu\left(\frac{\zeta}{\kappa}\right)^{\frac{5}{2}}\operatorname{csch}^3\left(\sqrt{\frac{\zeta}{\kappa}}x\right)\sinh^4\left(\frac{1}{2}\sqrt{\frac{\zeta}{\kappa}}x\right)\right)\frac{t^{\beta}}{\Gamma(\beta+1)},\\
\epsilon^2 &: \mathbf{J}_2(x,t) = \frac{t^{\varsigma}\zeta^4}{32\kappa^3\Gamma(2\varsigma+1)\Gamma(\varsigma+\beta+1)}\left(8\nu t^{\beta}\mu\left(2 + \cosh\left(\sqrt{\frac{\zeta}{\kappa}}x\right) - \cosh\left(2\sqrt{\frac{\zeta}{\kappa}}x\right)\right)\Gamma(2\varsigma+1)\right.\\
&\kappa t^{\varsigma}\left(40 - 32\nu + (-345 + 104\nu)\cosh\left(\sqrt{\frac{\zeta}{\kappa}}x\right) - 8(-15 + 4\nu)\cosh\left(2\sqrt{\frac{\zeta}{\kappa}}x\right) + \cosh\left(3\sqrt{\frac{\zeta}{\kappa}}x\right)\right)\\
&\left.\Gamma(\varsigma+\beta+1)\right)\operatorname{sech}^8\left(\frac{1}{2}\sqrt{\frac{\zeta}{\kappa}}x\right),\\
\epsilon^2 &: \mathbf{K}_2(x,t) = \frac{-1}{8\sqrt{\kappa}\kappa^{\frac{7}{2}}\Gamma(2\beta+1)\Gamma(\varsigma+\beta+1)}\left(\mu\zeta^4 t^{\beta}\operatorname{sech}\left(\frac{1}{2}\sqrt{\frac{\zeta}{\kappa}}x\right)\left(-\mu t^{\beta}\left(9 - 14\cosh\left(\sqrt{\frac{\zeta}{\kappa}}x\right) + \right.\right.\right.\\
&\left.\left.\left.\cosh\left(2\sqrt{\frac{\zeta}{\kappa}}x\right)\right)\Gamma(\varsigma+\beta+1) - 12\kappa t^{\varsigma}\left(7 - 2\nu + \cosh\left(\sqrt{\frac{\zeta}{\kappa}}x\right)\right)\Gamma(2\beta+1)\tanh^2\left(\frac{1}{2}\sqrt{\frac{\zeta}{\kappa}}x\right)\right)\right),\\
&\dots
\end{aligned}$$

The solution we obtained is taken in series form as

$$\mathbf{J}(x,t) = \mathbf{J}_0(x,t) + \mathbf{J}_1(x,t) + \mathbf{J}_2(x,t) + \cdots$$

$$\mathbf{J}(x,t) = \frac{\zeta}{\kappa}\left(\text{sech}\left(\frac{1}{2}\sqrt{\frac{\zeta}{\kappa}}x\right)\right)^2 + \left(\frac{1}{2}\varsigma\left(\frac{\zeta}{\kappa}\right)^{\frac{3}{2}}\left(7 - 2\nu + \cosh\left(\sqrt{\frac{\zeta}{\kappa}}x\right)\right)\text{sech}^4\left(\frac{1}{2}\sqrt{\frac{\zeta}{\kappa}}x\right)\right.$$
$$\left.\tanh\left(\frac{1}{2}\sqrt{\frac{\zeta}{\kappa}}x\right)\right)\frac{t^{\varsigma}}{\Gamma(\varsigma+1)} + \frac{t^{\varsigma}\zeta^4}{32\kappa^3\Gamma(2\varsigma+1)\Gamma(\varsigma+\beta+1)}\left(8\nu t^{\beta}\mu\left(2 + \cosh\left(\sqrt{\frac{\zeta}{\kappa}}x\right) - \cosh\left(2\sqrt{\frac{\zeta}{\kappa}}x\right)\right)\right.$$
$$\Gamma(2\varsigma+1)\kappa t^{\varsigma}\left(40 - 32\nu + (-345 + 104\nu)\cosh\left(\sqrt{\frac{\zeta}{\kappa}}x\right) - 8(-15 + 4\nu)\cosh\left(2\sqrt{\frac{\zeta}{\kappa}}x\right) + \cosh\left(3\sqrt{\frac{\zeta}{\kappa}}x\right)\right)$$
$$\left.\Gamma(\varsigma+\beta+1)\right)\text{sech}^8\left(\frac{1}{2}\sqrt{\frac{\zeta}{\kappa}}x\right) + \cdots$$

$$\mathbf{K}(x,t) = \mathbf{K}_0(x,t) + \mathbf{K}_1(x,t) + \mathbf{K}_2(x,t) + \cdots$$

$$\mathbf{K}(x,t) = \frac{\zeta}{\sqrt{2\kappa}}\left(\text{sech}\left(\frac{1}{2}\sqrt{\frac{\zeta}{\kappa}}x\right)\right)^2 + \left(4\sqrt{2}\sqrt{\kappa}\mu\left(\frac{\zeta}{\kappa}\right)^{\frac{5}{2}}\text{csch}^3\left(\sqrt{\frac{\zeta}{\kappa}}x\right)\sinh^4\left(\frac{1}{2}\sqrt{\frac{\zeta}{\kappa}}x\right)\right)\frac{t^{\beta}}{\Gamma(\beta+1)} +$$
$$\frac{-1}{8\sqrt{\kappa}\kappa^{\frac{7}{2}}\Gamma(2\beta+1)\Gamma(\varsigma+\beta+1)}\left(\mu\zeta^4 t^{\beta}\,\text{sech}\left(\frac{1}{2}\sqrt{\frac{\zeta}{\kappa}}x\right)\left(-\mu t^{\beta}\left(9 - 14\cosh\left(\sqrt{\frac{\zeta}{\kappa}}x\right) + \cosh\left(2\sqrt{\frac{\zeta}{\kappa}}x\right)\right)\right.\right.$$
$$\left.\left.\Gamma(\varsigma+\beta+1) - 12\kappa t^{\varsigma}\left(7 - 2\nu + \cosh\left(\sqrt{\frac{\zeta}{\kappa}}x\right)\right)\Gamma(2\beta+1)\tanh^2\left(\frac{1}{2}\sqrt{\frac{\zeta}{\kappa}}x\right)\right)\right) + \cdots$$

Case II: Solution by YTDM

Computing the YT, we obtain

$$\begin{aligned} Y\left[\frac{\partial^{\varsigma}\mathbf{J}}{\partial t^{\varsigma}}\right] &= Y\left[-\kappa\mathbf{J}_{xxx}(x,t) - 6\kappa\mathbf{J}(x,t)\mathbf{J}_x(x,t) + 2\nu\mathbf{K}(x,t)\mathbf{K}_x(x,t)\right], \\ Y\left[\frac{\partial^{\beta}\mathbf{K}}{\partial t^{\beta}}\right] &= Y\left[-\mu\mathbf{J}_{xxx}(x,t) - 3\mu\mathbf{J}(x,t)\mathbf{K}_x(x,t)\right]. \end{aligned} \tag{35}$$

After that, we have

$$\begin{aligned} \frac{1}{u^{\varsigma}}\{M(u) - u\mathbf{J}(0)\} &= Y\left[-\kappa\mathbf{J}_{xxx}(x,t) - 6\kappa\mathbf{J}(x,t)\mathbf{J}_x(x,t) + 2\nu\mathbf{K}(x,t)\mathbf{K}_x(x,t)\right], \\ \frac{1}{u^{\beta}}\{M(u) - u\mathbf{K}(0)\} &= Y\left[-\mu\mathbf{J}_{xxx}(x,t) - 3\mu\mathbf{J}(x,t)\mathbf{K}_x(x,t)\right], \end{aligned} \tag{36}$$

$$\begin{aligned} M(u) &= u\mathbf{J}(0) + u^{\varsigma}\left[-\kappa\mathbf{J}_{xxx}(x,t) - 6\kappa\mathbf{J}(x,t)\mathbf{J}_x(x,t) + 2\nu\mathbf{K}(x,t)\mathbf{K}_x(x,t)\right], \\ M(u) &= u\mathbf{K}(0) + u^{\beta}\left[-\mu\mathbf{J}_{xxx}(x,t) - 3\mu\mathbf{J}(x,t)\mathbf{K}_x(x,t)\right]. \end{aligned} \tag{37}$$

Operating the inverse YT, we have

$$\begin{aligned}
\mathbf{J}(x,t) &= \mathbf{J}(0) + Y^{-1}\left[u^{\varsigma}\left\{Y\left(-\kappa\mathbf{J}_{xxx}(x,t) - 6\kappa\mathbf{J}(x,t)\mathbf{J}_x(x,t) + 2\nu\mathbf{K}(x,t)\mathbf{K}_x(x,t)\right)\right\}\right],\\
\mathbf{K}(x,t) &= \mathbf{K}(0) + Y^{-1}\left[u^{\beta}\left\{Y\left(-\mu\mathbf{J}_{xxx}(x,t) - 3\mu\mathbf{J}(x,t)\mathbf{K}_x(x,t)\right)\right\}\right],\\
\mathbf{J}(x,t) &= \frac{\zeta}{\kappa}\left(\operatorname{sech}\left(\frac{1}{2}\sqrt{\frac{\zeta}{\kappa}}x\right)\right)^2 + Y^{-1}\left[u^{\varsigma}\left\{Y\left(-\kappa\mathbf{J}_{xxx}(x,t) - 6\kappa\mathbf{J}(x,t)\mathbf{J}_x(x,t) + 2\nu\mathbf{K}(x,t)\mathbf{K}_x(x,t)\right)\right\}\right],\\
\mathbf{K}(x,t) &= \frac{\zeta}{\sqrt{2\kappa}}\left(\operatorname{sech}\left(\frac{1}{2}\sqrt{\frac{\zeta}{\kappa}}x\right)\right)^2 + Y^{-1}\left[u^{\beta}\left\{Y\left(-\mu\mathbf{J}_{xxx}(x,t) - 3\mu\mathbf{J}(x,t)\mathbf{K}_x(x,t)\right)\right\}\right].
\end{aligned} \tag{38}$$

Thus, the required solution in terms of infinite series form is

$$\mathbf{J}(x,t) = \sum_{m=0}^{\infty}\mathbf{J}_m(x,t), \mathbf{K}(x,t) = \sum_{m=0}^{\infty}\mathbf{K}_m(x,t). \tag{39}$$

Assume the nonlinear terms by the Adomian polynomial as $\mathbf{J}(x,t)\mathbf{J}_x(x,t) = \sum_{m=0}^{\infty}\mathcal{A}_m, \mathbf{K}(x,t)$ $\mathbf{K}_x(x,t) = \sum_{m=0}^{\infty}\mathcal{B}_m, \mathbf{J}(x,t)\mathbf{K}_x(x,t) = \sum_{m=0}^{\infty}\mathcal{C}_m$. *So, we obtain*

$$\begin{aligned}
\sum_{m=0}^{\infty}\mathbf{J}_m(x,t) &= \mathbf{J}(x,0) + Y^{-1}\left[u^{\varsigma}Y\left[-\kappa\mathbf{J}_{xxx}(x,t) - 6\kappa\sum_{m=0}^{\infty}\mathcal{A}_m + 2\nu\sum_{m=0}^{\infty}\mathcal{B}_m\right]\right],\\
\sum_{m=0}^{\infty}\mathbf{K}_m(x,t) &= \mathbf{K}(x,0) + Y^{-1}\left[u^{\varsigma}Y\left[-\mu\mathbf{J}_{xxx}(x,t) - 3\mu\sum_{m=0}^{\infty}\mathcal{C}_m\right]\right],\\
\sum_{m=0}^{\infty}\mathbf{J}_m(x,t) &= \frac{\zeta}{\kappa}\left(\operatorname{sech}\left(\frac{1}{2}\sqrt{\frac{\zeta}{\kappa}}x\right)\right)^2 + Y^{-1}\left[u^{\varsigma}Y\left[-\kappa\mathbf{J}_{xxx}(x,t) - 6\kappa\sum_{m=0}^{\infty}\mathcal{A}_m + 2\nu\sum_{m=0}^{\infty}\mathcal{B}_m\right]\right],\\
\sum_{m=0}^{\infty}\mathbf{K}_m(x,t) &= \frac{\zeta}{\sqrt{2\kappa}}\left(\operatorname{sech}\left(\frac{1}{2}\sqrt{\frac{\zeta}{\kappa}}x\right)\right)^2 + Y^{-1}\left[u^{\varsigma}Y\left[-\mu\mathbf{J}_{xxx}(x,t) - 3\mu\sum_{m=0}^{\infty}\mathcal{C}_m\right]\right].
\end{aligned} \tag{40}$$

By equating both sides, we obtain

$$\mathbf{J}_0(x,t) = \frac{\zeta}{\kappa}\left(\operatorname{sech}\left(\frac{1}{2}\sqrt{\frac{\zeta}{\kappa}}x\right)\right)^2,$$

$$\mathbf{K}_0(x,t) = \frac{\zeta}{\sqrt{2\kappa}}\left(\operatorname{sech}\left(\frac{1}{2}\sqrt{\frac{\zeta}{\kappa}}x\right)\right)^2.$$

On $m = 0$

$$\mathbf{J}_1(x,t) = \left(\frac{1}{2}\zeta\left(\frac{\zeta}{\kappa}\right)^{\frac{3}{2}}\left(7 - 2\nu + \cosh\left(\sqrt{\frac{\zeta}{\kappa}}x\right)\right)\operatorname{sech}^4\left(\frac{1}{2}\sqrt{\frac{\zeta}{\kappa}}x\right)\tanh\left(\frac{1}{2}\sqrt{\frac{\zeta}{\kappa}}x\right)\right)\frac{t^{\varsigma}}{\Gamma(\varsigma+1)},$$

$$\mathbf{K}_1(x,t) = \left(4\sqrt{2}\sqrt{\kappa}\mu\left(\frac{\zeta}{\kappa}\right)^{\frac{5}{2}}\operatorname{csch}^3\left(\sqrt{\frac{\zeta}{\kappa}}x\right)\sinh^4\left(\frac{1}{2}\sqrt{\frac{\zeta}{\kappa}}x\right)\right)\frac{t^{\beta}}{\Gamma(\beta+1)}.$$

On $m=1$

$$\mathbf{J}_2(x,t)=\frac{t^{\varsigma}\zeta^4}{32\kappa^3\Gamma(2\varsigma+1)\Gamma(\varsigma+\beta+1)}\Bigg(8\nu t^{\beta}\mu\Bigg(2+\cosh\Bigg(\sqrt{\frac{\zeta}{\kappa}}x\Bigg)-\cosh\Bigg(2\sqrt{\frac{\zeta}{\kappa}}x\Bigg)\Bigg)\Gamma(2\varsigma+1)$$
$$\kappa t^{\varsigma}\Bigg(40-32\nu+(-345+104\nu)\cosh\Bigg(\sqrt{\frac{\zeta}{\kappa}}x\Bigg)-8(-15+4\nu)\cosh\Bigg(2\sqrt{\frac{\zeta}{\kappa}}x\Bigg)+\cosh\Bigg(3\sqrt{\frac{\zeta}{\kappa}}x\Bigg)\Bigg)$$
$$\Gamma(\varsigma+\beta+1)\Bigg)\operatorname{sech}^8\Bigg(\frac{1}{2}\sqrt{\frac{\zeta}{\kappa}}x\Bigg),$$

$$\mathbf{K}_2(x,t)=\frac{-1}{8\sqrt{\kappa}\kappa^{\frac{7}{2}}\Gamma(2\beta+1)\Gamma(\varsigma+\beta+1)}\Bigg(\mu\zeta^4t^{\beta}\operatorname{sech}\Bigg(\frac{1}{2}\sqrt{\frac{\zeta}{\kappa}}x\Bigg)\Bigg(-\mu t^{\beta}\Bigg(9-14\cosh\Bigg(\sqrt{\frac{\zeta}{\kappa}}x\Bigg)+$$
$$\cosh\Bigg(2\sqrt{\frac{\zeta}{\kappa}}x\Bigg)\Bigg)\Gamma(\varsigma+\beta+1)-12\kappa t^{\varsigma}\Bigg(7-2\nu+\cosh\Bigg(\sqrt{\frac{\zeta}{\kappa}}x\Bigg)\Bigg)\Gamma(2\beta+1)\tanh^2\Bigg(\frac{1}{2}\sqrt{\frac{\zeta}{\kappa}}x\Bigg)\Bigg)\Bigg).$$

In this manner, we can easily obtain the other terms for $(m\geq 3)$, *so*

$$\mathbf{J}(x,t)=\mathbf{J}_0(x,t)+\mathbf{J}_1(x,t)+\mathbf{J}_2(x,t)+\cdots$$
$$\mathbf{J}(x,t)=\frac{\zeta}{\kappa}\Bigg(\operatorname{sech}\Bigg(\frac{1}{2}\sqrt{\frac{\zeta}{\kappa}}x\Bigg)\Bigg)^2+\Bigg(\frac{1}{2}\zeta\Bigg(\frac{\zeta}{\kappa}\Bigg)^{\frac{3}{2}}\Bigg(7-2\nu+\cosh\Bigg(\sqrt{\frac{\zeta}{\kappa}}x\Bigg)\Bigg)\operatorname{sech}^4\Bigg(\frac{1}{2}\sqrt{\frac{\zeta}{\kappa}}x\Bigg)$$
$$\tanh\Bigg(\frac{1}{2}\sqrt{\frac{\zeta}{\kappa}}x\Bigg)\Bigg)\frac{t^{\varsigma}}{\Gamma(\varsigma+1)}+\frac{t^{\varsigma}\zeta^4}{32\kappa^3\Gamma(2\varsigma+1)\Gamma(\varsigma+\beta+1)}\Bigg(8\nu t^{\beta}\mu\Bigg(2+\cosh\Bigg(\sqrt{\frac{\zeta}{\kappa}}x\Bigg)-\cosh\Bigg(2\sqrt{\frac{\zeta}{\kappa}}x\Bigg)\Bigg)$$
$$\Gamma(2\varsigma+1)\kappa t^{\varsigma}\Bigg(40-32\nu+(-345+104\nu)\cosh\Bigg(\sqrt{\frac{\zeta}{\kappa}}x\Bigg)-8(-15+4\nu)\cosh\Bigg(2\sqrt{\frac{\zeta}{\kappa}}x\Bigg)+\cosh\Bigg(3\sqrt{\frac{\zeta}{\kappa}}x\Bigg)\Bigg)$$
$$\Gamma(\varsigma+\beta+1)\Bigg)\operatorname{sech}^8\Bigg(\frac{1}{2}\sqrt{\frac{\zeta}{\kappa}}x\Bigg)+\cdots$$
$$\mathbf{K}(x,t)=\mathbf{K}_0(x,t)+\mathbf{K}_1(x,t)+\mathbf{K}_2(x,t)+\cdots$$
$$\mathbf{K}(x,t)=\frac{\zeta}{\sqrt{2\kappa}}\Bigg(\operatorname{sech}\Bigg(\frac{1}{2}\sqrt{\frac{\zeta}{\kappa}}x\Bigg)\Bigg)^2+\Bigg(4\sqrt{2}\sqrt{\kappa}\mu\Bigg(\frac{\zeta}{\kappa}\Bigg)^{\frac{5}{2}}\operatorname{csch}^3\Bigg(\sqrt{\frac{\zeta}{\kappa}}x\Bigg)\sinh^4\Bigg(\frac{1}{2}\sqrt{\frac{\zeta}{\kappa}}x\Bigg)\Bigg)\frac{t^{\beta}}{\Gamma(\beta+1)}+$$
$$\frac{-1}{8\sqrt{\kappa}\kappa^{\frac{7}{2}}\Gamma(2\beta+1)\Gamma(\varsigma+\beta+1)}\Bigg(\mu\zeta^4t^{\beta}\operatorname{sech}\Bigg(\frac{1}{2}\sqrt{\frac{\zeta}{\kappa}}x\Bigg)\Bigg(-\mu t^{\beta}\Bigg(9-14\cosh\Bigg(\sqrt{\frac{\zeta}{\kappa}}x\Bigg)+\cosh\Bigg(2\sqrt{\frac{\zeta}{\kappa}}x\Bigg)\Bigg)$$
$$\Gamma(\varsigma+\beta+1)-12\kappa t^{\varsigma}\Bigg(7-2\nu+\cosh\Bigg(\sqrt{\frac{\zeta}{\kappa}}x\Bigg)\Bigg)\Gamma(2\beta+1)\tanh^2\Bigg(\frac{1}{2}\sqrt{\frac{\zeta}{\kappa}}x\Bigg)\Bigg)\Bigg)+\cdots$$

Inserting $\varsigma=\beta=1$, *we have*

$$\mathbf{J}(x,t)=\frac{\zeta}{\kappa}\Bigg(\operatorname{sech}\Bigg(\frac{1}{2}\sqrt{\frac{\zeta}{\kappa}}(x-\zeta t)\Bigg)\Bigg)^2,\ \mathbf{K}(x,t)=\frac{\zeta}{\sqrt{2\kappa}}\Bigg(\operatorname{sech}\Bigg(\frac{1}{2}\sqrt{\frac{\zeta}{\kappa}}(x-\zeta t)\Bigg)\Bigg)^2. \tag{41}$$

Example 2. *Let us assume fractional coupled KdV Equation (1) with* $\boldsymbol{a}=-1,\boldsymbol{b}=-6,\boldsymbol{c}=3$, $\boldsymbol{d}=-1$, *and* $\boldsymbol{e}=3$, *having initial condition*

$$\mathbf{J}(x,0)=\frac{4\varrho^2e^{\varrho x}}{(1+e^{\varrho x})^2},\mathbf{K}(x,0)=\frac{4\varrho^2e^{\varrho x}}{(1+e^{\varrho x})^2}.$$

Case I: Solution by HPTM

Computing the YT, we obtain

$$\begin{aligned} Y\left[\frac{\partial^{\varsigma}\mathbf{J}}{\partial t^{\varsigma}}\right] &= Y\left[-\mathbf{J}_{xxx}(x,t) - 6\mathbf{J}(x,t)\mathbf{J}_{x}(x,t) + 3\mathbf{K}(x,t)\mathbf{K}_{x}(x,t)\right], \\ Y\left[\frac{\partial^{\beta}\mathbf{K}}{\partial t^{\beta}}\right] &= Y\left[-\mathbf{J}_{xxx}(x,t) - 3\mathbf{J}(x,t)\mathbf{K}_{x}(x,t)\right]. \end{aligned} \tag{42}$$

After that, we have

$$\begin{aligned} \frac{1}{u^{\varsigma}}\{M(u) - u\mathbf{J}(0)\} &= Y\left[-\mathbf{J}_{xxx}(x,t) - 6\mathbf{J}(x,t)\mathbf{J}_{x}(x,t) + 3\mathbf{K}(x,t)\mathbf{K}_{x}(x,t)\right], \\ \frac{1}{u^{\beta}}\{M(u) - u\mathbf{K}(0)\} &= Y\left[-\mathbf{J}_{xxx}(x,t) - 3\mathbf{J}(x,t)\mathbf{K}_{x}(x,t)\right], \end{aligned} \tag{43}$$

$$\begin{aligned} M(u) &= u\mathbf{J}(0) + u^{\varsigma}\left[-\mathbf{J}_{xxx}(x,t) - 6\mathbf{J}(x,t)\mathbf{J}_{x}(x,t) + 3\mathbf{K}(x,t)\mathbf{K}_{x}(x,t)\right], \\ M(u) &= u\mathbf{K}(0) + u^{\beta}\left[-\mathbf{J}_{xxx}(x,t) - 3\mathbf{J}(x,t)\mathbf{K}_{x}(x,t)\right]. \end{aligned} \tag{44}$$

Operating the inverse YT, we have

$$\begin{aligned} \mathbf{J}(x,t) &= \mathbf{J}(0) + Y^{-1}\left[u^{\varsigma}\left\{Y\left(-\mathbf{J}_{xxx}(x,t) - 6\mathbf{J}(x,t)\mathbf{J}_{x}(x,t) + 3\mathbf{K}(x,t)\mathbf{K}_{x}(x,t)\right)\right\}\right], \\ \mathbf{K}(x,t) &= \mathbf{K}(0) + Y^{-1}\left[u^{\beta}\left\{Y\left(-\mathbf{J}_{xxx}(x,t) - 3\mathbf{J}(x,t)\mathbf{K}_{x}(x,t)\right)\right\}\right], \\ \mathbf{J}(x,t) &= \frac{4\varrho^{2}e^{\varrho x}}{(1+e^{\varrho x})^{2}} + Y^{-1}\left[u^{\varsigma}\left\{Y\left(-\mathbf{J}_{xxx}(x,t) - 6\mathbf{J}(x,t)\mathbf{J}_{x}(x,t) + 3\mathbf{K}(x,t)\mathbf{K}_{x}(x,t)\right)\right\}\right], \\ \mathbf{K}(x,t) &= \frac{4\varrho^{2}e^{\varrho x}}{(1+e^{\varrho x})^{2}} + Y^{-1}\left[u^{\beta}\left\{Y\left(-\mathbf{J}_{xxx}(x,t) - 3\mathbf{J}(x,t)\mathbf{K}_{x}(x,t)\right)\right\}\right]. \end{aligned} \tag{45}$$

By means of the homotopy perturbation method, we have

$$\begin{aligned} \sum_{k=0}^{\infty}\epsilon^{k}\mathbf{J}_{k}(x,t) &= \frac{4\varrho^{2}e^{\varrho x}}{(1+e^{\varrho x})^{2}} + \epsilon\left(Y^{-1}\left[u^{\varsigma}Y\left[-\left(\sum_{k=0}^{\infty}\epsilon^{k}\mathbf{J}_{k}(x,t)\right)_{xxx} - 6\left(\sum_{k=0}^{\infty}\epsilon^{k}H_{k}(x,t)\right) + \right.\right.\right. \\ &\left.\left.\left. 3\left(\sum_{k=0}^{\infty}\epsilon^{k}H_{k}(x,t)\right)\right]\right]\right), \\ \sum_{k=0}^{\infty}\epsilon^{k}\mathbf{K}_{k}(x,t) &= \frac{4\varrho^{2}e^{\varrho x}}{(1+e^{\varrho x})^{2}} + \epsilon\left(Y^{-1}\left[u^{\beta}Y\left[-\left(\sum_{k=0}^{\infty}\epsilon^{k}\mathbf{J}_{k}(x,t)\right)_{xxx} - 3\left(\sum_{k=0}^{\infty}\epsilon^{k}H_{k}(x,t)\right)\right]\right]\right). \end{aligned} \tag{46}$$

Equating the similar components of ϵ, we obtain

$$\epsilon^0 : \mathbf{J}_0(x,t) = \frac{4\varrho^2 e^{\varrho x}}{(1+e^{\varrho x})^2},$$
$$\epsilon^0 : \mathbf{K}_0(x,t) = \frac{4\varrho^2 e^{\varrho x}}{(1+e^{\varrho x})^2},$$
$$\epsilon^1 : \mathbf{J}_1(x,t) = \left(\frac{4\varrho^5 e^{\varrho x}(-1+e^{\varrho x})}{(1+e^{\varrho x})^3}\right)\frac{t^{\varsigma}}{\Gamma(\varsigma+1)},$$
$$\epsilon^1 : \mathbf{K}_1(x,t) = \left(\frac{4\varrho^5 e^{\varrho x}(-1+e^{\varrho x})}{(1+e^{\varrho x})^3}\right)\frac{t^{\beta}}{\Gamma(\beta+1)},$$
$$\epsilon^2 : \mathbf{J}_2(x,t) = \frac{1}{(1+e^{\varrho x})^6\Gamma(2\varsigma+1)\Gamma(\varsigma+\beta+1)}\Bigg(4\varrho^8 e^{\varrho x} t^{\varsigma}\Bigg(-24e^{\varrho x}(1-3e^{\varrho x}+e^{2\varrho x})\,t^{\beta}\Gamma(2\varsigma+1)+$$
$$(1+22e^{\varrho x}-78e^{2\varrho x}+22e^{3\varrho x}+e^{4\varrho x})\,t^{\varsigma}\Gamma(\varsigma+\beta+1)\Bigg)\Bigg),$$
$$\epsilon^2 : \mathbf{K}_2(x,t) = \frac{1}{(1+e^{\varrho x})^6\Gamma(2\beta+1)\Gamma(\varsigma+\beta+1)}\Bigg(4\varrho^8 e^{\varrho x} t^{\beta}\Bigg((1-14e^{\varrho x}+18e^{2\varrho x}-14e^{3\varrho x}+e^{4\varrho x})\,t^{\beta}$$
$$\Gamma(\varsigma+\beta+1)+12e^{\varrho x}(1+e^{\varrho x})^2 t^{\varsigma}\Gamma(2\beta+1)\Bigg)\Bigg),$$
$$\cdots$$

The solution we obtained is taken in series form as

$$\mathbf{J}(x,t) = \mathbf{J}_0(x,t) + \mathbf{J}_1(x,t) + \mathbf{J}_2(x,t) + \cdots$$
$$\mathbf{J}(x,t) = \frac{4\varrho^2 e^{\varrho x}}{(1+e^{\varrho x})^2} + \left(\frac{4\varrho^5 e^{\varrho x}(-1+e^{\varrho x})}{(1+e^{\varrho x})^3}\right)\frac{t^{\varsigma}}{\Gamma(\varsigma+1)} + \frac{1}{(1+e^{\varrho x})^6\Gamma(2\varsigma+1)\Gamma(\varsigma+\beta+1)}\Bigg(4\varrho^8 e^{\varrho x} t^{\varsigma}$$
$$\Bigg(-24e^{\varrho x}(1-3e^{\varrho x}+e^{2\varrho x})\,t^{\beta}\Gamma(2\varsigma+1) + (1+22e^{\varrho x}-78e^{2\varrho x}+22e^{3\varrho x}+e^{4\varrho x})\,t^{\varsigma}\Gamma(\varsigma+\beta+1)\Bigg)\Bigg) + \cdots$$
$$\mathbf{K}(x,t) = \mathbf{K}_0(x,t) + \mathbf{K}_1(x,t) + \mathbf{K}_2(x,t) + \cdots$$
$$\mathbf{K}(x,t) = \frac{4\varrho^2 e^{\varrho x}}{(1+e^{\varrho x})^2} + \left(\frac{4\varrho^5 e^{\varrho x}(-1+e^{\varrho x})}{(1+e^{\varrho x})^3}\right)\frac{t^{\beta}}{\Gamma(\beta+1)} + \frac{1}{(1+e^{\varrho x})^6\Gamma(2\beta+1)\Gamma(\varsigma+\beta+1)}\Bigg(4\varrho^8 e^{\varrho x} t^{\beta}$$
$$\Bigg((1-14e^{\varrho x}+18e^{2\varrho x}-14e^{3\varrho x}+e^{4\varrho x})\,t^{\beta}\Gamma(\varsigma+\beta+1) + 12e^{\varrho x}(1+e^{\varrho x})^2 t^{\varsigma}\Gamma(2\beta+1)\Bigg)\Bigg) + \cdots$$

Case II: Solution by YTDM
Computing the YT, we obtain

$$Y\left[\frac{\partial^{\varsigma}\mathbf{J}}{\partial t^{\varsigma}}\right] = Y\Big[-\mathbf{J}_{xxx}(x,t) - 6\mathbf{J}(x,t)\mathbf{J}_x(x,t) + 3\mathbf{K}(x,t)\mathbf{K}_x(x,t)\Big],$$
$$Y\left[\frac{\partial^{\beta}\mathbf{K}}{\partial t^{\beta}}\right] = Y\Big[-\mathbf{J}_{xxx}(x,t) - 3\mathbf{J}(x,t)\mathbf{K}_x(x,t)\Big]. \tag{47}$$

After that, we have

$$
\begin{aligned}
&\frac{1}{u^{\varsigma}}\{M(u)-u\mathbf{J}(0)\}=Y\Big[-\mathbf{J}_{xxx}(x,t)-6\mathbf{J}(x,t)\mathbf{J}_x(x,t)+3\mathbf{K}(x,t)\mathbf{K}_x(x,t)\Big],\\
&\frac{1}{u^{\beta}}\{M(u)-u\mathbf{K}(0)\}=Y\Big[-\mathbf{J}_{xxx}(x,t)-3\mathbf{J}(x,t)\mathbf{K}_x(x,t)\Big],
\end{aligned}
\tag{48}
$$

$$
\begin{aligned}
M(u)&=u\mathbf{J}(0)+u^{\varsigma}\Big[-\mathbf{J}_{xxx}(x,t)-6\mathbf{J}(x,t)\mathbf{J}_x(x,t)+3\mathbf{K}(x,t)\mathbf{K}_x(x,t)\Big],\\
M(u)&=u\mathbf{K}(0)+u^{\beta}\Big[-\mathbf{J}_{xxx}(x,t)-3\mathbf{J}(x,t)\mathbf{K}_x(x,t)\Big].
\end{aligned}
\tag{49}
$$

Operating the inverse YT, we have

$$
\begin{aligned}
\mathbf{J}(x,t)&=\mathbf{J}(0)+Y^{-1}\Big[u^{\varsigma}\Big\{Y\Big(-\mathbf{J}_{xxx}(x,t)-6\mathbf{J}(x,t)\mathbf{J}_x(x,t)+3\mathbf{K}(x,t)\mathbf{K}_x(x,t)\Big)\Big\}\Big],\\
\mathbf{K}(x,t)&=\mathbf{K}(0)+Y^{-1}\Big[u^{\beta}\Big\{Y\Big(-\mathbf{J}_{xxx}(x,t)-3\mathbf{J}(x,t)\mathbf{K}_x(x,t)\Big)\Big\}\Big],\\
\mathbf{J}(x,t)&=\frac{4\varrho^2e^{\varrho x}}{(1+e^{\varrho x})^2}+Y^{-1}\Big[u^{\varsigma}\Big\{Y\Big(-\mathbf{J}_{xxx}(x,t)-6\mathbf{J}(x,t)\mathbf{J}_x(x,t)+3\mathbf{K}(x,t)\mathbf{K}_x(x,t)\Big)\Big\}\Big],\\
\mathbf{K}(x,t)&=\frac{4\varrho^2e^{\varrho x}}{(1+e^{\varrho x})^2}+Y^{-1}\Big[u^{\beta}\Big\{Y\Big(-\mathbf{J}_{xxx}(x,t)-3\mathbf{J}(x,t)\mathbf{K}_x(x,t)\Big)\Big\}\Big].
\end{aligned}
\tag{50}
$$

Thus, the required solution in terms of infinite series form is

$$
\mathbf{J}(x,t)=\sum_{m=0}^{\infty}\mathbf{J}_m(x,t),\mathbf{K}(x,t)=\sum_{m=0}^{\infty}\mathbf{K}_m(x,t). \tag{51}
$$

Assume the nonlinear terms by the Adomian polynomial as $\mathbf{J}(x,t)\mathbf{J}_x(x,t)=\sum_{m=0}^{\infty}\mathcal{A}_m,\mathbf{K}(x,t)\mathbf{K}_x(x,t)=\sum_{m=0}^{\infty}\mathcal{B}_m,\mathbf{J}(x,t)\mathbf{K}_x(x,t)=\sum_{m=0}^{\infty}\mathcal{C}_m$. *So, we get*

$$
\begin{aligned}
\sum_{m=0}^{\infty}\mathbf{J}_m(x,t)&=\mathbf{J}(x,0)+Y^{-1}\Big[u^{\varsigma}Y\Big[-\mathbf{J}_{xxx}(x,t)-6\sum_{m=0}^{\infty}\mathcal{A}_m+3\sum_{m=0}^{\infty}\mathcal{B}_m\Big]\Big],\\
\sum_{m=0}^{\infty}\mathbf{K}_m(x,t)&=\mathbf{K}(x,0)+Y^{-1}\Big[u^{\varsigma}Y\Big[-\mathbf{J}_{xxx}(x,t)-3\sum_{m=0}^{\infty}\mathcal{C}_m\Big]\Big],\\
\sum_{m=0}^{\infty}\mathbf{J}_m(x,t)&=\frac{4\varrho^2e^{\varrho x}}{(1+e^{\varrho x})^2}+Y^{-1}\Big[u^{\varsigma}Y\Big[-\mathbf{J}_{xxx}(x,t)-6\sum_{m=0}^{\infty}\mathcal{A}_m+3\sum_{m=0}^{\infty}\mathcal{B}_m\Big]\Big],\\
\sum_{m=0}^{\infty}\mathbf{K}_m(x,t)&=\frac{4\varrho^2e^{\varrho x}}{(1+e^{\varrho x})^2}+Y^{-1}\Big[u^{\varsigma}Y\Big[-\mathbf{J}_{xxx}(x,t)-3\sum_{m=0}^{\infty}\mathcal{C}_m\Big]\Big].
\end{aligned}
\tag{52}
$$

By equating both sides, we obtain

$$
\mathbf{J}_0(x,t)=\frac{4\varrho^2e^{\varrho x}}{(1+e^{\varrho x})^2},
$$

$$
\mathbf{K}_0(x,t)=\frac{4\varrho^2e^{\varrho x}}{(1+e^{\varrho x})^2}.
$$

On $m = 0$

$$\mathbf{J}_1(x,t) = \left(\frac{4\varrho^5 e^{\varrho x}(-1+e^{\varrho x})}{(1+e^{\varrho x})^3}\right)\frac{t^{\varsigma}}{\Gamma(\varsigma+1)},$$

$$\mathbf{K}_1(x,t) = \left(\frac{4\varrho^5 e^{\varrho x}(-1+e^{\varrho x})}{(1+e^{\varrho x})^3}\right)\frac{t^{\beta}}{\Gamma(\beta+1)}.$$

On $m = 1$

$$\mathbf{J}_2(x,t) = \frac{1}{(1+e^{\varrho x})^6\Gamma(2\varsigma+1)\Gamma(\varsigma+\beta+1)}\Bigg(4\varrho^8 e^{\varrho x} t^{\varsigma}\Bigg(-24e^{\varrho x}(1-3e^{\varrho x}+e^{2\varrho x})\,t^{\beta}\Gamma(2\varsigma+1)+$$
$$(1+22e^{\varrho x}-78e^{2\varrho x}+22e^{3\varrho x}+e^{4\varrho x})\,t^{\varsigma}\Gamma(\varsigma+\beta+1)\Bigg)\Bigg),$$

$$\mathbf{K}_2(x,t) = \frac{1}{(1+e^{\varrho x})^6\Gamma(2\beta+1)\Gamma(\varsigma+\beta+1)}\Bigg(4\varrho^8 e^{\varrho x} t^{\beta}\Bigg((1-14e^{\varrho x}+18e^{2\varrho x}-14e^{3\varrho x}+e^{4\varrho x})\,t^{\beta}$$
$$\Gamma(\varsigma+\beta+1)+12e^{\varrho x}(1+e^{\varrho x})^2 t^{\varsigma}\Gamma(2\beta+1)\Bigg)\Bigg).$$

In this manner, we can easily obtain the other terms for $(m \geq 3)$, *so*

$$\mathbf{J}(x,t) = \mathbf{J}_0(x,t) + \mathbf{J}_1(x,t) + \mathbf{J}_2(x,t) + \cdots$$
$$\mathbf{J}(x,t) = \frac{4\varrho^2 e^{\varrho x}}{(1+e^{\varrho x})^2} + \left(\frac{4\varrho^5 e^{\varrho x}(-1+e^{\varrho x})}{(1+e^{\varrho x})^3}\right)\frac{t^{\varsigma}}{\Gamma(\varsigma+1)} + \frac{1}{(1+e^{\varrho x})^6\Gamma(2\varsigma+1)\Gamma(\varsigma+\beta+1)}\Bigg(4\varrho^8 e^{\varrho x} t^{\varsigma}$$
$$\Bigg(-24e^{\varrho x}(1-3e^{\varrho x}+e^{2\varrho x})\,t^{\beta}\Gamma(2\varsigma+1) + (1+22e^{\varrho x}-78e^{2\varrho x}+22e^{3\varrho x}+e^{4\varrho x})\,t^{\varsigma}\Gamma(\varsigma+\beta+1)\Bigg)\Bigg)+\cdots$$
$$\mathbf{K}(x,t) = \mathbf{K}_0(x,t) + \mathbf{K}_1(x,t) + \mathbf{K}_2(x,t) + \cdots$$
$$\mathbf{K}(x,t) = \frac{4\varrho^2 e^{\varrho x}}{(1+e^{\varrho x})^2} + \left(\frac{4\varrho^5 e^{\varrho x}(-1+e^{\varrho x})}{(1+e^{\varrho x})^3}\right)\frac{t^{\beta}}{\Gamma(\beta+1)} + \frac{1}{(1+e^{\varrho x})^6\Gamma(2\beta+1)\Gamma(\varsigma+\beta+1)}\Bigg(4\varrho^8 e^{\varrho x} t^{\beta}$$
$$\Bigg((1-14e^{\varrho x}+18e^{2\varrho x}-14e^{3\varrho x}+e^{4\varrho x})\,t^{\beta}\Gamma(\varsigma+\beta+1) + 12e^{\varrho x}(1+e^{\varrho x})^2 t^{\varsigma}\Gamma(2\beta+1)\Bigg)\Bigg)+\cdots$$

Inserting $\varsigma = \beta = 1$ *we have*

$$\mathbf{J}(x,t) = \mathbf{K}(x,t) = \frac{4\varrho^2 e^{\varrho(x-\varrho^2 t)}}{(1+e^{\varrho(x-\varrho^2 t)})^2}. \quad (53)$$

6. Results Discussion

The graphical and numerical analysis presented in this section offers valuable insights into the behavior and accuracy of our proposed solution method for the coupled Korteweg-de Vries (KdV) equations. Figure 1a depict the behavior of the exact solution and Figure 1b depict the behavior of our approaches solution for $\mathbf{J}(x,t)$ at $\varsigma = 1$. Figure 2a,b show the outcomes of suggested techniques at different orders of $\varsigma = 0.80, 0.60$. The graphs in Figure 3a,b illustrate the nature of the precise and proposed approaches solution for $\mathbf{K}(x,t)$ at $\varsigma = 1$ at $\varsigma = 1$. The approximate solutions using the suggested methods are depicted in Figure 4 in both 3D and 2D graphs, with distinct values of fractional order $\varsigma = 0.40$, 0.60, 0.80, 1. Table 1 displays the accurate and proposed methods estimated solution at various values of ς for $\mathbf{J}(x,t)$. Table 2 displays the accurate and proposed methods estimated solution at various values of ς for $\mathbf{K}(x,t)$. Figure 5a depict the behavior of the exact solution and Figure 5b depict the behavior of our approaches solution for $\mathbf{J}(x, \mathrm{t})$ and $\mathbf{K}(x, \mathrm{t})$ at $\varsigma = 1$. Figure 6a,b explore the behavior of our approaches solutions at different orders of $\varsigma = 0.80, 0.60$ for $\mathbf{J}(x, \mathrm{t})$ and $\mathbf{K}(x, \mathrm{t})$. Similarly, Figure 7a,b show the outcomes of suggested techniques through 3D and 2D graphs, with distinct values of fractional order $\varsigma = 0.40, 0.60, 0.80, 1$. Table 3 displays the accurate and proposed methods estimated solution at various values of ς for $\mathbf{J}(x, \mathrm{t})$. In summary, our graphical and numerical analysis demonstrates the effectiveness of our proposed methods in approximating the solutions of coupled KdV equations. It has been proven that the suggested approaches are the most effective means of resolving FPDEs.

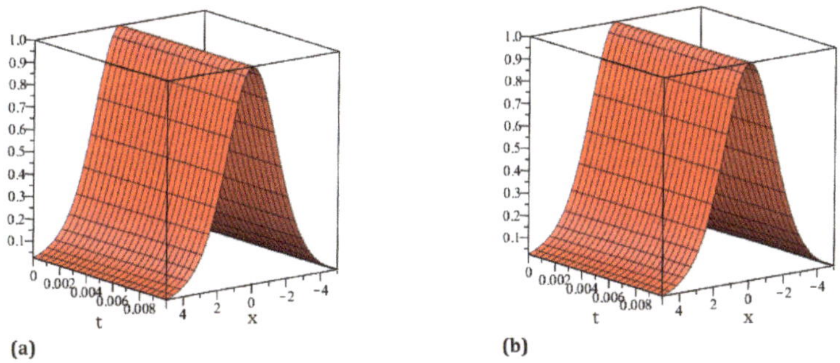

Figure 1. Graph (**a**) demonstrating the accurate solution, (**b**) demonstrating our technique's solution for $\mathbf{J}(x, \mathrm{t})$.

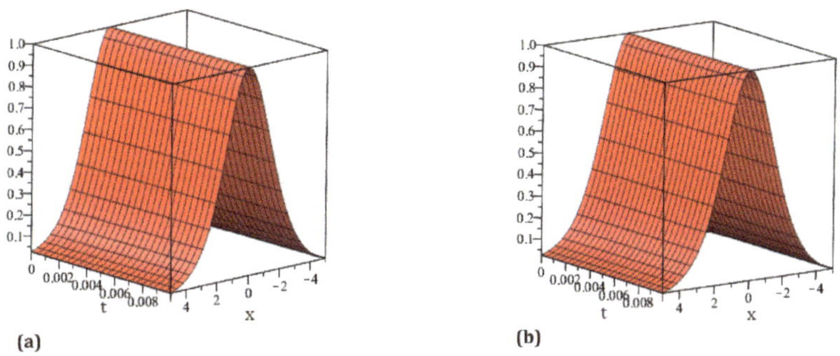

Figure 2. Graph (**a**) demonstrating our solution at $\varsigma = 0.8$, (**b**) demonstrating our solution at $\varsigma = 0.6$ for $\mathbf{J}(x, \mathrm{t})$.

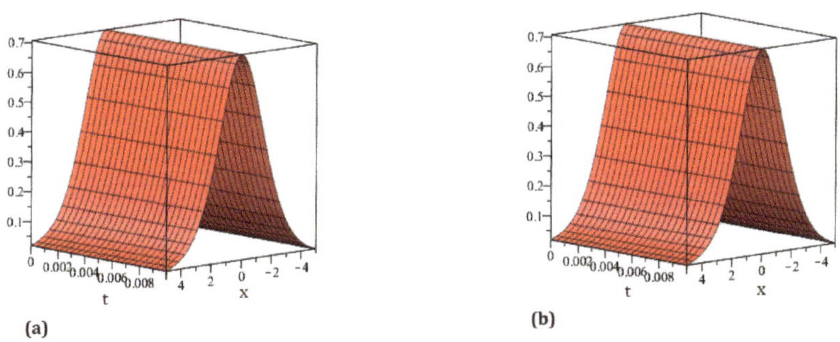

Figure 3. Graph (**a**) demonstrating the accurate solution, (**b**) demonstrating our technique's solution for $\mathbf{K}(x, \mathrm{t})$.

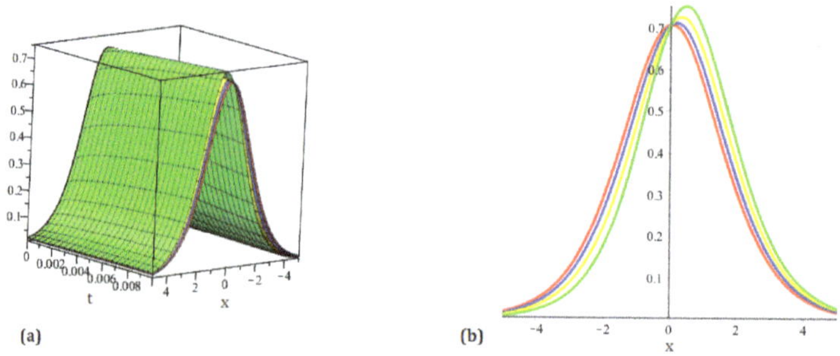

Figure 4. Graph demonstrating our technique's solution for various order of ς for $\mathbf{K}(x, \mathtt{t})$.

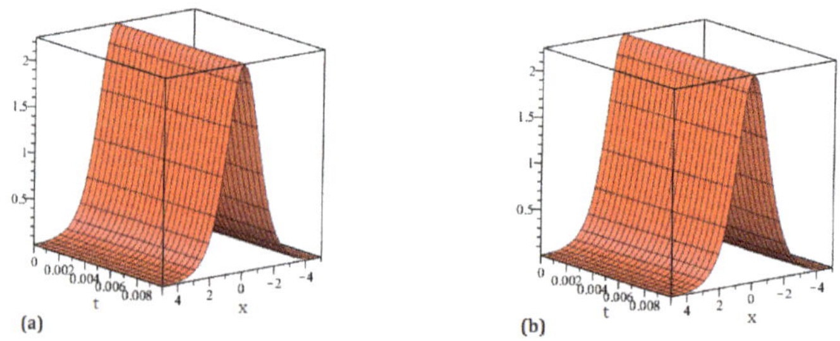

Figure 5. Graph (**a**) demonstrating the accurate solution, (**b**) demonstrating our technique's solution for $\mathbf{J}(x, \mathtt{t})$ and $\mathbf{K}(x, \mathtt{t})$.

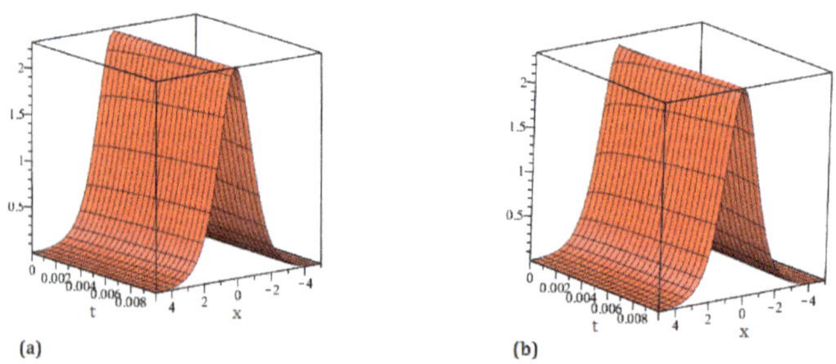

Figure 6. Graph (**a**) demonstrating our solution at $\varsigma = 0.8$, (**b**) demonstrating our solution at $\varsigma = 0.6$ for $\mathbf{J}(x, \mathtt{t})$ and $\mathbf{K}(x, \mathtt{t})$.

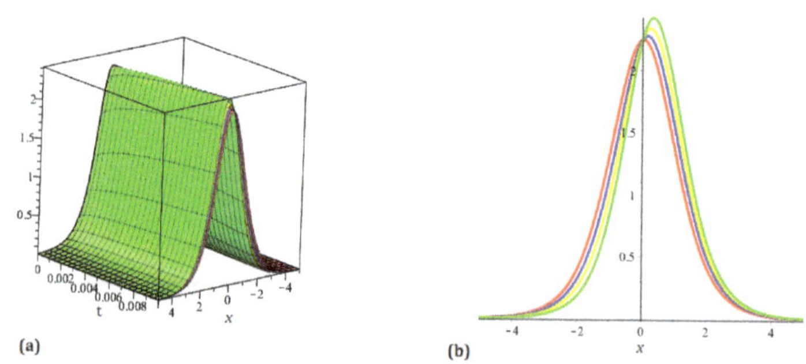

Figure 7. Graph demonstrating our technique's solution various order of ς for $\mathbf{J}(x, \mathtt{t})$ and $\mathbf{K}(x, \mathtt{t})$.

Table 1. Analysis of the exact and our technique's solution at numerous orders of ς for $\mathbf{J}(x, t)$.

ς	$\varsigma = 0.85$	$\varsigma = 0.90$	$\varsigma = 0.95$	$\varsigma = 1\ (Appro)$	$\varsigma = 1\ (Exact)$
0.0	1.00000000	1.00000000	1.00000000	1.00000000	0.99999975
0.1	0.99765268	0.99760754	0.99757599	0.99755399	0.99755374
0.2	0.99036039	0.99027100	0.99020853	0.99016496	0.99016472
0.3	0.97826716	0.97813527	0.97804311	0.97797883	0.97797860
0.4	0.96160834	0.96143650	0.96131642	0.96123266	0.96123245
0.5	0.94070103	0.94049247	0.94034673	0.94024507	0.94024488
0.6	0.91593153	0.91569002	0.91552126	0.91540355	0.91540338
0.7	0.88774061	0.88747037	0.88728152	0.88714980	0.88714966
0.8	0.85660774	0.85631323	0.85610742	0.85596388	0.85596376
0.9	0.82303486	0.82272069	0.82250115	0.82234803	0.82234793
1.0	0.78753093	0.78720170	0.78697163	0.78681116	0.78681109

Table 2. Analysis of the exact and our technique's solution at numerous orders of ς for $\mathbf{K}(x, t)$.

ς	$\varsigma = 0.85$	$\varsigma = 0.90$	$\varsigma = 0.95$	$\varsigma = 1\ (Appro)$	$\varsigma = 1\ (Exact)$
0.1	0.70565703	0.70556126	0.70549434	0.70544766	0.70537701
0.2	0.70070648	0.70051685	0.70038434	0.70029191	0.70015219
0.3	0.69235298	0.69207321	0.69187771	0.69174135	0.69153530
0.4	0.68075931	0.68039479	0.68014006	0.67996239	0.67969398
0.5	0.66614650	0.66570406	0.66539490	0.66517925	0.66485353
0.6	0.64878509	0.64827277	0.64791477	0.64766507	0.64728793
0.7	0.62898482	0.62841154	0.62801094	0.62773152	0.62730954
0.8	0.60708344	0.60645870	0.60602213	0.60571762	0.60525778
0.9	0.58343532	0.58276886	0.58230315	0.58197832	0.58148780
1.0	0.55840034	0.55770193	0.55721388	0.55687347	0.55635945

Table 3. Analysis of the exact and our technique's solution at numerous orders of ς for $\mathbf{J}(x, t)$ and $\mathbf{K}(x, t)$.

ς	$\varsigma = 0.85$	$\varsigma = 0.90$	$\varsigma = 0.95$	$\varsigma = 1\ (Appro)$	$\varsigma = 1\ (Exact)$
0.0	1.00000000	1.00000000	1.00000000	1.00000000	0.99999974
0.1	0.99765268	0.99760754	0.99757599	0.99755399	0.99755374
0.2	0.99036039	0.99027100	0.99020853	0.99016496	0.99016472
0.3	0.97826716	0.97813527	0.97804311	0.97797883	0.97797860
0.4	0.96160834	0.96143650	0.96131642	0.96123266	0.96123245
0.5	0.94070103	0.94049247	0.94034673	0.94024507	0.94024488
0.6	0.91593153	0.91569002	0.91552126	0.91540355	0.91540338
0.7	0.88774061	0.88747037	0.88728152	0.88714980	0.88714966
0.8	0.85660773	0.85631323	0.85610742	0.85596388	0.85596376
0.9	0.82303486	0.82272069	0.82250115	0.82234803	0.82234793
1.0	0.78753093	0.78720170	0.78697163	0.78681116	0.78681109

7. Conclusions

The YTDM and HPTM have been successfully used in this study to approximate the solution of the time-fractional coupled KdV equation. This study highlights the significance of fractional derivatives and the methods for handling the recurrence relation. The results obtained provide the highest degree of agreement regarding the exact solutions to the test issues. By using the suggested approaches to test issues, it was confirmed that the mathematical model of arbitrary order could interpret any experimental data more accurately than the model of integer-order. The series solutions are consequently executed by employing both techniques. With the aid of the MAPLE 2015 software, all iterations were computed. Tables and graphs are also used to present the numerical solutions. We have seen that the results of the arbitrary order converge to the integer-order solution for the test issues as the arbitrary order approaches integer order. These methods prove useful for a wide range of nonlinear fractional differential equations in science and engineering, as shown by the solution graphs and tables. This strategy could be expanded in future studies to address diverse nonlinear obstacle issues.

Author Contributions: Conceptualization, M.M.A., A.H.G. and A.K.; Methodology and Software, A.K.; Formal analysis and Editing, A.H.G.; Investigation, A.K.; Writing—original draft, A.K.; Supervision, A.H.G.; Project administration, M.M.A.; Funding acquisition, M.M.A. All authors have read and agreed to the published version of the manuscript.

Funding: This project funded by Prince Sattam bin Abdulaziz University through the project number PSAU/2023/01/25377.

Data Availability Statement: The numerical data used to support the findings of this study are included within the article.

Acknowledgments: We are thankful to the reviewers for the comments, that improved the presentation of the paper. Also, the authors extend their appreciation to Prince Sattam bin Abdulaziz University for funding this research work through the project number PSAU/2023/01/25377.

Conflicts of Interest: The authors declare no conflict of interest.

Abbreviations

The following abbreviations are used in this article:

FC	Fractional calculus
KdV	Korteweg–De Vries
FPDEs	Fractional-order partial differential equations
YT	Yang transform
YTDM	Yang transform decomposition method
HPTM	Homotopy perturbation transform method
x	Independent variable
$\mathtt{t}$	Time
$\mathbf{J}(x,\mathtt{t})$	Dependent function representing the physical quantity
ς, β	Fractional order
Y	Yang transform
Y^{-1}	Inverse Yang transform
ϵ	Perturbation parameter

References

1. Mainardi, F. *Fractional Calculus and Waves in Linear Viscoelasticity: An Introduction to Mathematical Models*; Imperial College Press: London, UK, 2022.
2. Li, C.; Deng, W. Remarks on fractional derivatives. *Appl. Math. Comput.* **2007**, *187*, 777–784. [CrossRef]
3. Alam, M.N.; Ilhan, O.A.; Manafian, J.; Asjad, M.I.; Rezazadeh, H.; Baskonus, H.M. New Results of Some of the Conformable Models Arising in Dynamical Systems. *Adv. Math. Phys.* **2022**, *2022*, 7753879. [CrossRef]
4. Alam, M.N.; Ilhan, O.A.; Uddin, M.S.; Rahim, M.A. Regarding on the Results for the Fractional Clannish Random Walker's Parabolic Equation and the Nonlinear Fractional Cahn-Allen Equation. *Adv. Math. Phys.* **2022**, *2022*, 5635514. [CrossRef]

5. Podlubny, I. *Fractional Differential Equations: An Introduction to Fractional Derivatives, Fractional Differential Equations, to Methods of Their Solution and Some of their Applications*; Academic Press: New York, NY, USA, 1999; 368p.
6. Oldham, K.; Spanier, J. *The Fractional Calculus Theory and Applications of Differentiation and Integration to Arbitrary Order*; Elsevier: Amsterdam, The Netherlands, 1974.
7. Klafter, J.; Lim, S.C.; Metzler, R. *Fractional Dynamics: Recent Advances*; World Scientific: Singapore; Hackensack, NJ, USA, 2012.
8. Tarasov, V.E. *Fractional Dynamics: Applications of Fractional Calculus to Dynamics of Particles, Fields and Media*; Higher Education Press Springer: Beijing, China; London, UK, 2010.
9. Kilbas, A.A.; Srivastava, H.M.; Trujillo, J.J. *Theory and Applications of Fractional Differential Equations*; Elsevier Science Inc., 655 Avenue of the Americas: New York, NY, USA, 2006; Volume 204.
10. Magin, R. Fractional calculus in bioengineering, part 1. *Crit. Rev. Biomed. Eng.* **2004**, *32*, 104.
11. Hilfer, R. (Ed.) *Applications of Fractional Calculus in Physics*; World Scientific: Singapore, 2000.
12. Arqub, O.A.; El-Ajou, A. Solution of the fractional epidemic model by homotopy analysis method. *J. King Saud-Univ.-Sci.* **2013**, *25*, 73–81. [CrossRef]
13. Bhrawy, A.H.; Ezz-Eldien, S. A new Legendre operational technique for delay fractional optimal control problems. *Calcolo* **2016**, *53*, 521–543. [CrossRef]
14. Jassim, H.K. Analytical solutions for system of fractional partial differential equations by homotopy perturbation transform method. *Int. J. Adv. Appl. Math. Mech.* **2015**, *3*, 36–40.
15. Thabet, H.; Kendre, S.; Chalishajar, D. New analytical technique for solving a system of nonlinear fractional partial differential equations. *Mathematics* **2017**, *5*, 47. [CrossRef]
16. Mamchuev, M.O. Cauchy problem in nonlocal statement for a system of fractional partial differential equations. *Differ. Equ.* **2012**, *48*, 354–361. [CrossRef]
17. El-Ajou, A.; Shqair, M.; Ghabar, I.; Burqan, A.; Saadeh, R. A solution for the neutron diffusion equation in the spherical and hemispherical reactors using the residual power series. *Front. Phys.* **2023**, *11*, 1229142. [CrossRef]
18. Zayed, E.M.; Amer, Y.A.; Al-Nowehy, A.G. The modified simple equation method and the multiple exp-function method for solving nonlinear fractional Sharma-Tasso-Olver equation. *Acta Math. Appl. Sin. Engl. Ser.* **2016**, *32*, 793–812. [CrossRef]
19. Ayati, Z.; Badiepour, A. Two New Modifications of the Exp-Function Method for Solving the Fractional-Order Hirota-Satsuma Coupled KdV. *Adv. Math. Phys.* **2022**, *2022*, 6304896. [CrossRef]
20. Alaoui, M.K.; Fayyaz, R.; Khan, A.; Shah, R.; Abdo, M.S. Analytical investigation of Noyes-Field model for time-fractional Belousov-Zhabotinsky reaction. *Complexity* **2021**, *2021*, 3248376. [CrossRef]
21. Sunthrayuth, P.; Alyousef, H.A.; El-Tantawy, S.A.; Khan, A.; Wyal, N. Solving fractional-order diffusion equations in a plasma and fluids via a novel transform. *J. Funct. Spaces* **2022**, *2022*, 1899130. [CrossRef]
22. Zayed, E.M.; Amer, Y.A.; Shohib, R.M. The fractional complex transformation for nonlinear fractional partial differential equations in the mathematical physics. *J. Assoc. Arab. Univ. Basic Appl. Sci.* **2016**, *19*, 59–69. [CrossRef]
23. Li, Z.B.; Zhu, W.H.; He, J.H. Exact solutions of time-fractional heat conduction equation by the fractional complex transform. *Therm. Sci.* **2012**, *16*, 335–338. [CrossRef]
24. Areshi, M.; Khan, A.; Shah, R.; Nonlaopon, K. Analytical investigation of fractional-order Newell-Whitehead-Segel equations via a novel transform. *Aims Math.* **2022**, *7*, 6936–6958. [CrossRef]
25. Alomari, A.K.; Noorani, M.S.M.; Nazar, R.; Li, C.P. Homotopy analysis method for solving fractional Lorenz system. *Commun. Nonlinear Sci. Numer. Simul.* **2010**, *15*, 1864–1872. [CrossRef]
26. Khan, N.A.; Jamil, M.; Ara, A. Approximate solutions to time-fractional Schrödinger equation via homotopy analysis method. *Int. Sch. Res. Not.* **2012**, *2012*, 197068. [CrossRef]
27. Jin, B.; Lazarov, R.; Zhou, Z. Error estimates for a semidiscrete finite element method for fractional order parabolic equations. *SIAM J. Numer. Anal.* **2013**, *51*, 445–466. [CrossRef]
28. Deng, W. Finite element method for the space and time fractional Fokker-Planck equation. *SIAM J. Numer. Anal.* **2009**, *47*, 204–226. [CrossRef]
29. Sahoo, S.; Ray, S.S. Improved fractional sub-equation method for (3+ 1)-dimensional generalized fractional KdV-Zakharov-Kuznetsov equations. *Comput. Math. Appl.* **2015**, *70*, 158–166. [CrossRef]
30. Goswami, A.; Singh, J.; Kumar, D. Numerical simulation of fifth order KdV equations occurring in magneto-acoustic waves. *Ain Shams Eng. J.* **2018**, *9*, 2265–2273. [CrossRef]
31. Djidjeli, K.; Price, W.G.; Twizell, E.H.; Wang, Y. Numerical methods for the solution of the third-and fifth-order dispersive Korteweg-de Vries equations. *J. Comput. Appl. Math.* **1995**, *58*, 307–336. [CrossRef]
32. Drazin, P.G.; Johnson, R.S. *Solitons: An Introduction*; Cambridge University Press: Cambridge, UK, 1989; Volume 2.
33. Zahran, M.A.; El-Shewy, E.K. Contribution of Higher-Order Dispersion to Nonlinear Electron-Acoustic Solitary Waves in a Relativistic Electron Beam Plasma System. *Phys. Scr.* **2008**, *78*, 431–442.
34. Seadawy, A.R. New exact solutions for the KdV equation with higher order nonlinearity by using the variational method. *Comput. Math. Appl.* **2011**, *62*, 3741–3755. [CrossRef]
35. Shi, Y.; Xu, B.; Guo, Y. Numerical solution of Korteweg-de Vries-Burgers equation by the compact-type CIP method. *Adv. Differ. Equ.* **2015**, *2015*, 19. [CrossRef]

36. Yang, X.J.; Baleanu, D.; Srivastava, H.M. *Local Fractional Integral Transforms and Their Applications*; Academic Press: New York, NY, USA, 2015.
37. Adomian, G. A review of the decomposition method in applied mathematics. *J. Math. Anal. Appl.* **1988**, *135*, 501–544. [CrossRef]
38. Adomian, G. *Solving Frontier Problems of Physics: The Decomposition Method*; Springer Science & Business Media: Berlin/Heidelberg, Germany, 2013; Volume 60.
39. Zidan, A.M.; Khan, A.; Shah, R.; Alaoui, M.K.; Weera, W. Evaluation of time-fractional Fisher's equations with the help of analytical methods. *Aims Math.* **2022**, *7*, 18746–18766. [CrossRef]
40. Mishra, N.K.; AlBaidani, M.M.; Khan, A.; Ganie, A.H. Two Novel Computational Techniques for Solving Nonlinear Time-Fractional Lax's Korteweg-de Vries Equation. *Axioms* **2023**, *12*, 400. [CrossRef]
41. Mishra, N.K.; AlBaidani, M.M.; Khan, A.; Ganie, A.H. Numerical Investigation of Time-Fractional Phi-Four Equation via Novel Transform. *Symmetry* **2023**, *15*, 687. [CrossRef]
42. Sunthrayuth, P.; Ullah, R.; Khan, A.; Shah, R.; Kafle, J.; Mahariq, I.; Jarad, F. Numerical analysis of the fractional-order nonlinear system of Volterra integro-differential equations. *J. Funct. Spaces* **2021**, *2021*, 1537958. [CrossRef]
43. Ganie, A.H.; Mofarreh, F.; Khan, A. A Fractional Analysis of Zakharov-Kuznetsov Equations with the Liouville-Caputo Operator. *Axioms* **2023**, *12*, 609. [CrossRef]
44. He, J.H. A coupling method of a homotopy technique and a perturbation technique for non-linear problems. *Int. J.-Non-Linear Mech.* **2000**, *35*, 37–43. [CrossRef]
45. Ghorbani, A. Beyond Adomian polynomials: He polynomials. *Chaos Solitons Fractals* **2009**, *39*, 1486–1492. [CrossRef]

fractal and fractional

Article

Qualitative Aspects of a Fractional-Order Integro-Differential Equation with a Quadratic Functional Integro-Differential Constraint

Ahmed M. A. El-Sayed [1], Antisar A. A. Alhamali [2,*], Eman M. A. Hamdallah [1] and Hanaa R. Ebead [1]

[1] Faculty of Science, Alexandria University, Alexandria 21521, Egypt; amasayed@alexu.edu.eg (A.M.A.E.-S.); eman.hamdallah@alexu.edu.eg (E.M.A.H.); hanaarezqalla@alexu.edu.eg (H.R.E.)

[2] Faculty of Science, Al-Zaytoonah University, Bani Walid 38645, Libya

* Correspondence: entisar.alhammali_pg@alexu.edu.eg

Abstract: This manuscript investigates a constrained problem of an arbitrary (fractional) order quadratic functional integro-differential equation with a quadratic functional integro-differential constraint. We demonstrate that there is at least one solution $x \in C[0,T]$ to the problem. Moreover, we outline the necessary demands for the solution's uniqueness. In addition, the continuous dependence of the solution and the Hyers–Ulam stability of the problem are analyzed. In order to illustrate our results, we provide some particular cases and instances.

Keywords: constrained problem; functional integro-differential equation; fractional order; Schauder fixed-point theorem; continuous dependence

1. Introduction

Fractional-order differential and integral equations have a wide range of applications across various fields with examples in physics, engineering, and biomedical engineering. The nonlocal conditions are often encountered in mathematical and physical problems, where the behavior of a system depends on different factors or parameters; see [1–10].

In recent years, several scholars have concentrated their efforts on constrained integral equations. Their findings about functional integral equations have been expanded to include a particular set of constrained integral equations on a bounded interval (see [11–13]) and unbounded intervals (see [14]). Constrained problems are essential in the mathematical depiction of real-world situations, where such problems are transformed into mathematical models [15–17]. The relevance of handling constraints or control variables arises from the unanticipated elements that persistently disrupt biological systems in the real world; biological traits like survival rates might change as a result. The question of whether an ecosystem can survive those erratic, disruptive occurrences that happen for a short while is of practical significance to ecology. The disturbance functions are what we refer to as control variables in the context of control variables. Numerous papers address this type of problem; for instance, in [18], the authors discussed a nonlinear constrained problem involving a nonlinear functional integral equation. They also examined the appropriate conditions for the solution's uniqueness and its continuous dependence on certain parameters. The authors applied Schauder's fixed-point theorem to prove the existence of solutions. In [14], the authors studied the solvability of a constrained problem involving a nonlinear-delay functional equation subject to a quadratic functional integral constraint. By applying the De Blasi measure of noncompactness, they studied nondecreasing solutions in the bounded interval $L_1[0,T]$ and nonincreasing solutions in the unbounded interval $L_1(R+)$.

Problems with a feedback control or control variable have great importance in numerous fields due to unforeseen factors that disrupt ecosystems in the real world. It could lead to changes in biological characteristics like survival rates; see [19–22]. Furthermore, ecology faces a practical challenge in determining whether an ecosystem can withstand unpredictable, disruptive events; see [15,23–25]. In addition, feedback control problems are crucial to establishing the solutions to delay population models; see [26–29]. In [23], the authors investigated the effect of feedback control on chemostat models; they studied a sufficient condition for the existence of a positive periodic solution tp the model. In [30], the author discussed a positive periodic solution to a nonlinear neutral delay population equation with feedback control. In [12], the authors studied fractional-order models of thermostats; they proved the existence of a solution and the continuous dependence of the unique solution on the control variable. In [13], the author investigated the solvability and the asymptotic stability of a class of nonlinear functional-integral equations with feedback control. For further relevant works, see [12,31–35].

Fixed-point theorems are a great tool for discussing the solvability of differential equation problems that have been studied in a number of monographs and publications; see [6,31,36–40].

Inspired by the above, we consider the constrained problem

$$\frac{dx}{dt} = f\left(t, g_1(t, D^{\zeta}x(t)) \cdot \int_0^{\vartheta(t)} g_2(s, D^{\gamma}x(s))ds\right), \quad \zeta, \gamma \in (0,1), \ t \in (0,T] \tag{1}$$

with the quadratic functional integro-differential constrained

$$x(\tau) = x_0 + \int_0^{T-\tau} h(s, x(s) \cdot D^{\eta}x(s))ds, \quad \eta \in (0,1), \ \tau \in [0,T]. \tag{2}$$

Our aim in this paper is to examine the existence of a solution $x \in C(0,T]$ to the constrained problems (1) and (2). A sufficient hypothesis for the solution's uniqueness will be given. Furthermore, we prove the Hyers–Ulam stability of the problem. The continuous dependence of the solution on the fractional-order derivative $D^{\zeta}x(t)$, the parameter x_0, and the function h will be studied. To highlight our results, we present several examples and special cases. This study establishes conditions for the existence and uniqueness of the solution according to Schauder's fixed-point theorem.

2. Main Result

2.1. Formulation of the Problem

Consider the constrained problem (1) and (2) under the next hypothesis. Let $I = [0,T]$.

(i) $\vartheta : I \to I$ is continuous function such that $\vartheta(t) \leq t$.

(ii) f, h and g_i, $i = 1,2 : I \times R \to R$ are Caratheodry functions [41]. There exist bounded measurable functions [42] a and $a_i : I \to R$ and a positive constants b and b_i such that

$$\begin{aligned} |f(t,x)| &\leq |a(t)| + b|x| \leq a^* + b|x|, \quad a^* = \sup_{t\in I}|a(t)|. \\ |g_i(t,x)| &\leq |a_i(t)| + b_i|x| \leq a_i^* + b_i|x|, \quad a_i^* = \sup_{t\in I}|a_i(t)|, i = 1,2. \\ |h(t,x)| &\leq |a_3(t)| + b_3|x|, \quad \sup_{s\in I}\int_0^{T-\tau}|a_3(s)|ds \leq N. \end{aligned}$$

(iii) The following algebraic equation has a real positive root r_1.

$$bb_1b_2T^{2-\gamma}r_1^2 + (a^*b_2T^{2-\gamma} + ba_1^*b_2T^{2-\gamma} + bb_1a_2^*T^{2-\zeta} - 1)r_1 + a^*a_2^*T^{2-\zeta} + ba_1^*a_2^*T^{2-\zeta} = 0.$$

(iv) $r_1b_3T^{\zeta-\eta+1} < 1$.

The next lemma demonstrates the equivalence between the constrained problem (1) and (2) and its corresponding integral equations.

Lemma 1. *If the solution to (1) and (2) exists, then it can be expressed by*

$$x(t) = x_0 + \int_0^{T-\tau} \Big(h(s, x(s) \cdot I^{\zeta-\eta} y(s)) \Big) ds - I^{\zeta} y(\tau) + I^{\zeta} y(t) \tag{3}$$

and

$$y(t) = I^{1-\zeta} f\Big(t, g_1(t, y(t)) \cdot \int_0^{\vartheta(t)} g_2(s, I^{\zeta-\gamma} y(s)) ds \Big). \tag{4}$$

Proof. Let x be the solution to (1) and (2). Operating by $I^{1-\zeta}$ in on both sides of (1), we obtain

$$D^{\zeta} x(t) = I^{1-\zeta} \frac{dx}{dt} = I^{1-\zeta} \Big(f(t, g_1(t, D^{\zeta} x(t)) \cdot \int_0^{\vartheta(t)} g_2(s, D^{\gamma} x(s)) ds \Big).$$

Taking $D^{\zeta} x(t) = y(t)$, then,

$$x(t) = x(0) + I^{\zeta} y(t). \tag{5}$$

And we can deduce that

$$\begin{aligned} I^{\zeta-\gamma} y(t) &= I^{\zeta-\gamma} D^{\zeta} x(t) = I^{\zeta-\gamma} I^{1-\zeta} \frac{dx}{dt} \\ &= I^{1-\gamma} \frac{dx}{dt} = D^{\gamma} x(t), \end{aligned} \tag{6}$$

and similarly,

$$\begin{aligned} I^{\zeta-\eta} y(t) &= I^{\zeta-\eta} D^{\zeta} x(t) = I^{\zeta-\eta} I^{1-\zeta} \frac{dx}{dt} \\ &= I^{1-\eta} \frac{dx}{dt} = D^{\eta} x(t). \end{aligned} \tag{7}$$

Substituting from (5)–(7) in (1) and (2), we obtain (4) and (3). Conversely, let x be a solution to (3). Differentiating (3), we obtain

$$\begin{aligned} \frac{dx}{dt} &= \frac{d}{dt}[x_0 + \int_0^{T-\tau} \Big(h(s, x(s) \cdot I^{\zeta-\eta} y(s)) \Big) ds - I^{\zeta} y(\tau) + I^{\zeta} y(t)]. \\ &= \frac{d}{dt} I^{\zeta} y = \frac{d}{dt} I^{\zeta} I^{1-\zeta} f(t, g_1(t, D^{\zeta} x(t)) \cdot \int_0^{\vartheta(t)} g_2(s, D^{\gamma} x(s)) ds \\ &= f(t, g_1(t, D^{\zeta} x(t)) \cdot \int_0^{\vartheta(t)} g_2(s, D^{\gamma} x(s)) ds \end{aligned}$$

This proves the equivalence between the two systems (1) and (2) and (3) to (4). □

2.2. Existence of the Solution

Here, we prove the existence of the continuous solution $x \in C(I)$ of (1) and (2). For this purpose, we present the next theorem.

Theorem 1. *Assume that the hypotheses (i)–(iv) are satisfied; then, the solution $x \in C(I)$ of (1) and (2) exists.*

Proof. Define the closed sphere Q_{r_1} and the operator F_1 with

$$Q_{r_1} = \{y \in C(I) : \|y\| \le r_1\}.$$

and

$$F_1y(t) = I^{1-\zeta}f\left(t, g_1(t, y(s)) \cdot \int_0^{\vartheta(t)} g_2(s, I^{\zeta-\gamma}y_2(s))ds\right).$$

Let $y \in Q_{r_1}$; then, for $t \in [0, T]$, and assumptions (i)–(ii), we obtain

$$\begin{aligned}
|F_1y(t)| &= \left|I^{1-\zeta}f\left(t, g_1(t, y(s)) \cdot \int_0^{\vartheta(t)} g_2(s, I^{\zeta-\gamma}y_2(s))ds\right)\right| \\
&\leq I^{1-\zeta}\left(a^* + b(a_1^* + b_1|y(s)|) \cdot \int_0^t (a_2^* + b_2 I^{\zeta-\gamma}|y(s)|)ds\right) \\
&\leq (a^* + b(a_1^* + b_1 r_1))(I^{2-\zeta}a_2^* + I^{2-\gamma}b_2 r_1) \\
&\leq (a^* + b(a_1^* + b_1 r_1))\left(\frac{a_2^* t^{2-\zeta}}{\Gamma(3-\zeta)} + \frac{b_2 r_1 t^{2-\gamma}}{\Gamma(3-\gamma)}\right) \\
&\leq (a^* + b(a_1^* + b_1 r_1))(a_2^* T^{2-\zeta} + b_2 r_1 T^{2-\gamma}) = r_1.
\end{aligned}$$

From assumption (iii), we obtain

$$\|F_1y\| \leq (a^* + b(a_1^* + b_1 r_1))(a_2^* T^{2-\zeta} + b_2 r_1 T^{2-\gamma}) = r_1.$$

This proves that $\{F_1 y\}$ is uniformly bounded on Q_{r_1}. Let $y \in Q_{r_1}, t_1, t_2 \in I$ such that $t_2 > t_1$ and $| t_1 - t_2 |\leq \delta$. By using assumption (ii), then,

$$\begin{aligned}
&|F_1y(t_2) - F_1y(t_1)| = \\
&\left|\int_0^{t_2} \frac{(t_2-s)^{-\zeta}}{\Gamma(1-\zeta)}\left(f(s, g_1(s, y(s)) \cdot \int_0^{\vartheta(s)} g_2(\theta, I^{\zeta-\gamma}y(\theta))d\theta\right)ds\right. \\
-& \left.\int_0^{t_1} \frac{(t_1-s)^{-\zeta}}{\Gamma(1-\zeta)}\left(f(s, g_1(s, y(s)) \cdot \int_0^{\vartheta(s)} g_2(\theta, I^{\zeta-\gamma}y(\theta))d\theta\right)ds\right| \\
\leq& \left|\int_0^{t_1} \frac{(t_2-s)^{-\zeta}}{\Gamma(1-\zeta)}\left(f(s, g_1(s, y(s)) \cdot \int_0^{\vartheta(s)} g_2(\theta, I^{\zeta-\gamma}y(\theta))d\theta\right)ds\right. \\
+& \int_{t_1}^{t_2} \frac{(t_2-s)^{-\zeta}}{\Gamma(1-\zeta)}\left(f(s, g_1(s, y(s)) \cdot \int_0^{\vartheta(s)} g_2(\theta, I^{\zeta-\gamma}y(\theta))d\theta\right)ds \\
-& \left.\int_0^{t_1} \frac{(t_1-s)^{-\zeta}}{\Gamma(1-\zeta)}\left(f(s, g_1(s, y(s)) \cdot \int_0^{\vartheta(s)} g_2(\theta, I^{\zeta-\gamma}y(\theta))d\theta\right)ds\right| \\
\leq& \left|\int_0^{t_1} \frac{(t_2-s)^{-\zeta}}{\Gamma(1-\zeta)} - \frac{(t_1-s)^{-\zeta}}{\Gamma(1-\zeta)}(a^* + b(a_1^* + b_1 r_1))(a_2^* T^{2-\zeta} + b_2 r_1 T^{2-\gamma}))ds\right. \\
+& \left.\int_{t_1}^{t_2} \frac{1}{\Gamma(1-\zeta)(t_2-s)^{\zeta}}(a^* + b(a_1^* + b_1 r_1))(a_2^* T^{2-\zeta} + b_2 r_1 T^{2-\gamma}))ds\right| \\
\leq& \int_0^{t_1} \left|\frac{(t_2-s)^{\zeta} - (t_1-s)^{\zeta}}{\Gamma(1-\zeta)(t_1-s)^{\zeta}(t_2-s)^{\zeta}}\right|(a^* + b(a_1^* + b_1 r_1))(a_2^* T^{2-\zeta} + b_2 r_1 T^{2-\gamma}))ds \\
+& \int_{t_1}^{t_2} \frac{1}{\Gamma(1-\zeta)(t_2-s)^{\zeta}}(a^* + b(a_1^* + b_1 r_1))(a_2^* T^{2-\zeta} + b_2 r_1 T^{2-\gamma}))ds.
\end{aligned}$$

This proves that $F_1 : Q_{r_1} \to Q_{r_1}$ and that $\{F_1 y\}$ is equi-continuous on Q_{r_1}. From [41], $\{F_1 y\}$ is relatively compact. Hence, the operator F_1 is compact.
Let $\{y_n\} \subset Q_{r_1}$ be such that $y_n \to y$; then,

$$F_1 y_n(t) = I^{1-\zeta} f\Big(t, g_1(t, y_n(t)) \cdot \int_0^{\vartheta(t)} g_2(s, I^{\zeta-\gamma} y_n(s)) ds\Big),$$

Thus, by taking the limits for both sides and in view of Lebesgues dominated convergence Theorem [41] and assumption (ii), we obtain

$$\begin{aligned}
\lim_{n\to\infty} F_1 y_n(t) &= \lim_{n\to\infty} I^{1-\zeta} f\Big(t, g_1(t, y_n(t)) \cdot \int_0^{\vartheta(t)} g_2(s, I^{\zeta-\gamma} y_n(s)) ds\Big) \\
&= I^{1-\zeta} f\Big(t, g_1(t, \lim_{n\to\infty} y_n(t)) \cdot \int_0^{\vartheta(t)} g_2(s, I^{\zeta-\gamma} \lim_{n\to\infty} y_n(s)) ds\Big) \\
&= I^{1-\zeta} f\Big(t, g_1(t, y(t)) \cdot \int_0^{\vartheta(t)} g_2(s, I^{\zeta-\gamma} y(s)) ds\Big) \\
&= F_1 y(t),
\end{aligned}$$

Hence, F_1 is continuous and the solution to (4) exists.

Now, for the validity of solutions $x \in C(I)$ of (3), let the assumptions (i)–(iv) be satisfied. Define Q_{r_2} as the closed sphere

$$Q_{r_2} = \{x \in C(I) : \|x\| \le r_2\}, \; r_2 = \frac{|x_0| + N + 2r_1 T^{\zeta}}{1 - b_3 r_1 T^{\zeta-\eta+1}}$$

and define the operator F_2 as

$$F_2 x(t) = x_0 + \int_0^{T-\tau} \Big(h(s, x(s) \cdot I^{\zeta-\eta} y(s))\Big) ds - I^{\zeta} y(\tau) + I^{\zeta} y(t).$$

Let $x \in Q_{r_2}$; then, by using assumption (ii), we obtain

$$\begin{aligned}
|F_2 x(t)| &= \left| x_0 + \int_0^{T-\tau} h(s, x(s) \cdot I^{\zeta-\eta} y(s)) ds - I^{\zeta} y(\tau) + I^{\zeta} y(t) \right| \\
&\le |x_0| + \int_0^{T-\tau} |h(s, x(s) \cdot I^{\zeta-\eta} y(s)| ds + I^{\zeta} |y(\tau)| + I^{\zeta} |y(t)| \\
&\le |x_0| + \int_0^{T-\tau} \Big(|a_3(s)| + b_3(|x(s) I^{\zeta-\eta} y(s)|\Big) ds + 2r_1 I^{\zeta} \\
&\le |x_0| + \int_0^{T-\tau} \Big(a_3 + b_3 r_1 r_2 \frac{T^{\zeta-\eta}}{\Gamma(\zeta-\eta+1)}\Big) ds + \frac{2r_1 T^{\zeta}}{\Gamma(\zeta+1)} \\
&\le |x_0| + N + \frac{r_1 r_2 b_3 T^{\zeta-\eta}}{\Gamma(\zeta-\eta+1)} + \frac{2r_1 T^{\zeta}}{\Gamma(\zeta+1)}
\end{aligned}$$

and from assumption (iv), we obtain

$$\|F_2 x\| \le |x_0| + N + r_1 r_2 b_3 T^{\zeta-\eta} + 2r_1 T^{\zeta} = r_2.$$

This shows that $\{F_2x\}$ is uniformly bounded on Q_{r_2}. Now, for $x \in Q_{r_2}$ and $t_1,\ t_2 \in I$, where $t_2 > t_1$ and $\mid t_1 - t_2 \mid \leq \delta$, we obtain

$$\begin{aligned}
|F_2x(t_2) - F_2x(t_1)| &= \Big| x_0 + \int_0^{T-\tau} h(s, x(s) \cdot I^{\zeta-\eta}y(s))ds - I^{\zeta}y(\tau) + I^{\zeta}y(t_2) \\
&- x_0 + \int_0^{T-\tau} h(s, x(s) \cdot I^{\zeta-\eta}y(s))ds - I^{\zeta}y(\tau) + I^{\zeta}y(t_1) \Big| \\
&\leq \int_0^{t_2} |f\Big(s, g_1(s, y(s)) \cdot \int_0^{\vartheta(t)} g_2(s, I^{\zeta-\gamma}y(s))ds\Big)|ds \\
&- \int_0^{t_1} |f\Big(s, g_1(s, y(s)) \cdot \int_0^{\vartheta(t)} g_2(s, I^{\zeta-\gamma}y(s))ds\Big)|ds \\
&\leq \int_{t_1}^{t_2} |f\Big(s, g_1(s, y(s)) \cdot \int_0^{\vartheta(t)} g_2(s, I^{\zeta-\gamma}y(s))ds\Big)|ds.
\end{aligned}$$

This means that $F_2 : Q_{r_2} \to Q_{r_2}$ and that $\{F_2x\}$ is equi-continuous on Q_{r_2}. From [41], $\{F_2x\}$ is relatively compact. Hence, F_2 is compact.
Assuming that $\{x_n\} \subset Q_{r_2}$, where $x_n \to x$, then,

$$F_2x_n(t) = x_0 + \int_0^{T-\tau} h(s, x_n(s) \cdot I^{\zeta-\eta}y(s))ds - I^{\zeta}y(\tau) + I^{\zeta}y(t)$$

and by passing the limit, we have

$$\lim_{n\to\infty} F_2x_n(t) = \lim_{n\to\infty} \left(x_0 + \int_0^{T-\tau} h(s, x_n(s) \cdot I^{\zeta-\eta}y(s))ds - I^{\zeta}y(\tau) + I^{\zeta}y(t) \right)$$

Applying the Lebesgue dominated convergence Theorem [41], then,

$$\begin{aligned}
\lim_{n\to\infty} F_2x_n(t) &= x_0 + \int_0^{T-\tau} h(s, \lim_{n\to\infty} x(s) \cdot I^{\zeta-\eta}y(s))ds - I^{\zeta}y(\tau) + I^{\zeta}y(t) \\
&= x_0 + \int_0^{T-\tau} h(s, x(s) \cdot I^{\zeta-\eta}y(s))ds - I^{\zeta}y(\tau) + I^{\zeta}y(t) = F_2x(t).
\end{aligned}$$

This means that $F_2x_n(t) \to F_2x(t)$. Therefore, F_2 is continuous. From [41], the solution $x \in C(I)$ of (3) exists. As a result, the solution $x \in C[0,T]$ to Problem (1) and (2) exists. □

3. Uniqueness of the Solution

Consider the next additional hypothesis:

$(i)^*$ f, h and $g_i : I \times R \to R$ are measurable in $t \in I,\ \forall x \in R$ and satisfy the Lipschitz condition [43]

$$\begin{aligned}
|f(t,x) - f(t,y)| &\leq b|x-y|, \\
|g_i(t,x) - g_i(t,y)| &\leq b_i|x-y| \\
|h(t,x) - h(t,y)| &\leq b_3|x-y|
\end{aligned}$$

with Lipschitz constants $b,\ b_i,\ b_3 > 0$ and $t \in I,\ x,\ y \in R,\ i = 1,2$.

Remark 1. *From assumption $(i)^*$, we deduce assumption (ii) as follows:*

$$|f(t,x)| \leq |f(t,0)| + b|x|,$$

$$|f(t,x)| \leq a + b|x|, \quad \textit{where } a = \sup_{t\in I} |f(t,0)|.$$

Also,

$$|g_i(t,x)| \leq |g_i(t,0)| + b_i|x|,$$

$$|g_i(t,x)| \leq a_i + b_i|x|, \quad where \ a_i = \sup_{t\in I} |g_i(t,0)|, \quad i = 1,2.$$

and

$$|h(t,x)| \leq |h(t,0)| + b_3|x|,$$

$$|h(t,x)| \leq a_3 + b_3|x|, \quad where \ a_3 = \sup_{t\in I} |h(t,0)|.$$

Theorem 2. *Let the hypotheses (i)–(iv) and (i*) be valid. If*

$$(a^*b_2 + bb_2(a_1^* + b_1r_1))T^{2-\gamma} + bb_1(a_2^*T^{2-\zeta} + r_1b_2T^{2-\gamma}) < 1,$$

Hence, the solution to (1) and (2) is unique.

Proof. It is clear that all hypotheses of Theorem 1 are valid, and thus, the solution to (4) exists. Now, assume that y_1, y_2 are two solutions of (4); then,

$$\begin{aligned}
& |y_2(t) - y_1(t)| \\
= & \Big| I^{1-\zeta} f\Big(t, g_1(t, y_2(s)) \cdot \int_0^{\vartheta(t)} g_2(s, I^{\zeta-\gamma} y_2(s)) ds\Big) \\
- & I^{1-\zeta} f\Big(t, g_1(t, y_1(s)) \cdot \int_0^{\vartheta(t)} g_2(s, I^{\zeta-\gamma} y_1(s)) ds\Big)\Big| \\
= & \Big| I^{1-\zeta} f\Big(t, g_1(t, y_2(s)) \cdot \int_0^{\vartheta(t)} g_2(s, I^{\zeta-\gamma} y_2(s)) ds\Big) \\
- & I^{1-\zeta} f\Big(t, g_1(t, y_2(s)) \cdot \int_0^{\vartheta(t)} g_2(s, I^{\zeta-\gamma} y_1(s)) ds\Big) \\
+ & I^{1-\zeta} f\Big(t, g_1(t, y_2(s)) \cdot \int_0^{\vartheta(t)} g_2(s, I^{\zeta-\gamma} y_1(s)) ds\Big) \\
- & I^{1-\zeta} f\Big(t, g_1(t, y_1(s)) \cdot \int_0^{\vartheta(t)} g_2(s, I^{\zeta-\gamma} y_1(s)) ds\Big)\Big| \\
\leq & I^{1-\zeta} |f(t, g_1(t, y_2(t)))| \cdot \int_0^{\vartheta(t)} |g_2(s, I^{\zeta-\gamma} y_2(s)) - g_2(s, I^{\zeta-\gamma} y_1(s))| ds \\
+ & I^{1-\zeta} \Big(|f(t, g_1(t, y_2(t)) - f(t, g_1(t, y_1(t)))| \Big) \cdot \int_0^{\vartheta(t)} |g_2(s, I^{\zeta-\gamma} y_1(s))| ds \\
\leq & I^{1-\zeta} (a^* + b(a_1^* + b_1 r_1)) \cdot b_2 \int_0^t I^{\zeta-\gamma} |y_2(s) - y_1(s)| ds \\
+ & I^{1-\zeta} \Big(bb_1 |y_2(s) - y_1(s)| \int_0^t (a_2^* + b_2 I^{\zeta-\gamma} |y(s)|) ds \Big) \\
\leq & (a^* + b(a_1^* + b_1 r_1)) \cdot b_2 I^{2-\gamma} \|y_2 - y_1\| + bb_1(a_2^* T^{2-\zeta} + r_1 b_2 T^{2-\gamma}) \|y_2 - y_1\|.
\end{aligned}$$

Hence,

$$\|y_2 - y_1\| \Big(1 - \big[(a^*b_2 + bb_2(a_1^* + b_1r_1))T^{2-\gamma} + bb_1(a_2^*T^{2-\zeta} + r_1b_2T^{2-\gamma})\big] \Big) \leq 0.$$

Since

$$(a^*b_2 + bb_2(a_1^* + b_1r_1))T^{2-\gamma} + bb_1(a_2^*T^{2-\zeta} + r_1b_2T^{2-\gamma}) < 1.$$

Then, the solution of (4) is unique.

Now, for every solution $y \in C(I)$ to (4), there exists a unique solution $x \in C(I)$ of (3). Let $y \in C(I)$ be a solution to (4), and let x_1, x_2 be two solutions to Equation (3); then,

$$\begin{aligned}
|x_2(t) - x_1(t)| &= \Big| x_0 + \int_0^{T-\tau} h(s, x_2(s) \cdot I^{\zeta-\eta} y(s)) ds - I^{\zeta} y(\tau) + I^{\zeta} y(t) \\
&- x_0 - \int_0^{T-\tau} h(s, x_1(s) \cdot I^{\zeta-\eta} y(s)) ds + I^{\zeta} y(\tau) - I^{\zeta} y(t) \Big|. \\
&\le \int_0^{T-\tau} \Big| h(s, x_2(s) \cdot I^{\zeta-\eta} y(s)) - h(s, x_1(s). I^{\zeta-\eta} y(s)) \Big| ds \\
&\le r_1 b_3 \int_0^{T-\tau} |x_2(s) - x_1(s)| \, I^{\zeta-\eta} ds, \\
&\le r_1 b_3 \|x_2 - x_1\| \frac{T^{\zeta-\eta+1}}{\Gamma(1+\zeta-\eta)},
\end{aligned}$$

from assumption (iv), we obtain

$$\|x_2 - x_1\| (1 - (\frac{r_1 b_3 T^{\zeta-\eta+1}}{\Gamma(1+\zeta-\eta)})) \le 0.$$

Thus, there is only one solution to (3). As a result, there is only one solution to (1) and (2). □

4. Hyers–Ulam Stability

Definition 1. [44] *Let the solution to (1) and (2) exist. The constrained problem (1) and (2) is Hyers–Ulam-stable if* $\forall \epsilon > 0$, $\exists \, \delta(\epsilon) > 0$ *such that, for any solution* $x_s \in C[0, T]$ *of (1) and (2) satisfying*

$$\left| \frac{dx_s}{dt} - f(t, g_1(t, D^{\zeta} x_s(t)) \cdot \int_0^{\vartheta(t)} g_2(s, D^{\gamma} x_s(s))) \right| \le \delta. \tag{8}$$

Then

$$\|x - x_s\|_c \le \epsilon.$$

Theorem 3. *Assume that the hypothesis of Theorem 2 is satisfied; then, problem (1) and (2) is Hyers–Ulam-stable.*

Proof. Let the condition of Equation (8) be satisfied; then, we have

$$\begin{aligned}
-\delta &\le \frac{dx_s(t)}{dt} - f(t, g_1(t, D^{\zeta} x_s(t)) \cdot \int_0^{\vartheta(t)} g_2(s, D^{\gamma} x_s(s)) ds) \le \delta, \\
-\tfrac{T^{1-\zeta}\delta}{\Gamma(2-\zeta)} &\le I^{1-\zeta} \frac{dx_s(t)}{dt} - I^{1-\zeta} f(t, g_1(t, D^{\zeta} x_s(t)) \cdot \int_0^{\vartheta(t)} g_2(s, D^{\gamma} x_s(s)) ds) \le \frac{T^{1-\zeta}\delta}{\Gamma(2-\zeta)}, \\
-\delta_1 &\le y_s(t) - I^{1-\zeta} f(t, g_1(t, y_s(t)) \cdot \int_0^{\vartheta(t)} g_2(s, I^{\zeta-\gamma} y_s(s)) ds) \le \delta_1.
\end{aligned}$$

Now,

$$
\begin{aligned}
&|y(t) - y_s(t)| = \\
&\left| I^{1-\zeta} f(t, g_1(t, y(t)) \cdot \int_0^{\vartheta(t)} g_2(s, I^{\zeta-\gamma} y(s)) ds) - y_s(t) \right. \\
- \quad & I^{1-\zeta} f(t, g_1(t, y_s(t)) \cdot \int_0^{\vartheta(t)} g_2(s, I^{\zeta-\gamma} y_s(s)) ds) \\
+ \quad & \left. I^{1-\zeta} f(t, g_1(t, y_s(t)) \cdot \int_0^{\vartheta(t)} g_2(s, I^{\zeta-\gamma} y_s(s)) ds) \right| \\
\leq \quad & \left| I^{1-\zeta} f(t, g_1(t, y(t)) \cdot \int_0^{\vartheta(t)} g_2(s, I^{\zeta-\gamma} y(s)) ds) \right. \\
- \quad & \left. I^{1-\zeta} f(t, g_1(t, y_s(t)) \cdot \int_0^{\vartheta(t)} g_2(s, I^{\zeta-\gamma} y_s(s)) ds) \right| \\
+ \quad & \left| I^{1-\zeta} f(t, g_1(t, y_s(t)) \cdot \int_0^{\vartheta(t)} g_2(s, I^{\zeta-\gamma} y_s(s)) ds) - y_s(t) \right| \\
\leq \quad & I^{1-\zeta} |f(t, g_1(t, y(t))| \cdot \int_0^{\vartheta(t)} |g_2(s, I^{\zeta-\gamma} y(s)) - g_2(s, I^{\zeta-\gamma} y_s(s)))| ds \\
+ \quad & I^{1-\zeta} |f(t, g_1(t, y(t)) - f(t, g_1(t, y_s(t))| \cdot \int_0^{\vartheta(t)} |g_2(s, I^{\zeta-\gamma} y_s(s))| ds + \delta_1 \\
\leq \quad & I^{1-\zeta} (a^* + b(a_1^* + b_1 r_1)) \cdot b_2 \int_0^t I^{\zeta-\gamma} |y(s) - y_s(s)| ds. \\
+ \quad & I^{1-\zeta} b b_1 |y(s) - y_s(s)| \cdot \int_0^t (a_2^* + b_2 I^{\zeta-\gamma} |y_s|) ds + \delta_1 \\
\leq \quad & (a^* + b(a_1^* + b_1 r_1)) \cdot b_2 T^{2-\gamma} \|y - y_s\| + b_1 b (a_2^* T^{2-\zeta} + r_1 . b_2 T^{2-\gamma}) \|y - y_s\| + \delta_1.
\end{aligned}
$$

Hence,

$$
\|y - y_s\| \left(1 - \left[(a^* + b(a_1^* + b_1 r_1)) \cdot b_2 T^{2-\gamma} + b_1 b (a_2^* T^{2-\zeta} + r_1 \cdot b_2 T^{2-\gamma}) \right] \right) \leq \delta_1
$$

and

$$
\|y - y_s\| \leq \frac{\delta_1}{1 - \left[(a^* + b(a_1^* + b_1 r_1)) \cdot b_2 T^{2-\gamma} + b_1 b (a_2^* T^{2-\zeta} + r_1 \cdot b_2 T^{2-\gamma}) \right]}.
$$

Since

$$
(a^* + b(a_1^* + b_1 r_1)) \cdot b_2 T^{2-\gamma} + b_1 b (a_2^* T^{2-\zeta} + r_1 \cdot b_2 T^{2-\gamma}) < 1,
$$

then

$$
\|y - y_s\| < \epsilon.
$$

Also, using assumption (iv), we obtain

$$\begin{aligned}|x(t)-x_s(t)| &= \Big|x_0+\int_0^{T-\tau} h(s,x(s)\cdot I^{\zeta-\eta}y(s))ds - I^{\zeta}y(\tau)+I^{\zeta}y(t)\\ &- x_0-\int_0^{T-\tau} h(s,x_s(s)\cdot I^{\zeta-\eta}y_s(s))ds + I^{\zeta}y_s(\tau)-I^{\zeta}y_s(t)\Big|\\ &\leq \int_0^{T-\tau} |h(s,x(s)\cdot I^{\zeta-\eta}y(s)) - h(s,x_s(s)\cdot I^{\zeta-\eta}y_s(s))|ds + 2I^{\zeta}\|y-y_s\|\\ &\leq b_3\int_0^{T-\tau}(|x(s)-x_s(s)|\, I^{\zeta-\eta}|y(s)| + I^{\zeta-\eta}|y(s)-y_s(s)|\,|x_s|)ds + \frac{2T^{\zeta}}{\Gamma(\zeta+1)}\epsilon\\ &\leq \frac{r_1 b_3 T^{\zeta-\eta+1}}{\Gamma(\zeta-\eta+1)}\|x-x_s\| + \frac{r_2 b_3 T^{\zeta-\eta+1}}{\Gamma(\zeta-\eta+1)}\epsilon + \frac{2T^{\zeta}}{\Gamma(\zeta+1)}\epsilon,\end{aligned}$$

$$\|x-x^*\| \leq \frac{\left(\frac{r_2 b_3 T^{\zeta-\eta+1}}{\Gamma(\zeta-\eta+1)} + \frac{2T^{\zeta}}{\Gamma(\zeta+1)}\right)\epsilon}{1-\left(\frac{r_1 b_3 T^{\zeta-\eta+1}}{\Gamma(\zeta-\eta+1)}\right)}.$$

Since

$$\frac{r_1 b_3 T^{\zeta-\eta+1}}{\Gamma(\zeta-\eta+1)} < 1,$$

thus,

$$\|x-x^*\| \leq \epsilon.$$

Then, the problem (1) and (2) is Hyers–Ulam-stable. □

5. Continuous Dependence

Definition 2. *The solution to (1) and (2) depends continuously on $y = D^{\zeta}x$, h and x_0, and if $\forall\, \epsilon > 0, \exists\, \delta(\epsilon) > 0$ such that*

$$\max\{\|y-\check{y}\|, \|h-\check{h}\|, |x_0-\check{x}_0| \leq \delta\} \Rightarrow \|x-\check{x}\| \leq \epsilon,$$

where $\check{x}$ and $\check{y}$ are the solutions to

$$\check{x}(t) = \check{x}_0 + \int_0^{T-\tau} \check{h}(s,\check{x}(s)\cdot I^{\zeta-\eta}\check{y}(s))ds - I^{\zeta}\check{y}(\tau) + I^{\zeta}\check{y}(t), \tag{9}$$

$$\check{y}(t) = I^{1-\zeta}f\Big(t, g_1(t,\check{y}(t))\cdot\int_0^{\vartheta(t)} g_2(s, I^{\zeta-\gamma}\check{y}(s))ds\Big). \tag{10}$$

Theorem 4. *Suppose that the hypotheses of Theorem 2 are satisfied; then, the solution to (1) and (2) depends continuously on y, h, and x_0.*

Proof. If $x(t)$ and $\check{x}(t)$ are the solutions to (3) and (9), respectively, using assumption $(i)^*$, we obtain

$$\begin{aligned}
& |x(t)-\check{x}(t)| \\
= & \left|x_0+\int_0^{T-\tau} h(s,x(s)\cdot I^{\zeta-\eta}y(s))ds - I^{\zeta}y(\tau)+I^{\zeta}y(t)\right. \\
- & \left.\check{x_0}-\int_0^{T-\tau} \check{h}(s,\check{x}(s)I^{\zeta-\eta}\check{y}(s))ds + I^{\zeta}\check{y}(\tau)-I^{\zeta}\check{y}(t)\right| \\
\leq & |x-\check{x_0}|+\left|\int_0^{T-\tau}\Big(h(s,x(s)\cdot I^{\zeta-\eta}y(s))-\check{h}(s,\check{x}(s)\cdot I^{\zeta-\eta}\check{y}(s))ds\Big)ds\right. \\
+ & \left. I^{\zeta}(y(\tau)-\check{y}(\tau))+I^{\zeta}(y(t)-\check{y}(t))\right| \\
\leq & |x-\check{x_0}|+\int_0^{T-\tau}\Big|h(s,x(s)\cdot I^{\zeta-\eta}y(s))-h(s,\check{x}(s)\cdot I^{\zeta-\eta}\check{y}(s)) \\
+ & h(s,\check{x}(s)\cdot I^{\zeta-\eta}\check{y}(s))-\check{h}(s,\check{x}(s)\cdot I^{\zeta-\eta}\check{y}(s))\Big|ds+2I^{\zeta}\|y-\check{y}\| \\
\leq & |x-\check{x_0}|+b_3\int_0^{T-\tau}|x(s)I^{\zeta-\eta}y(s)-\check{x}(s)I^{\zeta-\eta}\check{y}(s)|ds \\
+ & b_3\int_0^{T-\tau}\|h-\check{h}\|ds+2I^{\zeta}\|y-\check{y}\| \\
\leq & |x-\check{x_0}|+b_3\int_0^{T-\tau}|x(s)I^{\zeta-\eta}y(s)-x(s)I^{\zeta-\eta}\check{y}(s) \\
+ & x(s)I^{\zeta-\eta}\check{y}(s)-\check{x}(s)I^{\zeta-\eta}\check{y}(s)|ds+b_3\|h-\check{h}\|T+\|y-\check{y}\|\frac{2T^{\zeta}}{\Gamma(\zeta+1)} \\
\leq & \delta+b_3\int_0^{T-\tau}|x(s)|I^{\zeta-\eta}|y(s)-\check{y}(s)|ds \\
+ & b_3\int_0^{T-\tau}|x(s)-\check{x}(s)|I^{\zeta-\eta}|\check{y}(s)|ds+b_3T\delta+\frac{2T^{\zeta}\delta}{\Gamma(\zeta+1)} \\
\leq & \delta+b_3\,r_2\|y-\check{y}\|\frac{T^{\zeta-\eta+1}}{\Gamma(\zeta-\eta+1)}+b_3\,r_1\|x-\check{x}\|\frac{T^{\zeta-\eta+1}}{\Gamma(\zeta-\eta+1)}+b_3\,T\delta+\frac{2\delta T^{\zeta}}{\Gamma(\zeta+1)} \\
\leq & \delta+b_3\,r_2\delta\frac{T^{\zeta-\eta+1}}{\Gamma(\zeta-\eta+1)}+b_3\,r_1\|x-\check{x}\|\frac{T^{\zeta-\eta+1}}{\Gamma(\zeta-\eta+1)}+b_3\,T\delta+\frac{2\delta T^{\zeta}}{\Gamma(\zeta+1)}.
\end{aligned}$$

Hence,

$$\|x-\check{x}\|\left(1-\frac{r_1b_3T^{\zeta-\eta+1}}{\Gamma(\zeta-\eta+1)}\right)\leq\left(1+\frac{r_2b_3T^{\zeta-\eta+1}}{\Gamma(\zeta-\eta+1)}+\frac{2T^{\zeta}}{\Gamma(\zeta+1)}+b_3T\right)\delta$$

and

$$\|x-\check{x}\|=\frac{\left(1+\frac{r_2b_3T^{\zeta-\eta+1}}{\Gamma(\zeta-\eta+1)}+\frac{2T^{\zeta}}{\Gamma(\zeta+1)}+b_3T\right)\delta}{1-\frac{r_1b_3T^{\zeta-\eta+1}}{\Gamma(\zeta-\eta+1)}}=\epsilon.$$

Since $\frac{r_1b_3T^{\zeta-\eta+1}}{\Gamma(\zeta-\eta+1)}<1$, therefore, the solution to (3) depends continuously on y,h,x_0. Consequently, the solution $x\in C[0,T]$ of (1) and (2) depends continuously on y,h,x_0. □

6. Special Cases and Examples

Corollary 1. *Let the hypothesis of Theorem 1 be valid; if we put $\tau = T$ in (2), then the backward problem*

$$\frac{dx}{dt} = f(t, g_1(t, D^{\zeta}x(t)) \int_0^{\vartheta(t)} g_2(s, D^{\gamma}x(s)ds)), \ \zeta, \gamma \in (0,1), \ t \in (0,T],$$

$$x(T) = x_0,$$

has a solution $x \in C[0,T]$. Consequently, if the hypotheses of Theorem 2 are valid, it has a unique solution $x \in C[0,T]$.

Corollary 2. *Let the hypothesis of Corollary 1 be valid. If $\tau = T$, $\gamma = 1 - \zeta$, then the backward problem*

$$\frac{dx}{dt} = f(t, g_1(t, D^{\zeta}x(t)) \int_0^{\vartheta(t)} g_2(s, D^{1-\zeta}x(s)ds)), \ \zeta \in (\frac{1}{2}, 1), \ t \in (0,T],$$

$$x(T) = x_0.$$

has a solution $x \in C[0,T]$. Consequently, if the hypotheses of Theorem 2 are valid, it has a unique solution $x \in C[0,T]$.

Example 1. *Consider the next problem,*

$$\frac{dx}{dt} = \frac{1}{2}(\frac{e^{-t}}{1+e^{-t}}) + \frac{1}{8}(\frac{t^2}{2} + \frac{1}{6}D^{\frac{1}{2}}x(t)) \cdot \int_0^{\rho t} (\frac{s^3}{4} + \frac{1}{3}D^{\frac{1}{2}}x(s))ds, \ t \in (0,1], \quad (11)$$

$$x(\tau) = \frac{1}{4} + \int_0^{1-\tau} (\frac{sins}{6} + \frac{1}{2}x(s) \cdot D^{\frac{1}{2}}x(s))ds, \quad (12)$$

where

$$\zeta = \eta = \gamma = \frac{1}{2}, \ \rho \in (0,1), \ x(0) = \frac{1}{4}.$$

Then

$$f\left(t, g_1(t, D^{\zeta}x(t)) \cdot \int_0^{\vartheta(t)} g_2(s, D^{\gamma}x(s)ds)\right)$$
$$= \frac{1}{2}(\frac{e^{-t}}{1+e^{-t}}) + \frac{1}{8}\left(\frac{t^2}{2} + \frac{1}{6}D^{\frac{1}{2}}x(t)\right) \cdot \int_0^{\rho t} (\frac{s^3}{4} + \frac{1}{3}D^{\frac{1}{2}}x(s))ds.$$

Set

$$g_1(t, D^{\zeta}x(t)) = \frac{t^2}{2} + \frac{1}{6}D^{\frac{1}{2}}x(t)$$
$$g_2(t, D^{\gamma}x(t)) = \frac{t^3}{4} + \frac{1}{3}D^{\frac{1}{2}}x(t)$$
$$h(t, x(t) \cdot D^{\eta}x(t)) = \frac{sint}{6} + \frac{1}{2}x(t) \cdot D^{\frac{1}{2}}x(t).$$

Here, we have

$$a^* = a_1^* = \frac{1}{2}, \ a_2^* = \frac{1}{4}, \ b = \frac{1}{8}, \ b_1 = \frac{1}{6}, \ b_2 = \frac{1}{3}, \ b_3 = \frac{1}{2}$$
$$N = \frac{1}{6}, \ r_1 \approx 0.2, \text{ and } r_2 \approx 0.9.$$

It is obvious that all the hypotheses of Theorem 1 are valid. Hence there exists at least one solution $x \in [0,1]$ of (15)–(12). Moreover, we have

$$a^* b_2 + bb_2(a_1^* + b_1 r_1)T^{2-\gamma} + bb_1(a_2^* T^{2-\zeta} + r_1 b_2 T^{2-\gamma}) = 0.1950 < 1.$$

Thus, all the hypotheses of Theorem 2 are valid, so the solution of Problem (15)–(12) is unique.

Example 2. *Consider the problem*

$$\frac{dx}{dt} = \frac{1}{4}e^{-t^2}\cos(2t) + \frac{1}{3}\left(\frac{1}{3}(\frac{1}{5-t} + D^{\frac{1}{3}}x(t)) \cdot \int_0^{\frac{1}{2}t} \frac{1}{5}(\frac{e^{-s}}{s+2} + D^{\frac{1}{4}}x(s))ds\right) \quad t \in [0,1], \tag{13}$$

$$x(\tau) = \frac{1}{5} + \int_0^{1-\tau} \left(\frac{1}{18}s^2(\sin(2s+1)) + \frac{1}{6}x(s)D^{\frac{1}{5}}x(s)\right)ds, \tag{14}$$

where

$$\zeta = \frac{1}{3},\ \eta = \frac{1}{5},\ \gamma = \frac{1}{4},\ t \in (0,1],\ x(0) = \frac{1}{5}.$$

Then,

$$\begin{aligned} & f(t, g_1(t, D^{\zeta}x(t)) \int_0^{\vartheta(t)} g_2(s, D^{\gamma}x(s)ds)) \\ = & \frac{1}{4}e^{-t^2}\cos(2t) + \frac{1}{3}(\frac{1}{3}\frac{1}{5-t} + D^{\frac{1}{3}}x(t)) \cdot \int_0^{\frac{1}{2}t} \frac{1}{5}(\frac{e^{-s}}{s+2} + D^{\frac{1}{4}}x(s))ds. \end{aligned}$$

Set

$$\begin{aligned} g_1(t, D^{\zeta}x(t)) &= \frac{1}{3}(\frac{1}{5-t} + D^{\frac{1}{3}}x(t)) \\ g_2(t, D^{\gamma}x(t)) &= \frac{1}{5}(\frac{e^{-t}}{t+2} + D^{\frac{1}{4}}x(t)) \\ h(t, x(t) \cdot D^{\eta}x(t)) &= \frac{1}{6}(\frac{1}{3}t^2(\sin(2t+1)) + x(t)D^{\frac{1}{5}}x(t)). \end{aligned}$$

Here, we have

$$\begin{aligned} a^* &= \frac{1}{4},\ a_1^* = \frac{1}{12},\ a_2^* = \frac{1}{10},\ b = b_1 = \frac{1}{3},\ b_2 = \frac{1}{5},\ b_3 = \frac{1}{6}, \\ N &= \frac{1}{18},\ r_1 = 0.3,\ r_2 = 0.05. \end{aligned}$$

It is obvious that all the hypotheses of Theorem 1 are valid. Hence the solution $x \in [0,T]$ of (13) and (14) exists. Moreover, we have

$$a^* b_2 + bb_2(a^* + b_1 r_1)t^{2-\gamma} + bb_1(a_2^* t^{2-\gamma} + r_1 b_2 t^{2-\gamma}) = 0.2314 < 1,$$

Thus, all the hypotheses of Theorem 2 are valid, and then the solution to (13)–(14) is unique.

Example 3. *Consider the next problem*

$$\frac{dx}{dt} = \frac{1}{4}(\frac{t}{t^3+1}) + \frac{1}{3}(\frac{7+3t}{16} + \frac{\ln(1+|D^{\frac{1}{5}}x(t)|)}{5t+7}) \cdot \int_0^{t^4} (\frac{1}{9-s} + \frac{(D^{\frac{1}{7}}x(s))^2}{6(1+|D^{\frac{1}{7}}x(s)|)})ds, \quad t \in (0, \frac{1}{3}], \tag{15}$$

$$x(\tau) = \frac{1}{4} + \int_0^{\frac{1}{3}-\tau} (\frac{s^2}{s^2+1} + \frac{\ln(1+|x(s)\cdot D^{\frac{1}{4}}x(s)|)}{8+s^2})ds. \tag{16}$$

Here, we have

$$x_0 = \frac{1}{4}, \zeta = \frac{1}{5}, \eta = \frac{1}{7}, \gamma = \frac{1}{4}, \vartheta(t) = t^4,$$

and

$$f\Big(t, g_1(t, D^{\zeta}x(t)) \cdot \int_0^{\vartheta(t)} g_2(s, D^{\eta}x(s)ds)\Big)$$
$$= \frac{1}{4}(\frac{t}{t^3+1}) + \frac{1}{3}(\frac{7+3t}{16} + \frac{\ln(1+|D^{\frac{1}{5}}x(t)|)}{5t+7}) \cdot \int_0^{t^4} (\frac{1}{9-s} + \frac{(D^{\frac{1}{7}}x(s))^2}{6(1+|D^{\frac{1}{7}}x(s)|)})ds.$$

Set

$$\begin{aligned}
&\vartheta(t) = t^4,\\
g_1(t, D^{\zeta}x(t)) &= \frac{7+3t}{16} + \frac{\ln(1+|D^{\frac{1}{5}}x(t)|)}{5t+7},\\
g_2(t, D^{\gamma}x(t)) &= \frac{1}{9-s} + \frac{(D^{\frac{1}{7}}x(s))^2}{6(1+|D^{\frac{1}{7}}x(s)|)},\\
h(t, x(t)\cdot D^{\eta}x(t)) &= \frac{t^2}{t^2+1} + \frac{\ln(1+|x(t)\cdot D^{\frac{1}{4}}x(t)|)}{8+t^2}.
\end{aligned}$$

Thus, we obtain

$$a^* = \frac{1}{12}, a_1^* = \frac{1}{2}, a_2^* = \frac{3}{26}, N = \frac{1}{9}, b = \frac{1}{3}, b_1 = \frac{1}{7}, b_2 = \frac{1}{6}, b_3 = \frac{1}{8},$$
$$r_1 \approx 0.03, \text{ and } r_2 \approx 0.42.$$

It is clear that all assumptions of Theorem 1 are satisfied. Hence, there exists at least one solution $x \in [0, T]$ of (12)–(15). Moreover, we have

$$a^*b_2 + bb_2(a_1^* + b_1r_1)t^{2-\gamma} + bb_1(a_2^*t^{2-\gamma} + r_1b_2t^{2-\gamma}) = 0.043 < 1.$$

Thus, all assumptions of Theorem 2 are satisfied, and then the solution of the problem (12)–(15) is unique.

7. Conclusions

In this manuscript, we considered the constrained problem of the fractional-order integro-differential equation (1) under the quadratic functional integro-differential constraint (2). We proved the existence of solutions to the problem (1) and (2). The sufficient conditions for the uniqueness of the solution have been presented. The Hyers–Ulam stability of the problem (1) and (2) has been analyzed. The continuous dependence of the unique solution on its fractional-order derivative $D^{\zeta}x(t)$, the parameter x_0, and the function h has been studied. We introduced several examples and special cases.

Author Contributions: A.M.A.E.-S., Formal analysis, Supervision; A.A.A.A., Methodology; E.M.A.H., Formal analysis; H.R.E., Methodology. All authors have read and agreed to the published version of this manuscript.

Funding: This research received no external funding.

Data Availability Statement: Data are contained within the article.

Conflicts of Interest: The authors declare no conflicts of interest.

References

1. Baleanu, D.; Etemad, S.; Rezapour, S. On a fractional hybrid integro-differential equation with mixed hybrid integral boundary value conditions by using three operators. *Alex. Eng. J.* **2020**, *59*, 3019–3027. [CrossRef]
2. Banaś, J.; Zajac, T. A new approach to the theory of functional integral equations of fractional order. *J. Math. Anal. Appl.* **2011**, *375*, 375–387. [CrossRef]
3. Boucherif, A.; Precup, R. On the nonlocal initial value problem for first order differential equations. *Fixed Point Theory* **2003**, *4*, 205–212.
4. Caponetto, R. Fractional order systems. In *Modeling and Control Applications*; World Scientific: Singapore, 2010, Volume 72.
5. Caputo, M. Linear model of dissipation whose Q is almost frequency independent-II. *Geophys. J. R. Astr. Soc.* **1967**, *13*, 529–539. [CrossRef]
6. Kazemi, M.; Yaghoobnia, A.R. Application of fixed point theorem to solvability of functional stochastic integral equations. *Appl. Math. Comput.* **2022**, *417*, 126759. [CrossRef]
7. Monje, C.A.; Chen, Y.; Vinagre, B.M.; Xue, D.; Feliu-Batlle, V. *Fractional-Order Systems and Controls: Fundamentals and Applications*; Springer Science & Business Media: Berlin/Heidelberg, Germany, 2010.
8. Podlubny, I. Fractional-order systems and fractional-order controllers. *Inst. Exp. Phys. Slovak Acad. Sci. Kosice* **1994**, *12.3*, 1–18.
9. Samko, S.G.; Kilbas, A.A.; Marichev, O.I. *Integrals and Derivatives of the Fractional Order and Some of Their Applications*; Nauka i Tehnika: Minsh, Belarus, 1987. (In Russian English Translation)
10. Schneider, W.R.; Wyss, W. Fractional diffusion and wave equations. *J. Math. Phys.* **1989**, *30*, 134. [CrossRef]
11. El-Sayed, A.M.A.; Alrashdi, M.A.H. On a functional integral equation with constraint existence of solution and continuous dependence. *Int. J. Differ. Eq. Appl.* **2019**, *18*, 37–48.
12. Al-Issa, S. M.; El-Sayed, A.M.A; Hashem, H.H.G. An Outlook on Hybrid Fractional Modeling of a Heat Controller with Multi-Valued Feedback Control. *Fractal Fract.* **2023**, *7*, 759. [CrossRef]
13. Nasertayoob, P. Solvability and asymptotic stability of a class of nonlinear functional-integral equation with feedback control. *Commun. Nonlinear Anal.* **2018**, *5*, 19–27.
14. El-Sayed, A.M.; Ba-Ali, M.M.; Hamdallah, E.M. An Investigation of a Nonlinear Delay Functional Equation with a Quadratic Functional Integral Constraint. *Mathematics* **2023**, *11*, 4475. [CrossRef]
15. De la Sen, M.; Alonso-Quesada, S. Control issues for the Beverton–Holt equation in ecology by locally monitoring the environment carrying capacity: Non-adaptive and adaptive cases. *Appl. Math. Comput.* **2009**, *215*, 2616–2633. [CrossRef]
16. Rezapour, S.; Etemad, S.; Agarwal, R.P.; Nonlaopon, K. On a Lyapunov-Type Inequality for Control of a y-Model Thermostat and the Existence of Its Solutions. *Mathematics* **2022**, *10*, 4023. [CrossRef]
17. Zhao, K. Stability of a nonlinear Langevin system of ML-Type fractional derivative affected by time-varying delays and differential feedback control. *Fractal Fract.* **2022**, *6*, 725. [CrossRef]
18. El-Sayed, A.M.A.; Hamdallah, E.A.; Ahmed, R.G. On a nonlinear constrained problem of a nonlinear functional integral equation. *Appl. Anal. Optim.* **2022**, *6*, 95–107.
19. Cosentino, C.; Bates, D. *Feedback Control in Systems Biology*; CRC Press: Boca Raton, FL, USA, 2011.
20. Cowan, N.J.; Ankarali, M.M.; Dyhr, J.P.; Madhav, M.S.; Roth, E.; Sefati, S.; Sponberg, S.; Stamper, S.A.; Fortune, E.S.; Daniel, T.L. Feedback control as a framework for understanding tradeoffs in biology. *Am. Zool.* **2014**, *54*, 223–237. [CrossRef] [PubMed]
21. Del Vecchio, D.; Dy, A. J.; Qian, Y. Control theory meets synthetic biology. *J. R. Soc. Interface* **2016** , *13*, 20160380. [CrossRef] [PubMed]
22. Peiffer, S.; Dan, T.B.B.; Frevert, T.; Cavari, B.Z. Survival of *E. coli* and enterococci in sediment-water systems of Lake Kinneret under (Feedback) controlled concentrations of hydrogen sulfide. *Water Res.* **1988**, *22*, 233–240. [CrossRef]
23. De Leenheer, P.; Smith, H. Feedback control for chemostat models. *J. Math. Biol.* **2003**, *46*, 48–70. [CrossRef]
24. Marshall, S.H.; Smith, D.R. Feedback control and the distribution of prime numbers. *Math. Mag.* **2013**, *86*, 189–203. [CrossRef]
25. Stewart, G.E.; Dimitry, M.G.; Dumont, G.A. Feedback controller design for a spatially distributed system: The paper machine problem. *IEEE Trans. Control. Syst. Technol.* **2003**, *11.5*, 612–628. [CrossRef]
26. Chen, F.; Lin, F.; Chen, X. Sufficient conditions for the existence positive periodic solutions of a class of neutral delay models with feedback control. *Appl. Math. Comput.* **2004**, *158*, 45–68. [CrossRef]
27. Matveeva, I. Exponential stability of solutions to nonlinear time-varying delay systems of neutral type equations with periodic coefficients. *Electron. J. Differ. Eq.* **2020**, *20*, 1–12. [CrossRef]
28. Saker, S.H. Periodic solutions, oscillation and attractivity of discrete nonlinear delay population model. *Math. Comput. Model.* **2008**, *47*, 278–297. [CrossRef]
29. Yang, Z. Positive periodic solutions of a class of single-species neutral models with state-dependent delay and feedback control. *Eur. J. Appl. Math.* **2006**, *17*, 735–757. [CrossRef]
30. Nasertayoob, P.; Vaezpour, S.M. Positive periodic solution for a nonlinear neutral delay population equation with feedback control. *J. Nonlinear Sci. Appl.* **2013**, *6*, 152–161. [CrossRef]
31. Ahmed, E.; El-Sayed, A.M.A.; El-Mesiry, A.E.M.; El-Saka, H.A.A. Numerical solution for the fractional replicator equation. *Int. J. Mod. Phys. C* **2005**, *16*, 1017–1026. [CrossRef]
32. Banaś, J.; Caballero, J.; Rocha, J.; Sadarangani, K. Monotonic solutions of a class of quadratic integral equations of Volterra type. *Comput. Math. Appl.* **2005**, *49*, 943–952. [CrossRef]

33. El-Sayed, A.M.A.; Gaafar, F.M. Fractional calculus and some intermediate physical processes. *J. A. Math.Comp.* **2033**, *144*, 117–126. [CrossRef]
34. Failla, G.; Zingales, M. Advanced materials modelling via fractional calculus: Challenges and perspectives. *Phil. Trans. R. Soc.* **2020**, *378*, 20200050. [CrossRef] [PubMed]
35. Sumelka, W. Fractional viscoplasticity. *Mech. Res. Commun.* **2014**, *56*, 31–36. [CrossRef]
36. Bader, R.; Papageorgiou, N.S. Nonlinear multivalued boundary value problems. *Discuss. Math. Differ. Inclusions Control. Optim.* **2001**, 21, 127–148. [CrossRef]
37. Debnath, P.; Srivastava, H.M.; Kumam, P.; Hazarika, B. *Fixed Point Theory and Fractional Calculus*; Springer Nature: Singapore, 2022.
38. Gasiński, L.; Papageorgiou, N.S. Nonlinear second-order multivalued boundary value problems. *Proc. Indian Acad. Sci. (Math. Sci.)* **2003**, *113*, 293–319. [CrossRef]
39. Kamenskii, M.; Obukhovskii, V.; Petrosyan, G.; Yao, J. Existence and approximation of solutions to nonlocal boundary value problems for fractional differential inclusions. *Fixed Point Theory Appl.* **2019**, *2019*, 2. [CrossRef]
40. Tidke, H.L.; Kharat, V.V.; More, G.N. Some results on nonlinear mixed fractional integro differential equations. *J. Adv. Math. Stud.* **2022**, *15*, 274–287.
41. Curtain, R.F.; Pritchard, A.J. *Functional Analysis in Modern Applied Mathematics*; Academic Press: Cambridge, MA, USA, 1977.
42. Dunford, N.; Schwartz, J.T. *Linear Operators, (Part 1), General Theory*; NewYork Interscience: New York, NY, USA, 1957.
43. Cobzaş, Ş.; Miculescu, R.; Nicolae, A. *Lipschitz Functions*; Springer International Publishing: Berlin/Heidelberg, Germany, 2019.
44. Jung, S.M. *Hyers-Ulam-Rassias Stability of Functional Equations in Nonlinear Analysis*; Springer Science & Business Media: Berlin/Heidelberg, Germany, 2011; Volume 48.

fractal and fractional

MDPI

Article

Radial Basis Functions Approximation Method for Time-Fractional FitzHugh–Nagumo Equation

Mehboob Alam [1,*], Sirajul Haq [1], Ihteram Ali [2], M. J. Ebadi [3,*] and Soheil Salahshour [4,5,6]

1 Faculty of Engineering Sciences, GIK Institute, Topi 23640, Pakistan; siraj@giki.edu.pk
2 Department of Mathematics and Statistics, Women University, Swabi 23430, Pakistan; ihteramali60@gmail.com
3 Department of Mathematics, Chabahar Maritime University, Chabahar 9971756499, Iran
4 Faculty of Engineering and Natural Sciences, Istanbul Okan University, Istanbul 34959, Turkey
5 Faculty of Engineering and Natural Sciences, Bahcesehir University, Istanbul 34353, Turkey
6 Department of Computer Science and Mathematics, Lebanese American University, Beirut P.O. Box 13-5053, Lebanon; soheil.salahshour@okan.edu.tr
* Correspondence: mehboobalam.ma92@gmail.com (M.A.); ebadi@cmu.ac.ir (M.J.E.)

Abstract: In this paper, a numerical approach employing radial basis functions has been applied to solve time-fractional FitzHugh–Nagumo equation. Spatial approximation is achieved by combining radial basis functions with the collocation method, while temporal discretization is accomplished using a finite difference scheme. To evaluate the effectiveness of this method, we first conduct an eigenvalue stability analysis and then validate the results with numerical examples, varying the shape parameter c of the radial basis functions. Notably, this method offers the advantage of being mesh-free, which reduces computational overhead and eliminates the need for complex mesh generation processes. To assess the method's performance, we subject it to examples. The simulated results demonstrate a high level of agreement with exact solutions and previous research. The accuracy and efficiency of this method are evaluated using discrete error norms, including L_2, L_∞, and L_{rms}.

Keywords: fractional differential equation; meshless method; radial basis functions; FitzHugh–Nagumo equation; stability

1. Introduction

In recent years, the FitzHugh–Nagumo equation has garnered significant attention among physicists and mathematicians due to its critical role in mathematical physics. This equation finds applications in diverse fields, such as flame propagation, logistic population growth, neurophysiology, branching Brownian motion processes, autocatalytic chemical reactions, and nuclear reactor theory [1]. The FitzHugh–Nagumo equation is a nonlinear reaction–diffusion equation given by

$$u_t = u_{xx} + u(u-\beta)(1-u), \quad t > 0,\ x \in \Omega. \tag{1}$$

In the context of modeling nerve-impulse propagation [2,3], u represents the electrical potential transmission across the cell membrane. This equation elegantly combines diffusion and nonlinearity, with the behavior governed by the term $u(u-\beta)(1-u)$.

Many researchers have extensively investigated FitzHugh–Nagumo Equation (1). Notably, Shih et al. [4] explored this equation, revealing its applications in the domains of population dynamics and circuit theory. Kawahara and Tanaka [5] obtained solutions for the FitzHugh–Nagumo equation through the Hirota method. Nucci and Clarkson [6] derived solutions employing Jacobi elliptic functions. Li and Guo [7] conducted an examination and discovered a novel series of exact solutions using the first integral technique. Furthermore, Abbasbandy [8] determined soliton solutions through the homotopy analysis scheme. The FitzHugh–Nagumo equation attracted the attention of Kakiuchi and

Tchizawa [9], who obtained an explicit duck solution and delay. Schonbek [10] delved into FitzHugh–Nagumo equation in the context of boundary value problems. Yanagida [11] studied the equation's stability concerning traveling front solutions. Jackson [12] explored semidiscrete estimates for the FitzHugh–Nagumo equation. Additionally, Gao and Wang [13] discussed the existence of wavefronts and impulses in FitzHugh–Nagumo models. Employing the pseudo-spectral technique, Olmos and Shizgal [14] examined the FitzHugh–Nagumo equation. Dehghan et al. [15] investigated the FitzHugh–Nagumo equation using semianalytical techniques. The trajectory of arbitrary (real or complex) ordered derivatives exhibits nonlocal behavior when interpreted as fractional derivatives with memory indices [16,17]. This finding implies that when modeling real-world problems using fractional-order derivatives and integrals, there is a memory effect. In other words, the future state of a system not solely is determined by its current state but also takes into account its past states [18,19]. Consequently, FitzHugh–Nagumo Equation (1), which deals with arbitrary-order derivatives, can be seen as an extension of the traditional FitzHugh–Nagumo Equation (1).

Numerous authors have highlighted the practicality and significance of fractional-order derivatives and integrals in mathematical modeling within various scientific and engineering domains [20–23]. Given the ongoing research in this field and its importance in scientific applications, we now consider the fractional extension of Equation (1). The fractional version of the FitzHugh–Nagumo equation is derived from the well-known equation by replacing the first-order time derivative with an arbitrary-order derivative in the Caputo sense. This fractional model of FitzHugh–Nagumo Equation (1) can be expressed as follows:

$$u_t^{\alpha} = u_{xx} + u(u-\beta)(1-u), \quad t > 0,\ x \in \Omega, \tag{2}$$

with initial conditions (ICs) and boundary conditions (BCs)

$$\begin{cases} u(0,x) = u_0(x), & x \in \Omega, \\ u(t,a) = u_1(t), \quad \text{and} \quad u(t,b) = u_2(t), & x \in \partial\Omega, \quad t > 0, \end{cases} \tag{3}$$

where u is a function of both t and x, i.e., $u = u(t,x)$; β is an arbitrary constant; Ω represents the domain; and $\partial\Omega$ denotes the boundary of the domain. The time domain is defined as $t \in [0, t_{max}]$, where t_{max} is a finite real number representing the final time. The functions $u_0(x)$, $u_1(t)$, and $u_2(t)$ are known continuous functions. From Equation (2), it is important to observe that

1. When $\beta = -1$, then Equation (2) converts into the well-known Newell–Whitehead equation
$$u_t^{\alpha} = u_{xx} + u(u+1)(1-u), \quad t > 0,\ x \in \Omega. \tag{4}$$
2. When $\beta = 1$, then Equation (2) converts into the nonlinear FitzHugh–Nagumo equation
$$u_t^{\alpha} = u_{xx} + u(u-1)(1-u), \quad t > 0,\ x \in \Omega. \tag{5}$$
3. When $\beta = 0$, then Equation (2) converts into Fisher's equation
$$u_t^{\alpha} = u_{xx} + u^2(1-u), \quad t > 0,\ x \in \Omega. \tag{6}$$

Recent scientific research has involved a comprehensive exploration of the FitzHugh–Nagumo equation, employing a variety of analytical, numerical, and semianalytical methods to obtain both exact and approximate solutions. For instance, Kumar et al. [24] conducted a numerical investigation of the FitzHugh–Nagumo equation, utilizing a combination of the q-homotopy analysis approach and the Laplace transform method. Patel and Patel [25] examined the FitzHugh–Nagumo equation by applying the fractional reduced differential transform method (FRDTM). Abdel-Aty et al. [26] studied the time-fractional FitzHugh–Nagumo equation, both computationally and numerically, employing the improved Riccati expansion method and the B-spline method with a focus on the Atangana–Baleanu derivative. Additionally, Prakash and Kaur [27] explored the fractional model of the FitzHugh–Nagumo equation, which is relevant to the transmission of nerve impulses. They developed a reliable and computationally effective numerical scheme that combines the homotopy perturbation method with the Laplace transform approach. Lastly, Deniz [28] investigated the modified fractional version of the FitzHugh–Nagumo equation using the optimal perturbation iteration method.

Over the past decade, mesh-free methods using radial basis functions (RBFs) have gained significant prominence. This surge in interest is attributed to the challenges associated with classical numerical methods, such as the finite difference method, finite element method, and finite volume method, especially when dealing with two- or three-dimensional problems that require mesh generation. In 1990, Kansa introduced a technique for solving PDEs through the collocation method employing RBFs [29]. This approach involves approximating the solution using RBFs, and the collocation method is used to compute the unknown coefficients. The RBFs commonly used in the literature for solving PDEs include Hardy's multiquadric (MQ), Duchon's thin plate splines (TPSs), Gaussians (GS), inverse multiquadric (IMQ), and inverse quadric (IQ). The existence, uniqueness, and convergence of the RBF-based technique have been discussed by Franke and Schaback [30], Madych and Nelson [31], and Micchelli [32]. Kansa presented the initial concept of using RBFs to solve PDEs, and Golberg et al. [33] later refined it. In the context of solving PDEs, these RBFs have a shape parameter that can be adjusted to produce the best accurate results.

One of the main challenges associated with the RBF collocation method, as reported in the literature, is the dense and ill-conditioned nature of the system matrix that arises during the collocation process. This ill conditioning typically arises from a large number of nodes or an inappropriate choice of the shape parameter. However, various remedies for this issue have been proposed, including the contour-Padé algorithm, RBF-QR algorithm, extended precision arithmetic, and Hilbert–Schmidt decomposition, among others [34–36].

The main objective of this study is to compute a numerical solution for FitzHugh–Nagumo Equations (2) and (3) using the RBF collocation method. The structure of the paper is as follows: The methodology and stability analysis for Equations (2) and (3) are described in Section 2. Section 3 presents a number of examples and related discussions in order to validate the suggested methodology. Finally, in Section 4, a brief conclusion summarizes the study's important findings and contributions.

2. Methodology

The suggested meshless technique for solving FitzHugh–Nagumo Equations (2) and (3) will be discussed in this part along with its methodology. We present the notation to streamline our conversation: $\mathrm{u}^n = \mathrm{u}(\mathrm{t}_n, \mathrm{x})$, where $\mathrm{t}_n = n\delta\mathrm{t}|_{n=0}^{\mathrm{M}}$. Here, $\delta\mathrm{t} = \mathrm{t}_{max}/\mathrm{M}$ represents the time-step size, and $\mathrm{h} = 1/\mathrm{N}$ is the space-step size, where N and M are the number of points in the intervals $[\mathrm{a}, \mathrm{b}]$ and $[0, \mathrm{t}_{\max}]$, respectively.

The time-fractional derivative in Equation (2) uses the Caputo fractional partial derivative of order $\alpha \in (0,1)$, defined as [16]

$$\frac{\partial^\alpha \mathrm{u}}{\partial \mathrm{t}^\alpha} = \frac{1}{\Gamma(1-\alpha)} \int_0^{\mathrm{t}} \frac{\partial \mathrm{u}}{\partial \mathrm{s}} (\mathrm{t}-\mathrm{s})^{-\alpha} ds.$$

2.1. Time-Fractional Derivative Approximation

In Equation (2), the temporal part is discretized using the method described in [37] as follows:

$$\begin{aligned}\frac{\partial^\alpha u^{n+1}}{\partial t^\alpha} =&\frac{(\delta t)^{-\alpha}}{\Gamma(2-\alpha)}\sum_{k=0}^{n}\left(u^{n+1-k}-u^{n-k}\right)\left((k+1)^{1-\alpha}-(k)^{1-\alpha}\right)+\mathcal{O}(\delta t^{2-\alpha})\\ =&\ell^*_\alpha\left(u^{n+1}-u^n\right)+\mathfrak{B}^n+\mathcal{O}(\delta t^{2-\alpha}),\end{aligned}$$

where

$$\mathfrak{B}^n=\ell^*_\alpha\sum_{k=1}^{n}\ell^{**}_\alpha(k)\left(u^{n+1-k}-u^{n-k}\right)$$

and

$$\ell^*_\alpha=\frac{(\delta t)^{-\alpha}}{\Gamma(2-\alpha)},\quad \ell^{**}_\alpha(k)=(k+1)^{1-\alpha}-(k)^{1-\alpha}.$$

It is important to observe that $\mathfrak{B}^n=0$ whenever $n=0$. With this consideration, the discretization formula can be expressed as follows:

$$\frac{\partial^\alpha u^{n+1}}{\partial t^\alpha}=\begin{cases}\ell^*_\alpha\left(u^{n+1}-u^n\right)+\mathfrak{B}^n+\mathcal{O}(\delta t^{2-\alpha}), & \alpha\in(0,1),\\ \dfrac{u^{n+1}-u^n}{\delta t}+\mathcal{O}(\delta t), & \alpha=1.\end{cases} \tag{7}$$

2.2. The θ-Weighted Scheme

Utilizing Equation (7) in conjunction with the θ-weighted scheme and neglecting the error term, we can express Equation (2) in their time-discretized form as follows:

$$\begin{aligned}&\ell^*_\alpha u^{n+1}-\theta\left(u^{n+1}_{xx}-\left(u^{n+1}\right)^3+(1+\beta)\left(u^{n+1}\right)^2-\beta u^{n+1}\right)\\ &=\ell^*_\alpha u^n-(\theta-1)\left(u^n_{xx}-(u^n)^3+(1+\beta)(u^n)^2-\beta u^n\right)-\mathfrak{B}^n.\end{aligned} \tag{8}$$

The nonlinear terms in Equation (8) can be linearized using the following approach:

$$\begin{cases}\left(u^{n+1}\right)^3=3(u^n)^2u^{n+1}-2(u^n)^3,\\ \left(u^{n+1}\right)^2=2u^nu^{n+1}-(u^n)^2.\end{cases} \tag{9}$$

By substituting the values from Equation (9) into Equation (8), the following expressions can be obtained after simplification:

$$\nu^n_1u^{n+1}-\theta u^{n+1}_{xx}=\nu^n_2u^n+(1-\theta)u^n_{xx}-\mathfrak{B}^n, \tag{10}$$

where

$$\nu^n_1=\ell^*_\alpha+\theta\left(\beta-2(1+\beta)u^n+3(u^n)^2\right)\quad\text{and}\quad \nu^n_2=\ell^*_\alpha+\beta(\theta-1)+(3\theta-1)(u^n)^2+(1+\beta-2\theta(1+\beta))u^n.$$

2.3. Radial Basis Function Approximation Scheme

Now, we move on to approximating the spatial component using RBFs and the collocation method. To do this, the collocation points are taken as $\{x_i\}_{i=1}^{N}$. Consequently, we can represent the solution at interior points by employing RBFs denoted as $\phi_{ij}=\phi(\|x_i-x_j\|)$ in the following manner:

$$u^{n+1}=\sum_{j=1}^{N}\lambda^{n+1}_j\phi_{ij}=\Phi\daleth^{n+1},\quad i=2,\ldots,N-1, \tag{11}$$

where $\daleth^{n+1} = [\lambda_1^{n+1}, \ldots, \lambda_N^{n+1}]^T$ represents a vector of unknown coefficients at the $(n+1)^{th}$ time level. $\Phi = [\phi_{ij}]_{1 \leqslant i,j \leqslant N}$ is the matrix of RBFs, and $\| \cdot \|$ denotes the Euclidean norm. The boundary conditions (3) are approximated as follows:

$$\sum_{j=1}^{N} \lambda_j^{n+1} \phi_{1j} = u_1^{n+1} \quad \text{and} \quad \sum_{j=1}^{N} \lambda_j^{n+1} \phi_{Nj} = u_2^{n+1}. \tag{12}$$

Furthermore, the spatial derivative at the interior points $x \in \Omega$ are given as follows:

$$u_{xx}^{n+1} = \Phi_{xx} \daleth^{n+1}. \tag{13}$$

By substituting Equations (11)–(13) into Equation (10) and performing simplifications, we arrive at the following equation:

$$\mathbf{A} \daleth^{n+1} = \mathbf{B} \daleth^{n} + \mathbf{Z}^{n+1}, \tag{14}$$

where

$$\mathbf{A} = \begin{cases} \nu_1^n [\Phi]_{ij} - \theta [\Phi_{xx}]_{ij}, & x_i \in \Omega, \\ [\Phi]_{ij}, & x_i \in \partial\Omega, \end{cases}$$

$$\mathbf{B} = \begin{cases} \nu_2^n [\Phi]_{ij} + (1-\theta) [\Phi_{xx}]_{ij}, & x_i \in \Omega, \\ 0, & x_i \in \partial\Omega, \end{cases}$$

$$\mathbf{Z} = \begin{cases} -\mathfrak{B}^n, & x_i \in \Omega, \\ \mathfrak{C}^{n+1}, & x_i \in \partial\Omega, \end{cases}$$

where $\mathfrak{C}^{n+1} = [u_1^{n+1}, 0, \cdots, 0, u_2^{n+1}]^T$. Now Equation (14) implies that

$$\daleth^{n+1} = \mathbf{A}^{-1} \mathbf{B} \daleth^{n} + \mathbf{A}^{-1} \mathbf{Z}^{n+1}. \tag{15}$$

From Equations (11) and (15), it follows that

$$u^{n+1} = \Phi \mathbf{A}^{-1} \mathbf{B} \Phi^{-1} u^n + \Phi \mathbf{A}^{-1} \mathbf{Z}^{n+1}. \tag{16}$$

The numerical solution at any given time level n using scheme (16) can be obtained. We initialize the initial value u^0 by incorporating the initial condition $u(0, x) = u_0(x)$. In the subsequent section, stability analysis of scheme (16) will be discussed.

2.4. Stability

To examine stability, we employ an approach outlined in [38]. For the error vector $\mathbb{E}$ defined as

$$\mathbb{E} = u_{exact} - u_{approx},$$

the relation in (16) can be expressed as

$$\mathbb{E}^{n+1} = \wp \mathbb{E}^n,$$

where $\wp = \Phi \mathbf{A}^{-1} \mathbf{B} \Phi^{-1}$ represents the amplification matrix. According to the Lax–Richtmyer criterion of stability, the present method can be considered stable if

$$\|\wp\| \leqslant 1.$$

It is important to note that the inequality

$$\rho(\wp) \leqslant \|\wp\|$$

always holds, where $\rho(\wp)$ represents the spectral radius of the matrix $\wp$.

3. Computational Results and Discussion

In this section, the implementation of the method for solving FitzHugh–Nagumo Equations (2) and (3) has been presented. Computer simulations have been carried out via MATLAB R2020a on a PC with the following configuration: processor: Intel (R) Core (TM) i7-4790 CPU @ 3.60 GHz 3.60 GHz, RAM 8.00 GB, and system type: 64-bit operating system, x64-based processor. The accuracy and efficiency of the method are assessed using the following error norms:

$$L_2 = \left[h \sum_{i=1}^{N} (u_{exact} - u_{approx})^2 \right]^{1/2}, \quad L_\infty = \max_i |u_{exact} - u_{approx}|,$$

$$L_{rms} = \left[\frac{1}{N} \sum_{i=1}^{N} (u_{exact} - u_{approx})^2 \right]^{1/2}, \quad \text{Absolute error} = |u_{exact} - u_{approx}|.$$

For the solution of FitzHugh–Nagumo Equations (2) and (3), the following RBFs have been used:

- $MQ : \phi_{ij} = \sqrt{r_{ij}^2 + c^2}$;
- $IMQ : \phi_{ij} = \left(r_{ij}^2 + c^2\right)^{-1/2}$;
- $IQ : \phi_{ij} = \left(r_{ij}^2 + c^2\right)^{-1}$;
- $GS : \phi_{ij} = \exp(-c^2 r_{ij}^2)$,

where $c > 0$ represents the shape parameter and $r_{ij} = |x_i - x_j|_{1 \leqslant i,j \leqslant N}$.

Selection of Shape Parameter

Determining the optimal value for the shape parameter c can be a challenging task. The random selection of c can be a limitation since many researchers choose c using suboptimal criteria. Therefore, in this study, we employ the extended Rippa algorithm to select the optimal shape parameter. Rippa's algorithm, as described by Rippa [39], estimates the cost function based on the norm of the error vector, which can be either the L_2 or L_∞ norm. The parameter c that minimizes this cost function is deemed satisfactory, as it results in an approximation quality comparable to that achieved with the optimal c. We also provide plots illustrating the best-suited values of c obtained using this algorithm.

Example 1. *Let us consider FitzHugh–Nagumo Equations* (2) *and* (3) *with* $\beta = 1$. *The exact solution is given by [25]*

$$u(t,x) = \frac{1}{2} + \frac{1}{2}\tanh\left(\frac{\sqrt{2}x - t}{4}\right).$$

The ICs and BCs are derived from the exact solution within the domain $x \in [0,1]$. *The approximate solution is obtained using various RBFs, such as MQ, IMQ, IQ, and GS, with parameters* $N = 10$ *and* $\delta t = 0.1$ *for different values of* α *(0.25, 0.5, 0.75, and 1). The present method is examined, and the results are recorded in Tables 1 and 2 for various nodal points* (x_i, t_n). *The results are then compared with FRDTM. The comparison reveals that the present method produces good accuracy, specially for fractional order with the best results obtained using GS, MQ, IMQ, and IQ. Additionally, error norms at various time levels using the mentioned RBFs are dispatched in Tables 3 and 4.*

Furthermore, stability and error norm plots are displayed in Figure 1 for MQ, IMQ, IQ, and GS RBFs against the shape parameter. These plots clearly demonstrate that the present method fully satisfies the Lax–Richtmyer stability criterion. Surface plots in Figure 2 illustrate that the computed solutions using these RBFs closely match the exact solution. Absolute errors at various time levels for $\alpha = 1$ *are shown in Figure 3, indicating reasonable accuracy. A comparison between the exact and computed solutions at the final time level is presented in Figure 4, confirming the high accuracy of the present method. Finally, in Figures 5–8, absolute errors for different values of α's at various time levels are shown using MQ, IMQ, IQ, and GS, respectively.*

Table 1. Comparison of computed values of the present method solution with FRDTM using MQ, IMQ, IQ, and GS RBFs for $\alpha = 0.25, 0.5$, $\beta = 1$, $N = 10$, $\theta = 0.5$, and $\delta t = 0.1$ corresponds to Example 1.

		$\alpha = 0.25$					$\alpha = 0.5$				
(x, t)	**Exact**	**[25]**	**MQ**	**IMQ**	**IQ**	**GS**	**[25]**	**MQ**	**IMQ**	**IQ**	**GS**
			$c = 6.824741$	$c = 8.12967$	$c = 5.34901$	$c = 0.251637$		$c = 5.8659$	$c = 6.88885$	$c = 5.18412$	$c = 0.25937$
(0.1, 0.2)	0.492678	0.427418	0.492029	0.492126	0.492364	0.492466	0.454935	0.492344	0.492386	0.492489	0.492564
(0.1, 0.4)	0.467723	0.411555	0.467129	0.467083	0.467582	0.467632	0.429688	0.467279	0.467401	0.467571	0.467645
(0.1, 0.6)	0.442927	0.401291	0.443115	0.442313	0.442917	0.442952	0.410894	0.442364	0.442535	0.442858	0.442910
(0.1, 0.8)	0.418414	0.393583	0.418856	0.418114	0.418463	0.418448	0.395550	0.418125	0.418259	0.418442	0.418426
(0.3, 0.2)	0.528004	0.461640	0.526474	0.526698	0.527298	0.527493	0.489905	0.527223	0.527325	0.527585	0.527735
(0.3, 0.4)	0.503033	0.445267	0.501595	0.501492	0.502762	0.502797	0.464133	0.501982	0.502252	0.502729	0.502842
(0.3, 0.6)	0.478047	0.434619	0.478461	0.476553	0.478071	0.478089	0.444777	0.476697	0.477079	0.477948	0.477992
(0.3, 0.8)	0.453171	0.426595	0.454236	0.452429	0.453300	0.453249	0.428860	0.452424	0.452737	0.453293	0.453186
(0.5, 0.2)	0.563051	0.496159	0.561223	0.561488	0.562257	0.562434	0.524966	0.562128	0.562253	0.562589	0.562736
(0.5, 0.4)	0.538313	0.479367	0.536561	0.536435	0.538071	0.538014	0.498899	0.537055	0.537363	0.538023	0.538083
(0.5, 0.6)	0.513385	0.468375	0.513874	0.511551	0.513484	0.513427	0.479131	0.511752	0.512181	0.513354	0.513312
(0.5, 0.8)	0.488390	0.460051	0.489708	0.487477	0.488573	0.488485	0.462744	0.487455	0.487818	0.488617	0.488400
(0.7, 0.2)	0.597480	0.530655	0.595947	0.596167	0.596862	0.596963	0.559780	0.596717	0.596823	0.597129	0.597225
(0.7, 0.4)	0.573214	0.513551	0.571727	0.571609	0.573089	0.572956	0.533657	0.572160	0.572409	0.573040	0.573026
(0.7, 0.6)	0.548590	0.502269	0.549021	0.547016	0.548741	0.548627	0.513645	0.547210	0.547543	0.548648	0.548530
(0.7, 0.8)	0.523726	0.493674	0.524882	0.522951	0.523912	0.523812	0.496910	0.522935	0.523224	0.523996	0.523734
(0.9, 0.2)	0.630974	0.564813	0.630322	0.630415	0.630735	0.630756	0.594013	0.630655	0.630700	0.630843	0.630870
(0.9, 0.4)	0.607400	0.547522	0.606766	0.606706	0.607385	0.607291	0.568079	0.606954	0.607057	0.607361	0.607325
(0.9, 0.6)	0.583315	0.536019	0.583518	0.582633	0.583413	0.583335	0.548003	0.582725	0.582855	0.583381	0.583293
(0.9, 0.8)	0.558825	0.527198	0.559346	0.558498	0.558922	0.558867	0.531062	0.558499	0.558612	0.558979	0.558831

Table 2. Comparison of computed values of the present method solution with FRDTM using MQ, IMQ, IQ, and GS RBFs for $\alpha = 0.75, 1$, $\beta = 1$, $N = 10$, $\theta = 0.5$, and $\delta t = 0.1$ corresponds to Example 1.

		$\alpha = 0.75$					$\alpha = 1$				
(x, t)	**Exact**	**[25]**	**MQ**	**IMQ**	**IQ**	**GS**	**[25]**	**MQ**	**IMQ**	**IQ**	**GS**
			$c = 5.80145$	$c = 4.48635$	$c = 5.38471$	$c = 0.26237$		$c = 6.78326$	$c = 7.23608$	$c = 7.88039$	$c = 0.16625$
(0.1, 0.2)	0.492678	0.477029	0.492540	0.492594	0.492594	0.492630	0.492678	0.492674	0.492676	0.492674	0.492666
(0.1, 0.4)	0.467723	0.449555	0.467487	0.467619	0.467623	0.467672	0.467722	0.467706	0.467716	0.467707	0.467642
(0.1, 0.6)	0.442927	0.425857	0.442690	0.442835	0.442856	0.442912	0.442927	0.442909	0.442918	0.442905	0.442841
(0.1, 0.8)	0.418414	0.404564	0.418328	0.418368	0.418407	0.418433	0.418416	0.418407	0.418406	0.418399	0.418391
(0.3, 0.2)	0.528004	0.512307	0.527682	0.527809	0.527819	0.527892	0.528003	0.527996	0.528000	0.527994	0.527975
(0.3, 0.4)	0.503033	0.484582	0.502475	0.502807	0.502828	0.502912	0.503030	0.502996	0.503019	0.502999	0.502881
(0.3, 0.6)	0.478047	0.460446	0.477457	0.477869	0.477926	0.478004	0.478035	0.478003	0.478026	0.477996	0.477887
(0.3, 0.8)	0.453171	0.438573	0.452937	0.453093	0.453193	0.453211	0.453136	0.453156	0.453153	0.453136	0.453114
(0.5, 0.2)	0.563051	0.547464	0.562671	0.562826	0.562848	0.562922	0.563051	0.563043	0.563047	0.563041	0.563015
(0.5, 0.4)	0.538313	0.519760	0.537643	0.538070	0.53811	0.538172	0.538308	0.53827	0.538298	0.538274	0.538165
(0.5, 0.6)	0.513385	0.495415	0.512658	0.513228	0.513305	0.513335	0.513362	0.513331	0.513361	0.513326	0.513249
(0.5, 0.8)	0.488390	0.473159	0.488089	0.488345	0.488474	0.488438	0.488322	0.488375	0.488370	0.488348	0.488328
(0.7, 0.2)	0.597480	0.582153	0.597165	0.597300	0.597326	0.597377	0.597479	0.597474	0.597477	0.597471	0.597446
(0.7, 0.4)	0.573214	0.554743	0.572650	0.573038	0.573084	0.573102	0.573207	0.573178	0.573202	0.573181	0.573113
(0.7, 0.6)	0.548590	0.530429	0.547972	0.548512	0.548585	0.548554	0.548558	0.548544	0.548571	0.548541	0.548522
(0.7, 0.8)	0.523726	0.508002	0.523469	0.523735	0.523852	0.523770	0.523629	0.523715	0.523709	0.523691	0.523680
(0.9, 0.2)	0.630974	0.616050	0.630841	0.630902	0.630917	0.630933	0.630973	0.630971	0.630972	0.630970	0.630957
(0.9, 0.4)	0.607400	0.589194	0.607160	0.607341	0.607365	0.607357	0.607392	0.607384	0.607395	0.607386	0.607368
(0.9, 0.6)	0.583315	0.565149	0.583053	0.583308	0.583343	0.583305	0.583277	0.583296	0.583307	0.583294	0.583305
(0.9, 0.8)	0.558825	0.542773	0.558721	0.558852	0.558906	0.558848	0.558707	0.558822	0.558818	0.558811	0.558809

Table 3. Error norms at various time levels using MQ, IMQ, IQ, and GS RBFs for $\alpha = 0.25, 0.5$, $\beta = 1$, $N = 10$, $\theta = 0.5$, and $\delta t = 0.1$ corresponds to Example 1.

RBFs	t	$\alpha = 0.25$			$\alpha = 0.5$		
		L_2	L_∞	L_{rms}	L_2	L_∞	L_{rms}
		c = 6.824741			c = 5.8659		
MQ	0.2	1.331×10^{-3}	1.828×10^{-3}	1.270×10^{-3}	6.715×10^{-4}	9.231×10^{-4}	6.402×10^{-4}
	0.4	1.272×10^{-3}	1.752×10^{-3}	1.213×10^{-3}	9.153×10^{-4}	1.259×10^{-3}	8.727×10^{-4}
	0.6	3.663×10^{-4}	4.893×10^{-4}	3.493×10^{-4}	1.187×10^{-3}	1.633×10^{-3}	1.132×10^{-3}
	0.8	9.663×10^{-4}	1.318×10^{-3}	9.214×10^{-4}	6.701×10^{-4}	9.350×10^{-4}	6.389×10^{-4}
	1	4.238×10^{-6}	7.006×10^{-6}	4.041×10^{-6}	7.414×10^{-6}	1.297×10^{-5}	7.069×10^{-6}
		c = 8.12967			c = 6.88885		
IMQ	0.2	1.138×10^{-3}	1.563×10^{-3}	1.085×10^{-3}	5.811×10^{-4}	7.983×10^{-4}	5.541×10^{-4}
	0.4	1.368×10^{-3}	1.879×10^{-3}	1.304×10^{-3}	6.897×10^{-4}	9.504×10^{-4}	6.576×10^{-4}
	0.6	1.334×10^{-3}	1.835×10^{-3}	1.272×10^{-3}	8.769×10^{-4}	1.204×10^{-3}	8.360×10^{-4}
	0.8	6.601×10^{-4}	9.134×10^{-4}	6.294×10^{-4}	4.089×10^{-4}	5.721×10^{-4}	3.899×10^{-4}
	1	1.199×10^{-6}	1.851×10^{-6}	1.143×10^{-6}	5.718×10^{-6}	9.971×10^{-6}	5.452×10^{-6}
		c = 5.34901			c = 5.18412		
IQ	0.2	5.766×10^{-4}	7.940×10^{-4}	5.498×10^{-4}	3.359×10^{-4}	4.623×10^{-4}	3.202×10^{-4}
	0.4	1.825×10^{-4}	2.724×10^{-4}	1.740×10^{-4}	2.147×10^{-4}	3.145×10^{-4}	2.047×10^{-4}
	0.6	9.193×10^{-5}	1.510×10^{-4}	8.765×10^{-5}	6.746×10^{-5}	1.006×10^{-4}	6.432×10^{-5}
	0.8	1.387×10^{-4}	1.929×10^{-4}	1.322×10^{-4}	1.804×10^{-4}	2.700×10^{-4}	1.720×10^{-4}
	1	5.465×10^{-6}	8.804×10^{-6}	5.211×10^{-6}	3.988×10^{-6}	6.707×10^{-6}	3.803×10^{-6}
		c = 0.251637			c = 0.25937		
GS	0.2	4.473×10^{-4}	6.166×10^{-4}	4.265×10^{-4}	2.279×10^{-4}	3.146×10^{-4}	2.173×10^{-4}
	0.4	2.152×10^{-4}	2.992×10^{-4}	2.052×10^{-4}	1.651×10^{-4}	2.302×10^{-4}	1.574×10^{-4}
	0.6	3.447×10^{-5}	4.323×10^{-5}	3.286×10^{-5}	5.054×10^{-5}	7.298×10^{-5}	4.819×10^{-5}
	0.8	7.107×10^{-5}	9.455×10^{-5}	6.776×10^{-5}	1.058×10^{-5}	1.617×10^{-5}	1.009×10^{-5}
	1	4.706×10^{-6}	7.906×10^{-6}	4.487×10^{-6}	4.625×10^{-6}	8.048×10^{-6}	4.410×10^{-6}

Table 4. Error norms at various time levels using MQ, IMQ, IQ, and GS RBFs for $\alpha = 0.75, 1$, $\beta = 1$, $N = 10$, $\theta = 0.5$, and $\delta t = 0.1$ corresponds to Example 1.

RBFs	t	$\alpha = 0.75$			$\alpha = 1$		
		L_2	L_∞	L_{rms}	L_2	L_∞	L_{rms}
		c = 5.80145			c = 6.78326		
MQ	0.2	2.769×10^{-4}	3.802×10^{-4}	2.640×10^{-4}	5.932×10^{-6}	8.084×10^{-6}	5.656×10^{-6}
	0.4	4.878×10^{-4}	6.702×10^{-4}	4.651×10^{-4}	3.153×10^{-5}	4.263×10^{-5}	3.006×10^{-5}
	0.6	5.258×10^{-4}	7.275×10^{-4}	5.013×10^{-4}	3.904×10^{-5}	5.393×10^{-5}	3.722×10^{-5}
	0.8	2.143×10^{-4}	3.014×10^{-4}	2.044×10^{-4}	1.143×10^{-5}	1.609×10^{-5}	1.090×10^{-5}
	1	4.401×10^{-6}	6.944×10^{-6}	4.196×10^{-6}	7.107×10^{-7}	1.410×10^{-6}	6.776×10^{-7}
		c = 4.48635			c = 7.23608		
IMQ	0.2	1.630×10^{-4}	2.249×10^{-4}	1.554×10^{-4}	2.886×10^{-6}	3.898×10^{-6}	2.751×10^{-6}
	0.4	1.759×10^{-4}	2.466×10^{-4}	1.678×10^{-4}	1.103×10^{-5}	1.490×10^{-5}	1.052×10^{-5}
	0.6	1.191×10^{-4}	1.785×10^{-4}	1.135×10^{-4}	1.739×10^{-5}	2.373×10^{-5}	1.658×10^{-5}
	0.8	4.659×10^{-5}	7.766×10^{-5}	4.442×10^{-5}	1.510×10^{-5}	2.085×10^{-5}	1.440×10^{-5}
	1	4.166×10^{-6}	6.616×10^{-6}	3.972×10^{-6}	4.264×10^{-7}	6.996×10^{-7}	4.065×10^{-7}

Table 4. *Cont.*

RBFs	t	$\alpha = 0.75$			$\alpha = 1$		
		L_2	L_∞	L_{rms}	L_2	L_∞	L_{rms}
		c = 5.38471			c = 7.88039		
IQ	0.2	1.476×10^{-4}	2.032×10^{-4}	1.407×10^{-4}	7.689×10^{-6}	1.021×10^{-5}	7.331×10^{-6}
	0.4	1.489×10^{-4}	2.155×10^{-4}	1.420×10^{-4}	2.877×10^{-5}	3.894×10^{-5}	2.743×10^{-5}
	0.6	7.313×10^{-5}	1.212×10^{-4}	6.972×10^{-5}	4.352×10^{-5}	5.947×10^{-5}	4.149×10^{-5}
	0.8	7.707×10^{-5}	1.263×10^{-4}	7.349×10^{-5}	3.045×10^{-5}	4.238×10^{-5}	2.903×10^{-5}
	1	1.266×10^{-6}	2.428×10^{-6}	1.207×10^{-6}	5.121×10^{-7}	8.217×10^{-7}	4.883×10^{-7}
		c = 0.26237			c = 0.16625		
GS	0.2	9.327×10^{-5}	1.287×10^{-4}	8.893×10^{-5}	2.726×10^{-5}	3.641×10^{-5}	2.599×10^{-5}
	0.4	1.016×10^{-4}	1.413×10^{-4}	9.682×10^{-5}	1.115×10^{-4}	1.571×10^{-4}	1.063×10^{-4}
	0.6	3.468×10^{-5}	5.034×10^{-5}	3.306×10^{-5}	1.060×10^{-4}	1.599×10^{-4}	1.011×10^{-4}
	0.8	3.649×10^{-5}	4.743×10^{-5}	3.479×10^{-5}	4.430×10^{-5}	6.206×10^{-5}	4.224×10^{-5}
	1	2.129×10^{-6}	2.664×10^{-6}	2.030×10^{-6}	5.164×10^{-6}	6.820×10^{-6}	4.924×10^{-6}

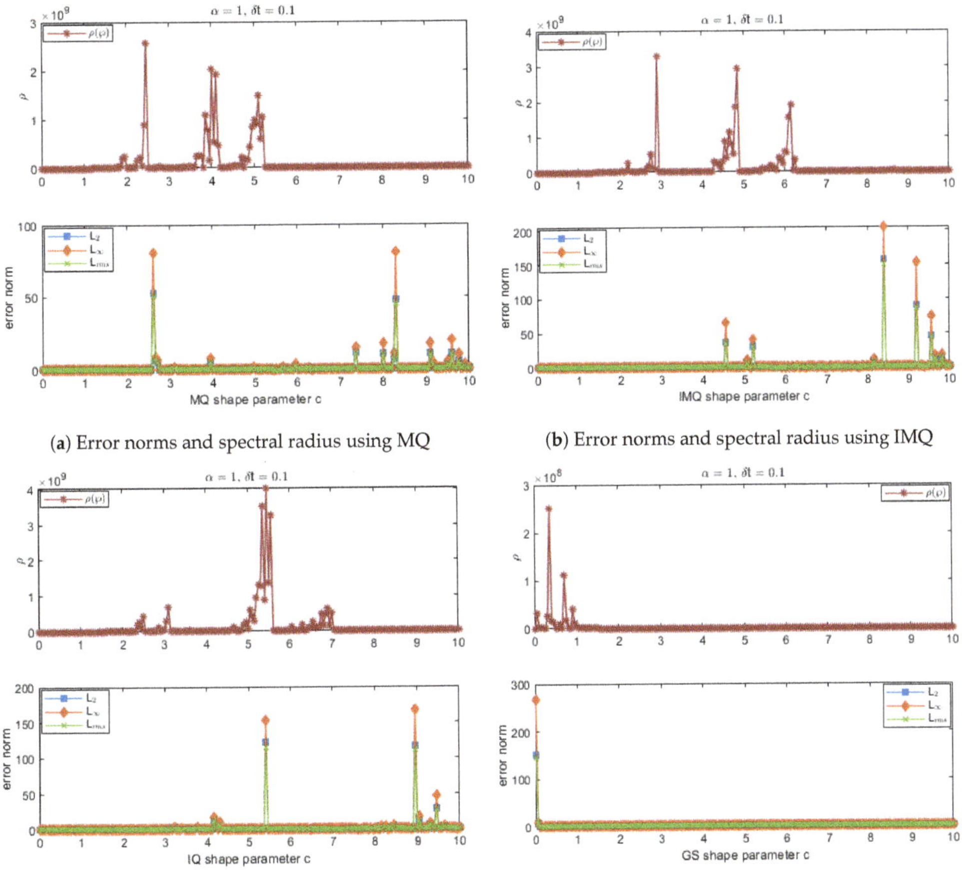

(**a**) Error norms and spectral radius using MQ (**b**) Error norms and spectral radius using IMQ

(**c**) Error norms and spectral radius against IQ (**d**) Error norms and spectral radius using GS

Figure 1. Error norms and spectral radius correspond to Example 1 when N = M = 10, $\theta = 0.5$ using MQ, IMQ, IQ, and GS RBFs.

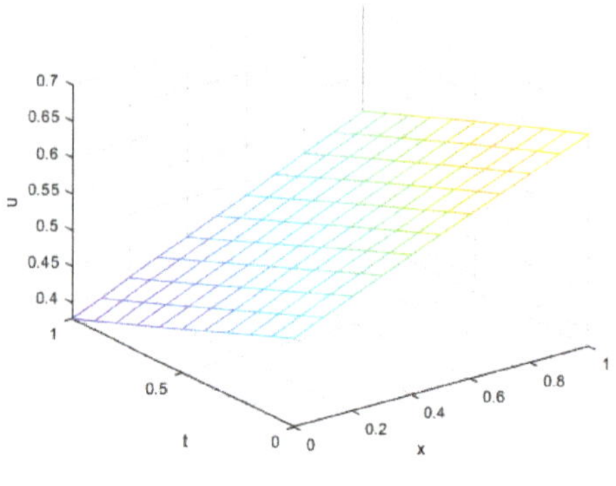

(**a**) Exact solution

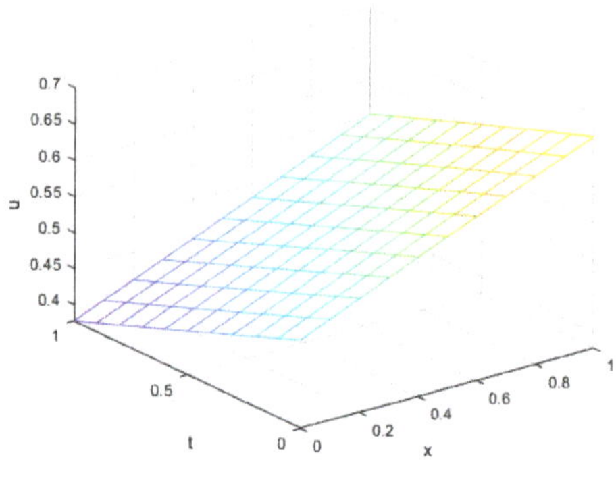

(**b**) Computed solution using MQ

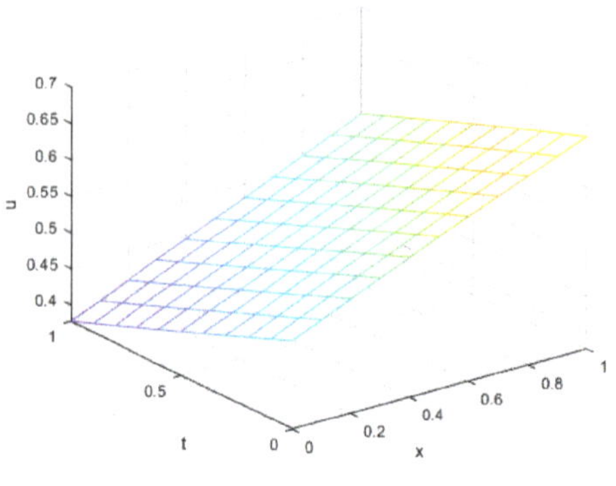

(**c**) Computed solution using IMQ

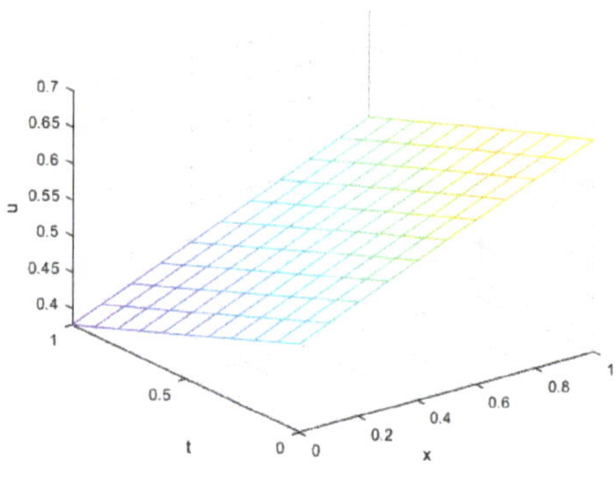

(**d**) Computed solution against IQ

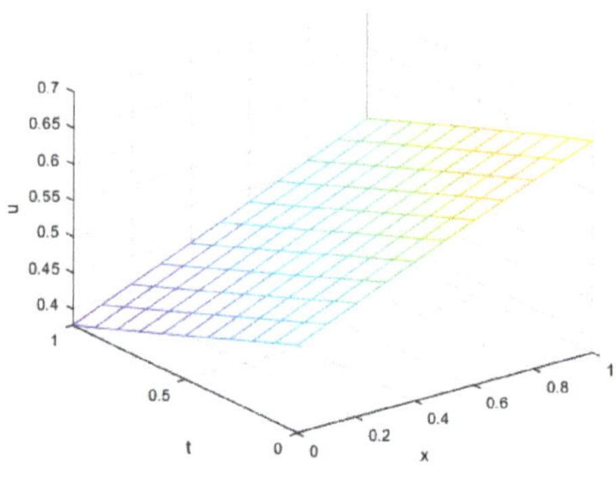

(**e**) Computed solution using GS

Figure 2. Exact vs. computed solution corresponds to Example 1 when $N = M = 10$, $\alpha = 1$ using MQ, IMQ, IQ, and GS RBFs.

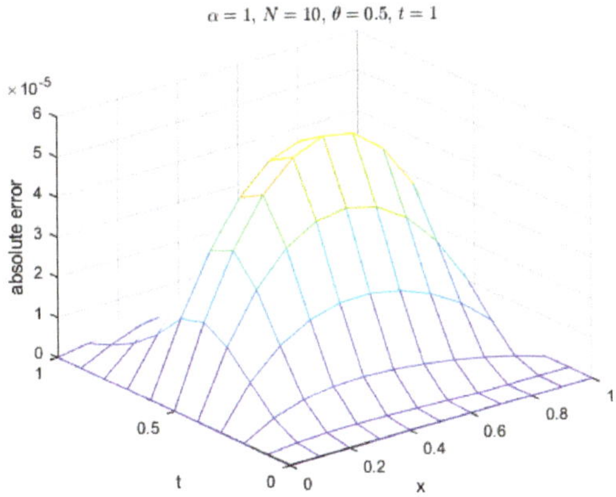

(**a**) Absolute error using MQ

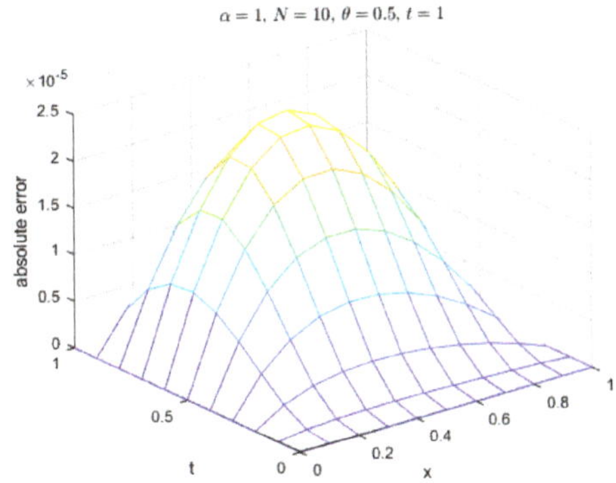

(**b**) Absolute error using IMQ

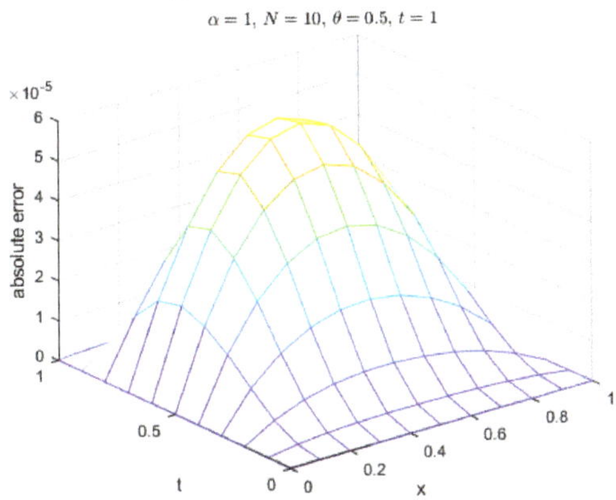

(**c**) Absolute error against IQ

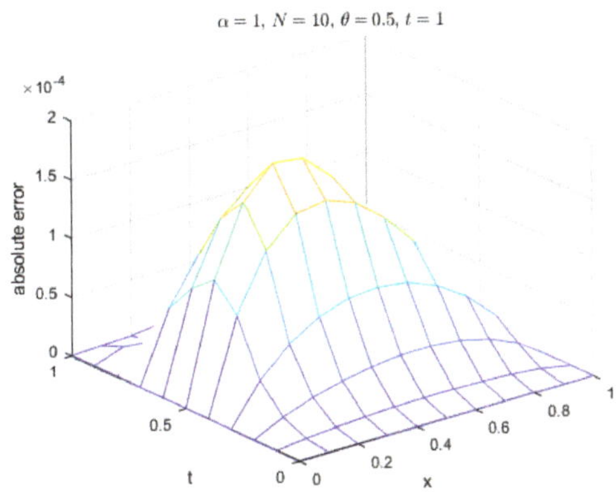

(**d**) Absolute error using GS

Figure 3. Absolute error of MQ, IMQ, IQ, and GS at t = 1 corresponds to Example 1.

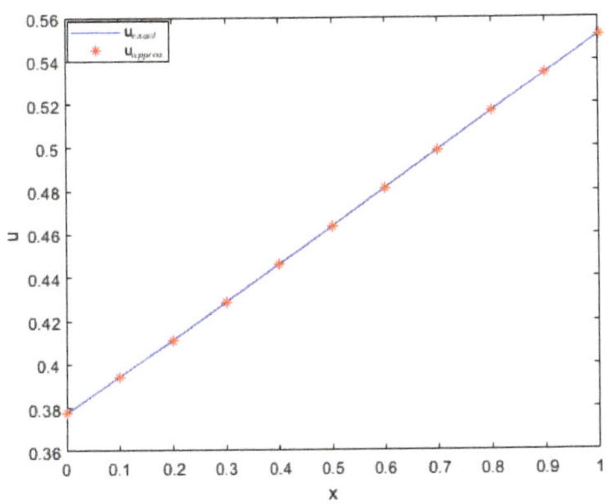

(**a**) Exact vs. numerical using MQ

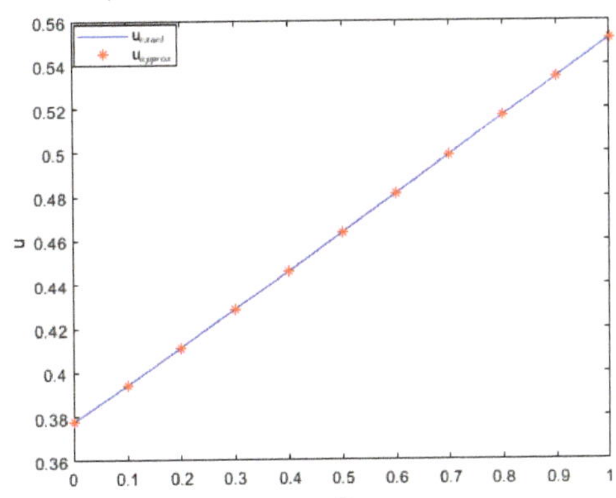

(**b**) Exact vs. numerical using IMQ

Figure 4. *Cont.*

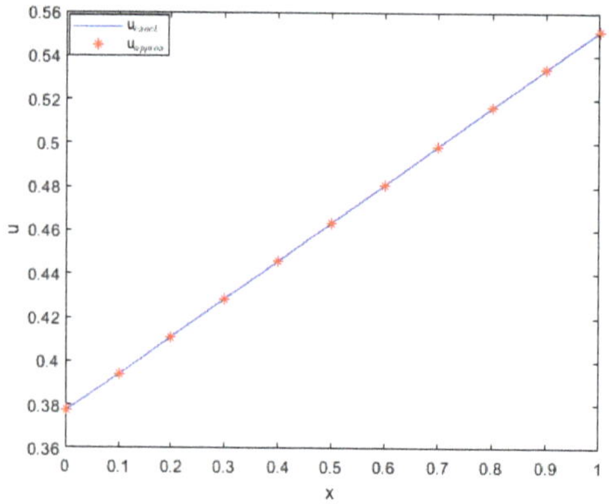

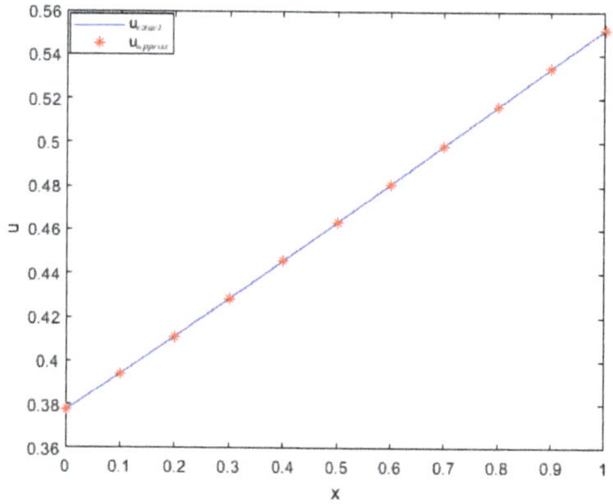

(**c**) Exact vs. numerical against IQ (**d**) Exact vs. numerical using GS

Figure 4. Comparison of exact and computed solution corresponds to Example 1 at t = 1 and $\alpha = 1$ using MQ, IMQ, IQ, and GS RBFs.

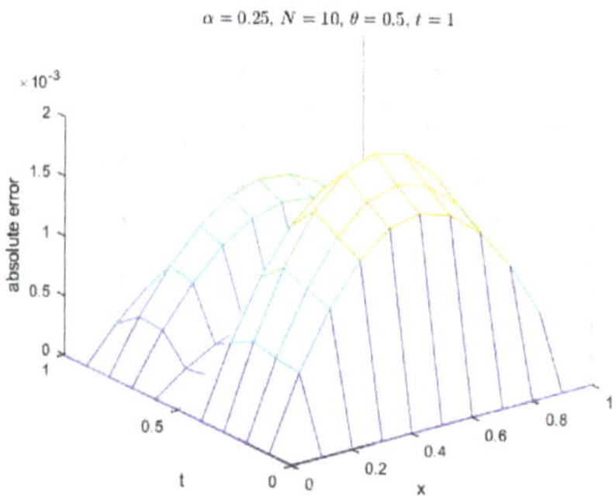

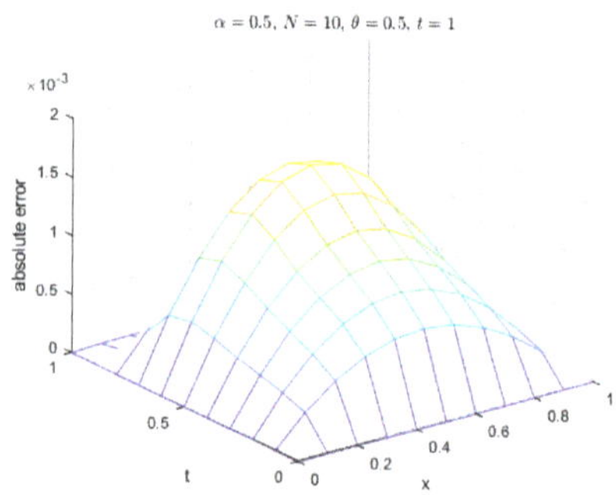

(**a**) Absolute error (**b**) Absolute error

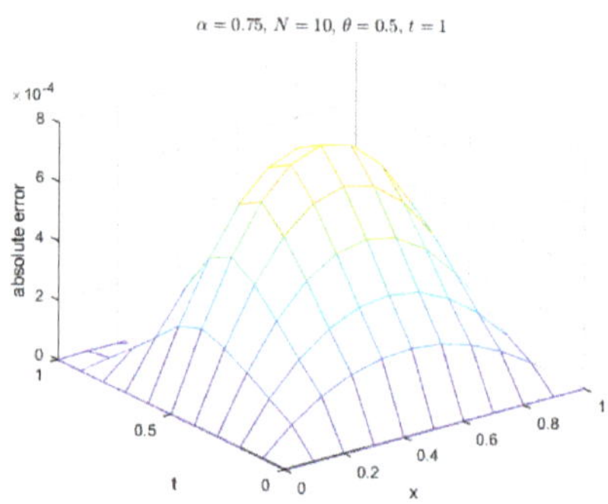

(**c**) Absolute error

Figure 5. Absolute errors for Example 1 with different values of α's using MQ RBF.

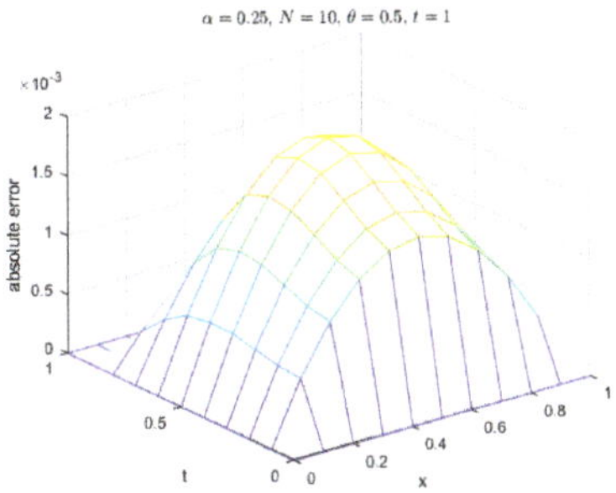

(**a**) Absolute error

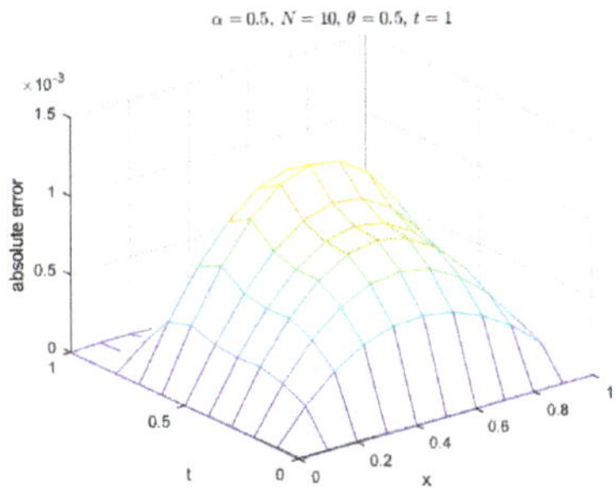

(**b**) Absolute error

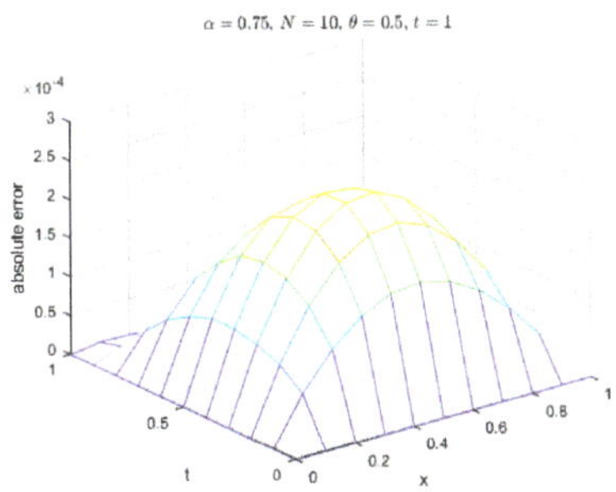

(**c**) Absolute error

Figure 6. Absolute errors for Example 1 with different values of α's using IMQ RBF.

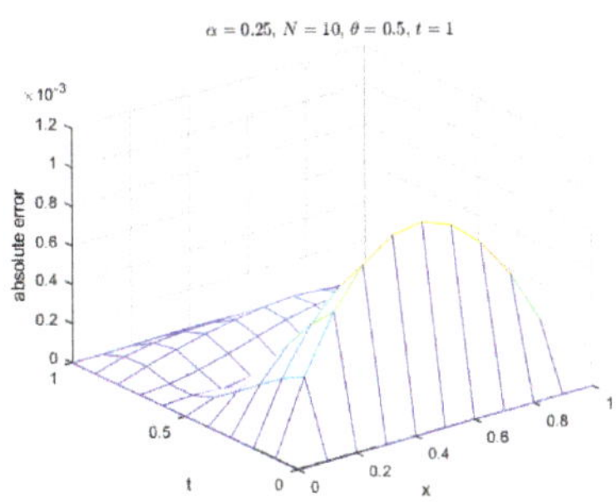

(**a**) Absolute error

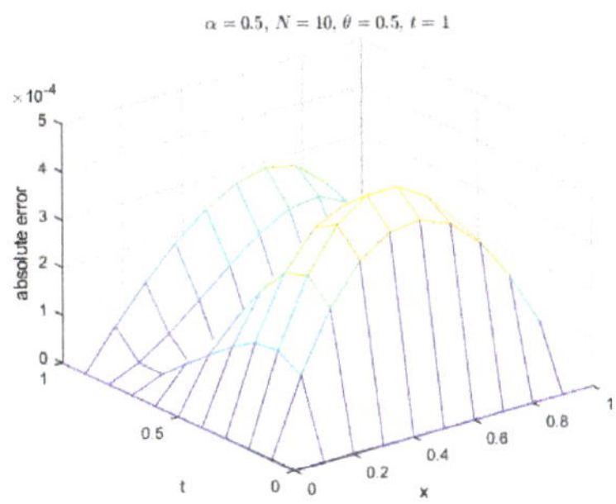

(**b**) Absolute error

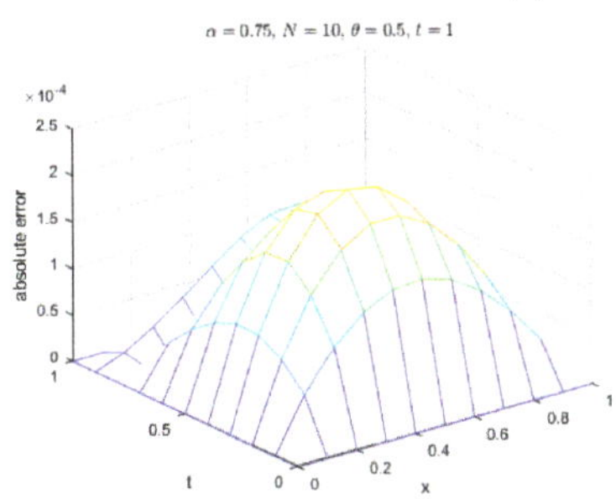

(**c**) Absolute error

Figure 7. Absolute errors for Example 1 with different values of α's using IQ RBF.

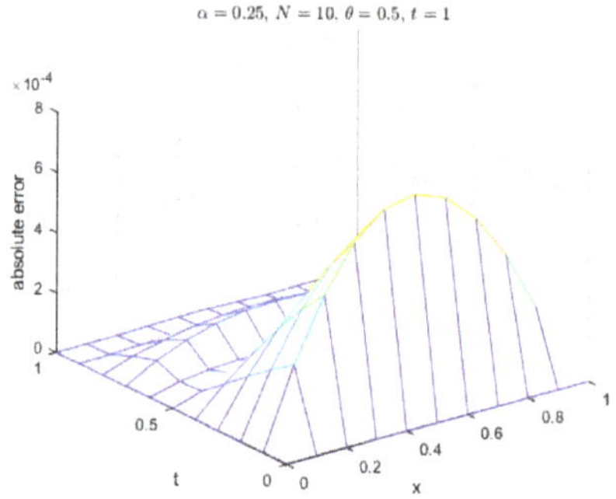

(**a**) Absolute error

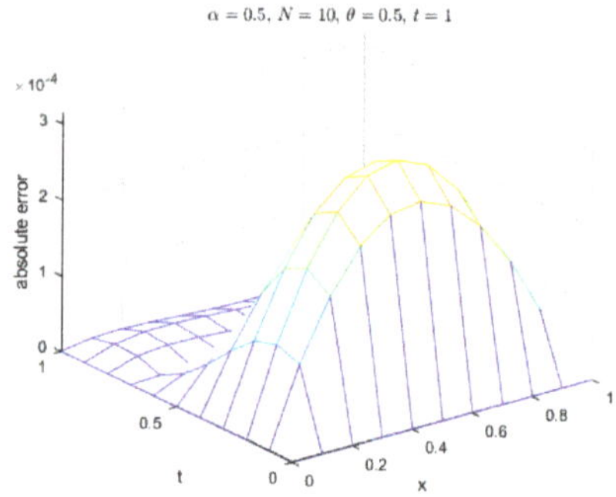

(**b**) Absolute error

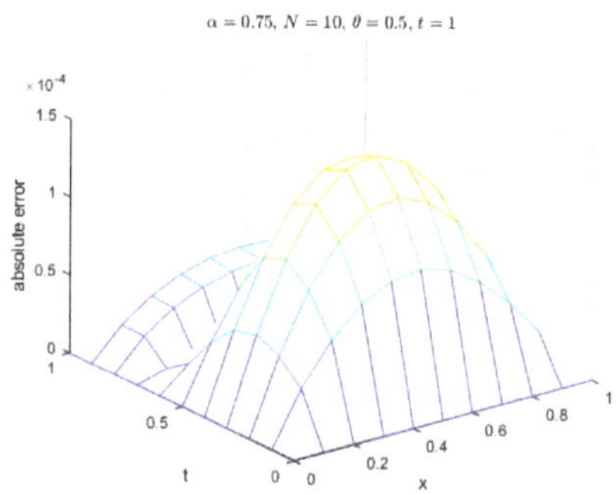

(**c**) Absolute error

Figure 8. Absolute errors for Example 1 with different values of α's using GS RBF.

Example 2. *Let us consider FitzHugh–Nagumo Equations* (2) *and* (3) *with* $\beta = -1$. *The exact solution is given by [25]*

$$u(t,x) = \frac{1}{2} + \frac{1}{2}\tanh\left(\frac{\sqrt{2}x + 3t}{4}\right).$$

The ICs and BCs are derived from the exact solution. The approximate solution is computed using various RBFs such as MQ, IMQ, IQ, and GS with parameters $N = 10$, $\delta t = 0.1$, $\theta = 0.5$, *and* $\alpha = 0.25, 0.5, 0.75, 1$. *The present method is evaluated, and the results are recorded in Tables 5 and 6 at various node points. These results are then compared with FRDTM. It can be seen that the computed solutions are more accurate than the cited method. All the RBFs exhibit good accuracy even for a small value of* α.

Furthermore, for $x \in [0,1]$, *error norms at various time levels are recorded in Tables 7 and 8 using MQ, IMQ, IQ, and GS RBFs with parameters* $N = 10$, $\delta t = 0.1$, *and* $\theta = 0.5$ *and for different values of* α *(0.25, 0.5, 0.75, and 1). Stability and error norm plots are displayed for MQ, IMQ, IQ, and GS RBFs against the shape parameter in Figure 9, which clearly show that the present method fully satisfies the Lax–Richtmyer stability criterion. Surface plots are presented in Figure 10, illustrating that the computed solutions using these RBFs closely match the exact solution. Absolute errors for* $\alpha = 1$ *at various time levels are shown in Figure 11, indicating reasonable accuracy. Additionally, in Figure 12, a comparison between the exact and computed solutions at the final time is displayed, demonstrating the good accuracy of the present method. Finally, Figures 13–16 present the absolute errors for different RBFs when considering fractional order, highlighting their performance.*

Table 5. Comparison of computed values of the present method solution with FRDTM using MQ, IMQ, IQ, and GS RBFs for $\alpha = 0.25, 0.5$, $\beta = -1$, $N = 10$, $\theta = 0.5$, and $\delta t = 0.1$ corresponds to Example 2.

		$\alpha = 0.25$					$\alpha = 0.5$				
(x,t)	Exact	[25]	MQ	IMQ	IQ	GS	[25]	MQ	IMQ	IQ	GS
			$c = 4.4666$	$c = 6.03186$	$c = 6.4267$	$c = 0.35958$		$c = 3.92393$	$c = 5.70391$	$c = 5.55183$	$c = 0.19219$
(0.1, 0.2)	0.591631	0.712693	0.593101	0.592493	0.592342	0.590743	0.685107	0.592535	0.592192	0.592074	0.591955
(0.1, 0.4)	0.661662	0.712224	0.663565	0.662685	0.662345	0.659307	0.727258	0.662760	0.662288	0.662272	0.661768
(0.1, 0.6)	0.725261	0.701487	0.727501	0.726615	0.726035	0.723119	0.741707	0.726324	0.725878	0.725984	0.725129
(0.1, 0.8)	0.780864	0.686791	0.782618	0.782556	0.781355	0.780438	0.739056	0.781578	0.781381	0.781398	0.780881
(0.3, 0.2)	0.625306	0.733926	0.628485	0.627149	0.626822	0.623410	0.712225	0.627311	0.626542	0.626279	0.626011
(0.3, 0.4)	0.692564	0.730566	0.696581	0.694651	0.693921	0.687425	0.748766	0.694919	0.693883	0.693797	0.692771
(0.3, 0.6)	0.752526	0.718291	0.757243	0.755312	0.754041	0.747581	0.758657	0.754761	0.753778	0.753975	0.752209
(0.3, 0.8)	0.804102	0.702703	0.807793	0.807757	0.805025	0.802687	0.752244	0.805574	0.805128	0.805201	0.804145
(0.5, 0.2)	0.657811	0.756506	0.661302	0.659809	0.659448	0.655772	0.738240	0.660064	0.659191	0.658895	0.658579
(0.5, 0.4)	0.721829	0.752516	0.726144	0.723992	0.723195	0.716165	0.770276	0.724394	0.723242	0.723087	0.722032
(0.5, 0.6)	0.777914	0.740736	0.782982	0.780841	0.779420	0.772144	0.777298	0.780297	0.779205	0.779384	0.777545
(0.5, 0.8)	0.825426	0.726144	0.829396	0.829500	0.826306	0.823317	0.769236	0.826965	0.826464	0.826587	0.825521
(0.7, 0.2)	0.688899	0.780077	0.691594	0.690419	0.690140	0.687381	0.763050	0.690677	0.689980	0.689747	0.689481
(0.7, 0.4)	0.749317	0.777418	0.752584	0.750893	0.750280	0.744958	0.791672	0.751279	0.750382	0.750211	0.749455
(0.7, 0.6)	0.801385	0.767864	0.805234	0.803562	0.802439	0.796670	0.797388	0.803170	0.802322	0.802430	0.801100
(0.7, 0.8)	0.844877	0.755857	0.847904	0.848125	0.845470	0.842806	0.789575	0.846004	0.845618	0.845751	0.845024
(0.9, 0.2)	0.718371	0.804119	0.719430	0.718959	0.718850	0.717810	0.786549	0.719084	0.718802	0.718709	0.718593
(0.9, 0.4)	0.774936	0.804312	0.776199	0.775521	0.775281	0.773242	0.812740	0.775698	0.775344	0.775256	0.774984
(0.9, 0.6)	0.822940	0.798295	0.824438	0.823772	0.823318	0.820985	0.818467	0.823620	0.823287	0.823318	0.822838
(0.9, 0.8)	0.862522	0.790062	0.863707	0.863865	0.862729	0.861527	0.812450	0.862941	0.862794	0.862864	0.862627

Table 6. Comparison of computed values of the present method solution with FRDTM using MQ, IMQ, IQ, and GS RBFs for $\alpha = 0.75, 1$, $\beta = -1$, $N = 10$, $\theta = 0.5$, and $\delta t = 0.1$ corresponds to Example 2.

		$\alpha = 0.75$					$\alpha = 1$				
(x,t)	Exact	[25]	MQ	IMQ	IQ	GS	[25]	MQ	IMQ	IQ	GS
			$c = 4.80554$	$c = 5.17758$	$c = 5.90952$	$c = 0.20069$		$c = 6.47961$	$c = 5.51787$	$c = 6.45128$	$c = 0.19927$
(0.1, 0.2)	0.591631	0.634779	0.591992	0.591864	0.591837	0.591767	0.591631	0.591628	0.591633	0.591632	0.591620
(0.1, 0.4)	0.661662	0.702543	0.662181	0.661959	0.661901	0.661733	0.661672	0.661649	0.661667	0.661662	0.661628
(0.1, 0.6)	0.725261	0.747913	0.725872	0.725535	0.725459	0.725237	0.725403	0.725246	0.725272	0.725258	0.725197
(0.1, 0.8)	0.780864	0.774078	0.781331	0.781026	0.781074	0.780806	0.781773	0.780862	0.780876	0.780859	0.780768
(0.3, 0.2)	0.625306	0.666335	0.626111	0.625833	0.625768	0.625606	0.625306	0.625302	0.625314	0.625312	0.625284
(0.3, 0.4)	0.692564	0.729310	0.693682	0.693228	0.693080	0.692711	0.692582	0.692538	0.692581	0.692572	0.692491
(0.3, 0.6)	0.752526	0.769312	0.753809	0.753125	0.752937	0.752464	0.752748	0.752494	0.752557	0.752531	0.752396
(0.3, 0.8)	0.804102	0.789838	0.805115	0.804456	0.804526	0.803957	0.805411	0.804095	0.804133	0.804104	0.803895
(0.5, 0.2)	0.657811	0.696497	0.658719	0.658414	0.658337	0.658141	0.657811	0.657808	0.657823	0.657821	0.657786
(0.5, 0.4)	0.721829	0.754683	0.723053	0.722590	0.722397	0.721980	0.721853	0.721803	0.721858	0.721849	0.721749
(0.5, 0.6)	0.777914	0.789950	0.779284	0.778586	0.778350	0.777837	0.778188	0.777881	0.777959	0.777936	0.777778
(0.5, 0.8)	0.825426	0.806094	0.826535	0.825827	0.825872	0.825257	0.826971	0.825416	0.825467	0.825446	0.825201
(0.7, 0.2)	0.688899	0.725094	0.689618	0.689385	0.689319	0.689149	0.688899	0.688896	0.688911	0.688910	0.688877
(0.7, 0.4)	0.749317	0.778610	0.750257	0.749934	0.749755	0.749423	0.749343	0.749298	0.749349	0.749342	0.749253
(0.7, 0.6)	0.801385	0.809841	0.802413	0.801920	0.801715	0.801324	0.801677	0.801361	0.801430	0.801416	0.801284
(0.7, 0.8)	0.844877	0.822859	0.845727	0.845204	0.845215	0.844750	0.846479	0.844868	0.844914	0.844909	0.844705
(0.9, 0.2)	0.718371	0.751995	0.718660	0.718571	0.718542	0.718465	0.718372	0.718370	0.718378	0.718377	0.718361
(0.9, 0.4)	0.774936	0.801046	0.775302	0.775193	0.775108	0.774973	0.774962	0.774928	0.774953	0.774950	0.774909
(0.9, 0.6)	0.822940	0.828936	0.823333	0.823160	0.823070	0.822918	0.823220	0.822932	0.822962	0.822959	0.822902
(0.9, 0.8)	0.862522	0.839976	0.862853	0.862662	0.862657	0.862479	0.864017	0.862518	0.862539	0.862542	0.862455

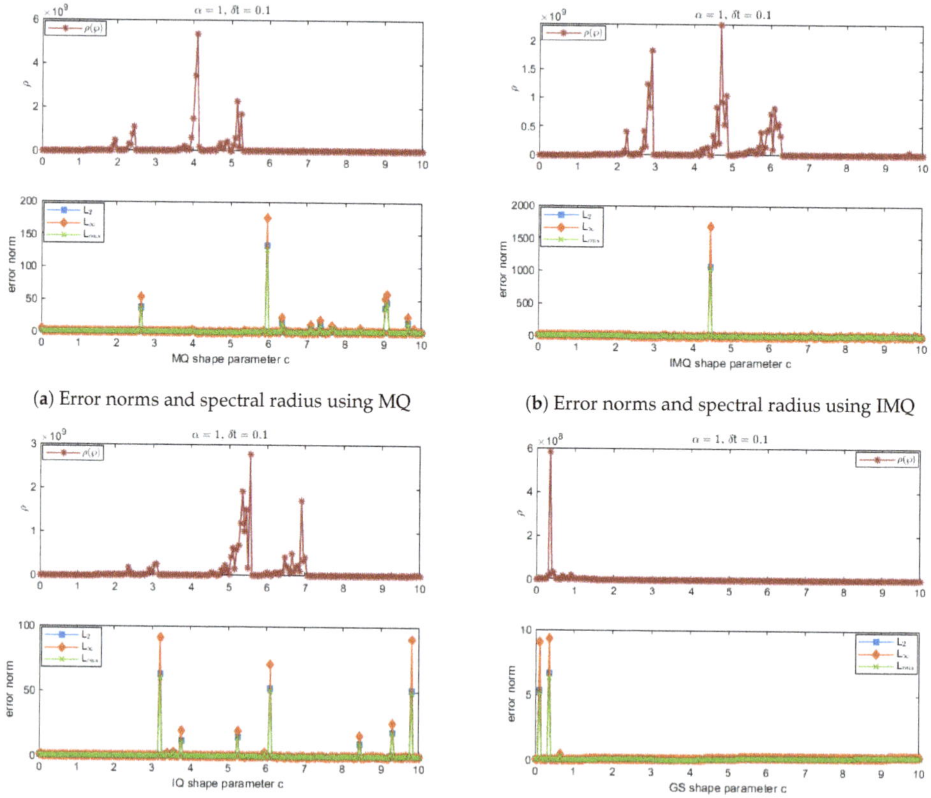

(**a**) Error norms and spectral radius using MQ

(**b**) Error norms and spectral radius using IMQ

(**c**) Error norms and spectral radius against IQ

(**d**) Error norms and spectral radius using GS

Figure 9. Error norms and spectral radius correspond to Example 2 when $N = M = 10$, $\theta = 0.5$ using MQ, IMQ, IQ, and GS RBFs.

Table 7. Error norms at various time levels using MQ, IMQ, IQ, and GS RBFs for $\alpha = 0.25, 0.5$, $\beta = -1$, $N = 10$, $\theta = 0.5$, and $\delta t = 0.1$ correspond to Example 2.

RBFs	t	$\alpha = 0.25$			$\alpha = 0.5$		
		L_2	L_∞	L_{rms}	L_2	L_∞	L_{rms}
		c = 4.4666			c = 3.92393		
MQ	0.2	2.56×10^{-3}	3.49×10^{-3}	2.44×10^{-3}	1.65×10^{-3}	2.25×10^{-3}	1.57×10^{-3}
	0.4	3.18×10^{-3}	4.36×10^{-3}	3.03×10^{-3}	1.88×10^{-3}	2.58×10^{-3}	1.80×10^{-3}
	0.6	3.74×10^{-3}	5.12×10^{-3}	3.56×10^{-3}	1.76×10^{-3}	2.42×10^{-3}	1.67×10^{-3}
	0.8	2.93×10^{-3}	4.01×10^{-3}	2.79×10^{-3}	1.14×10^{-3}	1.58×10^{-3}	1.09×10^{-3}
	1	3.66×10^{-5}	5.14×10^{-5}	3.49×10^{-5}	3.49×10^{-6}	5.48×10^{-6}	3.32×10^{-6}
		c = 6.03186			c = 5.70391		
IMQ	0.2	1.47×10^{-3}	2.01×10^{-3}	1.40×10^{-3}	1.01×10^{-3}	1.38×10^{-3}	9.63×10^{-4}
	0.4	1.61×10^{-3}	2.23×10^{-3}	1.53×10^{-3}	1.04×10^{-3}	1.43×10^{-3}	9.93×10^{-4}
	0.6	2.17×10^{-3}	2.99×10^{-3}	2.07×10^{-3}	9.59×10^{-4}	1.33×10^{-3}	9.14×10^{-4}
	0.8	3.00×10^{-3}	4.07×10^{-3}	2.86×10^{-3}	7.76×10^{-4}	1.08×10^{-3}	7.40×10^{-4}
	1	1.08×10^{-5}	1.83×10^{-5}	1.03×10^{-5}	5.36×10^{-6}	8.29×10^{-6}	5.11×10^{-6}

Table 7. *Cont.*

RBFs	t	$\alpha = 0.25$			$\alpha = 0.5$		
		L_2	L_∞	L_{rms}	L_2	L_∞	L_{rms}
			c = 6.4267			c = 5.55183	
IQ	0.2	1.20×10^{-3}	1.65×10^{-3}	1.15×10^{-3}	7.93×10^{-4}	1.08×10^{-3}	7.56×10^{-4}
	0.4	1.02×10^{-3}	1.43×10^{-3}	9.73×10^{-4}	9.34×10^{-4}	1.31×10^{-3}	8.91×10^{-4}
	0.6	1.13×10^{-3}	1.58×10^{-3}	1.08×10^{-3}	1.10×10^{-3}	1.53×10^{-3}	1.04×10^{-3}
	0.8	6.71×10^{-4}	9.45×10^{-4}	6.40×10^{-4}	8.61×10^{-4}	1.18×10^{-3}	8.21×10^{-4}
	1	1.45×10^{-5}	2.48×10^{-5}	1.38×10^{-5}	6.97×10^{-6}	1.10×10^{-5}	6.64×10^{-6}
			c = 0.35958			c = 0.19219	
GS	0.2	1.49×10^{-3}	2.06×10^{-3}	1.42×10^{-3}	5.62×10^{-4}	7.72×10^{-4}	5.36×10^{-4}
	0.4	4.14×10^{-3}	5.66×10^{-3}	3.95×10^{-3}	1.53×10^{-4}	2.16×10^{-4}	1.45×10^{-4}
	0.6	4.20×10^{-3}	5.77×10^{-3}	4.01×10^{-3}	2.63×10^{-4}	3.69×10^{-4}	2.51×10^{-4}
	0.8	1.54×10^{-3}	2.20×10^{-3}	1.47×10^{-3}	9.23×10^{-5}	1.46×10^{-4}	8.80×10^{-5}
	1	3.07×10^{-5}	5.19×10^{-5}	2.93×10^{-5}	1.25×10^{-5}	2.32×10^{-5}	1.19×10^{-5}

Table 8. Error norms at various time levels using MQ, IMQ, IQ, and GS RBFs for $\alpha = 0.75, 1$, $\beta = -1$, $N = 10$, $\theta = 0.5$, and $\delta t = 0.1$ correspond to Example 2.

RBFs	t	$\alpha = 0.75$			$\alpha = 1$		
		L_2	L_∞	L_{rms}	L_2	L_∞	L_{rms}
			c = 4.80554			c = 6.47961	
MQ	0.2	6.64×10^{-4}	9.08×10^{-4}	6.33×10^{-4}	2.74×10^{-6}	3.70×10^{-6}	2.61×10^{-6}
	0.4	8.97×10^{-4}	1.23×10^{-3}	8.56×10^{-4}	2.01×10^{-5}	2.76×10^{-5}	1.91×10^{-5}
	0.6	1.01×10^{-3}	1.39×10^{-3}	9.63×10^{-4}	2.46×10^{-5}	3.44×10^{-5}	2.35×10^{-5}
	0.8	8.12×10^{-4}	1.11×10^{-3}	7.74×10^{-4}	7.31×10^{-6}	1.02×10^{-5}	6.97×10^{-6}
	1	4.55×10^{-6}	7.31×10^{-6}	4.34×10^{-6}	5.95×10^{-7}	8.99×10^{-7}	5.67×10^{-7}
			c = 5.17758			c = 5.51787	
IMQ	0.2	4.41×10^{-4}	6.04×10^{-4}	4.20×10^{-4}	8.95×10^{-6}	1.28×10^{-5}	8.54×10^{-6}
	0.4	5.57×10^{-4}	7.60×10^{-4}	5.31×10^{-4}	2.21×10^{-5}	3.19×10^{-5}	2.10×10^{-5}
	0.6	4.93×10^{-4}	6.71×10^{-4}	4.70×10^{-4}	3.31×10^{-5}	4.66×10^{-5}	3.16×10^{-5}
	0.8	2.96×10^{-4}	4.01×10^{-4}	2.82×10^{-4}	2.96×10^{-5}	4.07×10^{-5}	2.82×10^{-5}
	1	1.30×10^{-6}	2.26×10^{-6}	1.24×10^{-6}	5.23×10^{-7}	8.30×10^{-7}	4.99×10^{-7}
			c = 5.90952			c = 6.45128	
IQ	0.2	3.84×10^{-4}	5.26×10^{-4}	3.66×10^{-4}	7.91×10^{-6}	1.14×10^{-5}	7.54×10^{-6}
	0.4	4.16×10^{-4}	5.68×10^{-4}	3.97×10^{-4}	1.58×10^{-5}	2.46×10^{-5}	1.51×10^{-5}
	0.6	3.23×10^{-4}	4.43×10^{-4}	3.08×10^{-4}	1.87×10^{-5}	3.05×10^{-5}	1.78×10^{-5}
	0.8	3.33×10^{-4}	4.54×10^{-4}	3.17×10^{-4}	1.88×10^{-5}	3.13×10^{-5}	1.80×10^{-5}
	1	1.29×10^{-6}	1.89×10^{-6}	1.23×10^{-6}	1.05×10^{-6}	1.81×10^{-6}	1.00×10^{-6}
			c = 0.20069			c = 0.19927	
GS	0.2	2.40×10^{-4}	3.31×10^{-4}	2.29×10^{-4}	1.90×10^{-5}	2.50×10^{-5}	1.81×10^{-5}
	0.4	1.11×10^{-4}	1.57×10^{-4}	1.06×10^{-4}	5.96×10^{-5}	8.05×10^{-5}	5.69×10^{-5}
	0.6	5.43×10^{-5}	7.71×10^{-5}	5.18×10^{-5}	1.02×10^{-4}	1.40×10^{-4}	9.67×10^{-5}
	0.8	1.19×10^{-4}	1.69×10^{-4}	1.14×10^{-4}	1.65×10^{-4}	2.26×10^{-4}	1.58×10^{-4}
	1	9.36×10^{-6}	1.59×10^{-5}	8.93×10^{-6}	5.69×10^{-6}	8.86×10^{-6}	5.43×10^{-6}

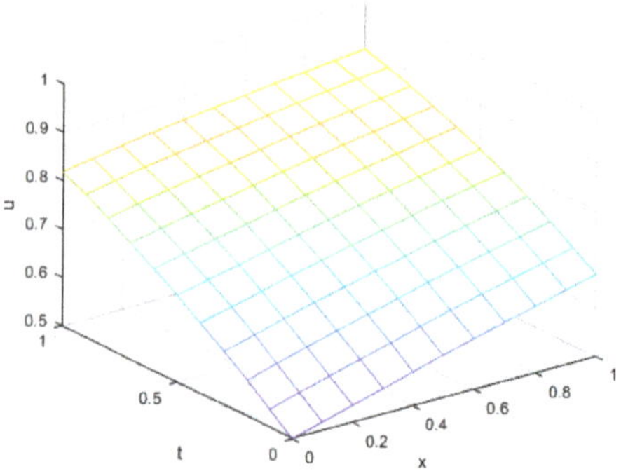

(**a**) Exact solution

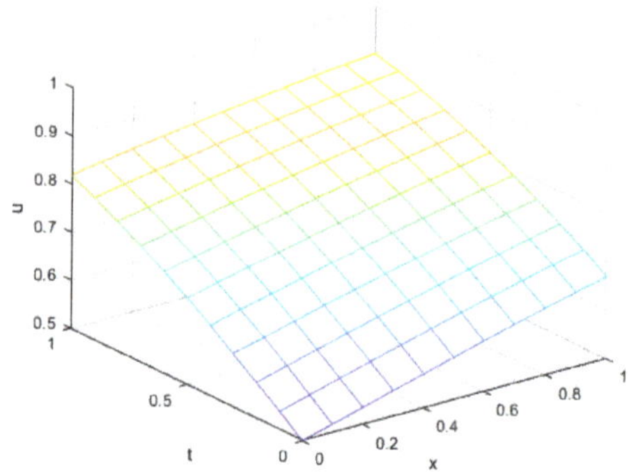

(**b**) Computed solution using MQ

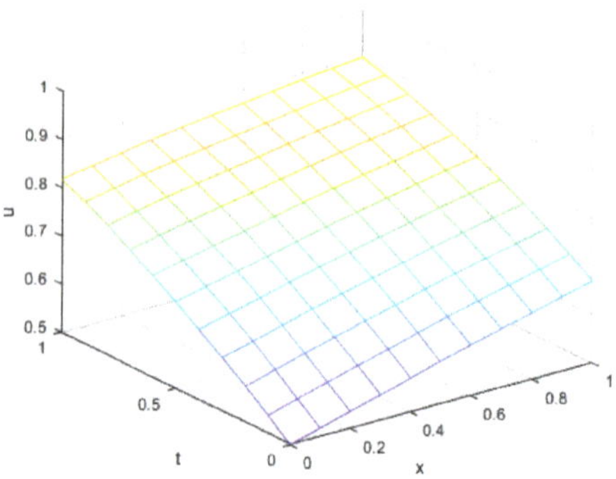

(**c**) Computed solution using IMQ

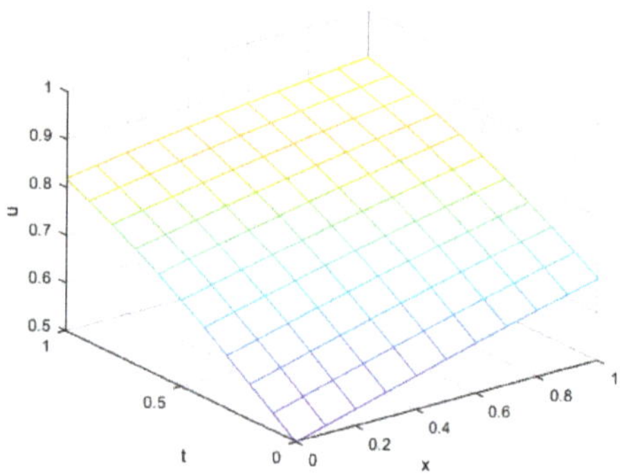

(**d**) Computed solution against IQ

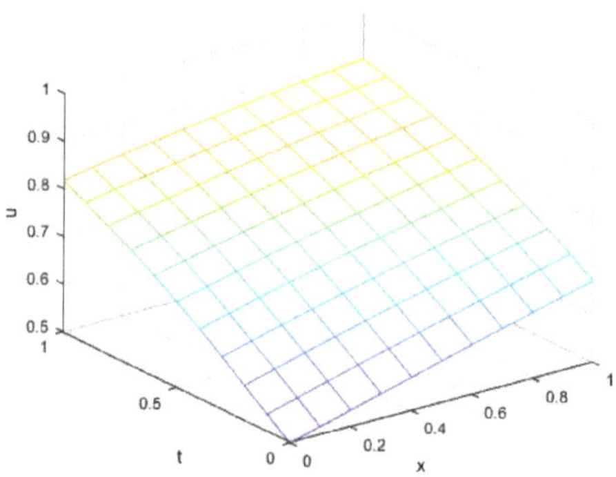

(**e**) Computed solution using GS

Figure 10. Exact vs. computed solution corresponds to Example 2 when $N = M = 10$, $\alpha = 1$ using MQ, IMQ, IQ, and GS RBFs.

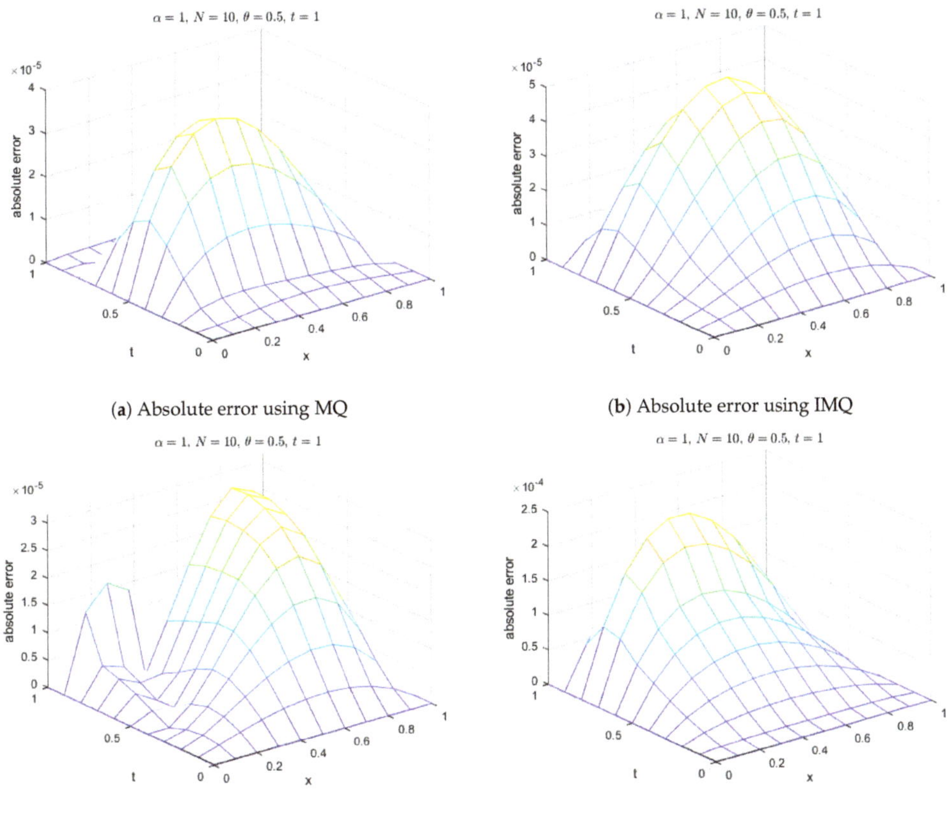

(**a**) Absolute error using MQ (**b**) Absolute error using IMQ

(**c**) Absolute error against IQ (**d**) Absolute error using GS

Figure 11. Absolute error of MQ, IMQ, IQ, and GS at $t_{max} = 1$ corresponds to Example 2.

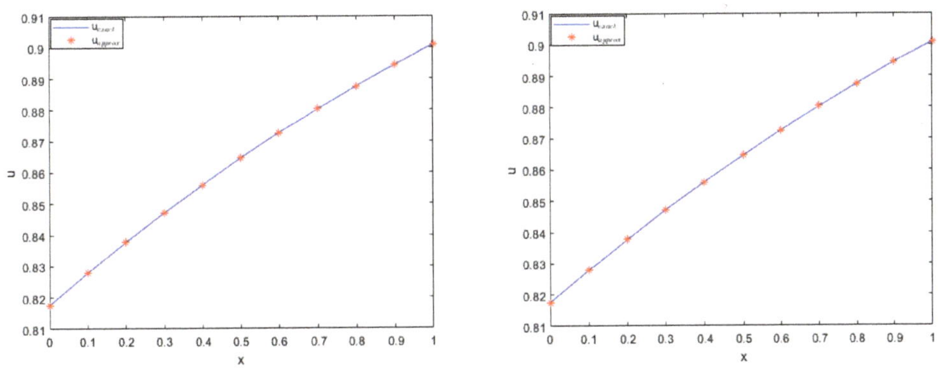

(**a**) Exact vs. numerical using MQ (**b**) Exact vs. numerical using IMQ

Figure 12. *Cont.*

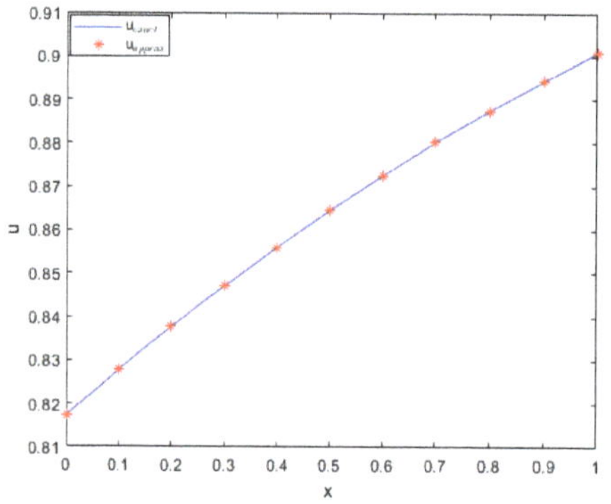

(c) Exact vs. numerical against IQ

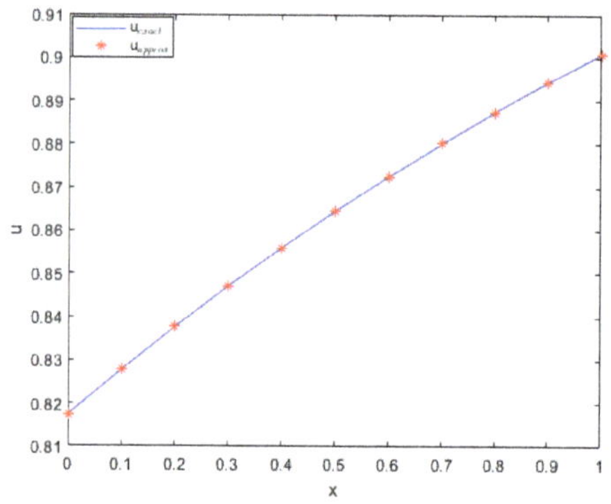

(d) Exact vs. numerical using GS

Figure 12. Comparison of exact and computed solution corresponds to Example 2 at $t_{max} = 1$ and $\alpha = 1$ using MQ, IMQ, IQ, and GS RBFs.

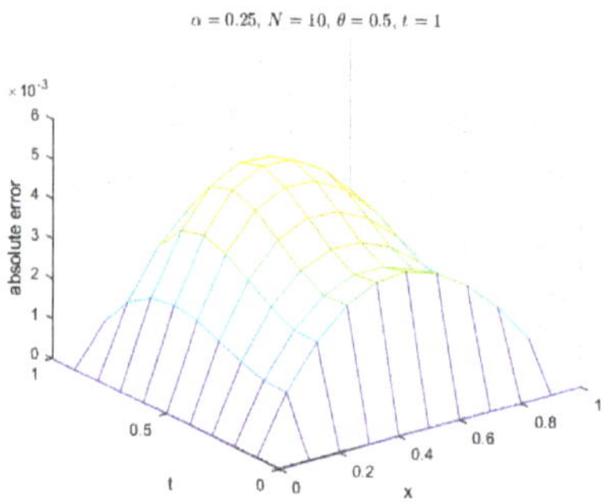

(a) Absolute error

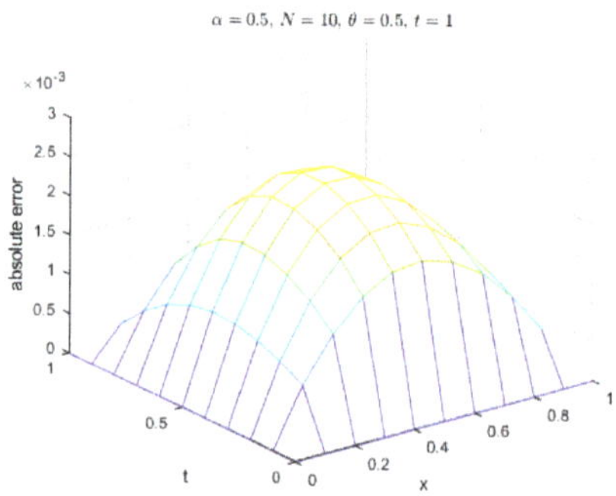

(b) Absolute error

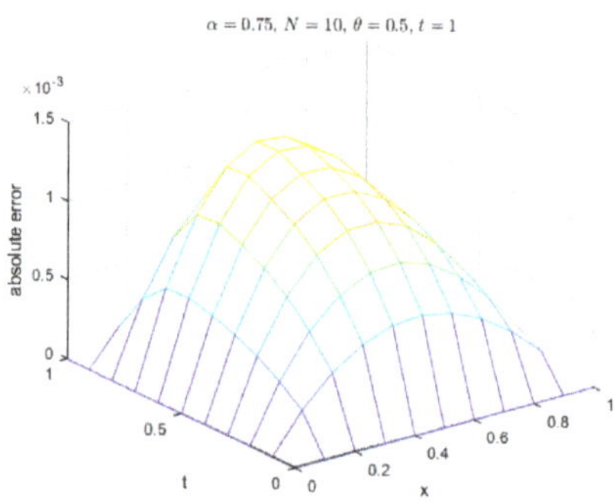

(c) Absolute error

Figure 13. Absolute errors for Example 3 with different values of α's using MQ RBF.

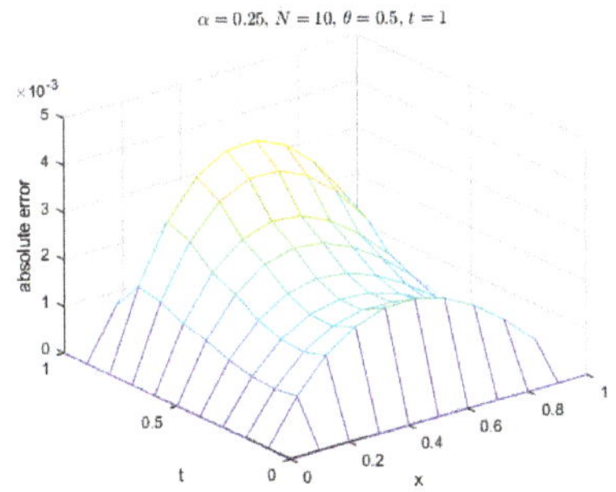

(**a**) Absolute error

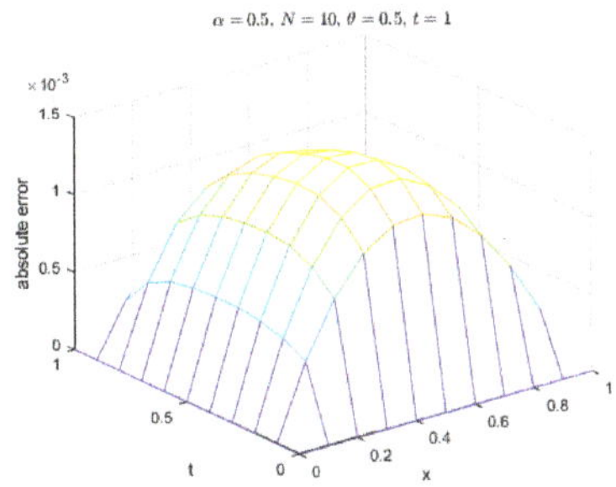

(**b**) Absolute error

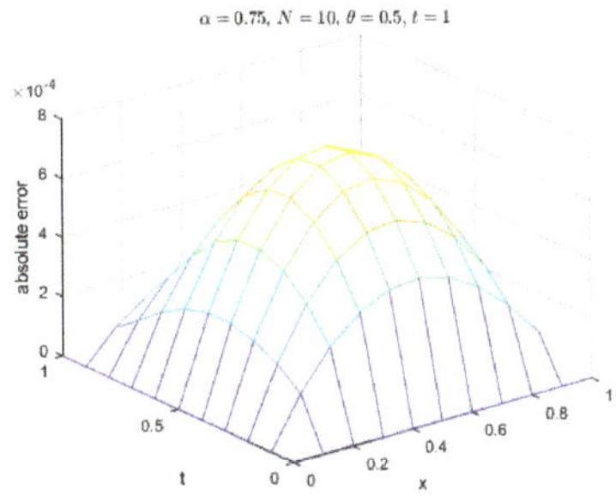

(**c**) Absolute error

Figure 14. Absolute errors for Example 3 with different values of α's using IMQ RBF.

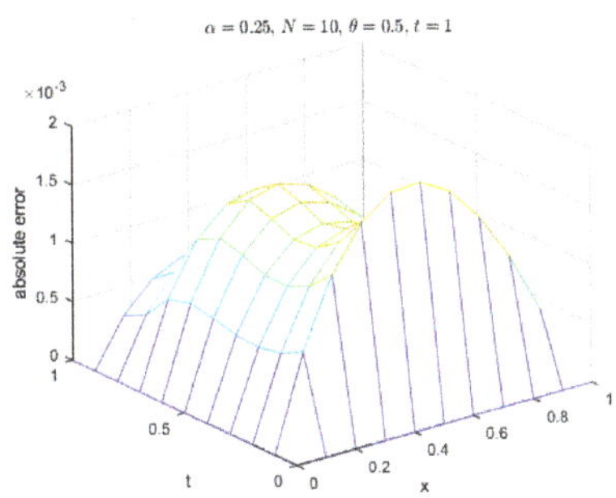

(**a**) Absolute error

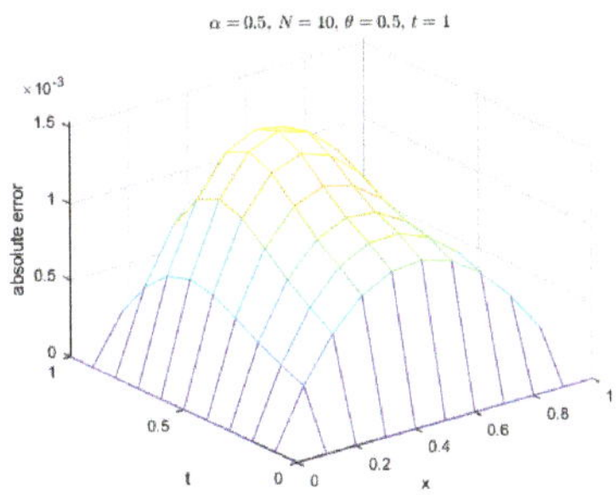

(**b**) Absolute error

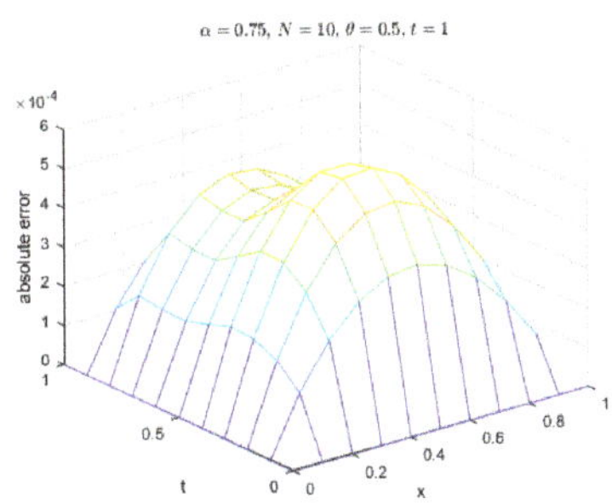

(**c**) Absolute error

Figure 15. Absolute errors for Example 3 with different values of α's using IQ RBF.

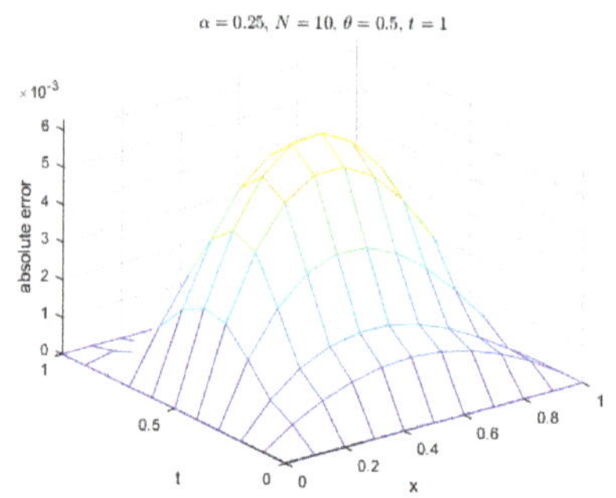

(**a**) Absolute error

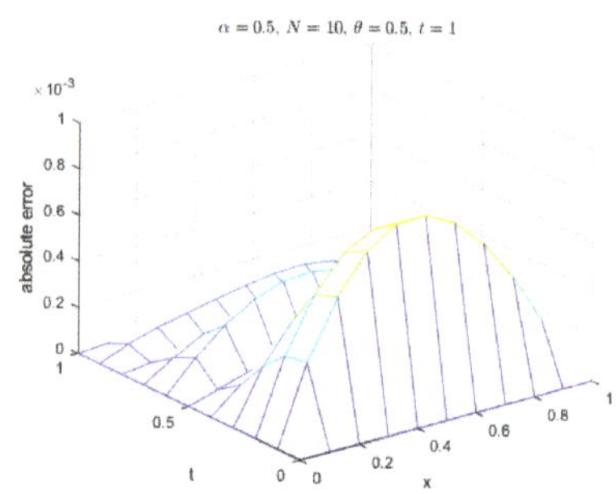

(**b**) Absolute error

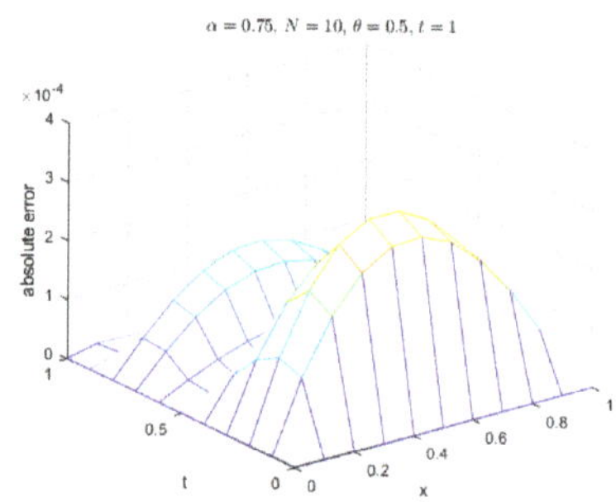

(**c**) Absolute error

Figure 16. Absolute errors for Example 3 with different values of α's using GS RBF.

Example 3. *Let us consider FitzHugh–Nagumo Equations (2) and (3) with $\beta = 0$. The exact solution is given by [25]*

$$u(t,x) = \frac{1}{2} + \frac{1}{2}\tanh\left(\frac{\sqrt{2}x + t}{4}\right).$$

We employ the ICs and BCs from this exact solution. Using this solution, we apply the present method to approximate the exact solution within the domain $x \in [0,1]$. RBFs such as MQ, IMQ, IQ, and GS are employed for the numerical approximation. We choose $N = 10$, $\delta t = 0.1$, and $\theta = 0.5$. The obtained results are presented in Tables 9 and 10 for different values of α $(0.25, 0.5, 0.75, 1)$.

The tables clearly indicate that the accuracy of the method is better than the FRDTM. Additionally, it can be seen that the accuracy improves as α approaches 1. Additionally, the chosen RBFs demonstrate comparable performance. Furthermore, the error norms at various time levels are recorded in Tables 11 and 12 for α values of 0.25, 0.5, 0.75, and 1, using the MQ, IMQ, IQ, and GS RBFs. The stability and error norm plots are presented in Figure 17, demonstrating that the present method consistently satisfies the Lax–Richtmyer stability criterion.

Additionally, surface plots in Figure 18 show that the computed solution using the selected RBFs closely matches the exact solution. The absolute errors for $\alpha = 1$ at various time levels are depicted in Figure 19, indicating reasonable accuracy. Figure 20 compares the exact and computed solutions at the final time, demonstrating the good accuracy of the present method. Finally, Figures 21–24 display the absolute errors for different fractional orders using different RBFs.

Table 9. Comparison of computed values of the present method solution with FRDTM using MQ, IMQ, IQ, and GS RBFs for $\alpha = 0.25, 0.5$, $\beta = 0$, $N = 10$, $\theta = 0.5$, and $\delta t = 0.1$ corresponds to Example 3.

(x, t)	Exact	$\alpha = 0.25$					$\alpha = 0.5$				
		[25]	MQ	IMQ	IQ	GS	[25]	MQ	IMQ	IQ	GS
			c = 3.68162	c = 6.61203	c = 8.81199	c = 0.36854		c = 6.48549	c = 7.63322	c = 6.9269	c = 0.33014
(0.1, 0.2)	0.542574	0.607541	0.543147	0.543015	0.542936	0.542301	0.579728	0.542826	0.542838	0.542813	0.542595
(0.1, 0.4)	0.567267	0.624171	0.567777	0.567728	0.567539	0.566309	0.604611	0.567451	0.567615	0.567554	0.567328
(0.1, 0.6)	0.591631	0.635373	0.592090	0.592066	0.591836	0.590916	0.623334	0.591672	0.591984	0.591826	0.591753
(0.1, 0.8)	0.615552	0.644106	0.615894	0.615880	0.615667	0.615606	0.638889	0.615523	0.615760	0.615571	0.615607
(0.3, 0.2)	0.577406	0.639862	0.578702	0.578408	0.578231	0.576967	0.613492	0.577980	0.578005	0.577953	0.577472
(0.3, 0.4)	0.601599	0.655466	0.602729	0.602641	0.602231	0.599800	0.637390	0.602020	0.602392	0.602265	0.601792
(0.3, 0.6)	0.625306	0.665857	0.626309	0.626280	0.625790	0.623770	0.655204	0.625410	0.626117	0.625769	0.625657
(0.3, 0.8)	0.648427	0.673883	0.649148	0.649157	0.648699	0.648556	0.669886	0.648373	0.648923	0.648480	0.648661
(0.5, 0.2)	0.611484	0.670946	0.612968	0.612638	0.612435	0.611202	0.646202	0.612144	0.612174	0.612119	0.611584
(0.5, 0.4)	0.634960	0.685416	0.636223	0.636155	0.635702	0.633346	0.668940	0.635440	0.635874	0.635739	0.635255
(0.5, 0.6)	0.657811	0.694923	0.658913	0.658914	0.658388	0.656165	0.685729	0.657930	0.658750	0.658358	0.658312
(0.5, 0.8)	0.679952	0.702183	0.680713	0.680772	0.680279	0.680129	0.699451	0.679896	0.680535	0.680019	0.680357
(0.7, 0.2)	0.644506	0.700614	0.645694	0.645439	0.645271	0.644477	0.677605	0.645032	0.645063	0.645023	0.644609
(0.7, 0.4)	0.667073	0.713905	0.668059	0.668036	0.667684	0.666161	0.699052	0.667449	0.667813	0.667710	0.667379
(0.7, 0.6)	0.688899	0.722509	0.689742	0.689775	0.689383	0.687690	0.714740	0.688986	0.689660	0.689347	0.689393
(0.7, 0.8)	0.709916	0.728997	0.710468	0.710559	0.710191	0.710100	0.727453	0.709870	0.710385	0.709969	0.710363
(0.9, 0.2)	0.676207	0.728724	0.676688	0.676590	0.676519	0.676287	0.707489	0.676418	0.676435	0.676422	0.676262
(0.9, 0.4)	0.697706	0.740845	0.698094	0.698100	0.697961	0.697504	0.727556	0.697851	0.698010	0.697969	0.697863
(0.9, 0.6)	0.718371	0.748576	0.718695	0.718725	0.718578	0.717935	0.742105	0.718399	0.718684	0.718556	0.718617
(0.9, 0.8)	0.738154	0.754327	0.738351	0.738410	0.738273	0.738255	0.753800	0.738134	0.738342	0.738175	0.738393

Table 10. Comparison of computed values of the present method solution with FRDTM using MQ, IMQ, IQ, and GS RBFs for $\alpha = 0.75, 1$, $\beta = 0$, $N = 10$, $\theta = 0.5$, and $\delta t = 0.1$ corresponds to Example 3.

(x, t)	Exact	$\alpha = 0.75$					$\alpha = 1$				
		[25]	MQ	IMQ	IQ	GS	[25]	MQ	IMQ	IQ	GS
			c = 6.20135	c = 7.82578	c = 6.73987	c = 0.333513		c = 5.79129	c = 6.46003	c = 8.05516	c = 0.22009
(0.1, 0.2)	0.542574	0.558029	0.542671	0.542661	0.542670	0.542575	0.542574	0.542576	0.542575	0.542570	0.542596
(0.1, 0.4)	0.567267	0.585031	0.567267	0.567359	0.567431	0.567193	0.567267	0.567272	0.567265	0.567252	0.567332
(0.1, 0.6)	0.591631	0.608198	0.591550	0.591683	0.591797	0.591527	0.591626	0.591638	0.591632	0.591658	0.591702
(0.1, 0.8)	0.615552	0.628969	0.615483	0.615541	0.615611	0.615522	0.615532	0.615559	0.615549	0.615646	0.615591
(0.3, 0.2)	0.577406	0.592512	0.577628	0.577605	0.577625	0.577403	0.577406	0.577409	0.577407	0.577397	0.577451
(0.3, 0.4)	0.601599	0.618758	0.601608	0.601811	0.601981	0.601363	0.601598	0.601610	0.601598	0.601567	0.601745
(0.3, 0.6)	0.625306	0.641090	0.625128	0.625431	0.625694	0.624963	0.625302	0.625322	0.625313	0.625358	0.625473
(0.3, 0.8)	0.648427	0.660973	0.648272	0.648398	0.648570	0.648301	0.648409	0.648443	0.648426	0.648650	0.648523
(0.5, 0.2)	0.611484	0.626109	0.611740	0.611714	0.611741	0.611473	0.611484	0.611487	0.611487	0.611475	0.611535
(0.5, 0.4)	0.634960	0.651378	0.634968	0.635204	0.635411	0.634600	0.634959	0.634972	0.634963	0.634927	0.635130
(0.5, 0.6)	0.657811	0.672710	0.657602	0.657954	0.658267	0.657287	0.657807	0.657830	0.657824	0.657873	0.658009
(0.5, 0.8)	0.679952	0.691573	0.679774	0.679907	0.680117	0.679745	0.679938	0.679971	0.679957	0.680214	0.680069
(0.7, 0.2)	0.644506	0.658533	0.644709	0.644690	0.644717	0.644489	0.644506	0.644509	0.644509	0.644499	0.644550
(0.7, 0.4)	0.667073	0.682643	0.667064	0.667266	0.667449	0.666697	0.667072	0.667083	0.667079	0.667048	0.667216
(0.7, 0.6)	0.688899	0.702841	0.688718	0.689008	0.689272	0.688366	0.688896	0.688914	0.688914	0.688963	0.689063
(0.7, 0.8)	0.709916	0.720587	0.709770	0.709863	0.710039	0.709701	0.709906	0.709931	0.709924	0.710127	0.710012
(0.9, 0.2)	0.676207	0.689541	0.676288	0.676281	0.676296	0.676195	0.676207	0.676209	0.676209	0.676204	0.676228
(0.9, 0.4)	0.697706	0.712345	0.697691	0.697781	0.697866	0.697510	0.697705	0.697710	0.697710	0.697697	0.697768
(0.9, 0.6)	0.718371	0.731313	0.718289	0.718410	0.718525	0.718106	0.718370	0.718378	0.718380	0.718410	0.718440
(0.9, 0.8)	0.738154	0.747877	0.738093	0.738123	0.738198	0.738049	0.738149	0.738160	0.738160	0.738238	0.738194

Table 11. Error norms at various time levels using MQ, IMQ, IQ, and GS RBFs for $\alpha = 0.25, 0.5$, $\beta = 0$, $N = 10$, $\theta = 0.5$, and $\delta t = 0.1$ correspond to Example 3.

RBFs	t	$\alpha = 0.25$			$\alpha = 0.5$		
		L_2	L_∞	L_{rms}	L_2	L_∞	L_{rms}
			c = 3.68162			c = 6.48549	
MQ	0.2	1.081×10^{-3}	1.484×10^{-3}	1.031×10^{-3}	4.795×10^{-4}	6.599×10^{-4}	4.572×10^{-4}
	0.4	9.220×10^{-4}	1.264×10^{-3}	8.791×10^{-4}	3.476×10^{-4}	4.805×10^{-4}	3.314×10^{-4}
	0.6	8.053×10^{-4}	1.103×10^{-3}	7.678×10^{-4}	8.368×10^{-5}	1.193×10^{-4}	7.978×10^{-5}
	0.8	5.578×10^{-4}	7.776×10^{-4}	5.319×10^{-4}	4.336×10^{-5}	5.738×10^{-5}	4.134×10^{-5}
	1	2.992×10^{-6}	4.995×10^{-6}	2.853×10^{-6}	2.723×10^{-6}	3.734×10^{-6}	2.597×10^{-6}
			c = 6.61203			c = 7.63322	
IMQ	0.2	8.418×10^{-4}	1.154×10^{-3}	8.027×10^{-4}	5.035×10^{-4}	6.907×10^{-4}	4.801×10^{-4}
	0.4	8.722×10^{-4}	1.195×10^{-3}	8.316×10^{-4}	6.669×10^{-4}	9.148×10^{-4}	6.358×10^{-4}
	0.6	8.053×10^{-4}	1.103×10^{-3}	7.679×10^{-4}	6.838×10^{-4}	9.390×10^{-4}	6.519×10^{-4}
	0.8	5.980×10^{-4}	8.194×10^{-4}	5.702×10^{-4}	4.202×10^{-4}	5.823×10^{-4}	4.007×10^{-4}
	1	1.530×10^{-6}	2.163×10^{-6}	1.458×10^{-6}	3.049×10^{-6}	5.391×10^{-6}	2.907×10^{-6}
			c = 8.81199			c = 6.9269	
IQ	0.2	6.924×10^{-4}	9.508×10^{-4}	6.602×10^{-4}	4.630×10^{-4}	6.348×10^{-4}	4.414×10^{-4}
	0.4	5.406×10^{-4}	7.424×10^{-4}	5.154×10^{-4}	5.671×10^{-4}	7.799×10^{-4}	5.407×10^{-4}
	0.6	4.209×10^{-4}	5.776×10^{-4}	4.013×10^{-4}	3.965×10^{-4}	5.470×10^{-4}	3.780×10^{-4}
	0.8	2.383×10^{-4}	3.268×10^{-4}	2.272×10^{-4}	4.684×10^{-5}	6.663×10^{-5}	4.466×10^{-5}
	1	7.249×10^{-7}	1.173×10^{-6}	6.912×10^{-7}	2.578×10^{-6}	3.610×10^{-6}	2.458×10^{-6}
			c = 0.36854			c = 0.33014	
GS	0.2	2.642×10^{-4}	4.388×10^{-4}	2.519×10^{-4}	7.528×10^{-5}	1.068×10^{-4}	7.178×10^{-5}
	0.4	1.233×10^{-3}	1.803×10^{-3}	1.175×10^{-3}	2.218×10^{-4}	3.161×10^{-4}	2.115×10^{-4}
	0.6	1.202×10^{-3}	1.671×10^{-3}	1.146×10^{-3}	3.722×10^{-4}	5.227×10^{-4}	3.549×10^{-4}
	0.8	1.376×10^{-4}	1.881×10^{-4}	1.312×10^{-4}	3.090×10^{-4}	4.497×10^{-4}	2.946×10^{-4}
	1	9.904×10^{-6}	1.513×10^{-5}	9.443×10^{-6}	6.429×10^{-6}	1.094×10^{-5}	6.130×10^{-6}

Table 12. Error norms at various time levels using MQ, IMQ, IQ, and GS RBFs for $\alpha = 0.75, 1$, $\beta = 0$, $N = 10$, $\theta = 0.5$, and $\delta t = 0.1$ correspond to Example 3.

RBFs	t	$\alpha = 0.75$			$\alpha = 1$		
		L_2	L_∞	L_{rms}	L_2	L_∞	L_{rms}
			c = 6.20135			c = 5.79129	
MQ	0.2	1.854×10^{-4}	2.561×10^{-4}	1.768×10^{-4}	2.754×10^{-6}	3.671×10^{-6}	2.626×10^{-6}
	0.4	9.181×10^{-6}	1.560×10^{-5}	8.754×10^{-6}	9.160×10^{-6}	1.245×10^{-5}	8.734×10^{-6}
	0.6	1.553×10^{-4}	2.091×10^{-4}	1.481×10^{-4}	1.392×10^{-5}	1.900×10^{-5}	1.327×10^{-5}
	0.8	1.306×10^{-4}	1.781×10^{-4}	1.245×10^{-4}	1.335×10^{-5}	1.841×10^{-5}	1.273×10^{-5}
	1	1.342×10^{-6}	2.211×10^{-6}	1.280×10^{-6}	4.507×10^{-7}	7.729×10^{-7}	4.298×10^{-7}
			c = 7.82578			c = 6.46003	
IMQ	0.2	1.672×10^{-4}	2.305×10^{-4}	1.594×10^{-4}	2.380×10^{-6}	3.590×10^{-6}	2.269×10^{-6}
	0.4	1.765×10^{-4}	2.442×10^{-4}	1.683×10^{-4}	3.844×10^{-6}	6.398×10^{-6}	3.665×10^{-6}
	0.6	1.025×10^{-4}	1.434×10^{-4}	9.769×10^{-5}	1.029×10^{-5}	1.545×10^{-5}	9.806×10^{-6}
	0.8	3.666×10^{-5}	5.292×10^{-5}	3.495×10^{-5}	5.069×10^{-6}	8.448×10^{-6}	4.833×10^{-6}
	1	8.111×10^{-7}	1.714×10^{-6}	7.733×10^{-7}	5.708×10^{-7}	7.934×10^{-7}	5.443×10^{-7}

Table 12. *Cont.*

RBFs	t	$\alpha = 0.75$			$\alpha = 1$		
		L_2	L_∞	L_{rms}	L_2	L_∞	L_{rms}
		c = 6.73987			c = 8.05516		
IQ	0.2	1.874×10^{-4}	2.569×10^{-4}	1.787×10^{-4}	6.647×10^{-6}	8.712×10^{-6}	6.337×10^{-6}
	0.4	3.295×10^{-4}	4.515×10^{-4}	3.141×10^{-4}	2.459×10^{-5}	3.395×10^{-5}	2.344×10^{-5}
	0.6	3.312×10^{-4}	4.562×10^{-4}	3.157×10^{-4}	5.053×10^{-5}	6.511×10^{-5}	4.817×10^{-5}
	0.8	1.167×10^{-4}	1.641×10^{-4}	1.112×10^{-4}	1.887×10^{-4}	2.612×10^{-4}	1.799×10^{-4}
	1	3.197×10^{-6}	4.250×10^{-6}	3.048×10^{-6}	1.895×10^{-6}	3.064×10^{-6}	1.806×10^{-6}
		c = 0.333513			c = 0.22009		
GS	0.2	1.039×10^{-5}	1.683×10^{-5}	9.904×10^{-6}	3.868×10^{-5}	5.120×10^{-5}	3.688×10^{-5}
	0.4	2.716×10^{-4}	3.860×10^{-4}	2.589×10^{-4}	1.255×10^{-4}	1.707×10^{-4}	1.197×10^{-4}
	0.6	3.887×10^{-4}	5.566×10^{-4}	3.706×10^{-4}	1.440×10^{-4}	1.978×10^{-4}	1.373×10^{-4}
	0.8	1.526×10^{-4}	2.234×10^{-4}	1.455×10^{-4}	8.383×10^{-5}	1.163×10^{-4}	7.993×10^{-5}
	1	5.527×10^{-6}	1.015×10^{-5}	5.270×10^{-6}	6.293×10^{-6}	9.884×10^{-6}	6.000×10^{-6}

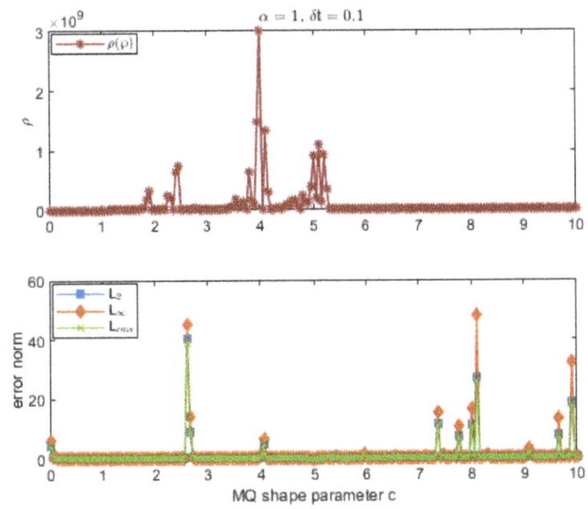

(**a**) Error norms and spectral radius using MQ

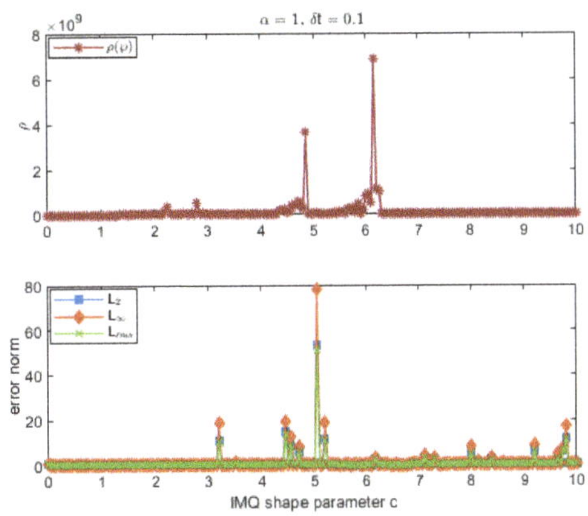

(**b**) Error norms and spectral radius using IMQ

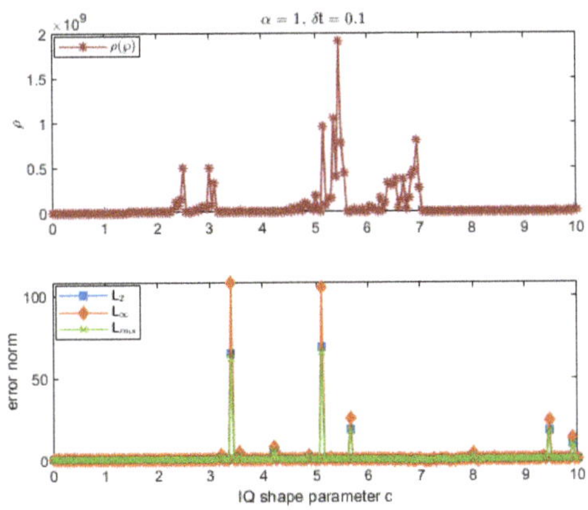

(**c**) Error norms and spectral radius against IQ

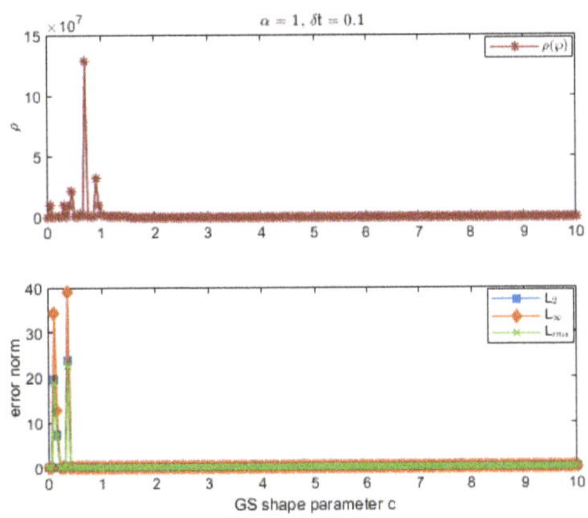

(**d**) Error norms and spectral radius using GS

Figure 17. Error norms and spectral radius correspond to Example 3 when N = M = 10, $\alpha = 1$ using MQ, IMQ, IQ, and GS RBFs.

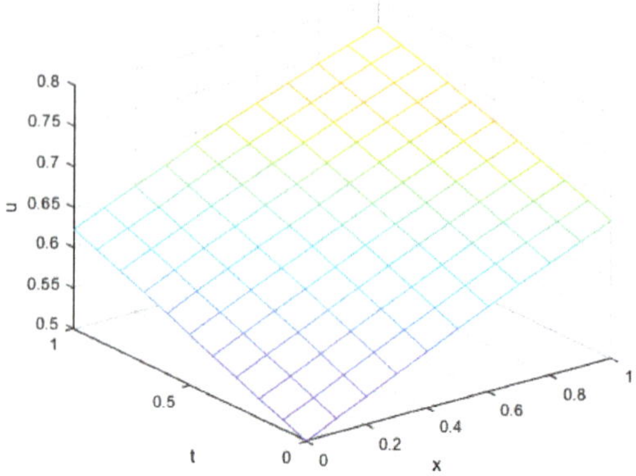

(**a**) Exact solution

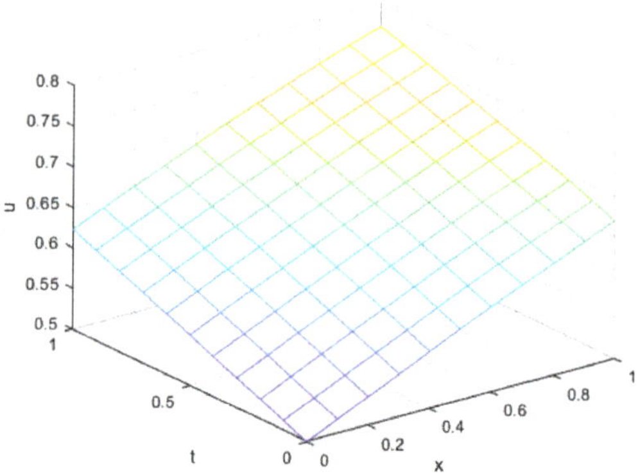

(**b**) Computed solution using MQ

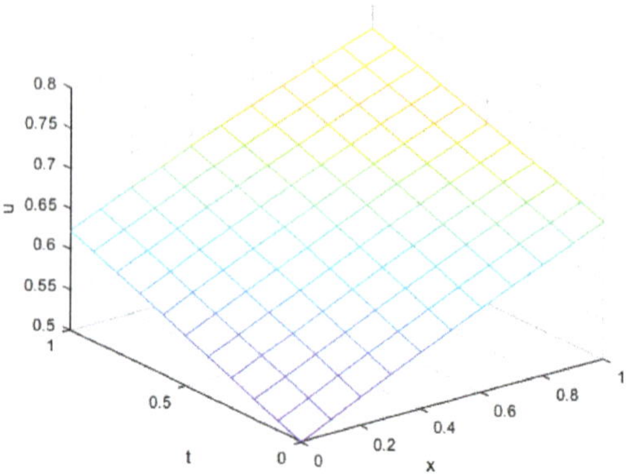

(**c**) Computed solution using IMQ

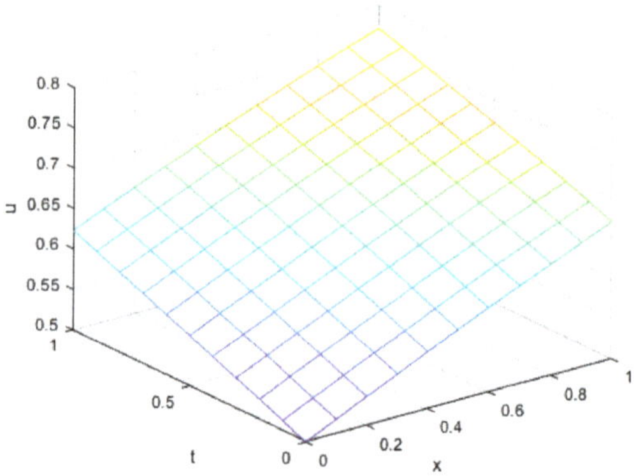

(**d**) Computed solution against IQ

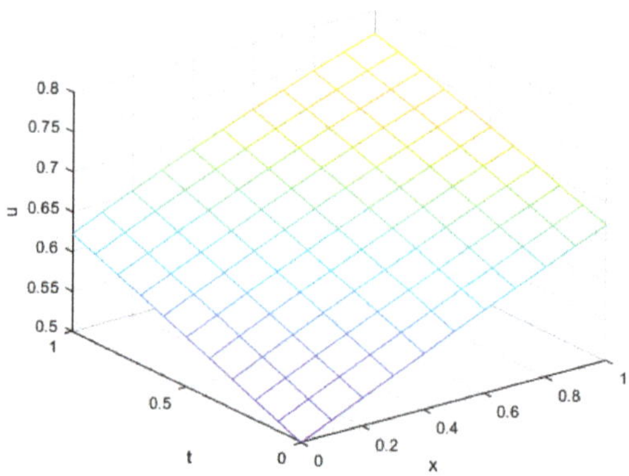

(**e**) Computed solution using GS

Figure 18. Exact vs. computed solution corresponds to Example 3 when $N = M = 10$, $\alpha = 1$ using MQ, IMQ, IQ, and GS RBFs.

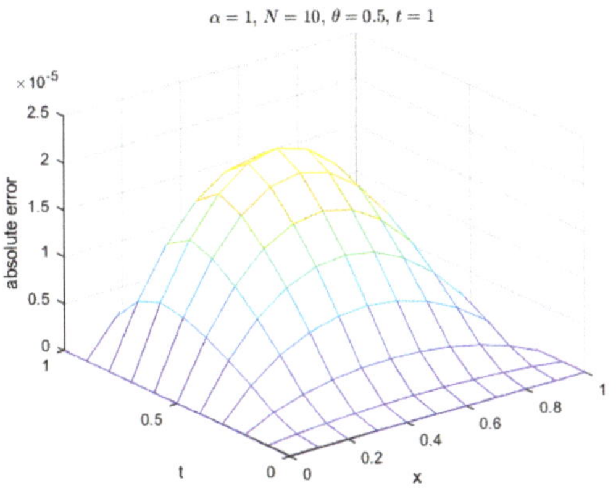

(**a**) Absolute error using MQ

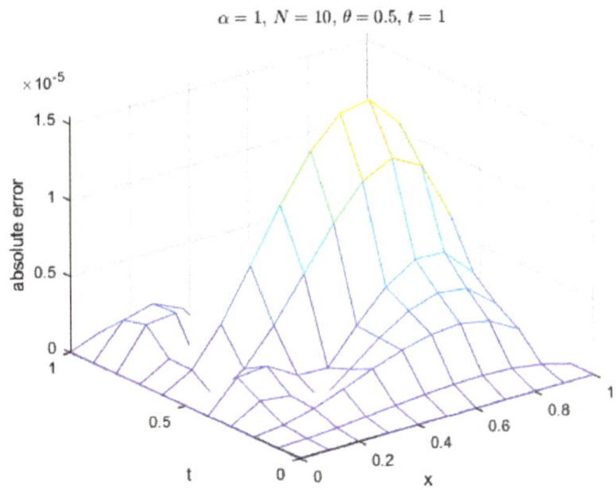

(**b**) Absolute error using IMQ

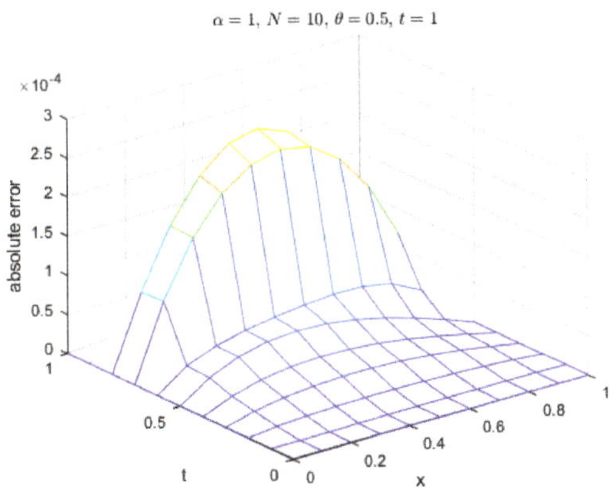

(**c**) Absolute error against IQ

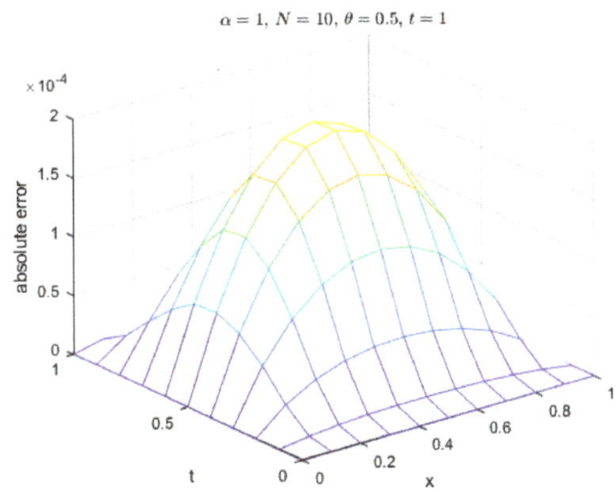

(**d**) Absolute error using GS

Figure 19. Absolute error of MQ, IMQ, IQ, and GS at t = 1×10^{-4} corresponds to Example 3.

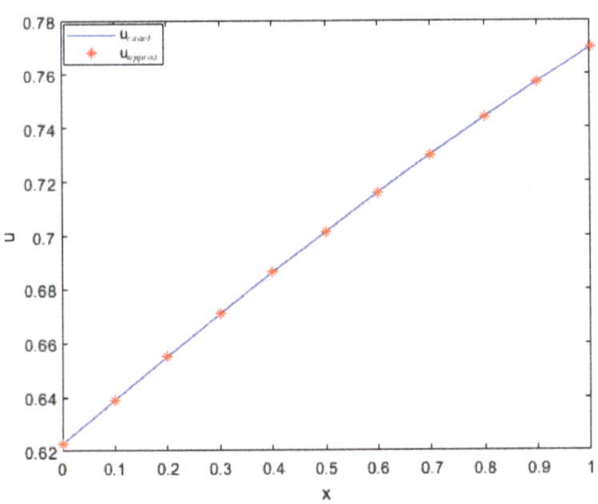

(**a**) Exact vs. numerical using MQ

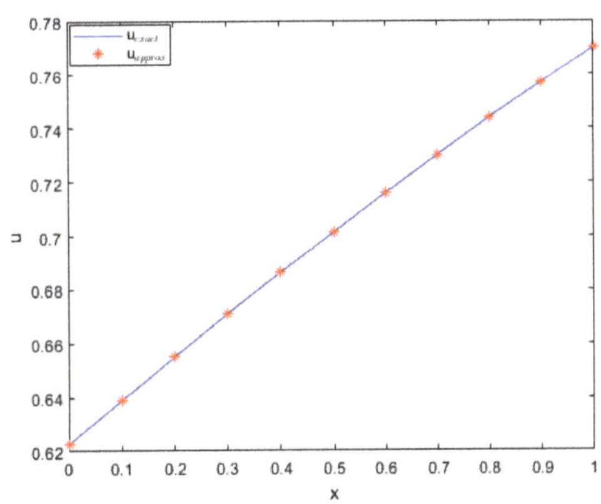

(**b**) Exact vs. numerical using IMQ

Figure 20. *Cont.*

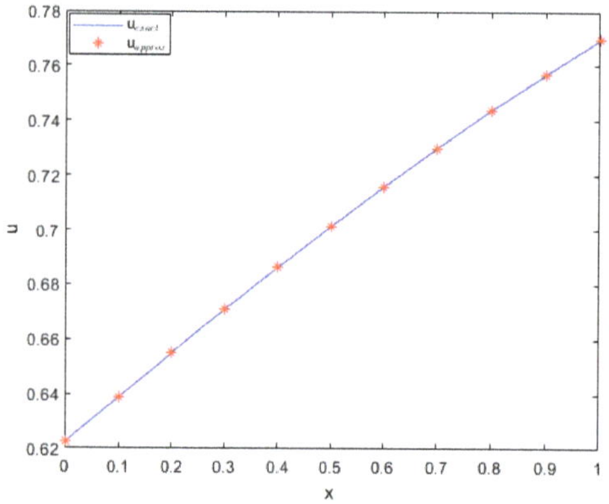

(**c**) Exact vs. numerical against IQ

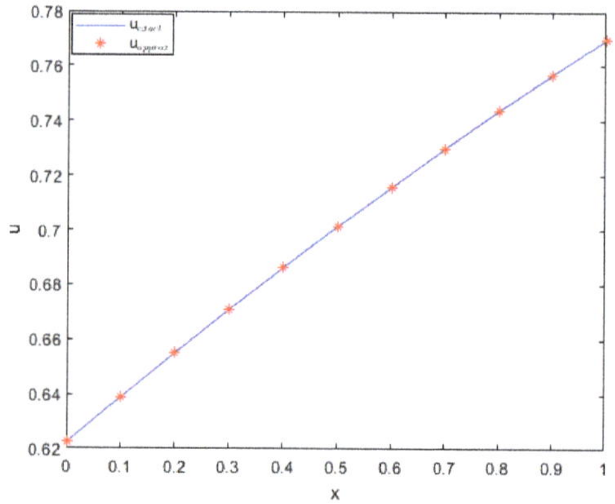

(**d**) Exact vs. numerical using GS

Figure 20. Comparison of exact and computed solution corresponds to Example 3 at t = 1 × 10^{-4} and $\alpha = 1$ using MQ, IMQ, IQ, and GS RBFs.

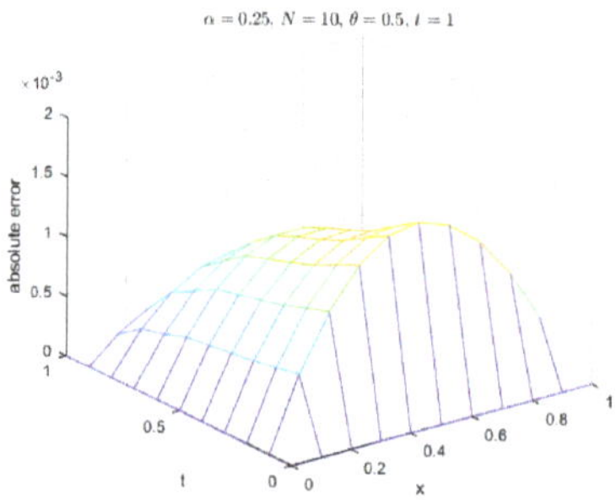

(**a**) Absolute error

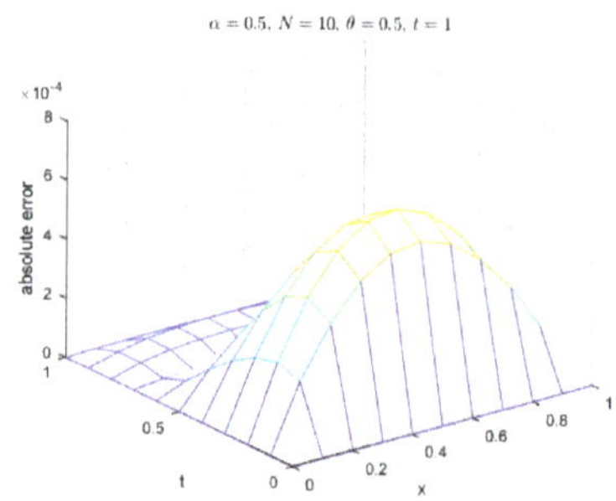

(**b**) Absolute error

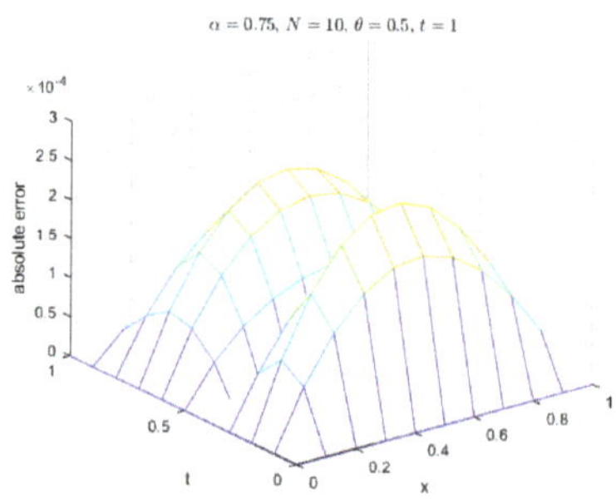

(**c**) Absolute error

Figure 21. Absolute errors for Example 3 with different values of α's using MQ RBF.

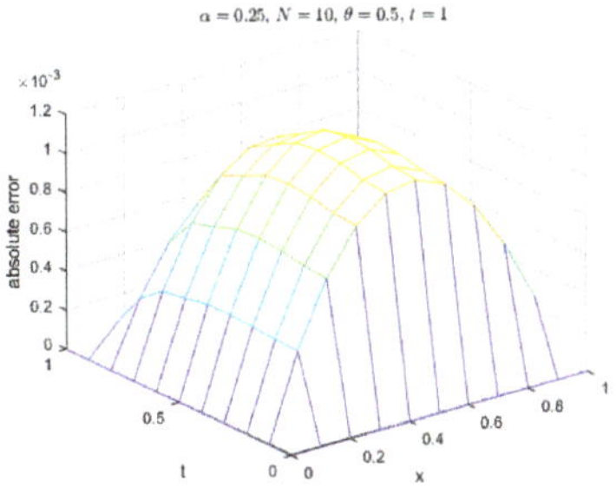

(**a**) Absolute error

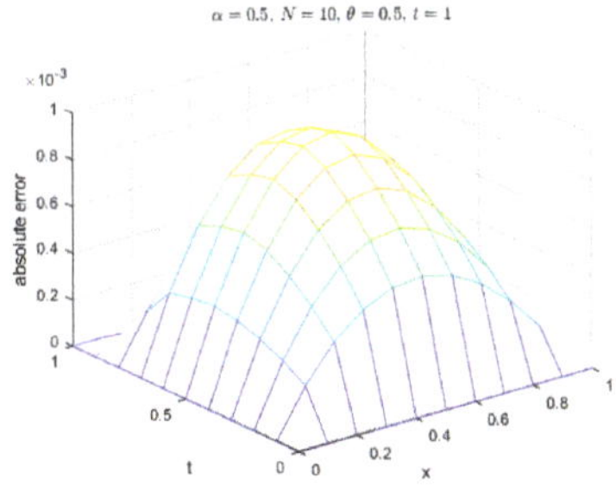

(**b**) Absolute error

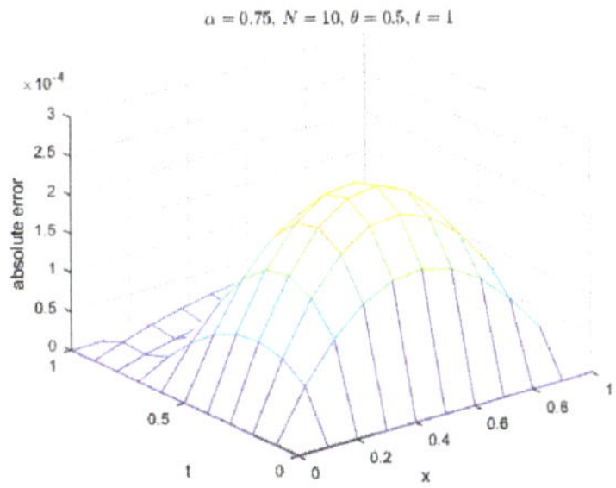

(**c**) Absolute error

Figure 22. Absolute errors for Example 3 with different values of α's using IMQ RBF.

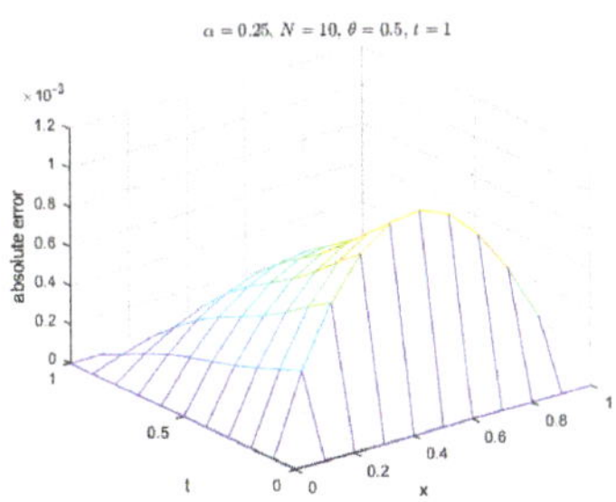

(**a**) Absolute error

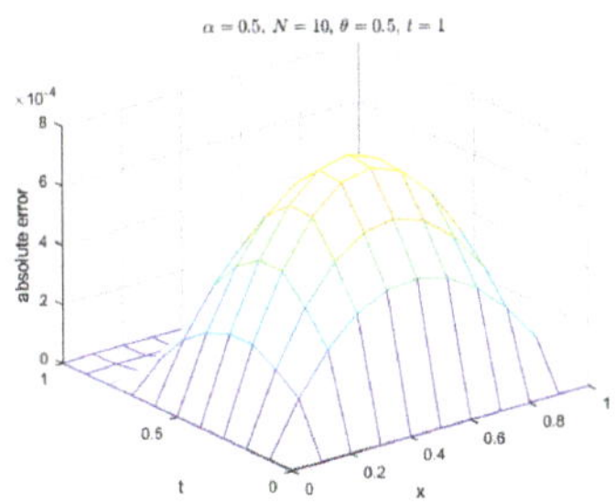

(**b**) Absolute error

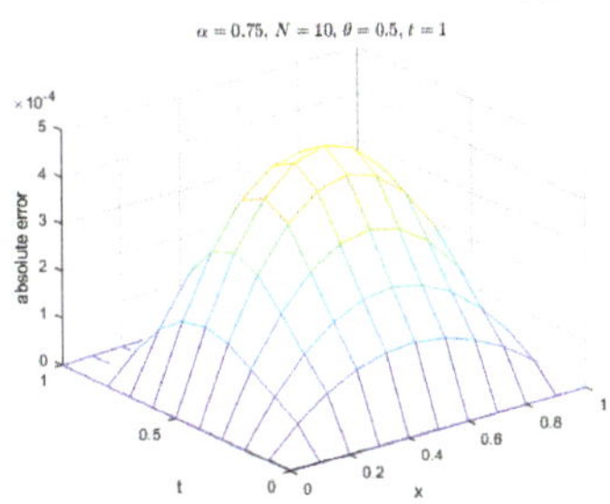

(**c**) Absolute error

Figure 23. Absolute errors for Example 3 with different values of α's using IQ RBF.

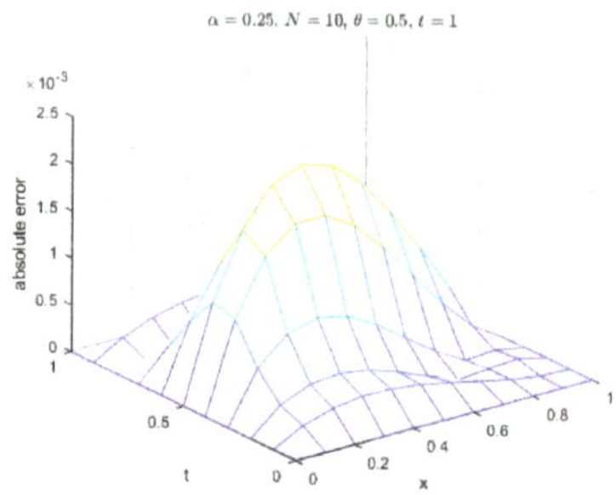

(**a**) Absolute error

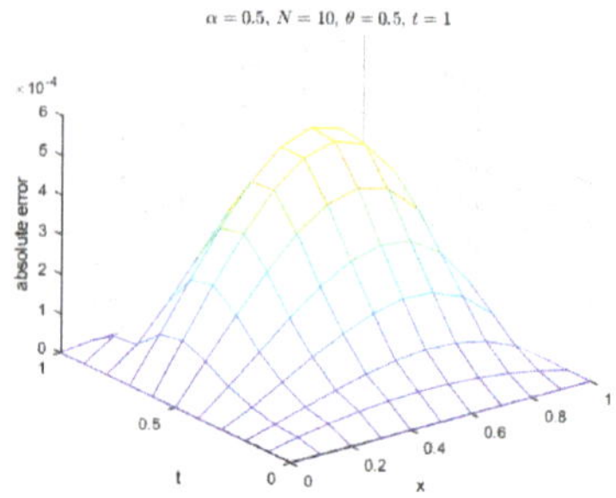

(**b**) Absolute error

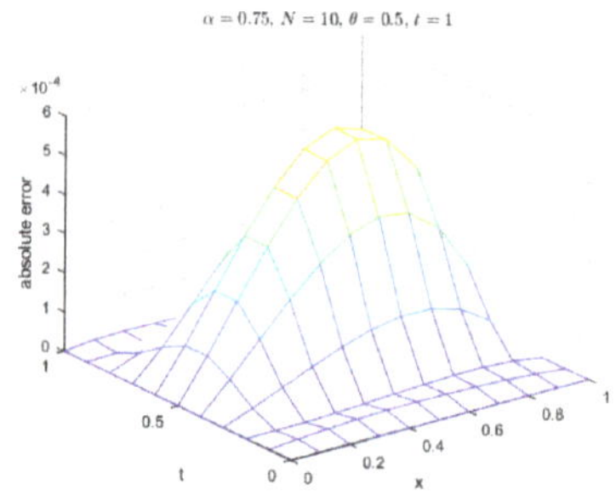

(**c**) Absolute error

Figure 24. Absolute errors for Example 3 with different values of α's using GS RBF.

Example 4. *Let us consider FitzHugh–Nagumo Equations* (2) *and* (3). *For* $\alpha = 1$, *the exact solution, as given in [27], is described by the following expression:*

$$u(t,x) = \frac{1}{1+e^{\left(\frac{-x}{\sqrt{2}}+yt\right)}}, \quad \textit{where} \quad y = \frac{1}{\sqrt{2}} - \sqrt{2}\beta,$$

where β *represents an arbitrary constant. We employ the ICs and BCs from this exact solution. Using this solution, we apply the present method to approximate the exact solution within the domain* $x \in [0,1]$. *RBFs such as MQ, IMQ, IQ, and GS are employed for the numerical approximation. We choose* $N = 10$, $\delta t = 0.001$, $\theta = 0.5$, *and* $\beta = -1$. *The obtained results, in terms of absolute errors, are presented in Table 13 for* $\alpha = 1$. *The table clearly indicates that the accuracy of the present method is better than that of the homotopy perturbation transform technique (HPTT). Additionally, the comparison of the present method with HPTT is presented in Table 14 for* $\beta = 0.45$ *and* $\alpha = 0.5$ *while keeping the other parameters the same. The comparison shows that the results of the present method using different RBFs are more accurate than those of HPTT. Furthermore, the error norms at various time levels are recorded in Tables 15 and 16 for* α *values of* 0.5 *and* 1 *using the MQ, IMQ, IQ, and GS RBFs.*

The stability and error norm plots are presented in Figures 25 and 26 for $\alpha = 1$ *and* 0.5 *and* $\beta = -1$ *and* $\beta = 0.45$, *respectively, for* $N = 10$, $\theta = 0.5$, *and* $\delta t = 0.001$, *demonstrating that the present method consistently satisfies the Lax–Richtmyer stability criterion. Additionally, the surface plots in Figures 27 and 28 show that the computed solution using the selected RBFs closely matches the exact solution. The absolute errors for* $\alpha = 1$ *and* 0.5 *at various time levels are depicted in Figures 29 and 30, respectively, indicating reasonable accuracy. Finally, Figures 31 and 32 compare the exact and computed solutions at the final time, demonstrating the good accuracy of the present method.*

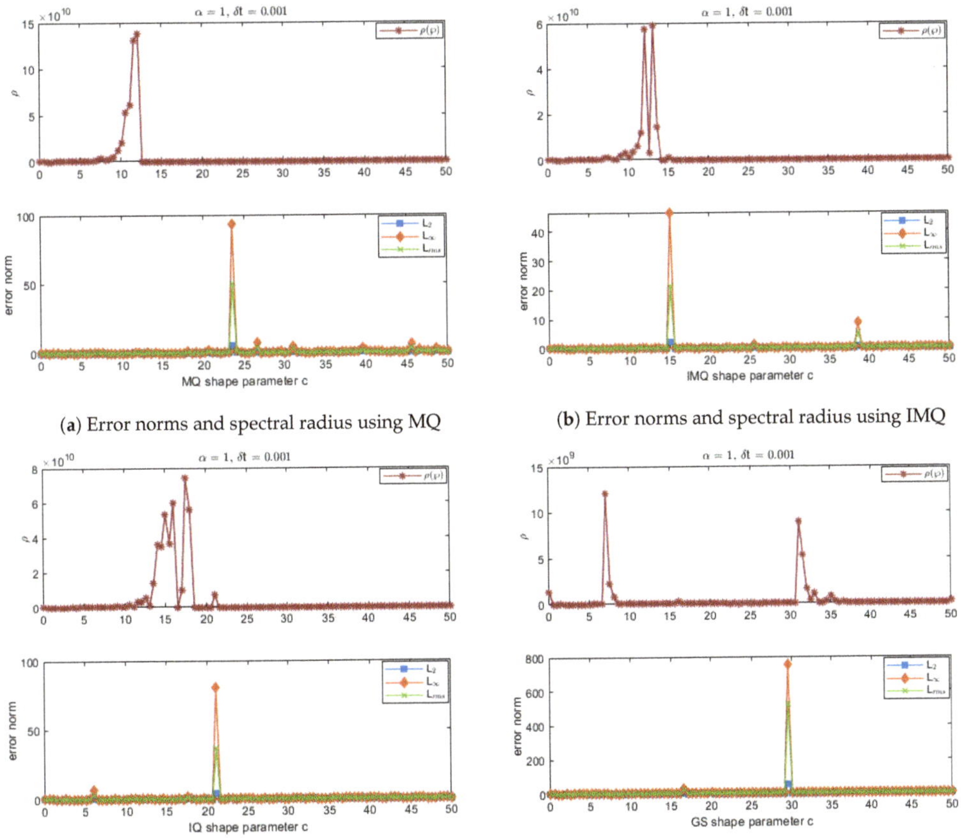

(**a**) Error norms and spectral radius using MQ

(**b**) Error norms and spectral radius using IMQ

(**c**) Error norms and spectral radius against IQ

(**d**) Error norms and spectral radius using GS

Figure 25. Error norms and spectral radius correspond to Example 4 when N = M = 10, $\alpha = 1$ using MQ, IMQ, IQ, and GS RBFs.

Table 13. Comparison of absolute errors of the present method solution with HPTT using MQ, IMQ, IQ, and GS RBFs for $\alpha = 1$, $\beta = -1$, N = 10, $\theta = 0.5$, and $\delta t = 0.001$ corresponds to Example 4.

x	t	[27]	MQ	IMQ	IQ	GS
			c = 18.6452	c = 15.3437	c = 19.0984	c = 0.3839
0.001	0.001	1.5×10^{-3}	2.604×10^{-9}	1.507×10^{-9}	1.243×10^{-9}	1.019×10^{-9}
0.002	0.002	3.0×10^{-3}	1.287×10^{-8}	3.875×10^{-9}	4.379×10^{-9}	8.782×10^{-11}
0.003	0.003	4.5×10^{-3}	1.573×10^{-8}	1.229×10^{-8}	9.328×10^{-9}	1.306×10^{-9}
0.004	0.004	6.0×10^{-3}	9.833×10^{-9}	6.037×10^{-9}	9.718×10^{-9}	3.324×10^{-9}
0.005	0.005	7.5×10^{-3}	1.269×10^{-8}	7.529×10^{-9}	2.312×10^{-8}	4.515×10^{-9}
0.006	0.006	9.1×10^{-3}	9.864×10^{-9}	6.832×10^{-9}	3.217×10^{-9}	5.898×10^{-9}
0.007	0.007	1.0×10^{-2}	2.049×10^{-9}	5.261×10^{-9}	6.513×10^{-9}	1.112×10^{-8}
0.008	0.008	1.2×10^{-2}	4.631×10^{-10}	5.446×10^{-9}	4.356×10^{-10}	1.287×10^{-8}
0.009	0.009	1.3×10^{-2}	3.879×10^{-9}	5.513×10^{-11}	1.102×10^{-9}	6.502×10^{-9}
0.010	0.010	1.5×10^{-2}	9.973×10^{-10}	8.579×10^{-10}	1.403×10^{-10}	1.438×10^{-9}

Table 14. Comparison of absolute errors of the present method solution with HPTT using MQ, IMQ, IQ, and GS RBFs for $\alpha = 0.5$, $\beta = 0.45$, $N = 10$, $\theta = 0.5$, and $\delta t = 0.001$ corresponds to Example 4.

x	t	[27]	MQ	IMQ	IQ	GS
			c = 5.8849	**c = 46.8122**	**c = 21.9648**	**c = 0.01313**
0.001	0.001	2.8×10^{-2}	5.428×10^{-10}	2.256×10^{-9}	8.790×10^{-11}	8.717×10^{-10}
0.002	0.002	4.1×10^{-2}	3.680×10^{-10}	2.810×10^{-9}	3.522×10^{-10}	4.335×10^{-10}
0.003	0.003	5.3×10^{-2}	6.547×10^{-10}	2.313×10^{-9}	2.294×10^{-12}	1.436×10^{-8}
0.004	0.004	6.2×10^{-2}	3.745×10^{-10}	4.687×10^{-9}	1.209×10^{-9}	6.656×10^{-9}
0.005	0.005	6.9×10^{-2}	2.766×10^{-10}	1.804×10^{-9}	5.891×10^{-10}	1.806×10^{-9}
0.006	0.006	8.0×10^{-2}	5.124×10^{-11}	4.929×10^{-9}	1.687×10^{-9}	4.174×10^{-9}
0.007	0.007	8.7×10^{-2}	2.419×10^{-11}	5.098×10^{-10}	1.065×10^{-9}	2.086×10^{-9}
0.008	0.008	9.4×10^{-2}	3.764×10^{-11}	8.220×10^{-10}	2.522×10^{-10}	3.540×10^{-10}
0.009	0.009	1.0×10^{-2}	2.451×10^{-11}	3.408×10^{-10}	1.441×10^{-9}	7.412×10^{-10}
0.010	0.010	1.1×10^{-2}	1.957×10^{-11}	4.644×10^{-10}	9.778×10^{-11}	1.064×10^{-9}

Table 15. Error norms at various time levels using MQ, IMQ, IQ, and GS RBFs for $\beta = -1$, $N = 10$, $\theta = 0.5$, and $\delta t = 0.001$ corresponds to Example 4.

RBFs	t	$\alpha = 0.5$			$\alpha = 1$		
		L_2	L_∞	L_{rms}	L_2	L_∞	L_{rms}
			c = 2.2759			c = 18.6452	
MQ	0.002	1.826×10^{-9}	2.695×10^{-8}	1.741×10^{-8}	1.506×10^{-9}	2.005×10^{-8}	1.436×10^{-8}
	0.004	3.987×10^{-10}	7.487×10^{-9}	3.801×10^{-9}	8.064×10^{-10}	1.239×10^{-8}	7.688×10^{-9}
	0.006	3.952×10^{-10}	6.265×10^{-9}	3.768×10^{-9}	7.224×10^{-10}	9.868×10^{-9}	6.888×10^{-9}
	0.008	1.206×10^{-10}	2.755×10^{-9}	1.150×10^{-9}	1.338×10^{-10}	2.402×10^{-9}	1.276×10^{-9}
	0.01	8.903×10^{-11}	1.567×10^{-9}	8.488×10^{-10}	8.692×10^{-11}	1.269×10^{-9}	8.287×10^{-10}
			c = 35.2365			c = 15.3437	
IMQ	0.002	1.410×10^{-9}	2.428×10^{-8}	1.344×10^{-8}	5.814×10^{-10}	9.810×10^{-9}	5.543×10^{-9}
	0.004	9.698×10^{-10}	1.670×10^{-8}	9.247×10^{-9}	3.875×10^{-10}	7.351×10^{-9}	3.695×10^{-9}
	0.006	2.074×10^{-9}	3.516×10^{-8}	1.977×10^{-8}	5.499×10^{-10}	7.665×10^{-9}	5.243×10^{-9}
	0.008	1.188×10^{-9}	1.630×10^{-8}	1.133×10^{-8}	5.216×10^{-10}	7.340×10^{-9}	4.973×10^{-9}
	0.01	7.080×10^{-10}	1.068×10^{-8}	6.751×10^{-9}	1.326×10^{-10}	2.486×10^{-9}	1.264×10^{-9}
			c = 22.2965			c = 19.0984	
IQ	0.002	4.624×10^{-9}	6.265×10^{-8}	4.409×10^{-8}	4.838×10^{-10}	6.599×10^{-9}	4.613×10^{-9}
	0.004	9.319×10^{-9}	1.256×10^{-7}	8.885×10^{-8}	7.086×10^{-10}	1.217×10^{-8}	6.757×10^{-9}
	0.006	2.882×10^{-9}	5.671×10^{-8}	2.748×10^{-8}	6.541×10^{-10}	1.277×10^{-8}	6.237×10^{-9}
	0.008	5.201×10^{-9}	7.886×10^{-8}	4.959×10^{-8}	1.535×10^{-10}	3.069×10^{-9}	1.463×10^{-9}
	0.01	1.441×10^{-9}	2.486×10^{-8}	1.374×10^{-8}	7.404×10^{-11}	1.420×10^{-9}	7.059×10^{-10}
			c = 0.2654			c = 0.3839	
GS	0.002	2.842×10^{-9}	3.915×10^{-8}	2.710×10^{-8}	1.096×10^{-10}	1.716×10^{-9}	1.045×10^{-9}
	0.004	5.743×10^{-9}	7.859×10^{-8}	5.476×10^{-8}	2.960×10^{-10}	4.213×10^{-9}	2.822×10^{-9}
	0.006	4.834×10^{-9}	7.845×10^{-8}	4.609×10^{-8}	4.196×10^{-10}	5.898×10^{-9}	4.001×10^{-9}
	0.008	5.551×10^{-9}	1.224×10^{-7}	5.292×10^{-8}	1.245×10^{-9}	1.639×10^{-8}	1.187×10^{-8}
	0.01	1.994×10^{-9}	3.734×10^{-8}	1.901×10^{-8}	1.991×10^{-10}	2.787×10^{-9}	1.898×10^{-9}

Table 16. Error norms at various time levels using MQ, IMQ, IQ, and GS RBFs for $\beta = 0.45$, $N = 10$, $\theta = 0.5$, and $\delta t = 0.001$ correspond to Example 4.

RBFs	t	$\alpha = 0.5$			$\alpha = 1$		
		L_2	L_∞	L_{rms}	L_2	L_∞	L_{rms}
		$c = 5.8849$			$c = 4.46$		
MQ	0.002	3.997×10^{-11}	6.588×10^{-10}	3.811×10^{-10}	3.832×10^{-11}	5.612×10^{-10}	3.654×10^{-10}
	0.004	2.543×10^{-11}	4.185×10^{-10}	2.425×10^{-10}	4.074×10^{-11}	6.447×10^{-10}	3.885×10^{-10}
	0.006	2.687×10^{-11}	4.331×10^{-10}	2.562×10^{-10}	3.552×10^{-11}	5.081×10^{-10}	3.387×10^{-10}
	0.008	2.878×10^{-11}	5.097×10^{-10}	2.744×10^{-10}	1.383×10^{-11}	1.986×10^{-10}	1.318×10^{-10}
	0.01	1.573×10^{-11}	2.450×10^{-10}	1.500×10^{-10}	9.560×10^{-12}	1.679×10^{-10}	9.115×10^{-11}
		$c = 46.8122$			$c = 47.0019$		
IMQ	0.002	1.732×10^{-10}	2.901×10^{-9}	1.652×10^{-9}	4.734×10^{-11}	7.761×10^{-10}	4.513×10^{-10}
	0.004	3.925×10^{-10}	5.261×10^{-9}	3.742×10^{-9}	4.022×10^{-11}	7.685×10^{-10}	3.835×10^{-10}
	0.006	3.585×10^{-10}	5.686×10^{-9}	3.418×10^{-9}	6.586×10^{-11}	1.284×10^{-9}	6.280×10^{-10}
	0.008	2.187×10^{-10}	3.579×10^{-9}	2.085×10^{-9}	7.760×10^{-11}	1.417×10^{-9}	7.399×10^{-10}
	0.01	4.236×10^{-11}	6.657×10^{-10}	4.038×10^{-10}	2.589×10^{-11}	3.952×10^{-10}	2.468×10^{-10}
		$c = 21.9648$			$c = 15.2317$		
IQ	0.002	2.981×10^{-11}	4.302×10^{-10}	2.842×10^{-10}	6.390×10^{-11}	1.053×10^{-9}	6.092×10^{-10}
	0.004	7.874×10^{-11}	1.499×10^{-9}	7.508×10^{-10}	4.657×10^{-11}	9.039×10^{-10}	4.441×10^{-10}
	0.006	1.340×10^{-10}	1.833×10^{-9}	1.278×10^{-9}	4.018×10^{-11}	7.631×10^{-10}	3.831×10^{-10}
	0.008	3.544×10^{-11}	6.846×10^{-10}	3.379×10^{-10}	1.035×10^{-10}	1.417×10^{-9}	9.868×10^{-10}
	0.01	4.529×10^{-11}	8.046×10^{-10}	4.318×10^{-10}	2.827×10^{-11}	4.326×10^{-10}	2.695×10^{-10}
		$c = 0.01313$			$c = 0.17158$		
GS	0.002	7.714×10^{-11}	1.385×10^{-9}	7.355×10^{-10}	1.530×10^{-11}	3.216×10^{-10}	1.459×10^{-10}
	0.004	1.041×10^{-9}	2.445×10^{-8}	9.924×10^{-9}	5.598×10^{-11}	7.387×10^{-10}	5.338×10^{-10}
	0.006	5.649×10^{-10}	9.973×10^{-9}	5.386×10^{-9}	3.017×10^{-11}	5.142×10^{-10}	2.876×10^{-10}
	0.008	2.462×10^{-10}	3.775×10^{-9}	2.348×10^{-9}	1.693×10^{-11}	2.656×10^{-10}	1.615×10^{-10}
	0.01	1.223×10^{-10}	1.844×10^{-9}	1.166×10^{-9}	2.405×10^{-11}	5.014×10^{-10}	2.293×10^{-10}

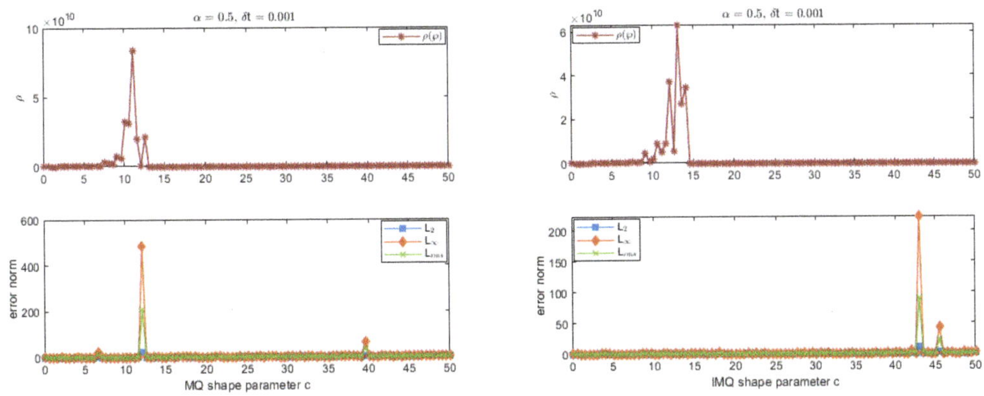

(**a**) Error norms and spectral radius using MQ

(**b**) Error norms and spectral radius using IMQ

Figure 26. *Cont.*

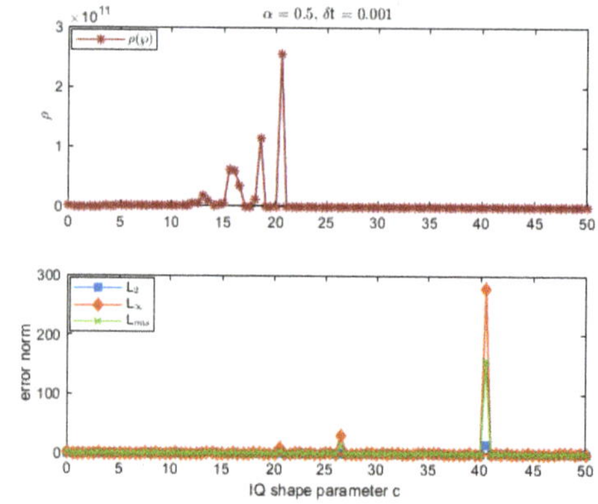

(**c**) Error norms and spectral radius against IQ

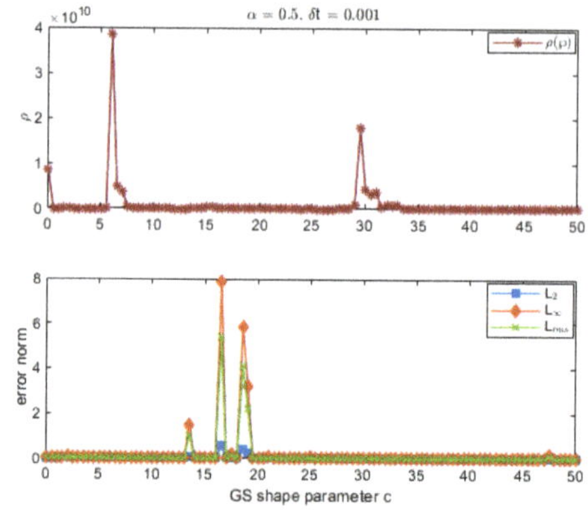

(**d**) Error norms and spectral radius using GS

Figure 26. Error norms and spectral radius correspond to Example 4 when N = M = 10, $\alpha = 0.5$ using MQ, IMQ, IQ, and GS RBFs.

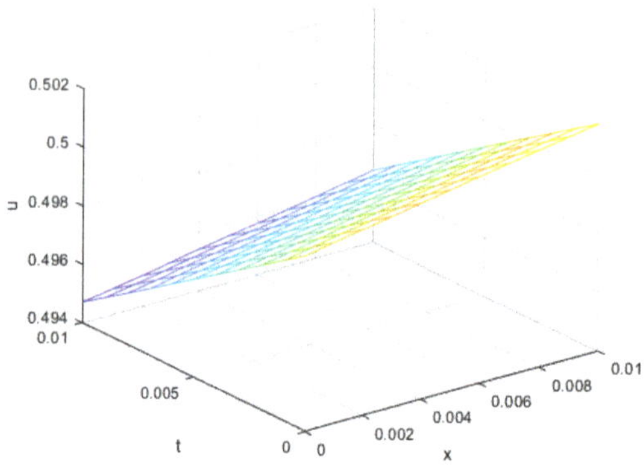

(**a**) Exact solution

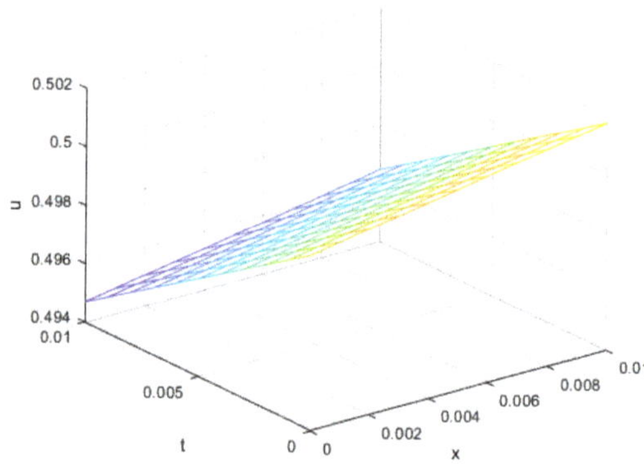

(**b**) Computed solution using MQ

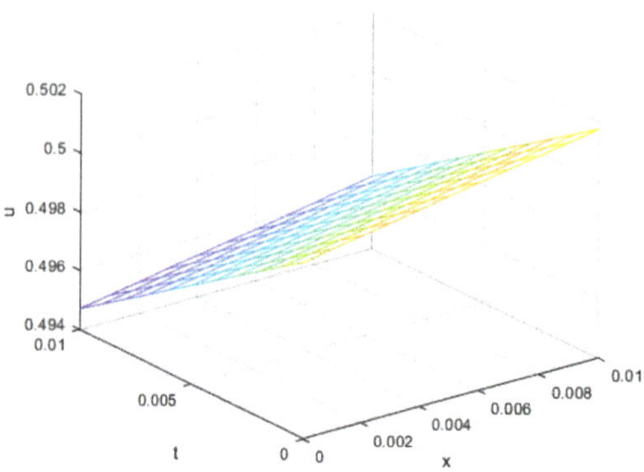

(**c**) Computed solution using IMQ

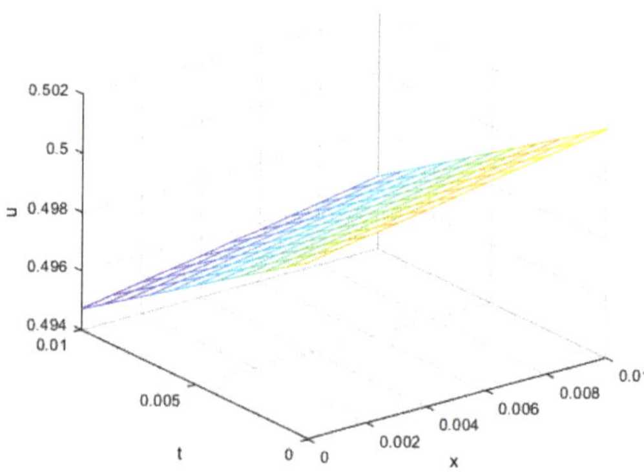

(**d**) Computed solution against IQ

Figure 27. *Cont.*

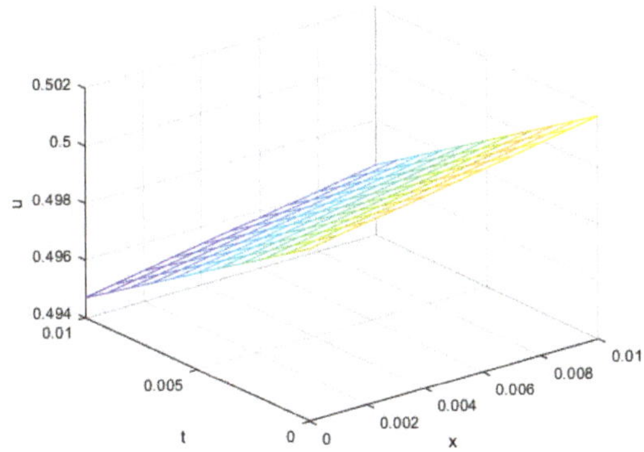

(**e**) Computed solution using GS

Figure 27. Exact vs. computed solution corresponds to Example 4 when $N = M = 10$, $\alpha = 1$ using MQ, IMQ, IQ, and GS RBFs.

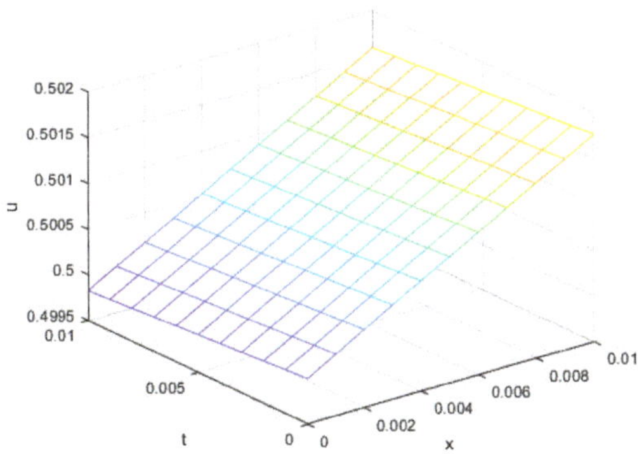

(**a**) Exact solution

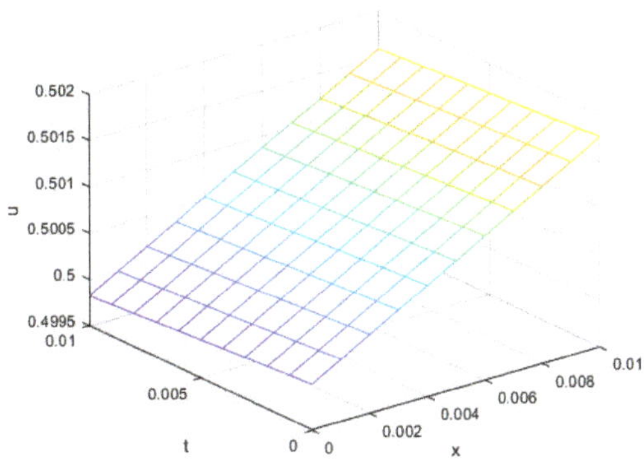

(**b**) Computed solution using MQ

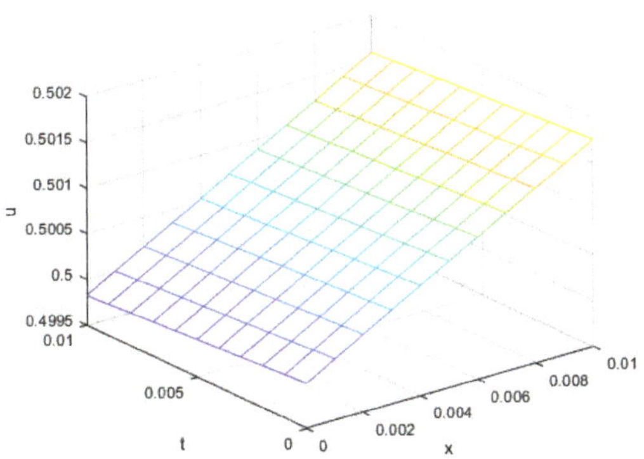

(**c**) Computed solution using IMQ

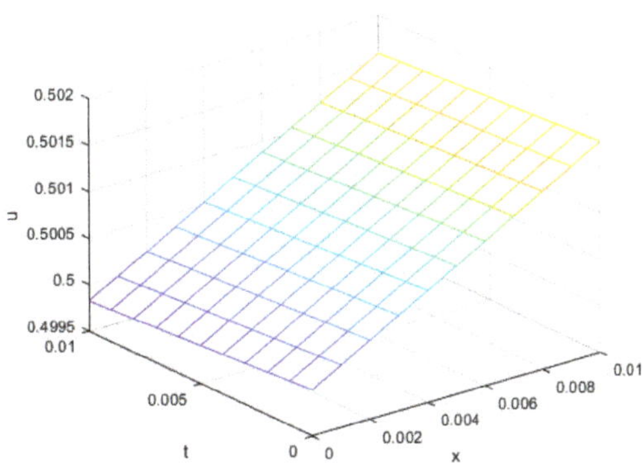

(**d**) Computed solution against IQ

Figure 28. *Cont.*

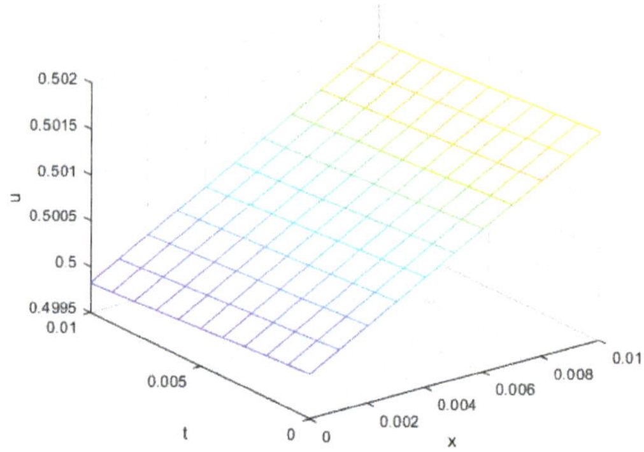

(**e**) Computed solution using GS

Figure 28. Exact vs. computed solution corresponds to Example 4 when N = M = 10, $\alpha = 0.5$ using MQ, IMQ, IQ, and GS RBFs.

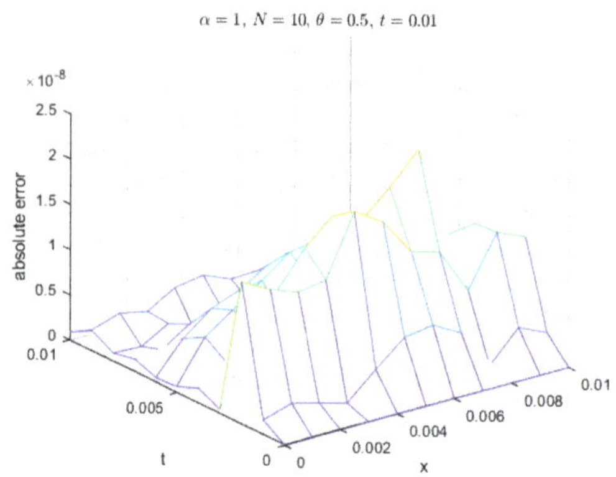

(**a**) Absolute error using MQ

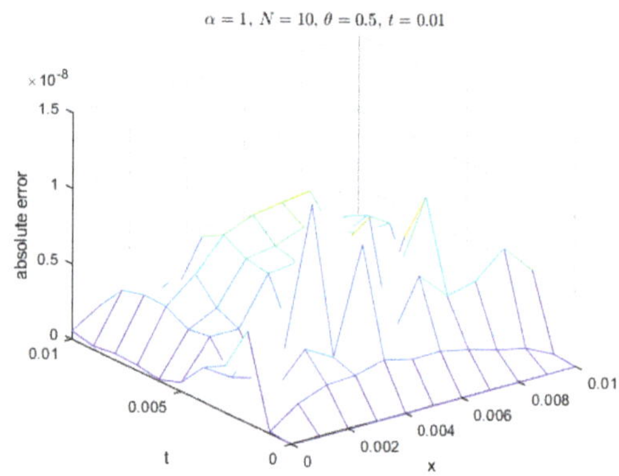

(**b**) Absolute error using IMQ

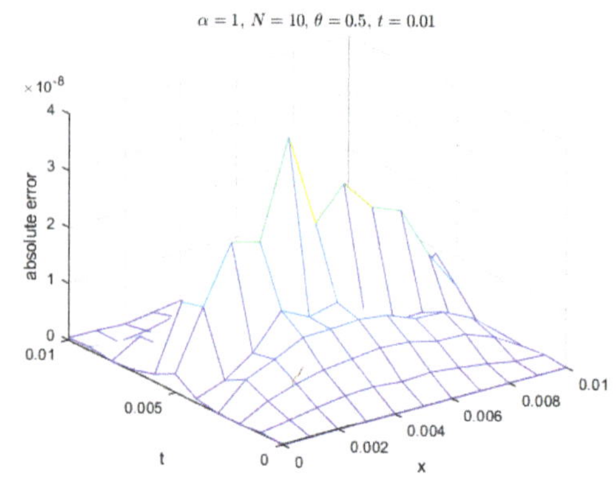

(**c**) Absolute error against IQ

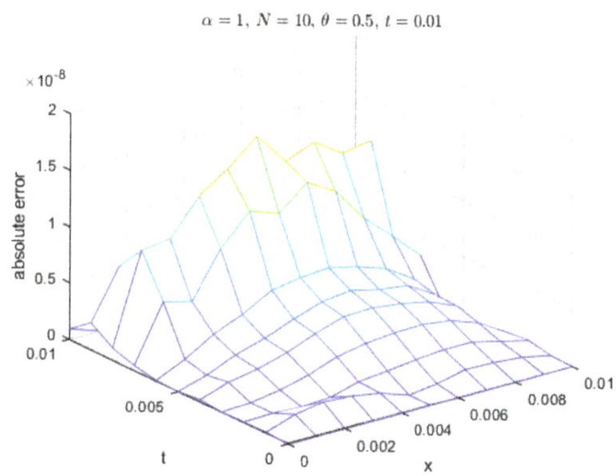

(**d**) Absolute error using GS

Figure 29. Absolute error of MQ, IMQ, IQ, and GS at t = 0.01 corresponds to Example 4.

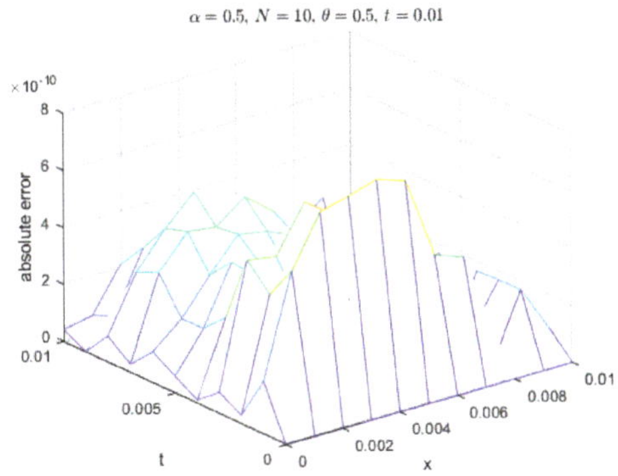

(a) Absolute error using MQ

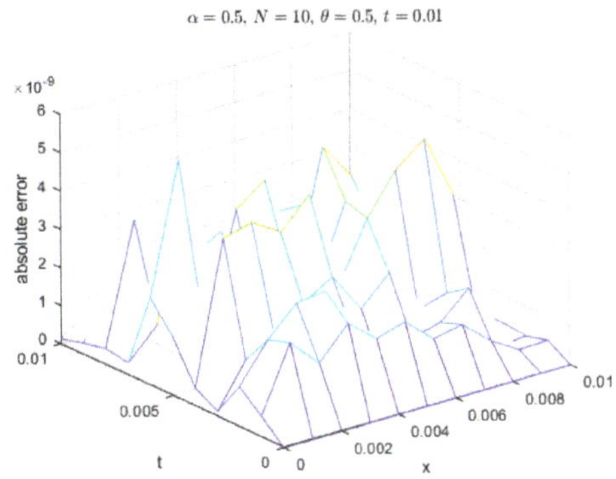

(b) Absolute error using IMQ

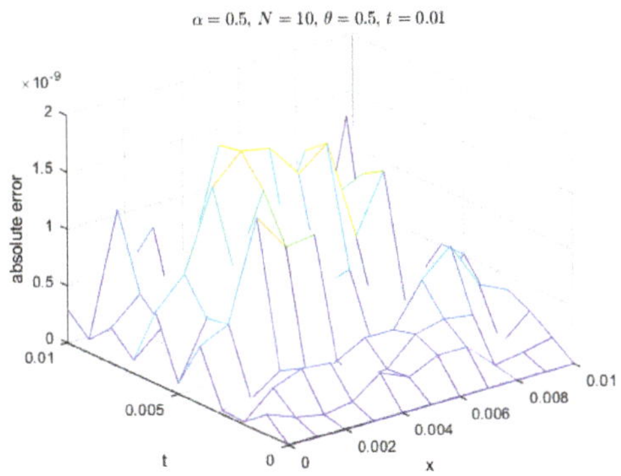

(c) Absolute error against IQ

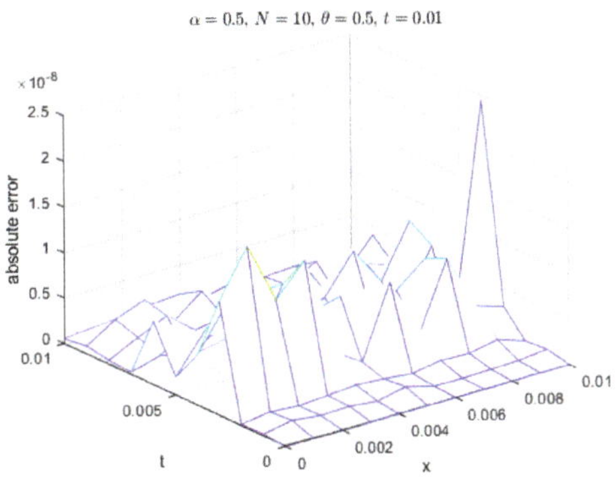

(d) Absolute error using GS

Figure 30. Absolute error of MQ, IMQ, IQ, and GS at t = 0.01 corresponds to Example 4.

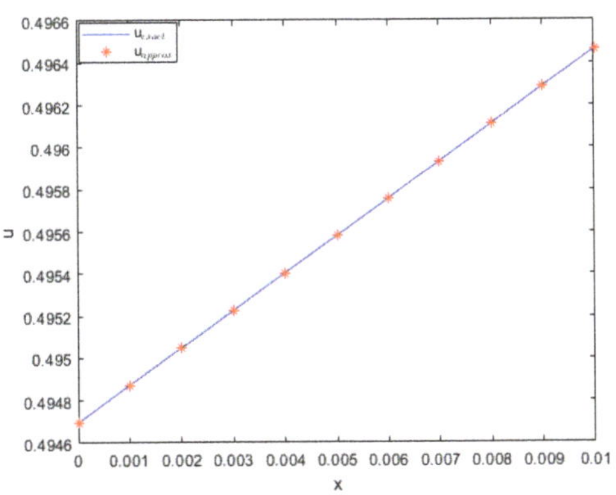

(a) Exact vs. numerical using MQ

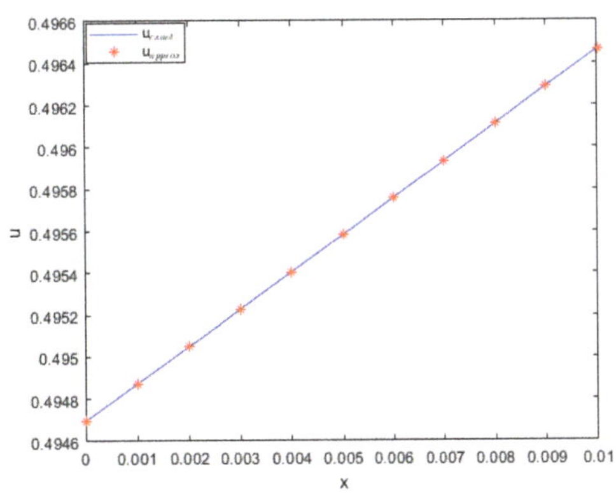

(b) Exact vs. numerical using IMQ

Figure 31. *Cont.*

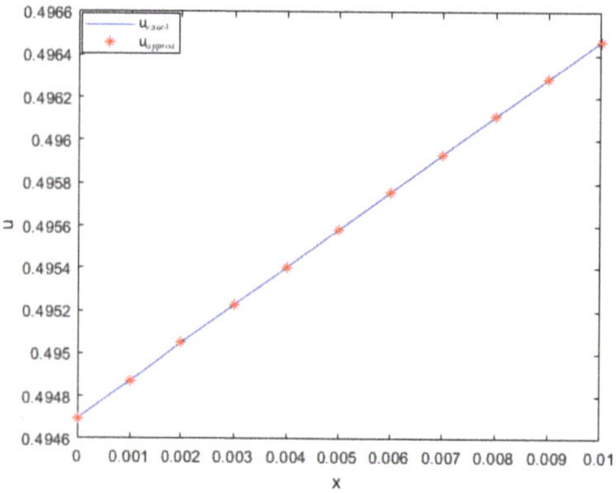

(**c**) Exact vs. numerical against IQ

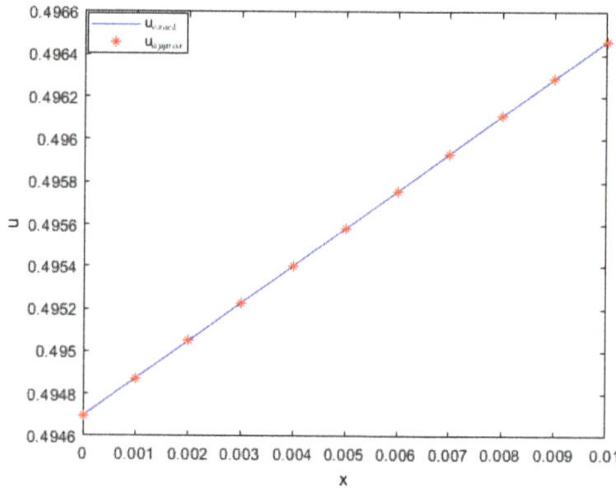

(**d**) Exact vs. numerical using GS

Figure 31. Comparison of exact and computed solution corresponds to Example 4 at t = 0.01 and $\alpha = 1$ using MQ, IMQ, IQ, and GS RBFs.

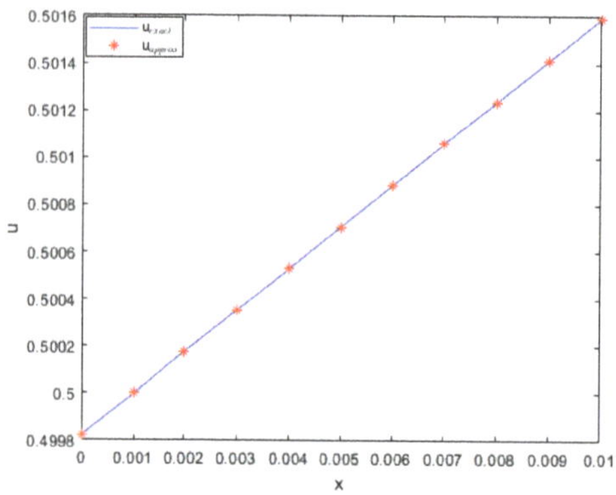

(**a**) Exact vs. numerical using MQ

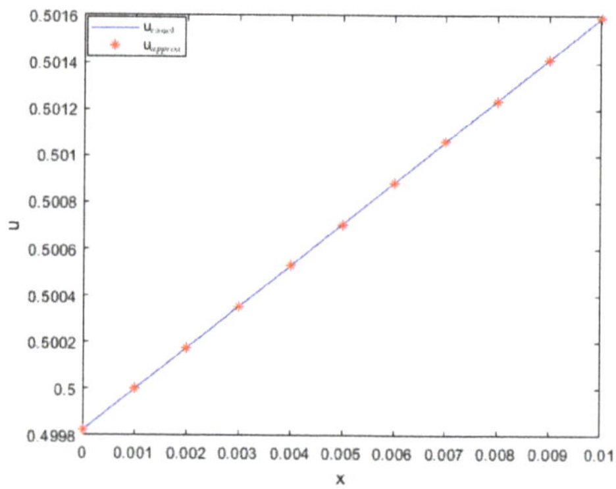

(**b**) Exact vs. numerical using IMQ

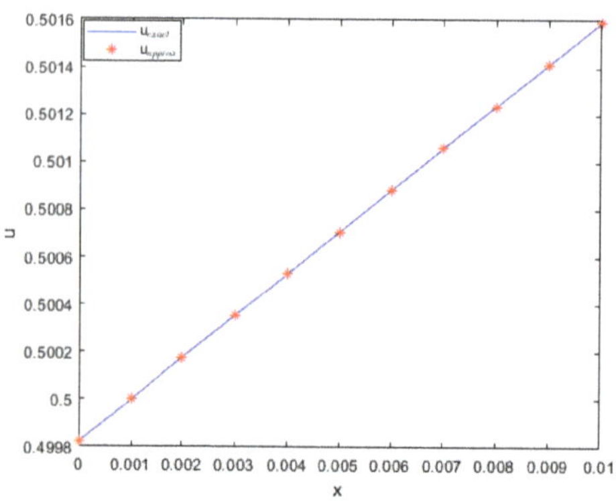

(**c**) Exact vs. numerical against IQ

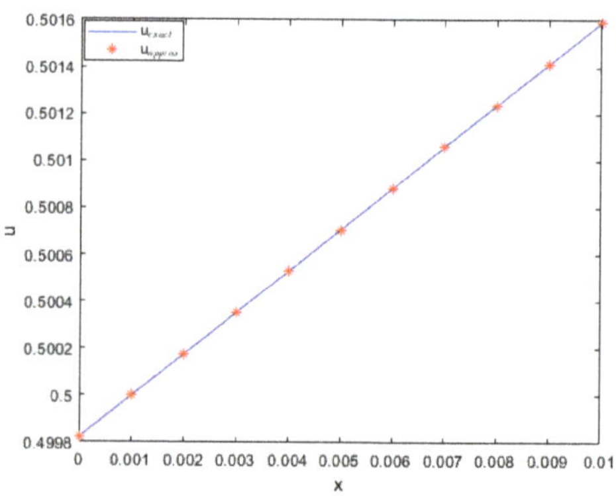

(**d**) Exact vs. numerical using GS

Figure 32. Comparison of exact and computed solution corresponds to Example 4 at t = 0.01 and $\alpha = 0.5$ using MQ, IMQ, IQ, and GS RBFs.

4. Conclusions

The RBF collocation method has been employed to numerically solve a range of FitzHugh–Nagumo Equations (2) and (3). The computed solutions exhibit excellent agreement with exact solutions across various parameter values. The accuracy of this method was rigorously assessed using different error norms. The results unequivocally establish that the proposed approach is highly effective in handling fractional PDE. Furthermore, the stability of the proposed algorithm was demonstrated through eigenvalue analysis, particularly focusing on the MQ, IMQ, IQ, and GS RBFs' shape parameter, denoted as c. From a computational standpoint, it is evident that the present method offers significant efficiency benefits, as it requires a minimal number of nodes and allows for fine-tuning of the RBF shape parameter to achieve satisfactory accuracy. Building on these achievements, several promising avenues for future research emerge.

- Investigate the use of locally supported RBFs to enhance adaptability to intricate spatial structures, improving accuracy in localized phenomena.
- Extend the methodology to incorporate time–space fractional derivatives, deepening understanding and expanding applicability to a broader range of real-world problems.
- The present study focuses on one-dimensional scenarios, and broadening its scope to handle multidimensional systems would significantly enhance its utility in practical applications.
- Exploring parallelization methods tailored for distributed memory systems would augment the adaptability and practical relevance of the presented techniques. Addressing these aspects not only demonstrates the methods' capacity to handle resource-intensive challenges but also enriches our understanding of their real-world applicability.

Author Contributions: Conceptualization, M.A.; methodology, M.A.; software, M.A., S.H., I.A., M.J.E. and S.S.; validation, M.A., S.H., I.A., M.J.E. and S.S.; formal analysis, M.A.; investigation, M.A.; writing—original draft preparation, M.A.; writing—review and editing, S.H., I.A., M.J.E. and S.S.; supervision, S.H.; funding acquisition, M.J.E. All authors have read and agreed to the published version of the manuscript.

Funding: This research received no external funding.

Data Availability Statement: The data used to support the findings of this study are available from the first author upon request.

Acknowledgments: The first author would like to express gratitude to the GIK Institute for their support during his MS studies. The authors would like to express their sincere thanks to the Department of Mathematics, Chabahar Maritime University, Chabahar, Iran, for the financial support.

Conflicts of Interest: The authors declare that they have no conflict of interest.

References

1. Bhrawy, A.H. A Jacobi–Gauss–Lobatto collocation method for solving generalized Fitzhugh–Nagumo equation with time-dependent coefficients. *Appl. Math. Comput.* **2013**, *222*, 255–264. [CrossRef]
2. Fitzhugh, R. Impulses and physiological states in models of nerve membrane. *Biophys. J.* **1961**, *1*, 445–466. [CrossRef]
3. Nagumo, J.; Arimoto, S.; Yoshizawa, S. An active pulse transmission line simulating nerve axon. *Proc. Ire* **1962**, *50*, 2061–2070. [CrossRef]
4. Shih, M.; Momoniat, E.; Mahomed, F. Approximate conditional symmetries and approximate solutions of the perturbed Fitzhugh–Nagumo equation. *J. Math. Phys.* **2005**, *46*, 023503. [CrossRef]
5. Kawahara, T.; Tanaka, M. Interactions of traveling fronts: An exact solution of a nonlinear diffusion equation. *Phys. Lett. A* **1983**, *97*, 311–314. [CrossRef]
6. Nucci, M.C.; Clarkson, P. The nonclassical method is more general than the direct method for symmetry reductions. An example of the Fitzhugh-Nagumo equation. *Phys. Lett. A* **1992**, *164*, 49–56. [CrossRef]
7. Li, H.; Guo, Y. New exact solutions to the Fitzhugh–Nagumo equation. *Appl. Math. Comput.* **2006**, *180*, 524–528. [CrossRef]
8. Abbasbandy, S. Soliton solutions for the Fitzhugh–Nagumo equation with the homotopy analysis method. *Appl. Math. Model.* **2008**, *32*, 2706–2714. [CrossRef]
9. Kakiuchi, N.; Tchizawa, K. On an explicit duck solution and delay in the Fitzhugh–Nagumo equation. *J. Differ. Equ.* **1997**, *141*, 327–339. [CrossRef]

10. Schonbek, M.E. Boundary value problems for the FitzHugh-Nagumo equations. *J. Differ. Equ.* **1978**, *30*, 119–147. [CrossRef]
11. Yanagida, E. Stability of travelling front solutions of the FitzHugh-Nagumo equations. *Math. Comput. Model.* **1989**, *12*, 289–301. [CrossRef]
12. Jackson, D. Error estimates for the semidiscrete Galerkin approximations of the FitzHugh-Nagumo equations. *Appl. Math. Comput.*, **1992**, *50*, 93–114. [CrossRef]
13. Gao, W.; Wang, J. Existence of wavefronts and impulses to FitzHugh–Nagumo equations. *Nonlinear Anal. Theory Methods Appl.* **2004**, *57*, 667–676. [CrossRef]
14. Olmos, D.; Shizgal, B.D. Pseudospectral method of solution of the Fitzhugh–Nagumo equation. *Math. Comput. Simul.* **2009**, *79*, 2258–2278. [CrossRef]
15. Dehghan, M.; Heris, J.M.; Saadatmandi, A. Application of semi-analytic methods for the Fitzhugh–Nagumo equation, which models the transmission of nerve impulses. *Math. Methods Appl. Sci.* **2010**, *33*, 1384–1398. [CrossRef]
16. Podlubny, I. *Fractional Differential Equations: An Introduction to Fractional Derivatives, Fractional Differential Equations, to Methods of Their Solution and Some of Their Applications*; Elsevier: Amsterdam, The Netherlands, 1998.
17. Kilbas, A.A.; Srivastava, H.M.; Trujillo, J.J. Theory and applications of fractional differential equations. In *North-Holland Mathematics Studies*; Elsevier Science B.V.: Amsterdam, The Netherlands, 2006; Volume 204, p. 540.
18. Singh, J.; Kumar, D.; Nieto, J.J. A reliable algorithm for a local fractional tricomi equation arising in fractal transonic flow. *Entropy* **2016**, *18*, 206. [CrossRef]
19. Hristov, J. Transient heat diffusion with a non-singular fading memory: From the Cattaneo constitutive equation with Jeffrey's kernel to the Caputo-Fabrizio time-fractional derivative. *Therm. Sci.* **2016**, *20*, 757–762. [CrossRef]
20. Zhao, D.; Singh, J.; Kumar, D.; Rathore, S.; Yang, X.J. An efficient computational technique for local fractional heat conduction equations in fractal media. *J. Nonlinear Sci. Appl. (JNSA)* **2017**, *10*, 1478–1486. [CrossRef]
21. Zaky, M.A.; Machado, J.T. On the formulation and numerical simulation of distributed-order fractional optimal control problems. *Commun. Nonlinear Sci. Numer. Simul.* **2017**, *52*, 177–189. [CrossRef]
22. Ahmadian, A.; Ismail, F.; Salahshour, S.; Baleanu, D.; Ghaemi, F. Uncertain viscoelastic models with fractional order: A new spectral tau method to study the numerical simulations of the solution. *Commun. Nonlinear Sci. Numer. Simul.* **2017**, *53*, 44–64. [CrossRef]
23. Carvalho, A.; Pinto, C.M. A delay fractional order model for the co-infection of malaria and HIV/AIDS. *Int. J. Dyn. Control* **2017**, *5*, 168–186. [CrossRef]
24. Kumar, D.; Singh, J.; Baleanu, D. A fractional model of convective radial fins with temperature-dependent thermal conductivity. *Rom. Rep. Phys.* **2017**, *69*, 103.
25. Patel, H.S.; Patel, T. Applications of Fractional Reduced Differential Transform Method for Solving the Generalized Fractional-order Fitzhugh–Nagumo Equation. *Int. J. Appl. Comput. Math.* **2021**, *7*, 188. [CrossRef]
26. Abdel-Aty, A.-H.; Khater, M.M.; Baleanu, D.; Khalil, E.; Bouslimi, J.; Omri, M. Abundant distinct types of solutions for the nervous biological fractional FitzHugh–Nagumo equation via three different sorts of schemes. *Adv. Differ. Equ.* **2020**, *2020*, 476. [CrossRef]
27. Prakash, A.; Kaur, H. A reliable numerical algorithm for a fractional model of Fitzhugh-Nagumo equation arising in the transmission of nerve impulses. *Nonlinear Eng.* **2019**, *8*, 719–727. [CrossRef]
28. Deniz, S. Optimal perturbation iteration method for solving fractional FitzHugh-Nagumo equation. *Chaos Solitons Fractals* **2021**, *142*, 110417. [CrossRef]
29. Kansa, E.J. Multiquadrics—A scattered data approximation scheme with applications to computational fluid-dynamics-I surface approximations and partial derivative estimates. *Comput. Math. Appl.* **1990**, *19*, 127–145. [CrossRef]
30. Franke, C.; Schaback, R. Convergence order estimates of meshless collocation methods using radial basis functions. *Adv. Comput. Math.* **1998**, *8*, 381–399. [CrossRef]
31. Madych, W.; Nelson, S. Multivariate interpolation and conditionally positive definite functions II. *Math. Comput.* **1990**, *54*, 211–230. [CrossRef]
32. Micchelli, C.A. Interpolation of Scattered Data: Distance Matrices and Conditionally Positive Definite Functions. *Constr. Approx.* **1986**, *2*, 11–22. [CrossRef]
33. Golberg, M.A.; Chen, C.-S.; Karur, S.R. Improved multiquadric approximation for partial differential equations. *Eng. Anal. Bound. Elem.* **1996**, *18*, 9–17. [CrossRef]
34. Sarra, S.A.; Kansa, E.J. Multiquadric radial basis function approximation methods for the numerical solution of partial differential equations. *Adv. Comput. Mech.* **2009**, *2*, 220.
35. Kansa, E.J.; Holoborodko, P. On the ill-conditioned nature of C^∞ RBF strong collocation. *Eng. Anal. Bound. Elem.* **2017**, *78*, 26–30. [CrossRef]
36. Fasshauer, G.E.; McCourt, M.J. *Kernel-Based Approximation Methods Using Matlab*; World Scientific Publishing Company: Singapore, 2015; Volume 19.
37. Uddin, M.; Haq, S. RBFs approximation method for time fractional partial differential equations *Commun. Nonlinear Sci. Numer. Simul.* **2011**, *16*, 4208–4214. [CrossRef]

38. Hussain, M.; Haq, S.; Ghafoor, A. Meshless RBFs method for numerical solutions of two-dimensional high order fractional Sobolev equations. *Comput. Math. Appl.* **2020**, *79*, 802–816. [CrossRef]
39. Rippa, S. An algorithm for selecting a good value for the parameter c in radial basis function interpolation. *Adv. Comput. Math.* **1999**, *11*, 193–210. [CrossRef]

fractal and fractional

Article

Modeling the Dispersion of Waves in a Multilayered Inhomogeneous Membrane with Fractional-Order Infusion

Ali M. Mubaraki [1], Rahmatullah Ibrahim Nuruddeen [2], Rab Nawaz [3,*] and Tayyab Nawaz [4]

[1] Department of Mathematics and Statistics, College of Science, Taif University, P.O. Box 11099, Taif 21944, Saudi Arabia; alimobarki@tu.edu.sa
[2] Department of Mathematics, Faculty of Science, Federal University Dutse, Dutse P.O. Box 7156, Jigawa State, Nigeria; rahmatullah.n@fud.edu.ng
[3] Center for Applied Mathematics and Bioinformatics (CAMB), Gulf University for Science and Technology, Hawally 32093, Kuwait
[4] Department of Mathematics, University of Illinois, Urbana Champaign, Urbana, IL 61801, USA; tnawaz2@illinois.edu
* Correspondence: nawaz.r@gust.edu.kw

Abstract: The dispersion of elastic shear waves in multilayered bodies is a topic of extensive research due to its significance in contemporary science and engineering. Anti-plane shear motion, a two-dimensional mathematical model in solid mechanics, effectively captures shear wave propagation in elastic bodies with relative mathematical simplicity. This study models the vibration of elastic waves in a multilayered inhomogeneous circular membrane using the Helmholtz equation with fractional-order infusion, effectively leveraging the anti-plane shear motion equation to avoid the computational complexity of universal plane motion equations. The method of the separation of variables and the conformable Bessel equation are utilized for the analytical examination of the model's resulting vibrational displacements, as well as the dispersion relation. Additionally, the influence of various wave phenomena, including the dependencies of the wavenumber on the frequency and the phase speed on the wavenumber, respectively, with the variational effect of the fractional order on wave dispersion is considered. Numerical simulations of prototypical cases validate the formulated model, illustrating its applicability and effectiveness. The study reveals that fractional-order infusion significantly impacts the dispersion of elastic waves in both single- and multilayer membranes. The effects vary depending on the membrane's structure and the wave propagation regime (long-wave vs. short-wave). These findings underscore the potential of fractional-order parameters in tailoring wave behavior for diverse scientific and engineering applications.

Keywords: Helmholtz equation; multilayered membrane; fractional order infusion; composite media; vibration; Bessel equation

MSC: 26A33; 35R11; 34A08; 49M41

1. Introduction

The vibration of elastic waves is among the burning areas of great concern in elasticity, and it is repeatedly encountered in a variety of processes and applications [1,2]. In particular, the vibration of waves in circular elastic shells and membranes has been comprehensively examined in both the past and present times, including the incorporation of external forces and excitations; see [3,4] and the references therein. Further, the vibration of elastic waves in cylindrical media under the assumption of an anti-plane motion is presided over by the following equation of motion [5]

$$r^2\frac{\partial^2 v}{\partial r^2} + r\frac{\partial v}{\partial r} + \frac{\partial^2 v}{\partial \theta^2} - \frac{1}{c^2}r^2\frac{\partial^2 v}{\partial t^2} = 0, \qquad c = \sqrt{\frac{\mu}{\rho}}, \tag{1}$$

where $v = v(r, \theta, t)$ is the wave vibrational displacement and c is the transverse speed, with μ and ρ representing the material constant and density, respectively. Furthermore, with a time-harmonic solution assumption of the form

$$v(r, \theta, t) = u(r, \theta)e^{i\omega t},$$

where ω is the dimensional frequency and $i = \sqrt{-1}$. Equation (1) then becomes

$$r^2\frac{\partial^2 u}{\partial r^2} + r\frac{\partial u}{\partial r} + \frac{\partial^2 u}{\partial \theta^2} + k^2r^2u = 0, \tag{2}$$

where $k = \frac{\omega}{c}$. In fact, Equation (2) is the celebrated Helmholtz equation in a cylindrical coordinate system [6] that has vast applications in the theory of thermoelasticity and electromagnetism, to mention a few.

In addition, in an attempt to generalize the classical derivative, Khalil et al. [7] conformably gave a definition of the fractional-order derivative β as follows:

$$D^\beta(v(r)) = \lim_{\varepsilon \to 0} \frac{v^{(\lceil\beta\rceil-1)}(r + \varepsilon r^{(\lceil\beta\rceil-\beta)}) - v^{(\lceil\beta\rceil-1)}(r)}{\varepsilon}, \quad \beta \in (w, w+1], \ w \in \mathbb{N}\cup\{0\}, \tag{3}$$

where $\lceil\beta\rceil$ is the smallest integer $\geq \beta$. Consequently, Khalil et al. [7] further related the above fractional-order derivative with the classical integer-order derivative using

$$D^\beta(v)(r) = r^{(\lceil\beta\rceil-\beta)}v^{\lceil\beta\rceil}(r), \quad \beta \in (w, w+1], \ w \in \mathbb{N}\cup\{0\}, \tag{4}$$

where v is $(w+1)$-differentiable at $r > 0$; for more on the fractional-order calculus and various submission of definitions, one may read [8–10] and the references therein. However, this study aims to make use of the Helmholtz equation, Equation (2), with a fractional infusion based on the definition put forward in Equation (3) to model the vibration of elastic waves in a multilayered inhomogeneous circular membrane. The separation of variable method [11], a simple yet efficient classical method, would be deployed for the analytical examination of the model, alongside the application of the recently devised conformable Bessel equation [12]. In essence, this study entails modeling the dispersion of waves in a multilayered body with fractional-order infusion to examine how the fractional order optimizes the long-wave and low-frequency propagation [13–15]. Certainly, when such propagation is achieved, the fractional order can then serve to effectively control and optimize wave dispersion in various engineering applications. Furthermore, the choice of the infused fractional operator is conformable [7], thereby giving Bessel equations in the reduced model, which favors its advantage in describing processes in cylindrical media. In contrast, the known Riemann–Liouville and Caputo fractional operators [2,8–10] will result in the acquisition of complicated reduced singular equations that cannot be examined analytically.

Moreover, the study of the dispersion of elastic shear waves in multilayered bodies has been comprehensively examined deeply in the literature in relation to their vast relevance in contemporary science and engineering applications. When shear waves are propagating on an elastic body, the scenario is perfectly captured using the anti-plane shear motion, which is indeed "an interesting two-dimensional mathematical model arising in solid mechanics involving a single second-order linear or quasi-linear partial differential equation. This model has the virtue of relative mathematical simplicity without loss of essential physical relevance. Anti-plane shear deformations are one of the simplest classes of deformations that solids can undergo" [16]. In view of the quoted statement, it is therefore very obvious that the equation of anti-plane shear motion can be utilized to model some sophisticated wave problems without the exploitation of the universal equations for plane motions that are computationally expensive and indirect. Certainly, the dispersion of elastic shear waves in multilayered bodies is vital in science and engineering. Previous studies, such as the one by Wang et al. [17] on complex dynamic behaviors in coupled systems and the one by Ba et al. [18] on multilayered structures under stress, provide foundational insights. Liu et al. [19] highlighted the efficacy of fractional-order parameters in dynamic systems, aligning with our approach to wave dispersion. The theoretical models by Kai et al. [20] offer precise frameworks for analyzing wave behavior in non-homogeneous media, which is essential for our research. Advancements in material sciences, as shown by Wang et al. [21] in electromagnetic wave manipulation, demonstrate the broad applicability of wave propagation studies, while Mubaraki et al. [22] portray the application of approximation method in the chlorine flow in multilayered channels via the shear equation of motion, to state but a few. In addition, the action of external forces in the system, including the action of the thermal effect, rotational frame, gravity, magnetic field presence, and viscoelasticity, to mention just a few, can be seen in various studies such as [23–32] and the references therein for up-to-date findings on wave dispersion in multilayered media. More precisely, in this study, the expected vibrational displacements in the respective layers of the structure will be determined, in addition to the determination of the consequential dispersion relation. Furthermore, we will deeply examine certain prototypical cases of the structure graphically—by numerically simulating the resulting dispersion relations—to validate the formulated model. This communication is organized as follows: Section 2 portrays the model formulation. Section 3 analytically tackles the formulated model. Section 4 gives the derivation of the resulting dispersion relation, and Section 5 gives the application and the numerical results and discussion. Section 6 outlines some concluding remarks.

2. Problem Formulation

We consider an isotropic multilayered inhomogeneous circular membrane—see Figure 1—which is modeled using the Helmholtz equations in a cylindrical coordinate system from Equation (4) as follows:

$$r^2\frac{\partial^2 u_i}{\partial r^2}+r\frac{\partial u_i}{\partial r}+\frac{\partial^2 u_i}{\partial \theta^2}+k_i^2r^2u_i=0, \qquad 0 \quad i=1,2,\ldots,m, \tag{5}$$

where

$$k_i=\frac{\omega}{c_i}, \quad c_i=\sqrt{\frac{\mu_i}{\rho_i}},$$

where $u_i = u_i(r,\theta)$ are the out-of-plane vibrational fields in the respective layers of the multilayered membrane for $i = 1,2,\ldots,m$, with r as the radial variable and θ as the azimuthal variable. Moreover, the precise ranges for definitions of the individual membranes are expressed as follows:

$$u_i := \left\{ u_i(r,\theta) : r \in \begin{cases} 0 < r \leq \alpha_1, & i=1, \\ \alpha_{(i-1)} \leq r \leq \alpha_i, & i \neq 1, \end{cases} \right. \quad -\pi < \theta < \pi, \quad i=1,2,\ldots,m, \tag{6}$$

where α_1 is the radius of the innermost membrane and α_i, for $i = 2,3,\ldots,m$ are the thicknesses of the subsequent membranes.

Furthermore, we impose suitable boundary conditions at $\theta = -\pi$ and $\theta = \pi$ as follows:

$$\begin{cases} u_i(r,-\pi) = u_i(r,\pi), \\ \frac{\partial u_i}{\partial \theta}(r,-\pi) = \frac{\partial u_i}{\partial \theta}(r,\pi), \end{cases} \quad i=1,2,\ldots,m, \tag{7}$$

while the following boundary data are defined along the circumferential length, precisely at $r=0$ and $r=\alpha_m$, as follows :

$$\begin{cases} u_1(0,\theta) \text{ is bounded,} \\ u_m(\alpha_m,\theta) = f_m(\theta), \end{cases} \tag{8}$$

where $f_m(\theta)$ is a θ-dependent vibrational field, virtually, a prescribed entire function.

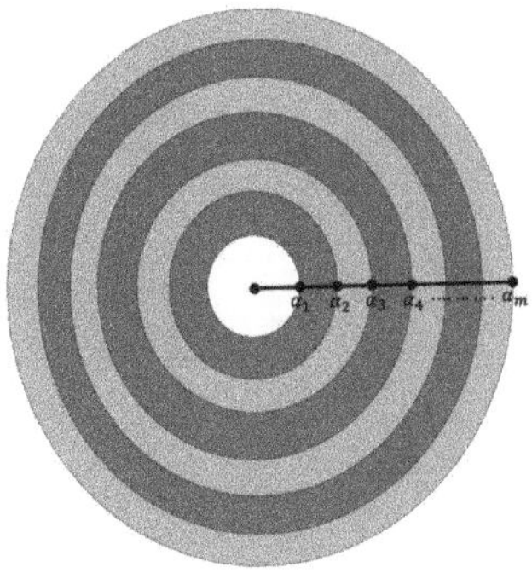

Figure 1. Multilayered inhomogeneous circular membrane.

Additionally, we further assume perfect continuity conditions in the respective interfaces of the multilayered membrane by equating the related vibrational fields u_i and the stresses $\sigma^i_{rz} = \mu_i \frac{\partial u_i}{\partial r}$ at the interfaces, $r = \alpha_i$, as follows

$$\begin{cases} u_i(\alpha_i, \theta) = u_{i+1}(\alpha_i, \theta), \\ \mu_i \frac{\partial u_i}{\partial r}(\alpha_i, \theta) = \mu_{i+1} \frac{\partial u_{i+1}}{\partial r}(\alpha_i, \theta), \end{cases} \quad i = 1, 2, \ldots, m, \tag{9}$$

where μ_i values, for $i = 1, 2, \ldots, m$, are the material constants in the respective layers of the multilayered membrane.

3. Problem Solution

To solve the governing problem, an analytical approach applying the method of separation of variables [11] is employed. Thus, the solution of Equation (5) is considered to admit the following solution pattern:

$$u_i(r, \theta) = R_i(r) Q(\theta), \qquad i = 1, 2, \ldots, m, \tag{10}$$

where $R_i(r)$ values are the respective radial solutions, while $Q(\theta)$ is the corresponding azimuthal solution. Further, upon substituting the latter equation into Equation (5), one obtains

$$-\left(r^2 \frac{R_i''}{R_i} + r \frac{R_i'}{R_i} + k_i^2 r^2 \right) = \frac{Q''}{Q} = -\lambda, \tag{11}$$

which is subsequently separated into the following boundary-value problem (BVP):

$$Q'' + \lambda Q = 0, \quad Q(-\pi) = Q(\pi), \quad Q'(-\pi) = Q'(\pi), \tag{12}$$

which admits the following solution:

$$Q(\theta) = C_{1n} \cos(n\theta) + C_{2n} \sin(n\theta), \tag{13}$$

where the eigenvalues take the form $\lambda_n = n^2$, for $n = 0, 1, 2, \ldots$ and further yield the following radial equation in terms of a Bessel differential equation:

$$r^2 R_i'' + r R_i' + (k_i^2 r^2 - n^2) R_i = 0, \qquad i = 1, 2, \ldots, m. \tag{14}$$

Most importantly, it is our aim to infuse a fractional-order derivative in the governing model; thus, we feel it is very relevant to fractionalize Equation (14) by considering the recently proposed conformable Bessel fractional differential equation by Hammad et al. [12] as follows:

$$r^{2\beta} D^\beta D^\beta R_i + \beta r^\beta D^\beta R_i + (k_i^2 r^{2\beta} - \beta^2 n^2) R_i = 0, \quad 0 < \beta \leq 1, \quad i = 1, 2, \ldots, m. \tag{15}$$

Certainly, when the fractional-order β takes the integer-order, that is, when $\beta = 1$, Equation (15) is completely reduced to Equation (14). In addition, the radial solutions $R_i(r)$ are further obtained by solving Equation (15) to obtain

$$R_i(r) = \begin{cases} {}^1C_3 J_{\beta n}(k_1 r), & 0 < r \le \alpha_1, \quad i = 1, \\ {}^iC_3 J_{\beta n}(k_i r) + {}^iC_4 J_{-\beta n}(k_i r), & \alpha_{(i-1)} \le r \le \alpha_i, \quad i \ne 1, \end{cases} \quad i = 1,2,\dots,m, \tag{16}$$

where

$$J_{\pm\beta n}(k_i r) = \sum_{s=0}^{\infty} (-1)^s \frac{(k_i r)^{2\beta s \pm \beta n}}{(2\beta)^{2s \pm n} s! \Gamma(s \pm n + 1)}, \quad i = 1,2,\dots,m,$$

is the conformable fractional Bessel function of the first kind of order βn; ${}^iC_3$, and ${}^iC_4$ values for $i = 1,2,\dots,m$, are constants to be determined. Furthermore, ${}^1C_4$ vanishes at the innermost membrane, that is, when $i = 1$ due to the boundedness condition at $r = 0$ that was prescribed in the first part of Equation (8). Also, when $\beta n = y$, for some integer y in Equation (16), $J_y(.)$ becomes the classical Bessel function of the first kind of order y, while $\Gamma(.)$ in the latter expression is the well-known gamma function.

Hence, the overall solution without the involvement of the continuity and boundary conditions, which was earlier expressed in Equation (10), is now rewritten using Equations (13) and (16) as follows:

$$u_i(r,\theta) = \begin{cases} \sum_{n=0}^{\infty} \{ {}^1a_n J_{\beta n}(k_1 r) \cos(n\theta) + {}^1b_n J_{\beta n}(k_1 r) \sin(n\theta) \}, & i = 1, \\ \sum_{n=0}^{\infty} \{ ({}^ia_n J_{\beta n}(k_i r) + {}^i\bar{a}_n J_{-\beta n}(k_i r)) \cos(n\theta) + \\ \qquad ({}^ib_n J_{\beta n}(k_i r) + {}^i\bar{b}_n J_{-\beta n}(k_i r)) \sin(n\theta) \}, & i \ne 1, \end{cases} \tag{17}$$

where

$$C_{1n}{}^1C_3 = {}^1a_n, \quad C_{2n}{}^1C_3 = {}^1b_n, \quad C_{1n}{}^iC_3 = {}^ia_n,$$
$$C_{1n}{}^iC_4 = {}^i\bar{a}_n, \quad C_{2n}{}^iC_3 = {}^ib_n, \quad C_{2n}{}^iC_4 = {}^i\bar{b}_n,$$

Moreover, in order to determine the explicit solution of the governing model, we now employ the prescribed second boundary condition in Equation (8) and the interfacial conditions given in Equation (5). Thus, we begin by substituting the interfacial conditions at $r = \alpha_i$ for $i = 1,2,\dots,m$ into the acquired solution in Equation (17) to obtain the following system of algebraic equations:

$$\begin{cases} \text{at} \quad r = \alpha_1, \\ {}^1a_n J_{\beta n}(k_1\alpha_1) = {}^2a_n J_{\beta n}(k_2\alpha_1) + {}^2\bar{a}_n J_{-\beta n}(k_2\alpha_1), \\ {}^1b_n J_{-\beta n}(k_1\alpha_1) = {}^2b_n J_{\beta n}(k_2\alpha_1) + {}^2\bar{b}_n J_{-\beta n}(k_2\alpha_1), \\ \mu_1 {}^1a_n J'_{\beta n}(k_1\alpha_1) = \mu_2({}^2a_n J'_{\beta n}(k_2\alpha_1) + {}^2\bar{a}_n J'_{-\beta n}(k_2\alpha_1)), \\ \mu_1 {}^1b_n J'_{-\beta n}(k_1\alpha_1) = \mu_2({}^2b_n J'_{\beta n}(k_2\alpha_1) + {}^2\bar{b}_n J'_{-\beta n}(k_2\alpha_1)), \end{cases}$$
$$\begin{cases} \text{at} \quad r = \alpha_j,\ j = 2,3,\dots,(m-1), \\ {}^ja_n J_{\beta n}(k_j\alpha_j) + {}^j\bar{a}_n J_{-\beta n}(k_j\alpha_j) = {}^{j+1}a_n J_{\beta n}(k_{j+1}\alpha_j) + {}^{j+1}\bar{a}_n J_{-\beta n}(k_{j+1}\alpha_j), \\ {}^jb_n J_{\beta n}(k_j\alpha_j) + {}^j\bar{b}_n J_{-\beta n}(k_j\alpha_j) = {}^{j+1}b_n J_{\beta n}(k_{j+1}\alpha_j) + {}^{j+1}\bar{b}_n J_{-\beta n}(k_{j+1}\alpha_j), \\ \mu_j({}^ja_n J'_{\beta n}(k_j\alpha_j) + {}^j\bar{a}_n J'_{-\beta n}(k_j\alpha_j)) = \mu_{j+1}({}^{j+1}a_n J'_{\beta n}(k_{j+1}\alpha_j) + {}^{j+1}\bar{a}_n J'_{-\beta n}(k_{j+1}\alpha_j)), \\ \mu_j({}^jb_n J'_{\beta n}(k_j\alpha_j) + {}^j\bar{b}_n J'_{-\beta n}(k_j\alpha_j)) = \mu_{j+1}({}^{j+1}b_n J'_{\beta n}(k_{j+1}\alpha_j) + {}^{j+1}\bar{b}_n J'_{-\beta n}(k_{j+1}\alpha_j)), \\ \text{for} \quad j = 2,3,\dots,(m-1), \end{cases} \tag{18}$$

where

$$J'_{\pm\beta n}(k_i r) = \frac{1}{2} k_i (J_{\pm n\beta - 1}(k_i r) - J_{\pm n\beta + 1}(k_i r)) \Big|_{r=\alpha_i}, \quad i = 1,2,\dots,m. \tag{19}$$

Lastly, upon deploying the second boundary condition in Equation (8) when $r = \alpha_m$, one systematically obtains

$$f_m(\theta) = \sum_{n=0}^{\infty}\{({}^{m}a_n J_{\beta n}(k_m\alpha_m) + {}^{m}\bar{a}_n J_{-\beta n}(k_m\alpha_m))\cos(n\theta) + ({}^{m}b_n J_{\beta n}(k_m\alpha_m) + {}^{m}\bar{b}_n J_{-\beta n}(k_m\alpha_m))\sin(n\theta)\}, \tag{20}$$

which, upon employing the application of Fourier's series [15], then yields the explict expressions for the involving coefficients as follows:

$$\begin{aligned} {}^{m}a_n J_{\beta n}(k_m\alpha_m) + {}^{m}\bar{a}_n J_{-\beta n}(k_m\alpha_m) &= \frac{1}{\pi}\int_{-\pi}^{\pi} f_m(\theta)\cos(n\theta)d\theta, \\ {}^{m}b_n J_{\beta n}(k_m\alpha_m) + {}^{m}\bar{b}_n J_{-\beta n}(k_m\alpha_m) &= \frac{1}{\pi}\int_{-\pi}^{\pi} f_m(\theta)\sin(n\theta)d\theta. \end{aligned} \tag{21}$$

Furthermore, the overall general solution is plainly determined when solving the $(m+4)\times(m+4)$ coupled algebraic system of equations in Equations (18) and (21) for ${}^{i}a_n$, ${}^{i}b_n$, ${}^{s}\bar{a}_n$, and ${}^{s}\bar{b}_n$ when $i = 1,2,\dots,m$ and $s = 2,3,\dots,m$.

4. Dispersion Relation

To derive the resulting dispersion relation, we revisit the governing Helmholtz equations for the vibration of waves in a multilayered inhomogeneous circular membrane expressed in Equation (5). In fact, u_i will further be conveniently represented by $u_i = R_i(r)\cos(\gamma\theta)$, where γ is the dimensional wavenumber. Moreover, the resultant infused conformable Bessel fractional differential equations for the inhomogeneous media then take the following form:

$$r^{2\beta}D^{\beta}D^{\beta}R_i + \beta r^{\beta}D^{\beta}R_i + (k_i^2 r^{2\beta} - \beta^2\gamma^2)R_i = 0, \quad 0 < \beta \leq 1, \quad i = 1,2,\dots,m, \tag{22}$$

which then admit the following solutions

$$R_i(r) = {}^{i}E_1 J_{\beta\gamma}(k_i r) + {}^{i}E_2 J_{-\beta\gamma}(k_i r), \ \alpha_i \leq r \leq \alpha_{(i+1)}, \qquad i = 1,2,\dots,m, \tag{23}$$

where $J_{\pm\beta\gamma}(.)$ is the conformable fractional Bessel function of the first kind of order $\beta\gamma$; ${}^{i}E_1$ and ${}^{i}E_2$ for $i = 1,2,\dots,m$ are constants. Notably, we mention here that the solution obtained above is for a hollow multilayered inhomogeneous membrane. Certainly, this is for the sake of a practical scenario. Thus, the prescribed interfacial conditions in Equation (9) are shifted starting from $i = 2,3,\dots,(m-1)$, while the prescribed boundary conditions at $r = \alpha_1$ and $r = \alpha_m$ are traction-free conditions, that is,

$$\sigma_{rz}^{1}|_{r=\alpha_1} = 0, \qquad \text{and} \qquad \sigma_{rz}^{m}|_{r=\alpha_{m+1}} = 0.$$

Further, with this development, one obtains the following dispersion equations:

$$\begin{cases} \text{at} \quad r = \alpha_1, \\ {}^{1}E_1 J'_{\beta\gamma}(k_1\alpha_1) + {}^{1}E_2 J'_{-\beta\gamma}(k_1\alpha_1) = 0, \\ \\ \text{at} \quad r = \alpha_j, \quad \text{for} \quad j = 2,3,\dots,(m-1), \\ {}^{j}E_1 J_{\beta\gamma}(k_j\alpha_j) + {}^{j}E_2 J_{-\beta\gamma}(k_j\alpha_j) = {}^{j+1}E_1 J_{\beta\gamma}(k_{j+1}\alpha_j) + {}^{j+1}E_2 J_{-\beta\gamma}(k_{j+1}\alpha_j), \\ \mu_j({}^{j}E_1 J'_{\beta\gamma}(k_j\alpha_j) + {}^{j}E_2 J'_{-\beta\gamma}(k_j\alpha_j)) = \mu_{j+1}({}^{j+1}E_1 J'_{\beta\gamma}(k_{j+1}\alpha_j) + {}^{j+1}E_2 J'_{-\beta\gamma}(k_{j+1}\alpha_j)), \\ \\ \text{at} \quad r = \alpha_m, \\ {}^{m}E_1 J'_{\beta\gamma}(k_m\alpha_m) + {}^{1}E_2 J'_{-\beta\gamma}(k_m\alpha_m) = 0, \end{cases} \tag{24}$$

where $J'_{\pm\beta\gamma}(.)$ follows from Equation (19). Moreover, the resulting dispersion relation will then be determined upon equating the determinant of the coefficient matrix of the above dispersion system of equations to zero.

5. Application

The present section considers two prototypical multilayered circular membranes as an application of the governing generalized multilayered inhomogeneous circular membrane that was successfully examined in the above section. More precisely, we will determine the consequential vibrational fields and the dispersion relations in two- and three-layered inhomogeneous membranes (Figure 2).

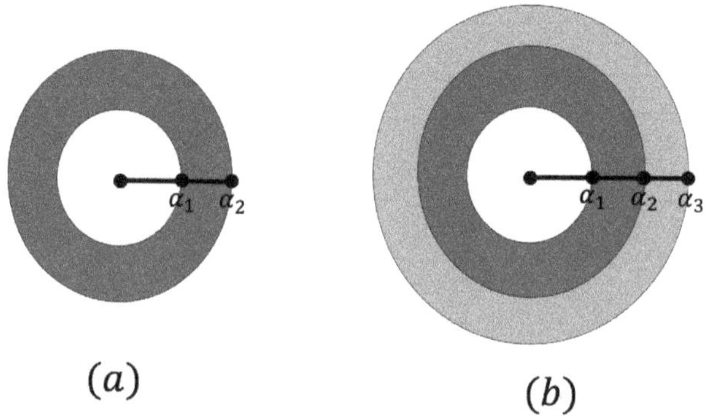

Figure 2. Prototype schema for (**a**) a two-layered inhomogeneous membrane, and (**b**) a three-layered inhomogeneous membrane.

5.1. Vibrational Displacement

This subsection undeniably presents the consequential vibrational fields for the prototype structures under consideration.

5.1.1. Two-Layered Inhomogeneous Membrane

In this regard, the explicit expressions for the resulting vibrational fields associated with the a two-layered membrane for $i = 2$ are obtained in the respective layers from Equation (17) as follows

$$\begin{aligned} u_1(r,\theta) &= \sum_{n=0}^{\infty}\{{}^1a_n J_{\beta n}(k_1 r)\cos(n\theta) + {}^1b_n J_{\beta n}(k_1 r)\sin(n\theta)\}, \\ u_2(r,\theta) &= \sum_{n=0}^{\infty}\{({}^2a_n J_{\beta n}(k_2 r) + {}^2\bar{a}_n J_{-\beta n}(k_2 r))\cos(n\theta) + \\ &\qquad ({}^2b_n J_{\beta n}(k_2 r) + {}^2\bar{b}_n J_{-\beta n}(k_2 r))\sin(n\theta)\}, \end{aligned} \tag{25}$$

where the involving coefficients ${}^1a_n, {}^1b_n, {}^2a_n, {}^2\bar{a}_n, {}^2b_n$, and ${}^2\bar{b}_n$ are determined from Equations (18) and (20); see Appendix A for their explicit expressions.

Particular case: singled-layered homogeneous membrane

Deducibly, when the second membrane is removed, thereby leaving behind a singled-layered hollow membrane, the solution found in Equation (25) reduces to the following

$$u_1(r,\theta) = \sum_{n=0}^{\infty}\{{}^1a_n J_{\beta n}(k_1 r)\cos(n\theta) + {}^1b_n J_{\beta n}(k_1 r)\sin(n\theta)\}, \tag{26}$$

where the coefficients involved, ${}^1a_n$ and ${}^1b_n$, are determined from Equation (21) as follows:

$$ {}^1a_n = \frac{1}{\pi J_{\beta n}(k_1\alpha_1)} \int_{-\pi}^{\pi} f_1(\theta)\cos(n\theta)d\theta, \qquad {}^1b_n = \frac{1}{\pi J_{\beta n}(k_1\alpha_1)} \int_{-\pi}^{\pi} f_1(\theta)\sin(n\theta)d\theta. $$

5.1.2. Three-Layered Inhomogeneous Membrane

As we proceed, the explicit expressions for the resulting vibrational fields in this regard for $i = 3$ are obtained from Equation (17) as follows:

$$ \begin{aligned} u_1(r,\theta) &= \sum_{n=0}^{\infty} \{ {}^1a_n J_{\beta n}(k_1 r)\cos(n\theta) + {}^1b_n J_{\beta n}(k_1 r)\sin(n\theta) \}, \\ u_2(r,\theta) &= \sum_{n=0}^{\infty} \{ ({}^2a_n J_{\beta n}(k_2 r) + {}^2\bar{a}_n J_{-\beta n}(k_2 r))\cos(n\theta) + \\ &\qquad ({}^2b_n J_{\beta n}(k_2 r) + {}^2\bar{b}_n J_{-\beta n}(k_2 r))\sin(n\theta) \}, \\ u_3(r,\theta) &= \sum_{n=0}^{\infty} \{ ({}^3a_n J_{\beta n}(k_3 r) + {}^3\bar{a}_n J_{-\beta n}(k_3 r))\cos(n\theta) + \\ &\qquad ({}^3b_n J_{\beta n}(k_3 r) + {}^3\bar{b}_n J_{-\beta n}(k_3 r))\sin(n\theta) \}, \end{aligned} \tag{27} $$

where the coefficients involved, ${}^1a_n, {}^1b_n, {}^2a_n, {}^2\bar{a}_n, {}^2b_n, {}^2\bar{b}_n, {}^3a_n, {}^3\bar{a}_n, {}^3b_n$, and ${}^3\bar{b}_n$, can equally be determined from Equations (18) and (20); see Appendix B for their explicit expressions.

5.2. Dispersion Relation

The subsection irrefutably derives the resulting dispersion relations with regard to the governing prototyped multilayered circular membranes.

5.2.1. Two-Layered Inhomogeneous Membrane

Upon considering the prototype for the two-layered inhomogeneous membrane, the obtained generalized equations for the dispersion relation in Equation (24) yield the consequential dispersion matrix in this regard as follows:

$$ A_1 = \begin{pmatrix} J'_{\beta\gamma}(k_1\alpha_1) & J'_{-\beta\gamma}(k_1\alpha_1) & 0 & 0 \\ J_{\beta\gamma}(k_1\alpha_2) & J_{-\beta\gamma}(k_1\alpha_2) & -J_{\beta\gamma}(k_2\alpha_2) & J_{-\beta\gamma}(k_2\alpha_2) \\ J'_{\beta\gamma}(k_1\alpha_2) & J'_{-\beta\gamma}(k_1\alpha_2) & -\frac{\mu_2}{\mu_1}J'_{\beta\gamma}(k_2\alpha_2) & -\frac{\mu_2}{\mu_1}J'_{-\beta\gamma}(k_2\alpha_2) \\ 0 & 0 & J'_{\beta\gamma}(k_2\alpha_3) & J'_{-\beta\gamma}(k_2\alpha_3) \end{pmatrix}, \tag{28} $$

upon which the dispersion equation is obtained by setting the resulting determinant of the above dispersion matrix to zero.

Particular case: singled-layered homogeneous membrane

It can be deduced that, when the second membrane is removed, thereby leaving behind a singled-layered hollow membrane with traction-free boundary conditions on both surfaces, the above dispersion matrix thus reduces to the following:

$$ A_2 = \begin{pmatrix} J'_{\beta\gamma}(k_1\alpha_1) & J'_{-\beta\gamma}(k_1\alpha_1) \\ J'_{\beta\gamma}(k_1\alpha_2) & J'_{-\beta\gamma}(k_1\alpha_2) \end{pmatrix}, \tag{29} $$

which reveals the following reduced and easy dispersion relation

$$ J'_{-\beta\gamma}(k_1\alpha_2)J'_{\beta\gamma}(k_1\alpha_1) - J'_{-\beta\gamma}(k_1\alpha_1)J'_{\beta\gamma}(k_1\alpha_2) = 0. \tag{30} $$

5.2.2. Three-Layered Inhomogeneous Membrane

Accordingly, the three-layered inhomogeneous membrane reveals from Equation (24) the following dispersion matrix:

$$A_3 = \begin{pmatrix} J'_{\beta\gamma}(k_1\alpha_1) & J'_{-\beta\gamma}(k_1\alpha_1) & 0 & 0 & 0 & 0 \\ J_{\beta\gamma}(k_1\alpha_2) & J_{-\beta\gamma}(k_1\alpha_2) & -J_{\beta\gamma}(k_2\alpha_2) & J_{-\beta\gamma}(k_2\alpha_2) & 0 & 0 \\ J'_{\beta\gamma}(k_1\alpha_2) & J'_{-\beta\gamma}(k_1\alpha_2) & -\frac{\mu_2}{\mu_1}J'_{\beta\gamma}(k_2\alpha_2) & -\frac{\mu_2}{\mu_1}J'_{-\beta\gamma}(k_2\alpha_2) & 0 & 0 \\ 0 & 0 & J_{\beta\gamma}(k_2\alpha_3) & J_{-\beta\gamma}(k_2\alpha_3) & a_{45} & a_{46} \\ 0 & 0 & J'_{\beta\gamma}(k_2\alpha_3) & J'_{-\beta\gamma}(k_2\alpha_3) & a_{55} & a_{56} \\ 0 & 0 & 0 & 0 & a_{65} & a_{66} \end{pmatrix}, \tag{31}$$

where

$$\begin{aligned} a_{45} &= -J_{\beta\gamma}(k_3\alpha_3), \quad a_{46} = -J_{-\beta\gamma}(k_3\alpha_3), \quad a_{55} = -\frac{\mu_3}{\mu_2}J'_{\beta\gamma}(k_3\alpha_3), \\ a_{65} &= J'_{\beta\gamma}(k_3\alpha_4), \quad a_{66} = J'_{-\beta\gamma}(k_3\alpha_4), \quad a_{56} = -\frac{\mu_3}{\mu_2}J'_{-\beta\gamma}(k_3\alpha_3). \end{aligned} \tag{32}$$

upon which the dispersion equation is obtained by setting the resulting determinant of the dispersion matrix to zero.

6. Numerical Results and Discussion

This section simulates and then discusses the obtained results numerically with the help of computational software. Indeed, in the numerical simulation, we consider the prototype two- and three-layered inhomogeneous membrane cases for brevity. Further, we deduce the result of the singled-layered homogeneous membrane by varnishing the outer layer of the two-layered membrane while imposing traction-free conditions on both sides of the hollow bodies.

6.1. *Two- and Three-Layered Inhomogeneous Membranes*

In this regard, the resulting dimensionless dispersion relation of the two-layered inhomogeneous membrane is obtained from Equation (28) as follows:

$$|A_1| = 0, \tag{33}$$

where the new dimensional structural parameters take the following expressions:

$$\mu = \frac{\mu_1}{\mu_2}, \quad \rho = \frac{\rho_1}{\rho_2}, \quad \alpha = \frac{\alpha_3}{\alpha_2}, \quad \alpha' = \frac{\alpha_1}{\alpha_2}, \tag{34}$$

where μ is the dimensionless material constant, ρ is the dimensionless density, and α, and α' are the respective dimensionless thicknesses. In addition, we also have the following dimensionless quantities:

$$W = \frac{\omega\alpha_2}{c_2}, \quad \Phi = \gamma\alpha_2, \quad \chi = \frac{c_2}{c_1}, \quad \tau = \frac{\beta}{\alpha_2}, \tag{35}$$

where W is the dimensionless frequency, Φ is the dimensionless wavenumber, χ is the shear speed ratio, which is also dimensionless; and τ is the scaled dimensionless fractional-order. Furthermore, the influence of the scaled fractional-order τ on the dispersion of elastic waves in the media in a bi-elastic inhomogeneous hollow membrane has been shown in Figure 3a,b, for the long-wave and short-wave propagations, respectively [33], with regard to the relationship between the phase-speed $\Theta(= W/\Phi)$ and the speed ratio $\chi(= c_2/c_1)$. In fact, we depict the harmonic curves, that is, the relationship between the dimensionless phase speed and the dimensionless speed ratio with respect to the variation in the scaled fractional-order τ in Figure 3a,b. Notably, in both Figure 3a,b, it is vividly obvious that an increase in the fractional-order τ partially/halfway stretches the harmonic curves backward, thereby implying a delay or rather a decrease in the propagation.

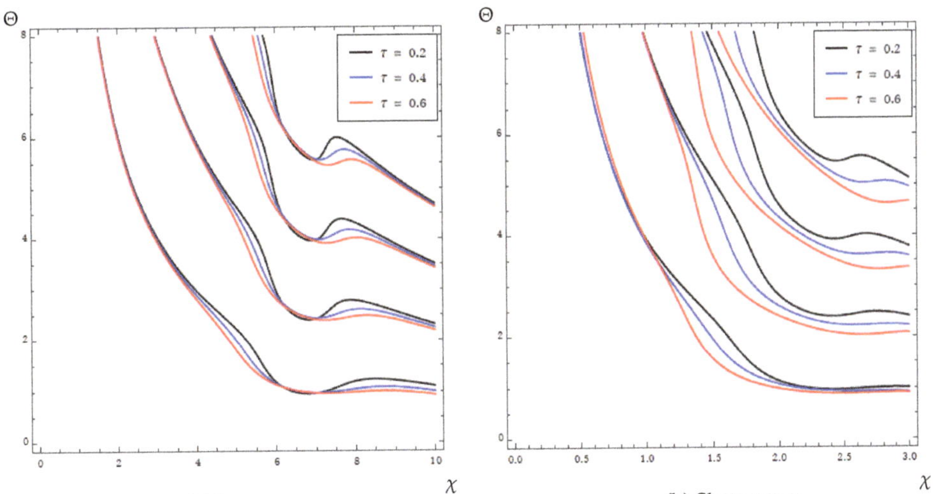

(a) Long-wave. (b) Short-wave.

Figure 3. Harmonic curves: relationship between the dimensionless phase-speed Θ and dimensionless speed ratio χ with respect to the variation of the scaled fractional-order τ for the two-layered inhomogeneous membrane when $\alpha_1 = 0.05$, $\alpha_2 = 0.15$, and $\alpha_3 = 0.2$ while fixing the dimensionless wavenumber to be (**a**) $\Phi = 0.4$ and (**b**) $\Phi = 1.2$.

Figure 4a portrays the harmonic curves via the relationship between the dimensionless phase-speed Θ and wavenumber Φ with respect to the variation in the scaled fractional-order τ for the two-layeredinhomogenous membrane. It is noted that an increase in the fractional order decreases the respective harmonic modes. Furthermore, it is equally noted that the disparity with regard to the effects of the fractional order becomes clearer as the wavenumber Φ tilts towards the short-wave region; remember that short-wave propagation occurs when $\Phi \geq 1$. Additionally, Figure 4b portrays the relationship between the frequency W and the wavenumber Φ within the estimate of long-wave and low-frequency propagation, that is, when $\Phi \ll 1$ and $W \ll 1$. Remember that the vibration and dispersion of surface waves and their likes under the assumption of a long-wave and low-frequency have been expansively studied with regards to their vast applications in wave analysis and vibration control, for more on the linked findings, one may consult [23–33] and the references therein. Hence, from Figure 4b, it is noted that only the fundamental mode is able to satisfy the long-wave and low-frequency conditions. Further, it was noted that an increase in the fractional-order τ uplifts the dispersion fundamental curve; indeed, this then shrinks the range of Φ to perfectly suit the long-wave range.

Accordingly, the three-layered inhomogeneous membrane case is analyzed in Figures 5 and 6, where harmonic curves, depicting the relationship between the dimensionless phase-speed and the dimensionless speed ratio with respect to the variation of the scaled fractional-order τ is shown in Figure 5 for long and short waves, respectively. In addition, Figure 4 portrays the harmonic curves via Figure 6a, which shows the relationship between the dimensionless phase-speed Θ and wavenumber Φ, while Figure 6b portrays the relationship between the frequency W and the wavenumber Φ; all with respect to the variation of the scaled fractional-order τ for the three-layered inhomogenous membrane. Moreover, the same interpretation with the two-layered case is applied here. Thus, we leave it for brevity. In addition, the fixed parameter values in the case of a two-layered membrane are extended and further used for plotting the results for the three-layered scenario. Moreover, in making the plots in the three-layered membrane, a consideration of alternating layers has been made for simplicity, where $\rho_1 = \rho_3$ and $\mu_1 = \mu_3$. In addition, beyond the dimensionless quantities in the two-layered case, this case discovered new dimensionless quantities, including $\alpha'' = \alpha_4/\alpha_2$, upon which we numerically consider $\alpha_4 = 0.2$. Notably, we can conclude from these figures that the lower the number of layers, the more modes observed concerning both the Θ vs. χ and also Θ vs. Φ scenarios; however, the fractional infusion has been noted to have the same effect in both the two- and three-layered membranes concerning the W vs. Φ relationship.

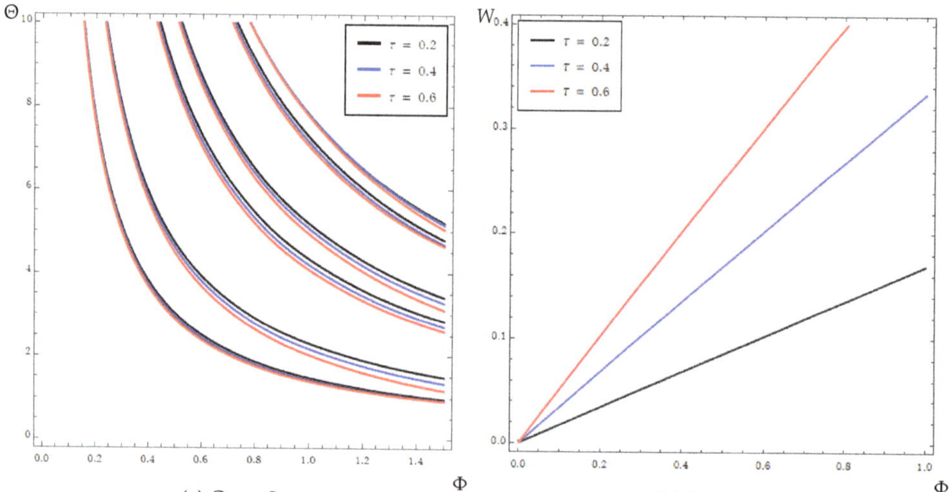

(a) Θ vs. Φ. (b) W vs. Φ.

Figure 4. Harmonic curves: the relationship between the (**a**) dimensionless phase-speed Θ and wavenumber Φ and (**b**) dimensionless frequency W and wavenumber Φ with respect to the variation in the scaled fractional-order τ for the two-layered inhomogeneous membrane when $\mu = 0.3$, $\rho = 0.3$, $\alpha = 1.3333$, $\alpha' = 0.3333$.

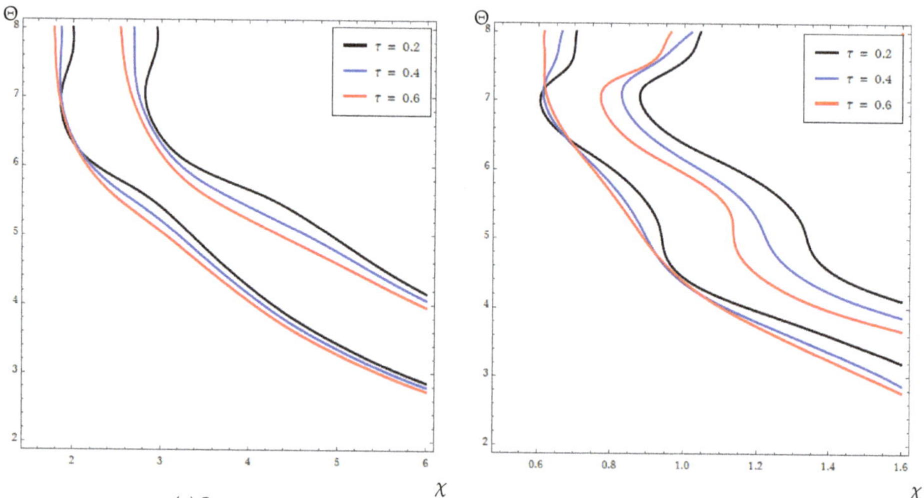

(a) Long-wave. (b) Short-wave.

Figure 5. Harmonic curves: the relationship between the dimensionless phase-speed Θ and dimensionless speed ratio χ with respect to the variation of the scaled fractional-order τ for the three-layered inhomogenous membrane while fixing the dimensionless wavenumber to (**a**) $\Phi = 0.4$ and (**b**) $\Phi = 1.2$.

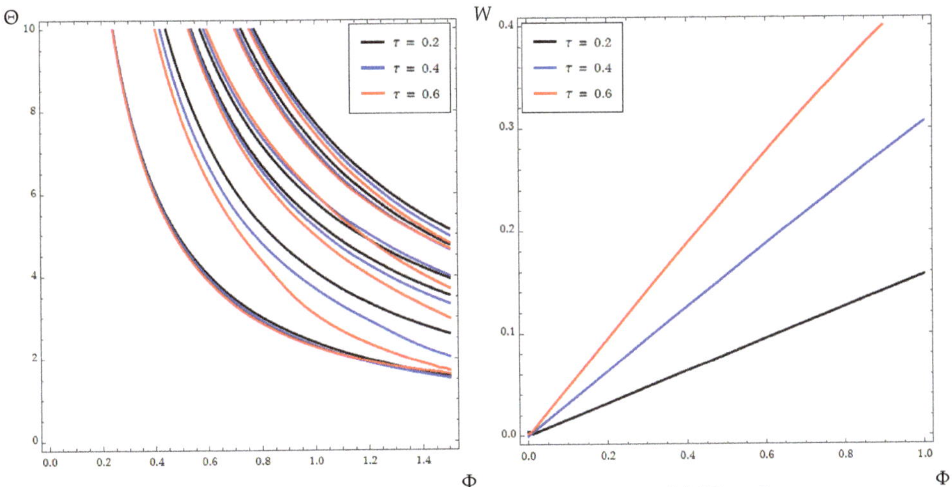

(a) Θ vs. Φ. (b) W vs. Φ.

Figure 6. Harmonic curves: the relationship between the (**a**) dimensionless phase-speed Θ and wavenumber Φ and (**b**) dimensionless frequency W and wavenumber Φ with respect to the variation of the scaled fractional-order τ for the three-layered inhomogenous membrane.

6.2. Singled-Layered Homogeneous Membrane

In the same manner, the reduced dimensionless dispersion relation for the singled-layered homogeneous membrane was obtained in Equation (30) as follows:

$$J'_{-\tau\Phi}(W)J'_{\tau\Phi}(W\alpha') - J'_{\tau\Phi}(W)J'_{-\tau\Phi}(W\alpha') = 0, \tag{36}$$

or equally, after explicitly expanding $J'_{\pm}(.)$ as in Equation (19), as follows

$$\begin{aligned}&(J_{-\tau\Phi-1}(W) - J_{1-\tau\Phi}(W))(J_{\tau\Phi-1}(W\alpha') - J_{\tau\Phi+1}(W\alpha')) - \\ &(J_{\tau\Phi-1}(W) - J_{\tau\Phi+1}(W))(J_{-\tau\Phi-1}(W\alpha') - J_{1-\tau\Phi}(W\alpha')) = 0,\end{aligned} \tag{37}$$

where τ, Φ and α' are already given in Equations (34) and (35), while W now takes the expression $W = \omega\alpha_2/c_1$ since c_2 is not present in the reduced body.

Further, the dispersion of elastic waves in the reduced medium with respect to the variation in the scaled fractional-order τ is depicted in Figure 7a, portraying the harmonic curves via the relationship between the dimensionless phase-speed Θ and wavenumber Φ with respect to the variation in the scaled fractional-order τ for the single-layered homogenous membrane. Indeed, the opposite has been noted here in comparison with the two-layered inhomogenous membrane. Precisely, an increase in the fractional order increases the respective harmonic modes. In addition, Figure 7b portrays the relationship between the frequency and the wavenumber equally within the estimate of long-wave and low-frequency propagation. Thus, without further delay, it is noted from Figure 7b that the fundamental mode increases with an increase in the fractional order. Furthermore, the fixed parameter values in the case of a two-layeredmembrane are systematically used here for plotting the corresponding reduced one-layeredcase.

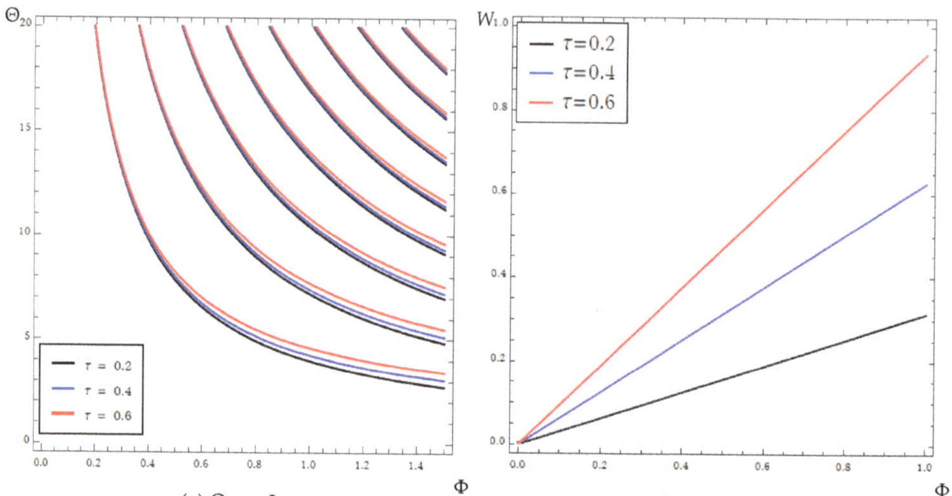

(a) Θ vs. Φ. (b) W vs. Φ.

Figure 7. Harmonic curves: the relationship between the (**a**) dimensionless phase-speed Θ and wavenumber Φ and (**b**) dimensionless frequency W and wavenumber Φ with respect to the variation of the scaled fractional-order τ for the single-layered homogenous membrane.

7. Conclusions

This research utilized the Helmholtz equation to model the dispersion of elastic waves in a multilayered inhomogeneous circular membrane with fractional infusion. Ideal continuity conditions were applied between membrane layers, with fixed conditions on the outermost layer, and traction-free conditions at the endpoints of the composite membrane. Numerical simulations of the wave expressions conclusively showed that fractional infusion significantly affected the dispersion of elastic waves in the medium. The key findings are summarized as follows:

1. The study shows that increasing the fractional-order parameter in a bi-elastic inhomogeneous hollow membrane stretches the harmonic curves backward, resulting in a delay or decrease in wave propagation. This effect is observed consistently in both long-wave and short-wave propagations.
2. For both the two- and three-layered inhomogeneous membranes, an increase in the fractional order leads to a decrease in the respective harmonic modes. This effect becomes more pronounced in the short-wave region, indicating that fractional-order parameters significantly influence short-wave propagation.
3. In the context of long-wave and low-frequency propagation, only the fundamental mode satisfies the condition; this cuts across the three prototype cases. An increase in the fractional order raises the fundamental dispersion curve, effectively shrinking the range of the wavenumber suitable for long-wave propagation. This highlights the importance of fractional-order parameters in tuning the wave behavior for specific applications.
4. In a single-layered homogeneous membrane, an increase in the fractional order results in an increase in the respective harmonic modes, contrasting with the behavior observed in the two- and three-layered inhomogeneous membranes. This indicates that the structural composition of the membrane (single vs. multilayered) plays a crucial role in determining how fractional-order parameters affect wave dispersion.
5. For both single- and multi-layered membranes, the fundamental mode increases with an increase in the fractional-order, especially within the long-wave and low-frequency propagation range. This suggests that fractional-order infusion can be effectively used to control and optimize wave dispersion in various engineering applications.

Author Contributions: Conceptualization, A.M.M. and R.I.N.; Methodology, A.M.M., R.I.N., R.N. and T.N.; Software, R.I.N. and T.N.; Validation, R.N.; Formal analysis, R.I.N., R.N. and T.N.; Investigation, A.M.M., R.N. and T.N.; Resources, T.N.; Writing—original draft, R.I.N.; Writing—review & editing, A.M.M., R.N. and T.N.; Visualization, A.M.M., R.N. and T.N.; Supervision, R.I.N.; Project administration, A.M.M. All authors have read and agreed to the published version of the manuscript.

Funding: This research was funded by Taif University, Taif, Saudi Arabia (TU-DSPP-2024-231).

Data Availability Statement: All data generated or analysed during this study are included in this published article.

Acknowledgments: The authors extend their appreciation to Taif University, Saudi Arabia, for supporting this work through project number (TU-DSPP-2024-231).

Conflicts of Interest: The authors declare no conflicts of interest.

Appendix A

The explicit form for the coefficients ${}^1a_n, {}^1b_n, {}^2a_n, {}^2\bar{a}_n, {}^2b_n,$ and ${}^2\bar{b}_n$ ubvikved in Equation (25) are found from Equations (18) and (20) as follows:

$$\begin{aligned}
{}^1a_n &= \mu_2\Big(J_{n\beta}(k_2\alpha_1)J'_{-n\beta}(k_2\alpha_1) - J_{-n\beta}(k_2\alpha_1)J'_{n\beta}(k_2\alpha_1)\Big)w_1(n),\\
{}^1b_n &= \mu_2\Big(J_{n\beta}(k_2\alpha_1)J'_{-n\beta}(k_2\alpha_1) - J_{-n\beta}(k_2\alpha_1)J'_{n\beta}(k_2\alpha_1)\Big)w_2(n),\\
{}^2a_n &= \Big(\mu_1 J_{-n\beta}(k_2\alpha_1)J'_{n\beta}(k_1\alpha_1) - \mu_2 J_{n\beta}(k_1\alpha_1)J'_{-n\beta}(k_2\alpha_1)\Big)w_1(n),\\
{}^2b_n &= \Big(\mu_1 J_{-n\beta}(k_2\alpha_1)J'_{-n\beta}(k_1\alpha_1) - \mu_2 J_{-n\beta}(k_1\alpha_1)J'_{-n\beta}(k_2\alpha_1)\Big)w_2(n),\\
{}^2\bar{a}_n &= \Big(\mu_1 J_{n\beta}(k_2\alpha_1)J'_{n\beta}(k_1\alpha_1) - \mu_2 J_{n\beta}(k_1\alpha_1)J'_{n\beta}(k_2\alpha_1)\Big)w_1(n),\\
{}^2\bar{b}_n &= \Big(\mu_1 J_{n\beta}(k_2\alpha_1)J'_{-n\beta}(k_1\alpha_1) - \mu_2 J_{-n\beta}(k_1\alpha_1)J'_{n\beta}(k_2\alpha_1)\Big)w_2(n),
\end{aligned}$$

where $w_1(n)$ and $w_2(n)$ appearing above are expressed as

$$w_1(n) = \frac{1}{\pi\zeta_1}\int_{-\pi}^{\pi} f_2(\theta)\cos(n\theta)d\theta, \qquad w_2(n) = \frac{1}{\pi\zeta_2}\int_{-\pi}^{\pi} f_2(\theta)\sin(n\theta)d\theta,$$

with ζ_1 and ζ_2 appearing above expressed as follows

$$\begin{aligned}
\zeta_1 = {} & \mu_1\big(J_{-n\beta}(k_2\alpha_2)J_{n\beta}(k_2\alpha_1) - J_{-n\beta}(k_2\alpha_1)J_{n\beta}(k_2\alpha_2)\big)J'_{n\beta}(k_1\alpha_1)\\
& + \mu_2 J_{n\beta}(k_1\alpha_1)\Big(J_{n\beta}(k_2\alpha_2)J'_{-n\beta}(k_2\alpha_1) - J_{-n\beta}(k_2\alpha_2)J'_{n\beta}(k_2\alpha_1)\Big),
\end{aligned}$$

$$\begin{aligned}
\zeta_2 = {} & \mu_1\big(J_{-n\beta}(k_2\alpha_2)J_{n\beta}(k_2\alpha_1) - J_{-n\beta}(k_2\alpha_1)J_{n\beta}(k_2\alpha_2)\big)J'_{-n\beta}(k_1\alpha_1)\\
& + \mu_2 J_{-n\beta}(k_1\alpha_1)\Big(J_{n\beta}(k_2\alpha_2)J'_{-n\beta}(k_2\alpha_1) - J_{-n\beta}(k_2\alpha_2)J'_{n\beta}(k_2\alpha_1)\Big).
\end{aligned}$$

Appendix B

The explicit expressions for ${}^1a_n, {}^1b_n, {}^2a_n, {}^2\bar{a}_n, {}^2b_n, {}^2\bar{b}_n, {}^3a_n, {}^3\bar{a}_n, {}^3b_n,$ and ${}^3\bar{b}_n$ with regard to the three-layered membrane appearing in Equation (27) are determined accordingly as follows:

$$\begin{aligned}
{}^1a_n = {} & \mu_2\mu_3\Big(J_{n\beta}(k_2\alpha_1)J'_{-n\beta}(k_2\alpha_1) - J_{-n\beta}(k_2\alpha_1)J'_{n\beta}(k_2\alpha_1)\Big)\times\\
& \Big(J_{n\beta}(k_3\alpha_2)J'_{-n\beta}(k_3\alpha_2) - J_{-n\beta}(k_3\alpha_2)J'_{n\beta}(k_3\alpha_2)\Big)w_1(n),\\
{}^1b_n = {} & \mu_2\mu_3\Big(J_{n\beta}(k_2\alpha_1)J'_{-n\beta}(k_2\alpha_1) - J_{-n\beta}(k_2\alpha_1)J'_{n\beta}(k_2\alpha_1)\Big)\times\\
& \Big(J_{n\beta}(k_3\alpha_2)J'_{-n\beta}(k_3\alpha_2) - J_{-n\beta}(k_3\alpha_2)J'_{n\beta}(k_3\alpha_2)\Big)w_2(n),
\end{aligned}$$

$$
\begin{aligned}
{}^{2}a_n &= -\mu_3\Big(J_{n\beta}(k_3\alpha_2)J'_{-n\beta}(k_3\alpha_2) - J_{-n\beta}(k_3\alpha_2)J'_{n\beta}(k_3\alpha_2)\Big)\times\\
&\quad\Big(\mu_1 J_{-n\beta}(k_2\alpha_1)J'_{n\beta}(k_1\alpha_1) - \mu_2 J_{n\beta}(k_1\alpha_1)J'_{-n\beta}(k_2\alpha_1)\Big)w_1(n),\\
{}^{2}b_n &= -\mu_3\Big(J_{n\beta}(k_3\alpha_2)J'_{-n\beta}(k_3\alpha_2) - J_{-n\beta}(k_3\alpha_2)J'_{n\beta}(k_3\alpha_2)\Big)\times\\
&\quad\Big(\mu_1 J_{-n\beta}(k_2\alpha_1)J'_{-n\beta}(k_1\alpha_1) - \mu_2 J_{-n\beta}(k_1\alpha_1)J'_{-n\beta}(k_2\alpha_1)\Big)w_2(n),\\
{}^{2}\bar{a}_n &= \mu_3\Big(J_{n\beta}(k_3\alpha_2)J'_{-n\beta}(k_3\alpha_2) - J_{-n\beta}(k_3\alpha_2)J'_{n\beta}(k_3\alpha_2)\Big)\times\\
&\quad\Big(\mu_1 J_{n\beta}(k_2\alpha_1)J'_{n\beta}(k_1\alpha_1) - \mu_2 J_{n\beta}(k_1\alpha_1)J'_{n\beta}(k_2\alpha_1)\Big)w_1(n),\\
{}^{2}\bar{b}_n &= \mu_3\Big(J_{n\beta}(k_3\alpha_2)J'_{-n\beta}(k_3\alpha_2) - J_{-n\beta}(k_3\alpha_2)J'_{n\beta}(k_3\alpha_2)\Big)\times\\
&\quad\Big(\mu_1 J_{n\beta}(k_2\alpha_1)J'_{-n\beta}(k_1\alpha_1) - \mu_2 J_{-n\beta}(k_1\alpha_1)J'_{n\beta}(k_2\alpha_1)\Big)w_2(n),\\
{}^{3}a_n &= \quad(\mu_1 X_1 J'_{n\beta}(k_1\alpha_1) + \mu_2 Z_1 J_{n\beta}(k_1\alpha_1))w_1(n),\\
{}^{3}b_n &= -\Big(\mu_1 X_2 J'_{-n\beta}(k_1\alpha_1) + \mu_2 Z_2 J_{-n\beta}(k_1\alpha_1)\Big)w_2(n),\\
{}^{3}\bar{a}_n &= -\Big(\mu_1 X_3 J'_{-n\beta}(k_1\alpha_1) + \mu_2 Z_3 J_{-n\beta}(k_1\alpha_1)\Big)w_1(n),\\
{}^{3}\bar{b}_n &= \quad(\mu_1 X_4 J'_{-n\beta}(k_1\alpha_1) + \mu_2 Z_4 J_{-n\beta}(k_1\alpha_1))w_2(n),
\end{aligned}
$$

where X_j, and Z_j, for $j = 1,2,3,4$ appearing in the later expressions are expressed as follows:

$$
\begin{aligned}
X_1 &= \mu_2 J_{-n\beta}(k_3\alpha_2)\Big(J_{-n\beta}(k_2\alpha_1)J'_{n\beta}(k_2\alpha_2) - J_{n\beta}(k_2\alpha_1)J'_{-n\beta}(k_2\alpha_2)\Big)\\
&\quad+\mu_3(J_{-n\beta}(k_2\alpha_2)J_{n\beta}(k_2\alpha_1) - J_{-n\beta}(k_2\alpha_1)J_{n\beta}(k_2\alpha_2))J'_{-n\beta}(k_3\alpha_2),\\
Z_1 &= \mu_2 J_{-n\beta}(k_3\alpha_2)\Big(J'_{-n\beta}(k_2\alpha_2)J'_{n\beta}(k_2\alpha_1) - J'_{-n\beta}(k_2\alpha_1)J'_{n\beta}(k_2\alpha_2)\Big)\\
&\quad+\mu_3 J'_{-n\beta}(k_3\alpha_2)\Big(J_{n\beta}(k_2\alpha_2)J'_{-n\beta}(k_2\alpha_1) - J_{-n\beta}(k_2\alpha_2)J'_{n\beta}(k_2\alpha_1)\Big),\\
X_2 &= \mu_2 J_{-n\beta}(k_3\alpha_2)\Big(J_{n\beta}(k_2\alpha_1)J'_{-n\beta}(k_2\alpha_2) - J_{-n\beta}(k_2\alpha_1)J'_{n\beta}(k_2\alpha_2)\Big)\\
&\quad+\mu_3(J_{-n\beta}(k_2\alpha_1)J_{n\beta}(k_2\alpha_2) - J_{-n\beta}(k_2\alpha_2)J_{n\beta}(k_2\alpha_1))J'_{-n\beta}(k_3\alpha_2),\\
Z_2 &= \mu_2 J_{-n\beta}(k_3\alpha_2)\Big(J'_{-n\beta}(k_2\alpha_1)J'_{n\beta}(k_2\alpha_2) - J'_{-n\beta}(k_2\alpha_2)J'_{n\beta}(k_2\alpha_1)\Big)\\
&\quad+\mu_3 J'_{-n\beta}(k_3\alpha_2)\Big(J_{-n\beta}(k_2\alpha_2)J'_{n\beta}(k_2\alpha_1) - J_{n\beta}(k_2\alpha_2)J'_{-n\beta}(k_2\alpha_1)\Big),\\
X_3 &= \mu_2 J_{-n\beta}(k_3\alpha_2)\Big(J_{n\beta}(k_2\alpha_1)J'_{-n\beta}(k_2\alpha_2) - J_{-n\beta}(k_2\alpha_1)J'_{n\beta}(k_2\alpha_2)\Big)\\
&\quad+\mu_3(J_{-n\beta}(k_2\alpha_1)J_{n\beta}(k_2\alpha_2) - J_{-n\beta}(k_2\alpha_2)J_{n\beta}(k_2\alpha_1))J'_{-n\beta}(k_3\alpha_2),\\
Z_3 &= \mu_2 J_{-n\beta}(k_3\alpha_2)\Big(J'_{-n\beta}(k_2\alpha_1)J'_{n\beta}(k_2\alpha_2) - J'_{-n\beta}(k_2\alpha_2)J'_{n\beta}(k_2\alpha_1)\Big)\\
&\quad+\mu_3 J'_{-n\beta}(k_3\alpha_2)\Big(J_{-n\beta}(k_2\alpha_2)J'_{n\beta}(k_2\alpha_1) - J_{n\beta}(k_2\alpha_2)J'_{-n\beta}(k_2\alpha_1)\Big),\\
X_4 &= \mu_2 J_{n\beta}(k_3\alpha_2)\Big(J_{n\beta}(k_2\alpha_1)J'_{-n\beta}(k_2\alpha_2) - J_{-n\beta}(k_2\alpha_1)J'_{n\beta}(k_2\alpha_2)\Big)\\
&\quad+\mu_3(J_{-n\beta}(k_2\alpha_1)J_{n\beta}(k_2\alpha_2) - J_{-n\beta}(k_2\alpha_2)J_{n\beta}(k_2\alpha_1))J'_{n\beta}(k_3\alpha_2),\\
Z_4 &= \mu_2 J_{n\beta}(k_3\alpha_2)\Big(J'_{-n\beta}(k_2\alpha_1)J'_{n\beta}(k_2\alpha_2) - J'_{-n\beta}(k_2\alpha_2)J'_{n\beta}(k_2\alpha_1)\Big)\\
&\quad+\mu_3 J'_{n\beta}(k_3\alpha_2)\Big(J_{-n\beta}(k_2\alpha_2)J'_{n\beta}(k_2\alpha_1) - J_{n\beta}(k_2\alpha_2)J'_{-n\beta}(k_2\alpha_1)\Big),
\end{aligned}
$$

while $w_1(n)$ and $w_2(n)$ take the following expressions:

$$
w_1(n) = \frac{1}{\pi\chi_1}\int_{-\pi}^{\pi} f_3(\theta)\cos(n\theta)d\theta, \quad w_2(n) = \frac{1}{\pi\chi_2}\int_{-\pi}^{\pi} f_3(\theta)\sin(n\theta)d\theta,
$$

with χ_1 and χ_2 in the above integrals expressed as follows:

$$\chi_1 = \mu_1 X_5 J'_{n\beta}(k_1\alpha_1) + \mu_2 Z_5 J_{n\beta}(k_1\alpha_1),$$
$$\chi_2 = \mu_1 X_5 J'_{-n\beta}(k_1\alpha_1) + \mu_2 Z_5 J_{-n\beta}(k_1\alpha_1),$$

along with X_5, and Z_5 in the latter expression found as follows:

$$\begin{aligned} X_5 = {} & \mu_2 (J_{-n\beta}(k_3\alpha_3) J_{n\beta}(k_3\alpha_2) - J_{-n\beta}(k_3\alpha_2) J_{n\beta}(k_3\alpha_3)) \times \\ & \left(J_{n\beta}(k_2\alpha_1) J'_{-n\beta}(k_2\alpha_2) - J_{-n\beta}(k_2\alpha_1) J'_{n\beta}(k_2\alpha_2) \right) \\ & + \mu_3 (J_{-n\beta}(k_2\alpha_2) J_{n\beta}(k_2\alpha_1) - J_{-n\beta}(k_2\alpha_1) J_{n\beta}(k_2\alpha_2)) \times \\ & \left(J_{n\beta}(k_3\alpha_3) J'_{-n\beta}(k_3\alpha_2) - J_{-n\beta}(k_3\alpha_3) J'_{n\beta}(k_3\alpha_2) \right), \\ Z_5 = {} & \mu_3 \left(J_{n\beta}(k_2\alpha_2) J'_{-n\beta}(k_2\alpha_1) - J_{-n\beta}(k_2\alpha_2) J'_{n\beta}(k_2\alpha_1) \right) \times \\ & \left(J_{n\beta}(k_3\alpha_3) J'_{-n\beta}(k_3\alpha_2) - J_{-n\beta}(k_3\alpha_3) J'_{n\beta}(k_3\alpha_2) \right) \\ & - \mu_2 (J_{-n\beta}(k_3\alpha_3) J_{n\beta}(k_3\alpha_2) - J_{-n\beta}(k_3\alpha_2) J_{n\beta}(k_3\alpha_3)) \times \\ & \left(J'_{-n\beta}(k_2\alpha_2) J'_{n\beta}(k_2\alpha_1) - J'_{-n\beta}(k_2\alpha_1) J'_{n\beta}(k_2\alpha_2) \right). \end{aligned}$$

References

1. Ewing, W.M.; Jardetzky, W.S.; Press, F.; Beiser, A. Elastic Waves in Layered Media. *Phys. Today* **1957**, *10*, 27–28. [CrossRef]
2. Asghar, S.; Zaman, F.; Masud, A. Dispersion of Love-type waves in a vertically inhomogeneous intermediate layer. *J. Phys. Earth* **1990**, *38*, 213–221. [CrossRef]
3. Mubaraki, A.M.; Althobaiti, S.; Nuruddeen, R.I. Heat and wave interactions in a thermoelastic coaxial solid cylinder driven by laser heating sources. *Case Stud. Therm. Eng.* **2022**, *38*, 102338. [CrossRef]
4. Althobaiti, S.; Mubaraki, A.; Nuruddeen, R.I.; Gomez-Aguilar, J.F. Wave propagation in an elastic coaxial hollow cylinder when exposed to thermal heating and external load. *Results Phys.* **2022**, *38*, 105582. [CrossRef]
5. Nuruddeen, R.I.; Nawaz, R.; Zaigham Zia, Q.M. Asymptotic approach to anti-plane dynamic problem of asymmetric three-layered composite plate. *Math. Methods Appl. Sci.* **2021**, *44*, 10933–10947. [CrossRef]
6. Wolfram MathWorld Helmholtz Differential Equation-Circular Cylindrical Coordinates. Available online: https://mathworld.wolfram.com/HelmholtzDifferentialEquationCircularCylindricalCoordinates.html (accessed on 24 September 2023).
7. Khalil, R.; Al Horani, M.; Yousef, A.; Sababheh, M. A new definition of fractional derivative. *J. Comput. Appl. Math.* **2014**, *264*, 65–701. [CrossRef]
8. Kukla, S.; Siedlecka, U. Time-fractional heat conduction in a finite composite cylinder with heat source. *J. Appl. Math. Comput. Mech.* **2020**, *19*, 85–94. [CrossRef]
9. Iyiola, O.S.; Zaman, F.D. A note on analytical solutions of nonlinear fractional 2-D heat equation with non-local integral terms. *Pramana* **2016**, *87*, 1–6. [CrossRef]
10. Anwar, A.M.O.; Jarad, F.; Baleanu, D.; Ayaz, F. Fractional Caputo heat equation within the double Laplace transform. *Rom. J. Phys.* **2013**, *58*, 15–22.
11. Haberman, R. *Elementary Applied Differential Equations*; A Paramaout Communication Company: Englewood Cliffs, NJ, USA, 1987.
12. Hammad, M.A.; AlSharif, S.; Khalil, R.; Shmasneh, A. Fractional Bessel differential equation and fractional Bessel functions. *Ital. J. Pure Appl. Math.-N* **2022**, *47*, 521–531.
13. Dai, H.-H.; Kaplunov, J.; Prikachikov, D.A. Long-wave model for the surface wave in a coated half-space. *Proc. R. Soc. A Math. Phy. Eng. Sci.* **2010**, *466*, 3097–3116. [CrossRef]
14. Kaplunov, J.; Prikazchikova, L.; Alkinidri, M. Antiplane shear of an asymmetric sandwich plate. *Contin. Mech. Thermodyn.* **2021**, *33*, 1247–1262. [CrossRef]
15. Mubaraki, A.; Prikazchikov, D.; Kudaibergenov, A. Explicit model for surface waves on an elastic half-space coated by a thin vertically inhomogeneous layer. *Dyn. Syst. Theo. Appl.* **2019**, 267–275. .77306-9_23. [CrossRef]
16. Horgan, C.O. Anti-plane shear deformations in linear and nonlinear solid mechanics. *SIAM Rev.* **1995**, *37*, 53–81. [CrossRef]
17. Wang, Z.; Chen, M.; Xi, X.; Tian, H.; Yang, R. Multi-chimera states in a higher-order network of FitzHugh–Nagumo oscillators. *Eur. Phys. J. Spec. Top.* **2024**, *233*, 779–786. [CrossRef]
18. Ba, Z.; Wu, M.; Liang, J. 3D dynamic responses of a multi-layered transversely isotropic saturated half-space under concentrated forces and pore pressure. *Appl. Math. Model.* **2020**, *80*, 859–878. [CrossRef]
19. Liu, L.; Zhang, S.; Zhang, L.; Pan, G.; Yu, J. Multi-UUV maneuvering counter-game for dynamic target scenario based on fractional-order recurrent neural network. *IEEE Trans. Cybern.* **2023**, *53*, 4015–4028. [CrossRef] [PubMed]

20. Kai, Y.; Chen, S.; Zhang, K.; Yin, Z. Exact solutions and dynamic properties of a nonlinear fourth-order time-fractional partial differential equation. *Waves Random Complex Media* **2022**, 1–12. [CrossRef]
21. Wang, C.; Wen, P.; Huang, Y.; Chen, K.; Xu, K. Terahertz dual-band bandpass filter based on spoof surface plasmon polaritons with wide upper stopband suppression. *Opt. Express* **2024**, *32*, 22748–22758. [CrossRef]
22. Mubaraki, A.M.; Nuruddeen, R.I.; Gomez-Aguilar, J.F. Closed-form asymptotic solution for the transport of chlorine concentration in composite pipes. *Phys. Scr.* **2024**, *99*, 075201. [CrossRef]
23. Sahin, O.; Erbas, B.; Kaplunov, J.; Savsek, T. The lowest vibration modes of an elastic beam composed of alternating stiff and soft components. *Arch. Appl. Mech.* **2020**, *90*, 339–352. [CrossRef]
24. Abd-Alla, A.M.; Abo-Dahab, S.M.; Khan, A. Rotational effects on magneto-thermoelastic Stoneley, Love, and Rayleigh waves in fibre-reinforced anisotropic general viscoelastic media of higher order. *Comput. Mater. Contin.* **2017**, *53*, 49–72. [CrossRef]
25. Ebrahimi, F.; Seyfi, A. A wave propagation study for porous metal foam beams resting on an elastic foundation. *Waves Random Complex Media* **2021**, *31*, 1–15. [CrossRef]
26. Liu, Z.; Qi, H. Dynamic anti-plane behavior of rare earth giant magnetostrictive medium with a circular cavity defect in semi-space. *Sci. Rep.* **2021**, *11*, 13442. [CrossRef] [PubMed]
27. Mandi, A.; Kundu, S.; Chandra, P.; Pati, P. An analytic study on the dispersion of Love wave propagation in double layers lying over inhomogeneous half-space. *J. Solid Mech.* **2019**, *11*, 570–580. [CrossRef]
28. Zenkour, A.M.; Radwan, A.F. Analysis of multilayered composite plates resting on elastic foundations in thermal environment using a hyperbolic model. *J. Braz. Soc. Mech. Sci.* **2017**, *39*, 2801–2816. [CrossRef]
29. Afsar, H.; Peiwei, G.; Alshamrani, A.; Aldandani, M.; Alam, M.M.; Aljohani, A.F. Dimensionless dynamics: Multipeak and envelope solitons in perturbed nonlinear Schrodinger equation with Kerr law nonlinearity. *AIP Phys. Fluids* **2024**, *36*, 067126. [CrossRef]
30. Erbas, B.; Kaplunov, J.; Nobili, A.; Kilic, G. Dispersion of elastic waves in a layer interacting with a Winkler foundation. *J. Acoust Soc. Am.* **2018**, *144*, 2918–2925. [CrossRef] [PubMed]
31. Ahmad, F.; Zaman, F.D. Exact and asymptotic solutions of the elastic wave propagation problem in a rod. *Int. J. Pure Appl. Math.* **2006**, *27*, 123–127.
32. Afsar, H.; Akbar, Y. Energy distribution of bifurcated waveguide structure with planar and non-planar surfaces. *Math. Mech. Solids* **2022**, *28*, 1155–1169. [CrossRef]
33. Kaplunov, J.D.; Kossovich, L.Y.; Nolde, E.V. *Dynamics of Thin Walled Elastic Bodies*; Academic Press: San Diego, CA, USA, 1998.

fractal and fractional

MDPI

Article

Theoretical Results on the pth Moment of ϕ-Hilfer Stochastic Fractional Differential Equations with a Pantograph Term

Abdelhamid Mohammed Djaouti [1,*,†] and Muhammad Imran Liaqat [2,†]

1 Department of Mathematics and Statistics, Faculty of Sciences, King Faisal University, Hofuf 31982, Saudi Arabia
2 Abdus Salam School of Mathematical Sciences, Government College University, 68-B, New Muslim Town, Lahore 54600, Pakistan; imran_liaqat_22@sms.edu.pk
* Correspondence: adjaout@kfu.edu.sa
† These authors contributed equally to this work.

Abstract: Here, we establish significant results on the well-posedness of solutions to stochastic pantograph fractional differential equations (SPFrDEs) with the ϕ-Hilfer fractional derivative. Additionally, we prove the smoothness theorem for the solution and present the averaging principle result. Firstly, the contraction mapping principle is applied to determine the existence and uniqueness of the solution. Secondly, continuous dependence findings are presented under the condition that the coefficients satisfy the global Lipschitz criteria, along with regularity results. Thirdly, we establish results for the averaging principle by applying inequalities and interval translation techniques. Finally, we provide numerical examples and graphical results to support our findings. We make two generalizations of these findings. First, in terms of the fractional derivative, our established theorems and lemmas are consistent with the Caputo operator for $\phi(t) = t$, $\alpha = 1$. Our findings match the Riemann–Liouville fractional operator for $\phi(t) = t$, $\alpha = 0$. They agree with the Hadamard and Caputo–Hadamard fractional operators when $\phi(t) = \ln(t)$, $\alpha = 0$ and $\phi(t) = \ln(t)$, $\alpha = 1$, respectively. Second, regarding the space, we are make generalizations for the case $\mathfrak{p} = 2$.

Keywords: continuous dependence; Hölder's inequality; well-posedness; pth moment; ϕ-Hilfer fractional operator; stochastic differential equation

MSC: 34K20; 34K30; 34K40

1. Introduction

The literature contains various types of fractional operators; the most important and commonly used are the Caputo and Riemann–Liouville derivatives. In 2000, Hilfer generalized the Riemann–Liouville derivative, which is known as the Hilfer fractional derivative (HFrD). In 2018, Sousa and Oliveira further generalized HFrD, defining it with respect to an increasing function $\phi(t)$ to enhance the precision of objective modeling.

Various authors have utilized the ϕ-HFrD with fractional differential equations (FDEs) and fractional stochastic differential equations (FSDEs) to analyze multiple concepts. For example, Raheem et al. [1] presented controllability results for FSDEs and discussed the existence of a solution. Lavanya et al. [2] also explored controllability for FSDEs with the Rosenblatt process. Gokul and Udhayakumar [3] examined approximate controllability through sectorial operators. The authors [4] have presented stability results for FDEs with

ϕ-HFrD and established various concepts related to the solutions of fractional integro-differential equations. Kucche and Mali [5] proved the existence of solutions for FDEs with ϕ-HFrD, while Bonilla et al. [6] investigated the solvability of such equations. Additionally, Lima et al. [7] provided results on Ulam–Hyers stability for FDEs with delay in the context of ϕ-HFrD. Abdo et al. [8] studied a fractional system in the sense of ϕ-HFrD and explored various concepts. Finally, the authors [9] established the approximate controllability of FDEs with ϕ-HFrD.

The Riemann–Liouville fractional integral of order $\mathfrak{q}$ with respect to an increasing, non-vanishing, and monotonic function $\phi(t)$ for a continuous function $f : [\mathfrak{u}, \mathfrak{g}] \to \Re$, as given below [10]:

$$\mathcal{I}_{\mathfrak{u}}^{\mathfrak{q},\phi} f(t) = \frac{1}{\Gamma(\mathfrak{q})} \int_{\mathfrak{u}}^{t} \phi'(\varpi)(\phi(t) - \phi(\varpi))^{\mathfrak{q}-1} f(\varpi) d\varpi. \tag{1}$$

The Riemann–Liouville fractional operator of order $\mathfrak{q}$ for $\phi(t)$ is given as follows [10]:

$$\begin{aligned} \mathcal{T}_{\mathfrak{u}^+}^{\mathfrak{q},\phi} f(t) &= \left(\frac{1}{\phi'(t)}\frac{d}{dt}\right)^{\delta} \mathcal{I}_{a}^{\delta-\mathfrak{q},\phi} f(t) \\ &= \frac{1}{\Gamma(\delta-\mathfrak{q})} \left(\frac{1}{\phi'(t)}\frac{d}{dt}\right)^{\delta} \int_{\mathfrak{u}}^{t} \phi'(\varpi)(\phi(t) - \phi(\varpi))^{\delta-\mathfrak{q}-1} f(\varpi) d\varpi. \end{aligned} \tag{2}$$

where $\mathfrak{q} \in (\delta - 1, \delta)$.

The ϕ-HFrD of order $\mathfrak{q}$ and type $\mathfrak{a}$ for the function $f(t)$ is defined as [11]:

$$^{H}\mathcal{T}_{\mathfrak{u}^+}^{\mathfrak{q},\mathfrak{a},\phi} f(t) = \mathcal{I}_{\mathfrak{u}^+}^{\mathfrak{a}(\delta-\mathfrak{q}),\phi} \left(\frac{1}{\phi'(t)}\frac{d}{dt}\right)^{\delta} \mathcal{I}_{\mathfrak{u}^+}^{(1-\mathfrak{a})(\delta-\mathfrak{q}),\phi} f(t), \tag{3}$$

where $\delta = [\mathfrak{q}] + 1$, $\delta \in \mathbf{N}$, and ϕ is an increasing function.

Stochastic differential equations with fractional calculus have drawn a lot of interest and have been used in a number of study fields, such as quantitative finance, option pricing, and disease transmission. Numerous scholars have investigated various important results related to FSDEs, such as the existence and uniqueness (EU) of the solution, stability, regularity, controllability, and averaging principle (AP). Some important works include the use of the Picard approach by the authors in [12] to examine the stability and EU of solutions for FSDEs. Their results were developed in the $\mathcal{L}^2$ space, and they established the results with the Caputo fractional derivative (CFD). The Hadamard operator was used in [13] to establish results on a number of different features, including stability and EU, with findings expressed in the $\mathcal{L}^2$ space. The EU of FSDEs containing fractional derivatives of a variable order was the main emphasis of Moualkia and Xu [14]. Babaei et al. [15] used the collocation approach with CFD to find solutions for FSDEs. FSDEs were solved using the Taylor series method by Asai and Kloeden [16]. The Picard approach with CFD was used by the authors in [17] to establish the EU results. In their study, Zhang et al. [18] investigated EU for FSDEs with delay while taking the CFD into account. Using the Hadamard operator, Lavanya and Vadivoo [19] examined the controllability of FSDEs with fractional Brownian motion. The Euler–Maruyama method was used to develop solutions for FSDEs in [20], along with stability and EU results. The Euler–Maruyama method's strong convergence was examined by Yang et al. [21]. In [22], the authors looked at EU and controllability for FSDEs with CFD. A large portion of the literature has been developed inside the framework of $\mathcal{L}^2$ space. The authors of [23] presented some important results for the stochastic Burgers system.

The concept of the AP was introduced by Khasminskii [24], who demonstrated that the average and original solutions of a system coincided under suitable restrictions. Using the AP tool, complex systems can be studied by approximating an average system, making it easier to analyze systems that are otherwise difficult to study directly. In the literature,

AP results have been proven for various types of systems under appropriate conditions, with some of the most significant being: Mao et al. [25] proved a result for the AP using jumps for delay stochastic systems. Xu et al. [26] discussed AP for FSDEs with the Caputo operator with a mean square. Guo et al. [27] established a theorem for AP under weak conditions. Liu and Xu [28] studied AP for impulsive FSDEs with the Caputo operator. Liu et al. [29] presented a result on AP for partial FSDEs with the Caputo operator with a mean square. Ahmed and Zhu [30] also proved a theorem for FSDEs with Poisson jumps under the Hilfer operator. Xu et al. [31] further explored AP for FSDEs with a mean square. Additionally, the authors investigated AP for backward stochastic system in $\mathcal{L}^2$ space. Jing and Li [32] discussed the AP for the stochastic model in the mean square sense. Guo et al. [33] also presented a result for the AP in the mean square sense. In the sense of the Caputo fractional operator, Mouy et al. [34] also worked on AP with the Caputo–Hadamard fractional operator in the mean square sense. In [35], Shen et al. discussed the AP for the fractional heat system. The authors [36,37] also established results regarding AP in the $\mathcal{L}^2$ space. For further results on AP regarding fractional operators and space, see [38–40].

In this research, we present significant results concerning the EU, continuous dependence, regularity, and AP for SPFrDEs with ϕ-HFrD in the $\mathfrak{p}$th moment. Using the contraction mapping principle, we establish the EU result for the solutions of SPFrDEs, then prove the results for continuous dependence under the condition that the coefficients satisfy the global Lipschitz criteria. Additionally, we prove regularity results and, by applying various inequalities and the interval translation approach, derive results for the AP. Finally, we provide numerical examples and graphical representations to support our findings.

This study makes notable contributions in the following ways:

1. To the best of our knowledge, this is the first research work to establish results regarding well-posedness, regularity, and AP for SPFrDEs concerning ϕ-HFrD.
2. The majority of results in the literature concerning the EU and AP for FSDEs were developed in the mean square sense; however, we derived these results using the $\mathfrak{p}$th moment. Consequently, our research expanded the findings about regularity, well-posedness, and the AP for SPFrDEs to $\mathfrak{p} = 2$.
3. For $\phi(\mathfrak{t}) = \mathfrak{t}$, $\mathfrak{a} = 1$ our established results align with the FSDEs of CFD. For $\phi(\mathfrak{t}) = \mathfrak{t}$, $\mathfrak{a} = 0$ our results correspond to the FSDEs of the Riemann–Liouville fractional operator. When $\phi(\mathfrak{t}) = \ln(\mathfrak{t})\mathfrak{a} = 0$, and $\phi(\mathfrak{t}) = \ln(\mathfrak{t})\mathfrak{a} = 1$, they align with the Hadamard and Caputo–Hadamard, respectively.
4. We present some numerical problems and their graphical results to prove the validity of our established theoretical results.

We examine the following SPFrDEs:

$$\begin{cases} {}^{H}\mathcal{T}_{\mathfrak{t}}^{\mathfrak{q},\mathfrak{a},\phi}\mathfrak{f}(\mathfrak{t}) = \mathcal{D}(\mathfrak{t},\mathfrak{f}(\mathfrak{t}),\mathfrak{f}(\mathfrak{s}\mathfrak{t})) + \Xi(\mathfrak{t},\mathfrak{f}(\mathfrak{t}),\mathfrak{f}(\mathfrak{s}\mathfrak{t}))\frac{d\mathcal{W}(\mathfrak{t})}{d\mathfrak{t}}, \\ \mathcal{I}_{0^+}^{(1-\mathfrak{q})(1-\mathfrak{a}),\phi}\mathfrak{f}(0) = \mathfrak{c}. \end{cases} \tag{4}$$

where $\mathfrak{s} \in (0,1)$, ϕ is an increasing function, and ${}^{H}\mathcal{T}_{\mathfrak{t}}^{\mathfrak{q},\mathfrak{a},\phi}$ represents the ϕ-HFrD with $\mathfrak{q} \in \left(\frac{1}{2},1\right)$ and $0 \leq \mathfrak{a} \leq 1$, the functions $\mathcal{D}: [0,\mathfrak{g}] \times \mathfrak{R}^{\varkappa} \times \mathfrak{R}^{\varkappa} \to \mathfrak{R}^{\varkappa}$ and $\Xi: [0,\mathfrak{g}] \times \mathfrak{R}^{\varkappa} \times \mathfrak{R}^{\varkappa} \to \mathfrak{R}^{\varkappa\times\mathfrak{b}}$ are measurable continuous mappings.

This research includes several essential components: In the following section, we outline the fundamental concepts and assumptions. Subsequently, we discuss the well-posedness and regularity of solutions and the AP results for SPFrDEs concerning ϕ-HFrD in Sections 3 and 4, respectively. The next four examples, along with the graphical results, are presented. Finally, our conclusions are summarized in Section 6.

2. Preliminaries

We now outline the definitions and assumptions that underpin the findings of this research study.

Lemma 1 ([41]). *Let $f_1(t) \in \mathcal{L}^p$ and $f_2(t) \in \mathcal{L}^q$. Then, Hölder's inequality is defined as follows:*

$$\| f_1 f_2 \|_1 \leq \| f_1 \|_p \| f_2 \|_q,$$

where $\frac{1}{p} + \frac{1}{q} = 1$.

Lemma 2 ([42]). *Assume that there are real numbers $\beta_1, \beta_2, \beta_3, \cdots, \beta_n (n \in N)$ with $\beta_\iota \geq 0$, $(\iota = 1, 2, 3, \cdots n)$. Then, Jensen's inequality is as follows:*

$$\left(\sum_{\iota=1}^{n} \beta_\iota \right)^p \leq n^{p-1} \sum_{\iota=1}^{n} \beta_\iota^p, \ \forall p > 1.$$

where $\frac{1}{p} + \frac{1}{q} = 1$.

Definition 1 ([43]). *Let $\mathbb{G} : \mathbb{X} \to \mathbb{R}$ be a measurable function on a measure space $(\mathbb{X}, \Sigma, \mathbb{U})$. The essential supremum of $\mathbb{G}$, denoted as is the smallest real number $\mathbb{Q}$, such that $\mathbb{G}(\tau) \leq \mathbb{Q}$ almost everywhere, meaning:*

$$\mathbb{U}(\{\tau \in \mathbb{X} \setminus \mathbb{G}(\tau) > \mathbb{Q}\}) = 0.$$

A measurable procedure $f(t) : [0, \mathfrak{g}] \to \mathcal{L}^p(\Omega, F, p)$ is an $\mathbb{F}-$adapted process when $f(t) \in \mathcal{Z}_t^p$ with $t \geq 0$. The integral form of (4) is as follows:

$$\begin{aligned} f(t) &= c\frac{(\phi(t)-\phi(0))^{(1-q)(1-a)}}{\Gamma(a(1-q)+a)} + \frac{1}{\Gamma(q)} \int_0^t (\phi(t) - \phi(\varpi))^{q-1} \phi'(\varpi) \mathcal{D}(\varpi, f(\varpi), f(s\varpi)) d\varpi \\ &+ \frac{1}{\Gamma(q)} \int_0^t (\phi(t) - \phi(\varpi))^{q-1} \phi'(\varpi) \Xi(\varpi, f(\varpi), f(s\varpi)) d\mathcal{W}(\varpi). \end{aligned} \quad (5)$$

For $\mathfrak{M}$ and $\mathfrak{B}$, we assume the following Lipschitz conditions, which are a fundamental criterion for proving the EU of solutions to differential equations.

1. $(\xi_1) \forall \mathfrak{A}_1, \mathfrak{A}_2, \nu_1, \nu_2 \in \mathfrak{R}^\varkappa$ there are $\mathfrak{T}_1 > 0$ and $\mathfrak{T}_2 > 0$, such as

$$\| \mathcal{D}(t, \mathfrak{A}_1, \mathfrak{A}_2) - \mathcal{D}(t, \nu_1, \nu_2) \|_p \leq \mathfrak{T}_1 \Big(\| \mathfrak{A}_1 - \nu_1 \|_p + \| \mathfrak{A}_2 - \nu_2 \|_p \Big).$$

$$\| \Xi(t, \mathfrak{A}_1, \mathfrak{A}_2) - \Xi(t, \nu_1, \nu_2) \|_p \leq \mathfrak{T}_2 \Big(\| \mathfrak{A}_1 - \nu_1 \|_p + \| \mathfrak{A}_2 - \nu_2 \|_p \Big).$$

2. (ξ_2) The $\mathcal{D}(t, 0, 0)$ and $\Xi(t, 0, 0)$ are essential bounded, so

$$\underset{t \in [0,\mathfrak{g}]}{esssup} \| \mathcal{D}(t, 0, 0) \|_p < \gamma, \ \underset{t \in [0,\mathfrak{g}]}{esssup} \| \Xi(t, 0, 0) \|_p < \gamma. \quad (6)$$

Now, assume the following:

1. $(\xi_3) : \forall \mathfrak{A}_1, \mathfrak{A}_2, \nu_1, \nu_2 \in \mathfrak{R}^\varkappa$, $t \in [0, \mathfrak{g}]$ there is a $\mathfrak{T}_3 > 0$, such that:

$$\begin{aligned} \| \mathcal{D}(t, \mathfrak{A}_1, \mathfrak{A}_2) - & \ \mathcal{D}(t, \nu_1, \nu_2) \| \vee \| \Xi(t, \mathfrak{A}_1, \mathfrak{A}_2) - \Xi(t, \nu_1, \nu_2) \| \\ & \leq \mathfrak{T}_3 (\| \mathfrak{A}_1 - \nu_1 \| + \| \mathfrak{A}_2 - \nu_2 \|). \end{aligned}$$

2. (ξ_4) : For $\forall \mathfrak{A}, \nu \in \mathfrak{R}^\varkappa$, $t \in [0, \mathfrak{g}]$, there is $\mathfrak{T}_4 > 0$, such as satisfy the following:

$$\| \mathcal{D}(t, \mathfrak{A}, \nu) \| \vee \| \Xi(t, \mathfrak{A}, \nu) \| \leq \mathfrak{T}_4 (1 + \| \mathfrak{A} \| + \| \nu \|).$$

3. (ξ_5) : For $\mathfrak{g}_1 \in [0,\mathfrak{g}]$, $t \in [0,\mathfrak{g}]$, and $p \geq 2$, we have

$$\frac{1}{\mathfrak{g}_1}\int_0^{\mathfrak{g}_1} \| \mathcal{D}(t,\mathfrak{A},\nu)-\widetilde{\mathcal{D}}(t,\mathfrak{A},\nu) \|^p dt \leq \mathbb{D}_1(\mathfrak{g}_1)(1+\| \mathfrak{A} \|^p + \| \nu \|^p),$$

$$\frac{1}{\mathfrak{g}_1}\int_0^{\mathfrak{g}_1} \| \Xi(t,\mathfrak{A},\nu)-\widetilde{\Xi}(t,\mathfrak{A},\nu) \|^p dt \leq \mathbb{D}_2(\mathfrak{g}_1)(1+\| \mathfrak{A} \|^p + \| \nu \|^p),$$

where $\lim_{\mathfrak{g}_1\to\infty} \mathbb{D}_1(\mathfrak{g}_1) = 0$, $\lim_{\mathfrak{g}_1\to\infty} \mathbb{D}_2(\mathfrak{g}_1) = 0$ and $\mathbb{D}_1(\mathfrak{g}_1)$, $\mathbb{D}_2(\mathfrak{g}_1)$ are positively bounded functions.

3. Significant Outcomes

We prove the well-posedness and regularity for the solution of SPFrDEs in this section.

3.1. Well-Posedness

In this sub-section, we prove EU for the solution of SPFrDEs by using the contraction mapping principle, and then we prove that the solution depends continuously on the fractional and initial values. Assume that $\mathcal{H}^p(0,\mathfrak{g})$ is the space of the $\mathbb{F}_\mathfrak{g}-$adapted process, where $\mathbb{F}_\mathfrak{g} = (F_t)_{t\in[0,\mathfrak{g}]}$, and we have

$$\| f \|_{\mathcal{H}^p} = \underset{t\in[0,\mathfrak{g}]}{esssup} \| f(t) \|_p < \infty.$$

Clearly, $(\mathcal{H}^p(0,\mathfrak{g}), \| \cdot \|_{\mathcal{H}^p})$ is a Banach space. Let $\psi_c : \mathcal{H}^p(0,\mathfrak{g}) \to \mathcal{H}^p(0,\mathfrak{g})$ with $\psi_c(f(0)) = c$ and

$$\begin{aligned}\psi_c(f(t)) &= c\frac{(\phi(t)-\phi(0))^{(1-q)(1-a)}}{\Gamma(a(1-q)+a)} \\ &+\frac{1}{\Gamma(q)}\int_0^t (\phi(t)-\phi(\varpi))^{q-1}\phi'(\varpi)\mathcal{D}(\varpi,f(\varpi),f(s\varpi))d\varpi \\ &+\frac{1}{\Gamma(q)}\int_0^t (\phi(t)-\phi(\varpi))^{q-1}\phi'(\varpi)\Xi(\varpi,f(\varpi),f(s\varpi))d\mathcal{W}(\varpi).\end{aligned} \tag{7}$$

The following lemma is very important in order to prove various results.

$$\| f_1 + f_2 \|_p^p \leq 2^{p-1}\Big(\| f_1 \|_p^p + (\| f_2 \|_p^p)\Big), \ \forall f_1, f_2 \in \mathfrak{R}^{\varkappa}. \tag{8}$$

Lemma 3. *Let ξ_1 and ξ_2 hold. Then, ψ_c is well-defined.*

Proof. Suppose $f(t) \in \mathcal{H}^p[0,\mathfrak{g}]$ and $\forall t \in [0,\mathfrak{g}]$. From (7) and (8), we have

$$\begin{aligned}\| \psi_c(f(t)) \|_p^p \leq & 2^{p-1} \| c\frac{(\phi(t)-\phi(0))^{(1-q)(1-a)}}{\Gamma(a(1-q)+a)} \|_p^p \\ &+ \frac{2^{2p-2}}{(\Gamma(q))^p} \| \int_0^t (\phi(t)-\phi(\varpi))^{q-1}\mathcal{D}(\varpi,f(\varpi),f(s\varpi))\phi'(\varpi)d\varpi \|_p^p \\ &+ \frac{2^{2p-2}}{(\Gamma(q))^p} \| \int_0^t (\phi(t)-\phi(\varpi))^{q-1}\Xi(\varpi,f(\varpi),f(s\varpi))\phi'(\varpi)d\mathcal{W}(\varpi) \|_p^p .\end{aligned} \tag{9}$$

By Hölder's inequality (HI) we have

$$
\begin{aligned}
&\| \int_0^t (\phi(t)-\phi(\varpi))^{q-1}\mathcal{D}(\varpi,f(\varpi),f(s\varpi))\phi'(\varpi)d\varpi \|_p^p = \\
&\sum_{\iota=1}^m \mathbf{E}\Big(\int_0^t (\phi(t)-\phi(\varpi))^{q-1}\Big|\mathcal{D}_\iota(\varpi,f(\varpi),f(s\varpi))\Big|\phi'(\varpi)d\varpi\Big)^p \\
&\le \sum_{\iota=1}^m \mathbf{E}\Bigg(\Big(\int_0^t (\phi(t)-\phi(\varpi))^{\frac{(q-1)p}{(p-1)}}(\phi'(\varpi))^{\frac{p}{p-1}}d\varpi\Big)^{p-1}\int_0^t\Big|\mathcal{D}_\iota(\varpi,f(\varpi),f(s\varpi))\Big|_p d\varpi\Bigg) \\
&\le \sum_{\iota=1}^m \mathbf{E}\Bigg(\Big(\sup_{0<\varpi\le t}(\phi'(\varpi))^{\frac{1}{p-1}}\Big)^{p-1}\Big(\int_0^t (\phi(t)-\phi(\varpi))^{\frac{(q-1)p}{(p-1)}}\phi'(\varpi)d\varpi\Big)^{p-1} \\
&\int_0^t\Big|\mathcal{D}_\iota(\varpi,f(\varpi),f(s\varpi))\Big|_p d\varpi\Bigg) \\
&\le \Im^{p-1}\Big((\phi(\varpi)-\phi(0))^{\frac{qp-1}{p-1}}\Big)^{p-1}\Big(\frac{p-1}{qp-1}\Big)^{p-1}\int_0^t \| \mathcal{D}(\varpi,f(\varpi),f(s\varpi)) \|_p^p d\varpi.
\end{aligned} \tag{10}
$$

where $\Im = \sup_{0<\varpi\le t}(\phi'(\varpi))^{\frac{1}{p-1}}$.

The detailed methodology used to simplify (10) is outlined in Appendix A.1. So, from (10), we have

$$
\begin{aligned}
&\| \int_0^t (\phi(t)-\phi(\varpi))^{q-1}\mathcal{D}(\varpi,f(\varpi),f(s\varpi))\phi'(\varpi)d\varpi \|_p^p \le \Im^{p-1} \\
&\Big((\phi(\varpi)-\phi(0))^{\frac{(qp-1)}{p-1}}\Big)^{p-1}\Big(\frac{p-1}{qp-1}\Big)^{p-1}2^{p-1}(\mathfrak{T}_1^p\mathfrak{g}(\| f(\varpi) \|_{\mathcal{H}^p}^p + \| f(s\varpi) \|_{\mathcal{H}^p}^p) + \mathfrak{g}\gamma^p).
\end{aligned} \tag{11}
$$

By the Burkholder–Davis–Gundy inequality (BDGI) and HI, we obtain

$$
\begin{aligned}
&\| \int_0^t (\phi(t)-\phi(\varpi))^{q-1}\Xi(\varpi,f(\varpi),f(s\varpi))\phi'(\varpi)d\mathcal{W}(\varpi) \|_p^p \\
&= \sum_{\iota=1}^m \mathbf{E}\Big|\int_0^t (\phi(t)-\phi(\varpi))^{q-1}(\Xi_\iota(\varpi,f(\varpi),f(s\varpi))\phi'(\varpi)d\mathcal{W}(\varpi)\Big|^p \\
&\le \sum_{\iota=1}^m \mathcal{C}_p\mathbf{E}\Big|\int_0^t (\phi(t)-\phi(\varpi))^{2q-2}\Big|\Xi_\iota(\varpi,f(\varpi),f(s\varpi))\Big|_2(\phi'(\varpi))^2 d\varpi\Big|^{\frac{p}{2}} \\
&\le \sum_{\iota=1}^m \mathcal{C}_p\mathbf{E}\int_0^t (\phi(t)-\phi(\varpi))^{2q-2}\Big|\Xi_\iota(\varpi,f(\varpi),f(s\varpi))\Big|_p(\phi'(\varpi))^2 d\varpi \\
&\Big(\int_0^t (\phi(t)-\phi(\varpi))^{2q-2}(\phi'(\varpi))^2 d\varpi\Big)^{\frac{p-2}{2}} \\
&\le \sum_{\iota=1}^m \mathcal{C}_p\mathbf{E}\int_0^t (\phi(t)-\phi(\varpi))^{2q-2}\Big|\Xi_\iota(\varpi,f(\varpi),f(s\varpi))\Big|_p(\phi'(\varpi))^2 d\varpi \\
&\Big(\sup_{0<\varpi\le t}\phi'(\varpi)\int_0^t (\phi(t)-\phi(\varpi))^{2q-2}\phi'(\varpi)d\varpi\Big)^{\frac{p-2}{2}} \\
&\le \mathbf{G}^{\frac{p-2}{2}}\mathcal{C}_p\Big(\frac{(\phi(t)-\phi(0))^{2q-1}}{2q-1}\Big)^{\frac{p-2}{2}} \\
&\int_0^t (\phi(t)-\phi(\varpi))^{2q-2} \| \Xi(\varpi,f(\varpi,f(s\varpi)) \|_p^p (\phi'(t))^2 d\varpi,
\end{aligned} \tag{12}
$$

where $\mathbf{G} = \sup_{0<\varpi\le t}\phi'(\varpi)$ and $\mathcal{C}_p = \Big(\frac{p^{p+1}}{2(p-1)^{p-1}}\Big)^{\frac{p}{2}}$.

The detailed methodology used to simplify (12) is outlined in Appendix A.2. Thus, from (12), we obtain

$$
\begin{aligned}
&\int_0^t (\phi(t)-\phi(\varpi))^{2q-2} \quad \| \Xi(\varpi,f(\varpi),f(s\varpi)) \|_p^p (\phi'(\varpi))^2 d\varpi \le \frac{2^{p-1}(\phi(\varpi)-\phi(0))^{(2q-1)}}{(2q-1)}\mathbf{G} \\
&\Big(\mathfrak{T}_2^p\Big(\| f(\varpi) \|_{\mathcal{H}_p}^p + \| f(s\varpi) \|_{\mathcal{H}_p}^p\Big) + \gamma^p\Big).
\end{aligned} \tag{13}
$$

Using (13) in (12), we obtain

$$\begin{aligned} &\| \int_0^t (\phi(t)-\phi(\varpi))^{q-1} \Xi(\varpi, f(\varpi), f(s\varpi))\phi'(\varpi) d\mathcal{W}(\varpi) \|_p^p \leq \mathbf{G}^{\frac{p-2}{2}} \\ &\mathcal{C}_p \left(\frac{(\phi(\varpi)-\phi(0))^{(2q-1)}}{(2q-1)} \right)^{\frac{p-2}{2}} \frac{2^{p-1}(\phi(\varpi)-\phi(0))^{(2q-1)}}{(2q-1)} \\ &\mathbf{G}\left(\mathfrak{T}_2^p \left(\| f(\varpi) \|_{\mathcal{H}_p}^p + \| f(s\varpi) \|_{\mathcal{H}_p}^p \right) + \gamma^p \right). \end{aligned} \tag{14}$$

Hence $\| \psi(f(t)) \|_{\mathcal{H}p} < \infty$. So, ψ_c is well-defined. □

The following lemma is important for EU.

Lemma 4. *Assume* $q, Y > 0$, *and* $\forall t \in [0, g]$, *then*

$$\mathbb{I}_{0^+}^{q,\phi} \exp(Y(\phi(\varpi)-\phi(0))) \leq \frac{\exp(Y(\phi(\varpi)-\phi(0)))}{Y^q}.$$

Proof. From (1), we obtain:

$$\mathbb{I}_{0^+}^{q,\phi} \exp(Y(\phi(\varpi)-\phi(0))) = \frac{1}{\Gamma(q)} \int_0^t (\phi(t)-\phi(\varpi))^{q-1} \exp(Y(\phi(\varpi)-\phi(0)))\phi'(\varpi) d\varpi.$$

By $\mathbb{K} = \phi(t) - \phi(\varpi)$,

$$\mathbb{I}_{0^+}^{q,\phi} \exp(Y(\phi(\varpi)-\phi(0))) = \frac{(Y(\phi(\varpi)-\phi(0)))}{\Gamma(q)} \int_0^{\phi(t)-\phi(0)} \mathbb{K}^{q-1} \exp(-Y\mathbb{K}) d\mathbb{K}. \tag{15}$$

Apply $\mathcal{V} = Y\mathbb{K}$ in (15),

$$\begin{aligned} \mathbb{I}_{0^+}^{q,\phi} \exp(Y(\phi(\varpi)-\phi(0))) &= \frac{\exp(Y(\phi(\varpi)-\phi(0)))}{Y^q \Gamma(q)} \int_0^{Y(\phi(\varpi)-\phi(0))} \mathcal{V}^{q-1} \exp(-\mathcal{V}) d\mathcal{V} \\ &\leq \frac{\exp(Y(\phi(\varpi)-\phi(0)))}{Y^q \Gamma(q)} \int_0^{\infty} \mathcal{V}^{q-1} \exp(-\mathcal{V}) d\mathcal{V} \\ &= \frac{\exp(Y(\phi(\varpi)-\phi(0)))}{Y^q}. \end{aligned}$$

Thus, we have

$$\frac{1}{\Gamma(q)} \int_0^t (\phi(t)-\phi(\varpi))^{q-1} \exp(Y(\phi(\varpi)-\phi(0))) d\varpi \leq \frac{\exp(Y(\phi(\varpi)-\phi(0)))}{Y^q}. \tag{16}$$

□

Now, the EU of solution is demonstrated by proving that the operator ψ_c is contractive with respect to an appropriate weighted norm.

Theorem 1. *Suppose* (ξ_1) *and* (ξ_2) *hold; then, system (4) has a unique solution.*

Proof. Taking Y as

$$Y^{2q-1} > 2\mathbb{Z}\Gamma(2q-1), \tag{17}$$

where

$$\begin{aligned} \mathbb{Z} &= \frac{2^{p-1}}{(\Gamma(q))^p} \left(\digamma^{p-1} \frac{\mathfrak{T}_1^p (\phi(\varpi)-\phi(0))^{(pq-2q+1)} (p-1)^{p-1}}{(pq-2q+1)^{p-1}} \mathbf{G} + \right. \\ &\left. \mathbf{G}^{\frac{p-2}{2}} \left(\frac{(\phi(\varpi)-\phi(0))^{(2q-1)}}{(2q-1)} \right)^{\frac{p-2}{2}} \mathfrak{T}_2^p \mathcal{C}_p \mathbf{G} \right). \end{aligned} \tag{18}$$

The $\|\cdot\|_{\Upsilon}$ is

$$\| f(t) \|_{\Upsilon} = \underset{t\in[0,g]}{esssup}\left(\frac{\| f(t) \|_{p}^{p}}{\exp(\Upsilon(\phi(\varpi)-\phi(0)))}\right)^{\frac{1}{p}},\ \forall f(t)\in\mathcal{H}^{p}([0,g]). \tag{19}$$

As the norms $\|\cdot\|_{\mathcal{H}^p}$ and $\|\cdot\|_{\Upsilon}$ are equivalent. So, $(\mathcal{H}^p(0,g),\|\cdot\|_{\Upsilon})$ is also a Banach space.

For $f(t)$ and $\tilde{f}(t)$, we obtain

$$\begin{aligned}\| \psi_c(f(t)) &-\psi_c\left(\tilde{f}(t)\right) \|_p^p \leq \\ &\frac{2^{p-1}}{(\Gamma(q))^p} \| \int_0^t(\phi(t)-\phi(\varpi))^{q-1}\left(\mathcal{D}(\varpi,f(\varpi),f(s\varpi))-\mathcal{D}\left(\varpi,\tilde{f}(\varpi),\tilde{f}(s\varpi)\right)\right)\phi'(\varpi)d\varpi \|_p^p + \\ &\frac{2^{p-1}}{(\Gamma(q))^p} \| \int_0^t(\phi(t)-\phi(\varpi))^{q-1}\left(\Xi(\varpi,f(\varpi),f(s\varpi))-\Xi\left(\varpi,\tilde{f}(\varpi),\tilde{f}(s\varpi)\right)\right)\phi'(\varpi)d\mathcal{W}(\varpi) \|_p^p .\end{aligned} \tag{20}$$

Using the HI and (ξ_1), we obtain

$$\begin{aligned}&\| \int_0^t(\phi(t)-\phi(\varpi))^{q-1}\left(\mathcal{D}(\varpi,f(\varpi),f(s\varpi))-\mathcal{D}\left(\varpi,\tilde{f}(\varpi),\tilde{f}(s\varpi)\right)\right)\phi'(\varpi)d\varpi \|_p^p \\ =\ & \sum_{\iota=1}^m \mathbf{E}\left(\int_0^t(\phi(t)-\phi(\varpi))^{q-1}\left(\mathcal{D}_\iota(\varpi,f(\varpi),f(s\varpi))-\mathcal{D}_\iota\left(\varpi,\tilde{f}(\varpi),\tilde{f}(s\varpi)\right)\right)\phi'(\varpi)d\varpi\right)^p \\ \leq\ & \sum_{\iota=1}^m \mathbf{E}\left(\left(\int_0^t(\phi(t)-\phi(\varpi))^{\frac{(q-1)(p-2)}{p-1}}(\phi'(\varpi))^{\frac{p-2}{p-1}}d\varpi\right)^{p-1}\right. \\ &\left.\left(\int_0^t(\phi(t)-\phi(\varpi))^{2q-2}\left|\mathcal{D}_\iota(\varpi,f(\varpi),f(s\varpi))-\mathcal{D}_\iota\left(\varpi,\tilde{f}(\varpi),\tilde{f}(s\varpi)\right)\right|\phi'(\varpi)d\varpi\right)\right) \\ \leq\ & \sum_{\iota=1}^m \mathbf{E}\left(\left(\sup_{0<\varpi\leq t}(\phi'(\varpi))^{\frac{1}{1-p}}\int_0^t(\phi(t)-\phi(\varpi))^{\frac{(q-1)(p-2)}{p-1}}\phi'(\varpi)d\varpi\right)^{p-1}\right. \\ &\left.\left(\int_0^t(\phi(t)-\phi(\varpi))^{2q-2}\left|\mathcal{D}_\iota(\varpi,f(\varpi),f(s\varpi))-\mathcal{D}_\iota\left(\varpi,\tilde{f}(\varpi),\tilde{f}(s\varpi)\right)\right|(\phi'(\varpi))^2d\varpi\right)\right) \\ \leq\ & \digamma^{p-1}\frac{\mathfrak{T}_1^p(\phi(\varpi)-\phi(0))^{(pq-2q+1)}(p-1)^{p-1}}{(pq-2q+1)^{p-1}} \\ &\sup_{0<\varpi\leq t}\phi'(\varpi)\int_0^t(\phi(t)-\phi(\varpi))^{2q-2}\left(\| f(\varpi)-\tilde{f}(\varpi)) \|_p^p+\| f(s\varpi)-\tilde{f}(s\varpi)\right) \|_p^p\Big)\phi'(\varpi)d\varpi.\end{aligned} \tag{21}$$

where $\digamma = \sup_{0<\varpi\leq t}(\phi'(\varpi))^{\frac{1}{1-p}}$.

Hence, we have

$$\begin{aligned}&\| \int_0^t(\phi(t)-\phi(\varpi))^{q-1}\left(\mathcal{D}(\varpi,f(\varpi),f(s\varpi))-\mathcal{D}\left(\varpi,\tilde{f}(\varpi),\tilde{f}(s\varpi)\right)\right)\phi'(\varpi)d\varpi \|_p^p \\ \leq\ & \mathbf{G}\digamma^{p-1}\frac{\mathfrak{T}_1^p(\phi(\varpi)-\phi(0))^{(pq-2q+1)}(p-1)^{p-1}}{(pq-2q+1)^{p-1}} \\ &\int_0^t(\phi(t)-\phi(\varpi))^{2q-2}\left(\| f(\varpi)-\tilde{f}(\varpi)) \|_p^p+\| f(s\varpi)-\tilde{f}(s\varpi)\right) \|_p^p\Big)\phi'(\varpi)d\varpi.\end{aligned} \tag{22}$$

Now, using (ξ_1) and the BDGI, we have

$$
\begin{aligned}
& \| \int_0^t (\phi(t)-\phi(\varpi))^{q-1}\Big(\Xi(\varpi,f(\varpi),f(s\varpi)) - \Xi\Big(\varpi,\widetilde{f}(\varpi),\widetilde{f}(s\varpi)\Big)\Big)\phi'(\varpi)d\mathcal{W}(\varpi) \|_p^p \\
= & \sum_{\imath=1}^m \mathbf{E}\Big|\int_0^t (\phi(t)-\phi(\varpi))^{q-1}\Big(\Xi_\imath(\varpi,f(\varpi),f(s\varpi)) - \Xi_\imath\Big(\varpi,\widetilde{f}(\varpi),\widetilde{f}(s\varpi)\Big)\Big)\phi'(\varpi)d\mathcal{W}(\varpi)\Big|^p \\
\leq & \sum_{\imath=1}^m \mathcal{C}_p\mathbf{E}\Big|\int_0^t (\phi(t)-\phi(\varpi))^{2q-2}\Big|\Xi_\imath(\varpi,f(\varpi),f(s\varpi)) - \Xi_\imath\Big(\varpi,\widetilde{f}(\varpi),\widetilde{f}(s\varpi)\Big)\Big|_2(\phi'(\varpi))^2 d\varpi\Big|^{\frac{p}{2}} \\
\leq & \sum_{\imath=1}^m \mathcal{C}_p\mathbf{E}\int_0^t (\phi(t)-\phi(\varpi))^{2q-2}\Big|\Xi_\imath(\varpi,f(\varpi),f(s\varpi)) - \Xi_\imath\Big(\varpi,\widetilde{f}(\varpi),\widetilde{f}(s\varpi)\Big)\Big|_p(\phi'(\varpi))^2 d\varpi \\
& \left(\int_0^t (\phi(t)-\phi(\varpi))^{2q-2}(\phi'(\varpi))^2 d\varpi\right)^{\frac{p-2}{2}} \\
\leq & \sum_{\imath=1}^m \mathcal{C}_p\mathbf{E}\int_0^t (\phi(t)-\phi(\varpi))^{2q-2}\Big|\Xi_\imath(\varpi,f(\varpi),f(s\varpi)) - \Xi_\imath\Big(\varpi,\widetilde{f}(\varpi),\widetilde{f}(s\varpi)\Big)\Big|_p(\phi'(\varpi))^2 d\varpi \\
& \left(\sup_{0<\varpi\leq t}(\phi'(\varpi))\int_0^t (\phi(t)-\phi(\varpi))^{2q-2}\phi'(\varpi)d\varpi\right)^{\frac{p-2}{2}} \\
\leq & \mathbf{G}^{\frac{p-2}{2}}\left(\frac{(\phi(\varpi)-\phi(0))^{(2q-1)}}{(2q-1)}\right)^{\frac{p-2}{2}} \mathfrak{T}_2^p\mathcal{C}_p\int_0^t (\phi(t)-\phi(\varpi))^{2q-2}\Big(\| f(\varpi)-\widetilde{f}(\varpi)\|_p^p + \| f(s\varpi)-\widetilde{f}(s\varpi)\|_p^p\Big) \\
& (\phi'(\varpi))^2 d\varpi. \\
\leq & \mathbf{G}^{\frac{p-2}{2}}\left(\frac{(\phi(\varpi)-\phi(0))^{(2q-1)}}{(2q-1)}\right)^{\frac{p-2}{2}} \mathfrak{T}_2^p\mathcal{C}_p\sup_{0<\varpi\leq t}\phi'(\varpi)\int_0^t (\phi(t)-\phi(\varpi))^{2q-2} \\
& \Big(\| f(\varpi)-\widetilde{f}(\varpi)\|_p^p + \| f(s\varpi)-\widetilde{f}(s\varpi)\|_p^p\Big)\phi'(\varpi)d\varpi.
\end{aligned}
$$

From the above, we have

$$
\begin{aligned}
& \| \int_0^t (\phi(t)-\phi(\varpi))^{q-1}\Big(\Xi(\varpi,f(\varpi),f(s\varpi)) - \Xi\Big(\varpi,\widetilde{f}(\varpi),\widetilde{f}(s\varpi)\Big)\Big)\phi'(\varpi)d\mathcal{W}(\varpi) \|_p^p \\
\leq & \mathbf{G}^{\frac{p-2}{2}}\left(\frac{(\phi(\varpi)-\phi(0))^{(2q-1)}}{(2q-1)}\right)^{\frac{p-2}{2}} \mathfrak{T}_2^p\mathcal{C}_p\mathbf{G}\int_0^t (\phi(t)-\phi(\varpi))^{2q-2}\Big(\| f(\varpi)-\widetilde{f}(\varpi)\|_p^p + \| f(s\varpi)-\widetilde{f}(s\varpi)\|_p^p\Big) \\
& \phi'(\varpi)d\varpi.
\end{aligned} \tag{23}
$$

Thus, $\forall t \in [0,\mathfrak{g}]$, we have

$$
\| \psi_c(f(t)) - \psi_c\Big(\widetilde{f}(t)\Big)\|_p^p \leq \mathbb{Z}\int_0^t\Big(\| f(\varpi)-\widetilde{f}(\varpi)\|_p^p + \| f(s\varpi)-\widetilde{f}(s\varpi)\|_p^p\Big)(\phi(t)-\phi(\varpi))^{2q-2}\phi'(\varpi)d\varpi, \tag{24}
$$

So,

$$
\begin{aligned}
& \frac{\|\psi_c f(t)-\psi_c\widetilde{f}(t)\|_p^p}{\exp(Y(\phi(\varpi)-\phi(0)))} \leq \frac{1}{\exp(Y(\phi(\varpi)-\phi(0)))}\mathbb{Z}\int_0^t(\phi(t)-\phi(\varpi))^{2q-2} \\
& \left(\exp(Y(\phi(\varpi)-\phi(0))))\frac{\|f(\varpi)-\widetilde{f}(\varpi)\|_p^p}{\exp(Y(\phi(\varpi)-\phi(0)))} + \exp(Ys(\phi(\varpi)-\phi(0)))\frac{\|f(s\varpi)-\widetilde{f}(s\varpi)\|_p^p}{\exp(Ys(\phi(\varpi)-\phi(0)))}\right) \\
& \phi'(\varpi)d\varpi \\
\leq & \frac{1}{\exp(Y(\phi(\varpi)-\phi(0)))}\mathbb{Z}\int_0^t(\phi(t)-\phi(\varpi))^{2q-2}\left(\exp(Y(\phi(\varpi)-\phi(0)))\operatorname*{esssup}_{\varpi\in[0,\mathfrak{g}]}\left(\frac{\|f(\varpi)-\widetilde{f}(\varpi)\|_p^p}{\exp(Y(\phi(\varpi)-\phi(0)))}\right)\right. \\
+ & \left.\exp(Ys(\phi(\varpi)-\phi(0)))\operatorname*{esssup}_{\varpi\in[0,\mathfrak{g}]}\left(\frac{\|f(s\varpi)-\widetilde{f}(s\varpi)\|_p^p}{\exp(Ys(\phi(\varpi)-\phi(0)))}\right)\right)\phi'(\varpi)d\varpi \\
\leq & \frac{\|f(\varpi)-\widetilde{f}(\varpi)\|_Y^p}{\exp(Y(\phi(\varpi)-\phi(0)))}\mathbb{Z}\int_0^t(\phi(t)-\phi(\varpi))^{2q-2}(\exp(Y(\phi(\varpi)-\phi(0)))+\exp(Ys(\phi(\varpi)-\phi(0)))) \\
& \phi'(\varpi)d\varpi \\
\leq & \frac{2\|f(\varpi)-\widetilde{f}(\varpi)\|_Y^p}{\exp(Y(\phi(\varpi)-\phi(0)))}\mathbb{Z}\int_0^t(\phi(t)-\phi(\varpi))^{2q-2}\exp(Y(\phi(\varpi)-\phi(0)))\phi'(\varpi)d\varpi.
\end{aligned} \tag{25}
$$

Now, replace q by $2q-1$ in (16).

$$
\frac{1}{\Gamma(2q-1)}\int_0^t(\phi(t)-\phi(\varpi))^{2q-2}\exp(Y(\phi(\varpi)-\phi(0)))\phi'(\varpi)d\varpi \leq \frac{\exp(Y(\phi(\varpi)-\phi(0)))}{Y^{2q-1}}.
$$

From above

$$
\int_0^t(\phi(t)-\phi(\varpi))^{2q-2}\exp(Y(\phi(\varpi)-\phi(0)))\phi'(\varpi)d\varpi \leq \frac{\Gamma(2q-1)\exp(Y(\phi(\varpi)-\phi(0)))}{Y^{2q-1}}.
$$

So,

$$\| \psi_{\mathfrak{c}}(\mathfrak{f}(\mathfrak{t})) - \psi_{\mathfrak{c}}\left(\tilde{\mathfrak{f}}(\mathfrak{t})\right) \|_{\Upsilon} \leq \left(\frac{2\mathbb{Z}\Gamma(2\mathfrak{q}-1)}{\Upsilon^{2\mathfrak{q}-1}}\right)^{\frac{1}{\mathfrak{p}}} \| \mathfrak{f}(\varpi) - \tilde{\mathfrak{f}}(\varpi) \|_{\Upsilon}. \tag{26}$$

From (17), we have $\frac{\mathbb{Z}\Gamma(2\mathfrak{q}-1)}{\Upsilon^{2\mathfrak{q}-1}} < 1$. □

Theorem 2. *Suppose ξ_1 and ξ_2 hold, then*

$$\lim_{\mathfrak{q}\to\tilde{\mathfrak{q}}} \underset{\mathfrak{t}\in[0,\mathfrak{g}]}{esssup} \| \mathcal{B}_{\mathfrak{q}}(\mathfrak{t},\mathfrak{c}) - \mathcal{B}_{\tilde{\mathfrak{q}}}(\mathfrak{t},\mathfrak{c}) \|_{\mathfrak{p}} = 0, \tag{27}$$

where $\mathcal{B}_{\mathfrak{q}}(\mathfrak{t},\mathfrak{c})$ is the solution.

Proof. Suppose $\mathfrak{q}, \tilde{\mathfrak{q}} \in \left(\frac{1}{2},1\right)$. We obtain the following:

$$\begin{aligned}
\mathcal{B}_{\mathfrak{q}}(\mathfrak{t},\mathfrak{c}) - \mathcal{B}_{\tilde{\mathfrak{q}}}(\mathfrak{c},\mathfrak{t}) &= \frac{1}{\Gamma(\mathfrak{q})}\int_0^{\mathfrak{t}} (\phi(\mathfrak{t})-\phi(\varpi))^{\mathfrak{q}-1}(\mathcal{D}(\varpi,\mathcal{B}_{\mathfrak{q}}(\varpi,\mathfrak{c})) - \mathcal{D}(\varpi,\mathcal{B}_{\tilde{\mathfrak{q}}}(\varpi,\mathfrak{c})))\phi'(\varpi)d\varpi \\
&+\int_0^{\mathfrak{t}}\left(\frac{(\phi(\mathfrak{t})-\phi(\varpi))^{\mathfrak{q}-1}}{\Gamma(\mathfrak{q})} - \frac{(\phi(\mathfrak{t})-\phi(\varpi))^{\tilde{\mathfrak{q}}-1}}{\Gamma(\tilde{\mathfrak{q}})}\right)\mathcal{D}(\varpi,\mathcal{B}_{\tilde{\mathfrak{q}}}(\varpi,\mathfrak{c}))\phi'(\varpi)d\varpi \\
&+\frac{1}{\Gamma(\mathfrak{q})}\int_0^{\mathfrak{t}} (\phi(\mathfrak{t})-\phi(\varpi))^{\mathfrak{q}-1}(\Xi(\varpi,\mathcal{B}_{\mathfrak{q}}(\varpi,\mathfrak{c})) - \Xi(\varpi,\mathcal{B}_{\tilde{\mathfrak{q}}}(\varpi,\mathfrak{c})))\phi'(\varpi)d\mathcal{W}(\varpi) \\
&+\int_0^{\mathfrak{t}}\left(\frac{(\phi(\mathfrak{t})-\phi(\varpi))^{\mathfrak{q}-1}}{\Gamma(\mathfrak{q})} - \frac{(\phi(\mathfrak{t})-\phi(\varpi))^{\tilde{\mathfrak{q}}-1}}{\Gamma(\tilde{\mathfrak{q}})}\right)\Xi(\varpi,\mathcal{B}_{\tilde{\mathfrak{q}}}(\varpi,\mathfrak{c}))\phi'(\varpi)d\mathcal{W}(\varpi).
\end{aligned} \tag{28}$$

We extract the subsequent outcome from (28) employing (8).

$$\begin{aligned}
\| \mathcal{B}_{\mathfrak{q}}(\mathfrak{t},\mathfrak{c}) - \mathcal{B}_{\tilde{\mathfrak{q}}}(\mathfrak{t},\mathfrak{c}) \|_{\mathfrak{p}}^{\mathfrak{p}} &\leq 2^{\mathfrak{p}-1}\mathbb{Z}\int_0^{\mathfrak{t}}(\phi(\mathfrak{t})-\phi(\varpi))^{2\mathfrak{q}-2} \| \mathcal{B}_{\mathfrak{q}}(\mathfrak{t},\mathfrak{c}) - \mathcal{B}_{\tilde{\mathfrak{q}}}(\mathfrak{c},\mathfrak{t}) \|_{\mathfrak{p}}^{\mathfrak{p}} d\varpi \\
&+2^{2\mathfrak{p}-2} \| \int_0^{\mathfrak{t}}\left(\frac{(\phi(\mathfrak{t})-\phi(\varpi))^{\mathfrak{q}-1}}{\Gamma(\mathfrak{q})} - \frac{(\phi(\mathfrak{t})-\phi(\varpi))^{\tilde{\mathfrak{q}}-1}}{\Gamma(\tilde{\mathfrak{q}})}\right)\mathcal{D}(\varpi,\mathcal{B}_{\tilde{\mathfrak{q}}}(\varpi,\mathfrak{c}))\phi'(\varpi)d\varpi \|_{\mathfrak{p}}^{\mathfrak{p}} \\
&+2^{2\mathfrak{p}-2} \| \int_0^{\mathfrak{t}}\left(\frac{(\phi(\mathfrak{t})-\phi(\varpi))^{\mathfrak{q}-1}}{\Gamma(\mathfrak{q})} - \frac{(\phi(\mathfrak{t})-\phi(\varpi))^{\tilde{\mathfrak{q}}-1}}{\Gamma(\tilde{\mathfrak{q}})}\right)\Xi(\varpi,\mathcal{B}_{\tilde{\mathfrak{q}}}(\varpi,\mathfrak{c}))\phi'(\varpi)d\mathcal{W}(\varpi) \|_{\mathfrak{p}}^{\mathfrak{p}}.
\end{aligned} \tag{29}$$

Assume

$$\mathcal{A}(\mathfrak{t},\varpi,\mathfrak{q},\tilde{\mathfrak{q}},\phi) = \left|\frac{(\phi(\mathfrak{t})-\phi(\varpi))^{\mathfrak{q}-1}}{\Gamma(\mathfrak{q})} - \frac{(\phi(\mathfrak{t})-\phi(\varpi))^{\tilde{\mathfrak{q}}-1}}{\Gamma(\tilde{\mathfrak{q}})}\right|\phi'(\varpi). \tag{30}$$

By HI, (ξ_1), (ξ_2), and (8), we have

$$\begin{aligned}
&\| \int_0^{\mathfrak{t}}\left(\frac{(\phi(\mathfrak{t})-\phi(\varpi))^{\mathfrak{q}-1}}{\Gamma(\mathfrak{q})} - \frac{(\phi(\mathfrak{t})-\phi(\varpi))^{\tilde{\mathfrak{q}}-1}}{\Gamma(\tilde{\mathfrak{q}})}\right)\mathcal{D}(\varpi,\mathcal{B}_{\tilde{\mathfrak{q}}}(\varpi,\mathfrak{c})\phi'(\varpi)d\varpi \|_{\mathfrak{p}}^{\mathfrak{p}} \\
&=\sum_{\iota=1}^{m}\mathbf{E}\left(\int_0^{\mathfrak{t}}\mathcal{A}(\mathfrak{t},\varpi,\mathfrak{q},\tilde{\mathfrak{q}},\phi)\left|\mathcal{D}_{\iota}(\varpi,\mathcal{B}_{\tilde{\mathfrak{q}}}(\varpi,\mathfrak{c}))\right|d\varpi\right)^{\mathfrak{p}} \\
&\leq\sum_{\iota=1}^{m}\mathbf{E}\left(\left(\int_0^{\mathfrak{t}}(\mathcal{A}(\mathfrak{t},\varpi,\mathfrak{q},\tilde{\mathfrak{q}},\phi))^{\frac{\mathfrak{p}}{\mathfrak{p}-1}}\right)^{\mathfrak{p}-1}\int_0^{\mathfrak{t}}|\mathcal{D}_{\iota}(\varpi,\mathcal{B}_{\tilde{\mathfrak{q}}}(\varpi,\mathfrak{c})|_{\mathfrak{p}}d\varpi\right) \\
&\leq\left(\int_0^{\mathfrak{t}}(\mathcal{A}(\mathfrak{t},\varpi,\mathfrak{q},\tilde{\mathfrak{q}},\phi))^2\right)^{\frac{\mathfrak{p}}{2}}\left(\int_0^{\mathfrak{t}}1d\varpi\right)^{\frac{\mathfrak{p}-2}{2}}\int_0^{\mathfrak{t}}\| \mathcal{D}(\varpi,\mathcal{B}_{\tilde{\mathfrak{q}}}(\varpi,\mathfrak{c}) \|_{\mathfrak{p}}^{\mathfrak{p}} d\varpi \\
&\leq\left(\int_0^{\mathfrak{t}}(\mathcal{A}(\mathfrak{t},\varpi,\mathfrak{q},\tilde{\mathfrak{q}},\phi))^2\right)^{\frac{\mathfrak{p}}{2}}\mathfrak{g}^{\frac{\mathfrak{p}-2}{2}}\int_0^{\mathfrak{t}}2^{\mathfrak{p}-1}\left(\mathfrak{T}_1^{\mathfrak{p}}\| \mathcal{B}_{\tilde{\mathfrak{q}}}(\varpi,\mathfrak{c}) \|_{\mathfrak{p}}^{\mathfrak{p}}) + \| \mathcal{D}(\varpi,0) \|_{\mathfrak{p}}^{\mathfrak{p}}\right) \\
&\leq\left(\int_0^{\mathfrak{t}}(\mathcal{A}(\mathfrak{t},\varpi,\mathfrak{q},\tilde{\mathfrak{q}},\phi))^2\right)^{\frac{\mathfrak{p}}{2}}\mathfrak{g}^{\frac{\mathfrak{p}}{2}}2^{\mathfrak{p}-1}\left(\mathfrak{T}_1^{\mathfrak{p}}\underset{\mathfrak{t}\in[0,\mathfrak{g}]}{esssup}\| \mathcal{B}_{\tilde{\mathfrak{q}}}(\varpi,\mathfrak{c}) \|_{\mathfrak{p}}^{\mathfrak{p}}) + \gamma^{\mathfrak{p}}\right).
\end{aligned} \tag{31}$$

Utilizing (30), (ξ_1), and (ξ_2) in (29).

$$
\begin{aligned}
&\| \int_0^t \left(\frac{(\phi(t)-\phi(\varpi))^{q-1}}{\Gamma(q)} - \frac{(\phi(t)-\phi(\varpi))^{\tilde{q}-1}}{\Gamma(\tilde{q})} \right) \Xi(\varpi, \mathcal{B}_{\tilde{q}}(\varpi,\mathfrak{c}))\phi'(\varpi) d\mathcal{W}(\varpi) \|_p^p \\
&= \sum_{\iota=1}^m \mathbf{E} \left| \int_0^t \mathcal{A}(t,\varpi,q,\tilde{q},\phi) \Xi_\iota(\varpi, \mathcal{B}_{\tilde{q}}(\varpi,\mathfrak{c})) d\mathcal{W}(\varpi) \right|^p \\
&\le \sum_{\iota=1}^m \mathcal{C}_p \mathbf{E} \left| \int_0^t \mathcal{A}(t,\varpi,q,\tilde{q},\phi)^2 \left| \Xi_\iota(\varpi, \mathcal{B}_{\tilde{q}}(\varpi,\mathfrak{c})) \right|_2 d\mathcal{W}(\varpi) \right|^{\frac{p}{2}} \\
&\le \sum_{\iota=1}^m \mathcal{C}_p \mathbf{E} \left[\left(\int_0^t \mathcal{A}(t,\varpi,q,\tilde{q},\phi)^2 \left| \Xi_\iota(\varpi, \mathcal{B}_{\tilde{q}}(\varpi,\mathfrak{c})) \right|_p d\varpi \right)^{\frac{2}{p}} \left(\int_0^t (\mathcal{A}(t,\varpi,q,\tilde{q},\phi))^2 d\varpi \right)^{\frac{p-2}{p}} \right]^{\frac{p}{2}} \\
&= \mathcal{C}_p \int_0^t \mathcal{A}(t,\varpi,q,\tilde{q},\phi)^2 \| \Xi(\varpi, \mathcal{B}_{\tilde{q}}(\varpi,\mathfrak{c})) \|_p^p \, d\varpi \left(\int_0^t (\mathcal{A}(t,\varpi,q,\tilde{q},\phi))^2 d\varpi \right)^{\frac{p-2}{p}} \\
&\le \mathcal{C}_p \left(\int_0^t \mathcal{A}(t,\varpi,q,\tilde{q},\phi)^2 d\varpi \right)^{\frac{p}{2}} 2^{p-1} \left(\mathfrak{T}_2^p \operatorname*{esssup}_{t\in[0,\mathfrak{g}]} \| \mathcal{B}_{\tilde{q}}(\varpi,\mathfrak{c}) \|_p^p + \gamma^p \right).
\end{aligned} \tag{32}
$$

Thus, we obtain

$$
\begin{aligned}
&\frac{\| \mathcal{B}_q(t,\mathfrak{c}) - \mathcal{B}_{\tilde{q}}(t,\mathfrak{c}) \|_p^p}{\exp(Y(\phi(\varpi)-\phi(0)))} \\
&\le \frac{\mathbb{Z} 2^{p-1} \int_0^t (\phi(t)-\phi(\varpi))^{2q-2} \frac{\| \mathcal{B}_q(\varpi,\mathfrak{c}) - \mathcal{B}_{\tilde{q}}(\varpi,\mathfrak{c}) \|_p^p}{\exp(Y(\phi(\varpi)-\phi(0)))} \exp(Y(\phi(\varpi)-\phi(0)))}{\exp(Y(\phi(\varpi)-\phi(0)))} \\
&+ 2^{3p-3} \left(\mathfrak{T}_1^p \operatorname*{esssup}_{t\in[0,\mathfrak{g}]} \| \mathcal{B}_{\tilde{q}}(\varpi,\mathfrak{c}) \|_p^p + \gamma^p \right) \left(\int_0^t (\mathcal{A}(t,\varpi,q,\tilde{q},\phi))^2 d\varpi \right)^{\frac{p}{2}} \mathfrak{g}^{\frac{p}{2}} \\
&+ 2^{3p-3} \left(\mathfrak{T}_2^p \operatorname*{esssup}_{t\in[0,\mathfrak{g}]} \| \mathcal{B}_{\tilde{q}}(\varpi,\mathfrak{c}) \|_p^p + \gamma^p \right) \mathcal{C}_p \left(\int_0^t (\mathcal{A}(t,\varpi,q,\tilde{q},\phi))^2 d\varpi \right)^{\frac{p}{2}}
\end{aligned} \tag{33}
$$

$$
\begin{aligned}
&\le \frac{\mathbb{Z} 2^{p-1} \Gamma(2q-1)}{Y} \| \mathcal{B}_q(t,\mathfrak{c}) - \mathcal{B}_{\tilde{q}}(t,\mathfrak{c}) \|_Y^p \\
&+ 2^{3p-3} \left(\mathfrak{T}_1^p \operatorname*{esssup}_{t\in[0,\mathfrak{g}]} \| \mathcal{B}_{\tilde{q}}(\varpi,\mathfrak{c}) \|_p^p + \gamma^p \right) \left(\int_0^t (\mathcal{A}(t,\varpi,q,\tilde{q},\phi))^2 d\varpi \right)^{\frac{p}{2}} \mathfrak{g}^{\frac{p}{2}} \\
&+ 2^{3p-3} \left(\mathfrak{T}_2^p \operatorname*{esssup}_{t\in[0,\mathfrak{g}]} \| \mathcal{B}_{\tilde{q}}(\varpi,\mathfrak{c}) \|_p^p + \gamma^p \right) \mathcal{C}_p \left(\int_0^t (\mathcal{A}(t,\varpi,q,\tilde{q},\phi))^2 d\varpi \right)^{\frac{p}{2}}.
\end{aligned} \tag{34}
$$

So

$$
\begin{aligned}
&\left(1 - \frac{\mathbb{Z} 2^{p-1} \Gamma(2q-1)}{Y}\right) \| \mathcal{B}_q(t,\mathfrak{c}) - \mathcal{B}_{\tilde{q}}(t,\mathfrak{c}) \|_Y^p \le 2^{3p-3} \left(\mathfrak{T}_1^p \operatorname*{esssup}_{t\in[0,\mathfrak{g}]} \| \mathcal{B}_{\tilde{q}}(\varpi,\mathfrak{c}) \|_p^p + \gamma^p \right) \\
&\left(\int_0^t (\mathcal{A}(t,\varpi,q,\tilde{q},\phi))^2 d\varpi \right)^{\frac{p}{2}} \mathfrak{g}^{\frac{p}{2}} + 2^{3p-3} \left(\mathfrak{T}_2^p \operatorname*{esssup}_{t\in[0,\mathfrak{g}]} \| \mathcal{B}_{\tilde{q}}(\varpi,\mathfrak{c}) \|_p^p + \gamma^p \right) \\
&\mathcal{C}_p \left(\int_0^t (\mathcal{A}(t,\varpi,q,\tilde{q},\phi))^2 d\varpi \right)^{\frac{p}{2}}.
\end{aligned} \tag{35}
$$

Now we prove

$$
\lim_{\tilde{q}\to q} \sup_{t\in[0,\mathfrak{g}]} \int_0^t (\mathcal{A}(t,\varpi,q,\tilde{q},\phi))^2 d\varpi = 0.
$$

To see this note

$$\int_0^t (\mathcal{A}(t,\varpi,q,\tilde{q},\phi))^2 d\varpi = \int_0^t \frac{(\phi(t)-\phi(\varpi))^{2q-2}}{\Gamma^2(q)}(\phi'(\varpi))^2 d\varpi + \int_0^t \frac{(\phi(t)-\phi(\varpi))^{2\tilde{q}-2}}{\Gamma^2(\tilde{q})}(\phi'(\varpi))^2 d\varpi$$
$$-2\int_0^t \frac{(\phi(t)-\phi(\varpi))^{q+\tilde{q}-2}}{\Gamma(q)\Gamma(\tilde{q})}(\phi'(\varpi))^2 d\varpi$$
$$\leq \sup_{0<\varpi\leq t}\phi'(\varpi)\int_0^t \frac{(\phi(t)-\phi(\varpi))^{2q-2}}{\Gamma^2(q)}\phi'(\varpi)d\varpi + \sup_{0<\varpi\leq t}\phi'(\varpi)\int_0^t \frac{(\phi(t)-\phi(\varpi))^{2\tilde{q}-2}}{\Gamma^2(\tilde{q})}\phi'(\varpi)d\varpi \quad (36)$$
$$-2\sup_{0<\varpi\leq t}\phi'(\varpi)\int_0^t \frac{(\phi(t)-\phi(\varpi))^{q+\tilde{q}-2}}{\Gamma(q)\Gamma(\tilde{q})}\phi'(\varpi)d\varpi$$
$$=\mathbf{G}\left(\frac{(\phi(\varpi)-\phi(0))^{(2q-1)}}{(2q-1)}\right)\frac{1}{\Gamma^2(q)} + \mathbf{G}\left(\frac{(\phi(\varpi)-\phi(0))^{(2\tilde{q}-1)}}{(2\tilde{q}-1)}\right)\frac{1}{\Gamma^2(\tilde{q})} - \mathbf{G}\frac{2(\phi(\varpi)-\phi(0))^{(q+\tilde{q}-1)}}{(q+\tilde{q}-1)\Gamma(q)\Gamma(\tilde{q})}.$$

This therefore demonstrates the necessary outcome. □

Theorem 3. *For any* $\mathfrak{c}$, $\mathfrak{u}$, *we have*

$$\| \mathcal{B}_q(t,\mathfrak{c}) - \mathcal{B}_q(t,\mathfrak{u})|_p \leq \mathfrak{T}\| \mathfrak{c}-\mathfrak{u}\|_p, \ \forall\, t\in[0,\ \mathfrak{g}], \quad (37)$$

where $\mathcal{B}_q(t,\mathfrak{c})$ *is the solution.*

Proof. We have

$$\begin{aligned}\mathcal{B}_q(t,\mathfrak{c}) - \mathcal{B}_q(t,\mathfrak{u}) &= \mathfrak{c}\tfrac{(\phi(t)-\phi(0))^{(1-q)(1-a)}}{\Gamma(a(1-q)+a)} - \mathfrak{u}\tfrac{(\phi(t)-\phi(0))^{(1-q)(1-a)}}{\Gamma(a(1-q)+a)}\\ &+\tfrac{1}{\Gamma(q)}\int_0^t(\phi(t)-\phi(\varpi))^{q-1}(\mathcal{D}(\varpi,\mathcal{B}_q(\varpi,\mathfrak{c}))-\mathcal{D}(\varpi,\mathcal{B}_q(\varpi,\mathfrak{u})))\phi'(\varpi)d\varpi\\ &+\tfrac{1}{\Gamma(q)}\int_0^t(\phi(t)-\phi(\varpi))^{q-1}(\Xi(\varpi,\mathcal{B}_q(\varpi,\mathfrak{c}))-\Xi(\varpi,\mathcal{B}_q(\varpi,\mathfrak{u})))\phi'(\varpi)d\mathcal{W}(\varpi).\end{aligned} \quad (38)$$

Apply (8) and we have

$$\begin{aligned}\| \mathcal{B}_q(t,\ \mathfrak{c})-\mathcal{B}_q(t,\mathfrak{u})\|_p^p &\leq 2^{p-1}\| \mathfrak{c}\frac{(\phi(t)-\phi(0))^{(1-q)(1-a)}}{\Gamma(a(1-q)+a)} - \mathfrak{u}\frac{(\phi(t)-\phi(0))^{(1-q)(1-a)}}{\Gamma(a(1-q)+a)}\|_p^p\\ &+\frac{2^{2p-2}}{(\Gamma(q))^p}\| \int_0^t(\phi(t)-\phi(\varpi))^{q-1}(\mathcal{D}(\varpi,\mathcal{B}_q(\varpi,\mathfrak{c}))-\mathcal{D}(\varpi,\mathcal{B}_q(\varpi,\mathfrak{u})))\phi'(\varpi)d\varpi\|_p^p\\ &+\frac{2^{2p-2}}{(\Gamma(q))^p}\| \int_0^t(\phi(t)-\phi(\varpi))^{q-1}(\Xi(\varpi,\mathcal{B}_q(\varpi,\mathfrak{c})))-\Xi(\varpi,\mathcal{B}_q(\varpi,\mathfrak{c})))\phi'(\varpi)d\mathcal{W}(\varpi)\|_p^p.\end{aligned} \quad (39)$$

By HI and (ξ_1).

$$
\begin{aligned}
& \| \int_0^t (\phi(t)-\phi(\varpi))^{q-1}(\mathcal{D}(\varpi,\mathcal{B}_q(\varpi,c))-\mathcal{D}(\varpi,\mathcal{B}_q(\varpi,u)))\phi'(\varpi)d\varpi \|_p^p \\
= & \sum_{\imath=1}^m \mathbf{E}\Big(\int_0^t(\phi(t)-\phi(\varpi))^{q-1}(\mathcal{D}_\imath(\varpi,\mathcal{B}_q(\varpi,c))-\mathcal{D}_\imath(\varpi,\mathcal{B}_q(\varpi,u)))\phi'(\varpi)d\varpi\Big)^p \\
\leq & \sum_{\imath=1}^m \mathbf{E}\bigg(\Big(\int_0^t(\phi(t)-\phi(\varpi))^{\frac{(q-1)(p-2)}{p-1}}(\phi'(\varpi))^{\frac{p-2}{p-1}}d\varpi\Big)^{p-1} \\
& \Big(\int_0^t(\phi(t)-\phi(\varpi))^{2q-2}\Big|\mathcal{D}_\imath\Big(\varpi,\mathcal{B}_q(\varpi,c)\Big)-\mathcal{D}_\imath\Big(\varpi,\mathcal{B}_q(\varpi,u)\Big)\Big|(\phi'(\varpi))^2d\varpi\Big)\bigg) \\
\leq & \sum_{\imath=1}^m \mathbf{E}\bigg(\Big(\sup_{0<\varpi\leq t}(\phi'(\varpi))^{\frac{1}{1-p}}\int_0^t(\phi(t)-\phi(\varpi))^{\frac{(q-1)(p-2)}{p-1}}\phi'(\varpi)d\varpi\Big)^{p-1} \\
& \Big(\int_0^t(\phi(t)-\phi(\varpi))^{2q-2}\Big|\mathcal{D}_\imath\Big(\varpi,\mathcal{B}_q(\varpi,c)\Big)-\mathcal{D}_\imath\Big(\varpi,\mathcal{B}_q(\varpi,u)\Big)\Big|(\phi'(\varpi))^2d\varpi\Big)\bigg) \\
\leq & F^{p-1}\bigg(\frac{\mathfrak{T}_1^p(\phi(\varpi)-\phi(0))^{(pq-2q+1)}(p-1)^{p-1}}{(pq-2q+1)^{p-1}}\bigg)\int_0^t(\phi(t)-\phi(\varpi))^{2q-2}(\|\mathcal{B}_q(\varpi,c)-\mathcal{B}_q(\varpi,u)\|_p^p)(\phi'(\varpi))^2d\varpi. \\
\leq & F^{p-1}\bigg(\frac{\mathfrak{T}_1^p(\phi(\varpi)-\phi(0))^{(pq-2q+1)}(p-1)^{p-1}}{(pq-2q+1)^{p-1}}\bigg)\sup_{0<\varpi\leq t}\phi'(\varpi)\int_0^t(\phi(t)-\phi(\varpi))^{2q-2}(\|\mathcal{B}_q(\varpi,c)-\mathcal{B}_q(\varpi,u)\|_p^p) \\
& \phi'(\varpi)d\varpi \\
= & F^{p-1}\bigg(\frac{\mathfrak{T}_1^p(\phi(\varpi)-\phi(0))^{(pq-2q+1)}(p-1)^{p-1}}{(pq-2q+1)^{p-1}}\bigg)\mathbf{G}\int_0^t(\phi(t)-\phi(\varpi))^{2q-2}(\|\mathcal{B}_q(\varpi,c)-\mathcal{B}_q(\varpi,u)\|_p^p)\phi'(\varpi)d\varpi.
\end{aligned} \tag{40}
$$

Through (ξ_1), HI, and BDGI, we have

$$
\begin{aligned}
& \| \int_0^t (\phi(t)-\phi(\varpi))^{q-1}(\Xi(\varpi,\mathcal{B}_q(\varpi,c))-\Xi(\varpi,\mathcal{B}_q(\varpi,u)))\phi'(\varpi)d\mathcal{W}(\varpi) \|_p^p \\
= & \sum_{\imath=1}^m \mathbf{E}\Big|\int_0^t(\phi(t)-\phi(\varpi))^{q-1}\Big(\Xi_\imath(\varpi,\mathcal{B}_q(\varpi,c))-\Xi_\imath(\varpi,\mathcal{B}_q(\varpi,u))\Big)\phi'(\varpi)d\mathcal{W}(\varpi)\Big|^p \\
\leq & \sum_{\imath=1}^m \mathcal{C}_p\mathbf{E}\Big|\int_0^t(\phi(t)-\phi(\varpi))^{2q-2}\Big|\Xi_\imath\Big(\varpi,\mathcal{B}_q(\varpi,c)\Big)-\Xi_\imath(\varpi,\mathcal{B}_q(\varpi,u))\Big|_2(\phi'(\varpi))^2d\varpi\Big|^{\frac{p}{2}} \\
\leq & \sum_{\imath=1}^m \mathcal{C}_p\mathbf{E}\int_0^t(\phi(t)-\phi(\varpi))^{2q-2}\Big|\Xi_\imath\Big(\varpi,\mathcal{B}_q(\varpi,c)\Big)-\Xi_\imath(\varpi,\mathcal{B}_q(\varpi,u))\Big|_p(\phi'(\varpi))^2d\varpi \\
& \Big(\int_0^t(\phi(t)-\phi(\varpi))^{2q-2}(\phi'(\varpi))^2d\varpi\Big)^{\frac{p-2}{2}} \\
\leq & \sum_{\imath=1}^m \mathcal{C}_p\mathbf{E}\int_0^t(\phi(t)-\phi(\varpi))^{2q-2}\Big|\Xi_\imath\Big(\varpi,\mathcal{B}_q(\varpi,c)\Big)-\Xi_\imath(\varpi,\mathcal{B}_q(\varpi,u))\Big|_p(\phi'(\varpi))^2d\varpi \\
& \Big(\sup_{0<\varpi\leq t}\phi'(\varpi)\int_0^t(\phi(t)-\phi(\varpi))^{2q-2}\phi'(\varpi)d\varpi\Big)^{\frac{p-2}{2}} \\
\leq & \mathbf{G}^{\frac{p-2}{2}}\mathfrak{T}_2^p\mathcal{C}_p\bigg(\frac{(\phi(\varpi)-\phi(0))^{(2q-1)}}{(2q-1)}\bigg)^{\frac{p-2}{2}}\int_0^t(\phi(t)-\phi(\varpi))^{2q-2}(\|\mathcal{B}_q(\varpi,c)-\mathcal{B}_q(\varpi,u)\|_p^p)(\phi'(\varpi))^2d\varpi. \\
\leq & \mathbf{G}^{\frac{p-2}{2}}\mathfrak{T}_2^p\mathcal{C}_p\bigg(\frac{(\phi(\varpi)-\phi(0))^{(2q-1)}}{(2q-1)}\bigg)^{\frac{p-2}{2}}\sup_{0<\varpi\leq t}\phi'(\varpi)\int_0^t(\phi(t)-\phi(\varpi))^{2q-2}(\|\mathcal{B}_q(\varpi,c)-\mathcal{B}_q(\varpi,u)\|_p^p)\phi'(\varpi)d\varpi. \\
= & \mathbf{G}^{\frac{p-2}{2}}\mathfrak{T}_2^p\mathcal{C}_p\bigg(\frac{(\phi(\varpi)-\phi(0))^{(2q-1)}}{(2q-1)}\bigg)^{\frac{p-2}{2}}\mathbf{G}\int_0^t(\phi(t)-\phi(\varpi))^{2q-2}(\|\mathcal{B}_q(\varpi,c)-\mathcal{B}_q(\varpi,u)\|_p^p)\phi'(\varpi)d\varpi.
\end{aligned} \tag{41}
$$

From (39) using (40) and (41), we obtain

$$
\begin{aligned}
\|\mathcal{B}_q(t,c) \quad -\mathcal{B}_q(t,u)\|_p^p \leq & \, 2^{p-1}\| c\frac{(\phi(t)-\phi(0))^{(1-q)(1-a)}}{\Gamma(a(1-q)+a)}-u\frac{(\phi(t)-\phi(0))^{(1-q)(1-a)}}{\Gamma(a(1-q)+a)}\|_p^p \\
& +2^{p-1}\mathbb{Z}\int_0^t(\phi(t)-\phi(\varpi))^{2q-2}(\|\mathcal{B}_q(\varpi,c)-\mathcal{B}_q(\varpi,u)\|_p^p)\phi'(\varpi)d\varpi.
\end{aligned} \tag{42}
$$

Now, the Grönwall inequality, gives

$$\| \mathcal{B}_q(t,c) \quad -\mathcal{B}_q(t,u) \|_p^p \leq 2^{p-1} \exp\left(2^{p-1}\mathbb{Z} \int_0^t (\phi(t) - \phi(\varpi))^{2q-2} \phi'(\varpi) d\varpi\right)$$
$$\| c \frac{(\phi(t)-\phi(0))^{(1-q)(1-a)}}{\Gamma(a(1-q)+a)} - u \frac{(\phi(t)-\phi(0))^{(1-q)(1-a)}}{\Gamma(a(1-q)+a)} \|_p^p .$$

By ([44], [Lemma 7.1.1]), we have

$$\| \mathcal{B}_q(t,c) \quad -\mathcal{B}_q(t,u) \|_p^p \leq 2^{p-1}\mathbb{E}_{2q-1}\left(2^{p-1}\mathbb{Z}\Gamma(2q-1)\phi^{(2q-1)}\right)$$
$$\| c \frac{(\phi(t)-\phi(0))^{(1-q)(1-a)}}{\Gamma(a(1-q)+a)} - u \frac{(\phi(t)-\phi(0))^{(1-q)(1-a)}}{\Gamma(a(1-q)+a)} \|_p^p .$$

Hence,

$$\lim_{c \to u} \| \mathcal{B}_q(t,c) - \mathcal{B}_q(t,u) \|_p = 0.$$

□

3.2. Regularity

Next, we prove the smoothness of the solution of SPFrDEs.

Theorem 4. *Let* (ξ_1) *and* (ξ_2) *hold. Then, for* $\mathcal{U} > 0$ *that depends on* $q, \mathfrak{T}, \gamma, p, g, \phi$.

$$\| \mathcal{B}_q(c,t) - \mathcal{B}_q(c,\mathfrak{r}) \|_p \leq \mathcal{U}|t-\mathfrak{r}|^{q-\frac{1}{2}}, \ \forall t,\mathfrak{r} \in [0,g]. \quad (43)$$

Proof. For $t > \mathfrak{r}$, we achieve

$$\begin{aligned} \| \mathcal{B}_q(t,c) - \mathcal{B}_q(\mathfrak{r},c) \|_p^p \leq & \frac{1}{\Gamma^p(q)2^{2-2p}} \| \int_{\mathfrak{r}}^t (\phi(t) - \phi(\varpi))^{q-1} \mathcal{D}(\varpi, \mathcal{B}_q(\varpi,c))\phi'(\varpi)d\varpi \|_p^p \\ & + \frac{1}{\Gamma^p(q)2^{2-2p}} \| \int_{\mathfrak{r}}^t (\phi(t) - \phi(\varpi))^{q-1} \Xi(\varpi, \mathcal{B}_q(\varpi,c))\phi'(\varpi)d\mathcal{W}(\varpi) \|_p^p \\ & + \frac{1}{\Gamma^p(q)2^{2-2p}} \| \int_0^{\mathfrak{r}} \left|(\phi(t) - \phi(\varpi))^{q-1} - (\phi(\mathfrak{r}) - \phi(\varpi))^{q-1}\right| \mathcal{D}(\varpi, \mathcal{B}_q(\varpi,c))\phi'(\varpi)d\varpi \|_p^p \\ & + \frac{1}{\Gamma^p(q)2^{2-2p}} \| \int_0^{\mathfrak{r}} \left|(\phi(t) - \phi(\varpi))^{q-1} - (\phi(\mathfrak{r}) - \phi(\varpi))^{q-1}\right| \Xi(\varpi, \mathcal{B}_q(\varpi,c))\phi'(\varpi)d\mathcal{W} \|_p^p . \end{aligned} \quad (44)$$

Through HI and BDGI.

$$\Gamma^p(q)2^{2-2p} \| \mathcal{B}_q(t,c) - \mathcal{B}_q(\mathfrak{r},c) \|_p^p \leq \frac{(p-1)^{p-1}}{(pq-1)^{p-1}(\phi(t) - \phi(\mathfrak{r}))^{1-qp}} \int_{\mathfrak{r}}^t \| \mathcal{D}(\varpi, \mathcal{B}_q(\varpi,c)) \|_p^p d\varpi$$
$$+C_p\left(\int_{\mathfrak{r}}^t \| \Xi(\varpi, \mathcal{B}_q(\varpi,c)) \|_p^p (\phi(t) - \phi(\varpi))^{2q-2}(\phi'(\varpi))^2 d\varpi\right)\left(\int_{\mathfrak{r}}^t (\phi(t) - \phi(\varpi))^{2q-2}(\phi'(\varpi))^2 d\varpi\right)^{\frac{p-2}{2}}$$
$$+\frac{1}{(\phi(g) - \phi(0))^{\frac{2-p}{2}}} \int_0^{\mathfrak{r}} \| \mathcal{D}(\varpi, \mathcal{B}_q(\varpi,c)) \|_p^p d\varpi \left(\int_0^{\mathfrak{r}} \left|(\phi(t) - \phi(\varpi))^{q-1} - (\phi(\mathfrak{r}) - \phi(\varpi))^{q-1}\right|_2 (\phi'(\varpi))^2 d\varpi\right)^{\frac{p}{2}}$$
$$+C_p \int_0^{\mathfrak{r}} \left((\phi(t) - \phi(\varpi))^{q-1} - (\phi(\mathfrak{r}) - \phi(\varpi))^{q-1}\right)^2 \| \Xi(\varpi, \mathcal{B}_q(\varpi,c)) \|_p^p (\phi'(\varpi))^2 d\varpi$$
$$\times\left(\int_0^{\mathfrak{r}} \left((\phi(t) - \phi(\varpi))^{q-1} - (\phi(\mathfrak{r}) - \phi(\varpi))^{q-1}\right)^2 (\phi'(\varpi))^2 d\varpi\right)^{\frac{p-2}{2}}.$$

We obtain the following:

$$\| \mathcal{D}(\varpi, \mathcal{B}_q(\varpi,c)) \|_p^p \leq 2^{p-1}\left(\mathfrak{T}_1^p \| \mathcal{B}_q(\varpi,c)) \|_p^p + \| \mathcal{D}(\varpi,0) \|_p^p\right) \leq 2^{p-1}(\mathfrak{T}_1^p\gamma_1 + \gamma^p).$$

$$\| \Xi(\varpi, \mathcal{B}_q(\varpi,c)) \|_p^p \leq 2^{p-1}\left(\mathfrak{T}_2^p \| \mathcal{B}_q(\varpi,c)) \|_p^p + \| \Xi(\varpi,0) \|_p^p\right) \leq 2^{p-1}(\mathfrak{T}_2^p\gamma_1 + \gamma^p).$$

Furthermore,

$$\begin{aligned}
&\int_0^{\mathfrak{r}}((\phi(\mathfrak{t})- \phi(\varpi))^{\mathfrak{q}-1} - (\phi(\mathfrak{r}) - \phi(\varpi))^{\mathfrak{q}-1}\Big)^2(\phi'(\varpi))^2 d\varpi \\
&\quad \leq \sup_{0<\varpi\leq \mathfrak{t}} \phi'(\varpi) \int_0^{\mathfrak{r}}\Big((\phi(\mathfrak{t}) - \phi(\varpi))^{\mathfrak{q}-1} - (\phi(\mathfrak{r}) - \phi(\varpi))^{\mathfrak{q}-1}\Big)^2 \phi'(\varpi)d\varpi \\
&\quad \leq \mathbf{G}\int_0^{\mathfrak{r}}\Big((\phi(\mathfrak{r}) - \phi(\varpi))^{2\mathfrak{q}-2} - (\phi(\mathfrak{t}) - \phi(\varpi))^{2\mathfrak{q}-2}\Big)\phi'(\varpi)d\varpi \qquad (45)\\
&\quad = \frac{(\phi(\mathfrak{t}) - \phi(\mathfrak{r}))^{(2\mathfrak{q}-1)}}{(2\mathfrak{q}-1)} + \frac{(\phi(\mathfrak{r}))^{(2\mathfrak{q}-1)} - (\phi(\mathfrak{t}))^{(2\mathfrak{q}-1)}}{(2\mathfrak{q}-1)} \\
&\quad \leq \frac{(\phi(\mathfrak{t}) - \phi(\mathfrak{r}))^{(2\mathfrak{q}-1)}}{(2\mathfrak{q}-1)}.
\end{aligned}$$

So,

$$\begin{aligned}
\Gamma^{\mathfrak{p}}(\mathfrak{q})2^{2-2\mathfrak{p}} \parallel \mathcal{B}_{\mathfrak{q}}(\mathfrak{t},\mathfrak{c}) - \mathcal{B}_{\mathfrak{q}}(\mathfrak{r},\mathfrak{c}) \parallel_{\mathfrak{p}}^{\mathfrak{p}} \leq & \frac{(2\mathfrak{p}-2)^{\mathfrak{p}-1}}{(\mathfrak{p}\mathfrak{q}-1)^{\mathfrak{p}-1}}(\phi(\mathfrak{t}) - \phi(\mathfrak{r}))^{\frac{(2\mathfrak{q}-1)\mathfrak{p}}{2}}(\mathfrak{T}_1^{\mathfrak{p}}\gamma_1 + \gamma^{\mathfrak{p}})(\phi(\mathfrak{g}) - \phi(0))^{\frac{\mathfrak{p}}{2}} \\
& + \frac{1}{(2\mathfrak{q}-1)^{\frac{\mathfrak{p}}{2}}}(\phi(\mathfrak{t}) - \phi(\mathfrak{r}))^{\frac{(2\mathfrak{q}-1)\mathfrak{p}}{2}}(\mathfrak{T}_2^{\mathfrak{p}}\gamma_1 + \gamma^{\mathfrak{p}})2^{\mathfrak{p}-1}\mathcal{C}_{\mathfrak{p}} \\
& + \frac{2^{\mathfrak{p}-1}}{(2\mathfrak{q}-1)^{\mathfrak{p}-1}}(\phi(\mathfrak{t}) - \phi(\mathfrak{r}))^{\frac{(2\mathfrak{q}-1)\mathfrak{p}}{2}}(\mathfrak{T}_1^{\mathfrak{p}}\gamma_1 + \gamma^{\mathfrak{p}})(\phi(\mathfrak{g}) - \phi(0))^{\frac{\mathfrak{p}}{2}} \\
& + \frac{1}{(2\mathfrak{q}-1)^{\frac{\mathfrak{p}}{2}}}(\phi(\mathfrak{t}) - \phi(\mathfrak{r}))^{\frac{(2\mathfrak{q}-1)\mathfrak{p}}{2}}(\mathfrak{T}_2^{\mathfrak{p}}\gamma_1 + \gamma^{\mathfrak{p}})2^{\mathfrak{p}-1}\mathcal{C}_{\mathfrak{p}}.
\end{aligned}$$

Hence,

$$\parallel \mathcal{B}_{\mathfrak{q}}(\mathfrak{t},\mathfrak{c}) - \mathcal{B}_{\mathfrak{q}}(\mathfrak{r},\mathfrak{c}) \parallel_{\mathfrak{p}} \leq \mathcal{U}(\phi(\mathfrak{t}) - \phi(\mathfrak{r}))^{\mathfrak{p}\mathfrak{q}-\frac{1}{2}\mathfrak{p}},$$

where

$$\begin{aligned}
\mathcal{U}^{\mathfrak{p}} =& 2^{2\mathfrak{p}-2}\left(\frac{(2\mathfrak{p}-2)^{\mathfrak{p}-1}}{(\mathfrak{p}\mathfrak{q}-1)^{\mathfrak{p}-1}}(\mathfrak{T}_1^{\mathfrak{p}}\gamma_1 + \gamma^{\mathfrak{p}})(\phi(\mathfrak{g}) - \phi(0))^{\frac{\mathfrak{p}}{2}} + \frac{1}{(2\mathfrak{q}-1)^{\frac{\mathfrak{p}}{2}}}(\mathfrak{T}_2^{\mathfrak{p}}\gamma_1 + \gamma^{\mathfrak{p}})2^{\mathfrak{p}-1}\mathcal{C}_{\mathfrak{p}}\right)\frac{1}{\Gamma^{\mathfrak{p}}(\mathfrak{q})} \\
&+ 2^{2\mathfrak{p}-2}\left(\frac{2^{\mathfrak{p}-1}}{(2\mathfrak{q}-1)^{\mathfrak{p}-1}}(\mathfrak{T}_1^{\mathfrak{p}}\gamma_1 + \gamma^{\mathfrak{p}})(\phi(\mathfrak{g}) - \phi(0))^{\frac{\mathfrak{p}}{2}} + \frac{1}{(2\mathfrak{q}-1)^{\frac{\mathfrak{p}}{2}}}(\mathfrak{T}_2^{\mathfrak{p}}\gamma_1 + \gamma^{\mathfrak{p}})2^{\mathfrak{p}-1}\mathcal{C}_{\mathfrak{p}}\right)\Gamma^{\mathfrak{p}}(\mathfrak{q}).
\end{aligned}$$

Thus, we obtain the following:

$$\lim_{\mathfrak{r}\to\mathfrak{t}} \parallel \mathcal{B}_{\mathfrak{q}}(\mathfrak{t},\mathfrak{c}) - \mathcal{B}_{\mathfrak{q}}(\mathfrak{r},\mathfrak{c}) \parallel_{\mathfrak{p}} = 0.$$

□

4. Averaging Principle

Now, we establish generalized results in the $\mathfrak{p}$th moment concerning the AP for SPFrDEs within the framework of the ϕ-HFrD.

Lemma 5. *By utilizing* (ξ_4) *and* (ξ_5), *we have*

$$\parallel \widetilde{\Xi}(\mathfrak{A},\nu) \parallel^{\mathfrak{p}} \leq \mathfrak{T}_6(1 + \parallel \mathfrak{A} \parallel^{\mathfrak{p}} + \parallel \nu \parallel^{\mathfrak{p}}),$$

where $\mathfrak{T}_6 = (2^{\mathfrak{p}-1}\mathbb{D}_2(\mathfrak{g}_1) + 6^{\mathfrak{p}-1}\mathfrak{T}_4^{\mathfrak{p}})$.

Proof. By (ξ_4), (ξ_5) and (8).

$$\begin{aligned}\| \widetilde{\Xi}(\mathfrak{A},\nu) \|^{\mathrm{p}} &\leq \| \Xi(\mathrm{t},\mathfrak{A},\nu) - \widetilde{\Xi}(\mathfrak{A},\nu) \|^{\mathrm{p}} + 2^{\mathrm{p}-1} \| \Xi(\mathrm{t},\mathfrak{A},\nu) \|^{\mathrm{p}} 2^{\mathrm{p}-1} \\ &\leq 2^{\mathrm{p}-1}\mathbb{D}_2(\mathfrak{g}_1)(1 + \| \mathfrak{A} \|^{\mathrm{p}} + \| \nu \|^{\mathrm{p}}) + 2^{\mathrm{p}-1}\mathfrak{T}_4^{\mathrm{p}}(1 + \| \mathfrak{A} \| + \| \nu \|)^{\mathrm{p}} \\ &\leq (\mathbb{D}_2(\mathfrak{g}_1 2^{\mathrm{p}-1}) + 6^{\mathrm{p}-1}\mathfrak{T}_4^{\mathrm{p}})(1 + \| \mathfrak{A} \|^{\mathrm{p}} + \| \nu \|^{\mathrm{p}}).\end{aligned}$$

□

Now, we prove the time-scale change property to obtain the standard form for the AP of (4).

Lemma 6. *Assume* $\mathrm{t} = \varphi\hbar$, *then*

$${}^{\mathrm{H}}\mathcal{T}_{\hbar}^{\mathrm{q},\mathrm{a},\phi}\mathrm{f}(\varphi\hbar) = {}^{\mathrm{H}}\mathcal{T}_{\mathrm{t}}^{\mathrm{q},\mathrm{a},\widetilde{\phi}}\mathrm{f}(\mathrm{t}).$$

Proof. From (2), we have

$$\begin{aligned}{}^{\mathrm{H}}\mathcal{T}_{\hbar}^{\mathrm{q},\mathrm{a},\phi}\mathrm{f}(\varphi\hbar) = & \frac{1}{\Gamma(\mathrm{a}(1-\mathrm{q}))}\int_0^{\hbar}\frac{d}{d\varpi}\phi(\varpi)(\phi(\hbar)-\phi(\varpi))^{\mathrm{a}(1-\mathrm{q})-1}\frac{1}{\frac{d}{d\varpi}\phi(\varpi)}\frac{d}{d\varpi}d\varpi \\ & \frac{1}{\Gamma((1-\mathrm{a})(1-\mathrm{q}))}\int_0^{\hbar}\phi'(\varpi)(\phi(\hbar)-\phi(\varpi))^{(1-\mathrm{a})(1-\mathrm{q})-1} \\ & \mathrm{f}(\varphi\varpi)d\varpi.\end{aligned}$$

Let $\varphi\varpi = \theta$, $\varpi = \frac{\theta}{\varphi}$, and by the chain rule $\frac{d}{d\varpi} = \frac{d}{d\theta}\cdot\frac{d\theta}{d\varpi} = \frac{d}{d\theta}\cdot\frac{d}{d\varpi}(\varphi\varpi) = \varphi\frac{d}{d\theta}$.

So, we have

$$\begin{aligned}{}^{\mathrm{H}}\mathcal{T}_{\hbar}^{\mathrm{q},\mathrm{a},\phi}\mathrm{f}(\varphi\hbar) = & \frac{1}{\Gamma(\mathrm{a}(1-\mathrm{q}))}\int_0^{\varphi\hbar}\varphi\frac{d}{d\theta}\phi\left(\frac{\theta}{\varphi}\right)\left(\phi(\hbar)-\phi\left(\frac{\theta}{\varphi}\right)\right)^{\mathrm{a}(1-\mathrm{q})-1}\frac{1}{\varphi\frac{d}{d\theta}\phi\left(\frac{\theta}{\varphi}\right)}\varphi\frac{d}{d\theta} \\ & \frac{1}{\Gamma((1-\mathrm{a})(1-\mathrm{q}))}\int_0^{\varphi\hbar}\varphi\frac{d}{d\theta}\phi\left(\frac{\theta}{\varphi}\right)\left(\phi(\hbar)-\phi\left(\frac{\theta}{\varphi}\right)\right)^{(1-\mathrm{a})(1-\mathrm{q})-1} \\ & \mathrm{f}(\theta)\frac{d\theta}{\varphi}\frac{d\theta}{\varphi}.\end{aligned}$$

From above, we have $\varphi\hbar = \mathrm{t}$ and $\hbar = \frac{\mathrm{t}}{\varphi}$

$$\begin{aligned}{}^{\mathrm{H}}\mathcal{T}_{\hbar}^{\mathrm{q},\mathrm{a},\phi}\mathrm{f}(\varphi\hbar) = & \frac{1}{\Gamma(\mathrm{a}(1-\mathrm{q}))}\int_0^{\mathrm{t}}\frac{d}{d\theta}\phi\left(\frac{\theta}{\varphi}\right)\left(\phi\left(\frac{\mathrm{t}}{\varphi}\right)-\phi\left(\frac{\theta}{\varphi}\right)\right)^{\mathrm{a}(1-\mathrm{q})-1}\frac{1}{\frac{d}{d\theta}\phi\left(\frac{\theta}{\varphi}\right)}\frac{d}{d\theta} \\ & \frac{1}{\Gamma((1-\mathrm{a})(1-\mathrm{q}))}\int_0^{\mathrm{t}}\frac{d}{d\theta}\phi\left(\frac{\theta}{\varphi}\right)\left(\phi\left(\frac{\mathrm{t}}{\varphi}\right)-\phi\left(\frac{\theta}{\varphi}\right)\right)^{(1-\mathrm{a})(1-\mathrm{q})-1} \\ & \mathrm{f}(\theta)d\theta d\theta.\end{aligned}$$

$\phi\left(\frac{\theta}{\varphi}\right) = \widetilde{\phi}(\theta)$ and $\phi\left(\frac{\mathrm{t}}{\varphi}\right) = \widetilde{\phi}(\mathrm{t})$ or, equivalently,

$$\begin{aligned}{}^{\mathrm{H}}\mathcal{T}_{\hbar}^{\mathrm{q},\mathrm{a},\phi}\mathrm{f}(\varphi\hbar) = & \frac{1}{\Gamma(\mathrm{a}(1-\mathrm{q}))}\int_0^{\mathrm{t}}\frac{d}{d\theta}\widetilde{\phi}(\theta)(\widetilde{\phi}(\mathrm{t})-\widetilde{\phi}(\theta))^{\mathrm{a}(1-\mathrm{q})-1}\frac{1}{\frac{d}{d\theta}\widetilde{\phi}(\theta)}\frac{d}{d\theta} \\ & \frac{1}{\Gamma((1-\mathrm{a})(1-\mathrm{q}))}\int_0^{\mathrm{t}}\frac{d}{d\theta}\widetilde{\phi}(\theta)(\widetilde{\phi}(\mathrm{t})-\widetilde{\phi}(\theta))^{(1-\mathrm{a})(1-\mathrm{q})-1} \\ & \mathrm{f}(\theta)d\theta d\theta.\end{aligned}$$

So, we have the following result:

$${}^{\mathrm{H}}\mathcal{T}_{\hbar}^{\mathrm{q},\mathrm{a},\phi}\mathrm{f}(\varphi\hbar) = {}^{\mathrm{H}}\mathcal{T}_{\mathrm{t}}^{\mathrm{q},\mathrm{a},\widetilde{\phi}}\mathrm{f}(\mathrm{t}).$$

□

Remark 1. *For $\phi(t) = t$ and $a = 1$, our established time-scale change property aligns with CFD. Similarly, for $\phi(t) = t$ and $a = 0$, it aligns with the Riemann–Liouville fractional operator. When $\phi(t) = \ln(t)$ with $a = 0$, and $\phi(t) = \ln(t)$ with $a = 1$, the formulation corresponds to the Hadamard and Caputo–Hadamard fractional operators, respectively.*

Now, we establish the result regarding the AP of SPFrDEs for the generalized case. For this, first consider the following:

$$\begin{cases} {}^{H}\mathcal{T}_t^{q,a,\phi} f(t) = \mathcal{D}\left(\frac{t}{\varepsilon}, f(t), f(ts)\right) + \Xi\left(\frac{t}{\varepsilon}, f(t), f(st)\right)\frac{d\mathcal{W}(t)}{dt}, \\ \mathcal{I}_{0^+}^{(1-q)(1-a),\phi} f(0) = c. \end{cases} \tag{46}$$

Utilizing $\frac{t}{\varepsilon} = \Theta$, Lemma 6 in (46):

$${}^{H}\mathcal{T}_t^{q,a,\widetilde{\phi}} f(\varepsilon\Theta) = \mathcal{D}(\Theta, f(\varepsilon\Theta), f(s\varepsilon\Theta)) + \Xi(\Theta, f(\varepsilon\Theta), f(s\varepsilon\Theta))\frac{d\mathcal{W}(\varepsilon\Theta)}{\varepsilon d\Theta}.$$

Hence

$${}^{H}\mathcal{T}_t^{q,a,\widetilde{\phi}} f_\varepsilon(\Theta) = \mathcal{D}(\Theta, f_\varepsilon(\Theta), f_\varepsilon(s\Theta)) + \varepsilon^{-\frac{1}{2}}\Xi(\Theta, f_\varepsilon(\Theta), f_\varepsilon(s\Theta))\frac{d\mathcal{W}(\Theta)}{d\Theta}.$$

So, we obtain

$$\begin{cases} {}^{H}\mathcal{T}_t^{q,a,\widetilde{\phi}} f_\varepsilon(t) = \mathcal{D}(t, f_\varepsilon(t), f_\varepsilon(st)) + \varepsilon^{-\frac{1}{2}}\Xi(t, f_\varepsilon(t), f_\varepsilon(st))\frac{d\mathcal{W}(t)}{dt}, \\ \mathcal{I}_{0^+}^{(1-q)(1-a),\widetilde{\phi}} f_\varepsilon(0) = c. \end{cases} \tag{47}$$

Thus, (47) can be expressed integrally as

$$\begin{aligned} f_\varepsilon(t) &= c\frac{\left(\widetilde{\phi}(t)-\widetilde{\phi}(0)\right)^{(1-q)(1-a)}}{\Gamma(a(1-q)+a)} \\ &+\frac{1}{\Gamma(q)}\int_0^t \widetilde{\phi}'(\varpi)\left(\widetilde{\phi}(t)-\widetilde{\phi}(\varpi)\right)^{1-q}\mathcal{D}(\varpi, f_\varepsilon(\varpi), f_\varepsilon(s\varpi))d\varpi \\ &+\varepsilon^{-\frac{1}{2}}\frac{1}{\Gamma(q)}\int_0^t \widetilde{\phi}'(\varpi)\left(\widetilde{\phi}(t)-\widetilde{\phi}(\varpi)\right)^{1-q}\Xi(\varpi, f_\varepsilon(\varpi), f_\varepsilon(s\varpi))d\mathcal{W}(\varpi), \end{aligned} \tag{48}$$

when $\varepsilon \in (0, \varepsilon_0]$ with fixed point ε_0. From (48), we have

$$\begin{aligned} f_\varepsilon^*(t) &= c\frac{\left(\widetilde{\phi}(t)-\widetilde{\phi}(0)\right)^{(1-q)(1-a)}}{\Gamma(a(1-q)+a)} \\ &+\frac{1}{\Gamma(q)}\int_0^t \widetilde{\phi}'(\varpi)\left(\widetilde{\phi}(t)-\widetilde{\phi}(\varpi)\right)^{1-q}\widetilde{\mathcal{D}}(f_\varepsilon^*(\varpi), f_\varepsilon^*(s\varpi))d\varpi \\ &+\varepsilon^{-\frac{1}{2}}\frac{1}{\Gamma(q)}\int_0^t \widetilde{\phi}'(\varpi)\left(\widetilde{\phi}(t)-\widetilde{\phi}(\varpi)\right)^{1-q}\widetilde{\Xi}(f_\varepsilon^*(\varpi), f_\varepsilon^*(s\varpi))d\mathcal{W}(\varpi), \end{aligned} \tag{49}$$

where $\widetilde{\mathcal{D}} : \mathfrak{R}^{\varkappa} \times \mathfrak{R}^{\varkappa} \to \mathfrak{R}^{\varkappa}, \widetilde{\Xi} : \mathfrak{R}^{\varkappa} \times \mathfrak{R}^{\varkappa} \to \mathfrak{R}^{\varkappa \times b}$.

Theorem 5. *When (ξ_3) to (ξ_5) are valid. When $\mho > 0$, $\varrho > 0$, and $\varepsilon_1 \in (0, \varepsilon_0]$ with $\eta \in \left(0, qp - \frac{p}{2}\right)$, then*

$$\mathbf{E}\left[\sup_{t\in[0,\, \varrho\varepsilon^{-\eta}]} \| f_\varepsilon(t) - f_\varepsilon^*(t) \|^p\right] \leq \mho, \ \varepsilon \in (0, \varepsilon_1]. \tag{50}$$

Proof. Using (48) and (49),

$$
\begin{aligned}
&\mathrm{f}_\varepsilon(\mathrm{t}) - \mathrm{f}^*_\varepsilon(\mathrm{t}) \\
&= \mathrm{c}\frac{\left(\widetilde{\phi}(\mathrm{t})-\widetilde{\phi}(0)\right)^{(1-\mathrm{q})(1-\mathrm{a})}}{\Gamma(\mathrm{a}(1-\mathrm{q})+\mathrm{a})} - \mathrm{c}\frac{\left(\widetilde{\phi}(\mathrm{t})-\widetilde{\phi}(0)\right)^{(1-\mathrm{q})(1-\mathrm{a})}}{\Gamma(\mathrm{a}(1-\mathrm{q})+\mathrm{a})} \\
&+\frac{1}{\Gamma(\mathrm{q})}\int_0^{\mathrm{t}}(\widetilde{\phi}(\mathrm{t}) - \widetilde{\phi}(\varpi))^{\mathrm{q}-1}\Big(\mathcal{D}(\varpi,\mathrm{f}_\varepsilon(\varpi),\mathrm{f}_\varepsilon(\mathrm{s}\varpi)) - \widetilde{\mathcal{D}}(\mathrm{f}^*_\varepsilon(\varpi),\mathrm{f}^*_\varepsilon(\mathrm{s}\varpi))\Big)\widetilde{\phi}'(\varpi)d\varpi \\
&+\varepsilon^{-\frac{1}{2}}\frac{1}{\Gamma(\mathrm{q})}\int_0^{\mathrm{t}}(\widetilde{\phi}(\mathrm{t}) - \widetilde{\phi}(\varpi))^{\mathrm{q}-1}\Big(\Xi(\varpi,\mathrm{f}_\varepsilon(\varpi),\mathrm{f}_\varepsilon(\mathrm{s}\varpi)) - \widetilde{\Xi}(\mathrm{f}^*_\varepsilon(\varpi),\mathrm{f}^*_\varepsilon(\mathrm{s}\varpi))\Big) \\
&\widetilde{\phi}'(\varpi)d\mathcal{W}(\varpi).
\end{aligned}
\tag{51}
$$

Via Jensen's inequality (JI), we have

$$
\begin{aligned}
&\| \mathrm{f}_\varepsilon(\mathrm{t}) - \mathrm{f}^*_\varepsilon(\mathrm{t}) \|^{\mathrm{p}} \leq 2^{\mathrm{p}-1} \\
&\| \frac{1}{\Gamma(\mathrm{q})}\int_0^{\mathrm{t}}(\widetilde{\phi}(\mathrm{t}) - \widetilde{\phi}(\varpi))^{\mathrm{q}-1}\Big(\mathcal{D}(\varpi,\mathrm{f}_\varepsilon(\varpi),\mathrm{f}_\varepsilon(\mathrm{s}\varpi)) - \widetilde{\mathcal{D}}(\mathrm{f}^*_\varepsilon(\varpi),\mathrm{f}^*_\varepsilon(\mathrm{s}\varpi))\Big)\widetilde{\phi}'(\varpi)d\varpi \|^{\mathrm{p}} \\
&+2^{\mathrm{p}-1} \\
&\| \varepsilon^{-\frac{1}{2}}\frac{1}{\Gamma(\mathrm{q})}\int_0^{\mathrm{t}}(\widetilde{\phi}(\mathrm{t}) - \widetilde{\phi}(\varpi))^{\mathrm{q}-1}\Big(\Xi(\varpi,\mathrm{f}_\varepsilon(\varpi),\mathrm{f}_\varepsilon(\mathrm{s}\varpi)) - \widetilde{\Xi}(\mathrm{f}^*_\varepsilon(\varpi),\mathrm{f}^*_\varepsilon(\mathrm{s}\varpi))\Big)\widetilde{\phi}'(\varpi)d\mathcal{W}(\varpi) \|^{\mathrm{p}} \\
&\leq \frac{1}{\Gamma^{\mathrm{p}}(\mathrm{q})}2^{\mathrm{p}-1} \\
&\| \int_0^{\mathrm{t}}(\widetilde{\phi}(\mathrm{t}) - \widetilde{\phi}(\varpi))^{\mathrm{q}-1}\Big(\mathcal{D}(\varpi,\mathrm{f}_\varepsilon(\varpi),\mathrm{f}_\varepsilon(\mathrm{s}\varpi)) - \widetilde{\mathcal{D}}(\mathrm{f}^*_\varepsilon(\varpi),\mathrm{f}^*_\varepsilon(\mathrm{s}\varpi))\Big)\widetilde{\phi}'(\varpi)d\varpi \|^{\mathrm{p}} \\
&+\frac{1}{\Gamma^{\mathrm{p}}(\mathrm{q})}2^{\mathrm{p}-1}\varepsilon^{\mathrm{p}(-\frac{1}{2})} \\
&\| \int_0^{\mathrm{t}}(\widetilde{\phi}(\mathrm{t}) - \widetilde{\phi}(\varpi))^{\mathrm{q}-1}\Big(\Xi(\varpi,\mathrm{f}_\varepsilon(\varpi),\mathrm{f}_\varepsilon(\mathrm{s}\varpi)) - \widetilde{\Xi}(\mathrm{f}^*_\varepsilon(\varpi),\mathrm{f}^*_\varepsilon(\mathrm{s}\varpi))\Big)\widetilde{\phi}'(\varpi)d\mathcal{W}(\varpi) \|_{\mathrm{p}}.
\end{aligned}
\tag{52}
$$

Utilizing (52) in (50).

$$
\begin{aligned}
&\mathbf{E}\Big[\sup_{0\leq \mathrm{t}\leq\vartheta} \| \mathrm{f}_\varepsilon(\mathrm{t}) - \mathrm{f}^*_\varepsilon(\mathrm{t}) \|^{\mathrm{p}}\Big] \\
&\leq \frac{1}{\Gamma^{\mathrm{p}}(\mathrm{q})}2^{\mathrm{p}-1} \\
&\mathbf{E}\Big[\sup_{0\leq \mathrm{t}\leq\vartheta} \| \int_0^{\mathrm{t}}(\widetilde{\phi}(\mathrm{t}) - \widetilde{\phi}(\varpi))^{\mathrm{q}-1}\Big(\mathcal{D}(\varpi,\mathrm{f}_\varepsilon(\varpi),\mathrm{f}_\varepsilon(\mathrm{s}\varpi)) - \widetilde{\mathcal{D}}(\mathrm{f}^*_\varepsilon(\varpi),\mathrm{f}^*_\varepsilon(\mathrm{s}\varpi))\Big)\widetilde{\phi}'(\varpi)d\varpi \|^{\mathrm{p}}\Big] \\
&+\frac{1}{\Gamma^{\mathrm{p}}(\mathrm{q})}2^{\mathrm{p}-1}\varepsilon^{\mathrm{p}(-\frac{1}{2})} \\
&\mathbf{E}\Big[\sup_{0\leq \mathrm{t}\leq\vartheta} \| \int_0^{\mathrm{t}}(\widetilde{\phi}(\mathrm{t}) - \widetilde{\phi}(\varpi))^{\mathrm{q}-1}\Big(\Xi(\varpi,\mathrm{f}_\varepsilon(\varpi),\mathrm{f}_\varepsilon(\mathrm{s}\varpi)) - \widetilde{\Xi}(\mathrm{f}^*_\varepsilon(\varpi),\mathrm{f}^*_\varepsilon(\mathrm{s}\varpi))\Big)\widetilde{\phi}'(\varpi)d\mathcal{W}(\varpi) \|^{\mathrm{p}}\Big] \\
&= j_1 + j_2.
\end{aligned}
\tag{53}
$$

From j_1

$$
\begin{aligned}
j_1 \leq\ &\frac{1}{\Gamma^{\mathrm{p}}(\mathrm{q})}2^{2\mathrm{p}-2} \\
&\mathbf{E}\Big[\sup_{0\leq \mathrm{t}\leq\vartheta} \| \int_0^{\mathrm{t}}(\widetilde{\phi}(\mathrm{t}) - \widetilde{\phi}(\varpi))^{\mathrm{q}-1}(\mathcal{D}(\varpi,\mathrm{f}_\varepsilon(\varpi),\mathrm{f}_\varepsilon(\mathrm{s}\varpi)) - \mathcal{D}(\varpi,\mathrm{f}^*_\varepsilon(\varpi),\mathrm{f}^*_\varepsilon(\mathrm{s}\varpi)))\widetilde{\phi}'(\varpi)d\varpi \|^{\mathrm{p}}\Big] \\
&+\frac{1}{\Gamma^{\mathrm{p}}(\mathrm{q})}2^{2\mathrm{p}-2} \\
&\mathbf{E}\Big[\sup_{0\leq \mathrm{t}\leq\vartheta} \| \int_0^{\mathrm{t}}(\widetilde{\phi}(\mathrm{t}) - \widetilde{\phi}(\varpi))^{\mathrm{q}-1}\Big(\mathcal{D}(\varpi,\mathrm{f}^*_\varepsilon(\varpi),\mathrm{f}^*_\varepsilon(\mathrm{s}\varpi)) - \widetilde{\mathcal{D}}(\mathrm{f}^*_\varepsilon(\varpi),\mathrm{f}^*_\varepsilon(\mathrm{s}\varpi))\Big)\widetilde{\phi}'(\varpi)d\varpi \|^{\mathrm{p}}\Big] \\
&= j_{11} + j_{12}.
\end{aligned}
\tag{54}
$$

By utilizing HI, JI, and (ξ_3) on j_{11}:

$$
\begin{aligned}
j_{11} \leq\ & \frac{1}{\Gamma^{p}(q)}2^{2p-2}\left(\int_0^{\vartheta}(\tilde{\phi}(\vartheta)-\tilde{\phi}(\varpi))^{\frac{(q-1)p}{p-1}}(\tilde{\phi}'(\varpi))^{\frac{p}{p-1}}d\varpi\right)^{p-1} \\
& \mathbf{E}\left[\sup_{0\leq t\leq\vartheta}\int_0^t \parallel \mathcal{D}(\varpi,f_{\varepsilon}(\varpi),f_{\varepsilon}(s\varpi))-\mathcal{D}(\varpi,f_{\varepsilon}^{*}(\varpi),f_{\varepsilon}^{*}(s\varpi)) \parallel^{p} d\varpi\right] \\
\leq\ & \frac{1}{\Gamma^{p}(q)}2^{2p-2}\left(\sup_{0<\varpi\leq\vartheta}(\tilde{\phi}'(\varpi))^{\frac{1}{p-1}}\int_0^{\vartheta}(\tilde{\phi}(\vartheta)-\tilde{\phi}(\varpi))^{\frac{(q-1)p}{p-1}}\tilde{\phi}'(\varpi)d\varpi\right)^{p-1} \\
& \mathbf{E}\left[\sup_{0\leq t\leq\vartheta}\int_0^t \parallel \mathcal{D}(\varpi,f_{\varepsilon}(\varpi),f_{\varepsilon}(s\varpi))-\mathcal{D}(\varpi,f_{\varepsilon}^{*}(\varpi),f_{\varepsilon}^{*}(s\varpi)) \parallel^{p} d\varpi\right] \\
\leq\ & \frac{1}{\Gamma^{p}(q)}2^{3p-3}\Im^{p-1}\mathfrak{T}_3^{p}\left((\tilde{\phi}(\vartheta)-\tilde{\phi}(0))^{\frac{(qp-1)}{p-1}}\right)^{p-1}\left(\frac{p-1}{qp-1}\right)^{p-1} \\
& \left(\mathbf{E}\left[\sup_{0\leq t\leq\vartheta}\int_0^t \parallel f_{\varepsilon}(\varpi)-f_{\varepsilon}^{*}(\varpi) \parallel^{p} d\varpi\right]+\mathbf{E}\left[\sup_{0\leq t\leq\vartheta}\int_0^t \parallel f_{\varepsilon}(s\varpi)-f_{\varepsilon}^{*}(s\varpi) \parallel^{p} d\varpi\right]\right) \\
=\ & \mathbb{Y}_{11}(\tilde{\phi}(\vartheta)-\tilde{\phi}(0))^{(qp-1)}\left(\int_0^{\vartheta}\mathbf{E}\left[\sup_{0\leq\rho\leq\varpi}\parallel f_{\varepsilon}(\rho)-f_{\varepsilon}^{*}(\rho)\parallel^{p}\right]d\varpi\right. \\
& \left.+\int_0^{\vartheta}\mathbf{E}\left[\sup_{0\leq\rho\leq\varpi}\parallel f_{\varepsilon}(\rho s)-f_{\varepsilon}^{*}(\rho s)\parallel^{p}\right]d\varpi\right),
\end{aligned}
\tag{55}
$$

where $\mathbb{Y}_{11}=\frac{1}{\Gamma^{p}(q)}2^{3p-3}\mathfrak{T}_3^{p}\left(\frac{p-1}{qp-1}\right)^{p-1}\Im^{p-1}$.

From j_{12} by applying HI, JI, and (ξ_5):

$$
\begin{aligned}
j_{12} \leq\ & \frac{1}{\Gamma^{p}(q)}2^{2p-2}\left(\int_0^{\vartheta}(\tilde{\phi}(\vartheta)-\tilde{\phi}(\varpi))^{\frac{(q-1)p}{p-1}}(\tilde{\phi}'(\varpi))^{\frac{p}{p-1}}d\varpi\right)^{p-1} \\
& \mathbf{E}\left[\sup_{0\leq t\leq\vartheta}\int_0^t \parallel \mathcal{D}(\varpi,f_{\varepsilon}^{*}(\varpi),f_{\varepsilon}^{*}(s\varpi))-\tilde{\mathcal{D}}(f_{\varepsilon}^{*}(\varpi),f_{\varepsilon}^{*}(s\varpi)) \parallel^{p}\ d\varpi\right] \\
\leq\ & \frac{1}{\Gamma^{p}(q)}2^{2p-2}\left(\sup_{0<\varpi\leq t}(\tilde{\phi}'(\varpi))^{\frac{1}{p-1}}\int_0^{\vartheta}(\tilde{\phi}(\vartheta)-\tilde{\phi}(\varpi))^{\frac{(q-1)p}{p-1}}\tilde{\phi}'(\varpi)d\varpi\right)^{p-1} \\
& \mathbf{E}\left[\sup_{0\leq t\leq\vartheta}\int_0^t \parallel \mathcal{D}(\varpi,f_{\varepsilon}^{*}(\varpi),f_{\varepsilon}^{*}(s\varpi))-\tilde{\mathcal{D}}(f_{\varepsilon}^{*}(\varpi),f_{\varepsilon}^{*}(s\varpi)) \parallel^{p}\ d\varpi\right] \\
\leq\ & \Im^{p-1}\frac{1}{\Gamma^{p}(q)}2^{2p-2}\left((\tilde{\phi}(\vartheta)-\tilde{\phi}(0))^{\frac{(qp-1)}{p-1}}\right)^{p-1}\left(\frac{p-1}{qp-1}\right)^{p-1}\mathbb{D}_1(\vartheta) \\
& \vartheta(1+\mathbf{E}\parallel f_{\varepsilon}^{*}(\varpi)\parallel^{p}+\mathbf{E}\parallel f_{\varepsilon}^{*}(s\varpi)\parallel^{p}) \\
=\ & \mathbb{Y}_{12}(\tilde{\phi}(\vartheta)-\tilde{\phi}(0))^{(qp-1)},
\end{aligned}
\tag{56}
$$

where $\mathbb{Y}_{12}=\vartheta\Im^{p-1}\frac{1}{\Gamma^{p}(q)}2^{2p-2}\left(\frac{p-1}{qp-1}\right)^{p-1}\mathbb{D}_1(\vartheta)(1+\mathbf{E}\parallel f_{\varepsilon}^{*}(\varpi)\parallel^{p}+\mathbf{E}\parallel f_{\varepsilon}^{*}(s\varpi)\parallel^{p})$.

The following is provided by j_2 via JI:

$$
\begin{aligned}
j_2 \leq\ & \frac{1}{\Gamma^{p}(q)}2^{2p-2}\varepsilon^{p(-\frac{1}{2})} \\
& \left(\mathbf{E}\left[\sup_{0\leq t\leq\vartheta}\parallel\int_0^t(\tilde{\phi}(t)-\tilde{\phi}(\varpi))^{q-1}[\Xi(\varpi,f_{\varepsilon}(\varpi),f_{\varepsilon}(s\varpi))-\Xi(\varpi,f_{\varepsilon}^{*}(\varpi),f_{\varepsilon}^{*}(s\varpi))]\tilde{\phi}'(\varpi)d\mathcal{W}(\varpi)\parallel^{p}\right]\right) \\
+\ & \frac{1}{\Gamma^{p}(q)}2^{2p-2}\varepsilon^{-\frac{1}{2})} \\
& \left(\mathbf{E}\left[\sup_{0\leq t\leq\vartheta}\parallel\int_0^t(\tilde{\phi}(t)-\tilde{\phi}(\varpi))^{q-1}\left[\Xi(\varpi,f_{\varepsilon}^{*}(\varpi),f_{\varepsilon}^{*}(s\varpi))-\tilde{\Xi}(f_{\varepsilon}^{*}(\varpi),f_{\varepsilon}^{*}(s\varpi))\right]\tilde{\phi}'(\varpi)d\mathcal{W}(\varpi)\parallel^{p}\right]\right) \\
=\ & j_{21}+j_{22}.
\end{aligned}
\tag{57}
$$

By employing (ξ_3), HI, and BDGI on j_{21}:

$$
\begin{aligned}
j_{21} \leq\ & \frac{1}{\Gamma^{\mathrm{p}}(\mathrm{q})}2^{2\mathrm{p}-2}\varepsilon^{\mathrm{p}(-\frac{1}{2})}\left(2(\mathrm{p}-1)^{1-\mathrm{p}}\mathrm{p}^{\mathrm{p}+1}\right)^{\frac{\mathrm{p}}{2}} \\
& \mathbf{E}\Big[\int_0^{\vartheta}(\widetilde{\phi}(\vartheta)-\widetilde{\phi}(\varpi))^{2\mathrm{q}-2}\|\ \Xi(\varpi,\mathrm{f}_\varepsilon(\varpi),\mathrm{f}_\varepsilon(\mathrm{s}\varpi))-\Xi(\varpi,\mathrm{f}^*_\varepsilon(\varpi),\mathrm{f}^*_\varepsilon(\mathrm{s}\varpi))\ \|^2(\widetilde{\phi}'(\varpi))^2 d\varpi\Big]^{\frac{\mathrm{p}}{2}} \\
& \leq \frac{1}{\Gamma^{\mathrm{p}}(\mathrm{q})}2^{2\mathrm{p}-2}\varepsilon^{\mathrm{p}(-\frac{1}{2})}(\widetilde{\phi}(\vartheta)-\widetilde{\phi}(0))^{\frac{\mathrm{p}}{2}-1}\left(\mathrm{p}^{\mathrm{p}+1}2(\mathrm{p}-1)^{1-\mathrm{p}}\right)^{\frac{\mathrm{p}}{2}} \\
& \mathbf{E}\Big[\int_0^{\vartheta}(\widetilde{\phi}(\vartheta)-\widetilde{\phi}(\varpi))^{(\mathrm{q}-1)\mathrm{p}}\|\ \Xi(\varpi,\mathrm{f}_\varepsilon(\varpi),\mathrm{f}_\varepsilon(\mathrm{s}\varpi))-\Xi(\varpi,\mathrm{f}^*_\varepsilon(\varpi),\mathrm{f}^*_\varepsilon(\mathrm{s}\varpi))\ \|^{\mathrm{p}}(\widetilde{\phi}'(\varpi))^{\mathrm{p}} d\varpi\Big] \\
& \leq \frac{1}{\Gamma^{\mathrm{p}}(\mathrm{q})}2^{3\mathrm{p}-3}\varepsilon^{\mathrm{p}(-\frac{1}{2})}(\widetilde{\phi}(\vartheta)-\widetilde{\phi}(0))^{\frac{\mathrm{p}}{2}-1}\mathfrak{T}_3^{\mathrm{p}}\left(\mathrm{p}^{\mathrm{p}+1}2(1-\mathrm{p})^{\mathrm{p}-1}\right)^{\frac{\mathrm{p}}{2}}\int_0^{\vartheta}(\widetilde{\phi}(\vartheta)-\widetilde{\phi}(\varpi))^{(\mathrm{q}-1)\mathrm{p}} \\
& \mathbf{E}\left[\sup_{0\leq\rho\leq\varpi}[\|\ \mathrm{f}_\varepsilon(\rho)-\mathrm{f}^*_\varepsilon(\rho)\ \|^{\mathrm{p}}+\|\ \mathrm{f}_\varepsilon(\rho \mathrm{s})-\mathrm{f}^*_\varepsilon(\rho \mathrm{s})\ \|^{\mathrm{p}}](\widetilde{\phi}'(\varpi))^{\mathrm{p}} d\varpi\right] \\
& \leq \frac{1}{\Gamma^{\mathrm{p}}(\mathrm{q})}2^{3\mathrm{p}-3}\varepsilon^{\mathrm{p}(-\frac{1}{2})}(\widetilde{\phi}(\vartheta)-\widetilde{\phi}(0))^{\frac{\mathrm{p}}{2}-1}\mathfrak{T}_3^{\mathrm{p}}\left(\mathrm{p}^{\mathrm{p}+1}2(1-\mathrm{p})^{\mathrm{p}-1}\right)^{\frac{\mathrm{p}}{2}}\sup_{0<\varpi\leq\vartheta}(\widetilde{\phi}'(\varpi))^{\mathrm{p}-1}\int_0^{\vartheta}(\widetilde{\phi}(\vartheta)-\widetilde{\phi}(\varpi))^{(\mathrm{q}-1)\mathrm{p}} \\
& \mathbf{E}\left[\sup_{0\leq\rho\leq\varpi}[\|\ \mathrm{f}_\varepsilon(\rho)-\mathrm{f}^*_\varepsilon(\rho)\ \|^{\mathrm{p}}+\|\ \mathrm{f}_\varepsilon(\rho \mathrm{s})-\mathrm{f}^*_\varepsilon(\rho \mathrm{s})\ \|^{\mathrm{p}}]\widetilde{\phi}'(\varpi)d\varpi\right] \\
& = \mathbb{Y}_{21}\varepsilon^{\mathrm{p}(-\frac{1}{2})}(\widetilde{\phi}(\vartheta)-\widetilde{\phi}(0))^{\frac{\mathrm{p}}{2}-1}\left(\int_0^{\vartheta}\left(\widetilde{\phi}(\vartheta)-\widetilde{\phi}(\varpi)\right)^{(\mathrm{q}-1)\mathrm{p}}\mathbf{E}\left[\sup_{0\leq\rho\leq\varpi}\|\ \mathrm{f}_\varepsilon(\rho)-\mathrm{f}^*_\varepsilon(\rho)\ \|^{\mathrm{p}}\right]\widetilde{\phi}'(\varpi)d\varpi\right. \\
& \left.+\int_0^{\vartheta}\left(\widetilde{\phi}(\vartheta)-\widetilde{\phi}(\varpi)\right)^{(\mathrm{q}-1)\mathrm{p}}\mathbf{E}\left[\sup_{0\leq\rho\leq\varpi}\|\ \mathrm{f}_\varepsilon(\rho \mathrm{s})-\mathrm{f}^*_\varepsilon(\rho \mathrm{s})\ \|^{\mathrm{p}}\right]\widetilde{\phi}'(\varpi)d\varpi\right),
\end{aligned} \tag{58}
$$

where $\mathbb{Y}_{21}=2^{3\mathrm{p}-3}\mathfrak{T}_3^{\mathrm{p}}\left(\frac{\mathrm{p}^{\mathrm{p}+1}}{2(\mathrm{p}-1)^{\mathrm{p}-1}}\right)^{\frac{\mathrm{p}}{2}}\frac{1}{\Gamma^{\mathrm{p}}(\mathrm{q})}\mathcal{Y}$ and $\mathcal{Y}=\sup_{0<\varpi\leq\vartheta}(\widetilde{\phi}'(\varpi))^{(\mathrm{p}-1)}$.

Utilizing HI and BDGI on j_{22}:

$$
\begin{aligned}
j_{22} \leq\ & \frac{1}{\Gamma^{\mathrm{p}}(\mathrm{q})}\varepsilon^{\mathrm{p}(-\frac{1}{2})}2^{2\mathrm{p}-2}\left(2(\mathrm{p}-1)^{1-\mathrm{p}}\mathrm{p}^{\mathrm{p}+1}\right)^{\frac{\mathrm{p}}{2}} \\
& \mathbf{E}\Big[\int_0^{\vartheta}\|\ \mathcal{D}(\varpi,\mathrm{f}^*_\varepsilon(\varpi),\mathrm{f}^*_\varepsilon(\mathrm{s}\varpi))-\widetilde{\Xi}(\varpi,\mathrm{f}^*_\varepsilon(\varpi),\mathrm{f}^*_\varepsilon(\mathrm{s}\varpi))\ \|^2(\widetilde{\phi}(\vartheta)-\widetilde{\phi}(\varpi))^{2\mathrm{q}-2}(\widetilde{\phi}'(\varpi))^2 d\varpi\Big]^{\frac{\mathrm{p}}{2}} \\
\leq\ & \frac{1}{\Gamma^{\mathrm{p}}(\mathrm{q})}2^{2\mathrm{p}-2}\varepsilon^{\mathrm{p}(-\frac{1}{2})}(\widetilde{\phi}(\vartheta)-\widetilde{\phi}(0))^{\frac{\mathrm{p}}{2}-1}\left(2(\mathrm{p}-1)^{\mathrm{p}-1}\mathrm{p}^{\mathrm{p}+1}\right)^{\frac{\mathrm{p}}{2}}\mathbf{E}\Big[\int_0^{\vartheta}\left(\widetilde{\phi}(\vartheta)-\widetilde{\phi}(\varpi)\right)^{(\mathrm{q}-1)\mathrm{p}} \\
& \left(\|\ \Xi(\varpi,\mathrm{f}^*_\varepsilon(\varpi),\mathrm{f}^*_\varepsilon(\mathrm{s}\varpi))\ \|^{\mathrm{p}}+\|\ \widetilde{\Xi}(\mathrm{f}^*_\varepsilon(\varpi),\mathrm{f}^*_\varepsilon(\mathrm{s}\varpi))\ \|^{\mathrm{p}}\right)(\widetilde{\phi}'(\varpi))^{\mathrm{p}} d\varpi\Big] \\
\leq\ & \frac{1}{\Gamma^{\mathrm{p}}(\mathrm{q})}2^{2\mathrm{p}-2}\varepsilon^{\mathrm{p}(-\frac{1}{2})}(\widetilde{\phi}(\vartheta)-\widetilde{\phi}(0))^{\frac{\mathrm{p}}{2}-1}\left(2(\mathrm{p}-1)^{\mathrm{p}-1}\mathrm{p}^{\mathrm{p}+1}\right)^{\frac{\mathrm{p}}{2}}\mathbf{E}\Big[\sup_{0<\varpi\leq\vartheta}(\widetilde{\phi}'(\varpi))^{(\mathrm{p}-1)} \\
& \int_0^{\vartheta}\left(\widetilde{\phi}(\vartheta)-\widetilde{\phi}(\varpi)\right)^{(\mathrm{q}-1)\mathrm{p}}\left(\|\ \Xi(\varpi,\mathrm{f}^*_\varepsilon(\varpi),\mathrm{f}^*_\varepsilon(\mathrm{s}\varpi))\ \|^{\mathrm{p}}+\|\ \widetilde{\Xi}(\mathrm{f}^*_\varepsilon(\varpi),\mathrm{f}^*_\varepsilon(\mathrm{s}\varpi))\ \|^{\mathrm{p}}\right)\widetilde{\phi}'(\varpi)d\varpi\Big] \\
\leq\ & \frac{1}{\Gamma^{\mathrm{p}}(\mathrm{q})}\frac{2^{3\mathrm{p}-3}3^{\mathrm{p}-1}\varepsilon^{\mathrm{p}(-\frac{1}{2})}(\widetilde{\phi}(\vartheta)-\widetilde{\phi}(0))^{((\mathrm{q}-1)\mathrm{p}+1)+\frac{\mathrm{p}}{2}-1}\mathfrak{T}_4^{\mathrm{p}}(\mathfrak{T}_4^{\mathrm{p}}+\mathfrak{T}_6)^{\mathrm{p}}}{((\mathrm{q}-1)\mathrm{p}+1)} \\
& \mathcal{Y}\left(2(\mathrm{p}-1)^{1-\mathrm{p}}\mathrm{p}^{\mathrm{p}+1}\right)^{\frac{\mathrm{p}}{2}}(1+\mathbf{E}[\|\ \mathrm{f}^*_\varepsilon(\varpi)\ \|^{\mathrm{p}}]+\mathbf{E}[\|\ \mathrm{f}^*_\varepsilon(\mathrm{s}\varpi)\ \|^{\mathrm{p}}]) \\
=\ & \mathbb{Y}_{22}\varepsilon^{\mathrm{p}(-\frac{1}{2})}(\widetilde{\phi}(\vartheta)-\widetilde{\phi}(0))^{((\mathrm{q}-1)\mathrm{p}+1)+\frac{\mathrm{p}}{2}-1},
\end{aligned} \tag{59}
$$

here

$$
\mathbb{Y}_{22}=2^{3\mathrm{p}-3}3^{\mathrm{p}-1}\mathfrak{T}_4^{\mathrm{p}}(\mathfrak{T}_4^{\mathrm{p}}+\mathfrak{T}_6)^{\mathrm{p}}\frac{1}{((\mathrm{q}-1)\mathrm{p}+1)}\mathcal{Y}\left(2(\mathrm{p}-1)^{1-\mathrm{p}}\mathrm{p}^{\mathrm{p}+1}\right)^{\frac{\mathrm{p}}{2}}(1+\mathbf{E}[\|\ \mathrm{f}^*_\varepsilon(\varpi)\ \|^{\mathrm{p}}]+\mathbf{E}[\|\ \mathrm{f}^*_\varepsilon(\mathrm{s}\varpi)\ \|^{\mathrm{p}}])\frac{1}{\Gamma^{\mathrm{p}}(\mathrm{q})}.
$$

From (54), (59), and (53).

$$\begin{aligned}&\mathbf{E}\left[\sup_{0\le t\le\vartheta}\parallel f_\varepsilon(t)-f^*_\varepsilon(t)\parallel^{p}\right]\le \mathbb{Y}_{12}(\widetilde{\phi}(\vartheta)-\widetilde{\phi}(0))^{(qp-1)}+\mathbb{Y}_{22}\varepsilon^{p(-\frac{1}{2})}(\widetilde{\phi}(\vartheta)-\widetilde{\phi}(0))^{((q-1)p+1)+\frac{p}{2}-1}\\&+\int_0^\vartheta\Big(\mathbb{Y}_{11}(\widetilde{\phi}(\vartheta)-\widetilde{\phi}(0))^{(qp-1)}+\mathbb{Y}_{21}\varepsilon^{p(-\frac{1}{2})}(\widetilde{\phi}(\vartheta)-\widetilde{\phi}(0))^{\frac{p}{2}-1}\big(\widetilde{\phi}(\vartheta)-\widetilde{\phi}(\varpi)\big)^{(q-1)p}\widetilde{\phi}'(\varpi)\Big)\\&\mathbf{E}\left[\sup_{0\le\rho\le\varpi}\parallel f_\varepsilon(\rho)-f^*_\varepsilon(\rho)\parallel^{p}\right]d\varpi+\int_0^\vartheta\Big(\mathbb{Y}_{11}(\widetilde{\phi}(\vartheta)-\widetilde{\phi}(0))^{(qp-1)}+\mathbb{Y}_{21}\varepsilon^{p(-\frac{1}{2})}(\widetilde{\phi}(\vartheta)-\widetilde{\phi}(0))^{\frac{p}{2}-1}\\&\big(\widetilde{\phi}(\vartheta)-\widetilde{\phi}(\varpi)\big)^{(q-1)p}\widetilde{\phi}'(\varpi)\Big)\mathbf{E}\left[\sup_{0\le\rho\le\varpi}\parallel f_\varepsilon(\rho s)-f^*_\varepsilon(\rho s)\parallel^{p}\right]d\varpi.\end{aligned} \tag{60}$$

From (60), we have

$$\begin{aligned}\mathbf{E}\left[\sup_{0\le t\le\vartheta}\parallel f_\varepsilon(t)-\right.&\left.f^*_\varepsilon(t)\parallel^{p}\right]\le\Big(\mathbb{Y}_{12}(\widetilde{\phi}(\vartheta)-\widetilde{\phi}(0))^{(qp-1)}+\mathbb{Y}_{22}\varepsilon^{p(-\frac{1}{2})}(\widetilde{\phi}(\vartheta)-\widetilde{\phi}(0))^{((q-1)p+1)+\frac{p}{2}-1}\Big)\\&\exp\Big(2\mathbb{Y}_{11}(\widetilde{\phi}(\vartheta)-\widetilde{\phi}(0))^{(qp-1)}\vartheta+\frac{2\mathbb{Y}_{21}}{((q-1)p+1)}\varepsilon^{p(-\frac{1}{2})}(\widetilde{\phi}(\vartheta)-\widetilde{\phi}(0))^{((q-1)p+1)+\frac{p}{2}-1}\Big).\end{aligned}$$

So, for $\varrho>0$, $\eta\in\left(0,qp-\frac{p}{2}\right)$, and $t\in[0,\varrho\varepsilon^{-\eta}]\subseteq[0,\mathfrak{g}]$, we have

$$\mathbf{E}\left[\sup_{0\le t\le\varrho\varepsilon^{-\eta}}\parallel f_\varepsilon(t)-f^*_\varepsilon(t)\parallel^{p}\right]\le\mathbb{A}\varepsilon^{1-\eta}, \tag{61}$$

where

$$\begin{aligned}\mathbb{A}=\;&\varepsilon^{\eta-1}\Big(\mathbb{Y}_{12}(\widetilde{\phi}(\varrho\varepsilon^{-\eta})-\widetilde{\phi}(0))^{(qp-1)}+\mathbb{Y}_{22}\varepsilon^{p(-\frac{1}{2})}(\widetilde{\phi}(\varrho\varepsilon^{-\eta})-\widetilde{\phi}(0))^{((q-1)p+1)+\frac{p}{2}-1}\Big)\\&\exp\Big(2\mathbb{Y}_{11}(\widetilde{\phi}(\varrho\varepsilon^{-\eta})-\widetilde{\phi}(0))^{(qp-1)}\varrho\varepsilon^{-\eta}+\frac{2\mathbb{Y}_{21}}{((q-1)p+1)}\varepsilon^{p(-\frac{1}{2})}(\widetilde{\phi}(\varrho\varepsilon^{-\eta})-\widetilde{\phi}(0))^{((q-1)p+1)+\frac{p}{2}-1}\Big).\end{aligned}$$

This concludes the proof. □

Corollary 1. *Suppose that the assumptions (ξ_3) to (ξ_4) are satisfied. When $\mho_1>0$ and $\varepsilon_1\in(0,\varepsilon_0)$, $\eta\in\left(0,qp-\frac{p}{2}\right)$, and $\varrho>0$, then $\forall\varepsilon\in(0,\varepsilon_1]$, we have:*

$$\lim_{\varepsilon\to0}\mathbb{P}\left[\sup_{t\in[0,\,\varrho\varepsilon^{-\eta}]}\parallel f_\varepsilon(t)-f^*_\varepsilon(t)\parallel>\mho_1\right]=0. \tag{62}$$

Proof. For $\mho_1>0$ by the Chebyshev–Markov inequality and Theorem 5,

$$\begin{aligned}\mathbb{P}\left[\sup_{t\in[0,\,\varrho\varepsilon^{-\eta}]}\parallel f_\varepsilon(t)-f^*_\varepsilon(t)\parallel>\mho_1\right]\le\;&\frac{1}{\mho_1^2}\mathbf{E}\left[\sup_{t\in[0,\,\varrho\varepsilon^{-\eta}]}\parallel f_\varepsilon(t)-f^*_\varepsilon(t)\parallel^2\right]\\\le\;&\frac{\mathbb{A}\varepsilon^{1-\eta}}{\mho_1^2}\\\le\;&0\text{ as }\varepsilon\to0.\end{aligned}$$

□

5. Numerical Problems

To better understand the theoretical results established in this research, we present numerical problems along with graphical comparisons of the original and averaged solutions. The Figures 1–4 show that the solutions of the original system and the average system overlap, demonstrating the effectiveness of our research study.

Problem 1. Take the system

$$\begin{cases} {}^{H}\mathcal{T}_{t}^{0.8,\alpha,\widetilde{\phi}} f_{\varepsilon}(t) = 6\sin^{2}(t)f_{\varepsilon}(t) + f_{\varepsilon}(t)\cos^{2}\left(\frac{1}{2}t\right) + \\ 3\varepsilon^{-\frac{1}{2}} f_{\varepsilon}(t)\cos^{2}(t)\sin(f_{\varepsilon}(t))\frac{d\mathcal{W}(t)}{dt}, \ t \in [0,\pi], \\ \mathcal{I}_{0^{+}}^{(1-0.8)(1-0.85),t^{\frac{1}{2}}} f(0) = c, \end{cases} \tag{63}$$

where $q = 0.8$, $s = \frac{1}{2}$, and

$$\mathcal{D}(t, f(t), f(ts)) = 6\sin^{2}(t)f_{\varepsilon}(t) + f_{\varepsilon}(t)\cos^{2}\left(\frac{1}{2}t\right),$$
$$\Xi(t, f(t), f(ts)) = 3f_{\varepsilon}(t)\cos^{2}(t)\sin(f_{\varepsilon}(t)).$$

The criteria of the EU are fulfilled by $6\sin^{2}(t)f_{\varepsilon}(t) + f_{\varepsilon}(t)\cos^{2}\left(\frac{1}{2}t\right)$ and $3f_{\varepsilon}(t)\cos^{2}(t)\sin(f_{\varepsilon}(t))$.

The $\mathcal{D}$ and Ξ are shown by the following expressions:

$$\widetilde{\mathcal{D}}(f(t), f(ts)) = \frac{1}{\pi}\int_{0}^{\pi}\left(6\sin^{2}(t)f_{\varepsilon}(t) + f_{\varepsilon}(t)\cos^{2}\left(\frac{1}{2}t\right)\right)dt = \frac{7}{2}f_{\varepsilon}(t),$$
$$\widetilde{\Xi}(f(t), f(ts)) = \frac{1}{\pi}\int_{0}^{\pi} 3f_{\varepsilon}(t)\cos^{2}(t)\sin(f_{\varepsilon}(t))dt = \frac{3}{2}f_{\varepsilon}(t)\sin(f_{\varepsilon}(t)).$$

Hence

$$\begin{cases} \mathcal{T}_{t}^{0.80,\alpha,\widetilde{\phi}} f_{\varepsilon}^{*}(t) = \frac{7}{2}f_{\varepsilon}(t) + \frac{3}{2}\varepsilon^{-\frac{1}{2}} f_{\varepsilon}(t)\sin(f_{\varepsilon}(t))\frac{d\mathcal{W}(t)}{dt}, \\ \mathcal{I}_{0^{+}}^{(1-0.80)(1-0.85),t^{\frac{1}{2}}} f(0) = c. \end{cases} \tag{64}$$

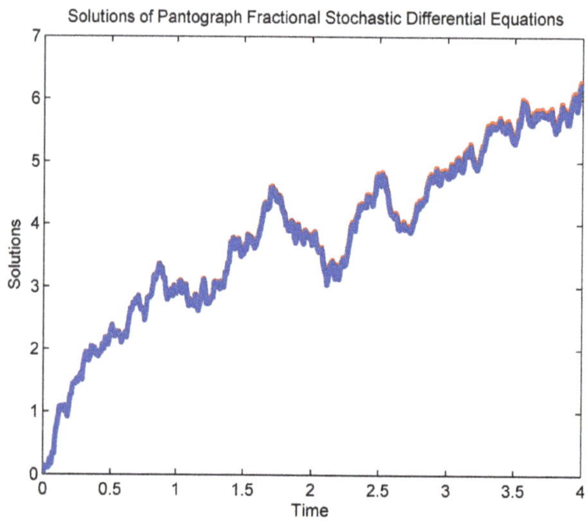

Figure 1. Red: original equation; blue: averaged equation for $\epsilon = 0.001$.

Problem 2. Consider SPFrDEs:

$$\begin{cases} {}^{H}\mathcal{T}_{t}^{0.95,\alpha,\widetilde{\phi}} f_{\varepsilon}(t) = 3\sin\left(f_{\varepsilon}\left(\frac{1}{2}t\right)\right)\sin^{2}(t)f_{\varepsilon}(t) + \varepsilon^{-\frac{1}{2}}\sin(f_{\varepsilon}(t))\cos(f_{\varepsilon}(t)) \\ \frac{d\mathcal{W}(t)}{dt}, \ t \in [0,\pi], \\ \mathcal{I}_{0^{+}}^{(1-0.95)(1-\alpha),\widetilde{\phi}} f(0) = c, \end{cases} \tag{65}$$

where $q = 0.95$, $s = \frac{1}{2}$, and

$$\mathcal{D}(t, f(t), f(ts)) = 3\sin\left(f_{\varepsilon}\left(\frac{1}{2}t\right)\right)\sin^2(t)f_{\varepsilon}(t),$$
$$\Xi(t, f(t), f(ts)) = \sin(f_{\varepsilon}(t))\cos(f_{\varepsilon}(t)).$$

The criteria of EU are fulfilled by $3\sin(f_{\varepsilon}(t))\sin^2(t)f_{\varepsilon}(t)$ and $\sin(f_{\varepsilon}(t))\cos(f_{\varepsilon}(t))$.

So,

$$\widetilde{\mathcal{D}}(f(t), f(ts)) = \frac{1}{\pi}\int_0^{\pi} 3\sin\left(f_{\varepsilon}\left(\frac{1}{2}t\right)\right)\sin^2(t)f_{\varepsilon}(t)dt = \frac{3}{2}\sin\left(f_{\varepsilon}\left(\frac{1}{2}t\right)\right)f_{\varepsilon}(t),$$
$$\widetilde{\Xi}(f(t), f(ts)) = \frac{1}{\pi}\int_0^{\pi} \sin(f_{\varepsilon}(t))\cos(f_{\varepsilon}(t))dt = \sin(f_{\varepsilon}(t))\cos(f_{\varepsilon}(t)).$$

Thus,

$$\begin{cases} \mathcal{T}_t^{0.95,\alpha,\widetilde{\phi}} f_{\varepsilon}^*(t) = \frac{3}{2}\sin\left(f_{\varepsilon}\left(\frac{1}{2}t\right)\right)f_{\varepsilon}(t) + \varepsilon^{-\frac{1}{2}}\sin(f_{\varepsilon}(t))\cos(f_{\varepsilon}(t))dt, \\ \mathcal{I}_{0^+}^{(1-0.95)(1-\alpha),\widetilde{\phi}} f(0) = c. \end{cases} \tag{66}$$

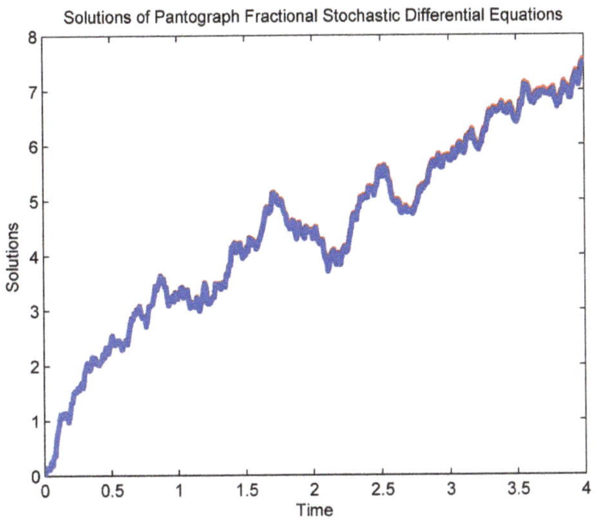

Figure 2. Red: original equation; blue: averaged equation for $\epsilon = 0.001$.

Problem 3. Consider SPFrDEs:

$$\begin{cases} {}^{H}\mathcal{T}_t^{0.9,\alpha,\widetilde{\phi}} f_{\varepsilon}(t) = \frac{1}{3}f_{\varepsilon}\left(\frac{1}{4}t\right)\cos\left(f_{\varepsilon}(t)\sin(f_{\varepsilon}(t)\right) + \frac{3\pi}{4}\varepsilon^{-\frac{1}{2}}\sin^3 t\cos(f_{\varepsilon}(t))\sin(f_{\varepsilon}(t))f_{\varepsilon}(t) \\ \frac{d\mathcal{W}(t)}{dt}, \ t \in [0, \pi], \\ \mathcal{I}_{0^+}^{(1-0.90)(1-\alpha),\widetilde{\phi}} f(0) = c, \end{cases} \tag{67}$$

where $q = 0.9$, $s = \frac{1}{4}$, and

$$\mathcal{D}(t, f(t), f(ts)) = \frac{1}{3}f_{\varepsilon}\left(\frac{1}{4}t\right)\cos(f_{\varepsilon}(t))\sin(f_{\varepsilon}(t)),$$
$$\Xi(t, f(t), f(ts)) = \frac{3\pi}{4}\sin^3 t\cos(f_{\varepsilon}(t))f_{\varepsilon}(t)\sin(f_{\varepsilon}(t)).$$

The criteria of EU are fulfilled by $\frac{1}{3}\mathrm{f}_\varepsilon\left(\frac{1}{4}\mathrm{t}\right)\cos(\mathrm{f}_\varepsilon(\mathrm{t}))\sin(\mathrm{f}_\varepsilon(\mathrm{t}))$ and $\frac{3\pi}{4}\sin^3\mathrm{t}\cos(\mathrm{f}_\varepsilon(\mathrm{t}))\mathrm{f}_\varepsilon(\mathrm{t})$ $\sin(\mathrm{f}_\varepsilon(\mathrm{t}))$.

The following equations display the $\mathcal{D}$ and Ξ averages:

$$\widetilde{\mathcal{D}}(\mathrm{f}(\mathrm{t}),\mathrm{f}(\mathrm{ts}))=\frac{1}{\pi}\int_0^\pi\frac{1}{3}\mathrm{f}_\varepsilon\left(\frac{1}{4}\mathrm{t}\right)\sin(\mathrm{f}_\varepsilon(\mathrm{t}))d\mathrm{q}=\frac{1}{3}\mathrm{f}_\varepsilon^*\left(\frac{1}{4}\mathrm{t}\right)\sin(\mathrm{f}_\varepsilon(\mathrm{t}))\cos(\mathrm{f}_\varepsilon(\mathrm{t})),$$
$$\widetilde{\Xi}(\mathrm{f}(\mathrm{t}),\mathrm{f}(\mathrm{ts}))=\frac{1}{\pi}\int_0^\pi\frac{3\pi}{4}\sin^3\mathrm{t}\cos(\mathrm{f}_\varepsilon(\mathrm{t}))\mathrm{f}_\varepsilon(\mathrm{t})\sin(\mathrm{f}_\varepsilon(\mathrm{t}))d\mathrm{q}=\sin(\mathrm{f}_\varepsilon(\mathrm{t}))\cos(\mathrm{f}_\varepsilon(\mathrm{t}))\mathrm{f}_\varepsilon^*(\mathrm{t}).$$

Hence

$$\begin{cases}\mathcal{T}_\mathrm{t}^{0.9,\mathfrak{a},\widetilde{\phi}}\mathrm{f}_\varepsilon^*(\mathrm{t})=\frac{1}{3}\mathrm{f}_\varepsilon^*\left(\frac{1}{4}\mathrm{t}\right)\sin(\mathrm{f}_\varepsilon(\mathrm{t}))\cos(\mathrm{f}_\varepsilon(\mathrm{t}))+\varepsilon^{-\frac{1}{2}}\cos(\mathrm{f}_\varepsilon(\mathrm{t}))\mathrm{f}_\varepsilon^*(\mathrm{t})\sin(\mathrm{f}_\varepsilon(\mathrm{t}))\frac{d\mathcal{W}(\mathrm{t})}{d\mathrm{t}},\\ \mathcal{I}_{0^+}^{(1-0.90)(1-\mathfrak{a}),\widetilde{\phi}}\mathrm{f}(0)=\mathfrak{c}.\end{cases} \tag{68}$$

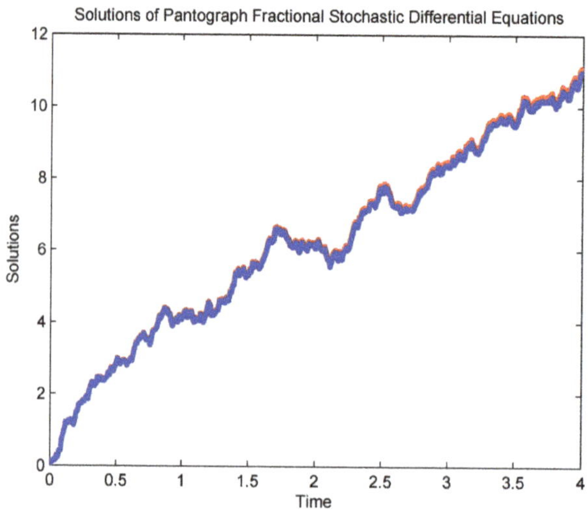

Figure 3. Red: original equation; blue: averaged equation for $\epsilon = 0.001$.

Problem 4. Consider SPFrDEs:

$$\begin{cases}{}^{\mathrm{H}}\mathcal{T}_\mathrm{t}^{0.95,\mathfrak{a},\widetilde{\phi}}\mathrm{f}_\varepsilon(\mathrm{t})=\frac{9}{2}\sin(\mathrm{f}_\varepsilon(\mathrm{t}))\cos(\mathrm{f}_\varepsilon(\mathrm{t}))\exp^{-\mathrm{t}}+\varepsilon^{-\frac{1}{2}}\sin(\mathrm{f}_\varepsilon(\mathrm{t}))\\ \mathrm{f}_\varepsilon\left(\frac{5}{3}\mathrm{t}\right)\cos(\mathrm{f}_\varepsilon(\mathrm{t}))\frac{d\mathcal{W}(\mathrm{t})}{d\mathrm{t}},\ \mathrm{t}\in[0,\pi],\\ \mathcal{I}_{0^+}^{(1-0.95)(1-\mathfrak{a}),\widetilde{\phi}}\mathrm{f}(0)=\mathfrak{c},\end{cases} \tag{69}$$

where $\mathrm{q} = 0.95, \mathrm{s} = \frac{5}{3}$, and

$$\mathcal{D}(\mathrm{t},\mathrm{f}(\mathrm{t}),\mathrm{f}(\mathrm{ts}))=\frac{9}{2}\sin(\mathrm{f}_\varepsilon(\mathrm{t}))\cos(\mathrm{f}_\varepsilon(\mathrm{t}))\exp^{-\mathrm{t}},$$
$$\Xi(\mathrm{t},\mathrm{f}(\mathrm{t}),\mathrm{f}(\mathrm{ts}))=\sin(\mathrm{f}_\varepsilon(\mathrm{t}))\mathrm{f}_\varepsilon\left(\frac{5}{3}\mathrm{t}\right)\cos(\mathrm{f}_\varepsilon(\mathrm{t})).$$

The $\frac{9}{2}\sin(\mathrm{f}_\varepsilon(\mathrm{t}))\cos(\mathrm{f}_\varepsilon(\mathrm{t}))\exp^{-\mathrm{t}}$ and $\sin(\mathrm{f}_\varepsilon(\mathrm{t}))\mathrm{f}_\varepsilon\left(\frac{5}{3}\mathrm{t}\right)\cos(\mathrm{f}_\varepsilon(\mathrm{t}))$ satisfies the needs of EU.

Hence,

$$\begin{aligned} \widetilde{\mathcal{D}}(\mathrm{f}(\mathrm{t}),\mathrm{f}(\mathrm{ts})) &= \frac{1}{\pi}\int_0^{\pi}\left(\frac{9}{2}\sin(\mathrm{f}_\varepsilon(\mathrm{t}))\cos(\mathrm{f}_\varepsilon(\mathrm{t}))\exp^{-\mathrm{t}}\right)dt \\ &= \frac{9}{2\pi}\sin(\mathrm{f}_\varepsilon(\mathrm{t}))\cos(\mathrm{f}_\varepsilon(\mathrm{t}))(1-\exp^{-\pi}), \\ \widetilde{\Xi}(\mathrm{f}(\mathrm{t}),\mathrm{f}(\mathrm{ts})) &= \frac{1}{\pi}\int_0^{\pi}\sin(\mathrm{f}_\varepsilon(\mathrm{t}))\mathrm{f}_\varepsilon\left(\frac{5}{3}\mathrm{t}\right)\cos(\mathrm{f}_\varepsilon(\mathrm{t}))dt \\ &= \sin(\mathrm{f}_\varepsilon(\mathrm{t}))\mathrm{f}_\varepsilon\left(\frac{5}{3}\mathrm{t}\right)\cos(\mathrm{f}_\varepsilon(\mathrm{t})). \end{aligned}$$

Thus, we have the corresponding averaged SPFrDEs

$$\begin{cases} \mathcal{T}_{\mathrm{t}}^{0.95,\mathfrak{a},\widetilde{\phi}}\mathrm{f}_\varepsilon^*(\mathrm{t}) = \frac{9}{2\pi}\sin(\mathrm{f}_\varepsilon(\mathrm{t}))\cos(\mathrm{f}_\varepsilon(\mathrm{t}))(1-\exp^{-\pi}) + \\ \varepsilon^{-\frac{1}{2}}\sin(\mathrm{f}_\varepsilon(\mathrm{t}))\mathrm{f}_\varepsilon\left(\frac{5}{3}\mathrm{t}\right)\cos(\mathrm{f}_\varepsilon(\mathrm{t}))\frac{d\mathcal{W}(\mathrm{t})}{dt}, \\ \mathcal{I}_{0^+}^{(1-0.95)(1-\mathfrak{a}),\widetilde{\phi}}\mathrm{f}(0) = \mathfrak{c}. \end{cases} \tag{70}$$

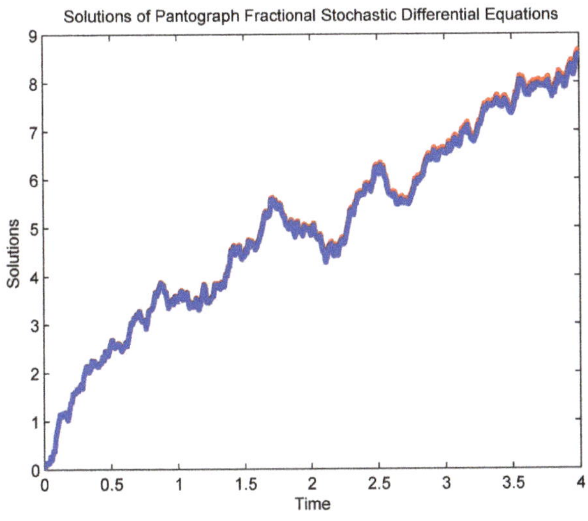

Figure 4. Red: original equation; blue: averaged equation for $\epsilon = 0.001$.

6. Conclusions

We prove the EU theorem using the contraction mapping principle and demonstrate that the solutions of SPFrDEs have continuous dependence on the fractional and initial values. Additionally, we establish that the solution satisfies the smoothness property by proving the regularity theorem. Using various inequalities, we prove the AP theorem. The primary tools employed in our proofs include the BDGI, JI, and HI. We prove the theorems and lemmas for FFrPSDEs under the ϕ-HFrD.

Our research work is important, for the following reasons: First, by proving the results of the EU, continuous dependence, regularity, and AP in the $\mathfrak{p}$th moment, we extend the outcomes for $\mathfrak{p} = 2$. Secondly, we construct theorems and lemmas in the context of ϕ-HFrD. In this way, we generalize the results of Caputo, Riemann–Liouville, and Hadamard and Caputo–Hadamard fractional operators. Third, we take into account SPFrDEs, which are a more widespread subclass of FSDEs.

Author Contributions: Conceptualization, A.M.D. and M.I.L.; methodology, A.M.D. and M.I.L.; software, A.M.D. and M.I.L.; validation, A.M.D. and M.I.L.; formal analysis, A.M.D. and M.I.L.; investigation, A.M.D. and M.I.L.; resources, A.M.D. writing—original draft preparation, A.M.D. and M.I.L.; writing—review and editing, A.M.D. and M.I.L.; visualization, A.M.D. and M.I.L.; funding acquisition, A.M.D. All authors have read and agreed to the published version of the manuscript.

Funding: This work was supported by the Deanship of Scientific Research, Vice Presidency for Graduate Studies and Scientific Research, King Faisal University, Saudi Arabia (Project No. KFU250687).

Data Availability Statement: No data were generated or analyzed during the current study.

Conflicts of Interest: The authors declare no conflicts of interest.

Abbreviations

The following abbreviations are used in this manuscript.

SPFrDEs	stochastic pantograph fractional differential equations
HFrD	Hilfer fractional derivative
AP	averaging principle
BDGI	Burkholder-Davis-Gundy inequality
FSDEs	Fractional stochastic differential equations
CFD	Caputo fractional derivative
HI	Hölder's inequality
JI	Jensen's inequality
FDEs	fractional differential equations

Appendix A

Appendix A.1

The detailed simplification of (10) is given below: From (ξ_1), we have

$$\begin{aligned} \| \mathcal{D}(\varpi, f(\varpi), f(s\varpi)) \|_p^p \leq & 2^{p-1}(\| \mathcal{D}(\varpi, f(\varpi), f(s\varpi)) - \mathcal{D}(\varpi,0,0) \|_p^p + \| \mathcal{D}(\varpi,0,0) \|_p^p) \\ \leq & 2^{p-1}(\mathfrak{T}_1^p(\| f(\varpi) \|_p^p + \| f(s\varpi) \|_p^p) + \| \mathcal{D}(\varpi,0,0) \|_p^p). \end{aligned} \tag{A1}$$

Therefore,

$$\begin{aligned} \int_0^t \| \mathcal{D}(\varpi, f(\varpi), f(s\varpi)) \|_p^p d\varpi \quad & \leq 2^{p-1}\mathfrak{T}_1^p\left(\left(\underset{\varpi\in[0,\mathfrak{g}]}{esssup} \| f(\varpi) \|_p\right)^p + \left(\underset{\varpi\in[0,\mathfrak{g}]}{esssup} \| f(s\varpi) \|_p\right)^p\right) \\ & \int_0^t 1 d\varpi + 2^{p-1}\int_0^t \| \mathcal{D}(\varpi,0,0) \|_p^p d\varpi \\ & \leq 2^{p-1}\mathfrak{g}\mathfrak{T}_1^p(\| f(\varpi) \|_{\mathcal{H}^p}^p + \| f(s\varpi) \|_{\mathcal{H}^p}^p) \\ & +2^{p-1}\int_0^t \| \mathcal{D}(\varpi,0,0) \|_p^p d\varpi. \end{aligned} \tag{A2}$$

From (10) and (A2), we get

$$\begin{aligned} & \| \int_0^t (\phi(t) - \phi(\varpi))^{q-1}\mathcal{D}(\varpi, f(\varpi), f(s\varpi))\phi'(\varpi)d\varpi \|_p^p \leq \Im^{p-1}\left((\phi(\varpi) - \phi(0))^{\frac{(qp-1)}{p-1}}\right)^{p-1} \\ & \left(\frac{p-1}{qp-1}\right)^{p-1} 2^{p-1}\left(\mathfrak{T}_1^p\mathfrak{g}(\| f(\varpi) \|_{\mathcal{H}^p}^p + \| f(s\varpi) \|_{\mathcal{H}^p}^p) + \int_0^t \| \mathcal{D}(\varpi,0,0) \|_p^p d\varpi\right). \end{aligned} \tag{A3}$$

Using (ξ_2), we obtain from (A3) that

$$\begin{aligned} & \| \int_0^t (\phi(t) - \phi(\varpi))^{q-1}\mathcal{D}(\varpi, f(\varpi), f(s\varpi))\phi'(\varpi)d\varpi \|_p^p \leq \Im^{p-1} \\ & \left((\phi(\varpi) - \phi(0))^{\frac{(qp-1)}{p-1}}\right)^{p-1} \left(\frac{p-1}{qp-1}\right)^{p-1} 2^{p-1}(\mathfrak{T}_1^p\mathfrak{g}(\| f(\varpi) \|_{\mathcal{H}^p}^p + \| f(s\varpi) \|_{\mathcal{H}^p}^p) + \mathfrak{g}\gamma^p). \end{aligned} \tag{A4}$$

Appendix A.2

The detailed simplification of (12) is given below: Thus, by using (ξ_1) and (ξ_2), we have

$$\begin{aligned} \| \Xi(\varpi, f(\varpi), f(s\varpi)) \|_p^p &\leq 2^{p-1}\mathfrak{T}_2^p(\| f(\varpi) \|_p^p + \| f(s\varpi) \|_p^p) + 2^{p-1} \| \Xi(\varpi,0,0) \|_p^p \\ &\leq 2^{p-1}\mathfrak{T}_2^p(\| f(\varpi) \|_p^p + \| f(s\varpi) \|_p^p) + 2^{p-1}\gamma^p. \end{aligned} \tag{A5}$$

So $\forall t \in [0, \mathfrak{g}]$, we have

$$\begin{aligned} &\int_0^t (\phi(t) - \phi(\varpi))^{2q-2} \| \Xi(\varpi, f(\varpi), f(s\varpi)) \|_p^p (\phi'(\varpi))^2 d\varpi \leq 2^{p-1}\mathfrak{T}_2^p \\ &\int_0^t (\phi(t) - \phi(\varpi))^{2q-2}\left(\left(\underset{\varpi\in[0,\mathfrak{g}]}{esssup} \| f(\varpi) \|_p\right)^p + \left(\underset{\varpi\in[0,\mathfrak{g}]}{esssup} \| f(s\varpi) \|_p\right)^p\right)(\phi'(\varpi))^2 d\varpi \\ + \;& 2^{p-1}\gamma^p \int_0^t (\phi(t) - \phi(\varpi))^{2q-2}(\phi'(\varpi))^2 d\varpi \\ \leq \;& 2^{p-1}\mathfrak{T}_2^p \sup_{0<\varpi\leq t} \phi'(\varpi) \int_0^t (\phi(t) - \phi(\varpi))^{2q-2}\left(\left(\underset{\varpi\in[0,\mathfrak{g}]}{esssup} \| f(\varpi) \|_p\right)^p\right. \\ + \;& \left.\left(\underset{\varpi\in[0,\mathfrak{g}]}{esssup} \| f(s\varpi) \|_p\right)^p\right)\phi'(\varpi)d\varpi + 2^{p-1}\gamma^p \sup_{0<\varpi\leq t} \phi'(\varpi) \int_0^t (\phi(t) - \phi(\varpi))^{2q-2}\phi'(\varpi)d\varpi \\ = \;& \mathbf{G}\frac{2^{p-1}(\phi(\varpi)-\phi(0))^{(2q-1)}}{(2q-1)}\left(\mathfrak{T}_2^p\left(\| f(\varpi) \|_{\mathcal{H}_p}^p + \| f(s\varpi) \|_{\mathcal{H}_p}^p\right) + \gamma^p\right). \end{aligned} \tag{A6}$$

Therefore, we obtain the following:

$$\begin{aligned} &\| \int_0^t (\phi(t) - \phi(\varpi))^{q-1}\Xi(\varpi, f(\varpi), f(s\varpi))\phi'(\varpi)d\mathcal{W}(\varpi) \|_p^p \leq \mathbf{G}^{\frac{p-2}{2}} \\ &\mathcal{C}_p\left(\frac{(\phi(\varpi)-\phi(0))^{(2q-1)}}{(2q-1)}\right)^{\frac{p-2}{2}} \frac{2^{p-1}(\phi(\varpi)-\phi(0))^{(2q-1)}}{(2q-1)} \\ &\mathbf{G}\left(\mathfrak{T}_2^p\left(\| f(\varpi) \|_{\mathcal{H}_p}^p + \| f(s\varpi) \|_{\mathcal{H}_p}^p\right) + \gamma^p\right). \end{aligned} \tag{A7}$$

References

1. Raheem, A.; Alamrani, F.M.; Akhtar, J.; Alatawi, A.; Alshaban, E.; Khatoon, A.; Khan, F.A. Study on Controllability for Ψ-Hilfer Fractional Stochastic Differential Equations. *Fractal Fract.* **2024**, *8*, 727. [CrossRef]
2. Lavanya, M.; Vadivoo, B.S.; Nisar, K.S. Controllability Analysis of neutral stochastic differential equation using Ψ-Hilfer fractional derivative with Rosenblatt process. *Qual. Theory Dyn. Syst.* **2025**, *24*, 19. [CrossRef]
3. Gokul, G.; Udhayakumar, R. Approximate Controllability Results of Ψ-Hilfer fractional neutral Hemivariational inequalities with infinite delay via almost sectorial operators. *Eur. Phys. J. Spec. Top.* **2024**, 1–19. [CrossRef]
4. Sousa, J.V.D.C.; Kucche, K.D.; De Oliveira, E.C. Stability of Ψ-Hilfer impulsive fractional differential equations. *Appl. Math. Lett.* **2019**, *88*, 73–80. [CrossRef]
5. Kucche, K.D.; Mali, A.D. On the Nonlinear Ψ-Hilfer hybrid fractional differential equations. *Comput. Appl. Math.* **2022**, *41*, 86. [CrossRef]
6. Montalvo Bonilla, M.; Vera Baca, J.; Torres Ledesma, C.E. Solvability of Ψ-Hilfer fractional differential equations in the space of summable functions. *Mediterr. J. Math.* **2024**, *21*, 204. [CrossRef]
7. Lima, K.B.; Vanterler da C. Sousa, J.; De Oliveira, E.C. Ulam–Hyers type stability for Ψ-Hilfer fractional differential equations with impulses and delay. *Comput. Appl. Math.* **2021**, *40*, 293. [CrossRef]
8. Abdo, M.S.; Panchal, S.K. Fractional integro-differential equations involving Ψ-Hilfer fractional derivative. *Adv. Appl. Math. Mech.* **2019**, *11*, 338–359. [CrossRef]
9. Varun Bose, C.S.; Udhayakumar, R.; Velmurugan, S.; Saradha, M.; Almarri, B. Approximate controllability of Ψ-Hilfer fractional neutral differential equation with infinite delay. *Fractal Fract.* **2023**, *7*, 537. [CrossRef]
10. Kilbas, A.A.; Srivastava, H.M.; Trujillo, J.J. *Theory and Applications of Fractional Differential Equations*; Elsevier: Amsterdam, The Netherlands, 2006; Volume 204.
11. Vanterler da C. Sousa, J.; Capelas de Oliveira, E. On the ψ-Hilfer fractional derivative. *Commun. Nonlinear Sci. Numer. Simul.* **2018**, *60*, 72–91. [CrossRef]
12. Umamaheswari, P.; Balachandran, K.; Annapoorani, N. Existence and stability results for Caputo fractional stochastic differential equations with Lévy noise. *Filomat* **2020**, *34*, 1739–1751. [CrossRef]

13. Ben, M.A.; Mchiri, L.; Rhaima, M.; Sallay, J. Hyers-Ulam stability of Hadamard fractional stochastic differential equations. *Filomat* **2023**, *37*, 10219–10228.
14. Moualkia, S.; Xu, Y. On the existence and uniqueness of solutions for multidimensional fractional stochastic differential equations with variable order. *Mathematics* **2021**, *9*, 2106. [CrossRef]
15. Babaei, A.; Banihashemi, S.; Moghaddam, B.P.; Dabiri, A.; Galhano, A. Efficient Solutions for Stochastic Fractional Differential Equations with a Neutral Delay Using Jacobi Poly-Fractonomials. *Mathematics* **2024**, *12*, 3273. [CrossRef]
16. Asai, Y.; Kloeden, P.E. Numerical schemes for ordinary delay differential equations with random noise. *Appl. Math. Comput.* **2019**, *347*, 306–318. [CrossRef]
17. Ali, A.; Hayat, K.; Zahir, A.; Shah, K.; Abdeljawad, T. Qualitative Analysis of Fractional Stochastic Differential Equations with Variable Order Fractional Derivative. *Qual. Theory Dyn. Syst.* **2024**, *23*, 120. [CrossRef]
18. Zhang, X.; Agarwal, P.; Liu, Z.; Peng, H.; You, F.; Zhu, Y. Existence and uniqueness of solutions for stochastic differential equations of fractional-order (q>1) with finite delays. *Adv. Differ. Equ.* **2017**, *2017*, 123. [CrossRef]
19. Lavanya, M.; Vadivoo, B.S. Analysis of controllability in Caputo-Hadamard stochastic fractional differential equations with fractional Brownian motion. *Int. J. Dyn. Control* **2024**, *12*, 15–23. [CrossRef]
20. Obradović, M.; Milošević, M. Stability of a class of neutral stochastic differential equations with unbounded delay and Markovian switching and the Euler-Maruyama method. *J. Comput. Appl. Math.* **2017**, *309*, 244–266. [CrossRef]
21. Yang, H.; Wu, F.; Kloeden, P.E.; Mao, X. The truncated Euler-Maruyama method for stochastic differential equations with Hölder diffusion coefficients. *J. Comput. Appl. Math.* **2020**, *366*, 112379. [CrossRef]
22. Muthukumar, P.; Thiagu, K. Existence of solutions and approximate controllability of fractional nonlocal stochastic differential equations of order $1 < q \leq 2$ with infinite delay and Poisson jumps. *Differ. Equ. Dyn. Syst.* **2018**, *26*, 15–36.
23. Zou, G.A.; Wang, B. Stochastic Burgers' equation with fractional derivative driven by multiplicative noise. *Comput. Math. Appl.* **2017**, *74*, 3195–3208. [CrossRef]
24. Khasminskij, R.Z. On the principle of averaging the Itov's stochastic differential equations. *Kybernetika* **1968**, *4*, 260–279.
25. Mao, W.; You, S.; Wu, X.; Mao, X. On the averaging principle for stochastic delay differential equations with jumps. *Adv. Differ. Equ.* **2015**, *2015*, 70. [CrossRef]
26. Xu, W.; Xu, W.; Lu, K. An averaging principle for stochastic differential equations of fractional order $0 < \alpha < 1$. *Fract. Calc. Appl. Anal.* **2020**, *23*, 908–919.
27. Guo, Z.; Lv, G.; Wei, J. Averaging principle for stochastic differential equations under a weak condition. *Chaos* **2020**, *30*, 1250014. [CrossRef] [PubMed]
28. Liu, J.; Xu, W. An averaging result for impulsive fractional neutral stochastic differential equations. *Appl. Math. Lett.* **2021**, *114*, 106892. [CrossRef]
29. Liu, J.; Xu, W.; Guo, Q. Averaging principle for impulsive stochastic partial differential equations. *Stoch. Dyn.* **2021**, *21*, 2150014. [CrossRef]
30. Ahmed, H.M.; Zhu, Q. The averaging principle of Hilfer fractional stochastic delay differential equations with Poisson jumps. *Appl. Math. Lett.* **2021**, *112*, 106755. [CrossRef]
31. Xu, W.; Xu, W.; Zhang, S. The averaging principle for stochastic differential equations with Caputo fractional derivative. *Appl. Math. Lett.* **2019**, *93*, 79–84. [CrossRef]
32. Jing, Y.; Li, Z. Averaging principle for backward stochastic differential equations. *Discret. Dyn. Nat. Soc.* **2021**, *2021*, 6615989. [CrossRef]
33. Guo, Z.; Xu, Y.; Wang, W.; Hu, J. Averaging principle for stochastic differential equations with monotone condition. *Appl. Math. Lett.* **2022**, *125*, 107705. [CrossRef]
34. Mouy, M.; Boulares, H.; Alshammari, S.; Alshammar, M.; Laskri, Y.; Mohammed, W.W. On averaging principle for Caputo–Hadamard fractional stochastic differential Pantograph equation. *Fractal Fract.* **2023**, *7*, 31. [CrossRef]
35. Shen, G.; Wu, J.L.; Yin, X. Averaging principle for fractional heat equations driven by stochastic measures. *Appl. Math. Lett.* **2020**, *106*, 106404. [CrossRef]
36. Liu, J.; Zhang, H.; Wang, J.; Jin, C.; Li, J.; Xu, W. A note on averaging principles for fractional stochastic differential equations. *Fractal Fract.* **2024**, *8*, 216. [CrossRef]
37. Liu, J.; Wei, W.; Wang, J.; Xu, W. Limit behavior of the solution of Caputo-Hadamard fractional stochastic differential equations. *Appl. Math. Lett.* **2023**, *140*, 108586. [CrossRef]
38. Yang, D.; Wang, J.; Bai, C. Averaging principle for Ψ-Caputo fractional stochastic delay differential equations with Poisson jumps. *Symmetry* **2023**, *15*, 1346. [CrossRef]
39. Djaouti, A.M.; Khan, Z.A.; Liaqat, M.I.; Al-Quran, A. Existence, uniqueness, and averaging principle of fractional neutral stochastic differential equations in the Lp space with the framework of the Ψ-Caputo derivative. *Mathematics* **2024**, *12*, 1037. [CrossRef]

40. Djaouti, A.M.; Liaqat, M.I. Qualitative analysis for the solutions of fractional stochastic differential equations. *Axioms* **2014**, *13*, 438. [CrossRef]
41. Albuquerque, N.; Araújo, G.; Pellegrino, D.; Seoane-Sepúlveda, J.B. Hölder's inequality: Some recent and unexpected applications. *Bull. Belg. Math. Soc.-Simon Stevin* **2017**, *24*, 199–225. [CrossRef]
42. Yang, Z.; Zheng, X.; Wang, H. Well-posedness and regularity of Caputo–Hadamard fractional stochastic differential equations. *Z. Angew. Math. Phys.* **2021**, *72*, 141. [CrossRef]
43. Kohler, M.; Krzyżak, A.; Walk, H. Estimation of the essential supremum of a regression function. *Stat. Probab. Lett.* **2011**, *81*, 685–693. [CrossRef]
44. Henry, D. *Geometric Theory of Semilinear Parabolic Equations*; Springer: Berlin/Heidelberg, Germany, 2006; Volume 840.

fractal and fractional

MDPI

Article

Existence and Hyers–Ulam Stability Analysis of Nonlinear Multi-Term Ψ-Caputo Fractional Differential Equations Incorporating Infinite Delay

Yating Xiong [1], Abu Bakr Elbukhari [1,2,3] and Qixiang Dong [1,*]

1 School of Mathematical Sciences, Yangzhou University, Yangzhou 225002, China; 221002131@stu.yzu.edu.cn (Y.X.); mrbakri123@hotmail.com (A.B.E.)
2 School of Information Engineering, Yangzhou University, Yangzhou 225003, China
3 Department of Mathematics, University of Khartoum, Omdurman, 406, Khartoum 11115, Sudan
* Correspondence: qxdong@yzu.edu.cn

Abstract: The aim of the paper is to prove the existence results and Hyers–Ulam stability to nonlinear multi-term Ψ-Caputo fractional differential equations with infinite delay. Some specified assumptions are supposed to be satisfied by the nonlinear item and the delayed term. The Leray–Schauder alternative theorem and the Banach contraction principle are utilized to analyze the existence and uniqueness of solutions for infinite delay problems. Some new inequalities are presented in this paper for delayed fractional differential equations as auxiliary results, which are convenient for analyzing Hyers–Ulam stability. Some examples are discussed to illustrate the obtained results.

Keywords: fractional differential equations; infinite delay; fixed-point theorem; existence and uniqueness; Hyers–Ulam stability

1. Introduction

Fractional differential equations (Fra-Diff-Equs) [1–5] are powerful tools for describing complex systems. In the early years, research was mainly focused on mathematical theoretical explorations, with less attention to time delays. They gained attention in the late 20th century and began to combine fractional calculus with time delays. Nowadays, fractional time delays have been applied in the fields of physics [6,7], solid mechanics [8], electromechanics [9], and finance [10], and chemistry [11], which help accurately describe the system dynamics, optimize the performance, improve the accuracy of the models, and assist in the decision-making process in these fields.

In order to ensure the solvability of the equations and to provide a prerequisite for numerical calculations, in recent years, scholars have devoted themselves to studying the properties of solutions of Fra-Diff-Equs [12–14]. Benchohra M et al. [15] explored the existence of solutions to Caputo Fra-Diff-Equs; Bao et al. [16] explored the existence results of solutions to neutral stochastic Fra-Diff-Equs in $\mathrm{Lp}(\Omega, Ch)$.

However, due to the constraints of the time-delay conditions, the study of the stability of Fra-Diff-Equs [17–22] is extremely difficult. It requires scholars attempt to prove new inequalities according to the requirements of the conditions. Over the past years, numerous articles have been dedicated to studying the Hyers–Ulam stability (Hs-Um-St) of Fra-Diff-Equs.

In [23], Dong et al. investigated a type of Riemann–Liouville Fra-Diff-Equs with time delay

$$\begin{cases} D^{\Theta}y(v) = f(v, \widehat{y_v}), & v \in (0, \flat], \\ \widehat{y_0} = \aleph \in \breve{\mathfrak{B}}, \end{cases}$$

where $\widehat{y}(v) = v^{1-\Theta}y(v)$, $0 < \Theta \leq 1$, $\breve{\mathfrak{B}}$ represents the phase space. For Fra-Diff-Equs with non-zero initial values, the weighted-delay method was employed to investigate the properties of the solutions. Dong et al. proved new Gronwall inequalities, which laid the foundation for the proof of Hs-Um-St.

In [24], Chen et al. investigated the existence, uniqueness, and Hs-Um-St of solutions for Fra-Diff-Equs with infinite delay

$$\begin{cases} {}_cD^{\Theta}y(v) - \mathfrak{a}\,{}_cD^{\varrho}y(v) = f(v, y_v), & v \in J = [0, \flat], \\ y(v) = \aleph(v), & v \in (-\infty, 0], \end{cases}$$

where $y_v(s) = y(v+s)$, $s \in (-\infty, 0]$, $v \in J$, ${}_cD^{\Theta}$ and ${}_cD^{\varrho}$ are a Caputo fractional derivative (Fr-De) with $0 < \varrho < \Theta \leq 1$, $f : J \times \breve{\mathfrak{B}} \to R$ is given that satisfies certain assumptions, the function $\aleph \in \breve{\mathfrak{B}}$.

Inspired by the works in the discussions above, in this paper, we conduct an in-depth study on a class of nonlinear Fra-Diff-Equs with infinite delay and featuring the Ψ-Caputo Fr-De

$$\begin{cases} {}^cD^{\Theta;\Psi}y(v) - \mathfrak{a}\,{}^cD^{\varrho;\Psi}y(v) = f(v, y_v), & v \in J = [0, \flat], \\ y(v) = \aleph(v), & v \in (-\infty, 0], \end{cases} \tag{1}$$

where ${}^cD^{\Theta;\Psi}$ and ${}^cD^{\varrho;\Psi}$ stand for Ψ-Caputo Fr-Des with $0 < \varrho < \Theta \leq 1$, $\mathfrak{a} \in R$ is a constant, and the function $f : J \times \breve{\mathfrak{B}} \to R$ satisfies the specified hypotheses, $\aleph \in \breve{\mathfrak{B}}$, and $\breve{\mathfrak{B}}$ is a phase space. y_v is a function defined on $(-\infty, \flat]$ as

$$y_v(s) = y(v+s), \quad s \in (-\infty, 0], \quad v \in J. \tag{2}$$

Our approach mainly focuses on transforming delayed differential equations into integral equations. Subsequently, these integral equations are properly extended within the phase space. We use the Leray–Schauder alternative and Banach fixed-point theorems to examine the existence and uniqueness of solutions. Furthermore, we initiate an exploration of the Hs-Um-St of the solution. It is worth noting that this exploration is faced with substantial challenges. These challenges mainly originate from the specific constraints caused by the delay conditions, which increase the complexity of analyzing the stability of the solution. Specifically, the difficulty lies in the fact that the original Gronwall inequality is inapplicable. To overcome this difficulty, we need to extend new inequalities.

In Section 2, a comprehensive review of some basic definitions and lemmas will be carried out. Section 3 is devoted to investigating the existence and uniqueness of the solutions. In Section 4, we discuss Hs-Um-St in detail. At the end of the article, two examples are provided to illustrate the conclusions.

2. Preliminaries and Lemmas

We first list several basic definitions and theorems. Subsequently, we proceed to prove a series of inequalities that are used to verify the Hs-Um-St. It should be emphasized that the function $\Psi([a, \flat] \to R_+)$ is increasing, positive, uniformly integrable, and $\Psi'(v) \neq 0$. This makes the subsequent proofs more rigorous.

Definition 1 ([25]). *Let $\Theta > 0$ and $n \in \mathbb{N}$ with $n = [\Theta] + 1$. The Riemann–Liouville Fr-De with respect to Ψ with the order Θ of y is defined by*

$$ {}^{RL}D_{a^+}^{\Theta;\Psi} y(v) := \left(\frac{1}{\Psi'(v)} \frac{d}{dv}\right)^n J_{a^+}^{n-\Theta;\Psi} y(v), \tag{3} $$

where $J_{a^+}^{\Theta;\Psi} y(v)$ is defined by

$$ J_{a^+}^{\Theta;\Psi} y(v) := \frac{1}{\Gamma(\Theta)} \int_a^v \Psi'(s)(\Psi(v) - \Psi(s))^{\Theta-1} y(s) ds. \tag{4} $$

Definition 2 ([26]). *Let $\Theta > 0$ and $n \in \mathbb{N}$. The Caputo-type Fr-De with respect to Ψ with the order Θ of y is defined by*

$$ {}^{c}D_{a^+}^{\Theta;\Psi} y(v) := {}^{RL}D_{a^+}^{\Theta;\Psi} [y(v) - \sum_{i=0}^{n-1} \frac{y_{\Psi}^{[i]}(a)}{i!} (\Psi(v) - \Psi(a))^i], \tag{5} $$

where $y \in C^{n-1}([a, \flat], R)$, ${}^{RL}D_{a^+}^{\Theta;\Psi} y(v)$ exists and

$$ y_{\Psi}^{[i]}(v) := \left(\frac{1}{\Psi'(v)} \frac{d}{dv}\right)^i y(v). $$

Theorem 1 ([27]). *Let $\Theta > 0$.*

(i) If the function $y : [a, \flat] \to R$ is continuous, then

$$ {}^{c}D_{a^+}^{\Theta;\Psi} J_{a^+}^{\Theta;\Psi} y(v) = y(v). $$

(ii) If $y \in C^{n-1}([a, \flat], R)$ and ${}^{RL}D_{a^+}^{\Theta;\Psi} y(v)$ exists, then

$$ J_{a^+}^{\Theta;\Psi} {}^{c}D_{a^+}^{\Theta;\Psi} y(v) = y(v) - \sum_{i=0}^{n-1} \frac{y_{\Psi}^{[i]}(a)}{i!} (\Psi(v) - \Psi(a))^i. $$

Definition 3 ([28]). *Let $\mathbb{X}$ be a Banach space. A linear topological space of functions from $(-\infty, 0]$ into $\mathbb{X}$, with the seminorm $\|\cdot\|_{\breve{\mathfrak{B}}}$, is said to be an admissible phase space if $\breve{\mathfrak{B}}$ has the following properties:*

(A1) There exists a constant $\mathbb{H} > 0$ and functions $\mathbb{K}(\cdot), \mathbb{M}(\cdot) : [0, +\infty) \to [0, +\infty)$, such that $\mathbb{K}$ is a continuous function and $\mathbb{M}$ is locally bounded, such that for any constant $a, \flat \in R$ with $\flat > a$, if the function $k : (-\infty, \flat] \to \mathbb{X}$, $k_a \in \breve{\mathfrak{B}}$ and function $k(\cdot)$ is continuous on $[a, \flat]$, then for every $v \in [a, \flat]$, the following conditions (i)-(iii) hold:

(i) $k_v \in \breve{\mathfrak{B}}$;

(ii) $\|k(v)\| \leq \mathbb{H}\|k_v\|_{\breve{\mathfrak{B}}}$;

(iii) $\|k_v\|_{\breve{\mathfrak{B}}} \leq \mathbb{K}(v - a) \sup_{a \leq s \leq v} \|k(s)\| + \mathbb{M}(v - a)\|k_a\|_{\breve{\mathfrak{B}}}$.

(A2) For the function $k(\cdot)$ in (A1), $v \mapsto k_v$ is a $\breve{\mathfrak{B}}$-valued continuous function for $v \in [a, \flat]$.

(B1) The space $\breve{\mathfrak{B}}$ is complete.

Definition 4 ([29]). *The problem (1) is said to be Hs-Um-St if there exists a real number $\mathfrak{r} > 0$, such that for each $\varepsilon > 0$ and for every solution $\beth(\cdot)$ of the inequalities*

$$ \begin{cases} |{}^{c}D^{\Theta;\Psi}\beth(v) - \mathfrak{a}\,{}^{c}D^{\varrho;\Psi}\beth(v) - f(v, \beth_v)| \leq \varepsilon, & v \in J = [0, \flat], \\ \beth(v) = \aleph(v), & v \in (-\infty, 0], \end{cases} \tag{6} $$

there exists a solution $\daleth(\cdot)$ of the problem (1) with

$$ |\beth(v) - \daleth(v)| \leq \mathfrak{r}\varepsilon, \qquad v \in J = [0, \flat]. $$

Lemma 1 ([30]). *(Leray–Schauder alternative) Let $\mathbb{X}$ be a Banach space, O is a subset of $\mathbb{X}$, and O is a closed and convex subset. Moreover, assume that $\mathcal{V}$ is an open subset of O with $0 \in \mathcal{V}$. Suppose $\tau : \overline{\mathcal{V}} \to O$ is a continuous and compact map. Then, either τ has a fixed point in $\mathcal{V}$, or there is a $s \in \partial\mathcal{V}$ and $\wp \in (0,1)$ with $s = \wp\nu(s)$.*

Next, for conveniently proving Theorem 5, we will extend certain properties of the Caputo derivative to the Ψ-Caputo derivative and introduce some integral inequalities that can be regarded as an extended version of the Gronwall inequality.

Lemma 2. *Suppose $\Theta > 0$, a function $f \in C[0,\flat]$, which is nonnegative and nondecreasing, and Ψ is an increasing function. Then, the function*

$$F(v) = J_{0^+}^{\Theta;\Psi} f(v) = \frac{1}{\Gamma(\Theta)} \int_0^v \Psi'(s)(\Psi(v) - \Psi(s))^{\Theta-1} f(s)\mathrm{d}s$$

is nondecreasing on $[0,\flat]$.

Proof. Assuming that the function f satisfies the conditions mentioned above, we can obtain that $f'(v) \geq 0$ for all $v \in [0,\flat]$. Let $\Psi(v) - \Psi(s) = \nu$. Then $s = \Psi^{-1}(\Psi(v) - \nu)$. It follows that

$$\begin{aligned} F'(v) = {} & \frac{f(0)}{\Gamma(\Theta)}\Psi'(v)(\Psi(v) - \Psi(0))^{\Theta-1} \\ & + \frac{1}{\Gamma(\Theta)} \int_0^{\Psi(v)-\Psi(0)} \nu^{\Theta-1} f'(\Psi^{-1}(\Psi(v) - \nu)) \frac{\mathrm{d}(\Psi^{-1}(\Psi(v) - \nu))}{\mathrm{d}v}\mathrm{d}\nu. \end{aligned} \tag{7}$$

Let $\theta(v) = \frac{f(0)}{\Gamma(\Theta)}\Psi'(v)(\Psi(v) - \Psi(0))^{\Theta-1}$, $\mu(v) = \Psi^{-1}(\Psi(v) - \nu)$. Then, $\theta(v) > 0$ because Ψ is increasing, and $\frac{\mathrm{d}\mu(v)}{\mathrm{d}v} > 0$ due to $\mu(\cdot)$ is nondecreasing. So, we have

$$F'(v) = \theta(v) + \frac{1}{\Gamma(\Theta)} \int_0^{\Psi(v)-\Psi(0)} \nu^{\Theta-1} f'(\mu(v)) \frac{\mathrm{d}\mu(v)}{\mathrm{d}v}\mathrm{d}\nu > 0$$

for all $v \in [0,\flat]$ and, hence, $F(\cdot)$ is nondecreasing on $[0,\flat]$. □

To study the problem of infinite delay, we extend Lemma 5 in [24] and prove the following inequality.

Lemma 3. *For any function $\omega \geq 0$ belonging to the space $C[a,\flat]$ and any $v \in [a,\flat]$, the following integral inequality*

$$\sup_{0\leq\nu\leq v} \int_0^\nu \Psi'(s)(\Psi(\nu) - \Psi(s))^{\Theta-1}\omega(s)\mathrm{d}s \leq \int_0^v \Psi'(s)(\Psi(v) - \Psi(s))^{\Theta-1} \sup_{0\leq\sigma\leq s} \omega(\sigma)\mathrm{d}s, \tag{8}$$

can be obtained.

Proof. Fix $v \in [a,\flat]$. Given the function $\omega(\cdot)$, which is nonnegative, and $\sup\limits_{0\leq\sigma\leq s} \omega(\sigma)$, which is nondecreasing, this results in $F(v) = \int_0^v \Psi'(s)(\Psi(v) - \Psi(s))^{\Theta-1} \sup\limits_{0\leq\sigma\leq s} \omega(\sigma)\mathrm{d}s$ also being nondecreasing according to Lemma 2. Then, for any $\nu \in [0,v]$, we have

$$\begin{aligned} \int_0^\nu \Psi'(s)(\Psi(\nu) - \Psi(s))^{\Theta-1}\omega(s)\mathrm{d}s & \leq \int_0^\nu \Psi'(s)(\Psi(\nu) - \Psi(s))^{\Theta-1} \sup_{0\leq\sigma\leq s} \omega(\sigma)\mathrm{d}s \\ & \leq \int_0^v \Psi'(s)(\Psi(v) - \Psi(s))^{\Theta-1} \sup_{0\leq\sigma\leq s} \omega(\sigma)\mathrm{d}s, \end{aligned}$$

therefore,

$$\sup_{0\le \nu\le v}\int_0^{\nu}\Psi'(s)(\Psi(\nu)-\Psi(s))^{\Theta-1}\omega(s)\mathrm{d}s\le\int_0^{v}\Psi'(s)(\Psi(v)-\Psi(s))^{\Theta-1}\sup_{0\le\sigma\le s}\omega(\sigma)\mathrm{d}s.$$

Thus, the proof is completed. □

Next, we extend the Lemma 2.6 in [1] to Ψ-Caputo calculus.

Lemma 4. *Let $\Theta>0$, $\hbar>0$. Consider $g(v,s)$ as a non-negative continuous function that is defined on the domain $[0,T]\times[0,T]$, where $g(v,s)\le\mathbb{M}$. The function $g(v,s)$ has the property of being non-decreasing in v and non-increasing in s. Let Ψ be an increasing and uniformly integrable function. Assume that the function $\varpi(t)$ is non-negative and integrable on the interval $[0,T]$ with*

$$\varpi(v)\le\hbar+\int_0^{v}g(v,s)\Psi'(s)(\Psi(v)-\Psi(s))^{\Theta-1}\varpi(s)\mathrm{d}s,\qquad v\in[0,T].$$

Then, we have

$$\varpi(v)\le\hbar+\hbar\int_0^{v}\sum_{n=1}^{\infty}\frac{(g(v,s)\Gamma(\Theta))^n}{\Gamma(n\Theta)}(\Psi(v)-\Psi(s))^{n\Theta-1}\Psi'(s)\mathrm{d}s.\tag{9}$$

Proof. Let $P\varpi(v)=\int_0^{v}g(v,s)\Psi'(s)(\Psi(v)-\Psi(s))^{\Theta-1}\varpi(s)\mathrm{d}s$, it follows that $\varpi(v)\le\hbar+P\varpi(v)$, which implies

$$\varpi(v)\le\sum_{k=0}^{n-1}P^k\ \hbar+P^n\varpi(v)\qquad(P^0\ \hbar=\hbar).\tag{10}$$

We now prove that

$$P^n\varpi(v)\le\int_0^{v}\frac{(g(v,s)\Gamma(\Theta))^n}{\Gamma(n\Theta)}(\Psi(v)-\Psi(s))^{n\Theta-1}\Psi'(s)\varpi(s)\mathrm{d}s.\tag{11}$$

For $n=1$, the demonstration is straightforward. Assume that Equation (11) is valid when $(n=k)$. Then, when $(n=k+1)$, we obtain

$$\begin{aligned}
&P^{k+1}\varpi(v)=P(P^k\varpi(v))\\
&=\int_0^{v}g(v,s)\Psi'(s)(\Psi(v)-\Psi(s))^{\Theta-1}P^k\varpi(s)\mathrm{d}s\\
&\le\int_0^{v}g(v,s)\Psi'(s)(\Psi(v)-\Psi(s))^{\Theta-1}\int_0^{s}\frac{(g(s,\nu)\Gamma(\Theta))^k}{\Gamma(k\Theta)}(\Psi(s)-\Psi(\nu))^{k\Theta-1}\Psi'(\nu)\varpi(\nu)\mathrm{d}\nu\mathrm{d}s\\
&\le\int_0^{v}g(v,\nu)\Psi'(s)\int_0^{s}\frac{(g(v,\nu)\Gamma(\Theta))^k}{\Gamma(k\Theta)}(\Psi(v)-\Psi(s))^{\Theta-1}(\Psi(s)-\Psi(\nu))^{k\Theta-1}\Psi'(\nu)\varpi(\nu)\mathrm{d}\nu\mathrm{d}s\\
&=\int_0^{v}g(v,\nu)^{k+1}\Big[\int_\nu^{v}\frac{\Gamma(\Theta)^k}{\Gamma(k\Theta)}(\Psi(v)-\Psi(s))^{\Theta-1}(\Psi(s)-\Psi(\nu))^{k\Theta-1}\Psi'(s)\mathrm{d}s\Big]\Psi'(\nu)\varpi(\nu)\mathrm{d}\nu\\
&=\int_0^{v}\frac{(g(v,\nu)\Gamma(\Theta))^{k+1}}{\Gamma((k+1)\Theta)}(\Psi(v)-\Psi(\nu))^{(k+1)\Theta-1}\Psi'(\nu)\varpi(\nu)\mathrm{d}\nu\\
&=\int_0^{v}\frac{(g(v,s)\Gamma(\Theta))^{k+1}}{\Gamma((k+1)\Theta)}(\Psi(v)-\Psi(s))^{(k+1)\Theta-1}\Psi'(s)\varpi(s)\mathrm{d}s.
\end{aligned}$$

Through the method of mathematical induction, inequality (11) holds for all $n\in\mathbb{N}$. Replacing $\varpi(v)$ with $\hbar$ in (11), we deduce that $P^k\ \hbar\le\hbar\int_0^{v}\frac{(g(v,s)\Gamma(\Theta))^k}{\Gamma(k\Theta)}(\Psi(v)-\Psi(s))^{k\Theta-1}\Psi'(s)\mathrm{d}s$, $k=1,2,\cdots$. Analogous to the proof process of Lemma 3.4 in [23], we are able to confirm that

$$P^n\varpi(v)\le\int_0^{v}\frac{(\mathbb{M}\Gamma(\Theta))^n}{\Gamma(n\Theta)}(\Psi(v)-\Psi(s))^{n\Theta-1}\Psi'(s)\varpi(s)\mathrm{d}s\to0$$

as n approaches infinity, uniformly in $v \in [0,T]$. Finally, letting n approach infinity in (10), we obtain

$$\varpi(v) \leq \sum_{n=0}^{\infty} P^n \not{\alpha} \leq \not{\alpha} + \not{\alpha} \int_0^v \sum_{n=1}^{\infty} \frac{(g(v,s)\Gamma(\Theta))^n}{\Gamma(n\Theta)} (\Psi(v)-\Psi(s))^{n\Theta-1}\Psi'(s)ds.$$

The lemma is proved. □

Lemma 5. *The solution of Equation* (1) *is*

$$y(v) = \mathfrak{a} J^{\Theta-\varrho;\Psi} y(v) + J^{\Theta;\Psi} f(v,y_v) + \vartheta(v), \quad v \in J = [0,\flat], \tag{12}$$

where $\vartheta(v) = y(0)(1 - \frac{\mathfrak{a}(\Psi(v)-\Psi(0))^{\Theta-\varrho}}{\Gamma(1+\Theta-\varrho)})$ *is a function.*

Proof. The proof is evident from Definition 1 and Theorem 1. □

3. Existence Results

In this part, we mainly use Lemma 1 and the Banach contraction principle to prove the existence results of solutions.

We list the following four assumptions.

(D1) The continuous function $f : [0,\flat] \times \breve{\mathfrak{B}} \to R$ has a bounded subset $W_0 \subset \breve{\mathfrak{B}}$, such that $f : [0,\flat] \times W_0$, on which it is uniformly continuous.

(D2) There exists a constant $\mathbb{L}$, such that $|f(v,\hbar) - f(v,\eth)| \leq \mathbb{L}\|\hbar - \eth\|_{\breve{\mathfrak{B}}}$ for each $v \in J$ and every $\hbar, \eth \in \breve{\mathfrak{B}}$.

(D3) There exist functions $g, l \in C(J, R^+)$, such that $|f(v,\hbar)| \leq g(v) + l(v)\|\hbar\|_{\breve{\mathfrak{B}}}$ for each $v \in J$ and every $\hbar \in \breve{\mathfrak{B}}$.

(D4) There exists a nonnegative function $\widetilde{\eta} \in \mathbb{L}^p[0,\flat]$ with $p > \frac{1}{\Theta}$ and a continuously non-decreasing function $\Omega : [0,+\infty) \to [0,+\infty)$, such that $|f(v,\hbar)| \leq \widetilde{\eta}(v)\Omega(\|\hbar\|_{\breve{\mathfrak{B}}})$ for all $v \in J$ and every $\hbar \in \breve{\mathfrak{B}}$.

Before the proof of the main result, let us initiate our analysis by transforming the problem of solutions into a fixed-point problem. According to Lemma 5, it is known that y is a solution to (1), precisely when y satisfies

$$y(v) = \begin{cases} \mathfrak{a} J^{\Theta-\varrho;\Psi} y(v) + J^{\Theta;\Psi} f(v,y_v) + \vartheta(v), & v \in [0,\flat], \\ \aleph(v), & v \in (-\infty, 0]. \end{cases}$$

For any $\aleph \in \breve{\mathfrak{B}}$, define the function $\widehat{\aleph}$ as

$$\widehat{\aleph}(v) = \begin{cases} \aleph(0), & v \in [0,\flat], \\ \aleph(v), & v \in (-\infty, 0]. \end{cases}$$

For $\Xi \in C([0,\flat], R)$, we define the function $\widehat{\Xi}$ as

$$\widehat{\Xi}(v) = \begin{cases} \Xi(v) - \aleph(0), & v \in [0,\flat], \\ 0, & v \in (-\infty, 0]. \end{cases}$$

We can decompose $y(\cdot)$ into the sum of two functions. For $v \in [0,\flat]$, we have $y(v) = \widehat{\aleph}(v) + \widehat{\Xi}(v)$. Moreover, for all $v \in [0,\flat]$, we can easily obtain that $y_v = \widehat{\aleph}_v + \widehat{\Xi}_v$, and note that $\Xi(\cdot)$ satisfies

$$\Xi(v) = \mathfrak{a} J^{\Theta-\varrho;\Psi} \Xi(v) + J^{\Theta;\Psi} f(v, \widehat{\aleph}_v + \widehat{\Xi}_v) + \vartheta(v).$$

Now, we define a set $C_0 = \{\Xi \in C([0,\flat], R) : \Xi(0) = \aleph(0)\}$. It is not difficult to see that the set C_0 is closed and, thus, completed. Based on this, we define an operator $T : C_0 \to C_0$ by

$$(T\Xi)(v) = \mathfrak{a} J^{\Theta-\varrho;\Psi}\Xi(v) + J^{\Theta;\Psi} f(v, \widehat{\aleph}_v + \widehat{\Xi}_v) + \vartheta(v). \tag{13}$$

Theorem 2. *Suppose that (D1) and (D2) are satisfied. If*

$$0 < \frac{|\,\mathfrak{a}\,|\,(\Psi(\flat) - \Psi(0))^{\Theta-\varrho}}{\Gamma(\Theta - \varrho + 1)} + \frac{\mathbb{L}\mathbb{K}_m(\Psi(\flat) - \Psi(0))^{\Theta}}{\Gamma(\Theta + 1)} < 1, \tag{14}$$

then Equation (1) *has a unique solution on* $(-\infty, \flat]$.

Proof. Let $T : C_0 \to C_0$ be given as (13). For any $\hbar, \eth \in C_0$ and each $v \in [0, \flat]$, we have

$$\begin{aligned}
&|\,(T\hbar)(v) - (T\eth)(v)\,| \\
&\leq \frac{|\,\mathfrak{a}\,|}{\Gamma(\Theta-\varrho)} \int_0^v \Psi'(s)(\Psi(v) - \Psi(s))^{\Theta-\varrho-1}\,|\,\hbar(s) - \eth(s)\,|\,ds \\
&+ \frac{1}{\Gamma(\Theta)} \int_0^v \Psi'(s)(\Psi(v) - \Psi(s))^{\Theta-1}\,|\,f(s, \widehat{\aleph}_s + \widehat{\hbar}_s) - f(s, \widehat{\aleph}_s + \widehat{\eth}_s)\,|\,ds \\
&\leq \frac{|\,\mathfrak{a}\,|\,(\Psi(\flat) - \Psi(0))^{\Theta-\varrho}}{\Gamma(\Theta-\varrho+1)} \|\hbar - \eth\| + \frac{\mathbb{L}}{\Gamma(\Theta)} \int_0^v \Psi'(s)(\Psi(v) - \Psi(s))^{\Theta-1} \left\|\widehat{\hbar}_s - \widehat{\eth}_s\right\|_{\breve{\mathfrak{B}}} ds.
\end{aligned}$$

As

$$\begin{aligned}
\left\|\widehat{\hbar}_s - \widehat{\eth}_s\right\|_{\breve{\mathfrak{B}}} &\leq \mathbb{K}(s) \sup_{0 \leq \nu \leq s} \left\|\widehat{\hbar}(\nu) - \widehat{\eth}(\nu)\right\| + \mathbb{M}(s) \left\|\widehat{\hbar}_0 - \widehat{\eth}_0\right\|_{\breve{\mathfrak{B}}} \\
&\leq \mathbb{K}_m \sup_{0 \leq \nu \leq s} \|\hbar(\nu) - \aleph(0) - \eth(\nu) + \aleph(0)\| \\
&\leq \mathbb{K}_m \|\hbar - \eth\|,
\end{aligned}$$

where $\mathbb{K}_m = sup\{|\mathbb{K}(v)| : v \in [a, \flat]\}$, we get

$$\|T\hbar - T\eth\| \leq \left(\frac{|\mathfrak{a}|(\Psi(\flat) - \Psi(0))^{\Theta-\varrho}}{\Gamma(\Theta-\varrho+1)} + \frac{\mathbb{L}\mathbb{K}_m(\Psi(\flat) - \Psi(0))^{\Theta}}{\Gamma(\Theta+1)}\right)\|\hbar - \eth\|.$$

Assumption (14) shows that T is a contraction. Applying the Banach contraction principle, we conclude that T has a unique fixed point. Then Equation (1) has a unique solution on $(-\infty, \flat]$. □

Theorem 3. *Suppose that (D1) and (D3) hold. Further, suppose that*

$$\frac{|\mathfrak{a}|(\Psi(\flat) - \Psi(0))^{\Theta-\varrho}}{\Gamma(\Theta-\varrho+1)} + \frac{\mathbb{K}_m(\Psi(\flat) - \Psi(0))^{\Theta}}{\Gamma(\Theta+1)} \|l\| < 1 \tag{15}$$

holds. Then, Equation (1) *has at least one solution on* $(-\infty, \flat]$.

Proof. To apply Lemma 1, we will demonstrate, through the subsequent steps, that the operator T is completely continuous.

Let $\{\Xi_n\}$ be a sequence, such that $\Xi_n \to \Xi$ in C_0. Then, for each $v \in [0, \flat]$, we have

$$\begin{aligned}
&|T\Xi_n(v) - T\Xi(v)| \\
&\leq \frac{|\,\mathfrak{a}\,|}{\Gamma(\Theta-\varrho)} \int_0^v \Psi'(s)(\Psi(v)-\Psi(s))^{\Theta-\varrho-1} \mid \Xi_n(s) - \Xi(s) \mid \mathrm{d}s \\
&+ \frac{1}{\Gamma(\Theta)} \int_0^v \Psi'(s)(\Psi(v)-\Psi(s))^{\Theta-1} \mid f(s, \widehat{\aleph}_s + \widehat{(\Xi_n)}_s) - f(s, \widehat{\aleph}_s + \widehat{\Xi}_s) \mid \mathrm{d}s.
\end{aligned}$$

Set $W_0 = \{(\Xi_n)_s : s \in [0, \flat], n \geq 1\} \subset \breve{\mathfrak{B}}$. From (D1), it can be observed that the function f is uniformly continuous with respect to $s \in [0, v]$. This means that for each $\varepsilon > 0$, there exists $\delta > 0$, such that for each $\Xi_1, \Xi_2 \in W_0$ with $|\Xi_1 - \Xi_2| < \delta$, we have $|f(s, \Xi_1) - f(s, \Xi_2)| < \varepsilon$. As $\Xi_n \to \Xi$, $N > 0$, such that for each $n > N$, we have $|\Xi_n - \Xi| < \delta$. Hence, $|f(s, \Xi_n) - f(s, \Xi)| < \varepsilon$ for all $s \in [0, v]$. Based on the previously introduced definition $\Xi_v = \widehat{\Xi}_v + \widehat{\aleph}_v$, it follows that $\left|f(s, \widehat{\aleph}_s + \widehat{(\Xi_n)}_s) - f(s, \widehat{\aleph}_s + \widehat{\Xi}_s)\right| < \varepsilon$, so we get

$$|T\Xi_n(v) - T\Xi(v)| \leq \frac{|\,\mathfrak{a}\,| \, (\Psi(\flat) - \Psi(0))^{\Theta-\varrho}}{\Gamma(\Theta-\varrho+1)} \|\Xi_n - \Xi\| + \frac{(\Psi(\flat) - \Psi(0))^{\Theta}\varepsilon}{\Gamma(\Theta+1)}.$$

Hence, $\|\Xi_n - \Xi\| \to 0$ as $\Xi_n \to \Xi$. Due to the arbitrariness of ε, we obtain that $|T\Xi_n(v) - T\Xi(v)| \to 0$, which implies that T is continuous.

We now show that T maps bounded subsets into bounded subsets in C_0. In fact, it is enough to prove that for any $r > 0$, there exists a positive constant ζ, such that for each $\Xi \in B_r = \{\Xi \in C_0 : \|\Xi\| \leq r\}$, we have $\|T\Xi(v)\| \leq \zeta$. Let $\Xi \in B_r$. As f is a continuous function, for each $v \in [0, \flat]$, we have

$$\begin{aligned}
|T\Xi(v)| &\leq \frac{|\mathfrak{a}|}{\Gamma(\Theta-\varrho)} \int_0^v \Psi'(s)(\Psi(v)-\Psi(s))^{\Theta-\varrho-1} |\Xi(s)| \mathrm{d}s \\
&+ \frac{1}{\Gamma(\Theta)} \int_0^v \Psi'(s)(\Psi(v)-\Psi(s))^{\Theta-1} \left| f(s, \widehat{\Xi}_s + \widehat{\aleph}_s) \right| \mathrm{d}s + |\vartheta(\flat)| \\
&\leq \frac{|\mathfrak{a}|(\Psi(\flat)-\Psi(0))^{\Theta-\varrho}}{\Gamma(\Theta-\varrho+1)} \|\Xi\| + \frac{1}{\Gamma(\Theta)} \int_0^v \Psi'(s)(\Psi(v)-\Psi(s))^{\Theta-1} \\
&(g(s) + l(s) \left\| \widehat{\Xi}_s + \widehat{\aleph}_s \right\|_{\breve{\mathfrak{B}}}) \mathrm{d}s + |\vartheta(\flat)|.
\end{aligned}$$

As

$$\begin{aligned}
\left\| \widehat{\Xi}_s + \widehat{\aleph}_s \right\|_{\breve{\mathfrak{B}}} &\leq \left\| \widehat{\Xi}_s \right\|_{\breve{\mathfrak{B}}} + \left\| \widehat{\aleph}_s \right\|_{\breve{\mathfrak{B}}} \\
&\leq \mathbb{K}(s) \sup_{0 \leq \nu \leq s} \left\| \widehat{\Xi}(\nu) \right\| + \mathbb{M}(s) \left\| \widehat{\Xi}_0 \right\|_{\breve{\mathfrak{B}}} + \mathbb{K}(s) \sup_{0 \leq \nu \leq s} \left\| \widehat{\aleph}(\nu) \right\| + \mathbb{M}(s) \left\| \widehat{\aleph}_0 \right\|_{\breve{\mathfrak{B}}} \\
&\leq \mathbb{K}_m \sup_{0 \leq \nu \leq s} \|\Xi(\nu) - \aleph(0)\| + \mathbb{K}_m \|\aleph(0)\| + \mathbb{M}_m \|\aleph\|_{\breve{\mathfrak{B}}} \\
&\leq \mathbb{K}_m r + 2\mathbb{K}_m \|\aleph(0)\| + \mathbb{M}_m \|\aleph\|_{\breve{\mathfrak{B}}} \\
&\leq \mathbb{K}_m r + 2\mathbb{K}_m \mathbb{H} \|\aleph\|_{\breve{\mathfrak{B}}} + \mathbb{M}_m \|\aleph\|_{\breve{\mathfrak{B}}} \\
&\leq \mathbb{K}_m r + (2\mathbb{K}_m \mathbb{H} + \mathbb{M}_m) \|\aleph\|_{\breve{\mathfrak{B}}} := r_0,
\end{aligned}$$

where $\mathbb{H} > 0$, $\mathbb{M}_m = \sup\{|\mathbb{M}(v)| : v \in [a, \flat]\}$, $\mathbb{K}_m = \sup\{|\mathbb{K}(v)| : v \in [a, \flat]\}$, we have

$$|T\Xi(v)| \leq \frac{|\mathfrak{a}|(\Psi(\flat)-\Psi(0))^{\Theta-\varrho}}{\Gamma(\Theta-\varrho+1)} r + \frac{(\Psi(\flat)-\Psi(0))^{\Theta}}{\Gamma(\Theta+1)} (\|g\| + \|l\| r_0) + |\vartheta(\flat)| := \zeta.$$

This can be proven.

Next, we prove that T maps bounded subsets into equicontinuous subsets of C_0. For all $\Xi \in B_r$ and $v_1, v_2 \in [0, \flat]$, $v_1 < v_2$, we have

$$
\begin{aligned}
&|(T\Xi)(v_2) - (T\Xi)(v_1)| \\
&\leq \frac{|\mathfrak{a}|\|\Xi\|}{\Gamma(\Theta-\varrho)}\Big|\int_0^{v_1}((\Psi(v_2)-\Psi(s))^{\Theta-\varrho-1} - (\Psi(v_1)-\Psi(s))^{\Theta-\varrho-1})\mathrm{d}\Psi(s) \\
&+ \int_{v_1}^{v_2}(\Psi(v_2)-\Psi(s))^{\Theta-\varrho-1}\mathrm{d}\Psi(s)\Big| \\
&+ \frac{1}{\Gamma(\Theta)}\Big|\int_0^{v_1}((\Psi(v_2)-\Psi(s))^{\Theta-1} - (\Psi(v_1)-\Psi(s))^{\Theta-1})f(s, \widehat{\Xi}_s + \widehat{\aleph}_s)\mathrm{d}\Psi(s) \\
&+ \int_{v_1}^{v_2}(\Psi(v_2)-\Psi(s))^{\Theta-1}f(s, \widehat{\Xi}_s + \widehat{\aleph}_s)\mathrm{d}\Psi(s)\Big| + |\vartheta(v_2) - \vartheta(v_1)| \\
&\leq \frac{|\mathfrak{a}|\|\Xi\|}{\Gamma(\Theta-\varrho+1)}((\Psi(v_2)-\Psi(0))^{\Theta-\varrho} - (\Psi(v_1)-\Psi(0))^{\Theta-\varrho} + 2(\Psi(v_2)-\Psi(v_1))^{\Theta-\varrho}) \\
&+ \frac{\|g\| + \|l\|r_0}{\Gamma(\Theta+1)}((\Psi(v_2)-\Psi(0))^{\Theta} - (\Psi(v_1)-\Psi(0))^{\Theta} \\
&+ 2(\Psi(v_2)-\Psi(v_1))^{\Theta}) + |\vartheta(v_2) - \vartheta(v_1)|.
\end{aligned}
$$

As $\Theta - \varrho > 0, \Theta > 0$, it is easy to see that $|(T\Xi)(v_2) - (T\Xi)(v_1)| \to 0$ as $v_1 - v_2 \to 0$. As a consequence, $T(B_r)$ is equicontinuous. According to the Arzela-Ascolli theorem, we can conclude that $T : C_0 \to C_0$ is a completely continuous mapping.

Now, we have to verify that there exists at least one fixed point Ξ of T. We assume that there exists an open set $\mathcal{V} \subseteq C_0$, such that for every $\Xi \in \partial\mathcal{V}$ and for each $\wp \in (0,1)$, the inequality $\Xi \neq \wp T(\Xi)$ holds. Define the set $\chi = \{\Xi \in C_0 : \|\Xi\| < N\}$. So, the operator $T : \overline{\chi} \to C_0$ satisfies the complete continuity. Assume

$$\Xi = \wp T\Xi$$

holds for some $\Xi \in \overline{\chi}$ and $\wp \in (0,1)$. Then, we obtain

$$
\begin{aligned}
|\Xi(v)| = |\wp T\Xi(v)| &\leq |T\Xi(v)| \\
&\leq \frac{|\mathfrak{a}|(\Psi(\flat)-\Psi(0))^{\Theta-\varrho}}{\Gamma(\Theta-\varrho+1)}\|\Xi\| \\
&+ \frac{(\Psi(\flat)-\Psi(0))^{\Theta}}{\Gamma(\Theta+1)}(\|g\| + \|l\|(\mathbb{K}_m\|\Xi\| + (2\mathbb{K}_m\mathbb{H} + \mathbb{M}_m)\|\aleph\|_{\mathfrak{B}})) + |\vartheta(\flat)|.
\end{aligned}
$$

Hence, the following inequalities can be obtained based on the conditions (15).

$$
\begin{aligned}
\|\Xi\| &\leq \frac{|\mathfrak{a}|(\Psi(\flat)-\Psi(0))^{\Theta-\varrho}}{\Gamma(\Theta-\varrho+1)}\|\Xi\| + \frac{(\Psi(\flat)-\Psi(0))^{\Theta}}{\Gamma(\Theta+1)}\mathbb{K}_m\|l\|\|\Xi\| \\
&+ \frac{(\Psi(\flat)-\Psi(0))^{\Theta}}{\Gamma(\Theta+1)}(\|g\| + \|l\|(2\mathbb{K}_m\mathbb{H} + \mathbb{M}_m)\|\aleph\|_{\mathfrak{B}}) + |\vartheta(\flat)| \\
&< N
\end{aligned}
$$

holds, which contradicts with the fact that $N = \|\Xi\|$. Thus, we obtain

$$\Xi \neq \wp T\Xi$$

for any $\Xi \in \overline{\chi}$ and $\wp \in (0,1)$.

Utilizing Lemma 1, we infer that there exists at least one fixed point Ξ of T. This completes the proof. □

Theorem 4. *Suppose that (D1) and (D4) hold. Additionally, suppose that*

$$\frac{|\mathfrak{a}|(\Psi(\flat)-\Psi(0))^{\Theta-\varrho}}{\Gamma(\Theta-\varrho+1)}+\frac{(\Psi(\flat)-\Psi(0))^{r_1}\|\widetilde{\eta}\|_p\mathbb{K}_m}{\Gamma(\Theta)r_2}\limsup_{r\to\infty}\frac{\Omega(r)}{r}<1 \tag{16}$$

holds, where $r_1=[(\Theta-1)q+1]/q$, $r_2=(1+(\Theta-1)q)^{\frac{1}{q}}$. *Then, the Equation* (1) *has at least one solution on* $(-\infty,\flat]$.

Proof. With the aid of the Lebesgue dominated convergence theorem, it is straightforward to confirm that T is continuous.

We now show that T maps bounded subsets into bounded subsets in C_0. Let $B_r=\{\Xi\in C_0:\|\Xi\|\le r\}$. Then, for any $\Xi\in B_r$ and $v\in[0,\flat]$, we have

$$\begin{aligned}|T\Xi(v)|\le&\frac{|\mathfrak{a}|}{\Gamma(\Theta-\varrho)}\int_0^v\Psi'(s)(\Psi(v)-\Psi(s))^{\Theta-\varrho-1}|\Xi(s)|\mathrm{d}s\\&+\frac{1}{\Gamma(\Theta)}\int_0^v\Psi'(s)(\Psi(v)-\Psi(s))^{\Theta-1}\Big|f(s,\widehat{\Xi}_s+\widehat{\aleph}_s)\Big|\mathrm{d}s+|\vartheta(\flat)|\\\le&\frac{|\mathfrak{a}|(\Psi(v)-\Psi(0))^{\Theta-\varrho}}{\Gamma(\Theta-\varrho+1)}\|\Xi\|+\frac{1}{\Gamma(\Theta)}\int_0^v\Psi'(s)(\Psi(v)-\Psi(s))^{\Theta-1}\\&\times\widetilde{\eta}(s)\Omega(\Big\|\widehat{\Xi}_s+\widehat{\aleph}_s\Big\|_{\mathfrak{B}})\mathrm{d}s+|\vartheta(\flat)|.\end{aligned}$$

As

$$\Big\|\widehat{\Xi}_s+\widehat{\aleph}_s\Big\|_{\mathfrak{B}}\le\mathbb{K}_m r+(2\mathbb{K}_m\mathbb{H}+\mathbb{M}_m)\|\aleph\|_{\mathfrak{B}}:=r_0,$$

where $\mathbb{M}_m=\sup\{|\mathbb{M}(v)|:v\in[a,\flat]\}$, $\mathbb{K}_m=\sup\{|\mathbb{K}(v)|:v\in[a,\flat]\}$ and $\mathbb{H}>0$ is a constant. By Hölder inequality, we have

$$\begin{aligned}|T\Xi(v)|\le&\frac{|\mathfrak{a}|(\Psi(\flat)-\Psi(0))^{\Theta-\varrho}}{\Gamma(\Theta-\varrho+1)}\|\Xi\|+\frac{\Omega(r_0)}{\Gamma(\Theta)}\int_0^v\Psi'(s)(\Psi(v)-\Psi(s))^{\Theta-1}\widetilde{\eta}(s)\mathrm{d}s+|\vartheta(\flat)|\\\le&\frac{|\mathfrak{a}|(\Psi(\flat)-\Psi(0))^{\Theta-\varrho}}{\Gamma(\Theta-\varrho+1)}\|\Xi\|+\frac{\Omega(r_0)}{\Gamma(\Theta)}(\int_0^v(\Psi(v)-\Psi(s))^{(\Theta-1)q}\mathrm{d}\Psi(s))^{\frac{1}{q}}\\&\times(\int_0^\flat\widetilde{\eta}^p(\Psi(s))\mathrm{d}\Psi(s))^{\frac{1}{p}}+|\vartheta(\flat)|\\\le&\frac{|\mathfrak{a}|(\Psi(\flat)-\Psi(0))^{\Theta-\varrho}}{\Gamma(\Theta-\varrho+1)}r+\frac{\Omega(r_0)(\Psi(\flat)-\Psi(0))^{r_1}}{\Gamma(\Theta)r_2}\|\widetilde{\eta}\|_p+|\vartheta(\flat)|=\zeta.\end{aligned}$$

where $r_1=[(\Theta-1)q+1]/q$, $r_2=(1+(\Theta-1)q)^{\frac{1}{q}}$, $\|\widetilde{\eta}\|_p=(\int_0^\flat|\widetilde{\eta}(s)|^p)^{\frac{1}{p}}$, $\frac{1}{p}+\frac{1}{q}=1$ and $(\Theta-1)>-1$.

Next, we prove that T maps bounded subsets into equicontinuous subsets of C_0. Consider the set $B_r = \{\Xi \in C_0 : \|\Xi\| \leq r\}$ and take an arbitrary $\Xi \in B_r$. Then, for $v_1, v_2 \in [0, b]$ with $v_1 < v_2$, we have

$$\begin{aligned}
&|(T\Xi)(v_2) - (T\Xi)(v_1)| \\
&\leq \frac{|\mathfrak{a}|\|\Xi\|}{\Gamma(\Theta-\varrho)}[\int_0^{v_1}((\Psi(v_2)-\Psi(s))^{\Theta-\varrho-1} - (\Psi(v_1)-\Psi(s))^{\Theta-\varrho-1})d\Psi(s) \\
&+ \int_{v_1}^{v_2}(\Psi(v_2)-\Psi(s))^{\Theta-\varrho-1}d\Psi(s)] \\
&+ \frac{1}{\Gamma(\Theta)}\left|\int_0^{v_1}((\Psi(v_2)-\Psi(s))^{\Theta-1} - (\Psi(v_1)-\Psi(s))^{\Theta-1})f(s,\widehat{\Xi}_s+\widehat{\aleph}_s)d\Psi(s)\right| \\
&+ \left|\int_{v_1}^{v_2}(\Psi(v_2)-\Psi(s))^{\Theta-1}f(s,\widehat{\Xi}_s+\widehat{\aleph}_s)d\Psi(s)\right| + |\vartheta(v_2)-\vartheta(v_1)| \\
&\leq \frac{|\mathfrak{a}|\|\Xi\|}{\Gamma(\Theta-\varrho+1)}((\Psi(v_2)-\Psi(0))^{\Theta-\varrho} - (\Psi(v_1)-\Psi(0))^{\Theta-\varrho} + 2(\Psi(v_2)-\Psi(v_1))^{\Theta-\varrho}) \\
&+ \frac{\Omega(r_0)}{\Gamma(\Theta)}(\int_0^{v_1}[(\Psi(v_2)-\Psi(s))^{\Theta-1} - (\Psi(v_1)-\Psi(s))^{\Theta-1}]^q d\Psi(s))^{\frac{1}{q}}(\int_0^{v_1}\widetilde{\eta}^p(\Psi(s))d\Psi(s))^{\frac{1}{p}} \\
&+ \frac{\Omega(r_0)}{\Gamma(\Theta)}(\int_{v_1}^{v_2}(\Psi(v_2)-\Psi(s))^{(\Theta-1)q}d\Psi(s))^{\frac{1}{q}}(\int_{v_1}^{v_2}\widetilde{\eta}^p(\Psi(s))d\Psi(s))^{\frac{1}{p}} + |\vartheta(v_2)-\vartheta(v_1)|.
\end{aligned}$$

As $n > 1$, $a > b$, $(a-b)^n < a^n - b^n$, we can obtain

$$\begin{aligned}
&|(T\Xi)(v_2) - (T\Xi)(v_1)| \\
&\leq \frac{|\mathfrak{a}|\|\Xi\|}{\Gamma(\Theta-\varrho+1)}((\Psi(v_2)-\Psi(0))^{\Theta-\varrho} - (\Psi(v_1)-\Psi(0))^{\Theta-\varrho} + 2(\Psi(v_2)-\Psi(v_1))^{\Theta-\varrho}) \\
&+ \frac{\Omega(r_0)}{\Gamma(\Theta)}(\int_0^{v_1}((\Psi(v_2)-\Psi(s))^{(\Theta-1)q} - (\Psi(v_1)-\Psi(s))^{(\Theta-1)q})d\Psi(s))^{\frac{1}{q}}\|\widetilde{\eta}\|_p \\
&+ \frac{(\Psi(v_2)-\Psi(v_1))^{r_1}}{r_2}\|\widetilde{\eta}\|_p + |\vartheta(v_2)-\vartheta(v_1)| \\
&\leq \frac{|\mathfrak{a}|\|\Xi\|}{\Gamma(\Theta-\varrho+1)}((\Psi(v_2)-\Psi(0))^{\Theta-\varrho} - (\Psi(v_1)-\Psi(0))^{\Theta-\varrho} + 2(\Psi(v_2)-\Psi(v_1))^{\Theta-\varrho}) \\
&+ \frac{\Omega(r_0)\|\widetilde{\eta}\|_p}{\Gamma(\Theta)r_2}((\Psi(v_2)-\Psi(0))^{r_1} - (\Psi(v_1)-\Psi(0))^{r_1} + 2(\Psi(v_2)-\Psi(v_1))^{r_1}) \\
&+ |\vartheta(v_2)-\vartheta(v_1)|,
\end{aligned}$$

where $r_1 = [(\Theta-1)q+1]/q$, $r_2 = (1+(\Theta-1)q)^{\frac{1}{q}}$, $r_0 = \mathbb{K}_m r + (2\mathbb{K}_m\mathbb{H} + \mathbb{M}_m)\|\aleph\|_{\mathfrak{B}}$. As $\Theta - \varrho > 0$, $r_1 > 0$, it is easy to see that $|(T\Xi)(v_2) - (T\Xi)(v_1)| \to 0$ as $v_1 - v_2 \to 0$. By the Arzela–Ascolli theorem, we can conclude that $T : C_0 \to C_0$ is a completely continuous mapping.

Now, we have to verify that there exists at least one fixed point Ξ of T. We assume that there exists an open set $\mathcal{V} \subseteq C_0$, such that for every $\Xi \in \partial\mathcal{V}$ and for each $\wp \in (0,1)$, the inequality $\Xi \neq \wp T(\Xi)$ holds. Define the set $\chi = \{\Xi \in C_0 : \|\Xi\| < N\}$. So, the operator $T : \overline{\chi} \to C_0$ satisfies the complete continuity. Assume

$$\Xi = \wp T\Xi$$

holds for some $\Xi \in \overline{\chi}$ and $\wp \in (0,1)$. Then, we obtain

$$\begin{aligned}|\Xi(v)| &= |\wp T\Xi(v)| \leq |T\Xi(v)| \\ &\leq \frac{|\mathfrak{a}|(\Psi(\flat) - \Psi(0))^{\Theta-\varrho}}{\Gamma(\Theta-\varrho+1)}\|\Xi\| \\ &+ \frac{\Omega(\mathbb{K}_m r + (2\mathbb{K}_m\mathbb{H} + \mathbb{M}_m)\|\aleph\|_{\mathfrak{B}})(\Psi(\flat) - \Psi(0))^{r_1}}{\Gamma(\Theta) r_2}\|\widetilde{\eta}\|_p + |\vartheta(\flat)|.\end{aligned}$$

Hence, the following inequalities can be obtained based on the conditions (16).

$$\|\Xi\| < N$$

holds, which contradicts $N = \|\Xi\|$. Thus,

$$\Xi \neq \wp T\Xi$$

for any $\Xi \in \overline{\chi}$ and $\wp \in (0,1)$.

As a consequence of Lemma 1, we deduce that there exists at least one fixed point Ξ of T. The proof is complete. □

4. Stability Analysis

In this section, we conduct an analysis of the Hs-Um-St of the Fra-Diff-Equs (1) with infinite delay.

Theorem 5. *Assume that all the conditions stated in Theorem 2 are met, and inequality* (6) *admits at least one solution. Under such circumstances, the problem* (1) *exhibits Hs-Um-St.*

Proof. For each $\varepsilon > 0$, and each function $\beth$ that satisfies the following inequalities

$$\left|{}^cD^{\Theta;\Psi}\beth(v) - \mathfrak{a}\,{}^cD^{\varrho;\Psi}\beth(v) - f(v,\beth_v)\right| \leq \varepsilon, \quad v \in [0,\flat],$$

let $g(v) = {}^cD^{\Theta;\Psi}\beth(v) - \mathfrak{a}\,{}^cD^{\varrho;\Psi}\beth(v) - f(v,\beth_v)$. Then we have

$$\beth(v) = \mathfrak{a}J^{\Theta-\varrho;\Psi}\beth(v) + J^{\Theta;\Psi}f(v,\beth_v) + J^{\Theta;\Psi}g(v) + \vartheta(v).$$

According to Theorem 2, there is a unique solution $\daleth(v)$ of problem (1), and the function $\daleth$ can be expressed as

$$\daleth(v) = \mathfrak{a}J^{\Theta-\varrho;\Psi}\daleth(v) + J^{\Theta;\Psi}f(v,\daleth_v) + \vartheta(v).$$

So, we have

$$\begin{aligned}|\beth(v) - \daleth(v)| \leq& \frac{|\mathfrak{a}|}{\Gamma(\Theta-\varrho)}\int_0^v \Psi'(s)(\Psi(v)-\Psi(s))^{\Theta-\varrho-1}|\beth(v) - \daleth(v)|\mathrm{d}s \\ &+ \frac{1}{\Gamma(\Theta)}\int_0^v \Psi'(s)(\Psi(v)-\Psi(s))^{\Theta-1}|f(s,\beth_s) - f(s,\daleth_s)|\mathrm{d}s \\ &+ \frac{1}{\Gamma(\Theta)}\int_0^v \Psi'(s)(\Psi(v)-\Psi(s))^{\Theta-1}|g(s)|\mathrm{d}s.\end{aligned}$$

As

$$|f(s,\beth_s) - f(s,\daleth_s)| \leq \mathbb{L}\|\beth_s - \daleth_s\|_{\mathfrak{B}},$$

together with Definition 3 , we obtain

$$
\begin{aligned}
\|\gimel_s-\daleth_s\|_{\breve{\mathfrak{B}}} &= \left\|(\hat{\gimel}_s+\hat{\aleph}_s)-(\hat{\daleth}_s+\hat{\aleph}_s)\right\|_{\breve{\mathfrak{B}}} = \left\|\hat{\gimel}_s-\hat{\daleth}_s\right\|_{\breve{\mathfrak{B}}} \\
&\leq \mathbb{K}(s)\sup_{0\leq\nu\leq s}\left\|\hat{\gimel}(\nu)-\hat{\daleth}(\nu)\right\| + \mathbb{M}(s)\left\|\hat{\gimel}_0-\hat{\daleth}_0\right\|_{\breve{\mathfrak{B}}} \\
&\leq \mathbb{K}_m\sup_{0\leq\nu\leq s}\|\gimel(\nu)-\aleph(0)-\daleth(\nu)+\aleph(0)\| \\
&= \mathbb{K}_m\sup_{0\leq\nu\leq s}|\gimel(\nu)-\daleth(\nu)|,
\end{aligned}
$$

which indicates that

$$
\begin{aligned}
|\gimel(v)-\daleth(v)| \leq& \frac{|\mathfrak{a}|}{\Gamma(\Theta-\varrho)}\int_0^v \Psi'(s)(\Psi(v)-\Psi(s))^{\Theta-\varrho-1}|\gimel(s)-\daleth(s)|ds \\
&+\frac{\mathbb{L}\mathbb{K}_m}{\Gamma(\Theta)}\int_0^v \Psi'(s)(\Psi(v)-\Psi(s))^{\Theta-1}\sup_{0\leq\sigma\leq s}|\gimel(\sigma)-\daleth(\sigma)|ds \\
&+\frac{(\Psi(\flat)-\Psi(0))^{\Theta}}{\Gamma(\Theta+1)}\varepsilon.
\end{aligned}
$$

According to Lemma 3,

$$
\begin{aligned}
&\sup_{0\leq\nu\leq v}|\gimel(\nu)-\daleth(\nu)| \\
&\leq \frac{|\mathfrak{a}|}{\Gamma(\Theta-\varrho)}\int_0^v \Psi'(s)(\Psi(v)-\Psi(s))^{\Theta-\varrho-1}\sup_{0\leq\sigma\leq s}|\gimel(\sigma)-\daleth(\sigma)|ds \\
&+\frac{\mathbb{L}\mathbb{K}_m}{\Gamma(\Theta)}\int_0^v \Psi'(s)(\Psi(v)-\Psi(s))^{\Theta-1}\sup_{0\leq\sigma\leq s}|\gimel(\sigma)-\daleth(\sigma)|ds+\frac{(\Psi(\flat)-\Psi(0))^{\Theta}}{\Gamma(\Theta+1)}\varepsilon \\
&=\int_0^v\left[|\mathfrak{a}|\frac{\Psi'(s)(\Psi(v)-\Psi(s))^{\Theta-\varrho-1}}{\Gamma(\Theta-\varrho)}+\frac{\mathbb{L}\mathbb{K}_m\Psi'(s)(\Psi(v)-\Psi(s))^{\Theta-1}}{\Gamma(\Theta)}\right]\sup_{0\leq\sigma\leq s}|\gimel(\sigma)-\daleth(\sigma)|ds \\
&+\frac{(\Psi(\flat)-\Psi(0))^{\Theta}}{\Gamma(\Theta+1)}\varepsilon.
\end{aligned}
$$

Let $\varphi(v):=\sup_{0\leq\nu\leq v}|\gimel(\nu)-\daleth(\nu)|$, $\mathbb{M}=\frac{(\Psi(b)-\Psi(0))^{\Theta}}{\Gamma(\Theta+1)}$, and $g(v,s)=\frac{|\mathfrak{a}|}{\Gamma(\Theta-\varrho)}+\frac{\mathbb{L}\mathbb{K}_b(\Psi(v)-\Psi(s))^{\varrho}}{\Gamma(\Theta)}\leq \mathbb{M}_0$. We can obtain

$$
\varphi(v)\leq \mathbb{M}\varepsilon+\int_0^v g(v,s)\Psi'(s)(\Psi(v)-\Psi(s))^{\Theta-\varrho-1}\varphi(s)ds.
$$

It is not difficult to show that

$$
\begin{aligned}
\varphi(v) &\leq \mathbb{M}\varepsilon+\mathbb{M}\varepsilon\int_0^v\sum_{n=1}^{\infty}\frac{(\mathbb{M}_0\Gamma(\Theta-\varrho))^n}{\Gamma(n(\Theta-\varrho))}(\Psi(v)-\Psi(s))^{n(\Theta-\varrho)-1}\Psi'(s)ds \\
&\leq \mathbb{M}\varepsilon+\mathbb{M}\varepsilon\sum_{n=1}^{\infty}\frac{(\mathbb{M}_0\Gamma(\Theta-\varrho))^n}{\Gamma(n(\Theta-\varrho)+1)}(\Psi(b)-\Psi(0))^{n(\Theta-\varrho)} \\
&= \varepsilon\mathbb{M}\left(1+\sum_{n=1}^{\infty}\frac{(\mathbb{M}_0\Gamma(\Theta-\varrho))^n}{\Gamma(n(\Theta-\varrho)+1)}(\Psi(b)-\Psi(0))^{n(\Theta-\varrho)}\right) \\
&= \varepsilon\mathbb{M}E_{\Theta-\varrho}(\mathbb{M}_0\Gamma(\Theta-\varrho)(\Psi(b)-\Psi(0))^{\Theta-\varrho}).
\end{aligned}
$$

Then, the inequality

$$
\varphi(v)\leq\mathfrak{r}\varepsilon
$$

holds for $\mathfrak{r}=\mathbb{M}E_{\Theta-\varrho}(\mathbb{M}_0\Gamma(\Theta-\varrho)(\Psi(b)-\Psi(0))^{\Theta-\varrho})$, which implies that the Hs-Um-St of problem (1) is proved. □

5. Examples

For any real constant $\Upsilon > 0$, we set

$$U_\Upsilon = \left\{ y \in C((-\infty, 0], R) : \lim_{\theta \to -\infty} e^{\Upsilon\theta} y(\theta) \ \ exist \ \ in \ \ R \right\},$$

and set

$$|y|_\Upsilon = \sup\left\{ e^{\Upsilon\theta} |y(\theta)| : -\infty < \theta \leq 0 \right\}.$$

By [31], U_Υ satisfies the conditions $\mathfrak{K} = \mathfrak{M} = \mathfrak{H} = 1$, and, hence, U_Υ is a phase space.

Example 1. *Consider the following nonlinear Ψ-Caputo-type Fra-Diff-Equs with infinite delay of the form*

$$\begin{cases} {}^c D^{0.7;\Psi} y(v) - \frac{1}{4}\, {}^c D^{0.4;\Psi} y(v) = e^{-\gamma v}(y_v + cos v), & v \in J = [0,1], \\ y(v) = \aleph(v) \in U_\gamma, \quad v \in (-\infty, 0], \end{cases} \tag{17}$$

where $\Psi(v) = \sqrt{1+v}$.

In this case, it is readily observable that (D1) and (D3) are satisfied with the function $l(v) = e^{-\Upsilon v}$. Due to

$$\begin{aligned} &\frac{|\mathfrak{a}|(\Psi(\mathfrak{b}) - \Psi(0))^{\Theta - \varrho}}{\Gamma(\Theta - \varrho + 1)} + \frac{\mathbb{K}_m (\Psi(\mathfrak{b}) - \Psi(0))^{\Theta}}{\Gamma(\Theta + 1)} \|l\| \\ &< \frac{(\sqrt{2} - 1)^{0.3}}{4\Gamma(1.3)} + \frac{(\sqrt{2} - 1)^{0.7}}{\Gamma(1.7)} \approx 0.7658 < 1. \end{aligned}$$

Thus, all the conditions of Theorem 3 hold. Therefore, the problem (17) has at least one solution on $(-\infty, 1]$.

Example 2. *Consider the following problem*

$$\begin{cases} {}^c D^{0.8;\Psi} y(v) - \frac{1}{5}\, {}^c D^{0.4;\Psi} y(v) = \frac{c' e^{-\Upsilon v + v} |y|_\Upsilon}{1 + |y|_\Upsilon}, & v \in J = [0,1], \\ y(v) = \aleph(v) \in U_\Upsilon, \quad v \in (-\infty, 0], \end{cases} \tag{18}$$

where $\Psi(v) = 2^v$, $c' > 0$. Set

$$f(v, x) = \frac{c' e^{-\Upsilon v + v} x}{1 + x}, \quad (v, x) \in [0,1] \times R^+.$$

Then, for any $x, y \in U_\Upsilon$, we have

$$\begin{aligned} |f(v,x) - f(v,y)| &= c' e^{-\Upsilon v + v} \left| \frac{x}{1+x} - \frac{y}{1+y} \right| \\ &\leq \frac{c' e^{-\Upsilon v + v} |x - y|}{(1+x)(1+y)} \leq c' e^{v} |x - y| \leq c' e |x - y|. \end{aligned}$$

Hence, $0 < c' < \frac{\Gamma(1.8)(5\Gamma(1.4) - 1)}{5e\Gamma(1.4)} \approx 0.2674$, condition (D2) holds. Thus, problem (18) has a unique solution to $(-\infty, 1]$ by applying Theorem 2.

Next, we discuss the Hs-Um-St of problem (18). For any $\varepsilon > 0$, and each function y that satisfies the following inequalities

$$\left| {}^{c}\mathcal{D}^{0.8;\Psi}y(v) - \frac{1}{5}\,{}^{c}\mathcal{D}^{0.4;\Psi}y(v) - \frac{c'e^{-\Upsilon v+v}|y|_{\Upsilon}}{1+|y|_{\Upsilon}} \right| \leq \varepsilon, \quad v \in J = [0,1],$$

let $g(v)$ represent the left side of the inequality above and let $\daleth(t)$ be the unique solution of problem (18); then, we have

$$\sup_{0\leq \nu\leq v} |y(\nu) - \daleth(\nu)| \leq \int_0^v \left[\frac{2^s \ln 2(2^v-2^s)^{-0.6}}{5\Gamma(0.4)} + \frac{c'2^s \ln 2(2^v-2^s)^{-0.2}}{\Gamma(0.8)}\right] \sup_{0\leq\sigma\leq s}|y(\sigma)-\daleth(\sigma)|ds + \frac{\varepsilon}{\Gamma(1.8)}$$

let $\varphi(v) := \sup\limits_{0\leq\nu\leq v} |y(\nu) - \daleth(\nu)|$, $\mathbb{M} = \frac{1}{\Gamma(1.8)}$, and $g(v,s) = \frac{1}{5\Gamma(0.4)} + \frac{c'(2^v-2^s)^{0.4}}{\Gamma(0.8)} \leq \frac{1}{5\Gamma(0.4)} + \frac{c'}{\Gamma(0.8)} = \mathbb{M}_0$. By Lemma 4,

$$\begin{aligned} \varphi(v) &\leq \mathbb{M}\varepsilon + \int_0^v g(v,s)\Psi'(s)(\Psi(v)-\Psi(s))^{\Theta-\varrho-1}\varphi(s)ds \\ &\leq \mathbb{M}\varepsilon + \mathbb{M}\varepsilon\sum_{n=1}^{\infty}\frac{(\mathbb{M}_0\Gamma(0.4))^n}{\Gamma(0.4n+1)} \\ &\leq \mathbb{M}\varepsilon E_{0.4}(\mathbb{M}_0\Gamma(0.4)), \end{aligned} \tag{19}$$

let $\mathfrak{r} = \mathbb{M}E_{0.4}(\mathbb{M}_0\Gamma(0.4)) = \frac{1}{\Gamma(1.8)}E_{0.4}(\frac{1}{5} + \frac{c'\Gamma(0.4)}{\Gamma(0.8)})$, it follows that $\varphi(v) \leq \mathfrak{r}\varepsilon$, which implies that the problem (18) is Hs-Um-St.

6. Conclusions

In this paper, we mainly discuss a class of nonlinear Fra-Diff-Equs with finite time delay. We first use the Leray–Schauder alternation theorem and the Banach fixed-point theorem to study the existence and uniqueness of solutions for this class of Ψ-Caputo Fra-Diff-Equs. Then, we study the Hs-Um-St of the Fra-Diff-Equs (1). With the aim of overcoming the difficulty in proving Hs-Um-St, some inequalities are obtained for delayed Fra-Diff-Equs. In addition, there are two examples listed to illustrate the conclusions. The findings of our study enhance and extend the results presented in [23,24].

Author Contributions: Conceptualization, Y.X.; Methodology, Q.D.; Formal analysis, A.B.E. and Q.D.; Investigation, Y.X.; Resources, A.B.E.; Data curation, Q.D.; Writing—original draft, Y.X.; writing—review and editing, Y.X., A.B.E. and Q.D. All authors have read and agreed to the published version of the manuscript.

Funding: This work was supported by the National Natural Science Foundations of China [Grant No. 12271469 and 12371140] and Jiangsu Students' Innovation and Entrepreneurship Training Program [202411117164Y].

Data Availability Statement: The data presented in this study are openly available in [WOS] at [10.3390/math10071013].

Acknowledgments: We sincerely express my gratitude to every editor and reviewer for their dedication. Wish you all a happy life.

Conflicts of Interest: The authors declare no conflict of interest.

References

1. Xu, L.; Dong, Q.; Li, G. Existence and Hyers–Ulam stability for three-point boundary value problems with Riemann–Liouville fractional derivatives and integrals. *Adv. Differ. Equ.* **2018**, *2018*, 458. [CrossRef]
2. Diethelm, K.; Ford, N.J. Analysis of fractional differential equations. *J. Math. Anal. Appl.* **2002**, *265*, 229–248. [CrossRef]
3. Plekhanova, M.V. Nonlinear equations with degenerate operator at fractional Caputo derivative. *Math. Methods Appl. Sci.* **2017**, *40*, 6138–6146. [CrossRef]
4. Fedorov, V.E.; Nagumanova, A.V.; Avilovich, A.S. A class of inverse problems for evolution equations with the Riemann-Liouville derivative in the sectorial case. *Math. Methods Appl. Sci.* **2021**, *44*, 11961–11969. [CrossRef]
5. Li, C.; Sarwar, S. Existence and continuation of solutions for Caputo type fractional differential equations. *Electron. J. Differ. Equ.* **2016**, *2016*, 1–14. [CrossRef]
6. Alzaidy, J. Fractional sub-equation method and its applications to the space-time fractional differential equations in mathematical physics. *Br. J. Math. Comput. Sci.* **2013**, *3*, 153–163. [CrossRef] [PubMed]
7. Sun, H.; Chang, A.; Zhang, Y.; Chen, W. A review on variable-order fractional differential equations: Mathematical foundations, physical models, numerical methods and applications. *Fract. Calc. Appl. Anal.* **2019**, *22*, 27–59. [CrossRef]
8. Rossikhin, Y.A.; Shitikova, M.V. Application of fractional calculus for dynamic problems of solid mechanics: Novel trends and recent results. *Appl. Mech. Rev.* **2010**, *63*, 010801. [CrossRef]
9. Abro, K.A.; Atangana, A. A comparative analysis of electromechanical model of piezoelectric actuator through Caputo–Fabrizio and Atangana–Baleanu fractional derivatives. *Math. Methods Appl. Sci.* **2020**, *43*, 9681–9691. [CrossRef]
10. Ali, I.; Khan, S.U. A dynamic competition analysis of stochastic fractional differential equation arising in finance via pseudospectral method. *Mathematics* **2023**, *11*, 1328. [CrossRef]
11. Maleknejad, K.; Hashemizadeh, E. Numerical solution of the dynamic model of a chemical reactor by hybrid functions. *Procedia Comput. Sci.* **2011**, *3*, 908–912. [CrossRef]
12. Gou, H.; Li, B. Existence of mild solutions for Sobolev-type Hilfer fractional evolution equations with boundary conditions. *Bound. Value Probl.* **2018**, *2018*, 1–25. [CrossRef]
13. Zhu, B.; Han, B.y.; Yu, W.G. Existence of mild solutions for a class of fractional non-autonomous evolution equations with delay. *Acta Math. Appl. Sin. Engl. Ser.* **2020**, *36*, 870–878. [CrossRef]
14. Wang, X.; Zhu, B. Existence Results for Fractional Semilinear Integrodifferential Equations of Mixed Type with Delay. *J. Funct. Spaces* **2021**, *2021*, 5519992. [CrossRef]
15. Benchohra, M.; Graef, J.R.; Hamani, S. Existence results for boundary value problems with non-linear fractional differential equations. *Appl. Anal.* **2008**, *87*, 851–863. [CrossRef]
16. Bao, H. Existence and uniqueness of solutions to neutral stochastic functional differential equations with infinite delay in L^p (\Omega, C_h). *Turk. J. Math.* **2010**, *34*, 45–58.
17. Yao, H.; Dong, Q. Hyers-Ulam-Rassias Stability of Ψ -Caputo Fractional Differential Equations. *J. Appl. Anal. Comput.* **2024**, *14*, 2903–2921.
18. Baleanu, D.; Ranjbar, A.; Sadati, S.; Delavari, R.; Abdeljawad, T. Lyapunov-Krasovskii stability theorem for fractional systems with delay. *Rom. J. Phys.* **2011**, *56*, 636–643.
19. Baleanu, D.; Sadati, S.; Ghaderi, R.; Ranjbar, A.; Abdeljawad, T.; Jarad, F. Razumikhin stability theorem for fractional systems with delay. In *Abstract and Applied Analysis*; Wiley Online Library: Hoboken, NJ, USA, 2010; Volume 2010, p. 124812.
20. Podlubny, I. Fractional Differential Equations, Mathematics in Science and Engineering; Science Direct: Amsterdam, The Netherlands, 1999.
21. Agarwal, R.P.; Hristova, S. Ulam-type stability for a boundary-value problem for multi-term delay fractional differential equations of Caputo type. *Axioms* **2022**, *11*, 742. [CrossRef]
22. Zada, A.; Shah, S.O. Hyers-Ulam stability of first-order non-linear delay differential equations with fractional integrable impulses. *Hacet. J. Math. Stat.* **2018**, *47*, 1196–1205. [CrossRef]
23. Dong, Q.; Liu, C.; Fan, Z. Weighted fractional differential equations with infinite delay in Banach spaces. *Open Math.* **2016**, *14*, 370–383. [CrossRef]
24. Chen, C.; Dong, Q. Existence and Hyers–Ulam stability for a multi-term fractional differential equation with infinite delay. *Mathematics* **2022**, *10*, 1013. [CrossRef]
25. Almeida, R. Fractional differential equations with mixed boundary conditions. *Bull. Malays. Math. Sci. Soc.* **2019**, *42*, 1687–1697. [CrossRef]
26. Almeida, R. A Caputo fractional derivative of a function with respect to another function. *Commun. Nonlinear Sci. Numer. Simul.* **2017**, *44*, 460–481. [CrossRef]
27. Sousa, J.V.d.C.; De Oliveira, E.C. On the ψ-Hilfer fractional derivative. *Commun. Nonlinear Sci. Numer. Simul.* **2018**, *60*, 72–91. [CrossRef]
28. Hino, Y.; Murakami, S.; Naito, T. *Functional Differential Equations with Infinite Delay*; Springer: Berlin/Heidelberg, Germany, 2006.

29. Sousa, J.V.d.C.; De Oliveira, E.C. Ulam–Hyers stability of a nonlinear fractional Volterra integro-differential equation. *Appl. Math. Lett.* **2018**, *81*, 50–56. [CrossRef]
30. Smart, D. *Fixed Point Theorems;* Cambridge University Press: Cambridge, UK, 1980.
31. Benchohra, M.; Henderson, J.; Ntouyas, S.; Ouahab, A. Existence results for fractional order functional differential equations with infinite delay. *J. Math. Anal. Appl.* **2008**, *338*, 1340–1350. [CrossRef]

fractal and fractional

MDPI

Article

On the Pseudospectral Method for Solving the Fractional Klein–Gordon Equation Using Legendre Cardinal Functions

Tao Liu [1], Bolin Ding [2], Behzad Nemati Saray [3,*], Davron Aslonqulovich Juraev [4,5] and Ebrahim E. Elsayed [6]

1 School of Mathematics and Statistics, Northeastern University at Qinhuangdao, Qinhuangdao 066004, China; liutao@neuq.edu.cn
2 Sydney Smart Technology College, Northeastern University at Qinhuangdao, Qinhuangdao 066004, China; 202319273@stu.neuq.edu.cn
3 Department of Mathematics, Institute for Advanced Studies in Basic Sciences (IASBS), Zanjan 45137-66731, Iran
4 Scientific Research Center, Baku Engineering University, Baku AZ0102, Azerbaijan; juraev_davron@ipu-edu.uz or juraevdavron12@gmail.com
5 Department of Scientific Research, Innovation and Training of Scientific and Pedagogical Staff, University of Economics and Pedagogy, Karshi 180100, Uzbekistan
6 Department of Electronics and Communication Engineering, Faculty of Engineering, Mansoura University, Mansoura 35516, El-Dakahilia, Egypt; engebrahem16@gmail.com or ebrahimeldesoky@gmail.com
* Correspondence: bn.saray@iasbs.ac.ir

Abstract: This work introduces the Legendre cardinal functions for the first time. Based on Jacobi and Lobatto grids, two approaches are employed to determine these basis functions. These functions are then utilized within the pseudospectral method to solve the fractional Klein–Gordon equation (FKGE). Two numerical schemes based on the pseudospectral method are considered. The first scheme reformulates the given equation into a corresponding integral equation and solves it. The second scheme directly addresses the problem by utilizing the matrix representation of the Caputo fractional derivative operator. We provide a convergence analysis and present numerical experiments to demonstrate the convergence of the schemes. The convergence analysis shows that convergence depends on the smoothness of the unknown function. Notable features of the proposed approaches include a reduction in computations due to the cardinality property of the basis functions, matrices representing fractional derivative and integral operators, and the ease of implementation.

Keywords: cardinal functions; pseudospectral method; Legendre polynomials; fractional partial differential equations; convergence

MSC: 54A25; 65M70; 42C10; 35R11; 65M12

1. Introduction

Fractional calculus and fractional differential equations (FDEs) have emerged as powerful mathematical tools with a profound impact on almost all fields of science and engineering. While classical calculus deals with integer-order derivatives and integrals, fractional calculus generalizes these operators to non-integer orders. As a result, systems with memory and hereditary properties can be modeled using fractional calculus. This capability is particularly valuable for describing entire classes of phenomena that exhibit anomalous diffusion, viscoelastic behavior, and long-range dependencies—features that often cannot be captured by traditional models. FDEs arise in a wide range of applications, including fluid dynamics, control theory, signal processing, and biological systems, where they provide a more realistic modeling of real processes compared to their classical counterparts. Fractional calculus is an important area of modern mathematics because it helps us understand complex systems and solve challenging problems.

Analytical and numerical methods are required to solve FDEs. Analytical methods include the Laplace transform, the Fourier transform, and expansions involving Mittag–Leffler functions, which provide exact solutions for certain classes of FDEs. However, it is commonly known these methods are usually limited to linear or simple nonlinear problems and are insufficient for handling more complicated or higher-dimensional fractional partial differential equations (FPDEs). If such methods exist to solve complicated problems, the literature is quite limited due to the associated difficulties. As a result, numerical methods have become essential tools for addressing FDEs. Numerical approximations for FPDEs, particularly for problems that are difficult to solve analytically, often rely on techniques such as the finite difference method [1], the spectral element method [2,3], the finite element method [4], nonuniform difference schemes [5], the Galerkin method [6,7], the collocation method [8,9], the fractional differential transform method [10], and the kernel-based pseudo-spectral method [11]. For further study, we refer readers to [12,13]. Such numerical approaches enable researchers to tackle real-world problems involving irregular domains, complex boundary conditions, and nonlinearities.

Given $\Omega = [a,b] \times [0,\tau]$, the fractional Klein–Gordon equation (FKGE) we consider in this paper reads

$$ {}_{a}^{C}\mathcal{D}_{t}^{\kappa} y(x,t) + d_1 \frac{\partial^2}{\partial x^2} y(x,t) + d_2 \mathcal{F}(x,t,y(x,t)) = g(x,t), \qquad \forall (x,t) \in \Omega, \kappa \in (1,2], \tag{1} $$

subjected to conditions

$$ y(x,0) = \phi_2(x), \quad \mathcal{D}_t\,(y(x,t))|_{t=0} = \phi_3(x), \quad x \in [a,b], \tag{2} $$

$$ y(a,t) = \phi_0(t), \quad y(b,t) = \phi_1(t), \quad t \in [0,\tau], \tag{3} $$

where d_1 and d_2 are constants, the functions g, $\mathcal{F}$ are sufficiently smooth functions, and ϕ_i for $i = 0,\ldots 3$ are known. Furthermore, the function $\mathcal{F}$ satisfies the Lipschitz condition

$$ |\mathcal{F}(x,t,y_1(x,t)) - \mathcal{F}(x,t,y_2(x,t))| \leq L|y_1(x,t) - y_2(x,t)|, \tag{4} $$

with Lipschitz constant L. The derivative operators ${}_{a}^{C}\mathcal{D}_{t}^{\kappa}$ and $\mathcal{D}_t$ refer to Caputo fractional derivative (CFD) and derivative with respect to variable t, respectively.

As we know, both linear and nonlinear Klein–Gordon equations play an important role in modeling various physical phenomena within a wide scope of applications: solitons, condensed matter physics, and classical and quantum mechanics [14] are only a few among others. Originally, the equation was proposed in 1926 by physicists Oskar Klein [15] and Walter Gordon [16] to model relativistic electrons. Given the importance of such equations, the study and determination of their solutions are quite significant [17]. Recently, much attention has been given to the FKGE. Essentially, it serves as a generalization of the integer-order Klein–Gordon equation and further extends the range of applicability. This equation also models non-locality in space and time with the help of power-law kernels [3]. Rapid developments have occurred in presented numerical methods for solving the FPDEs, and especially the FKGE, in recent years, including the following: the Sinc–Chebyshev collocation method [18], homotopy perturbation method [19], the third-kind Chebyshev collocation method [20], cubic B-spline method [21], meshless method [22], Fourier transform method [23], finite difference methods [24], and spectral collocation methods [25].

Essentially, the pseudospectral method among the spectral methods relies on the basic minimization of a residual function at some collocation points and is usually very accurate and efficient. Its simplicity and effectiveness arise from the fact that one is making sure the residual is minimized, and if well implemented, the method always outperforms many other numerical techniques. The method takes advantage of orthogonal polynomials or even trigonometric functions for approximations and realizes exponential convergence in problems with smooth solutions. The pseudospectral method is, therefore, seen as the best option in handling differential equations due to better accuracy and efficiency in computation, including those involving nonlinearities and high-dimensional cases [26].

Cardinal functions serve as a set of basis functions in numerical analysis and approximation theory. They play a critical role in constructing interpolants or approximating functions from discrete data points, making them particularly valuable in spectral and pseudospectral techniques. While some cardinal functions exhibit orthogonality, which streamlines computations in functional spaces, they are predominantly employed in spectral and pseudospectral methods as the bases. The significance of these bases can be examined from two perspectives:

Accuracy: Cardinal functions enable spectral accuracy in numerical approaches, delivering highly accurate approximations for solutions to differential equations. In scenarios demanding high accuracy, pseudospectral methods demonstrate superior performance compared to finite difference and finite element methods.

Computational Efficiency: The inherent sparsity or localized nature of certain cardinal functions reduces the computational cost of interpolation and quadrature, enhancing overall efficiency.

The outline of this paper is as follows. We introduce the Legendre cardinal function and its properties in the next section. In the section, the matrix form of fractional integral derivatives and the CFD is also presented. In Section 3, two numerical schemes based on the pseudospectral method are developed and implemented for solving FKGEs. The convergence analysis is also investigated. Some numerical experiments are implemented, and the results are reported in Section 4. In Section 5, we provide some final observations and conclusions.

2. Legendre Cardinal Functions

Legendre polynomials are specified as the eigenfunctions of the well-known Sturm–Liouville equation

$$\mathcal{D}_x\left(\left(1-x^2\right)\mathcal{D}_x(y(x))\right)+\lambda y(x)=0,$$

corresponding to the eigenvalues $\lambda_m = m(m+1)$. Here, $\mathcal{D}_x$ indicates the derivative operative with respect to the independent variable x. There are some explicit expressions of these polynomials; among them, the following formula can be mentioned:

$$L_m(x)=\frac{1}{2^m}\sum_{i=0}^{m}\binom{m}{i}^2(x+1)^i(x-1)^{m-i}. \tag{5}$$

This expression derivates Rodrigues' formula, obtained under the normalization $L_m(1)=1$. The three-term recurrence formula for these polynomials holds as follows:

$$\begin{aligned} L_0(x)&=1, \qquad L_1(x)=x,\\ (m+1)L_{m+1}(x)&=(2m+1)xL_m(x)-mL_{m-1}(x), \quad m\geq 1, \end{aligned}$$

These polynomials are orthogonal with respect to the L^2 norm on $[-1,1]$, viz.,

$$(L_m(x), L_{m'}(x))_2 = \int_{-1}^{1} L_m(x)L_{m'}(x)dx = \frac{2}{2m+1}\delta_{m,m'},$$

where $(.,.)$ states the inner product of $L^2[-1,1]$ and $\delta_{m,m'}$ specifies the Kronecker delta.

Note that the shifted Legendre polynomials on the generic interval $[a,b]$ can be introduced through the suitable variable change, i.e.,

$$L^*_m(x) = L_m\left(\frac{2(x-a)}{(b-a)} - 1\right), \qquad m = 0,1,\ldots,M. \tag{6}$$

Explicit expressions for the roots of Legendre polynomials do not exist, and thus numerical computation is required to find them. Generally, two effective algorithms are used for this: the eigenvalue method and the iterative procedure. All the roots of Legendre polynomials are simple, real, and lie in the interval $[-1,1]$. Based on the construction of the shifted Legendre polynomials, their roots can be determined using

$$x^*_m = a + \frac{(x_m+1)(b-a)}{2}, \qquad m = 0,1,\ldots,M. \tag{7}$$

Set the nodes $\{x^*_m\}_{m=0}^{M}$ as the shifted Legendre polynomial roots; the Legendre cardinal functions associated with these nodes are determined as

$$c_m(x) \equiv \frac{L^*_{M+1}(x)}{\mathcal{D}_x(L^*_{M+1}(x^*_m))(x-x^*_m)}, \qquad m = 0,1,\ldots,M, \quad x \in [a,b], \tag{8}$$

Another way to determine the Legendre cardinal functions is to take a grid specified by the extrema of the Legendre polynomial $L^*_M(x)$ and add the endpoints, namely,

$$\{x^*_m\}_{m=0}^{M} = \left\{\{\hat{x}^*_m\}_{m=0}^{M-2} \cup \{a,b\} \middle| \ \mathcal{D}_x(L^*_M(x))|_{\{\hat{x}^*_m\}_{m=0}^{M}} = 0\right\}.$$

This set of nodes is often called the Lobatto grid. Associated with this grid, called the Lobatto grid, the Legendre cardinal functions are defined as follows:

$$c_m(x) \equiv \frac{(1-x^2)\mathcal{D}_x(L^*_M(x))}{\mathcal{D}_x((1-x^{*2}_m)\mathcal{D}_x(L^*_M(x^*_m)))(x-x^*_m)}, \qquad m = 0,1,\ldots,M \quad x \in [a,b]. \tag{9}$$

The main characteristic of Legendre cardinal functions is

$$c_m(x^*_{\overline{m}}) = \delta_{m,\overline{m}}, \quad m,\overline{m} = 0,1,\ldots,M. \tag{10}$$

This property allows an M-degree polynomial to interpolate exactly $M+1$ data points of the function y. Strictly speaking, any function with $M+1$ data points is approximated by

$$y(x) \approx \mathcal{Q}_M(y(x)) = \sum_{m=0}^{M} y(x^*_m)c_m(x). \tag{11}$$

where $\mathcal{Q}_M : L^2[a,b] \to \Pi_M[a,b]$ is a projection operator and $\Pi_M[a,b]$ indicates the space of polynomials of degree less than M. This approximation is computationally significant because it avoids the integration when calculating expansion coefficients.

Given a two-dimensional function $y(x,t) \in L^2(\Omega)$ with $\Omega = [a,b] \times [0,\tau]$, one can approximate it as follows:

$$y(x,t) \approx \mathcal{Q}_M(y(x,t)) = \sum_{m=0}^{M} \sum_{m'=0}^{M} y_{m,m'} c_m(x) c_{m'}(t) \in \Pi_M^2(\Omega), \tag{12}$$

in which $y_{m,m'} = y(x_m^*, t_{m'}^*)$ and $\Pi_M^2(\Omega)$ states the space of the quadratic polynomial on Ω.

Given $w^{\alpha,\beta}(x) = (1-x)^\alpha(1+x)^\beta$ for $\alpha, \beta > -1$, let $\hat{w}^{\alpha,\beta}(x) = w^{\alpha,\beta}\left(\frac{2(x-a)}{(b-a)} - 1\right)$, $\hat{w}^{\alpha,\beta}(t) = w^{\alpha,\beta}\left(\frac{2t}{\eta} - 1\right)$ and $\hat{\mathbf{w}}^{\boldsymbol{\alpha},\boldsymbol{\beta}}(x,t) = \hat{w}^{\alpha_1,\beta_1}(x) \times \hat{w}^{\alpha_2,\beta_2}(t)$. Furthermore, assume that

$$\mathcal{F}_i = \left\{ \mathbf{n} \in \mathbb{N}_0^2 : 2 \leq n_i \leq n; n_j \in \{0,1\}, j \neq i; \sum_{i'=1}^{2} n_{i'} = n \right\}, \qquad 1 \leq i \leq 2.$$

We consider the space $\mathbf{B}^n_{\boldsymbol{\alpha},\boldsymbol{\beta}}(\Omega)$ for $n \geq 2$ as defined in [27], with the norm and semi-norm

$$\begin{aligned} |y|^2_{\mathbf{B}^n_{\boldsymbol{\alpha},\boldsymbol{\beta}}(\Omega)} &= \sum_{i=1}^{2} \sum_{\mathbf{n} \in \mathcal{F}_i} \| \mathcal{D}^{\mathbf{n}}_{\mathbf{x}}(y) \|^2_{\hat{\mathbf{w}}^{\boldsymbol{\alpha}+n_i e_i, \boldsymbol{\beta}+n_i e_i}}, \\ \| y \|^2_{\mathbf{B}^n_{\boldsymbol{\alpha},\boldsymbol{\beta}}(\Omega)} &= \| y \|^2_{\hat{\mathbf{w}}^{\boldsymbol{\alpha},\boldsymbol{\beta}}} + |y|^2_{\mathbf{B}^n_{\boldsymbol{\alpha},\boldsymbol{\beta}}(\Omega)}, \end{aligned} \tag{13}$$

where $\mathbf{x} = (x,t)$, $\boldsymbol{\alpha} = (\alpha_1, \alpha_2)$, $\boldsymbol{\beta} = (\beta_1, \beta_2)$, and e_i for $i = 1,2$ indicates the standard-basis vectors. Throughout the paper, we denote C as a positive constant, which can differ in various formulas.

Theorem 1 (cf. Theorem 8.6, [27])**.** *Let $\mathbf{0}$ indicates the zero vector. Given $\boldsymbol{\alpha}, \boldsymbol{\beta} = \mathbf{0}$, assume that $y \in \mathbf{B}^n_{\mathbf{0},\mathbf{0}}(\Omega)$. If $2 \leq n \leq M+1$, then*

$$\| \mathcal{Q}_M(y) - y \|_{L^2(\Omega)} \leq C \sqrt{\frac{(M+1-n)!}{M!}} (M+n)^{-(n+1)/2} \left(\frac{h_{\max}}{2}\right)^{2n} |y|_{\mathbf{B}^n_{\mathbf{0},\mathbf{0}}(\Omega)}, \tag{14}$$

where $h_{max} = max\{(b-a), \tau\}$.

2.1. Derivative Operator in the Matrix Form

This section presents a framework to show how the derivative operator acting on Legendre cardinal functions can be represented as a matrix. Recall that (see, e.g., [27]) the leading coefficients of Legendre polynomials $L^*_{M+1}(x)$ are given as

$$\eta_M = \frac{\Gamma(2M+1)}{(b-a)^M \Gamma(M+1)^2}, \tag{15}$$

and taking the derivative of it leads to

$$\mathcal{D}^k_x(L^*_{M+1})(x) = \rho_{M+1,k} L^*_{M+1-k}(x), \tag{16}$$

where the constant $\rho_{M+1,k}$ is equal to

$$\rho_{M+1,k} = \frac{\Gamma(M+k)}{2^{k-1}(b-a)\Gamma(M)}. \tag{17}$$

Taking into account Equations (15) and (17), an alternative representation of the Legendre cardinal functions (8) and (9) is available as follows:

$$c_m(x) = \sigma \prod_{\substack{i=0,\\ i\neq m}}^{M} (x - x_i^*), \qquad m = 0, 1, \ldots, M, \quad x \in [a, b], \tag{18}$$

where σ is equal to $\frac{\eta_M}{\mathcal{D}_x\left(L_{M+1}^*(x)\right)|_{x=x_m^*}}$ and $\frac{-4\rho_{M+1,1}\Gamma(2M-1)}{(M-2)(b-a)^M\Gamma(M+1)\mathcal{D}_x\left((1-x^2)\mathcal{D}_x\left(L_M^*(x)\right)\right)|_{x=x_m^*}}$ for (8) and (9), respectively.

Taking the derivative on both sides of (18) leads to

$$\mathcal{D}_x(c_m)(x) = \sigma \sum_{\substack{l=0\\ l\neq m}}^{M} \prod_{\substack{i=0\\ i\neq m,l}}^{M} (x - x_i^*) = \sum_{\substack{l=0\\ l\neq m}}^{M} \frac{c_m(x)}{(x - x_l^*)}, \quad m = 0, 1, \ldots, M. \tag{19}$$

If $\mathcal{D}_x(c_m(x))$ is estimated based on the Legendre cardinal functions $c_m(x)$, it is easy to verify that

$$\mathcal{D}_x(c_m(x)) \approx \sum_{m''=0}^{M} \mathcal{D}_x(c_m(x))|_{x=x_{m''}^*} c_{m''}(x), \quad m = 0, 1, \ldots, M. \tag{20}$$

Thus, it results from (19) and (20) that

$$\mathcal{D}_x(c_m(x))|_{x_{m''}^*} = \begin{cases} \sum\limits_{\substack{l=0\\ l\neq m}}^{M} \left(x_{m''}^* - x_l^*\right)^{-1}, & m = m'', \\ \sigma \prod\limits_{\substack{i=0\\ i\neq m,m''}}^{M} \left(x_{m''}^* - x_i^*\right), & m \neq m'', \end{cases} \qquad m = 0, 1, \ldots, M. \tag{21}$$

Assume that $\Psi_M(x)$ is a vector function whose elements are specified by

$$[\Psi_M]_{m+1}(x) = c_m(x), \qquad m = 0, 1, \ldots, M. \tag{22}$$

Using this vector function, the matrix form of derivative operator can be determined as

$$\mathcal{D}_x(\Psi_M(x)) \approx D\Psi_M(x), \tag{23}$$

in which the entries of $D \in \mathbb{R}^{(M+1)\times(M+1)}$ are determined by (21).

2.2. Fractional Integral Operator in Matrix Form

Firstly, a reformulation of Legendre cardinal functions is required to specify the matrix form of the fractional integral operator (FIO) [28,29], viz.,

$$\prod_{\substack{i=0\\ i\neq m}}^{M} (x - x_i^*) = \sum_{j=0}^{M} \varrho_{m,j} x^{M-j}, \tag{24}$$

in which

$$\varrho_{m,0} = 1, \quad \varrho_{m,j} = \frac{1}{j}\sum_{k=0}^{j} u_{m,k}\varrho_{m,j-k}, \quad u_{m,k} = \sum_{\substack{l=0\\ l\neq m}}^{M} (x_l^*)^k \quad m, j = 0, 1 \ldots, M.$$

Thus, an alternative formula of the Legendre cardinal functions can be determined as follows:

$$c_m(x) = \sigma \sum_{j=0}^{M} \varrho_{m,j} x^{M-j}, \qquad m = 0, 1, \ldots, M, \quad x \in [a, b]. \tag{25}$$

Given the value of "a" (the left endpoint of the generic interval $[a, b]$), two cases must be considered:

- If $a = 0$: Considering the definition of FIO and gamma function [30], one can prove that

$$\mathcal{I}_a^\kappa (x)^\vartheta = \frac{\Gamma(\vartheta + 1)}{\Gamma(\vartheta + \kappa + 1)} x^{\kappa+\vartheta}, \quad \kappa \in \mathbb{R}_+, x \in [a, b]. \tag{26}$$

  Given (26) and considering the reformulation (25), one obtains the result of acting FIO on the Legendre cardinal function, i.e.,

$$\mathcal{I}_a^\kappa (c_m(x)) = \sigma \mathcal{I}_a^\kappa \left(\sum_{j=0}^{M} \varrho_{m,j} x^{M-j} \right) = \sigma \sum_{j=0}^{M} \varrho_{m,j} \frac{\Gamma(M - j + 1)}{\Gamma(M - j + \kappa + 1)} x^{M-j+\kappa}, \quad m = 0, 1, \ldots, M. \tag{27}$$

- If $a \neq 0$, it results that

$$\begin{aligned} \mathcal{I}_a^\kappa (x)^\vartheta &= \frac{1}{\Gamma(\kappa)} \int_a^t (x - \xi)^{\kappa-1} \xi^\vartheta d\xi \\ &= \frac{(x-a)^\kappa a^\vartheta}{\Gamma(\kappa)} \int_0^1 (1-t)^{\kappa-1} \left(1 - t\left(1 - \frac{x}{a}\right)\right)^\vartheta dx \qquad (\xi = a + t(x-a)) \\ &= \frac{(x-a)^\kappa a^\vartheta}{\Gamma(\kappa)} B(1, \kappa)_2 F_1 \left(-\vartheta, 1; \kappa + 1; 1 - \frac{x}{a}\right), \end{aligned} \tag{28}$$

  (see e.g., ([31]), p.65),
  where B and 2_{F_1} state the beta and hypergeometric functions [31], respectively. Thus, it proves from (25) and (28) that

$$\mathcal{I}_a^\kappa (c_m(x)) = \frac{\sigma (x-a)^\kappa B(1, \kappa)}{\Gamma(\kappa)} \sum_{j=0}^{M} \varrho_{m,j} a^{M-j} 2_{F_1} \left(-(M-j), 1; \kappa + 1; 1 - \frac{x}{a}\right), \quad m = 0, \ldots M. \tag{29}$$

Now, everything is ready to present the matrix form of FIO based on Legendre cardinal functions, viz.,

$$\mathcal{I}_a^\kappa (c_m(x)) \approx \sum_{m'=0}^{M} \mathcal{I}_a^\kappa (c_m)(x_{m'}^*) c_{m'}(x), \quad m = 0, \ldots M, \tag{30}$$

where the coefficients $\mathcal{I}_a^\kappa (c_m)(x_{m'}^*)$ are calculated through (27) and (29). So, one can introduce a matrix $I_\vartheta \in \mathbb{R}^{(M+1)\times(M+1)}$ that satisfies

$$\mathcal{I}_a^\kappa (\Psi_M(x)) \approx I_\kappa \Psi_M(x), \tag{31}$$

and has elements

$$[I_\kappa]_{m+1, m'+1} = \mathcal{I}_a^\kappa (c_m)(x_{m'}^*), \quad m, m' = 0, \ldots M. \tag{32}$$

2.3. Caputo Fractional Derivative Operator in Matrix Form

Assume that $\kappa \in \mathbb{R}_+$ and $\nu = \lceil \kappa \rceil$ (where $\lceil . \rceil$ is the ceiling function). The CFD operator ${}_a^C\mathcal{D}_x^k$ is represented by $\mathcal{I}_a^{\nu-\kappa}\mathcal{D}^\nu$ when $\kappa \notin \mathbb{N}_0$. We aim to find a matrix $D_\kappa \in \mathbb{R}^{(M+1)\times(M+1)}$ that satisfies

$$ {}_a^C\mathcal{D}_x^k(\Psi_M(x)) \approx D_\kappa \Psi_M(x). \tag{33} $$

Replacing $\mathcal{I}_a^{\nu-\kappa}\mathcal{D}^\nu$ instead of ${}_a^C\mathcal{D}_x^k$ leads to

$$ {}_a^C\mathcal{D}_x^k(\Psi_M(x)) = \mathcal{I}_a^{\nu-\kappa}\mathcal{D}^\nu(\Psi_M(x)) \approx D^\nu I_{\nu-\kappa}\Psi_M(x). \tag{34} $$

Thus, without direct calculations, the matrix form of the CFD operator is obtained, viz.,

$$ D_\kappa := D^\nu I_{\nu-\kappa}. \tag{35} $$

3. Pseudospectral Method Based on Legendre Cardinal Functions

In the sequel, two numerical schemes based on the pseudospectral method are developed and implemented for solving Equation (1).

- **First scheme (PS1):** A traditional scheme to solve a fractional partial differential equation is to render it into a corresponding integral equation. Our first numerical scheme involves applying the pseudospectral method to solve the integral equation obtained from Equation (1):

$$ y(x,t) - y_0(x,t) + \mathcal{I}_a^\kappa\left(d_1 \frac{\partial^2}{\partial x^2} y(x,t) + d_2\mathcal{F}(x,t,y(x,t)) - g(x,t)\right) = 0, \tag{36} $$

$$ y(a,t) = \phi_0(t), \quad y(b,t) = \phi_1(t), \quad t \in [0,\tau], \tag{37} $$

where $y_0(x,t) = y(x,0) + \mathcal{D}_t\left(y(x,t)\right)|_{t=0}$. It is not difficult to prove that the solution to this integral equation is equivalent to the solution of (1) [30]. Let us approximate the unknown $y(x,t)$ using the expansion (12) based on Legendre cardinal functions, i.e.,

$$ y(x,t) \approx \mathcal{Q}_M(y(x,t)) = \sum_{m=0}^{M}\sum_{m'=0}^{M} y_{m,m'} c_m(x) c_{m'}(t) = \Psi^T(x) Y \Psi(t) \in \Pi_M^2(\Omega), \tag{38} $$

where $Y \in \mathbb{R}^{(M+1)\times(M+1)}$ whose elements must be found. Substituting the approximate solution $y_M(x,t) := \mathcal{Q}_M(y(x,t))$ into (36) instead of y leads to introducing the residual function

$$ r_1(x,t) = y_M(x,t) - y_0(x,t) + \mathcal{I}_a^\kappa\left(d_1 \frac{\partial^2}{\partial x^2} y_M(x,t) + d_2\mathcal{F}(x,t,y_M(x,t)) - g(x,t)\right). \tag{39} $$

Thanks to the matrix form of the derivative operator D and FIO I_κ in the Legendre cardinal functions, one can write

$$ \mathcal{Q}_M(r_1(x,t)) = \Psi^T(x)\left(Y - Y_0 + d_1 {D^2}^T Y I_\kappa + d_2 F I_\kappa - G I_\kappa\right)\Psi(t), \tag{40} $$

in which

$$ \begin{aligned} y_0(x,t) &\approx \mathcal{Q}_M(y_0(x,t)) = \Psi^T(x) Y_0 \Psi(t), \\ \mathcal{F}(x,t,y_M(x,t)) &\approx \mathcal{Q}_M(\mathcal{F}(x,t,y_M(x,t))) = \Psi^T(x) F \Psi(t). \\ g(x,t) &\approx \mathcal{Q}_M(g(x,t)) = \Psi^T(x) G \Psi(t), \end{aligned} \tag{41} $$

where Y_0, F, and G are $(M+1)\times(M+1)$ matrices.

The objective is to apply the pseudospectral method. Thus, the unknowns can be found by picking the Jacobi or Lobatto grids $\{x^*_m\}_{m=0}^M$, such that the residual is approximately zero at these points, i.e.,

$$\mathcal{Q}_M(r_1(x,t))|_{(x,t)=(x^*_m,x^*_{m'})} = 0, \qquad m,m' = 0,\ldots,M. \tag{42}$$

Equivalently, we have the nonlinear system

$$R(Y) = Y - Y_0 + d^2 D^{2^T} Y I_\kappa + d_2 F I_\kappa - G I_\kappa = 0. \tag{43}$$

First, to apply the boundary conditions (37), the functions $\phi_0(t)$ and $\phi_1(t)$ must be approximated by Legendre cardinal functions, viz.,

$$\begin{aligned}\phi_0(t) &\approx \mathcal{Q}_M(\phi_0(t)) = \Phi_0{}^T\Psi(t),\\ \phi_1(t) &\approx \mathcal{Q}_M(\phi_1(t)) = \Phi_1{}^T\Psi(t),\end{aligned} \tag{44}$$

where $\Phi_i \in \mathbb{R}^{M+1}$ for $i = 0,1$. By replacing the first and last rows of $R(Y)$ with vectors $\left(\psi^T(a)Y\right)^T - \Phi_0$ and $\left(\psi^T(b)Y\right)^T \Phi_1$, respectively, a new nonlinear system

$$\overline{R}(Y) = 0, \tag{45}$$

is obtained. Solving this system using Newton's method leads to specifying the unknowns Y.

- **Second scheme (PS2):** The second numerical scheme solves Equation (1) directly without rendering it to an integral equation. Taking into account the approximation (38) and using the matrix form of the CFD operator, one derives

$$^C_a\mathcal{D}^\kappa_t y_M(x,t) = \Psi^T(x) Y D_\kappa \Psi(t). \tag{46}$$

Furthermore, we have

$$\frac{\partial^2}{\partial x^2} y_M(x,t) = \Psi^T(x) D^{2^T} Y \Psi(t). \tag{47}$$

Substituting (41), (46), and (47) into (1) enables us to introduce the residual as follows:

$$r_2(x,t) = \Psi^T(x)\left(Y D_\kappa + d_1 D^{2^T} Y + d_2 F - G\right)\Psi(t) \tag{48}$$

Using collocation points $(x^*_m, x^*_{m'})$ for $m, m' = 0,\ldots,M$ is sufficient to apply the pseudospectral method, viz.,

$$R(Y) = Y D_\kappa + d_1 D^{2^T} Y + d_2 F - G. \tag{49}$$

It is necessary to approximate the initial conditions to apply the initial and boundary conditions (2) and (3), in addition to the approximations (44). For this purpose, we have the following:

$$\begin{aligned}\phi_2(x) &\approx \mathcal{Q}_M(\phi_2(x)) = \Phi_2{}^T\Psi(x),\\ \phi_3(x) &\approx \mathcal{Q}_M(\phi_3(x)) = \Phi_3{}^T\Psi(x),\end{aligned} \tag{50}$$

where $\Phi_i \in \mathbb{R}^{M+1}$ for $i = 2,3$. By replacing the first and last rows and columns of $R(Y)$ with vectors Φ_0, Φ_1, Φ_2, and Φ_3, respectively, a new nonlinear system

$$\overline{R}(Y) = 0. \tag{51}$$

Newton's method is applied to solve this nonlinear system.

Convergence Analysis

Theorem 2. *Let y be the exact solution of (36) and y_M the approximate solution obtained from PS1. If $y, g, \mathcal{F} \in \mathbf{B}^n_{0,0}(\Omega)$, $2 < n \leq M+1$, and $\mathcal{F}$ satisfies the Lipschitz condition (4), then it can be obtained that*

$$\| e_M \|_{L^2(\Omega)} \to 0, \qquad as \qquad M \to \infty,$$

where $e_M = y - y_M$.

Proof. Subtracting (36) from (42) leads to

$$y - y_M - (y_0 - \mathcal{Q}_M(y_0)) + \mathcal{I}_a^\kappa\left(d_1 \frac{\partial^2}{\partial x^2} y(x,t) + d_2 \mathcal{F}(x,t,y(x,t)) - g(x,t)\right)$$
$$- \mathcal{Q}_M\left(\mathcal{I}_a^\kappa\left(d_1 \frac{\partial^2}{\partial x^2} y_M(x,t) + d_2 \mathcal{F}(x,t,y_M(x,t)) - g(x,t)\right)\right) = 0.$$

Adding and subtracting some terms, we can rewrite this equation as

$$\begin{aligned} e_M =& (y_0 - \mathcal{Q}_M(y_0)) - d_1 \mathcal{I}_a^\kappa\left(\frac{\partial^2}{\partial x^2} e_M\right) - d_2 \mathcal{I}_a^\kappa(\mathcal{F}(x,t,y) - \mathcal{F}(x,t,y_M)) \\ &+ \mathcal{I}_a^\kappa(g - \mathcal{Q}_M(g)) + d_1(\mathcal{I} - \mathcal{Q}_M)\left(\mathcal{I}_a^\kappa\left(\frac{\partial^2}{\partial x^2} y_M\right)\right) \\ &+ d_2(\mathcal{I} - \mathcal{Q}_M)(\mathcal{I}_a^\kappa(\mathcal{F}(x,t,y_M))) - (\mathcal{I} - \mathcal{Q}_M)(\mathcal{I}_a^\kappa(\mathcal{Q}_M(g))), \end{aligned} \tag{52}$$

where $\mathcal{I}$ is identity operator. Taking the norm from both sides of (52) leads to

$$\begin{aligned} \| e_M \|_{L^2(\Omega)} \leq& \| (\mathcal{I} - \mathcal{Q}_M)(y_0) \|_{L^2(\Omega)} + d_1 \| \mathcal{I}_a^\kappa\left(\frac{\partial^2}{\partial x^2} e_M\right) \|_{L^2(\Omega)} + \| \mathcal{I}_a^\kappa(g - \mathcal{Q}_M(g)) \|_{L^2(\Omega)} \\ &+ d_2 \| \mathcal{I}_a^\kappa(\mathcal{F}(x,t,y) - \mathcal{F}(x,t,y_M)) \|_{L^2(\Omega)} + d_1 \| (\mathcal{I} - \mathcal{Q}_M)\left(\mathcal{I}_a^\kappa\left(\frac{\partial^2}{\partial x^2} y_M\right)\right) \|_{L^2(\Omega)} \\ &+ d_2 \| (\mathcal{I} - \mathcal{Q}_M)(\mathcal{I}_a^\kappa(\mathcal{F}(x,t,y_M))) \|_{L^2(\Omega)} + \| (\mathcal{I} - \mathcal{Q}_M)(\mathcal{I}_a^\kappa(\mathcal{Q}_M(g))) \|_{L^2(\Omega)}. \end{aligned} \tag{53}$$

Taking into account Theorem 1 and using the Lipschitz condition (4) and Lemma 2.1(a) [30], we have

$$\begin{aligned} \| \mathcal{I}_a^\kappa(\mathcal{F}(x,t,y) - \mathcal{F}(x,t,y_M)) \|_{L^2(\Omega)} \leq& L \| \mathcal{I}_a^\kappa(e_M) \|_{L^2(\Omega)} \leq L \frac{\tau}{\Gamma(\kappa+1)} \| e_M \|_{L^2(\Omega)} \\ \leq& CL \frac{\tau}{\Gamma(\kappa+1)} \sqrt{\frac{(M+1-n)!}{M!}} (M+n)^{-(n+1)/2} \left(\frac{h_{\max}}{2}\right)^{2n} |y|_{\mathbf{B}^n_{0,0}(\Omega)}. \end{aligned} \tag{54}$$

where $h_{\max} = \max\{(b-a), \tau\}$. Applying Theorems (3.40) and (8.6) [27] gives rise to writing

$$\begin{aligned} \| \mathcal{I}_a^\kappa\left(\frac{\partial^2}{\partial x^2} e_M\right) \|_{L^2(\Omega)} \leq& \frac{\tau}{\Gamma(\kappa+1)} \| \frac{\partial^2}{\partial x^2} e_M \|_{L^2(\Omega)} \\ \leq& C \frac{\tau}{\Gamma(\kappa+1)} \sqrt{\frac{(M+1-n)!}{M!}} (M+n)^{2-(n+1)/2} \left(\frac{h_{\max}}{2}\right)^{2n} |y|_{\mathbf{B}^n_{0,0}(\Omega)}, \end{aligned} \tag{55}$$

and

$$\begin{aligned} \| \mathcal{I}_a^\kappa(g - \mathcal{Q}_M(g)) \|_{L^2(\Omega)} \leq& \frac{\tau}{\Gamma(\kappa+1)} \| g - \mathcal{Q}_M(g) \|_{L^2(\Omega)} \\ \leq& C \frac{\tau}{\Gamma(\kappa+1)} \sqrt{\frac{(M+1-n)!}{M!}} (M+n)^{-(n+1)/2} \left(\frac{h_{\max}}{2}\right)^{2n} |g|_{\mathbf{B}^n_{0,0}(\Omega)}. \end{aligned} \tag{56}$$

For the rest of the norms in (53), applying Theorem 1, one can write

$$\| (\mathcal{I}-\mathcal{Q}_M)(z-z_M) \|_{L^2(\Omega)} \leq C\sqrt{\frac{(M+1-n)!}{M!}}(M+n)^{-(n+1)/2}\left(\frac{h_{\max}}{2}\right)^{2n}|z|_{\mathbf{B}^n_{0,0}(\Omega)}, \quad (57)$$

where $z \in \left\{y_0, \mathcal{I}^\kappa_a\left(\frac{\partial^2}{\partial x^2}y_M\right), \mathcal{I}^\kappa_a(\mathcal{F}(x,t,y_M)), \mathcal{I}^\kappa_a(\mathcal{Q}_M(g))\right\}$.

Considering (54)–(57), it follows from (53) that

$$\begin{aligned}\| e_M \|_{L^2(\Omega)} \leq & CL\frac{\tau}{\Gamma(\kappa+1)}\sqrt{\frac{(M+1-n)!}{M!}}(M+n)^{2-(n+1)/2}\left(\frac{h_{\max}}{2}\right)^{2n}|y|_{\mathbf{B}^n_{0,0}(\Omega)} \\ & +C\frac{\tau}{\Gamma(\kappa+1)}\sqrt{\frac{(M+1-n)!}{M!}}(M+n)^{-(n+1)/2}\left(\frac{h_{\max}}{2}\right)^{2n}|u|_{\mathbf{B}^n_{0,0}(\Omega)},\end{aligned} \quad (58)$$

in which

$$|u|_{\mathbf{B}^n_{0,0}(\Omega)} = \max\left\{|z|_{\mathbf{B}^n_{0,0}(\Omega)}, |g|_{\mathbf{B}^n_{0,0}(\Omega)}\right\}.$$

If $y, g, \mathcal{F} \in \mathbf{B}^n_{0,0}(\Omega)$ and $2 < n \leq M+1$, then it can be obtained that

$$\| e_M \|_{L^2(\Omega)} \to 0, \quad as \quad M \to \infty.$$

□

Theorem 3. *Let y be the exact solution of (1) and y_M the approximate solution obtained from PS2. If $\mathcal{F}, g$ are sufficiently smooth functions, $y \in \mathbf{B}^n_{0,0}(\Omega)$, $2 < n \leq M+1$, and $\mathcal{F}$ satisfies the Lipschitz condition (4), then it can be obtained that*

$$\| e_M \|_{L^2(\Omega)} \to 0, \quad as \quad M \to \infty,$$

where $e_M = y - y_M$.

Proof. Subtracting (1) from

$$\mathcal{Q}_M\left({}^C_a\mathcal{D}^\kappa_t y_M(x,t)\right) + d_1\mathcal{Q}_M\left(\frac{\partial^2}{\partial x^2}y_M(x,t)\right) + d_2\mathcal{Q}_M(\mathcal{F}(x,t,y_M(x,t))) = \mathcal{Q}_M(g(x,t)),$$

leads to

$$\begin{aligned}{}^C_a\mathcal{D}^\kappa_t e_M + d_1\frac{\partial^2}{\partial x^2}e_M + d_2(\mathcal{F}(x,t,y) - \mathcal{F}(x,t,y_M)) + (\mathcal{I}-\mathcal{Q}_M)\Big({}^C_a\mathcal{D}^\kappa_t y_M \\ +d_1\frac{\partial^2}{\partial x^2}y_M + d_2\mathcal{F}(x,t,y_M) - g\Big) = 0.\end{aligned} \quad (59)$$

For $(x,t) \in \Omega$, using the Cauchy–Schwarz inequality, one can write

$$\begin{aligned}e_M(x,t) = & \int_a^x \frac{\partial}{\partial s}e_M(s,t)ds \leq \int_a^x |\frac{\partial}{\partial s}e_M(s,t)|ds = \int_a^x \left|\frac{\partial}{\partial s}e_M(s,t).1\right|ds \\ & \leq \left(\int_a^b \left|\frac{\partial}{\partial s}e_M(s,t)\right|^2 ds\right)^{1/2} . \left(\int_a^b 1ds\right)^{1/2} = \sqrt{b-a}\left(\int_a^b \left|\frac{\partial}{\partial s}e_M(s,t)\right|^2 ds\right)^{1/2}.\end{aligned}$$

Integrating both sides over Ω after squaring them gives rise to

$$\int_0^\tau \int_a^b |e_M(x,t)|^2 dxdt \leq \int_0^\tau \int_a^b (b-a) \left| \left(\int_a^b \left| \frac{\partial}{\partial s} e_M(s,t) \right|^2 ds \right) \right|^2 dxdt$$
$$= (b-a)^2 \int_0^\tau \left(\int_a^b \left| \frac{\partial}{\partial s} e_M(s,t) \right|^2 ds \right) dt.$$

Hence,

$$\| e_M \|_{L^2(\Omega)} \leq (b-a) \| \frac{\partial}{\partial x} e_M \|_{L^2(\Omega)} \leq (b-a)^2 \| \frac{\partial^2}{\partial x^2} e_M \|_{L^2(\Omega)}. \tag{60}$$

Given

$$r(y_M) = {}_a^C\mathcal{D}_t^\kappa y_M + d_1 \frac{\partial^2}{\partial x^2} y_M + d_2 \mathcal{F}(x,t,y_M) - g.$$

Consider (59) and (60). Then, using the triangular inequality, we have

$$\begin{aligned} \frac{1}{(b-a)^2} \| e_M \|_{L^2(\Omega)} \leq & |d_1| \| \frac{\partial^2}{\partial x^2} e_M \|_{L^2(\Omega)} + |d_2| \| (\mathcal{F}(x,t,y) - \mathcal{F}(x,t,y_M)) \|_{L^2(\Omega)} \\ & + \| {}_a^C\mathcal{D}_t^\kappa e_M \|_{L^2(\Omega)} + \| (\mathcal{I} - \mathcal{Q}_M)(r(y_M)) \|_{L^2(\Omega)} \end{aligned} \tag{61}$$

Taking into account Theorem 1 and using the Lipschitz condition (4), one can obtain

$$\| (\mathcal{F}(x,t,y) - \mathcal{F}(x,t,y_M)) \|_{L^2(\Omega)} \leq C \sqrt{\frac{(M+1-n)!}{M!}} (M+n)^{-(n+1)/2} \left(\frac{h_{\max}}{2} \right)^{2n} |y|_{\mathbf{B}_{0,0}^n(\Omega)}. \tag{62}$$

Recall that ${}_a^C\mathcal{D}_t^\kappa := \mathcal{I}_a^{2-\kappa}\mathcal{D}^2$ where $1 < \kappa < 2$. Thus, utilizing Lemma 2.1(a) [30], we have

$$\| {}_a^C\mathcal{D}_t^\kappa e_M \|_{L^2(\Omega)} \leq \| \mathcal{I}_a^{2-\kappa}\mathcal{D}^2(e_M) \|_{L^2(\Omega)} \leq \frac{\tau}{\Gamma(3-\kappa)} \| \mathcal{D}^2(e_M) \|_{L^2(\Omega)}.$$

It follows from using Theorem 1 and Theorems (3.40) and (8.6) [27] that

$$\| {}_a^C\mathcal{D}_t^\kappa e_M \|_{L^2(\Omega)} \leq C \frac{\tau}{\Gamma(3-\kappa)} \sqrt{\frac{(M+1-n)!}{M!}} (M+n)^{2-(n+1)/2} \left(\frac{h_{\max}}{2} \right)^{2n} |y|_{\mathbf{B}_{0,0}^n(\Omega)}. \tag{63}$$

Using Equations (55) and (61)–(63), we have

$$\begin{aligned} \| e_M \|_{L^2(\Omega)} \leq & C \sqrt{\frac{(M+1-n)!}{M!}} (M+n)^{2-(n+1)/2} \left(\frac{h_{\max}}{2} \right)^{2n} |y|_{\mathbf{B}_{0,0}^n(\Omega)} \\ & + C \sqrt{\frac{(M+1-n)!}{M!}} (M+n)^{-(n+1)/2} \left(\frac{h_{\max}}{2} \right)^{2n} |r(y_M)|_{\mathbf{B}_{0,0}^n(\Omega)}. \end{aligned}$$

If $y \in \mathbf{B}_{0,0}^n(\Omega)$ and $2 < n \leq M+1$, then it can be obtained that

$$\| e_M \|_{L^2(\Omega)} \to 0, \quad as \quad M \to \infty.$$

□

4. Numerical Results

Example 1. *Consider the fractional Klein–Gordon equation*

$$ {}_{0}^{C}\mathcal{D}_t^{\kappa} y(x,t) - \frac{\partial^2}{\partial x^2} y(x,t) + sin(y(x,t)) = \sin\left(t^2 \sin(x)\right) + \left(\frac{2t^{2-\kappa}}{\Gamma(2-\kappa)} + t^2\right) \sin(x), $$

subjected to the following initial and boundary conditions:

$$ y(x,0) = 0, \quad \mathcal{D}_t\left(y(x,t)\right)|_{t=0} = 0, \quad x \in [0,1], $$

$$ y(0,t) = 0, \quad y(1,t) = t^2 \sin(1), \quad t \in [0,1]. $$

For this example, the exact solution $y(x,t) = t^2 \sin(x)$ is provided in [32].

Table 1 shows the efficiency and accuracy of the two proposed schemes based on Jacobi and Lobatto grids for different values of κ. To compare the proposed methods with existing ones, Table 2 presents comparisons with the implicit RBF meshless method [32]. The results confirm that our schemes yield better outcomes than the implicit RBF meshless method. The L^2-errors at different times are reported in Table 3 for PS1 with Jacobi grid, Table 4 for PS1 with Lobatto grid, Table 5 for PS2 with Jacobi grid, and Table 6 for PS2 with Lobatto grid. In all tables, the CPU times are also included. Figure 1 illustrates the convergence of the proposed schemes.

Table 1. The L^2-errors obtained by the proposed schemes, for Example 1, taking different collocation points and different choices of κ.

	M	9	11	13	15
$\kappa = 1.5$	PS1-Jacobi grid	2.155×10^{-5}	1.199×10^{-5}	7.355×10^{-6}	4.836×10^{-6}
	PS1-Lobatto grid	1.217×10^{-4}	6.301×10^{-5}	3.678×10^{-5}	2.333×10^{-5}
	PS2-Jacobi grid	2.229×10^{-11}	1.456×10^{-14}	6.514×10^{-18}	2.123×10^{-21}
	PS2-Lobatto grid	$\mathbf{7.642 \times 10^{-12}}$	$\mathbf{4.301 \times 10^{-15}}$	$\mathbf{1.712 \times 10^{-18}}$	$\mathbf{5.075 \times 10^{-22}}$
$\kappa = 1.15$	PS1-Jacobi grid	3.243×10^{-6}	1.374×10^{-6}	6.769×10^{-7}	3.719×10^{-7}
	PS1-Lobatto grid	1.361×10^{-5}	5.786×10^{-6}	2.853×10^{-6}	1.562×10^{-6}
	PS2-Jacobi grid	2.250×10^{-11}	1.469×10^{-14}	6.573×10^{-18}	2.142×10^{-21}
	PS2-Lobatto grid	$\mathbf{7.642 \times 10^{-12}}$	$\mathbf{4.301 \times 10^{-15}}$	$\mathbf{1.712 \times 10^{-18}}$	$\mathbf{5.075 \times 10^{-22}}$

Table 2. Comparison of the maximum errors between our numerical scheme and other existing methods for Example 1.

	Method	κ=1.15	κ=1.85
Proposed method (M = 15)	PS1-Jacobi grid	3.456×10^{-6}	5.382×10^{-5}
	PS1-Lobatto grid	4.278×10^{-6}	7.075×10^{-4}
	PS2-Jacobi grid	7.804×10^{-21}	7.818×10^{-21}
	PS2-Lobatto grid	$\mathbf{1.067 \times 10^{-21}}$	$\mathbf{1.031 \times 10^{-21}}$
Other Methods	Implicit RBF meshless method [32] ($\Delta t = 1/160, \Delta x = 1/50$)	8.66×10^{-4}	5.52×10^{-4}

Table 3. The L^2-errors obtained by PS1-Jacobi grid at various times using different values of M, taking $\kappa = 1.5$.

$t \backslash M$	6	8	10	12	14
0.1	8.974×10^{-5}	4.240×10^{-5}	2.817×10^{-5}	1.811×10^{-5}	1.081×10^{-5}
0.3	1.001×10^{-4}	4.208×10^{-5}	1.916×10^{-5}	1.356×10^{-5}	8.080×10^{-6}
0.5	2.734×10^{-5}	8.164×10^{-6}	6.436×10^{-6}	3.047×10^{-6}	2.392×10^{-6}
0.7	3.819×10^{-5}	6.014×10^{-6}	3.852×10^{-6}	3.099×10^{-6}	1.168×10^{-6}
0.9	1.864×10^{-5}	1.248×10^{-5}	7.379×10^{-6}	4.211×10^{-6}	2.071×10^{-6}
CPU time	1.938	15.687	65.140	227.844	697.969

Table 4. The L^2-errors obtained by PS1-Lobatto grid at various times using different values of M, taking $\kappa = 1.5$.

$t \backslash M$	6	8	10	12	14
0.1	1.040×10^{-3}	3.318×10^{-4}	1.178×10^{-4}	6.512×10^{-5}	5.137×10^{-5}
0.3	4.358×10^{-4}	2.133×10^{-4}	1.380×10^{-4}	5.232×10^{-5}	4.249×10^{-5}
0.5	7.634×10^{-4}	1.014×10^{-4}	1.936×10^{-5}	2.470×10^{-5}	8.000×10^{-6}
0.7	2.389×10^{-4}	9.775×10^{-5}	2.886×10^{-5}	1.491×10^{-5}	1.296×10^{-5}
0.9	4.219×10^{-4}	7.714×10^{-5}	3.403×10^{-5}	2.518×10^{-5}	1.454×10^{-5}
CPU time	2.250	14.656	69.046	256.766	873.187

Table 5. The L^2-errors obtained by PS2-Jacobi grid at various times using different values of M, taking $\kappa = 1.5$.

$t \backslash M$	6	8	10	12	14
0.1	3.618×10^{-9}	4.602×10^{-12}	3.815×10^{-15}	2.113×10^{-18}	3.729×10^{-22}
0.3	4.610×10^{-8}	6.679×10^{-11}	5.467×10^{-14}	2.935×10^{-17}	3.356×10^{-21}
0.5	1.701×10^{-7}	2.372×10^{-10}	1.931×10^{-13}	1.033×10^{-16}	9.360×10^{-21}
0.7	3.967×10^{-7}	5.504×10^{-10}	4.462×10^{-13}	2.383×10^{-16}	1.827×10^{-20}
0.9	7.374×10^{-7}	1.017×10^{-9}	8.238×10^{-13}	4.397×10^{-16}	3.021×10^{-20}
CPU time	0.610	1.797	6.437	19.672	49.031

Table 6. The L^2-errors obtained by PS2-Lobatto grid at various times using different values of M, taking $\kappa = 1.5$.

$t \backslash M$	6	8	10	12	14
0.1	3.113×10^{-9}	3.390×10^{-12}	2.324×10^{-15}	1.092×10^{-18}	3.729×10^{-22}
0.3	2.808×10^{-8}	3.053×10^{-11}	2.092×10^{-14}	9.826×10^{-18}	3.356×10^{-21}
0.5	7.840×10^{-8}	8.516×10^{-11}	5.835×10^{-14}	2.740×10^{-17}	9.360×10^{-21}
0.7	1.531×10^{-7}	1.663×10^{-10}	1.139×10^{-13}	5.350×10^{-17}	1.827×10^{-20}
0.9	2.531×10^{-7}	2.748×10^{-10}	1.883×10^{-13}	8.843×10^{-17}	3.021×10^{-20}
CPU time	0.484	1.859	6.859	23.344	72.063

Finally, the accuracy and efficiency of the proposed schemes are validated by the reported results. Additionally, the obtained results support the convergence analysis provided. Moreover, the second scheme yields more accurate results compared to the first scheme. Generally, the best results for this example are achieved by the second scheme using the Lobatto grid (specifically the PS2-Lobatto grid), while requiring less computational time.

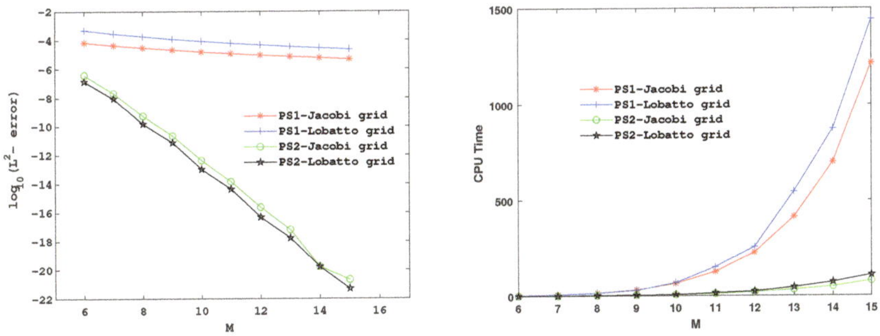

Figure 1. The plots of L^2-errors and CPU times, for Example 1, taking $\kappa = 1.5$.

Example 2. *Consider the fractional Klein–Gordon equation*

$$ {}^{C}_{0}\mathcal{D}^{\kappa}_{t} y(x,t) - \frac{\partial^2}{\partial x^2} y(x,t) + y(x,t) + \frac{3}{2} y(x,t)^3 = g(x,t), $$

subjected to conditions

$$ y(x,0) = 0, \quad \mathcal{D}_t\left(y(x,t)\right)|_{t=0} = 0, \quad x \in [0,1], $$

$$ y(0,t) = 0, \quad y(1,t) = t^{2+\kappa}\sin(\pi), \quad t \in [0,1], $$

where $g(x,t) = \frac{\sin \pi x}{2}\left(3\left(\sin^2(\pi x)\right)t^{6+3\kappa} + \Gamma(3+\kappa)t^2 + 2\pi^2 t^{2+\kappa} + 2t^{2+\kappa}\right)$.

For this example, the exact solution $y(x,t) = t^{2+\kappa}\sin(\pi x)$ is reported in [33].

Table 7 displays the accuracy of the two proposed schemes based on Jacobi and Lobatto grids for different values of κ. To compare the proposed methods with existing methods, Table 8 is presented. The variational iteration method [33] and Sinc–Chebyshev collocation method [18] are compared with our proposed schemes in this table. The results confirm that our schemes yield better outcomes than these methods. We compared the errors obtained using the different schemes proposed in this paper and plotted them in Figure 2, where CPU times are also reported.

The experimental results indicate that the first scheme is more accurate, while the second scheme executes faster.

Table 7. The L^2-errors obtained by the proposed schemes, for Example 2, taking different collocation points and different choices of κ.

	M	9	11	13	15
$\kappa = 1.5$	PS1-Jacobi grid	$\mathbf{3.748 \times 10^{-7}}$	$\mathbf{6.687 \times 10^{-8}}$	$\mathbf{1.707 \times 10^{-8}}$	$\mathbf{5.367 \times 10^{-9}}$
	PS1-Lobatto grid	5.155×10^{-7}	9.351×10^{-8}	2.323×10^{-8}	7.139×10^{-9}
	PS2-Jacobi grid	5.735×10^{-6}	1.682×10^{-6}	6.135×10^{-7}	2.601×10^{-7}
	PS2-Lobatto grid	1.762×10^{-6}	4.492×10^{-7}	1.503×10^{-7}	6.002×10^{-8}
$\kappa = 1.8$	PS1-Jacobi grid	$\mathbf{1.646 \times 10^{-7}}$	$\mathbf{2.190 \times 10^{-8}}$	$\mathbf{4.989 \times 10^{-9}}$	$\mathbf{1.428 \times 10^{-9}}$
	PS1-Lobatto grid	5.155×10^{-7}	9.351×10^{-8}	2.323×10^{-8}	7.139×10^{-9}
	PS2-Jacobi grid	1.039×10^{-5}	2.932×10^{-6}	1.047×10^{-6}	4.384×10^{-7}
	PS2-Lobatto grid	3.742×10^{-6}	9.701×10^{-7}	3.260×10^{-7}	1.302×10^{-7}

Table 8. Comparison of the maximum errors between our numerical scheme and other existing methods for Example 2.

(x, t)	VIM [33]	SCCM [18]	PS1		PS2	
			Jacobi Grid	Lobatto Grid	Jacobi Grid	Lobatto Grid
(0.1,0.1)	3.921×10^{-5}	2.381×10^{-5}	9.376×10^{-6}	4.636×10^{-6}	3.464×10^{-5}	2.327×10^{-5}
(0.2,0.2)	6.171×10^{-4}	5.264×10^{-5}	7.188×10^{-6}	2.455×10^{-5}	9.053×10^{-5}	3.438×10^{-5}
(0.3,0.3)	2.199×10^{-3}	6.019×10^{-6}	1.264×10^{-5}	1.452×10^{-5}	7.679×10^{-5}	1.746×10^{-5}
(0.4,0.4)	2.555×10^{-3}	6.664×10^{-5}	2.765×10^{-6}	2.157×10^{-7}	4.884×10^{-5}	2.300×10^{-5}
(0.5,0.5)	5.341×10^{-3}	4.001×10^{-5}	2.524×10^{-5}	4.955×10^{-5}	8.665×10^{-5}	8.397×10^{-5}
(0.6,0.6)	3.141×10^{-2}	1.584×10^{-4}	6.384×10^{-5}	6.122×10^{-5}	1.448×10^{-4}	1.319×10^{-5}
(0.7,0.7)	8.009×10^{-2}	9.192×10^{-4}	1.093×10^{-4}	1.437×10^{-4}	1.881×10^{-4}	1.083×10^{-4}
(0.8,0.8)	1.353×10^{-1}	2.908×10^{-3}	4.545×10^{-4}	3.518×10^{-4}	5.376×10^{-4}	3.827×10^{-4}
(0.9,0.9)	1.427×10^{-1}	3.873×10^{-3}	1.395×10^{-3}	1.232×10^{-3}	1.497×10^{-4}	9.042×10^{-5}

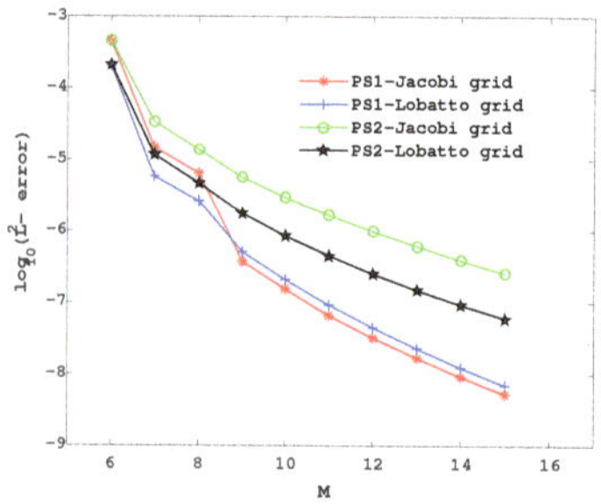

(**a**) L^2-errors with $\kappa = 1.5$

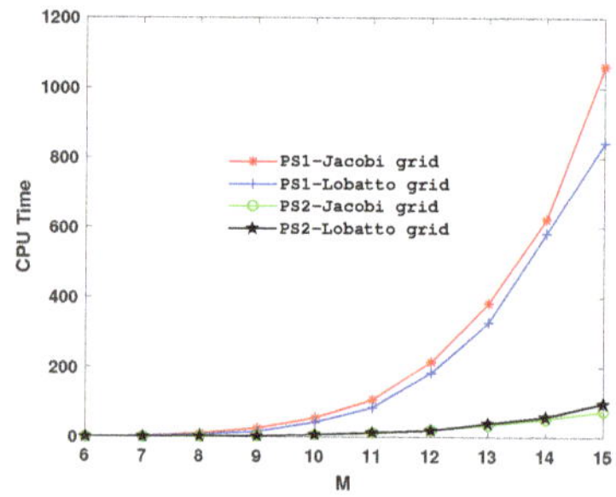

(**b**) CPU time for $\kappa = 1.5$

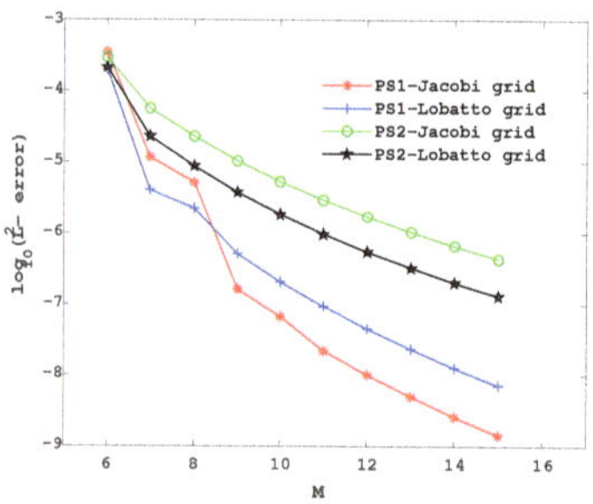

(**c**) L^2-errors with $\kappa = 1.8$

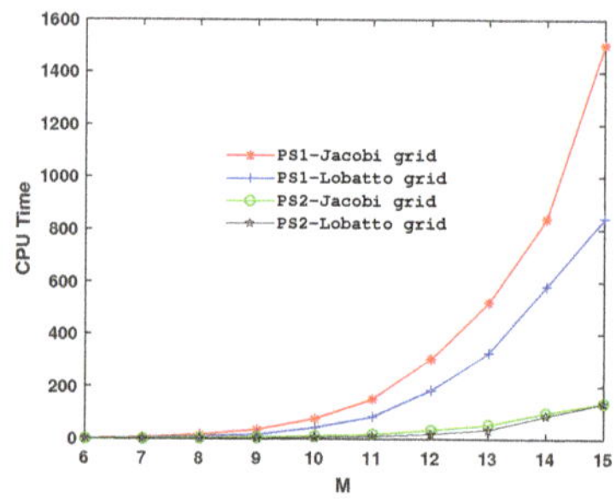

(**d**) CPU time for $\kappa = 1.8$

Figure 2. The plots of L^2-errors obtained from two schemes with different choices of collocation points, for Example 2.

Example 3. *Consider the fractional Klein–Gordon equation*

$$ {}_{0}^{C}\mathcal{D}_t^{\kappa} y(x,t) - \frac{\partial^2}{\partial x^2} y(x,t) + \sin(y(x,t)) = g(x,t), $$

subjected to conditions

$$ y(x,0) = e^x, \quad \mathcal{D}_t(y(x,t))|_{t=0} = 0, \quad x \in [0,1], $$

$$ y(0,t) = t^3 + t^2 + 1, \quad y(1,t) = e\left(t^3 + t^2 + 1\right), \quad t \in [0,1], $$

where $g(x,t) = \left(\frac{6t^{3-\kappa}}{\Gamma(4-\kappa)} + \frac{2t^{2-\kappa}}{\Gamma(3-\kappa)} - (t^3 + t^2 + 1) \right) e^x + \sin((t^3 + t^2 + 1)e^x)$.

For this example, the exact solution is $y(x,t) = (t^3 + t^2 + 1)e^x$.

Table 9 displays the accuracy of the two proposed schemes based on Jacobi and Lobatto grids for different values of M. We compared the errors obtained using the different schemes proposed in this paper and plotted them in Figure 3, where CPU times are also reported.

Table 9. The L^2-errors obtained by the proposed schemes, for Example 3, taking different collocation points.

	M	9	11	13	15
$\kappa = 1.5$	PS1-Jacobi grid	8.025×10^{-5}	4.512×10^{-5}	2.783×10^{-5}	1.836×10^{-5}
	PS1-Lobatto grid	5.493×10^{-4}	2.366×10^{-4}	1.390×10^{-4}	8.849×10^{-5}
	PS2-Jacobi grid	1.855×10^{-10}	1.234×10^{-13}	5.630×10^{-17}	1.869×10^{-20}
	PS2-Lobatto grid	$\mathbf{5.476 \times 10^{-11}}$	$\mathbf{3.076 \times 10^{-14}}$	$\mathbf{1.223 \times 10^{-17}}$	$\mathbf{3.622 \times 10^{-21}}$

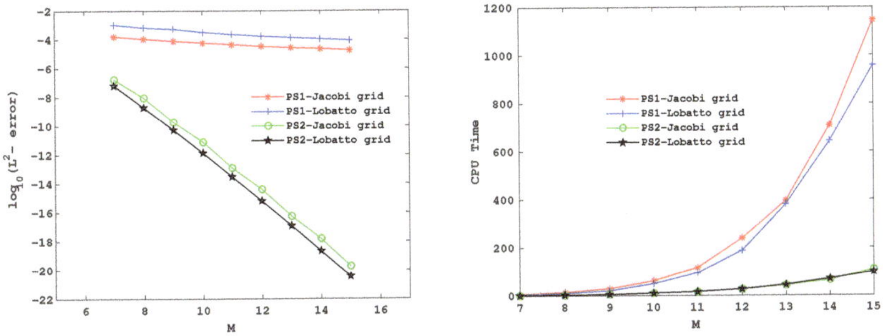

Figure 3. The plots of L^2-errors and CPU times, for Example 3, taking $\kappa = 1.5$.

5. Conclusions

This paper introduces the Legendre cardinal function for the first time and employs two numerical schemes to solve the fractional Klein–Gordon equation (FKGE). The paper addresses two main subjects: the introduction of the Legendre cardinal functions and the solution of the FKGE. The Legendre cardinal functions are determined using Jacobi and Lobatto grids, both of which satisfy the cardinality condition—a fundamental property of cardinal functions. We represent the fractional integral operator and the Caputo fractional derivative as matrices.

Two numerical schemes based on the pseudospectral method are considered. The first scheme reformulates the given equation into a corresponding integral equation for solving it. The second scheme directly tackles the problem by utilizing the matrix representation of the Caputo fractional derivative operator. The numerical examples validate our convergence analysis. All proposed methods result in accurate solutions. Comparisons with other methods demonstrate that the proposed schemes outperform existing approaches.

Some notable features of the proposed methods include a reduction in computational effort due to the cardinality property of the basis functions, matrices representing fractional derivative and integral operators, and ease of implementation. The presented approaches can be extended to solve higher-dimensional FKGEs. Additionally, these schemes can be used to address other fractional problems, including fractional differential equations, fractional partial differential equations, integral equations with weakly singular kernels, and fractional integro-differential equations.

Author Contributions: Conceptualization, T.L., B.D., B.N.S., D.A.J. and E.E.E.; Methodology, T.L., B.D., B.N.S., D.A.J. and E.E.E.; Software, B.N.S. and D.A.J.; Validation, T.L., B.D., B.N.S., D.A.J. and E.E.E.; Formal analysis, T.L., B.D., B.N.S., D.A.J. and E.E.E.; Investigation, B.N.S. and E.E.E.; Writing—original draft, B.N.S., D.A.J. and E.E.E.; Writing—review & editing, T.L., B.D., B.N.S., D.A.J. and E.E.E.; Visualization, B.N.S., D.A.J. and E.E.E.; Supervision, B.N.S.; Funding acquisition, T.L., B.D. and E.E.E. All authors have read and agreed to the published version of the manuscript.

Funding: This research was funded by the Open Fund Project of the Marine Ecological Restoration and Smart Ocean Engineering Research Center of Hebei Province (HBMESO2321), the Technical Service Project of the Eighth Geological Brigade of the Hebei Bureau of Geology and Mineral Resources Exploration (KJ2022-021), the Technical Service Project of Hebei Baodi Construction Engineering Co., Ltd. (KJ2024-012), the Natural Science Foundation of Hebei Province of China (A2020501007), and the Fundamental Research Funds for the Central Universities (N2123015).

Data Availability Statement: The original contributions presented in this study are included in the article. Further inquiries can be directed to the corresponding author.

Conflicts of Interest: The writers state that they have no known personal relationships or competing financial interests that could have appeared to affect the work reported in this work.

References

1. Zhang, Y. A finite difference method for fractional partial differential equation. *Appl. Math. Comput.* **2009**, *215*, 524–529. [CrossRef]
2. Asadzadeh, M.; Saray, B.N. On a multiwavelet spectral element method for integral equation of a generalized Cauchy problem. *BIT* **2022**, *62*, 383–1416. [CrossRef]
3. Liu, T.; Xue, R.; Ding, b.; Juraev, D.; Saray, B.N.; Soleymani, F. A Novel and Effective Scheme for Solving the Fractional Telegraph Problem via the Spectral Element Method. *Fractal Fract.* **2024**, *8*, 711. [CrossRef]
4. Ford, N.J.; Xiao, J.; Yan, Y. A finite element method for time fractional partial differential equations. *Fract. Calc. Appl. Anal.* **2011**, *14*, 454–474. [CrossRef]
5. Fardi, M.; Zaky, M.A.; Hendy, A.S. Nonuniform difference schemes for multi-term and distributed-order fractional parabolic equations with fractional Laplacian. *Math. Comput. Simulat.* **2023**, *206*, 614–635. [CrossRef]
6. Li, C.; Li, Z.; Wang, Z. Mathematical analysis and the local discontinuous Galerkin method for Caputo–Hadamard fractional partial differential equation. *J. Sci. Comput.* **2020**, *85*, 41. [CrossRef]
7. Mao, Z.; Shen, J. Efficient spectral–Galerkin methods for fractional partial differential equations with variable coefficients. *J. Comput. Phys.* **2016**, *307*, 243–261. [CrossRef]
8. Bonyadi, S.; Mahmoudi, Y.; Lakestani, M.; Jahangiri rad, M. Numerical solution of space-time fractional PDEs with variable coefficients using shifted Jacobi collocation method. *Comput. Methods Differ. Equ.* **2023**, *11*, 81–94.
9. Javidi, M. Chebyshev Spectral Collocation Method for Computing Numerical Solution of Telegraph Equation. *Comput. Methods Differ. Equ.* **2013**, *1*, 16–29.
10. Günerhan, H.; Çelik, E. Analytical and approximate solutions of fractional partial differential-algebraic equations. *Appl. Math. Nonlinear Sci.* **2020**, *5*, 109–120. [CrossRef]
11. Fardi, M. A kernel-based pseudo-spectral method for multi-term and distributed order time-fractional diffusion equations. *Numer. Methods Partial. Differ. Equ.* **2023**, *39*, 2630–2651. [CrossRef]
12. Juraev, D.A.; Shokri, A.; Marian, D. Solution of the ill-posed Cauchy problem for systems of elliptic type of the first order. *Fractal Fract.* **2022**, *6*, 358. [CrossRef]
13. Juraev, D.A.; Shokri, A.; Marian, D. On the approximate solution of the Cauchy problem in a multidimensional unbounded domain. *Fractal Fract.* **2022**, *6*, 403. [CrossRef]
14. Bussey, P.J. Improving our Understanding of the Klein–Gordon Equation. *Glob. J. Sci. Front. Res.* **2022**, *22*, 11–19.
15. Klein, O. Quantentheorie und fünfdimensionale Relativitätstheorie. *Z. Phys.* **1926**, *37*, 895–906. [CrossRef]
16. Gordon, W. Der Comptoneffekt nach der Schrödingerschen Theorie. *Z. Phys.* **1926**, *40*, 117–133. [CrossRef]
17. Aaqib, I.; Rashid, N.; Rashid, A.; Mehran; Fewster-Young, N.; Hina. Extension of optimal auxiliary function method to nonlinear Sine Gordon differential equations. *Partial. Differ. Equ. Appl. Math.* **2024**, *10*, 100735.
18. Nagy, A.M. Numerical solution of time fractional nonlinear Klein–Gordon equation using Sinc-Chebyshev collocation method. *Appl. Math. Comput.* **2017**, *310*, 139–148. [CrossRef]
19. Golmankhaneh, A.K.; Golmankhaneh, A.K.; Baleanu, D. On nonlinear fractional Klein–Gordon equation. *Signal Process* **2011**, *91*, 446–451. [CrossRef]

20. Singh, H.; Kumar, D.; Pandey, R.K. An Efficient Computational Method for the Time-Space Fractional Klein–Gordon Equation. *Front Phys.* **2020**, *8*, 281. [CrossRef]
21. Amin, M.; Abbas, M.; Iqbal, M.K.; Baleanu, D. Numerical treatment of time-fractional Klein–Gordon equation using redefined extended cubic B-spline functions. *Front Phys.* **2020**, *8*, 288. [CrossRef]
22. Gharian, D.; Ghaini, F.M.M.; Heydari, M.H.; Avazzadeh, Z. A meshless solution for the variable-order time fractional nonlinear Klein–Gordon equation. *Int. J. Appl. Comput. Math.* **2020**, *6*, 130. [CrossRef]
23. Mainardi, F. *Fractional Calculus and Waves in Linear Viscoelasticity*; World Scientific: Singapore, 2010.
24. Chen, S.; Liu, F.; Anh, V. Numerical analysis of the fractional Klein–Gordon equation. *J. Comput. Phys.* **2007**, *227*, 941–952.
25. Bhrawy, A.H.; Alghamdi, M.A. A shifted Jacobi-Gauss-Lobatto collocation method for solving nonlinear fractional differential equations. *Bound. Value Probl.* **2013**, *2013*, 62.
26. Boyd, J.P. *Chebyshev and Fourier Spectral Methods*, 2nd ed.; Dover Publications: Garden City, NY, USA, 2001; Revised.
27. Shen, J.; Tang, T.; Wang, L.L. *Spectral Methods: Algorithms. Analysis, Applications*; Springer: Berlin, Germany, 2011.
28. Sayevand, K.; Arab, H. An efficient extension of the Chebyshev cardinal functions for differential equations with coordinate derivatives of non-integer order. *Comput. Methods Differ. Equ.* **2018**, *6*, 339–352.
29. Shahriari, M.; Saray, B.N.; Mohammadalipour, B.; Saeidian, S. Pseudospectral method for solving the fractional one-dimensional Dirac operator using Chebyshev cardinal functions. *Phys. Scr.* **2023**, *98*, 055205. [CrossRef]
30. Kilbas, A.; Srivastava, H.M.; Trujillo, J.J. *Theory and Applications of Fractional Differential Equations*; Elsevier B. V.: Amsterdam, The Netherlands, 2006; p. 24.
31. Andrews, G.E.; Askey, R.; Roy, R. Special functions. In *Encyclopedia of Mathematics and its Applications*; Cambridge University Press: Cambridge, UK, 1999; Volume 71.
32. Dehghan, M.; Abbaszadeh, M.; Mohebbi, A. An implicit RBF meshless approach for solving the time fractional nonlinear sine-Gordon and Klein–Gordon equations. *Eng. Anal. Bound. Elem.* **2015**, *50*, 412–434. [CrossRef]
33. Odibat, Z.; Momani, S. The variational iteration method: An efficient scheme for handling fractional partial differential equations in fluid mechanics. *Comput. Math. Appl.* **2009**, *58*, 2199–2208. [CrossRef]

fractal and fractional

MDPI

Article

Stability Analysis of a Fractional Epidemic Model Involving the Vaccination Effect

Sümeyye Çakan

Department of Mathematics, İnönü University, 44280 Malatya, Türkiye; sumeyye.tay@inonu.edu.tr

Abstract: This paper, by constructing a fractional epidemic model, analyzes the transmission dynamics of some infectious diseases under the effect of vaccination, which is one of the most effective and common control measures. In the model, considering that antibody formation by vaccination may not cause permanent immunity, it has been taken into account that the protection period provided by the vaccine may be finite, in addition to the fact that this period may change according to individuals. The model differs from other $SVIR$ models given in the literature in its progressive process with a distributed delay in the loss of the protective effect provided by the vaccine. To explain this process, the model was constructed by using a system of distributed delay nonlinear fractional integro-differential equations. Thus, the model aims to present a realistic approach to following the course of the disease. Additionally, an analysis was conducted regarding the minimum vaccination ratio of new members required for the elimination of the disease in the population by using the vaccine free basic reproduction number ($\mathcal{R}_0^{vf}$). After providing examples for the selection of the distribution function, the variation of $\mathcal{R}_0$ was simulated for a specific selection of parameters in the model. Finally, the sensitivity indices of the parameters affecting $\mathcal{R}_0$ were calculated, and this situation is been visually supported.

Keywords: fractional model with vaccination; stability analysis; basic reproduction number; Lyapunov function; dulac criteria

1. Introduction

Compartmental models for infectious diseases separate a population into various classes according to the stages of infection. The reflected rates of transition between compartments are stated by time derivatives of the population sizes in each compartment, so such models are formulated by differential equations. Mathematical models in which the rates of transfer between compartments depend on the sizes of compartments in the past or at the moment of transfer require working with differential, integral, or integro-differential equations.

The early and foundational work on compartmental models in mathematical epidemiology is based on Kermack and McKendrick [1]. In 1927, they introduced a compartmental epidemic model based on basic transfers between divided groups in a population. To explain the compartments, they divided the population into three groups, designated S, I, and R, to describe the compartments. $S(t)$ denotes the number of individuals who are susceptible to the disease at time t, in other words, those who are not yet infected and do not have any immunity. $I(t)$ represents the number of infectious individuals, that is, members of $I(t)$ can spread the disease to susceptible individuals with effective contact. $R(t)$ shows the number of recovered individuals, who have immunity against the pathogen and there thus is no probability of spread of infection via these individuals.

Based on the model given by Kermack and McKendrick, mathematical epidemiology has been developed with numerous studies providing various contributions to the literature in this field (e.g., [2–4]).

Vaccination of susceptible individuals against infection is one of the effective control measures in the process related to the struggle with diseases. So far, numerous studies have been introduced explaining the effects of vaccination on the spread of diseases (see [5–8] and references therein).

Fractional order systems are modeled with fractional order differential equations containing derivatives of non-integer order. These systems make significant contributions to the study of the behavior of dynamic systems in many fields such as physics, electrochemistry, biology, engineering, mechanics, economics, mathematical epidemiology, and ecology.

The reason for choosing to work with these systems is that fractional order derivatives provide a better fit to real data in these application areas and overcome the limitations of classical integer order derivatives.

In this context, in recent times, studies on the necessity of using fractional order equations, including fractional order derivatives or integrals in order for model problems to better reflect the events in our daily lives and to establish more realistic models, have increased considerably [9–12].

For dynamical systems that reflect situations where memory effects are important, fractional order equations are more suitable than integer order equations. Due to the memory effect, the non-integer models integrate all previous information from the past that makes them able to predict and translate the epidemic models more accurately. For this reason, fractional order models are more reliable and helpful in real phenomena than the classical models [10]. To summarize, the fractional epidemic models are the generalizations of the integer-order models and provide useful information any time desired. Additionally, in the real-world explanation, the integer order derivative does not explore the dynamics between two different points. For example, there are many TB models in the literature that are based on ordinary (or delay) integer-order derivative. However, such models have some limitations, as they do not provide any information about the memory and learning mechanism. To deal with such failures of classical local differentiation, different concepts on differentiation with non-local or fractional orders have been developed in the existing literature. Thus, working with fractional equations offers a more realistic pathway to the epidemic models. Some authors have extended classical epidemic models to fractional-order epidemic systems and discussed the stability of equilibrium [9,13,14].

In recent years, some fractional-order differential equation models of infectious disease dynamics have been introduced with the Caputo derivation. In 2018, Saif Ullah et al. [10] proposed a fractional Caputo model of TB infection and validated it with the real data of TB incidence cases from 2002 to 2017 in the Khyber Pakhtunkhwa province of Pakistan. The authors then showed through numerical simulations that the proposed fractional model provides a better fit to real data than classical models.

Alqahtani et al. [15] introduced a Caputo Fractional Chlamydia pandemic model and investigated the stability analysis of the α-fractional order model along with the sensitivity analysis. Their simulations showed that memory effects, represented by the fractional order (α), significantly impact disease spread, with memory-driven acceleration increasing transmission potential.

El Hajji and Sayari [16] have investigated a $SVEIR$ model of infectious disease transmission in a chemostat and study on the model's local and global stabilities with a profound analysis.

Özdemir and colleagues [11] studied a $SVIR$ model under the influence of vaccination for an infectious disease by generalizing it with the Caputo fractional derivative. They focused on the effect of fractional parameter and noted that the increasing effect of vaccination was observed at decreasing values of the fractional order.

Gökbulut et al. [12] proposed a fractional order $SVIR$ model for studying the COVID-19 pandemic and used Caputo fractional derivatives with the purpose of observing a memory effect.

This paper reveals and analyzes a novel epidemic model, considering the vaccination effect on the spread of any disease. As is known, the immunity obtained through vaccination may not be permanent, and the immunization periods of vaccinated individuals may not be the same. Thus, even if they were vaccinated at the same time, while the immunity of some of the individuals may continue, the others may lose their immunity and become susceptible to the epidemic. This situation is particularly relevant for diseases such as pertussis or measles, where vaccine effectiveness may decrease over time. In this study, prepared by taking all these facts into consideration, a mathematical epidemic model reflecting that the protection period provided by the vaccine effect may vary from person to person, is presented. This novel $SVIR$ fractional epidemic model is formed by aid of a system of distributed delay nonlinear fractional integro-differential equations. Unlike conventional $SVIR$ models, which assume a uniform rate of immunity loss, this view taken into consideration in the proposed model accounts for individual heterogeneity in immune response, thereby offering a more detailed and realistic portrayal of population dynamics.

This study introduces significant innovation by integrating fractional calculus to enhance the explanatory capacity of the model. This approach allows for modeling non-local and memory effects often observed in immunological responses. Additionally, the study employs a distributed delay approach, which allows for a more realistic representation of immunity loss by considering the variability in how long individuals retain immunity post-vaccination, increasing the applicability of the models to real-world vaccination strategies. Furthermore, the expansion to include fractional-order derivatives of the classical SIR and $SVIR$ models provides greater flexibility in defining immunity loss, allowing for a finer-grained control over the rate of immunity loss and capturing subtle and non-linear dynamics often missed by classical models.

For model analysis, first, disease-free and endemic equilibrium points were determined. Then the basic reproduction number related to the model was obtained by using the next generation matrix method. It is also shown that the disease-free and the endemic equilibrium are locally and globally asymptotically stable for $\mathcal{R}_0 < 1$ and $\mathcal{R}_0 > 1$, respectively.

Local stabilities of equilibrium points have been researched by analyzing the corresponding characteristic equation. To prove global stabilities of equilibrium, the LaSalle Invariance Principle, associated with the Lyapunov function and Dulac Criteria, respectively, has been used.

Lastly, an assessment regarding the minimum vaccination ratio of new members required for the elimination of the disease in the population has been carried out. After providing examples for the selection of the distribution function, reflecting that the protection period provided by the vaccine effect, which may vary from person to person, the variation of $\mathcal{R}_0$ has been simulated for a specific selection of parameters in the model. Finally, the sensitivity indices of the parameters affecting $\mathcal{R}_0$ have been calculated, and this situation has also been visually supported.

2. Some Basic Mathematical Properties and Model Structure

The definitions of the fractional integral and Caputo fractional derivative are defined as follows [17].

Definition 1. *Suppose that $\alpha > 0$, $a \in \mathbb{R}$, $t > a$ and x is an integrable function. Then the fractional integral of x of order α is defined as*

$$I^{\alpha}_{a+}x(t) = \frac{1}{\Gamma(\alpha)} \int_a^t (t-s)^{\alpha-1} x(s) ds.$$

The Caputo fractional derivative of x of order α is defined as

$$^{C}D^{\alpha}_{a+}x(t) = \left(\frac{d}{dt}\right)^n I^{n-\alpha}_{a+}\left[x(t) - \sum_{k=0}^{n-1} \frac{x^{(k)}(a)}{k!}(t-a)^k\right],\ t > a,$$

where $n = [\alpha] + 1$. When α is an integer number, $^{C}D^{\alpha}_{a+}x$ is a usual derivative of order α of x. If x is a function of class C^n, its fractional derivative is represented by

$$^{C}D^{\alpha}_{a+}x(t) = \frac{1}{\Gamma(n-\alpha)} \int_a^t (t-s)^{n-\alpha-1} x^{(n)}(s) ds.$$

Specifically, we write $^{C}D^{\alpha}x$ instead of $^{C}D^{\alpha}_{0+}x$. It is obvious that the Caputo fractional derivative of order α of x is

$$^{C}D^{\alpha}x(t) = \frac{1}{\Gamma(1-\alpha)} \int_0^t \frac{x'(s)ds}{(t-s)^{\alpha}}$$

for $0 < \alpha < 1$.

On the other hand, let us recall some properties of Laplace transforms. The Laplace transform of the Caputo fractional derivative [9] is given by

$$\mathscr{L}\left\{^{C}D^{\alpha}x(t)\right\} = \lambda^{\alpha}\mathscr{L}\{x(t)\} - \sum_{k=0}^{n-1} x^{(k)}(0)\lambda^{\alpha-k-1}. \tag{1}$$

Additionally, the Laplace transform of the Mittag–Leffler function defined by the power series

$$E_{\alpha,\beta}(z) = \sum_{k=0}^{\infty} \frac{z^k}{\Gamma(\alpha k + \beta)}$$

holds the following equality [9]:

$$\mathscr{L}\left\{t^{\beta-1}E_{\alpha,\beta}(-at^{\alpha})\right\} = \frac{\lambda^{\alpha-\beta}}{\lambda^{\alpha} + a}. \tag{2}$$

Theorem 1. *The equilibrium solutions x^* of the Caputo fractional differential equations system are*

$$^{C}D^{\alpha}x(t) = f(t,x),\ x(t_0) = x_0$$

The Jacobian matrix $\frac{\partial f}{\partial x_j}$ evaluated at equilibrium points ensures local asymptotic stability if its eigenvalues λ_j satisfy [15,18]

$$|\arg(\lambda_j)| = \pi > \alpha\pi/2,\ 0 < \alpha < 1,\ j = 1,2,\cdots,n.$$

Theorem 2. *Let x^* be an equilibrium point for $^{C}D^{\alpha}x(t) = f(t,x)$, and let Ω be a domain containing x^*. Let $L : [0,\infty) \times \Omega \to \mathbb{R}$ be a continuously differentiable function such that*

$$W_1(x) \le L(t,x) \le W_2(x),$$

$$^{C}D^{\alpha}L(t,x) \le -W_3(x)$$

hold for all $t \geq 0$, $x \in \Omega$ and $\alpha \in (0,1)$, where functions W_i are continuous positive definite functions on Ω. Then the equilibrium point of system ${}^C D^\alpha x(t) = f(t,x)$ is uniformly asymptotically stable [13,14].

Model Structure

We introduce a new fractional $SVIR$ mathematical compartmental model expressed by the system of the following nonlinear fractional integro-differential equations, with all parameters being positive:

$$\begin{aligned} {}^C D^\alpha S(t) &= b - \beta S(t)I(t) - qS(t) - \mu S(t) \\ {}^C D^\alpha V(t) &= qS(t) - \beta q I(t) \int_0^\infty f(\theta) S(t-\theta) e^{-\mu\theta} d\theta - \mu V(t) \\ {}^C D^\alpha I(t) &= \beta S(t)I(t) + \beta q I(t) \int_0^\infty f(\theta) S(t-\theta) e^{-\mu\theta} d\theta - (\gamma + \delta + \mu) I(t) \\ {}^C D^\alpha R(t) &= \gamma I(t) - \mu R(t), \end{aligned} \tag{3}$$

where $\alpha \in (0,1]$ and functions $S(t)$, $V(t)$, $I(t)$, and $R(t)$ represent the numbers of the susceptible, vaccinated, infectious, and recovered individuals at time t, respectively. The total population size is $N(t)$ and $N(t) = S(t) + V(t) + I(t) + R(t)$ for all $t \geq 0$. Additionally, all these functions are non-negative.

In the model, all newborn individuals become involved in the population by entering to S at a constant rate b. β denotes the effective contact rate between infectious and susceptible or vaccinated individuals. μ is the natural death rate in each compartment, and δ is the death rate welded from the outbreak. The rate of vaccinated individuals within susceptible individuals is represented by q. Additionally, γ denotes the transition rate from the infectious compartment to compartment R.

Vaccination may not always be completely effective for individuals. Therefore, in this model, we suppose that the vaccine provides a temporary immunity effect or a permanent effect for some individuals. In this context, we use the distribution parameter θ to mean the protection period caused by vaccination. Essentially, the term θ designates the protection efficacy of the vaccine. That is, $\theta = 0$ means that the vaccine is completely ineffective. Additionally, $0 < \theta < \infty$ means that the vaccinated individuals have only partial protection. Otherwise, it means that the vaccine is wholly effective against the pathogen.

On the other hand, we assume that the protection provided by the vaccination may vary according to the individual. Therefore, we use a distribution function f to reflect this fact into the model. f is a distribution function, and $f(\theta)$ is the ratio of the individuals whose protection period provided by the vaccine is θ. Classically, it is supposed that $f(\theta)$ is non-negative for each θ and f is continuous on $\mathbb{R}_+$, and f satisfies $\int_0^\infty f(\theta) d\theta = 1$. The term $q \int_0^\infty f(\theta) S(t-\theta) e^{-\mu\theta} d\theta$ represents the number of surviving individuals at time t who have been vaccinated at time $t - \theta$ and have protection period θ.

Of course, since it is thought that the vaccine may not provide full protection, some vaccinated individuals may still be susceptible to infection. Therefore, as a result of a sufficiently effective contact with infectious individuals, a vaccinated individual who no longer has any protection enters the infectious compartment. To reflect this transition to the compartment I, the expression $\beta q I(t) \int_0^\infty f(\theta) S(t-\theta) e^{-\mu\theta} d\theta$ has been used in the model.

3. Analysis of the Model

In this part, for the model, the convenient and positive invariant region, equilibrium points and the basic reproduction number have been determined.

3.1. Feasible Region

Theorem 3. *For System (3), the set*

$$\Omega = \left\{(S,V,I,R) : S \in BC([-\theta,\infty),\mathbb{R}_+);\ V,I,R \in BC([0,\infty),\mathbb{R}_+) \text{ and } N(t) \leq \frac{b}{\mu}\right\} \tag{4}$$

is a positively invariant region in which the solutions of the model are bounded.

Proof. (Following [9]), adding the four equations in (3), we write

$$\begin{aligned} {}^{C}D^{\alpha}N(t) &= b-\mu(S(t)+V(t)+I(t)+R(t))-\delta I \\ &\leq b-\mu N(t). \end{aligned} \tag{5}$$

Then we can obtain

$$\lambda^{\alpha}\mathscr{L}\{N(t)\}-\lambda^{\alpha-1}N(0) \leq \frac{b}{\lambda}-\mu\mathscr{L}\{N(t)\} \tag{6}$$

from (1) and other properties of the Laplace transform. If we take $N(0) \leq b/\mu$ and consider the inequality (6), we obtain

$$(\lambda^{\alpha}+\mu)\mathscr{L}\{N(t)\} \leq \frac{b}{\lambda}+\lambda^{\alpha-1}N(0)$$

and

$$\begin{aligned} \mathscr{L}\{N(t)\} &\leq \frac{b}{\lambda(\lambda^{\alpha}+\mu)}+\left(\frac{\lambda^{\alpha-1}}{\lambda^{\alpha}+\mu}\right)\frac{b}{\mu} \\ &\leq \frac{b}{\lambda\mu}+\frac{b}{\mu}\mathscr{L}\left\{t^{\alpha-1}E_{\alpha,\alpha}(-\mu t^{\alpha})\right\}. \end{aligned} \tag{7}$$

Applying the inverse Laplace transform to (7) and considering the boundedness of Mittag–Leffler function $E_{\alpha,\alpha}(-\mu t^{\alpha})$ for all $t>0$, we can write

$$\begin{aligned} N(t) &\leq \frac{b}{\mu}\left(1+t^{\alpha-1}E_{\alpha,\alpha}(-\mu t^{\alpha})\right) \\ &\leq \frac{b}{\mu}\left(1+t^{\alpha-1}C\right), \end{aligned} \tag{8}$$

where C is a constant such that $E_{\alpha,\alpha}(-\mu t^{\alpha}) \leq C$ hold for all $t>0$.

Therefore, if $\alpha \in (0,1)$, we obtain $N(t) \leq b/\mu$ for all $t>0$ as $t \to \infty$ from (8). Additionally, if $\alpha=1$, then the solution of (5) comes with the solution of the differential equation $N'(t)+\mu N(t)=b$. If the integrating factor method is processed, it is obtained that $N(t)=b/\mu+ce^{-\mu t}$, so

$$N(t)=N(0)e^{-\mu t}+\frac{b}{\mu}(1-e^{-\mu t}) \tag{9}$$

is obtained for the initial condition $t=0$. The Standard Comparison Theorem [19] says that the right side of (9) is the maximal solution of Equation (5). Thus, the following inequality is reached:

$$N(t) \leq N(0)e^{-\mu t} + \frac{b}{\mu}(1 - e^{-\mu t})$$

for all $t \geq 0$.

Hence, when $N(0) \leq b/\mu$, we obtain $N(t) \leq b/\mu$ for all $t > 0$ and $\alpha \in (0,1]$. This means that Ω is positively invariant for System (3). □

Because the populations $V(t)$ and $R(t)$ do not feature in remainder equations of System (3), it will be enough to consider with the reduced System (10)

$$\begin{aligned} {}^{C}D^{\alpha}S(t) &= b - \beta S(t)I(t) - (q+\mu)S(t), \\ {}^{C}D^{\alpha}I(t) &= \beta S(t)I(t) + \beta q I(t)\int_0^{\infty} f(\theta)S(t-\theta)e^{-\mu\theta}d\theta - (\gamma+\delta+\mu)I(t). \end{aligned} \quad (10)$$

3.2. Existence of Solutions of the System

In this section, we focus on the existence of solution of the problem

$$\begin{aligned} {}^{C}D^{\alpha}x(t) &= h(x^t), t \geq 0 \\ x_0(t) &= g(t), -\theta \leq t < 0. \end{aligned} \quad (11)$$

where $g = (g_1(t), g_2(t))$ represents the initial functions of System (10) and $g \in C\left([-\theta,0), \left[0, \frac{b}{\mu}\right]^2\right)$. Additionally, let us take $h : \Psi \subset C\left([-\theta,0), \left[0, \frac{b}{\mu}\right]^2\right) \to \left[0, \frac{b}{\mu}\right]^2$, $x^t(s) = x(t+s)$ and $x \in \{(x_1, x_2) : (x_1, \cdot, x_2, \cdot) \in \Omega \text{ defined by (4)}\} \subset C\left([-\theta,\infty), \left[0, \frac{b}{\mu}\right]^2\right)$. If we choose the function h as $h = (h_1, h_2)$ such that

$$\begin{aligned} h_1(x) &= b - \beta x_1(0)x_2(0) - (q+\mu)x_1(0) \\ h_2(x) &= \beta x_1(0)x_2(0) + \beta q x_1(0)\int_0^{\infty} f(\theta)x_2(-\theta)e^{-\mu\theta}d\theta - (\gamma+\delta+\mu)x_1(0) \end{aligned} \quad (12)$$

and $x = (x_1, x_2) = (S, I)$, then we can say that finding the solution of the problem (11) is equivalent to solving System (10) or equivalently the following problem.

$$\begin{array}{ll} \begin{array}{c} {}^{C}D^{\alpha}S(t) = b - \beta S(t)I(t) - (q+\mu)S(t) \\ {}^{C}D^{\alpha}I(t) = \beta S(t)I(t) + \beta q I(t)\int_0^{\infty} f(\theta)S(t-\theta)e^{-\mu\theta}d\theta - (\gamma+\delta+\mu)I(t) \end{array}, & t \in [0,\infty) \\ \begin{array}{c} S(t) = g_1(t) \\ I(t) = g_2(t) \end{array}, & t \in [-\theta, 0) \end{array} \quad (13)$$

Additionally, we can say that Equation (11) has a unique solution if h is Lipschitz continuous in every compact subset $M \subset \Psi$. Indeed, this result depends on the Schauder fixed point theorem [20].

In this study, the fact that the set $C = C([-\theta,0), \mathbb{R}^2)$ is a Banach space with the norm

$$\|x\|_C = \sup\{|x_1(t)| + |x_2(t)| : -\theta \leq t \leq 0\}$$

is also taken into consideration.

Theorem 4. *There is a unique solution of System (13), or equivalently, of Equation (11) with* $h : \Psi \to \left[0, \frac{b}{\mu}\right]^2$*, defined by (12).*

Proof. The proof depends on the result in [20]. Therefore, it is sufficient to show that h is Lipschitz continuous in every compact subset $M \subset \Psi$. Let $x = (x_1, x_2) \in M$, and $y = (y_1, y_2) \in M$. Then, considering $|x_i(t)| \leq \frac{b}{\mu}$ and $|y_i(t)| \leq \frac{b}{\mu}$ for $-\tau \leq t \leq 0, i = 1,2$, we can write from the description of h

$$\begin{aligned}
& \|h(x) - h(y)\| \\
\leq\ & |h_1(x) - h_1(y)| + |h_2(x) - h_2(y)| \\
=\ & |\beta[y_1(0)y_2(0) - x_1(0)x_2(0)] + (q+\mu)[y_1(0) - x_1(0)]| \\
& + |\beta[x_1(0)x_2(0) - y_1(0)y_2(0)] + (\gamma+\delta+\mu)[y_1(0) - x_1(0)]| \\
& + \left|\beta q x_1(0)\int_0^\infty f(\theta)x_2(-\theta)e^{-\mu\theta}d\theta - \beta q y_1(0)\int_0^\infty f(\theta)y_2(-\theta)e^{-\mu\theta}d\theta\right| \\
=\ & |\beta[y_1(0)y_2(0) - y_1(0)x_2(0) + y_1(0)x_2(0) - x_1(0)x_2(0)] + (q+\mu)[y_1(0) - x_1(0)]| \\
& + |\beta[x_1(0)x_2(0) - x_1(0)y_2(0) + x_1(0)y_2(0) - y_1(0)y_2(0)] + (\gamma+\delta+\mu)[y_1(0) - x_1(0)]| \\
& + \left|\beta q x_1(0)\int_0^\infty f(\theta)x_2(-\theta)e^{-\mu\theta}d\theta - \beta q y_1(0)\int_0^\infty f(\theta)x_2(-\theta)e^{-\mu\theta}d\theta\right. \\
& \left. + \beta q y_1(0)\int_0^\infty f(\theta)x_2(-\theta)e^{-\mu\theta}d\theta - \beta q y_1(0)\int_0^\infty f(\theta)y_2(-\theta)e^{-\mu\theta}d\theta\right| \\
\leq\ & \beta(|y_1(0)||x_2(0) - y_2(0)| + |x_2(0)||x_1(0) - y_1(0)|) \\
& + \beta(|x_1(0)||x_2(0) - y_2(0)| + |y_2(0)||x_1(0) - y_1(0)|) \\
& + (q + 2\mu + \gamma + \delta)|y_1(0) - x_1(0)| \\
& + \beta q|x_1(0) - y_1(0)|\int_0^\infty f(\theta)|x_2(-\theta)|e^{-\mu\theta}d\theta \\
& + \beta q|y_1(0)|\int_0^\infty f(\theta)|x_2(-\theta) - y_2(-\theta)|e^{-\mu\theta}d\theta \\
\leq\ & 2\beta\frac{b}{\mu}(|x_1(0) - y_1(0)| + |x_2(0) - y_2(0)|) \\
& + (q + 2\mu + \gamma + \delta)|y_1(0) - x_1(0)| \\
& + \beta q\frac{b}{\mu}F(|x_1(0) - y_1(0)| + |x_2(-\theta) - y_2(-\theta)|) \\
\leq\ & \left(2\beta\frac{b}{\mu} + q + 2\mu + \gamma + \delta + \beta q\frac{b}{\mu}F\right)\|x - y\|_C.
\end{aligned}$$

Therefore, we conclude

$$\|h(x) - h(y)\| \leq \left(\frac{\beta b}{\mu}(2 + qF) + q + 2\mu + \gamma + \delta\right)\|x - y\|_C.$$

Thus, if we take

$$K \geq \frac{\beta b}{\mu}(2 + qF) + q + 2\mu + \gamma + \delta$$

then the inequality

$$\|h(x) - h(y)\| \leq K\|x - y\|_C$$

holds in every compact subset $M \subset \Psi$. As a result, it is concluded that there is only one solution of System (13) since h satisfies the Lipschitz inequality in every compact M subset of Ψ. □

3.3. Disease-Free Equilibria, Basic Reproduction Number

Since the equilibria of the proposed model are the solutions of the system (10), then the disease-free equilibrium point, which we will show with $P_{DF} = (S_0, I_0)$, provides the equations in the system.

Therefore, System (10) always has a disease-free equilibria

$$P_{DF} = (S_0, I_0) = \left(\frac{b}{q+\mu}, 0\right). \tag{14}$$

Now we will determine the threshold value $\mathcal{R}_0$ referred to as the basic reproduction number is the number of secondary infections caused by one infectious individual. This parameter allows us to have an idea about the dynamics of the epidemic and to make predictions. For this reason, it is a very important value in epidemiology. Using the next generation matrix method, the value of $\mathcal{R}_0$ related to the model (10) is calculated by the following terminology [21,22].

First of all, let us specify that the value of the integral $\int_0^\infty f(\theta)e^{-\mu\theta}d\theta$ briefly will be used in notation F, throughout the remainder of the text.

Let $X = (I, S)^T$. Then we can write System (10) in the form

$$\begin{bmatrix} {}^C D^\alpha I(t) \\ {}^C D^\alpha S(t) \end{bmatrix} = \underbrace{\begin{bmatrix} \beta S(t)I(t) + \beta q I(t) \int_0^\infty f(\theta)S(t-\theta)e^{-\mu\theta}d\theta \\ 0 \end{bmatrix}}_{\mathcal{M}(X)} - \underbrace{\begin{bmatrix} (\gamma+\delta+\mu)I(t) \\ \beta S(t)I(t) + (q+\mu)S(t) - b \end{bmatrix}}_{\mathcal{N}(X)},$$

that is

$${}^C D^\alpha X(t) = \mathcal{M}(X) - \mathcal{N}(X).$$

The values at P_{DF} of the derivatives of $\mathcal{M}(X)$ and $\mathcal{N}(X)$ with respect to I, S, respectively, appear with the following Jacobian matrices:

$$d\mathcal{M}(P_{DF}) = \begin{bmatrix} \beta S_0(1+qF) & \beta I_0(1+qF) \\ 0 & 0 \end{bmatrix},$$

$$d\mathcal{N}(P_{DF}) = \begin{bmatrix} \gamma+\delta+\mu & 0 \\ \beta S_0 & \beta I_0 + q + \mu \end{bmatrix}.$$

According to the terminology in Subheading 4.1 of reference [21], which explains the next-generation matrix method theoretically and with examples, the infected compartment for System (10) is I, giving $m = 1$. Since the next-generation matrix depends only on the infected equation, this results in the matrices M and N being $(1,1)$ entries of $\mathcal{M}$ and $\mathcal{N}$. Thus, we can write

$$d\mathcal{M}(P_{DF}) = \begin{bmatrix} M & 0 \\ 0 & 0 \end{bmatrix} \text{ and } d\mathcal{N}(P_{DF}) = \begin{bmatrix} N & 0 \\ \frac{b\beta}{q+\mu} & q+\mu \end{bmatrix}$$

and

$$M = [\beta S_0(1+qF)],$$
$$N = [\gamma+\delta+\mu].$$

Since N is a non-singular M-matrix, it is invertible. Therefore,

$$MN^{-1} = \left[\frac{\beta S_0(1+qF)}{\gamma+\delta+\mu}\right].$$

Therefore, by using the characteristic polynomial of MN^{-1}, we obtain the spectral radius as

$$\rho\left(MN^{-1}\right) = \frac{\beta S_0(1+qF)}{\gamma+\delta+\mu}.$$

Taking into account that S_0, the basic reproduction number of the System (10) is calculated in the form of

$$\mathcal{R}_0 = \rho\left(MN^{-1}\right) = \frac{b\beta(1+qF)}{(q+\mu)(\gamma+\delta+\mu)}.$$

In the following part, the results about stability dynamics belonging to the epidemic model (10) have been discussed under the titles "Disease-Free Case" and "Endemic Case", respectively.

3.4. Disease-Free Case

Under this title, we consider local and global stabilities of $P_{DF} = (S_0, I_0)$ for System (10).

Theorem 5. *P_{DF} is locally asymptotically stable for $\mathcal{R}_0 < 1$.*

Proof. The Jacobian matrix at $P_{DF} = (S_0, I_0)$ of System (10) is

$$J(P_{DF}) = \begin{bmatrix} -\beta I_0 - q - \mu & -\beta S_0 \\ \beta I_0(1+qF) & \beta S_0(1+qF) - (\gamma+\delta+\mu) \end{bmatrix}.$$

For the point $(S_0, I_0) = \left(\frac{b}{q+\mu}, 0\right)$, the characteristic equation for this matrix is

$$(\lambda+q+\mu)\left(\lambda - \frac{b\beta(1+qF)-(q+\mu)(\gamma+\delta+\mu)}{q+\mu}\right) = 0. \tag{15}$$

Using the notations λ_1 and λ_2 for the roots of Equation (15), we obtain

$$\lambda_1 = -(q+\mu)$$

and

$$\begin{aligned} \lambda_2 &= \frac{(q+\mu)(\gamma+\delta+\mu)\left(\frac{b\beta(1+qF)}{(q+\mu)(\gamma+\delta+\mu)} - 1\right)}{q+\mu} \\ &= (\gamma+\delta+\mu)(\mathcal{R}_0 - 1). \end{aligned}$$

When $\mathcal{R}_0 < 1$, two roots of Equation (15) are negative. Thus, nonzero both eigenvalues of the Jacobian matrix $J(P_{DF})$ are negative and satisfying $|\arg(\lambda_j)| = \pi > \alpha\pi/2, j = 1,2$. Since the eigenvalues lie outside the closed angular sector $|\arg(\lambda_j)| < \alpha\pi/2$. According to the theory developed by Matignon, we say that P_{DF} is locally asymptotically stable for $\mathcal{R}_0 < 1$ with the help of Theorem 1. □

Theorem 6. *P_{DF} is uniformly asymptotically stable for $\mathcal{R}_0 < 1$.*

Proof. Consider the nonnegative function L defined as

$$L(t, S, I) = I(t).$$

Computing the time derivative of L, we obtain

$$
\begin{aligned}
{}^{C}D^{\alpha}L(t,S,I) &= \beta S(t)I(t) + \beta q I(t)\int_0^{\infty} f(\theta)S(t-\theta)e^{-\mu\theta}d\theta - (\gamma+\delta+\mu)I(t) \\
&= \left(\beta S(t) + \beta q\int_0^{\infty} f(\theta)S(t-\theta)e^{-\mu\theta}d\theta - (\gamma+\delta+\mu)\right)I(t) \\
&\leq \left(\frac{b\beta}{q+\mu} + \frac{b\beta qF}{q+\mu} - (\gamma+\delta+\mu)\right)I(t) \\
&= (\gamma+\delta+\mu)\left(\frac{b\beta(1+qF)}{(q+\mu)(\gamma+\delta+\mu)} - 1\right)I(t) \\
&= (\gamma+\delta+\mu)(\mathcal{R}_0 - 1)I(t).
\end{aligned}
$$

When $\mathcal{R}_0 < 1$, we say that ${}^{C}D^{\alpha}L(t,S,I) \leq 0$ and ${}^{C}D^{\alpha}L(t,S,I) = 0$ for $S = S_0$, $I = I_0$. By Theorem 2, the disease free equilibrium P_{DF} is uniformly asymptotically stable in the interior of Ω, when $\mathcal{R}_0 < 1$. □

3.5. Endemic Case

In this part, firstly the existence and uniqueness of the endemic equilibrium point of the model has been shown. Then, in addition to the course of the disease when $\mathcal{R}_0 > 1$, the local and global stability of this equilibrium point has been investigated.

3.6. Existence of the Endemic Equilibria

Since ${}^{C}D^{\alpha}I^* = {}^{C}D^{\alpha}S^* = 0$, the endemic equilibria denoted by $P_E = (S^*, I^*)$ satisfies the algebraic equations with $I^* \neq 0$

$$
\begin{aligned}
0 &= b - \beta S^* I^* - (q+\mu)S^*, \\
0 &= \beta S^* I^* + \beta q S^* I^* \int_0^{\infty} f(\theta)e^{-\mu\theta}d\theta - (\gamma+\delta+\mu)I^*.
\end{aligned}
\tag{16}
$$

From the second equation of (16), we write

$$
0 = I^*(\beta S^* + \beta q F S^* - (\gamma+\delta+\mu)).
$$

Since $I^* \neq 0$, it must be $\beta S^* + \beta q F S^* - (\gamma+\delta+\mu) = 0$. Then the endemic equilibrium point comes with

$$
\begin{aligned}
P_E &= (S^*, I^*) \\
&= \left(\frac{\gamma+\delta+\mu}{\beta(1+qF)}, \frac{b-(q+\mu)S^*}{\beta S^*}\right).
\end{aligned}
$$

We say that P_E can be expressed as

$$
P_E = \left(\frac{b}{(q+\mu)\mathcal{R}_0}, \frac{(q+\mu)(\mathcal{R}_0 - 1)}{\beta}\right)
$$

in terms of $\mathcal{R}_0$. Additionally, it is seen clearly that System (10) has a unique endemic equilibria iff $\mathcal{R}_0 > 1$.

3.7. Course of the Disease for $\mathcal{R}_0 > 1$

Now, we will focus on how the disease will progress (whether it will disappear or not) in the population when $\mathcal{R}_0 > 1$. For this, we will assume the infectious population at the beginning exists, and we will try to see the course of the infectious population as time progresses for $\mathcal{R}_0 > 1$.

To do this, let us suppose $I(0) > 0$ and $\lim_{t\to\infty} I(t) = 0$. Then, for any given $\epsilon > 0$, there is a $T_1 > 0$ such that $I(t) < \epsilon$ holds for $t > T_1$. Specifically, we can choose an ϵ such that

$$0 < \epsilon < b\left(1 - \frac{1}{\mathcal{R}_0}\right), \tag{17}$$

and

$$I(t) \leq \frac{\epsilon\mu}{b\beta}$$

hold for all $t > T_1$.

Then

$$\begin{aligned} {}^{C}D^{\alpha}S(t) &= b - \beta S(t)I(t) - (q+\mu)S(t) \\ &\geq b - \frac{\beta b}{\mu}I(t) - (q+\mu)S(t) \\ &\geq b - \frac{\beta b\epsilon\mu}{\mu b\beta} - (q+\mu)S(t) \\ &= b - (q+\mu)S(t) - \epsilon. \end{aligned}$$

Therefore, we say that

$${}^{C}D^{\alpha}S(t) \geq b\left(1 - \frac{q+\mu}{b}\right)S(t) - \epsilon$$

for $t > T_1$. This requires

$$\liminf_{t\to\infty} S(t) \geq \frac{b}{q+\mu}\left(1 - \frac{\epsilon}{b}\right).$$

If we take into account the basic properties of limit inferior and remember the choosing (17), then we say that there is a $T_2 > 0$ such that

$$S(t) \geq \frac{b}{q+\mu}\left(1 - \frac{b\left(1 - \frac{1}{\mathcal{R}_0}\right)}{b}\right) = \frac{b}{(q+\mu)\mathcal{R}_0}$$

for all $t > T_2$. Thus,

$$S(t) \geq \frac{b}{(q+\mu)\mathcal{R}_0} \text{ and } S(t-\theta) \geq \frac{b}{(q+\mu)\mathcal{R}_0}$$

hold for all $t > T_2 + \theta$. If T is chosen as

$$T = \max\{T_1, T_2 + \theta\}$$

then

$$\begin{aligned} {}^{C}D^{\alpha}I(t) &= I(t)\left(\beta S(t) + \beta q\int_0^{\infty} f(\theta)S(t-\theta)e^{-\mu\theta}d\theta - (\gamma+\delta+\mu)\right) \\ &> I(t)\left(\beta\frac{b}{(q+\mu)\mathcal{R}_0} + \beta q\frac{b}{(q+\mu)\mathcal{R}_0}F - (\gamma+\delta+\mu)\right) \\ &= I(t)(\gamma+\delta+\mu)\left(\frac{b\beta(1+qF)}{(q+\mu)(\gamma+\delta+\mu)\mathcal{R}_0} - 1\right) \\ &= 0 \end{aligned}$$

for $t > T$. This result contradicts $\lim_{t\to\infty} I(t) = 0$. Moreover, the fact ${}^{C}D^{\alpha}I(t) > 0$ for $0 < \alpha < 1$ means that $I(t)$ is increasing [23]. However, when $\mathcal{R}_0 > 1$, it is not possible that

$\lim_{t\to\infty} I(t) = 0$ with the initial assumption $I(0) > 0$. All these imply that the disease will not disappear in the population when $\mathcal{R}_0 > 1$. This case is what should be happen for a consistent model and a meaningful threshold $\mathcal{R}_0$.

Now let us analyze the behavior of function I, which does not converge to zero when $\mathcal{R}_0 > 1$, and of the function S.

3.8. Local and Global Asymptotic Stability of the Endemic Equilibrium Point

Theorem 7. *P_E is locally asymptotically stable in Ω for $\mathcal{R}_0 > 1$ and $\alpha \in (0,1]$.*

Proof. The Jacobian matrix of System (10) at $P_E = (S^*, I^*)$ is

$$J(P_E) = \begin{bmatrix} -\beta I^* - q - \mu & -\beta S^* \\ \beta I^*(1+qF) & \beta S^*(1+qF) - (\gamma+\delta+\mu) \end{bmatrix}.$$

Herefrom, the characteristic equation of the matrix $J(P_E)$ forms with the determinant

$$\det(\lambda I_2 - J(P_E)) = \begin{vmatrix} -(q+\mu)\mathcal{R}_0 - \lambda & -\frac{b\beta}{(q+\mu)\mathcal{R}_0} \\ (q+\mu)(1+qF)(\mathcal{R}_0 - 1) & -\lambda \end{vmatrix} = 0.$$

After the rearrangements, this equation is written as

$$\lambda^2 + (q+\mu)\mathcal{R}_0\lambda + b\beta(1+qF)(\mathcal{R}_0 - 1) = 0. \tag{18}$$

Let two roots of Equation (18) be λ_1 and λ_2. Then

$$\lambda_1 + \lambda_2 = -(q+\mu)\mathcal{R}_0$$

and

$$\lambda_1\lambda_2 = b\beta(1+qF)(\mathcal{R}_0 - 1).$$

Therefore, we say that $\lambda_1\lambda_2 > 0$ and $\lambda_1 + \lambda_2 < 0$ for $\mathcal{R}_0 > 1$. In that case, two roots of Equation (18) are negative. Since all eigenvalues of the Jacobian matrix of System (10) at P_E have negative real parts, then $|\arg(\lambda_j)| = \pi > \alpha\pi/2, j = 1,2$.

Thus, $J(P_E)$ satisfies the Matignon's conditions. By Theorem 1, $P_E = (S^*, I^*)$ is locally asymptotically stable. □

Now, we will prove that P_E is globally stable for the special case $\alpha = 1$ by using the Dulac criterion and the Poincaré-Bendixson theorem.

Theorem 8. *P_E is globally asymptotically stable for $\mathcal{R}_0 > 1$ and $\alpha = 1$.*

Proof. We will show that (10) does not have any periodic solutions in the positive quadrant of the SI plane. Let us establish a continuous function $\Phi(S, I)$ defined by

$$\Phi(S,I) = \frac{1}{\beta SI}, \; S > 0, \; I > 0$$

for System (10). Setting G and H as

$$\begin{aligned} G(S,I) &= b-\beta S(t)I(t)-(q+\mu)S(t), \\ H(S,I) &= \beta S(t)I(t)+\beta qI(t)\int_0^\infty f(\theta)S(t-\theta)e^{-\mu\theta}d\theta-(\gamma+\delta+\mu)I(t), \end{aligned}$$

we obtain

$$\begin{aligned} \frac{\partial(\Phi G)}{\partial S}+\frac{\partial(\Phi H)}{\partial I} &= \frac{\partial}{\partial S}\left\{\frac{b}{\beta SI}-1-\frac{q+\mu}{\beta I}\right\} \\ &+ \frac{\partial}{\partial I}\left\{1+\frac{q\int_0^\infty f(\theta)S(t-\theta)e^{-\mu\theta}d\theta}{S}-1-\frac{\gamma+\delta+\mu}{\beta S}\right\} \\ &= -\frac{b\beta I}{(\beta SI)^2} \end{aligned}$$

for all $S>0$, $I>0$. We see the last expression is clearly negative. It has the same sign almost everywhere in the positive quadrant of the SI plane for the appropriate Dulac function Φ. According to the Bendixson–Dulac theorem [24], we can see that System (10) has no periodic orbits in the interior of the first quadrant. Thus, all solutions of System (10) tend to one of the equilibria. Here, this point is the endemic equilibrium point that only exists when $\mathcal{R}_0>1$. Hence, P_E is globally asymptotically stable in the interior of the first quadrant.

Consequently, while $\mathcal{R}_0>1$, System (10) has a unique endemic equilibrium $P_E=(S^*,I^*)$, which is globally asymptotically stable. □

3.9. A Brief Analysis on Vaccine Strategy

When the model (10) is considered without the vaccine (in this case, $q=0$), the vaccine free basic reproduction number for the formed model $\left(\mathcal{R}_0^{vf}\right)$ is

$$\mathcal{R}_0^{vf}=\frac{b\beta}{\mu(\gamma+\delta+\mu)}.$$

It can be easily seen that there is a relationship

$$\begin{aligned} \mathcal{R}_0 &= \frac{(1+qF)\mu}{(q+\mu)}\frac{b\beta}{\mu(\gamma+\delta+\mu)} \\ &= \left(1-\frac{q(1-\mu F)}{q+\mu}\right)\mathcal{R}_0^{vf} \end{aligned}$$

between $\mathcal{R}_0$ and $\mathcal{R}_0^{vf}$. Here, $\mathcal{R}_0<\mathcal{R}_0^{vf}$, and this mathematical result indicates that, obviously, vaccination has a crucial effect on disease control by decreasing the basic reproduction number. Thus, with the appropriate vaccination strategy, the disease can be eradicated in the population by keeping the value $\mathcal{R}_0$ below 1.

Therefore, starting from the goal of eliminating the disease, we obtain

$$\begin{aligned} \mathcal{R}_0 &< 1 \\ &\Leftrightarrow \left(\mathcal{R}_0^{vf}-\frac{q(1-\mu F)\mathcal{R}_0^{vf}}{q+\mu}\right)<1 \\ &\Leftrightarrow \mu\left(\mathcal{R}_0^{vf}-1\right)<q-\mu qF\mathcal{R}_0^{vf}. \end{aligned}$$

From here, the value $p_{\min}$ that comes with the inequality

$$p_{\min} > \frac{\mu\left(\mathcal{R}_0^{vf} - 1\right)}{1 - \mu F \mathcal{R}_0^{vf}} \tag{19}$$

is the minimum vaccination ratio of new members required for the elimination of the disease in the population.

4. Sensitivity Analysis

It is difficult to completely eradicate an epidemic in a population in a short period of time. Considering that many negative situations are brought about by the disease, attempts to reduce the spread of the disease have great importance. In this context, with various control measures to be implemented, lowering the $\mathcal{R}_0$ value is an important goals. Therefore, it is of great importance to examine the effect of parameters on the change of $\mathcal{R}_0$ and to apply control measures in this direction.

Now we will focus on the sensitivity analysis of $\mathcal{R}_0$. Sensitivity analysis clarifies how effective each parameter is to disease transmission. To observe whether the parameters that affect the basic reproduction number have a positive or negative effect, we will explore the normalized forward sensitivity index of $\mathcal{R}_0$. The normalized forward sensitivity index of the variable $\mathcal{R}_0$ with respect to the parameter ς is defined as

$$\chi_{\varsigma}^{\mathcal{R}_0} = \frac{\partial \mathcal{R}_0}{\partial \varsigma} \times \frac{\varsigma}{\mathcal{R}_0},$$

by using partial derivatives, where ς represents the basic parameters constituting $\mathcal{R}_0$.

Then

$$\chi_{\beta}^{\mathcal{R}_0} = \frac{\partial \mathcal{R}_0}{\partial \beta} \times \frac{\beta}{\mathcal{R}_0} = 1 > 0,$$

$$\begin{aligned} \chi_{q}^{\mathcal{R}_0} &= \frac{\partial \mathcal{R}_0}{\partial q} \times \frac{q}{\mathcal{R}_0} \\ &= -\frac{\mu q(1+F)}{(q+\mu)(1+qF)} < 0, \end{aligned}$$

$$\begin{aligned} \chi_{\gamma}^{\mathcal{R}_0} &= \frac{\partial \mathcal{R}_0}{\partial \gamma} \times \frac{\gamma}{\mathcal{R}_0} \\ &= -\frac{\gamma}{\gamma+\delta+\mu} < 0 \end{aligned}$$

and

$$\begin{aligned} \chi_{\delta}^{\mathcal{R}_0} &= \frac{\partial \mathcal{R}_0}{\partial \delta} \times \frac{\delta}{\mathcal{R}_0} \\ &= -\frac{\delta}{\gamma+\delta+\mu} < 0. \end{aligned}$$

Additionally, we have

$$\begin{aligned} \chi_{b}^{\mathcal{R}_0} &= \frac{\partial \mathcal{R}_0}{\partial b} \times \frac{b}{\mathcal{R}_0} \\ &= \frac{\beta(1+qF)}{(\mu+q)(\gamma+\delta+\mu)} \frac{b}{\mathcal{R}_0} \\ &= 1, \end{aligned}$$

$$
\begin{aligned}
\chi_{\mu}^{\mathcal{R}_0} &= \frac{\partial \mathcal{R}_0}{\partial \mu} \times \frac{\mu}{\mathcal{R}_0} \\
&= -\mathcal{R}_0 \frac{\mu}{\mathcal{R}_0} \\
&= -\mu
\end{aligned}
$$

and

$$
\begin{aligned}
\chi_{F}^{\mathcal{R}_0} &= \frac{\partial \mathcal{R}_0}{\partial F} \times \frac{F}{\mathcal{R}_0} \\
&= \frac{b\beta q}{(\mu+q)(\gamma+\delta+\mu)} \frac{F}{\mathcal{R}_0} \\
&= \frac{qF}{1+qF}.
\end{aligned}
$$

With increasing values of the parameters that have positive indices $(b,\ \beta,\ F)$, $\mathcal{R}_0$ increases, so the spread of the disease progresses in the population. On the other hand, the parameters in which its sensitivity indices are negative $(q,\ \gamma,\ \delta$ and $\mu)$ cause a decrease in $\mathcal{R}_0$. That is, the average number of secondary infection cases decreases, while these parameters increase, so the spread of the disease starts to decrease. In the next section, we will present an example for sensitivity analysis after choosing the distribution function.

5. Some Examples for Distribution Function and $\mathcal{R}_0$

Example 1. *If we take the distribution function f as $f(\theta) = e^{-\theta}$, then*

$$
\int_0^\infty f(\theta) d\theta = 1
$$

and

$$
\begin{aligned}
F &= \int_0^\infty f(\theta) e^{-\mu\theta} d\theta = \int_0^\infty e^{-(\mu+1)\theta} d\theta \\
&= \lim_{t\to\infty} \int_0^t e^{-(\mu+1)\theta} d\theta = \lim_{t\to\infty} \left(\frac{1-e^{-(\mu+1)t}}{\mu+1} \right) = \frac{1}{\mu+1}.
\end{aligned}
$$

Therefore, we obtain $\mathcal{R}_0$ as

$$
\mathcal{R}_0 = \frac{b\beta(\mu+q+1)}{(q+\mu)(\gamma+\delta+\mu)(\mu+1)}.
$$

Example 2. *If we take f as $f(\theta) = \theta e^{-\theta}$, then*

$$
\int_0^\infty f(\theta) d\theta = 1
$$

and we obtain

$$
\begin{aligned}
F &= \int_0^\infty f(\theta) e^{-\mu\theta} d\theta = \int_0^\infty \theta e^{-(\mu+1)\theta} d\theta \\
&= \lim_{t\to\infty} \int_0^t \theta e^{-(\mu+1)\theta} d\theta = \lim_{t\to\infty} \left(\frac{1-e^{-(\mu+1)t}(\mu t+t+1)}{(\mu+1)^2} \right) = \frac{1}{(\mu+1)^2}.
\end{aligned}
$$

Therefore, we can write $\mathcal{R}_0$ as

$$\mathcal{R}_0 = \frac{b\beta\left((\mu+1)^2+q\right)}{(q+\mu)(\gamma+\delta+\mu)(\mu+1)^2}.$$

Now we will focus on presenting the effect of the choice of distribution function on the number of secondary infections $\mathcal{R}_0$ with some simulations. For this, we will present the effect of the variables q, which is related to vaccination, and μ, which is decisive in the distribution function, which determine $\mathcal{R}_0$. The simulation below shows how the change in the parameters q and μ, respectively, affects $\mathcal{R}_0$ for two different distribution functions, keeping the other parameters that determine $\mathcal{R}_0$ constant except for these two parameters.

In the rest of the article, we will use the following parameters given in [25] (Table 1).

Table 1. Numerical values defined for Model (10). (The values based on the data are given in [25]).

Parameters:	q	γ	β	δ	b	μ
Values:	0.33	0.19	0.21	0.12	0.76	0.11

The Figures 1 and 2 represent the changes in $\mathcal{R}_0$ with respect to the q and μ variables depending on the choices of f.

As mentioned in the previous section, parameters q, γ, δ and μ exhibit negative indices, while β, F, b display positive indices. Table 2 and Figure 3 reflect this case.

A small example can be given to explain the meaning of these values. As can be seen in Table 2, sensitivity indices of γ and F are -0.4523 and 0.2291, respectively. This means that, if γ is increased by 10%, then $\mathcal{R}_0$ is decreased by 4.523%. Similary, a 10% increase in F results in a 2.291% increase in $\mathcal{R}_0$.

Table 2. Sensitivity indices of $\mathcal{R}_0$ with respect to the parameters, for $f(\theta) = e^{-\theta}$.

q	γ	β	δ	F	b	μ
−0.1208	−0.4523	1	−0.2857	0.2291	1	−0.11

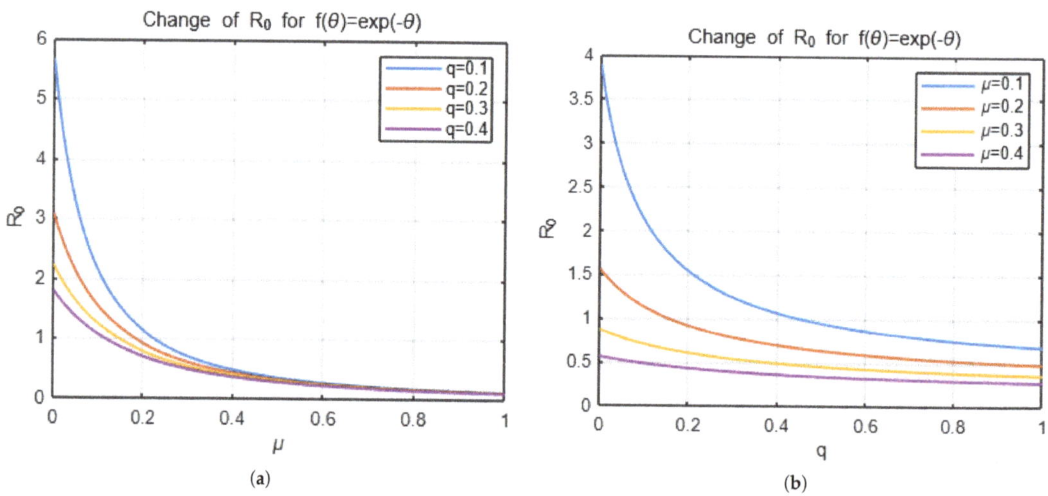

(a)

(b)

Figure 1. *Cont.*

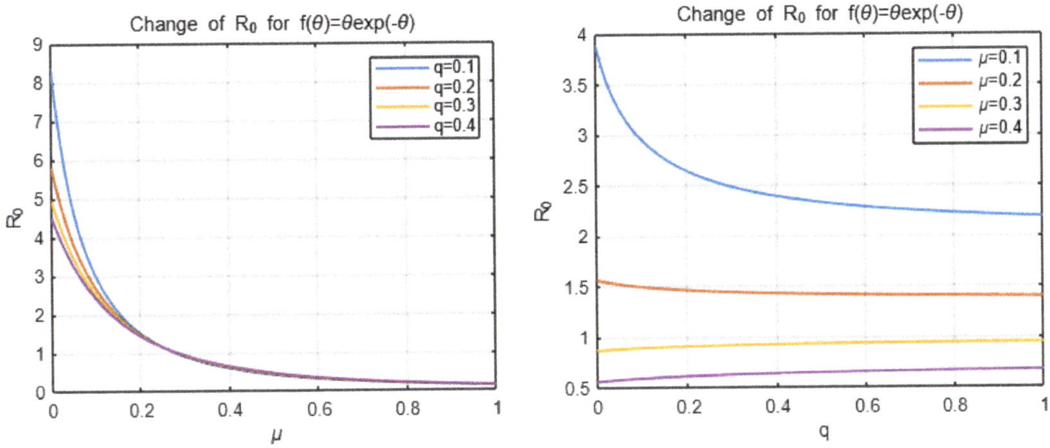

(c) (d)

Figure 1. The variation of $\mathcal{R}_0$ with respect to μ for different values of q for the selection of $f(\theta) = e^{-\theta}$ f is shown in Figure (**a**). Here, the exception of the q and μ parameters are taken from [25]. (**b**) shows the variation of $\mathcal{R}_0$ with respect to q for different values of μ. Additionally, for the $f(\theta) = \theta e^{-\theta}$, these variations are presented in the forms of (**c**,**d**), respectively.

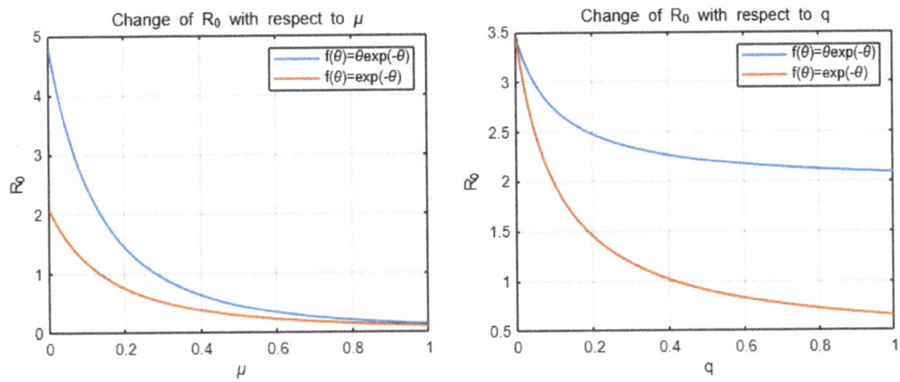

(a) (b)

Figure 2. (**a**,**b**) represent the change in $\mathcal{R}_0$, for the choices $f(\theta) = e^{-\theta}$ and $f(\theta) = \theta e^{-\theta}$, with respect to μ and q, respectively.

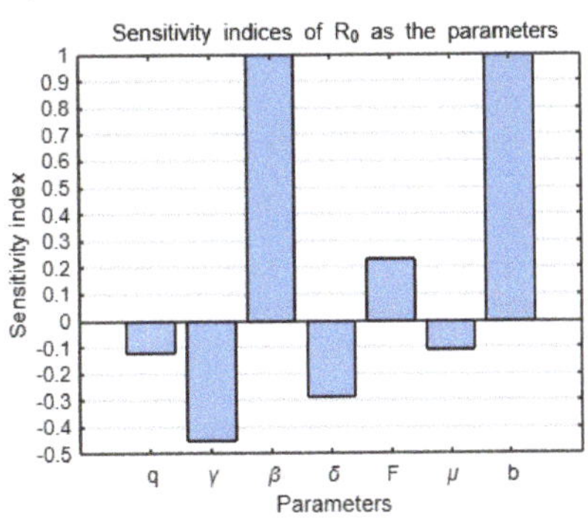

Figure 3. Plot represents the sensitivity of the parameters in the $\mathcal{R}_0$ of the model.

6. Conclusions

In this study, a mathematical epidemic model reflecting that the protection period provided by the vaccine effect may vary from person to person is presented with its analysis. This novel $SVIR$ fractional epidemic model is formed by the aid of a system of distributed delay nonlinear Caputo fractional integro-differential equations.

Firstly, equilibrium points of formed system are found and the basic reproduction number of the model are determined as

$$\mathcal{R}_0 = \frac{b\beta(1+qF)}{(q+\mu)(\gamma+\delta+\mu)}.$$

Thus, it is proved that System (10) has a unique disease-free equilibrium point P_{DF} when $\mathcal{R}_0 < 1$ and there is a unique endemic equilibrium P_E when $\mathcal{R}_0 > 1$. Moreover, it has been shown that, in a population with infectious individuals, the disease will never disappear when $\mathcal{R}_0 > 1$. Thus, it has been reinforced that the introduced model is consistent and that $\mathcal{R}_0$ is meaningful.

Additionally, the global behavior of System (10) was examined. Firstly, it is proved that all solutions of the system tend toward P_{DF} by constituting the appropriate Lyapunov function for $\mathcal{R}_0 < 1$. Then, when $\mathcal{R}_0 > 1$ and $\alpha = 1$, the proof of global stability of P_E has been presented by the Dulac criterion and the Poincaré–Bendixson theorem, which are commonly used in two-dimensional population models.

When the effect of the parameters in the model on $\mathcal{R}_0$, it can be seen that the parameters that can reduce $\mathcal{R}_0$ and can be controlled partially or completely are q and γ.

γ is the recovery (or treatment) rate, and q is the vaccination rate. Controlling the vaccination rate (q) is both easier and less costly than the recovery rate (γ). In addition, considering that vaccinating the entire population may not be possible in real terms and is costly, knowing the minimum vaccination level that must be achieved to eliminate the disease is extremely important. In this study, a result is also given regarding the minimum vaccination rate that must be achieved to eliminate the disease.

Possible future work could consist of adding the optimal control problem to the model or using other derivative definitions. Additionally, authors working in the field of applied mathematics can conduct numerical simulations for the model and their comparative analysis.

Funding: This research received no external funding.

Data Availability Statement: Data are contained within the article.

Conflicts of Interest: The author declares no conflicts of interest.

References

1. Kermack, W.O.; McKendrick, A.G. A contributions to the mathematical theory of epidemics. *Proc. Royal Soc. A* **1927**, *115*, 700–721.
2. Tyagi, S.; Martha, S.C.; Abbas, S.; Debbouche, A. Mathematical modeling and analysis for controlling the spread of infectious diseases. *Chaos Soliton Fract.* **2021**, *144*, 110707.
3. Çakan, S. Dynamic analysis of a mathematical model with health care capacity for COVID-19 pandemic. *Chaos Soliton Fract.* **2020**, *139*, 110033. [CrossRef]
4. Çakan, S. Mathematical analysis of local and global dynamics of a new epidemic model. *Turk. J. Math.* **2022**, *46*, 533–551.
5. Chauhan, S.; Misra, O.P.; Dhar, J. Stability Analysis of SIR Model with Vaccination. *Am. J. Comput. Math.* **2014**, *4*, 17–23.
6. Liu, X.; Takeuchi, Y.; Iwami, S. SVIR epidemic models with vaccination strategies. *J. Theor. Biol.* **2008**, *253*, 1–11.
7. Sekerci, Y.; Khoshnaw, S.H.A. The impact of vaccination strategy on the spatiotemporal pattern dynamics of a COVID-19 epidemic model. *Eur. Phys. J. Plus* **2024**, *139*, 1–15.
8. Gökçe, A.; Gürbüz, B.; Rendall, A.D. Dynamics of a mathematical model of virus spreading incorporating the effect of a vaccine. *Nonlinear Anal. Real World Appl.* **2024**, *78*, 104097. [CrossRef]
9. Hamdan, N.; Kılıçman, A. A fractional order SIR epidemic model for dengue transmission. *Chaos Soliton Fract.* **2018**, *114*, 55–62.
10. Ullah, S.; Khan, M.A.; Farooq, M. A fractional model for the dynamics of TB virus. *Chaos Soliton Fract.* **2018**, *116*, 63–71.

11. Özdemir, N.; Uçar, E.; Avcı, D. Dynamic analysis of a fractional SVIR system modeling an infectious disease. *Facta Univ. Ser. Math. Inform.* **2022**, *37*, 605–619.
12. Gökbulut, N.; Amilo, D. Kaymakamzade, B. Fractional SVIR Model for COVID-19 under Caputo Derivative. *J. Biometry Stud.* **2021**, *1*, 58–64.
13. Delavari, H.; Baleanu, D.; Sadati, J. Stability analysis of Caputo fractional-order nonlinear systems revisited. *Nonlinear Dyn.* **2012**, *67*, 2433–2439. [CrossRef]
14. Vargas-De-León, C. Volterra-type Lyapunov functions for fractional-order epidemic systems. *Commun. Nonlinear Sci. Numer. Simulat.* **2015**, *24*, 75–85. [CrossRef]
15. Alqahtani, Z.; Almuneef, A.; DarAssi, M.H.; AbuHour, Y.; Al-arydah, M.T.; Safi, M.A.; Al-Hdaibat, B. Mathematical analysis of fractional Chlamydia pandemic model. *Sci. Rep.* **2024**, *14*, 31113.
16. El Hajji, M.; Sayari, S. Analysis of a Fractional-order "SVEIR" Epidemic Model with a General Nonlinear Saturated Incidence Rate in a Continuous Reactor. *Asian Res. J. Math.* **2019**, *12*, 1–17.
17. Almeida, R. Analysis of a fractional SEIR model with treatment. *Appl. Math. Lett.* **2018**, *84*, 56–62.
18. Matignon, D. Stability results for fractional differential equations with applications to control processing. *Comput. Eng. Syst. Appl.* **1996**, *2*, 952–956.
19. Lakshmikantham, S.; Leela, S.; Martynyuk, A.A. *Stability Analysis of Nonlinear Systems*; Marcel Dekker, Inc.: New York, NY, USA, 1989.
20. Kuang, Y. *Delay Differential Equations: With Applications in Population Dynamics*; Academic Press: New York, NY, USA, 1993.
21. Driessche, P.V.D.; Watmough, J. Reproduction numbers and sub-threshold endemic equilibria for compartmental models of disease transmission. *Math. Biosci.* **2002**, *180*, 29–48.
22. Rothman, K.J.; Lash, T.L.; Greenland, S. *Modern Epidemiology*, 3rd ed.; Lippincott Williams & Wilkins: Philadelphia, PA, USA, 2013.
23. Diethelm, K. Monotonocity of functions and sign changes of their Caputo derivatives. *Fract. Calc. Appl. Anal.* **2016**, *19*, 561–566.
24. Dulac, H. Recherche des cycles limites. *C. R. Acad. Sci. Paris* **1937**, *204*, 1703–1706.
25. Ismail, H.; Debbouche, A.; Hariharan, S.; Shangerganesh, L.; Kashtanova, S.V. Stability and Optimality Criteria for an SVIR Epidemic Model with Numerical Simulation. *Mathematics* **2024**, *12*, 3231. [CrossRef]

fractal and fractional

MDPI

Article

Analysis of Large Membrane Vibrations Using Fractional Calculus

Nihar Ranjan Mallick [1], Snehashish Chakraverty [1,*] and Rajarama Mohan Jena [2]

1 Department of Mathematics, National Institute of Technology Rourkela, Rourkela 769008, India; niharranjanmallick273@gmail.com
2 Department of Mathematics, C.V. Raman Global University, Bhubaneswar 752054, India; rajarama1994@gmail.com
* Correspondence: sne_chak@yahoo.com

Abstract: The study of vibration equations of large membranes is crucial in various scientific and engineering fields. Analyzing the vibration equations of bridges, roofs, and spacecraft structures helps in designing structures that resist excessive oscillations and potential failures. Aircraft wings, parachutes, and satellite components often behave like large membranes. Understanding their vibration characteristics is essential for stability, efficiency, and durability. Studying large membrane vibration involves solving partial differential equations and eigenvalue problems, contributing to advancements in numerical methods and computational physics. In this paper, the Elzaki transformation decomposition method and the Shehu transformation decomposition method, along with inverse Elzaki and inverse Shehu transformations, are used to investigate the fractional vibration equation of a large membrane. The solutions are obtained in terms of Mittag–Leffler functions.

Keywords: Elzaki transform; Shehu transform; adomian decomposition method; fractional vibration equation; Caputo operator

1. Introduction

Investigating the Vibration Equation is both challenging and essential for various applications, as many modern devices, such as microphones and audio systems, rely on membranes, making it crucial to study their physics and wave propagation [1–4]. In bioengineering, physiological tissues are often modeled as membranes, and the human hearing system is understood through the physical properties of the eardrum's Vibration Equation. A deep understanding of membrane vibrations is vital for designing assistive devices for deaf people. Additionally, the vibration equation of a large membrane serves as a fundamental mathematical model describing two-dimensional wave propagation, playing a crucial role in fields such as acoustics, engineering, biomedical science, and astrophysics [5–8]. Mastering membrane vibrations enables the development of efficient systems in musical instruments, aerospace structures, and medical devices [9–11]. In recent years, fractional calculus has been viewed as an effective approach to modeling real-world scenarios with high precision and efficiency [12–16]. Fractional calculus [17–19] has emerged as a valuable tool for modeling complex and anomalous phenomena in various scientific and engineering fields.

Here, the time-fractional derivatives are included in the following equation. We have examined large membrane vibrations involving fractional derivatives in this article [20].

$$\frac{\partial^\gamma h}{\partial u^\gamma} = c^2\left(\frac{\partial^2 h}{\partial v^2} + \frac{1}{v}\frac{\partial h}{\partial v}\right), 1 < \gamma \leq 2$$

with initial conditions (IC)

$$h(v,0) = h_1(v), \qquad h_u(v,0) = c(h_2(v)),$$

where $D_u^{\gamma} h(v,u)$ represents the Liouville–Caputo fractional derivatives of a function $h(v,u)$ that describes the displacement of finding a particle at the point in time u, and c indicates the wave velocity of the free vibration.

Advancements in computational methods have also played a crucial role in the growing adoption of large membrane vibration equations involving fractional derivatives. The fractional vibration equation was investigated by using various methods such as q homotopy analysis transform method [20], Laplace decomposition method [20], Yang transform decomposition method [21], Yang transform perturbation method [21], Sumudu transform perturbation method [15], residual power series method [22], Operational matrix method [23], and so on.

Adomian decomposition method (ADM) is a semi-analytical technique first introduced by George Adomian [24]. The Elzaki transform (ET) and the ADM are used to create the Elzaki transformation decomposition method (ETDM). ETDM is one of the simple and efficient techniques for resolving fractional partial differential equations. Laplace and Sumudu transformations are modified in the ET. Differential equations having constant or non-constant coefficients can sometimes be solved using ET rather than Laplace or Sumudu transformations [25–27]. With the use of ET, researchers have been able to solve a variety of problems, including the Navier-Stokes equations [28], heat-like equations [29], advection equation [30], hyperbolic equations [30], and Fisher's equations [30]. The Shehu transformation decomposition method (STDM) is a combination of the Shehu transform (ST) and the ADM. The ST, which researchers frequently use for fractional-order differential equations [31–34], has recently attracted the attention of researchers. STDM has fewer variables than other analytical techniques, and due to the lack of discretion or linearization, it is the recommended method. Using the STDM and ETDM, we have examined the large membrane vibration equation with fractional derivative in the current article.

The structure of this paper is as follows. In Section 2, some basic features of fractional calculus related to the titled problems have been represented. Section 3 contains the methodology. Convergence analysis of these methods is developed in Section 4. Three example problems are included to validate the effectiveness and exactness of the proposed method in Section 5. A comparison of obtained results has been discussed in Section 6. Finally, the conclusion section is included in Section 7.

2. Preliminaries

The essential fractional calculus, the Elzaki transform, and the Shehu transform concepts that will be used throughout this study have been discussed in this part.

Definition 1. *The fractional Riemann Liouville integral operator of a function h is given as [35–37]*

$$J^{\alpha} h(u) = \frac{1}{\Gamma(\alpha)} \int_0^u (u-\eta)^{\alpha-1} h(\eta) d\eta, \ \ \alpha > 0, \ u > 0$$

and $J^0 h(u) = h(u)$.

Definition 2. *The Caputo fractional derivatives of a function h are presented as [38–40].*

$$D^{\alpha}h(u) = J^{k-\alpha}D^{k}h(u) = \begin{cases} \dfrac{1}{\Gamma(k-\alpha)}\int_0^u \dfrac{h^{(k)}(\eta)d\eta}{(u-\eta)^{\alpha+1-k}}, & k-1 < \alpha < k, \quad k \in N \\ \dfrac{d^k}{du^k}h(u), & \alpha = k, \quad k \in N \end{cases}$$

Definition 3. *The Mittag–Leffler (1902–1905) functions* E_{γ} *and* $E_{\gamma,\eta}$, *defined by the power series [36,41].*

$$E_{\gamma}(u) = \sum_{k=0}^{\infty} \frac{u^k}{\Gamma(k\gamma+1)}, \quad E_{\gamma,\eta}(u) = \sum_{k=0}^{\infty} \frac{u^k}{\Gamma(k\gamma+\eta)}, \quad \gamma, \eta > 0$$

Definition 4. *For* $u \in (0, \infty)$, *the Elzaki transform of* $h(u)$ *is given by [29,42].*

$$E(h(u)) = H(s) = s\int_0^{\infty} h(u)e^{-\frac{1}{s}u}du$$

Some of the useful Elzaki transforms which are applied in this paper, are as follows: For $E(h_1(u)) = H_1(s)$ and $E(h_2(u)) = H_2(s)$

$$E[h_1(u) + h_2(u)] = H_1(s) + H_2(s),$$

$$E\left[h^{(k)}(u)\right] = \frac{H(s)}{s^k} - \sum_{n=0}^{k-1} s^{2-k+n}h^n(0),$$

$$E\left[u^k\right] = k!\, s^{k+2}, \ k \in N,$$

$$E\{e^{-cu}\} = \frac{s^2}{1+cs},$$

$$E\{\sin(cu)\} = \frac{cs^3}{1+c^2s^2},$$

Lemma 1 ([26,42])**.** *Let* $B(s)$ *be the Laplace transform of* $h(u)$, *then Elzaki transform* $H(s)$ *is defined as* $H(s) = s\,B\left(\frac{1}{s}\right)$.

Lemma 2 ([42,43])**.** *The Elzaki transform of Caputo fractional derivatives of order* γ *can be obtained in the form of* $E[D^{\gamma}h(u)] = \frac{H(s)}{s^{\gamma}} - \sum_{n=0}^{k-1} s^{n-\gamma+2}h^{(n)}(0);\ k-1 < \gamma \leq k,\ k \in N$.

Definition 5 ([25,42])**.** *If we consider* $H(s)$ *is the Elzaki transform of function* $h(u)$ *then the inverse of* $H(s)$ *is* $h(u)$ *such that* $E^{-1}[H(s)] = h(u);\ \forall u > 0$.

Definition 6. *The Shehu transform for the function* $h(u)$ *is defined as [44],*

$$S(h(u)) = H(s,\sigma) = \int_0^{\infty} h(u)\, e^{\frac{-su}{\sigma}}\, du; \quad \sigma > 0, s > 0, u \geq 0.$$

Some of the useful Shehu transforms which are applied in this paper, are as follows:

For $S(h_1(u)) = H_1(s,\sigma)$ and $S(h_2(u)) = H_2(s,\sigma)$

$$S[Ah_1(u) + Bh_2(u)] = AH_1(s,\sigma) + BH_2(s,\sigma),$$

where A and B are constants.

$$S(1) = \frac{\sigma}{s},$$

$$S(u) = \frac{\sigma^2}{s^2},$$

$$S\left(e^{bu}\right) = \frac{\sigma}{s - b\sigma},$$

$$S(\sin(bu)) = \frac{b\sigma^2}{s^2 + b^2\sigma^2},$$

$$S(\cos(bu)) = \frac{\sigma s}{s^2 + b^2\sigma^2},$$

$$S\left(\frac{u^k}{k!}\right) = \left(\frac{\sigma}{s}\right)^{k+1} for\, k = 0, 1, 2, \ldots\ ,$$

$$S\left\{h^{(k)}(u)\right\} = \frac{s^k}{\sigma^k}H(s,\sigma) - \sum_{l=0}^{k-1}\left(\frac{s}{\sigma}\right)^{k-l-1} h^{(l)}(0).$$

Lemma 4. *The Shehu transform of Caputo fractional derivatives of order γ is expressed as [45]*

$$S\left\{h^{(\gamma)}(u)\right\} = \frac{s^\gamma}{\sigma^\gamma}H(s,\sigma) - \sum_{l=0}^{k-1}\left(\frac{s}{\sigma}\right)^{\gamma-l-1} h^{(l)}(0); 0 < \gamma \le k.$$

Definition 7 ([46]). *If we consider $H(s,\sigma)$ is the Shehu transform for a function $h(u)$ then the inverse of $H(s,\sigma)$ is $h(u)$ such that $S^{-1}[H(s,\sigma)] = h(u)$; $\forall u \ge 0$*

alternatively,

$$h(u) = S^{-1}[H(s,\sigma)] = \frac{1}{2\pi i}\int_{\psi-i\infty}^{\psi+i\infty} \frac{e^{-\frac{su}{\sigma}}}{\sigma} H(s,\sigma)ds.$$

Lemma 5 ([46]). *If $S^{-1}[H_1(s,\sigma)] = h_1(u)$ and $S^{-1}[H_2(s,\sigma)] = h_2(u)$,*

then

$$\begin{aligned} &S^{-1}[AH_1(s,\sigma) + BH_2(s,\sigma)] \\ &= AS^{-1}[H_1(s,\sigma)] + BS^{-1}[H_2(s,\sigma)] \\ &= Ah_1(u) + Bh_2(u) \end{aligned}.$$

where A and B are constants.

3. Methodology

The fractional partial differential equation problem of the vibration equation of a large membrane is considered as the following:

$$\frac{\partial^\gamma h}{\partial u^\gamma} = c^2\left(\frac{\partial^2 h}{\partial v^2} + \frac{1}{v}\frac{\partial h}{\partial v}\right) \quad (1)$$

with IC:

$$h(v,0) = h_1(v), \qquad h_u(v,0) = c(h_2(v)), \quad (2)$$

where $h(v,u)$ stand for displacement and c for free vibration wave velocity.

3.1. Case 1 (ETDM)

ET technique for Caputo fractional derivatives is applied to Equation (1) and gives

$$E\left(\frac{\partial^\gamma h}{\partial u^\gamma}\right) = E\left[c^2\left(\frac{\partial^2 h}{\partial v^2} + \frac{1}{v}\frac{\partial h}{\partial v}\right)\right].$$

This gives

$$\frac{E(h(v,u))}{s^\gamma} - \sum_{n=0}^{1} s^{n-\gamma+2} h^{(n)}(v,0) = E\left[c^2\left(h_{vv} + \frac{1}{v}h_v\right)\right] \tag{3}$$

Multiplying s^γ on both sides of Equation (3), we have

$$E(h(v,u)) = s^2 h(v,0) + s^3 h_u(v,0) + s^\gamma c^2\left[E\left(h_{vv} + \frac{1}{v}h_v\right)\right] \tag{4}$$

Applying inverse of ET on both sides of Equation (4) yields

$$h(v,u) = h_1(v) + uc(h_2(v)) + E^{-1}\left(s^\gamma c^2 E\left(h_{vv} + \frac{1}{v}h_v\right)\right) \tag{5}$$

The ETDM represents the solution as an infinite series of components as

$$h(v,u) = \sum_{k=0}^{\infty} h_k^{(E)}(v,u) \tag{6}$$

By substituting Equation (6) in Equation (5), one gets

$$\sum_{k=0}^{\infty} h_k^{(E)}(v,u) = h_1(v) + uc(h_2(v)) + E^{-1}\left(s^\gamma c^2\left(E\left(\sum_{k=0}^{\infty} h_k^{(E)}(v,u)\right)_{vv} + \frac{1}{v}\left(\sum_{k=0}^{\infty} h_k^{(E)}(v,u)\right)_v\right)\right) \tag{7}$$

By comparing both sides of Equation (7), we have

$$h_0^{(E)}(v,u) = h_1(v) + uc(h_2(v)) \tag{8}$$

$$h_n^{(E)}(v,u) = E^{-1}\left(s^\gamma c^2\left(E\left(h_{n-1}^{(E)}(v,u)\right)_{vv} + \frac{1}{v}\left(h_{n-1}^{(E)}(v,u)\right)_v\right)\right), \quad n \geq 1 \tag{9}$$

From Equations (8) and (9), we can determine the components $h_k^{(E)}(v,u)$ and hence, the series solution of $h(v,u)$ in Equation (6) can be obtained for the k term approximant as $Z_k{}^{(E)}(v,u) = \sum_{n=0}^{k} h_n^{(E)}(v,u)$.

3.2. Case 2 (STDM)

The ST procedure for Caputo fractional derivatives is applied to Equation (1) and gives

$$S\left(\frac{\partial^\gamma h}{\partial u^\gamma}\right) = S\left(c^2\left(\frac{\partial^2 h}{\partial v^2} + \frac{1}{v}\frac{\partial h}{\partial v}\right)\right), \quad 0 < \gamma \leq 2$$

This gives

$$\frac{s^\gamma}{\sigma^\gamma}H(s,\sigma) - \left(\frac{s}{\sigma}\right)^{\gamma-1} h(v,0) - \left(\frac{s}{\sigma}\right)^{\gamma-2} h_u(v,0) = S\left(c^2\left(\frac{\partial^2 h}{\partial v^2} + \frac{1}{v}\frac{\partial h}{\partial v}\right)\right) \tag{10}$$

Multiplying $\frac{\sigma^\gamma}{s^\gamma}$ on both sides of Equation (10), we have

$$H(s,\sigma) = \left(\frac{\sigma}{s}\right)h_1(v) + \left(\frac{\sigma}{s}\right)^2 ch_2(v) + \left(\frac{\sigma}{s}\right)^\gamma c^2\left(S\left(h_{vv} + \frac{1}{v}h_v\right)\right) \tag{11}$$

Applying inverse of ST on both sides of Equation (11) yields

$$h(v,u) = h_1(v) + ch_2(v)u + S^{-1}\left(\left(\frac{\sigma}{s}\right)^\gamma c^2\left(S\left(h_{vv} + \frac{1}{v}h_v\right)\right)\right)$$

The STDM represents the solution as an infinite series of components as

$$h(v,u) = \sum_{K=0}^{\infty} h_k^{(S)}(v,u) \tag{12}$$

By substituting Equation (12) in Equation (11), we get

$$\sum_{k=0}^{\infty} h_k^{(S)}(v,u) = h_1(v) + uc(h_2(v)) + S^{-1}\left(\left(\frac{\sigma}{s}\right)^\gamma c^2\left(S\left(\left(\sum_{K=0}^{\infty} h_k^{(S)}(v,u)\right)_{vv} + \frac{1}{v}\left(\sum_{K=0}^{\infty} h_k^{(S)}(v,u)\right)_v\right)\right)\right) \tag{13}$$

By comparing both sides of Equation (13), we have

$$h_0^{(S)}(v,u) = h_1(v) + uc(h_2(v)) \tag{14}$$

$$h_n^{(S)}(v,u) = S^{-1}\left(\left(\frac{\sigma}{s}\right)^\gamma c^2\left(S\left(h_{n-1}^{(S)}(v,u)\right)_{vv} + \frac{1}{v}\left(h_{n-1}^{(S)}(v,u)\right)_v\right)\right), \quad n \geq 1 \tag{15}$$

From Equations (14) and (15), we can determine the components $h_k^{(S)}(v,u)$ and hence, the series solution of $h(v,u)$ in Equation (12) can be obtained for the k term approximant as $Z_k{}^{(S)}(v,u) = \sum_{n=0}^{k} h_n^{(S)}(v,u)$.

4. Convergence Analysis

The fractional Klein Gordan equation's uniqueness and convergence of the solution using NTDM and STDM are provided in [47]; accordingly, in this section, we illustrate the uniqueness and convergence of the solution of the fractional vibration equation of large membrane by using ETDM and STDM.

Uniqueness and Convergence of ETDM and STDM for Large Membrane of Vibration Equation

Assume $|L(h(v,u)) - L(h^*(v,u))| < \omega|h(v,u) - h^*(v,u)|, \forall\, h(v,u), h^*(v,u) \in C[I]$, where $C[I]$ denotes continuous function on I and L specify the linear operator, i.e., $L(h(v,u)) = h(v,u)_{vv} + \frac{1}{v}h(v,u)_v$.

Theorem 1. *Uniqueness of the ETDM solution of Equation (6) occurs when* $0 < \omega\frac{u^{\gamma-2}}{\Gamma(\gamma-1)} < 1$.

Proof. Let us take a Banach space $(C[I], \|.\|)$ for all continuous function on I with the norm $\|.\|$. Let $F : C[I] \to C[I]$ is a mapping such that

$$F(h) = h_1(v) + uc(h_2(v)) + E^{-1}\left(s^\gamma c^2 E\left(h_{vv} + \frac{1}{v}h_v\right)\right)$$

$$\begin{aligned}
\|F(h)-F(h^*)\| &= \max_{u,v\in I}\left|E^{-1}\left(s^\gamma c^2 E(L(h(v,u)))\right)-E^{-1}\left(s^\gamma c^2 E(L(h^*(v,u)))\right)\right| \\
&= \max_{u,v\in I}\left|\tfrac{u^{\gamma-2}}{\Gamma(\gamma-1)}c^2(L(h(v,u))-L(h^*(v,u)))\right| \\
&\le c^2\omega\tfrac{u^{\gamma-2}}{\Gamma(\gamma-1)}\|h-h^*\| \\
&< c^2\|h-h^*\|
\end{aligned}$$

Hence, ETDM solution of Equation (6) is unique. □

Theorem 2. *The ETDM solution of Equation (6) is convergent when* $0 < c^2\omega\frac{u^{\gamma-2}}{\Gamma(\gamma-1)} < 1$.

Proof. Let us take a Banach space $(C[I], \|.\|)$ for all continuous function I with the norm $\|.\|$. For $Z_f^{(E)}, Z_g^{(E)} \in C[I]$ and $f, g \in N, f \ge g$,

$$\begin{aligned}
&\left\|Z_f^{(E)}-Z_g^{(E)}\right\| \\
&= \max_{u,v\in I}\left|Z_f^{(E)}(v,u)-Z_g^{(E)}(v,u)\right| \\
&= \max_{u,v\in I}\left|\sum_{k=g+1}^{f} h_k^{(E)}(v,u)\right| \\
&= \max_{u,v\in I}\left|\sum_{k=g+1}^{f} E^{-1}\left(s^\gamma c^2\left(E\left(L\left(h_{k-1}^{(E)}(v,u)\right)\right)\right)\right)\right| \\
&= \max_{u,v\in I}\left|E^{-1}\left(s^\gamma c^2\left(E\left(\sum_{k=g+1}^{f} L\left(h_{k-1}^{(E)}(v,u)\right)\right)\right)\right)\right| \\
&= \max_{u,v\in I}\left|E^{-1}\left(s^\gamma c^2\left(E\left(\sum_{k=g}^{f-1} L\left(h_{k}^{(E)}(v,u)\right)\right)\right)\right)\right| \\
&= \max_{u,v\in I}\left|E^{-1}\left(s^\gamma c^2\left(E\left(\sum_{k=0}^{f-1} L\left(h_{k}^{(E)}(v,u)\right)-\sum_{k=0}^{g-1} L\left(h_{k}^{(E)}(v,u)\right)\right)\right)\right)\right| \\
&= \max_{u,v\in I}\left|E^{-1}\left(s^\gamma c^2\left(E\left(L\left(Z_{f-1}^{(E)}(v,u)\right)-L\left(Z_{g-1}^{(E)}(v,u)\right)\right)\right)\right)\right| \\
&< \max_{u,v\in I}\left|\omega c^2\frac{u^{\gamma-2}}{\Gamma(\gamma-1)}\left(Z_{f-1}^{(E)}(v,u)-Z_{g-1}^{(E)}(v,u)\right)\right| \\
&< \omega c^2\frac{u^{\gamma-2}}{\Gamma(\gamma-1)}\left\|Z_{f-1}^{(E)}-Z_{g-1}^{(E)}\right\|
\end{aligned}$$

If $f = g+1$,

$$\left\|Z_{g+1}^{(E)}-Z_g^{(E)}\right\| < \omega c^2\frac{u^{\gamma-2}}{\Gamma(\gamma-1)}\left\|Z_g^{(E)}-Z_{g-1}^{(E)}\right\|$$

Let $b = \omega c^2\frac{u^{\gamma-2}}{\Gamma(\gamma-1)}$

$$\left\|Z_{g+1}^{(E)}-Z_g^{(E)}\right\| < b\left\|Z_g^{(E)}-Z_{g-1}^{(E)}\right\| < b^2\left\|Z_{g-1}^{(E)}-Z_{g-2}^{(E)}\right\| < \cdots < b^g\left\|Z_1^{(E)}-Z_0^{(E)}\right\|$$

$$\begin{aligned}
&\left\|Z_f^{(E)}-Z_g^{(E)}\right\| \\
&= \left\|\left(Z_f^{(E)}-Z_{f-1}^{(E)}\right)+\left(Z_{f-1}^{(E)}-Z_{f-2}^{(E)}\right)+\cdots\cdots+\left(Z_{g+1}^{(E)}-Z_g^{(E)}\right)\right\| \\
&\le \left\|Z_f^{(E)}-Z_{f-1}^{(E)}\right\|+\left\|Z_{f-1}^{(E)}-Z_{f-2}^{(E)}\right\|+\cdots\cdots+\left\|Z_{g+1}^{(E)}-Z_g^{(E)}\right\| \\
&< \left(b^{f-1}+b^{f-2}+\cdots\cdots+b^g\right)\left\|Z_1^{(E)}-Z_0^{(E)}\right\| \\
&\le b^g\frac{(1-b^{f-g})}{(1-b)}\left\|h_1^{(E)}\right\| \\
&< b^g\frac{1}{(1-b)}\left\|h_1^{(E)}\right\|
\end{aligned}$$

As $g \to \infty$, $b^g \to 0$. Therefore, $\left\|Z_f^{(E)}-Z_g^{(E)}\right\| \to 0$, when $g \to \infty$.

$\therefore$ The sequence $\left\{Z_k^{(E)}\right\}$ is a Cauchy sequence in Banach space $(C[I], \|.\|)$, and hence it is convergent. □

Theorem 3. *The STDM solution of Equation (12) is unique when* $0 < \omega \frac{u^{\gamma-1}}{\Gamma(\gamma)} < 1$.

Proof. Since this proof is similar to Theorem 1, it was omitted. □

Theorem 4. *The STDM solution of Equation (12) is convergent when* $0 < c^2 \omega \frac{u^{\gamma-1}}{\Gamma(\gamma)} < 1$.

Proof. Since this proof is similar to Theorem 2, it was omitted. □

5. Numerical Examples

This section comprises various numerical experiments to acquire an approximation of the solution to the vibration equations of large membranes comprising fractional derivative Equations (1) and (2). The adaptability of STDM and ETDM are shown by the computational results, which are used to assess the method's correctness in comparison to precise and/or computational results from earlier studies. The outcomes of our techniques implementation showcase that they are very competitive and that they are simple to use.

5.1. Example 1

Consider the following vibration equation of a large membrane with fractional derivative [20,22]

$$\frac{\partial^\gamma h}{\partial u^\gamma} = c^2 \left(\frac{\partial^2 h}{\partial v^2} + \frac{1}{v} \frac{\partial h}{\partial v} \right)$$

with IC:

$$h(v,0) = v^2, \qquad h_u(v,0) = cv$$

By employing ETDM, we get

$$h_0^{(E)}(v,u) = v^2 + ucv$$

$$h_1^{(E)}(v,u) = 4c^2 \frac{u^\gamma}{\Gamma(\gamma+1)} + \frac{c^3}{v} \frac{u^{\gamma+1}}{\Gamma(\gamma+2)}$$

$$h_2^{(E)}(v,u) = \frac{c^5}{v^3} \frac{u^{2\gamma+1}}{\Gamma(2\gamma+2)}$$

We obtain ETDM solution by incorporating $h_0^{(E)}(v,u), h_1^{(E)}(v,u), \cdots$, in Equation (6) as

$$\begin{aligned}
h(v,u) &= v^2 + ucv + 4c^2 \frac{u^\gamma}{\Gamma(\gamma+1)} + \frac{c^3}{v} \frac{u^{\gamma+1}}{\Gamma(\gamma+2)} + \frac{c^5}{v^3} \frac{u^{2\gamma+1}}{\Gamma(2\gamma+2)} + 9 \frac{c^7}{v^5} \frac{u^{3\gamma+1}}{\Gamma(3\gamma+2)} + 225 \frac{c^9}{v^7} \frac{u^{4\gamma+1}}{\Gamma(4\gamma+2)} + \cdots \\
&= v^2 + 4c^2 \frac{u^\gamma}{\Gamma(\gamma+1)} + ucv \left(1 + \frac{c^2}{v^2} \frac{u^\gamma}{\Gamma(\gamma+2)} + \frac{c^4}{v^4} \frac{u^{2\gamma}}{\Gamma(2\gamma+2)} + 9 \frac{c^6}{v^6} \frac{u^{3\gamma}}{\Gamma(3\gamma+2)} + 225 \frac{c^8}{v^8} \frac{u^{4\gamma}}{\Gamma(4\gamma+2)} + \cdots \right) \\
&= v^2 + 4c^2 \frac{u^\gamma}{\Gamma(\gamma+1)} + ucv\, E_{\gamma,2} \left(\frac{c^2}{v^2} T u^\gamma \right)
\end{aligned}$$

where $T^k = [1.3.5. \cdots \cdots .(2k-3)]^2$.

The solution obtained by the proposed method is found to be exactly as that of [22].

On the other hand, by employing STDM, we have,

$$h_0^{(S)}(v,u) = v^2 + ucv$$

$$h_1^{(S)}(v,u) = 4c^2 \frac{u^\gamma}{\Gamma(\gamma+1)} + \frac{c^3}{v} \frac{u^{\gamma+1}}{\Gamma(\gamma+2)}$$

$$h_2^{(S)}(v,u) = \frac{c^5}{v^3}\frac{u^{2\gamma+1}}{\Gamma(2\gamma+2)}$$

STDM solution is obtained by incorporating $h_0^{(S)}(v,u), h_1^{(S)}(v,u), \cdots$, in Equation (12) as

$$\begin{aligned}
h(v,u) &= v^2 + ucv + 4c^2\frac{u^\gamma}{\Gamma(\gamma+1)} + \frac{c^3}{v}\frac{u^{\gamma+1}}{\Gamma(\gamma+2)} + \frac{c^5}{v^3}\frac{u^{2\gamma+1}}{\Gamma(2\gamma+2)} + 9\frac{c^7}{v^5}\frac{u^{3\gamma+1}}{\Gamma(3\gamma+2)} + 225\frac{c^9}{v^7}\frac{u^{4\gamma+1}}{\Gamma(4\gamma+2)} + \cdots \\
&= v^2 + 4c^2\frac{u^\gamma}{\Gamma(\gamma+1)} + ucv\left(1 + \frac{c^2}{v^2}\frac{u^\gamma}{\Gamma(\gamma+2)} + \frac{c^4}{v^4}\frac{u^{2\gamma}}{\Gamma(2\gamma+2)} + 9\frac{c^6}{v^6}\frac{u^{3\gamma}}{\Gamma(3\gamma+2)} + 225\frac{c^8}{v^8}\frac{u^{4\gamma}}{\Gamma(4\gamma+2)} + \cdots\right) \\
&= v^2 + 4c^2\frac{u^\gamma}{\Gamma(\gamma+1)} + ucv\, E_{\gamma,2}\left(\frac{c^2}{v^2}Tu^\gamma\right),
\end{aligned}$$

where $T^k = [1.3.5.\cdots\cdots.(2k-3)]^2$.

It is found that the solution produced by the suggested approach is identical to that of [22].

5.2. Example 2

Next, consider the following large membrane of vibration equation involving fractional [20,22].

$$\frac{\partial^\gamma h}{\partial u^\gamma} = c^2\left(\frac{\partial^2 h}{\partial v^2} + \frac{1}{v}\frac{\partial h}{\partial v}\right)$$

with IC:

$$h(v,0) = v, \qquad h_u(v,0) = cv$$

From ETDM, we get

$$h_0^{(E)}(v,u) = v + ucv$$

$$h_1^{(E)}(v,u) = \frac{c^2}{v}\frac{u^\gamma}{\Gamma(\gamma+1)} + \frac{c^3}{v}\frac{u^{\gamma+1}}{\Gamma(\gamma+2)}$$

$$h_2^{(E)}(v,u) = \frac{c^4}{v^3}\frac{u^{2\gamma}}{\Gamma(2\gamma+1)} + \frac{c^5}{v^3}\frac{u^{2\gamma+1}}{\Gamma(2\gamma+2)}$$

ETDM solution then may be obtained by incorporating $h_0^{(E)}(v,u), h_1^{(E)}(v,u), \cdots$, in Equation (6) as

$$\begin{aligned}
h(v,u) &= v + ucv + \frac{c^2}{v}\frac{u^\gamma}{\Gamma(\gamma+1)} + \frac{c^3}{v}\frac{u^{\gamma+1}}{\Gamma(\gamma+2)} + \frac{c^4}{v^3}\frac{u^{2\gamma}}{\Gamma(2\gamma+1)} + \frac{c^5}{v^3}\frac{u^{2\gamma+1}}{\Gamma(2\gamma+2)} + \\
&\quad 9\frac{c^6}{v^5}\frac{u^{3\gamma}}{\Gamma(3\gamma+1)} + 9\frac{c^7}{v^5}\frac{u^{3\gamma+1}}{\Gamma(3\gamma+2)} + 225\frac{c^8}{v^7}\frac{u^{4\gamma}}{\Gamma(4\gamma+1)} + 225\frac{c^9}{v^7}\frac{u^{4\gamma+1}}{\Gamma(4\gamma+2)} + \cdots \\
&= v\left(1 + \frac{c^2}{v^2}\frac{u^\gamma}{\Gamma(\gamma+1)} + \frac{c^4}{v^4}\frac{u^{2\gamma}}{\Gamma(2\gamma+1)} + 9\frac{c^6}{v^6}\frac{u^{3\gamma}}{\Gamma(3\gamma+1)} + 225\frac{c^8}{v^8}\frac{u^{4\gamma}}{\Gamma(4\gamma+1)} + \cdots\right) \\
&\quad + ucv\left(1 + \frac{c^2}{v^2}\frac{u^\gamma}{\Gamma(\gamma+2)} + \frac{c^4}{v^4}\frac{u^{2\gamma}}{\Gamma(2\gamma+2)} + 9\frac{c^6}{v^6}\frac{u^{3\gamma}}{\Gamma(3\gamma+2)} + 225\frac{c^8}{v^8}\frac{u^{4\gamma}}{\Gamma(4\gamma+2)} + \cdots\right) \\
&= v\, E_\gamma\left(\frac{c^2}{v^2}Tu^\gamma\right) + ucv\, E_{\gamma,2}\left(\frac{c^2}{v^2}Tu^\gamma\right)
\end{aligned}$$

where $T^k = [1.3.5.\cdots\cdots.(2k-3)]^{.2}$.

The solution obtained by the proposed method is found to be exactly as that of [22].

For STDM, we have

$$h_0^{(S)}(v,u) = v + ucv$$

$$h_1^{(S)}(v,u) = \frac{c^2}{v}\frac{u^\gamma}{\Gamma(\gamma+1)} + \frac{c^3}{v}\frac{u^{\gamma+1}}{\Gamma(\gamma+2)}$$

$$h_2^{(S)}(v,u) = \frac{c^4}{v^3}\frac{u^{2\gamma}}{\Gamma(2\gamma+1)} + \frac{c^5}{v^3}\frac{u^{2\gamma+1}}{\Gamma(2\gamma+2)}$$

Finally, the STDM solution is found by incorporating $h_0^{(S)}(v,u), h_1^{(S)}(v,u), \cdots$, in Equation (12)

$$\begin{aligned}
h(v,u) &= v + ucv + \frac{c^2}{v}\frac{u^\gamma}{\Gamma(\gamma+1)} + \frac{c^3}{v}\frac{u^{\gamma+1}}{\Gamma(\gamma+2)} + \frac{c^4}{v^3}\frac{u^{2\gamma}}{\Gamma(2\gamma+1)} + \frac{c^5}{v^3}\frac{u^{2\gamma+1}}{\Gamma(2\gamma+2)} + \\
&\quad 9\frac{c^6}{v^5}\frac{u^{3\gamma}}{\Gamma(3\gamma+1)} + 9\frac{c^7}{v^5}\frac{u^{3\gamma+1}}{\Gamma(3\gamma+2)} + 225\frac{c^8}{v^7}\frac{u^{4\gamma}}{\Gamma(4\gamma+1)} + 225\frac{c^9}{v^7}\frac{u^{4\gamma+1}}{\Gamma(4\gamma+2)} + \cdots \\
&= v\left(1 + \frac{c^2}{v^2}\frac{u^\gamma}{\Gamma(\gamma+1)} + \frac{c^4}{v^4}\frac{u^{2\gamma}}{\Gamma(2\gamma+1)} + 9\frac{c^6}{v^6}\frac{u^{3\gamma}}{\Gamma(3\gamma+1)} + 225\frac{c^8}{v^8}\frac{u^{4\gamma}}{\Gamma(4\gamma+1)} + \cdots\right) \\
&+ucv\left(1 + \frac{c^2}{v^2}\frac{u^\gamma}{\Gamma(\gamma+2)} + \frac{c^4}{v^4}\frac{u^{2\gamma}}{\Gamma(2\gamma+2)} + 9\frac{c^6}{v^6}\frac{u^{3\gamma}}{\Gamma(3\gamma+2)} + 225\frac{c^8}{v^8}\frac{u^{4\gamma}}{\Gamma(4\gamma+2)} + \cdots\right) \\
&= v\, E_\gamma\left(\frac{c^2}{v^2}Tu^\gamma\right) + ucv\, E_{\gamma,2}\left(\frac{c^2}{v^2}Tu^\gamma\right),
\end{aligned}$$

where $T^k = [1.3.5. \cdots\cdots .(2k-3)]^2$.

It is found that the solution produced by the suggested approach is identical to that of [22].

5.3. Example 3

Finally, let us consider the following large membrane of vibration equation [20,22]

$$\frac{\partial^\gamma h}{\partial u^\gamma} = c^2\left(\frac{\partial^2 h}{\partial v^2} + \frac{1}{v}\frac{\partial h}{\partial v}\right)$$

with IC:

$$h(v,0) = v^2, \qquad h_u(v,0) = cv^2$$

Using ETDM, one may write

$$h_0^{(E)}(v,u) = v^2 + ucv^2$$

$$h_1^{(E)}(v,u) = 4c^2\frac{u^\gamma}{\Gamma(\gamma+1)} + 4c^3\frac{u^{\gamma+1}}{\Gamma(\gamma+2)}$$

$$h_2^{(E)}(v,u) = 0$$

Correspondingly, the ETDM solution will be obtained by introducing $h_0^{(E)}(v,u)$, $h_1^{(E)}(v,u), \cdots$, in Equation (6)

$$\begin{aligned}
h(v,u) &= v^2 + ucv^2 + 4c^2\frac{u^\gamma}{\Gamma(\gamma+1)} + 4c^3\frac{u^{\gamma+1}}{\Gamma(\gamma+2)} + 0 + \cdots \\
&= v^2 + ucv^2 + 4c^2\frac{u^\gamma}{\Gamma(\gamma+1)} + 4c^3\frac{u^{\gamma+1}}{\Gamma(\gamma+2)}
\end{aligned}$$

It is found that the solution produced by the suggested approach is identical to that of [22].

Further, by employing STDM, we have

$$h_0^{(S)}(v,u) = v^2 + ucv^2$$

$$h_1^{(S)}(v,u) = 4c^2\frac{u^\gamma}{\Gamma(\gamma+1)} + 4c^3\frac{u^{\gamma+1}}{\Gamma(\gamma+2)}$$

$$h_2^{(S)}(v,u) = 0$$

Similarly from STDM, the solution will be obtained by incorporating $h_0^{(S)}(v,u)$, $h_1^{(S)}(v,u),\cdots$, in Equation (12)

$$h(v,u) = v^2 + ucv^2 + 4c^2\frac{u^\gamma}{\Gamma(\gamma+1)} + 4c^3\frac{u^{\gamma+1}}{\Gamma(\gamma+2)} + 0 + \cdots$$
$$= v^2 + ucv^2 + 4c^2\frac{u^\gamma}{\Gamma(\gamma+1)} + 4c^3\frac{u^{\gamma+1}}{\Gamma(\gamma+2)}$$

It is found that the solution produced by the suggested approach is identical to that of [22].

6. Numerical Results and Discussion

This section determines displacement $h(v,u)$ for various values of time u and fractional time derivative γ for the above three different examples in Tables 1–3 and Figures 1–6 which are discussed below. Table 1, for example 1, shows that for c = 5, v = 6, and various values of u and γ present methods are in excellent agreement with the existing methods, i.e., LDM [20] and RPSM [22]. Similarly, by taking the same values of c, v, u, and γ as previously, term-wise solutions of vibration equation of large membrane with fractional derivative derived by ETDM and STDM, for example 1, are shown in Table 2. For c = 5 and v = 6, solutions of example 1, 2, and 3 for various values of u and γ are depicted in Table 3. Figure 1, Figure 3, and Figure 6 show that for c = 5, displacement increases with the increase of v and u. Figure 2, Figure 4, and Figure 6 show that for v = 3 and c = 5, displacement increases with the increase of u, whereas displacement decreases with the increase of γ. It has also been observed that the rate of change of displacement is higher when $h_1(v)$ and $h_2(v)$ are nonlinear than when $h_1(v)$ and $h_2(v)$ are linear. It comes from the observation that example 3 exhibits a higher rate of change of displacement than the other two examples. All the figures in this section are presented for STDM solutions. Similarly, the figures can be generated for ETDM solutions.

Table 1. Comparative analysis among LDM [20], RPSM [22], solution by ETDM and STDM for $h(v,u)$ at different values of u and γ when $c = 5$ and $v = 6$ for example 1.

u	γ	h_{LDM}	h_{RPSM}	h_{ETDM}	h_{STDM}
0.2	1.5	48.8406	48.8415	48.8415	48.8415
	2	44.0278	44.0278	44.0278	44.0278
0.4	1.5	67.6701	67.6820	67.6829	67.6829
	2	56.2234	56.2235	56.2234	56.2234
0.6	1.5	90.7471	90.7980	90.8153	90.8153
	2	72.7599	72.7598	72.7599	72.7599
0.8	1.5	117.5902	117.6890	117.8195	117.8195
	2	93.8217	93.8205	93.8216	93.8216
1	1.5	148.1551	148.0990	148.7224	148.7224
	2	119.6163	119.6060	119.6150	119.6150

Table 2. Comparative analysis among termwise solution of ETDM and STDM for $h(v,u)$ at different values of γ and u when $c = 5$ and $v = 6$ for example 1.

u	γ	1st Term		2nd Term		3rd Term		4th Term	
		h_{ETDM}	h_{STDM}	h_{ETDM}	h_{STDM}	h_{ETDM}	h_{STDM}	h_{ETDM}	h_{STDM}
0.2	1.5	48.8404	48.8404	48.8414	48.8414	48.8415	48.8415	48.8415	48.8415
	2	44.0277	44.0277	44.0278	44.0278	44.0278	44.0278	44.0278	44.0278
0.4	1.5	67.6650	67.6650	67.6804	67.6804	67.6824	67.6824	67.6829	67.6829
	2	56.2222	56.2222	56.2234	56.2234	56.2234	56.2234	56.2234	56.2234
0.6	1.5	90.7096	90.7096	90.7877	90.7877	90.8066	90.8066	90.8153	90.8153
	2	72.7500	72.7500	72.7593	72.7893	72.7598	72.7598	72.7599	72.7599
0.8	1.5	117.4152	117.4152	117.6621	117.6621	117.7542	117.7542	117.8195	117.8195
	2	93.7777	93.7777	93.8172	93.8172	93.8210	93.8210	93.8216	93.8216
1	1.5	147.4940	147.4940	148.0968	148.0968	148.4109	148.4109	148.7224	148.7224
	2	119.4722	119.4722	119.5927	119.5927	119.6107	119.6107	119.6150	119.6150

Table 3. Comparative analysis among solutions of ETDM and STDM for $h(v,u)$ at different values of γ and u when $c = 5$ and $v = 6$ for example 1, example 2, and example 3.

u	γ	Example 1		Example 2		Example 3	
		h_{ETDM}	h_{STDM}	h_{ETDM}	h_{STDM}	h_{ETDM}	h_{STDM}
0.2	1.5	48.8415	48.8415	12.3976	12.3976	81.4197	81.4197
	2	44.0278	44.0278	12.1113	12.1113	74.6667	74.6667
0.4	1.5	67.6829	67.6829	19.4835	19.4835	142.2552	142.2552
	2	56.2234	56.2234	18.5600	18.5600	121.3333	121.3333
0.6	1.5	90.8153	90.8153	27.4697	27.4697	220.9154	220.9154
	2	72.7599	72.7599	25.5268	25.5268	180.0000	180.0000
0.8	1.5	117.8195	117.8195	36.7233	36.7233	319.9498	319.9498
	2	93.8216	93.8216	33.2122	33.2122	254.6667	254.6667
1	1.5	148.7224	148.7224	47.8953	47.8953	441.6758	441.6758
	2	119.6150	119.6150	41.8518	41.8518	349.3333	349.3333

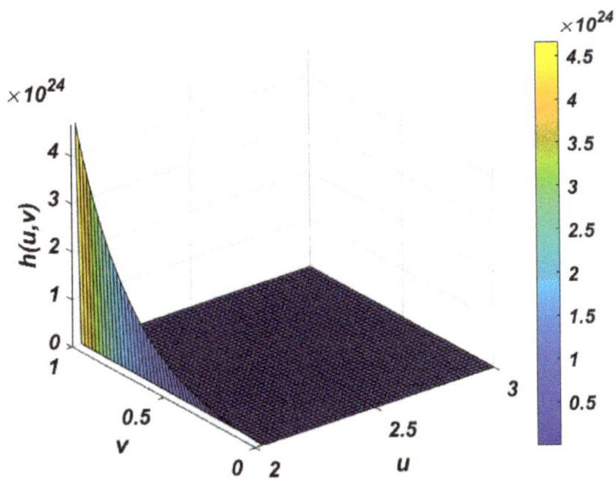

Figure 1. STDM solutions of example 1 for $\gamma = 2$ and $c = 5$.

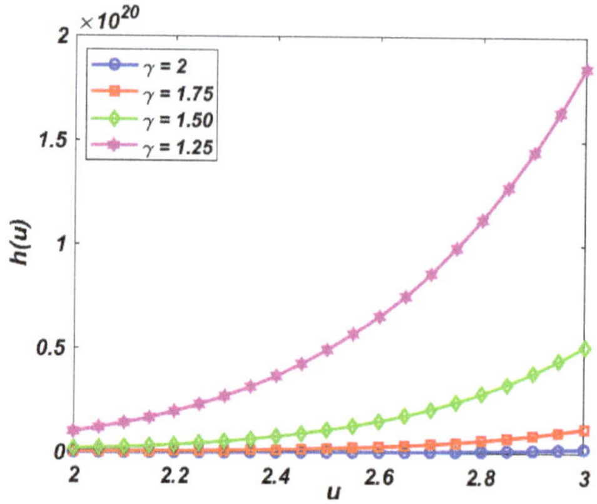

Figure 2. STDM solutions of example 1 for various values of γ, when $v = 3$ and $c = 5$.

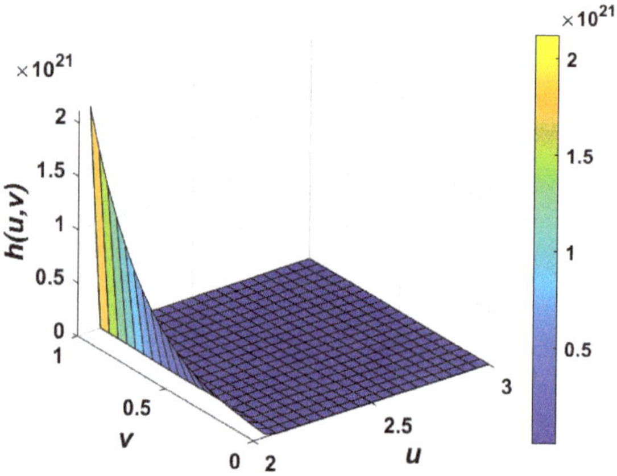

Figure 3. STDM solutions of example 2 for $\gamma = 2$ and $c = 5$.

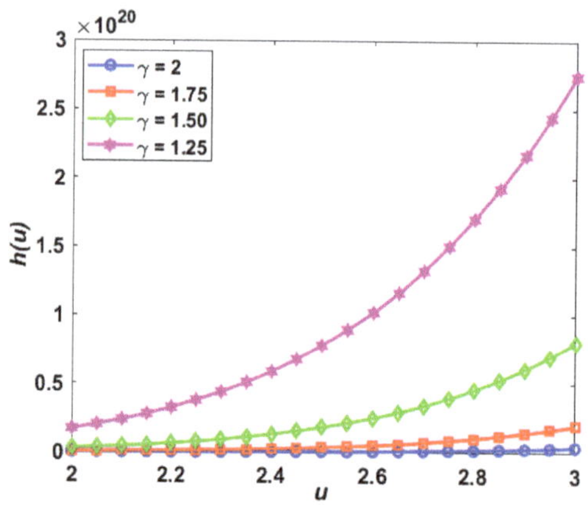

Figure 4. STDM solutions for example 2 for various value of γ, when $v = 3$ and $c = 5$.

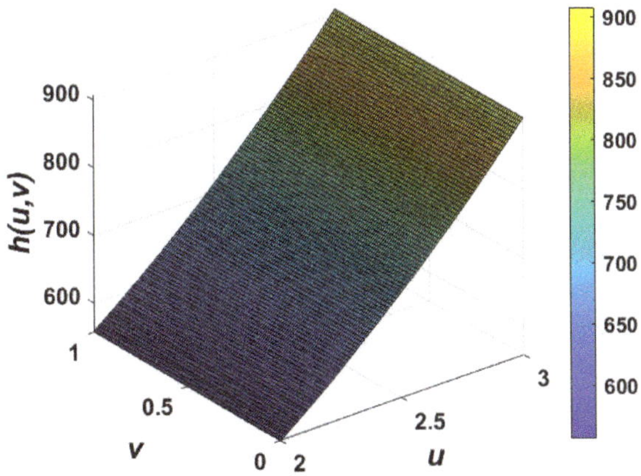

Figure 5. STDM solutions of example 3 for $\gamma = 2$ and $c = 5$.

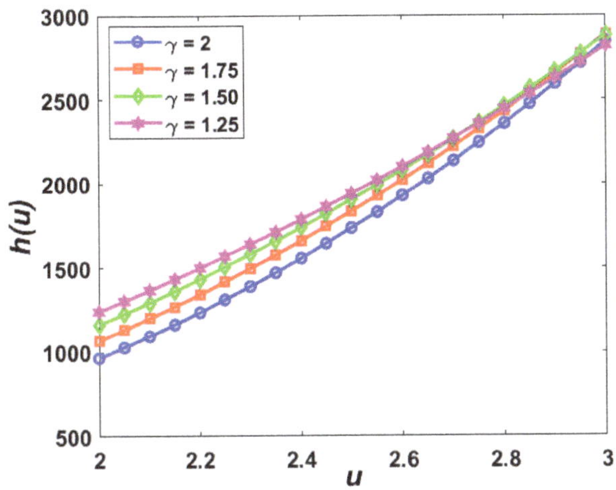

Figure 6. STDM solutions of example 3 for various value of γ, when $v = 3$ and $c = 5$.

7. Conclusions

The new modification of the decomposition method is a powerful tool that makes it easy to obtain analytical solutions for fractional differential equations. The main aim of this article is to provide a series of solutions to the differential equations of fractional order. In this article, ETDM and STDM are successfully implemented to examine the large membrane vibration equation involving fractional derivatives. The presented approach provides an efficient way of solving these kinds of vibration problems with fractional derivatives. Three example problems are addressed in order to validate and test the efficacy of the proposed method. The illustrative examples show that the method is easy to use and is an effective tool for solving fractional partial differential equations. Thus, it is concluded that ETDM and STDM are quite useful, convenient, and powerful analytical methods to find the solution to the fractional problems arising in mathematics and engineering. The superiority of these methods lies in their ability to provide faster convergence, reduced computational complexity, and explicit analytical solutions compared to conventional methods such as LDM, HAM, and RPSM, which often struggle with iterative complexity and convergence issues. Furthermore, unlike numerical techniques that introduce discretization errors,

ETDM and STDM yield solutions in terms of Mittag–Leffler functions, ensuring a more accurate representation of long-memory and nonlocal effects in fractional-order systems.

Author Contributions: Conceptualization, N.R.M., S.C. and R.M.J.; methodology, N.R.M., S.C. and R.M.J.; software, N.R.M.; validation, N.R.M., S.C. and R.M.J.; formal analysis, N.R.M.; investigation, N.R.M., S.C. and R.M.J.; resources, N.R.M.; data curation, N.R.M.; writing—original draft preparation, N.R.M.; writing—review and editing, S.C. and R.M.J.; visualization, N.R.M.; supervision, S.C. and R.M.J. All authors have read and agreed to the published version of the manuscript.

Funding: This research received no external funding.

Data Availability Statement: The original contributions presented in this study are included in the article. Further inquiries can be directed to the corresponding author.

Acknowledgments: The first author would like to express his gratitude to the University Grants Commission, New Delhi, India, for the fellowship to carry out this research work.

Conflicts of Interest: The authors declare no conflict of interest.

Abbreviations

ET	Elzaki transform
ST	Shehu transform
ETDM	Elzaki transformation decomposition method
STDM	Shehu transformation decomposition method
NTDM	Natural transformation decomposition method
RPSM	Residual power series method
LDM	Laplace decomposition method

References

1. Suleman, M.; Wu, Q.; Elzaki, T. Explicit Analytic Solution of Vibration Equation for large domain by mean of the Elzaki projected Differential Transform Method. *J. Adv. Math.* **2015**, *11*, 5244–5257. [CrossRef]
2. Chakraverty, S. *Vibration of Plates*; CRC Press: Boca Raton, FL, USA, 2008.
3. Sina, S.; Navazi, H.; Haddadpour, H. An analytical method for free vibration analysis of functionally graded beams. *Mater. Des.* **2009**, *30*, 741–747. [CrossRef]
4. Ke, L.-L.; Yang, J.; Kitipornchai, S. An analytical study on the nonlinear vibration of functionally graded beams. *Meccanica* **2010**, *45*, 743–752. [CrossRef]
5. Rao, P.; Mohapatra, D.; Chakraverty, S.; Roy, D. Vibration analysis of non-homogenous single-link flexible manipulator in uncertain environment. *Appl. Math. Model.* **2025**, *141*, 115939. [CrossRef]
6. Gartia, A.K.; Chakraverty, S. Free Vibration of Bi-Directional Functionally Graded Nanobeams Resting on Winkler–Pasternak Foundations. *J. Vib. Eng. Technol.* **2024**, *12* (Suppl. S2), 1929–1945. [CrossRef]
7. Ni, Z.; Zhu, F.; Fan, Y.; Yang, J.; Hang, Z.; Feng, C.; Yang, J. Numerical study on nonlinear vibration of FG-GNPRC circular membrane with dielectric properties. *Mech. Adv. Mater. Struct.* **2024**, *31*, 3756–3775. [CrossRef]
8. Gartia, A.K.; Chakraverty, S. Advanced computational modeling and mechanical behavior analysis of multi-directional functionally graded nanostructures: A comprehensive review. *Comput. Model. Eng. Sci.* **2025**, *142*, 2405–2455. [CrossRef]
9. Chen, X.; Han, M.; Yang, X.; Wang, B. Stability Analysis of Parametric Vibration in Overhead Conductors Under Time-Varying Tension. *Symmetry* **2025**, *17*, 464. [CrossRef]
10. Ye, Y.; Yin, Z.; Zhu, A. A Mixed Finite Element Method for Vibration Equations of Structurally Damped Beam and Plate. *Numer. Methods Partial. Differ. Equ.* **2025**, *41*, e70005. [CrossRef]
11. Qin, Z.; Lin, Y.; Han, M.; Han, X.; Zhang, X.; He, P.; Gao, X.; Feng, X. Experimental and theoretical investigation on the thermoacoustic-induced vibration in a centrally-staged combustor. *Combust. Flame* **2025**, *273*, 113890. [CrossRef]
12. Khatib, M.N.; Hatip, A. On Refined Netrusophic Fractional Calculus. *Int. J. Neutrosophic Sci.* **2024**, *24*, 8–18.
13. Hilfer, R.; Kleiner, T. Fractional calculus for distributions. *Fract. Calc. Appl. Anal.* **2024**, *27*, 2063–2123.
14. Sahoo, M.; Chakraverty, S. Solitary wave solution for time-fractional SMCH equation in fuzzy environment. In *Computation and Modeling for Fractional Order Systems*; Academic Press: New York, NY, USA, 2024; pp. 227–239.

15. Goyal, M.; Prakash, A.; Gupta, S. An efficient perturbation sumudu transform technique for the time-fractional vibration equation with a memory dependent fractional derivative in liouville–caputo sense. *Int. J. Appl. Comput. Math.* **2021**, *7*, 1–18. [CrossRef]
16. Meng, L.; Kexin, M.; Ruyi, X.; Mei, S.; Cattani, C. Haar wavelet transform and variational iteration method for fractional option pricing models. *Math. Methods Appl. Sci.* **2023**, *46*, 8408–8417. [CrossRef]
17. El-Ajou, A.; Abu Arqub, O.; Momani, S. Approximate analytical solution of the nonlinear fractional KdV–Burgers equation: A new iterative algorithm. *J. Comput. Phys.* **2015**, *293*, 81–95. [CrossRef]
18. Kumar, D.; Singh, J.; Baleanu, D. On the analysis of vibration equation involving a fractional derivative with Mittag-Leffler law. *Math. Methods Appl. Sci.* **2020**, *43*, 443–457. [CrossRef]
19. Singh, H. Approximate solution of fractional vibration equation using Jacobi polynomials. *Appl. Math. Comput.* **2018**, *317*, 85–100. [CrossRef]
20. Srivastava, H.; Kumar, D.; Singh, J. An efficient analytical technique for fractional model of vibration equation. *Appl. Math. Model.* **2017**, *45*, 192–204. [CrossRef]
21. Al-Sawalha, M.M.; Alshehry, A.S.; Nonlaopon, K.; Shah, R.; Ababneh, O.Y. Approximate analytical solution of time-fractional vibration equation via reliable numerical algorithm. *AIMS Math.* **2022**, *7*, 19739–19757. [CrossRef]
22. Jena, R.M.; Chakraverty, S. Residual power series method for solving time-fractional model of vibration equation of large membranes. *J. Appl. Comput. Mech.* **2019**, *5*, 603–615.
23. Aghchi, S.; Sun, H.; Fazli, H. Operational matrix approach for solving fractional vibration equation of large membranes with error estimation. *Filomat* **2024**, *38*, 2205–2216. [CrossRef]
24. Adomian, G. *Solving Frontier Problems of Physics: The Decomposition Method*; Springer Science & Business Media: Dordrecht, The Netherlands, 2013; Volume 60.
25. Elzaki, T.M. The new integral transform Elzaki transform. *Glob. J. Pure Appl. Math.* **2011**, *7*, 57–64.
26. Elzaki, T.M. On the connections between Laplace and Elzaki transforms. *Adv. Theor. Appl. Math.* **2011**, *6*, 1–11.
27. Elzaki, T.M. On The New Integral Transform "Elzaki Transform" Fundamental Properties Investigations and Applications. *Glob. J. Math. Sci. Theory Pract.* **2012**, *4*, 1–13.
28. Hajira Khan, H.; Khan, A.; Kumam, P.; Baleanu, D.; Arif, M. An approximate analytical solution of the Navier–Stokes equations within Caputo operator and Elzaki transform decomposition method. *Adv. Differ. Equ.* **2020**, *2020*, 1–23.
29. Sedeeg, A.K.H. A coupling Elzaki transform and homotopy perturbation method for solving nonlinear fractional heat-like equations. *Am. J. Math. Comput. Model* **2016**, *1*, 15–20.
30. Neamaty, A.; Agheli, B.; Darzi, R. Applications of homotopy perturbation method and Elzaki transform for solving nonlinear partial differential equations of fractional order. *J. Nonlin. Evolut. Equat. Appl.* **2015**, *2015*, 91–104.
31. Akinyemi, L.; Iyiola, O.S. Exact and approximate solutions of time-fractional models arising from physics via Shehu transform. *Math. Methods Appl. Sci.* **2020**, *43*, 7442–7464. [CrossRef]
32. Khalouta, A.; Kadem, A. A comparative study of Shehu variational iteration method and Shehu decomposition method for solving nonlinear Caputo time-fractional wave-like equations with variable coefficients. *Appl. Appl. Math. Int. J. (AAM)* **2020**, *15*, 24.
33. Maitama, S.; Zhao, W. Homotopy perturbation Shehu transform method for solving fractional models arising in applied sciences. *J. Appl. Math. Comput. Mech.* **2021**, *20*, 71–82. [CrossRef]
34. Shah, N.A.; Dassios, I.; El-Zahar, E.R.; Chung, J.D.; Taherifar, S. The Variational Iteration Transform Method for Solving the Time-Fractional Fornberg–Whitham Equation and Comparison with Decomposition Transform Method. *Mathematics* **2021**, *9*, 141. [CrossRef]
35. Podlubny, I. Fractional differential equations. *Math. Sci. Eng.* **1999**, *198*, 41–119.
36. Chakraverty, S.; Jena, R.M.; Jena, S.K. Time-fractional order biological systems with uncertain parameters. *Synth. Lect. Math. Stat.* **2020**, *12*, 1–160. [CrossRef]
37. Chakraverty, S.; Tapaswini, S.; Behera, D. *Fuzzy Arbitrary Order System: Fuzzy Fractional Differential Equations and Applications*; John Wiley & Sons: Hoboken, NJ, USA, 2016.
38. Kilbas, A.A.; Srivastava, H.M.; Trujillo, J.J. *Theory and Applications of Fractional Differential Equations*; Elsevier: Amsterdam, The Netherlands, 2006; Volume 204.
39. Miller, K.S.; Ross, B. *An Introduction to the Fractional Calculus and Fractional Differential Equations*; Wiley: Hoboken, NJ, USA, 1993.
40. Chakraverty, S.; Jena, R.M.; Jena, S.K. *Computational Fractional Dynamical Systems: Fractional Differential Equations and Applications*; John Wiley & Sons: Hoboken, NJ, USA, 2022.
41. Podlubny, I. *Fractional Differential Equations: An Introduction to Fractional Derivatives, Fractional Differential Equations, to Methods of Their Solution and Some of Their Applications*; Elsevier: Amsterdam, The Netherlands, 1998.
42. Jena, R.M.; Chakraverty, S. Solving time-fractional navier-stokes equations using homotopy perturbation elzaki transform. *SN Appl. Sci.* **2019**, *1*, 16. [CrossRef]

43. Khalid, M.; Sultana, M.; Zaidi, F.; Arshad, U. Application of Elzaki transform method on some fractional differential equations. *Math. Theory Model.* **2015**, *5*, 89–96.
44. Maitama, S.; Zhao, W. New integral transform: Shehu transform a generalization of sumudu and laplace transform for solving differential equations. *Int. J. Anal. Appl.* **2019**, *17*, 167–190. [CrossRef]
45. Belgacem, R.; Baleanu, D.; Bokhari, A. Shehu transform and applications to caputo-fractional differential equations. *Int. J. Anal. Appl.* **2019**, *17*, 917–927. [CrossRef]
46. Khalouta, A.; Kadem, A. A new method to solve fractional differential equations: Inverse fractional Shehu transform method. *Appl. Appl. Math. Int. J. (AAM)* **2019**, *14*, 19.
47. Kanth, A.R.; Aruna, K.; Raghavendar, K.; Rezazadeh, H.; Inc, M. Numerical solutions of nonlinear time fractional Klein-Gordon equation via natural transform decomposition method and iterative Shehu transform method. *J. Ocean Eng. Sci.* 2021, *in press*. [CrossRef]

fractal and fractional

MDPI

Article

A Suitable Algorithm to Solve a Nonlinear Fractional Integro-Differential Equation with Extended Singular Kernel in (2+1) Dimensions

Sameeha Ali Raad [1,*] and Mohamed Abdella Abdou [2]

[1] Mathematics Department, Faculty of Sciences, Umm Al-Qura University, Makkah 21955, Saudi Arabia
[2] Department of Mathematics, Faculty of Education, Alexandria University, Alexandria 21526, Egypt; abdella_777@yahoo.com
* Correspondence: saraad@uqu.edu.sa

Abstract: In this paper, the authors consider a problem with comprehensive properties in terms of form and content in the space $\mathcal{L}_2[(a,b)\times(\mathrm{c},\mathrm{d})]\times C[0,T], T<1$. In terms of time form, we assume that the time phase delay is implicitly contained in a nonlinear differential integral equation. The positional part is considered in two dimensions, and the position's kernel is a general singular kernel, many different forms of which will be derived. In terms of content, all of the previously established numerical techniques are only appropriate for studying special cases of the kernel separately but are not suitable for studying the general kernel. This led to the use of the Toeplitz matrix method, which deals with the kernel in its extended nonlinear form and the special kernels will be studied as applications of the method. Moreover, this method has the advantage of converting all single integrals into regular integrals that can be easily solved. Additionally, the researchers examine the solution's existence, uniqueness, and convergence in this paper. The error and its stability are also studied. At the end of the research, the authors studied some numerical applications of some of the singular kernels derived from the general kernel, examining the approximation error in each application separately.

Keywords: fractional integro-differential equations; fixed point theorem; error convergence; general singular kernel; nonlinear mixed integral equation; Toeplitz matrix method

1. Introduction

Interest in fractional equations and fractional integral equations has increased steadily in recent years due to their wide range of applications. The list of applications has become far more diverse and extensive in a short time. Fractional integro-differential equations (**FrI-DEs**) for electromagnetic waves in a dielectric medium were discovered by Tarasov [1]. Munusamy et al. [2] used the resolvent operator theory and the fixed-point theorem to examine the existence of a mild solution of the **FrI-DE** with nonlocal conditions. In [3], the existence of a solution to **FrI-DEs** was presented using the Banach principle and fixed-point theorems. After converting the Volterra–Fredholm integral equation (**V-FIE**) from **FrI-DE** using the Riemann–Liouville fractional integral, the existence of a unique solution was demonstrated using the Picard technique [4]. Alhazmi [5] employed a novel method based on the orthogonal polynomials method and variable separation to derive numerous spectral relationships from the mixed integral equation using the generalized potential kernel. The Legendre polynomials approach was used by Nemati et al. [6] to analyze the results of the second kind of two-dimensional (**2D**) Volterra integral model. Hafez and Youssri [7] discussed using the Legendre–Chebyshev polynomials to solve the **2D** integral model numerically based on the **V-FIE**. The existence of solutions for a coupled system of **FrI-DEs** with Riemann–Stieltjes integral conditions and nonlocal infinite-point was demonstrated by El-Sayed et al. [8]. **FrI-DEs** can be solved in a variety of ways, some of which are analytical. Using the Taylor expansion method, Huang et al. [9] provided a simple and closed solution to a class of **FrI-DEs**. Legendre wavelets were used to solve a class of **2-D FrI-DEs** in [10]. Using Babenko's method, Li and Plowman developed solutions for the generalized Abel's integral equations with variable coefficients [11]. In [12], Matoog applied the modified Taylor's technique to derive a nonlinear algebraic system from the Hammerstein–Volterra integral equation with a continuous kernel. In order to reach the approximate solution, Abusalim et al. [13] used hybrid and block-pulse functions to solve the **2-D** nonlinear integral equation with symmetric and nonsymmetric kernels. The separation of variables technique has been used to solve the mixed **V-FIE** [14]. By using the properties of a fractional integral, Jan [15] was able to conform the nonlinear mixed **FrI-DE** to the Volterra–Hammerstein integral equation. By using the extended cubic B-spline, Akram et al. [16] interpreted the collocation strategy for solving the partial **FrI-DE**. The approximate solution for variable-order **FrI-DEs** with a weakly singular kernel was obtained by Abdelkawy et al. [17] by applying the Jacobi–Gauss collocation method.

In the remainder of the paper, particularly in Section 3, the authors present a second-order nonlinear fractional differential equation under initial conditions. This equation carries physical implications, particularly since the kernel of the equation is completely singular in various ways. Under the conditions imposed on the equation, the authors were able to transform it into a mixed integral equation that is nonlinear in position and time. Also, in Section 4 of the paper, the authors consider special cases that can be derived from the imposed kernel. This section is of great importance and illustrates the overall significance of the paper in studying mixed integro-differential equations in position and time, where the kernel is generally singular in both dimensions. (This situation has not been previously investigated by researchers.) Furthermore, the compact matrix method used encompasses all special cases in a single, generalized form, which distinguishes this method from all other numerical methods. In addition, in Section 5, we use Banach's fixed point theorem to demonstrate why the solution exists and is unique in the space $\mathcal{L}_2[\omega] \times C[0,T] = \mathcal{L}_2([a,b] \times [c,d]) \times C[0,T]$ under specific conditions. Additionally, we will demonstrate in Section 6 how the unique solution converges. The error convergence will be demonstrated using one of the well-known theorems in Section 7. In Section 8, a system of nonlinear Fredholm integral equations (**SNFIEs**) in position with a time-dependent coefficient is then obtained from the **NMIE** using the separation of variables method. In Section 9, the Toeplitz matrix method (**TMM**) on an integral equation yields a nonlinear algebraic system (**NAS**). We will then use Mable 18 to present numerical results based on the kernel of the equation, which takes the logarithmic kernel, Carleman function, and Cauchy form in Section 10. Additionally, the related errors will be computed.

2. Fractional Calculus

Definitions and properties of fractional calculus theory, which will be applied throughout the article, are stated in this section.

Definition 1 ([18]). *The Riemann–Liouville fractional integral operator of order* $p \geq 0$ *with* $a \geq 0$ *is defined as*

$$I_a^p f(x) = \frac{1}{\Gamma(p)} \int_a^x (x-t)^{p-1} f(t) dt, \qquad I_a^0 f(x) = f(x), \tag{1}$$

where Γ is the gamma function.

In addition, we consider the following essential property for $n-1<\beta,\gamma\leq n, n\in\mathbb{N}$

$$\left(\left(I_a^{\gamma}I_a^{\beta}\right)h\right)(u)=\left(I_a^{\gamma+\beta}h\right)(u)=\frac{1}{\Gamma(\gamma+\beta)}\int_a^u(u-t)^{\gamma+\beta-1}h(t)dt,\quad(0<\gamma+\beta<1).\tag{2}$$

Moreover, we consider the famous integral relation

$$\int_0^t\int_0^{\tau_{n-1}}\dots\int_0^{\tau_2}\int_0^{\tau_1}h(\tau)d\tau d\tau_1\dots d\tau_{n-2}d\tau_{n-1}=\frac{1}{\Gamma(n)}\int_0^t(t-\tau)^{n-1}h(\tau)d\tau,\quad n\in\mathbb{N}.\tag{3}$$

Definition 2 ([19]). *The left- and right-sided Riemann–Liouville fractional derivative of order p; $(n-1)\leq p<n$ is*

$${}_aD_x^pf(x)=\frac{1}{\Gamma(n-p)}\frac{d^n}{dx^n}\int_a^x(x-t)^{n-p-1}f(t)dt.$$

$${}_xD_b^pf(x)=\frac{1}{\Gamma(n-p)}\left(-\frac{d}{dx}\right)^n\int_x^b(t-x)^{n-p-1}f(t)dt.$$

Definition 3 ([19]). *Caputo fractional derivative of order p; $(n-1)\leq p<n$ is defined as*

$${}_a^CD_x^pf(x)=\frac{1}{\Gamma(n-p)}\int_a^x(x-t)^{n-p-1}f^{(n)}(t)dt.$$

3. Problem Formulation and Basic Equations

Due to the importance of integral equations, with their different kinds, that can be used to simulate a wide range of problems in the basic sciences, many scientists have focused a great deal of attention on presenting the solutions to these systems. These equations have played a significant role in finding the solutions by using diverse methods, which is in line with the rapid development in finding the solutions to these problems originating from many sciences. Additionally, recent developments in fractional calculus have consequences for real-world applications in viscoelasticity, bioengineering, and biology.

Kernels offer a more general framework, allowing for non-local interactions, anomalous diffusion, and memory effects. By incorporating fractional derivatives and extended kernels, one can extend Keller–Segel models to account for more complex behaviors observed in biological systems, where interactions may occur over long distances and involve memory or non-local effects (see Columbu et al. [20]).

Here, we consider a nonlinear mixed integro-fractional differential equation (**NMI-FrDE**) in time and position in the space $\mathcal{L}_2[\omega]\times C[0,T], T<1$, under specific conditions in time.

$$\begin{gathered}\mu_0\psi(x,y;t)+\mu_1\frac{\partial^p\psi(x,y;t)}{\partial t^p}+\mu_2\frac{\partial^{p+1}\psi(x,y;t)}{\partial t^{p+1}}\\=f(x,y;t)+\lambda(t)\iint_{\omega}k(|x-\zeta|,|y-\eta|)\,\psi^{\alpha}(\zeta,\eta;t)\,d\zeta d\eta,\ 0<p<1,\end{gathered}\tag{4}$$

under the conditions

$$\psi(x,y;0)=\chi_1(x,y),\qquad\frac{\partial\psi(x,y;t)}{\partial t}\Big|_{t=0}=\chi_2(x,y),\tag{5}$$

where, for a linear type, $\alpha=1$ and for a nonlinear type, $\alpha=2,3,4,\dots N$. μ_0, μ_1 and μ_2 are constants.

The solution to Equation (4) in the linear case was discussed by the same authors in [21].

The unknown function to be found is $\psi(x,y;t)$, while the time function $\lambda(t)$ and free term $f(x,y;t)$ have been identified as known continuous functions. The kernel of position $k(|x-\zeta|,|y-\eta|)$ has several single forms, which will be discussed.

With the aid of (4), the fractional Riemann–Liouville integral (1), and relations (2), (3) will be applied to an initial value problem (4), yielding the following nonlinear mixed integral equation (**NMIE**) with a singular kernel in the position term and a continuous kernel in time

$$\begin{aligned}&\mu_2\,\psi(x,y;t)+\int_0^t\left[\frac{\mu_0\,p\,(t-s)^p}{\Gamma(p+1)}+\mu_1\right]\psi(x,y;s)\,ds\\&=\frac{1}{\Gamma(p+1)}\int_0^t\iint_\omega(t-s)^p\,\lambda(s)\;k(|x-\zeta|,|y-\eta|)\;\psi^\alpha(\zeta,\eta;s)\,d\zeta d\eta\,ds+F(x,y;t),\end{aligned}\tag{6}$$

where

$$F(x,y;t)=\frac{1}{\Gamma(p+1)}\int_0^t(t-\tau)^p f(x,y;\tau)d\tau+\mu_1\chi_1(x,y)+\mu_2\chi_2(x,y).\frac{t^p}{\Gamma(p+1)}.\tag{7}$$

Equation (6) will obviously meet the initial condition $\psi(x,y;0)=\chi_1(x,y)$ for $t=0$. Furthermore, this integral Equation (6) is equivalent to the **NMI-FrDE** (4) under consideration.

4. Special Cases from the Mixed Nonlinear Integral Equation and Its Extended Kernel

Equation (4) and the related one (6) are general formulas that include a variety of problems due to their form and kernel. These cases can be summarized as follows:

(I) Many special and new cases can be derived from NMI-FrDE

- If in Equation (4), we consider $\frac{\mu_1}{\mu_0}=\frac{q^p}{\Gamma(p+1)},\ \frac{\mu_2}{\mu_0}=\frac{q^{p+1}}{\Gamma(p+2)}$, after using the second order of Taylor expansion, we have the following equation

$$\psi(x,y;t+q)=f(x,y;t)+\lambda(t)\iint_\omega k(|x-\zeta|,|y-\eta|)\psi^\alpha(\zeta,\eta;t)d\zeta d\eta,\ \alpha=1,2,\ldots,N.\tag{8}$$

Formula (8) represents a nonlinear phase-lag mixed integral equation in (2+1) dimension.

The problem of phase delay in physical and engineering sciences, especially in nonlinear thermoelastic materials, plays an important role in establishing the important properties of these materials before using them. Therefore, studying this type of problem gives researchers a great benefit over the ionic bonds of these materials with each other.

Moreover, in (8), letting $\alpha=1$, we have the linear phase-lag mixed integral equation,

$$\psi(x,y;t+q)=f(x,y;t)+\lambda(t)\iint_\omega k(|x-\zeta|,|y-\eta|)\psi(\zeta,\eta;t)\,d\zeta d\eta.\tag{9}$$

The same equivalent equation to (9) is considered by the authors in [21].

- If in Equation (6) $\alpha=1$, we have the MI-FrDE in the form

$$\begin{aligned}&\mu_2\psi(x,y;t)+\int_0^t\left[\frac{\mu_0 p(t-s)^p}{\Gamma(p+1)}+\mu_1\right]\psi(x,y;s)\,ds\\&=\frac{1}{\Gamma(p+1)}\int_0^t(t-s)^p\lambda(s)\iint_\omega k(|x-\zeta|,|y-\eta|)\psi(\zeta,\eta;s)\,d\zeta d\eta\,ds+F(x,y;t).\end{aligned}$$

- If in Equation (6), $\mu_1=\mu_0=0$, and $\alpha=1,2,\ldots,N$, we have an NFIE of the second kind

$$\mu_2\psi(x,y;t)=\frac{1}{\Gamma(p+1)}\int_0^t (t-s)^p\lambda(s)\iint\limits_{\omega} k(|x-\zeta|,|y-\eta|)\psi^{\alpha}(\zeta,\eta;s)\,d\zeta d\eta\,ds+F(x,y;t),$$

where $F(x,y;t)$ in the last two cases is as in relation (7).

- If in Equation (6), $\mu_2=0$, we have the following first kind mixed integral equation

$$\int_0^t\left[\frac{\mu_0 p(t-s)^p}{\Gamma(p+1)}+\mu_1\right]\psi(x,y;s)\,ds$$
$$=\frac{1}{\Gamma(p+1)}\left[\int_0^t (t-s)^p\lambda(s)\iint\limits_{\omega} k(|x-\zeta|,|y-\eta|)\psi^{\alpha}(\zeta,\eta;s)\,d\zeta d\eta\,ds+\int_0^t (t-\tau)^p f(x,y;\tau)d\tau\right].$$

(II) Special cases from the kernel:

(II-1) we can consider the weak singular kernel from the general form as
Logarithmic kernel: $k(|x-\zeta|,|y-\eta|)=ln(|x-\zeta|)ln(|y-\eta|)$,
Carleman kernel: $k(|x-\zeta|,|y-\eta|)=|x-\zeta|^{-\alpha}|y-\eta|^{-\beta}, 0\le\alpha,\beta<1$,
Logarithmic and Carleman kernel: $k(|x-\zeta|,|y-\eta|)=ln(|x-\zeta|)|y-\eta|^{-\beta}$.
(II-2) Cauchy singular kernel: $k(|x-\zeta|,|y-\eta|)=\frac{1}{(|x-\zeta|)(|y-\eta|)}$,
Cauchy–logarithmic kernel: $k(|x-\zeta|,|y-\eta|)=\frac{ln(|y-\eta|)}{(|x-\zeta|)}$,
(f) Cauchy–Carleman kernel : $k(|x-\zeta|,|y-\eta|)=\frac{ln(|y-\eta|)}{(|x-\zeta|)}$.
(II-3) Strong singular kernel: $k(|x-\zeta|,|y-\eta|)=\frac{1}{(|x-\zeta|)^2(|y-\eta|)^2}$.
(II-4) Super-strong singular kernel: $k(|x-\zeta|,|y-\eta|)=\frac{1}{(|x-\zeta|)^{n}(|y-\eta|)^{m}}$, $(2<n, m\le N,M)$.

5. Existence of a Unique Solution of the Integro-Fractional Differential Equation

For this aim, we assume the following conditions:

(i) The kernel of position $k(|x-\zeta|,\ |y-\eta|)$ satisfies the discontinuity conditions in the space $\mathcal{L}_2([a,b]\times[c,d])$

$$\left\{\int_c^d\int_c^d\left\{\int_a^b\int_a^b k^2(|x-\zeta|,|y-\eta|)dxd\zeta\right\}dyd\eta\right\}^{\frac{1}{2}}\le\mathcal{M},\qquad(\mathcal{M}\text{ is aconstant})$$

(ii) The kernel $(t-s)^p\forall t,\ s\in[0,T],\ 0\le s\le t\le T<1$, satisfies for a continuous function $\lambda(t),\ |\lambda(t)|\le\xi$, the following integrals are continuous functions of t

$$\max_{0\le s\le T}\int_0^t (t-s)^p ds,\quad \int_{\tau_1}^{\tau_2}(t-s)^p\lambda(s)ds,\quad \int_0^t (t-s)^p\lambda(s)ds.$$

Consequently, we have

$$\left|\int_0^t (t-s)^p\lambda(s)ds\right|\le\frac{T^{p+1}\xi}{\Gamma(p+1)}, p\ne-1.$$

(iii) The norm of the function $F(x,y;t)$ in Equation (7) is defined as

$$\begin{aligned}\|F(x,y;t)\|&\le\left\|\frac{1}{\Gamma(p+1)}\int_0^t (t-\tau)^p f(x,y;\tau)d\tau+\left[\mu_1\,\chi_1(x,y)+\mu_2\,\chi_2(x,y)\frac{t^p}{\Gamma(p+1)}\right]\right\|\\&\le\frac{T^{p+1}\mathrm{f}}{\Gamma(p+2)}+\left[|\mu_1|\|\chi_1(x,y)\|+|\mu_2|\|\chi_2(x,y)\|\frac{|T^p|}{\Gamma(p+1)}\right]=Q,\end{aligned}\tag{10}$$

where $|f|\le\mathrm{f}.Q$ and f are constants.

(iv) The known function $\psi^{\alpha}(x,y;t)$, for the constant $\varepsilon > \max\{\varepsilon_1, \varepsilon_2\}$, satisfies

$$(iv-1)\quad |\psi^{\alpha}(x,y;t)| \le A_1(x,y;t)|\psi(x,y;t)| \le \varepsilon_1|\psi(x,y;t)| \le \varepsilon|\psi(x,y;t)|,$$

$$\varepsilon_1 = \max_{0\le s\le T}\int_0^t \left(\int_c^d\int_a^b A_1^2(x,y;s)\,dxdy\right)^{\frac{1}{2}} ds,$$

$$(iv-2)\quad |\psi_1^{\alpha}(x,y;t) - \psi_2^{\alpha}(x,y;t)| \le A_2(x,y;t)|\psi_1(x,y;t) - \psi_2(x,y;t)|$$
$$\le \varepsilon_2|\psi_1(x,y;t) - \psi_2(x,y;t)| \le \varepsilon|\psi_1(x,y;t) - \psi_2(x,y;t)|,$$

$$\varepsilon_2 = \max_{0\le s\le t}\int_0^t \left(\int_c^d\int_a^b A_2^2(x,y;s)\,dxdy\right)^{\frac{1}{2}} ds,$$

where $A_1(x,y;t)$, $A_2(x,y;t)$ are continuous functions in the domain of integration.

(v) The norm of any function $h(x,y;t)$ in $\mathcal{L}_2([a,b]\times[c,d])\times C[0,T]-$ space is defined as

$$\| h(x,y;t) \| = \max_{0\le t\le T}\left\{\int_0^t \left\{\int_c^d\int_a^b h^2(x,y;s)dxdy\right\}^{\frac{1}{2}} ds\right\}.$$

To discuss the analytic fundamentals of the NMIE (6), we write it in the integral operator form

$$\overline{W}\psi(x,y;t) = \frac{1}{\mu_2}[F(x,y;t) + W_1\psi(x,y;t) + W_2\psi(x,y;t)], \tag{11}$$

where

$$W_1\psi(x,y;t) = \frac{1}{\Gamma(p+1)}\int_0^t (t-s)^p\lambda(s)\int_c^d\int_a^b k(|x-\zeta|,|y-\eta|)\psi^m(\,|\zeta,\eta;s)\,d\zeta d\eta\,ds, \tag{12}$$

$$W_2\psi(x,y;t) = -\int_0^t \left[\frac{\mu_0 p(t-s)^p}{\Gamma(p+1)} + \mu_1\right]\psi(x,y;s)\,ds. \tag{13}$$

In our study of the existence of a unique solution using the fixed-point theory or the study of the convergence of the solution as well as studying the convergence of the error, the researcher must prove that the basic integral operator in Equation (11) is finite and continuous. Therefore, it should be formulated as follows.

Lemma 1. *The boundedness: Under the conditions (i)–(iv), the integral operators $W_1\psi(x,y;t)$ and $W_2\psi(x,y;t)$ are bounded. Accordingly, $\overline{W}\psi(x,y;t)$ is also bounded. Moreover, the integral operator $\overline{W}\psi(x,y;t)$ maps $\mathcal{L}_2([a,b]\times[c,d])\times C[0,T]$—space into itself.*

Proof. Using the relation's norm (12), and then applying the assumptions (i)–(iv-1) with Cauchy–Schwartz inequality, we obtain

$$\|W_1\psi(x,y;t)\| = \| \tfrac{1}{\Gamma(p+1)}\int_0^t (t-s)^p\,\lambda(s)\int_c^d\int_a^b k(|x-\zeta|,|y-\eta|)\psi^{\alpha}(\zeta,\eta;s)\,d\zeta d\eta\,ds \|$$
$$\le \tfrac{1}{\Gamma(p+1)}\left\|\left(\max_{0\le s\le t}\int_0^t (t-s)^p ds\right)|\lambda(t)|\left(\left\{\int_c^d\int_c^d\left\{\int_a^b\int_a^b k^2(|x-\zeta|,|y-\eta|)dxd\zeta\right\}dyd\eta\right\}^{\frac{1}{2}}\right)|\psi^{\alpha}(x,y;t)|\right\|$$
$$\le \tfrac{\xi M T^{p+1}\varepsilon}{\Gamma(p+2)}\left(\max_{0\le s\le t}\left\{\int_0^t\left\{\int_c^d\int_a^b \psi^2(x,y;s)dxdy\right\}^{\frac{1}{2}} ds\right\}\right) \le \tfrac{\xi M T^{p+1}\varepsilon}{\Gamma(p+2)} \| \psi(x,y;t) \| = \boldsymbol{\rho_1} \| \psi(x,y;t) \|.$$

However,

$$\| W_2\psi(x,y;t) \| = \| \int_0^t \left[\frac{\mu_0\, p(t-s)^p}{\Gamma(p+1)} + \mu_1\right]\psi(x,y;s)\,ds \| \le \left[\frac{\mu_0\, pT^{p+1}}{\Gamma(p+2)} + \mu_1 T\right]\|\psi(x,y;t)\| = \boldsymbol{\rho_2} \| \psi(x,y;t) \|$$

where $\rho_1 = \frac{\xi\,\mathcal{M}\,T^{p+1}\varepsilon}{\Gamma(p+2)}$, and $\rho_2 = \frac{\mu_0\,pT^{p+1}}{\Gamma(p+2)} + \mu_1 T$.

Therefore, use (11), with the aid of (10) to get

$$\|\ \overline{W}\Psi(x,y;t)\ \| \le \frac{1}{|\mu_2|}[Q + \rho\|\psi(x,y;t)\|], \qquad \rho = \frac{\rho_1+\rho_2}{|\mu_2|}.\ (\mu_2 \neq 0) \tag{14}$$

Inequality (14) indicates that the ball S_r is mapped into itself by the operator $\overline{W}$, where $r = \left\{\frac{Q}{\mu_2-\rho}\right\}$,

Thus, the radius of the boundedness of convergent is

$$\rho = \frac{\mathbf{1}}{|\mu_2|}\left[\frac{(\xi\,\mathcal{M}\,\varepsilon + \mu_0\,p)T^{p+1}}{\Gamma(p+2)} + \mu_1 T\right] < 1. \tag{15}$$

□

Lemma 2. *The integral operator (11) is continuous under the conditions (i)–(iv).*

Proof. Using conditions (i)–(iv), the integral operator (11) for the two functions $\psi_1(x,y;s)$ and $\psi_2(x,y;s)$ in the space $\mathcal{L}_2([a,b]\times[c,d])\times C[0,T]$ leads to

$$\begin{aligned}
&\|(\overline{W}\psi_1 - \overline{W}\psi_2)(x,y;t)\| \le \Big\|-\tfrac{1}{\mu_2}\textstyle\int_0^t \left[\frac{\mu_0\,p(t-s)^p}{\Gamma(p+1)} + \mu_1\right](\psi_1-\psi_2)(x,y;s)\,ds \\
&+\tfrac{1}{\mu_2\Gamma(p+1)}\textstyle\int_0^t (t-s)^p\lambda(s)\int_c^d\int_a^b k(|x-\zeta|,|y-\eta|)(\psi_1^\alpha-\psi_2^\alpha)(\zeta,\eta;s)\,d\zeta d\eta\,ds\Big\| \\
&\le \left|\tfrac{1}{\mu_2}\right|\Big\|\textstyle\int_0^t \left[\frac{\mu_0 p(t-s)^p}{\Gamma(p+1)} + \mu_1\right](\psi_1-\psi_2)(x,y;s)\,ds\Big\| \\
&+\left|\tfrac{1}{\mu_2\Gamma(\alpha+1)}\right|\Big\|\textstyle\int_0^t (t-s)^p\lambda(s)\int_c^d\int_a^b k(|x-\zeta|,|y-\eta|)(\psi_1^\alpha-\psi_2^\alpha)(\zeta,\eta;s)\,d\zeta d\eta\,ds\Big\| \\
&\quad\le \left|\tfrac{1}{\mu_2}\right|\left(\tfrac{(\xi\,\mathcal{M}\,\varepsilon+\mu_0\,p)T^{p+1}}{\Gamma(p+2)} + \mu_1 T\right)\|\psi_1(x,y;t)-\psi_2(x,y;t)\|,
\end{aligned}$$

which can be simplified as follows:

$$\|(\overline{W}\psi_1 - \overline{W}\psi_2)(x,y;t)\| \le \rho\ \|\psi_1(x,y;t)-\psi_2(x,y;t)\|. \tag{16}$$

□

Operator (11) is a continuous and bounded integral operator. Furthermore, operator (11) is a contraction mapping under the inequality (15). There, we can state the following:

Theorem 1. *The mixed integral Equation (6), with the aid of a Banach fixed point theorem, has a unique solution, under the condition (15).*

Proof. The proof of the theorem is directly obtained after applying Lemma 1 and Lemma 2. □

6. Stability of a General Solution

Lemma 3. *Under the conditions (i)–(iv), the infinite series $\sum_{i=0}^{\infty}\Psi_i(x,y;t)$ is uniformly convergent to a continuous solution function $\Psi(x,y;t)$.*

Proof. For this, construct the sequence of functions $\Psi(x,y;t) = \{\Psi_0, \Psi_1, \ldots, \Psi_{n-1}, \Psi_n, \ldots\} = \{\Psi_i\}_{i=0}^{\infty}$, then pick up two functions $\{\Psi_{n-1}, \Psi_n\}$ such that

$$\begin{aligned}
&\mu_2\Psi_n(x,y;t) + \textstyle\int_0^t \left[\frac{\mu_0\, p(t-s)^p}{\Gamma(p+1)} + \mu_1\right] \Psi_{n-1}(x,y;s)\, ds \\
&= \tfrac{1}{\Gamma(p+1)} \textstyle\int_0^t (t-s)^p \lambda(s) \int_c^d \int_a^b k(|x-\zeta|,|y-\eta|) \Psi_{n-1}^{\alpha}(\zeta,\eta;s)\, d\zeta d\eta\, ds + F(x,y;t), \\
&\mu_2\Psi_{n-1}(x,y;t) + \textstyle\int_0^t \left[\frac{\mu_0\, p(t-s)^p}{\Gamma(p+1)} + \mu_1\right] \Psi_{n-2}(x,y;s)\, ds \\
&= \tfrac{1}{\Gamma(p+1)} \textstyle\int_0^t (t-s)^p\, \lambda(s) \int_c^d \int_a^b k(|x-\zeta|,|y-\eta|)\, \Psi_{n-2}^{\alpha}(\zeta,\eta;s)\, d\zeta d\eta\, ds + F(x,y;t).
\end{aligned}$$

Hence, from the above we have

$$\mu_2(\Psi_n(x,y;t) - \Psi_{n-1}(x,y;t)) + \int_0^t \left[\frac{\mu_0\, p(t-s)^p}{\Gamma(p+1)} + \mu_1\right] (\Psi_{n-1}(x,y;s) - \Psi_{n-2}(x,y;s))\, ds$$

$$= \frac{1}{\Gamma(p+1)} \int_0^t (t-s)^p\, \lambda(s) \int_c^d \int_a^b k(|x-\zeta|,|y-\eta|)(\Psi_{n-1}^{\alpha}(\zeta,\eta;s) - \Psi_{n-2}^{\alpha}(\zeta,\eta;s))\, d\zeta d\eta\, ds.$$

Taking the norm, and applying conditions (i), (ii), and (iv), we follow

$$\begin{aligned}
\|\mu_2(\Psi_n(x,y;t) - \Psi_{n-1}(x,y;t))\| \leq \Big\| &\textstyle\int_0^t \left[\frac{\mu_0\, p(t-s)^p}{\Gamma(p+1)} + \mu_1\right] (\Psi_{n-1}(x,y;s) - \Psi_{n-2}(x,y;s))\, ds + \\
&\tfrac{1}{\Gamma(p+1)} \textstyle\int_0^t (t-s)^p\, \lambda(s) \int_c^d \int_a^b k(|x-\zeta|,|y-\eta|)\, (\Psi_{n-1}^{\alpha}(\zeta,\eta;s) - \Psi_{n-2}^{\alpha}(\zeta,\eta;s))\, d\zeta d\eta\, ds \Big\|.
\end{aligned}$$

Finally, we get

$$\|\, \Psi_n(x,y;t) - \Psi_{n-1}(x,y;t)\, \| \leq \rho\, \|\Psi_{n-1}(x,y;t) - \Psi_{n-2}(x,y;t)\|. \tag{17}$$

Now, assume

$$\Phi_n(x,y;t) = \Psi_n(x,y;t) - \Psi_{n-1}(x,y;t),$$

hence, we have

$$\Phi_0(x,y;t) = \Psi_0(x,y;t) = \frac{F(x,y;t)}{\mu_2}, \qquad \Psi_n(x,y;t) = \sum_{i=0}^{n} \Phi_i(x,y;t), \tag{18}$$

using the results of Equation (18) in inequality (17), we have

$$\|\, \Phi_n(x,y;t)\, \| \leq \frac{1}{|\mu_2|} \left[\frac{(\xi\, \mathcal{M}\, \varepsilon + \mu_0\, p) T^{p+1}}{\Gamma(p+2)} + \mu_1 T\right] \|\, \Phi_{n-1}(x,y;t)\, \| = \rho \|\, \Phi_{n-1}(x,y;t)\, \|.$$

Letting $n = 1$, we have

$$\|\, \Phi_1(x,y;t)\, \| \leq \frac{1}{|\mu_2|} \left[\frac{(\xi\, \mathcal{M}\, \varepsilon + \mu_0 p) T^{p+1}}{\Gamma(p+2)} + \mu_1 T\right] Q = \rho\, Q.$$

By induction, we have

$$\|\Psi_n(x,y;t)\| \leq Q\, \rho^n, \qquad \rho = \frac{1}{|\mu_2|} \left[\frac{(\xi\, \mathcal{M}\, \varepsilon + \mu_0 p)\, T^{p+1}}{\Gamma(p+2)} + \mu_1 T\right] < 1. \tag{19}$$

As we know

$$\Psi(x,y;t) = \lim_{n \to \infty} \Psi_n(x,y;t) = \sum_{i=0}^{\infty} \Phi_i(x,y;t).$$

Given that $Q > 0$ and ρ^n decrease as n increases. Hence, $\Psi_n(x,y;t)$ is a decreasing function. □

7. The Error Stability

When looking at approximate solutions in general, and using computer programs to determine the results, the basic idea must be understood; that is, the error in the calculation program. The behavioral matching between the error function and the unknown function must also be taken into consideration. The graph in applications will show that the two functions have the same convergence behavior.

Assume that there is a function $F_n(x,y;t)$ for $\psi_n(x,y;t)$, which is an approximate solution to Equation (6), in order to illustrate the convergence of the error. Consequently, we have:

$$\begin{aligned}&\mu_2\psi_n(x,y;t)+\int_0^t\left[\frac{\mu_0\,p(t-s)^p}{\Gamma(p+1)}+\mu_1\right]\psi_n(x,y;s)\,ds\\&=\frac{1}{\Gamma(p+1)}\int_0^t(t-s)^p\,\lambda(s)\iint_\omega k(|x-\zeta|,|y-\eta|)\,\psi_n^{\alpha}(\zeta,\eta;s)\,d\zeta d\eta\,ds+F_n(x,y;t).\end{aligned}\tag{20}$$

Hence, from (6) and (20) we have

$$\begin{aligned}R_n(x,y;t)&=\frac{\varepsilon}{\mu_2\Gamma(p+1)}\int_0^t(t-s)^p\,\lambda(s)\iint_\omega k(|x-\zeta|,|y-\eta|)\,R_n(\zeta,\eta;s)\,d\zeta d\eta\,ds\\&-\frac{1}{\mu_2}\int_0^t\left[\frac{\mu_0\,p(t-s)^p}{\Gamma(p+1)}+\mu_1\right]R_n(x,y;s)\,ds+\frac{1}{\mu_2}\varphi_n(x,y;t),(p\neq-1,\mu_2\neq0),\end{aligned}\tag{21}$$

where

$$R_n(x,y;t)=\psi(x,y;t)-\psi_n(x,y;t),\qquad\varphi_n(x,y;t)=F(x,y;t)-F_n(x,y;t).\tag{22}$$

To discuss the error's convergence, we perform the following: It is necessary to create the error equation sequence $\{(ER_n)_i(x,y;t)\}_{i=0}^{\infty}$. Next, the error functions $\{(R_n)_i(x,y;t),(R_n)_{i-1}(x,y;t)\}$ are picked up so that they match Equation (21). Thus, we have

$$\begin{aligned}(ER_n)_i(x,y;t)&=\frac{1}{\mu_2}\varphi_n(x,y;t)-\frac{1}{\mu_2}\int_0^t\left[\frac{\mu_0\,p(t-s)^p}{\Gamma(p+1)}+\mu_1\right](ER_n)_{i-1}(x,y;s)\,ds+\\&\frac{\varepsilon}{\mu_2\Gamma(p+1)}\int_0^t(t-s)^p\lambda(s)\iint_\omega k(|x-\zeta|,|y-\eta|)\,(ER_n)_{i-1}(\zeta,\eta;s)\,d\zeta d\eta\,ds,\end{aligned}\tag{23}$$

whereas

$$(ER_n)_i(x,y;t)=(R_n)_i(x,y;t)-(R_n)_{i-1}(x,y;t);(ER_n)_0(x,y;t)=\frac{1}{\mu_2}\varphi_n(x,y;t),$$

and

$$(R_n)_i(x,y;t)=\sum_{j=0}^{i}(ER_n)_j(x,y;t).\tag{24}$$

With the same time and position kernels, it is clear that the error relates to the same integral equation concept. Under the same assumptions of Theorem 1, we may discuss the error's convergence and uniqueness of the error as the following.

Lemma 4. *Considering conditions (i)–(iv), the infinite series $\sum_{i=0}^{\infty}(ER_n)_i(x,y;t)$, converges uniformly to R_n.*

Proof. Using Equation (23), taking the norm of both sides and following the same way of Lemma 3, we have

$$\|(ER_n)_i(x,y;t)\|\leq\rho\|(ER_n)_{i-1}(x,y;t)\|,\qquad\rho=\frac{T}{|\mu_2|}\left[\frac{(\xi\,\mathcal{M}\,\varepsilon+\mu_0p)T^p}{\Gamma(p+2)}+\mu_1\right].$$

By induction, we obtain

$$\|(ER_n)_i(x,y;t)\| \le \rho^i \frac{T^{p+1}\|f(x,y,t) - f_i(x,y,t)\|}{|\mu_2|\Gamma(p+2)}, \tag{25}$$

taking the sum for $i = 0 \to \infty$, we get

$$\sum_{i=0}^{\infty}\|(ER_n)_i(x,y;t)\| \le \frac{T^{p+1}\|f(x,y,t) - f_i(x,y,t)\|}{|\mu_2|\Gamma(p+2)}\sum_{i=0}^{\infty}\rho^i.$$

Finally, we have

$$\|R_n(x,y;t)\| \le (1-\rho)^{-1}\frac{T^{p+1}\|f(x,y,t) - f_i(x,y,t)\|}{|\mu_2|\Gamma(p+2)}, \tag{26}$$

which establishes the convergence of the error under the constraint $0 < \rho < 1$. □

Lemma 5. *As $n \to \infty$, the error $R_\infty(x,y;t) \to 0$.*

Proof. From inequality (26), since $f(x,y;t) = f_\infty(u,v;t)$, then the error $\|R_n(x,y;t)\| \to 0$ as $n \to \infty$. This led us to conclude that the error $R_n(x,y;t)$ Equation (26) has a unique representation.

Another way to prove the error's unique representation is to write the error equation in the integral operator form. And then to prove this integral operator is bounded and maps the space of integration $\mathcal{L}_2([a,b] \times [c,d]) \times C[0,T]$ into itself. In addition, we must prove that the integral operator is continuous and contraction-mapping. □

8. Technique of Separation of Variables

The separation of variables approach is straightforward, easy to understand, easy to solve, and simple and effective. It is an idea that the dependent variable is stated in the separable form as a multiple independent function of the independent variables. Many authors were able to approximate the unknown function of integral equations using the separation of variables approach for handling the mixed integral equation solution at a certain time.

For this, assume the following forms for the known function and the unknown function, respectively,

$$\psi(x,y;t) = \phi(x,y)\Upsilon(t)\,, F(x,y;t) = g(x,y)\Upsilon(t),\ \Upsilon(0) \ne 0, \tag{27}$$

where $T(t)$ is the known time function.

Using (27) in NMIE (6), we have

$$\begin{aligned}\phi(x,y)\Big\{\mu_2\Upsilon(t) + \textstyle\int_0^t \Big[\frac{\mu_0\, p(t-s)^p}{\Gamma(p+1)} + \mu_1\Big]\Upsilon(s)\,ds\Big\} &= \tfrac{1}{\Gamma(p+1)}\textstyle\int_0^t (t-s)^p\,\lambda(s)\Upsilon^\alpha(s)ds \\ \times \textstyle\int_c^d\int_a^b k(|x-\zeta|,|y-\eta|)\,\phi^\alpha(\zeta,\eta)\,d\zeta d\eta &+ g(x,y)\Upsilon(t),\end{aligned} \tag{28}$$

the above formula can be adapted in the form

$$\phi(x,y) = \frac{\gamma_2(t,p)}{\gamma_1(t,p)}\int_c^d\int_a^b k(|x-\zeta|,|y-\eta|)\,\phi^\alpha(\zeta,\eta)\,d\zeta d\eta + \frac{1}{\gamma_1(t,p)}g(x,y), \tag{29}$$

where

$$\gamma_1(t,p) = 1 + \frac{1}{\mu_2\Upsilon(t)}\int_0^t \left[\frac{\mu_0\,(t-s)^p}{\Gamma(p)} + \mu_1\right]\Upsilon(s)\,ds,$$

$$\gamma_2(t,p) = \frac{1}{\mu_2 \Gamma(p+1)\Upsilon(t)} \int_0^t (t-s)^p \, \lambda(s) \Upsilon^{\alpha}(s) \, ds. \tag{30}$$

Formula (29) represents a nonlinear Fredholm integral equation (NFIE), in two dimensions with respect to position, with coefficients depending on time and the fractional order.

9. The Toeplitz Matrix Method

The Toeplitz matrix approach for obtaining the numerical solution to the NFIE with a singular kernel is covered in this section. The goal of this approach is to produce a system of algebraic nonlinear equations that are easily solved. The Toeplitz matrix and a matrix with zero elements other than the first and end columns are the two matrices that make up the coefficient matrix.

After letting $h_1 = \frac{b-a}{N}, h_2 = \frac{d-c}{M}$, in Equation (29), the integral term will take the form

$$\begin{aligned} &\int_c^d \int_a^b k(|x-\zeta|, |y-\eta|) \, \phi^{\alpha}(\zeta,\eta) \, d\zeta d\eta \\ &= \sum_{m=-M}^{M-1} \sum_{n=-N}^{N-1} \int_{mh_2}^{mh_2+h_2} \int_{nh_1}^{nh_1+h_1} k(|x-\zeta|, |y-\eta|) \, \phi^{\alpha}(\zeta,\eta) \, d\zeta d\eta. \end{aligned} \tag{31}$$

Then, approximate the integral in the right-hand side of (31) by

$$\begin{aligned} &\int_{mh_2}^{mh_2+h_2} \int_{nh_1}^{nh_1+h_1} k(|x-\zeta|, |y-\eta|) \, \phi^{\alpha}(\zeta,\eta) \, d\zeta d\eta = \mho(x,y)\phi^{\alpha}(nh_1, mh_2) + \overline{\mho}(x,y) \\ &\times \phi^{\alpha}(nh_1, (m+1)h_2) + \hat{\mho}(x,y)\phi^{\alpha}((n+1)h_1, mh_2) + \tilde{\mho}(x,y)\phi^{\alpha}((n+1)h_1, (m+1)h_2) + R, \end{aligned} \tag{32}$$

where R is the estimate error; the weights of the integration $\mho, \overline{\mho}, \hat{\mho}$, and $\tilde{\mho}$ are continuous functions and will be determined. Using the principal idea of the Toeplitz matrix method, by assuming in (32), $\phi(x,y) = 1, x, y, xy$ respectively, in this case $R = 0$, hence, we have four formulas

$$\begin{aligned} I_1(x) &= \int_{mh_2}^{mh_2+h_2} \int_{nh_1}^{nh_1+h_1} k(|x-\zeta|, |y-\eta|) \, d\zeta d\eta = \mho + \overline{\mho} + \hat{\mho} + \tilde{\mho}, \\ I_2(x) &= \int_{mh_2}^{mh_2+h_2} \int_{nh_1}^{nh_1+h_1} \zeta^{\alpha} k(|x-\zeta|, |y-\eta|) \, d\zeta d\eta = (nh_1)^{\alpha} (\mho + \overline{\mho}) + (nh_1+h_1)^{\alpha} \left(\hat{\mho} + \tilde{\mho}\right), \\ I_3(x) &= \int_{mh_2}^{mh_2+h_2} \int_{nh_1}^{nh_1+h_1} \eta^{\alpha} k(|x-\zeta|, |y-\eta|) \, d\zeta d\eta = (mh_2)^{\alpha} (\mho + \hat{\mho}) + (mh_2+h_2)^{\alpha} \left(\overline{\mho} + \tilde{\mho}\right), \\ I_4(x) &= \int_{mh_2}^{mh_2+h_2} \int_{nh_1}^{nh_1+h_1} \zeta^{\alpha} \, \eta^{\alpha} k(|x-\zeta|, |y-\eta|) \, d\zeta d\eta = [nh_1 mh_2]^{\alpha} \mho \\ &\quad + [nh_1(m+1)h_2]^{\alpha} \overline{\mho} + [mh_2(n+1)h_1]^{\alpha} \hat{\mho} + [(n+1)h_1(m+1)h_2]^{\alpha} \tilde{\mho}. \end{aligned} \tag{33}$$

Now, by evaluating integrals, it is simple to compute weights $\mho, \overline{\mho}, \hat{\mho}$, and $\tilde{\mho}$ immediately

$$\mho(x,y) = \frac{(m^{\alpha} n^{\alpha} + n^{\alpha} + m^{\alpha} + 1) h_1^{\alpha} \, h_2^{\alpha} \, I_1 - (m^{\alpha}+1) \, h_2^{\alpha} \, I_2 - (n^{\alpha}+1) h_1^{\alpha} \, I_3 + I_4}{h_1^{\alpha} \, h_2^{\alpha}},$$

$$\overline{\mho}(x,y) = \frac{-(n^{\alpha}+1) m^{\alpha} h_1^{\alpha} \, h_2^{\alpha} \, I_1 + m^{\alpha} \, h_2^{\alpha} \, I_2 + (n^{\alpha}+1) h_1^{\alpha} I_3 - I_4}{h_1^{\alpha} \, h_2^{\alpha}},$$

$$\hat{\mho}(x,y) = \frac{-(m^{\alpha}+1) n^{\alpha} h_1^{\alpha} \, h_2^{\alpha} \, I_1 + (m^{\alpha}+1) \, h_2^{\alpha} \, I_2 + n^{\alpha} h_1^{\alpha} \, I_3 - I_4}{h_1^{\alpha} \, h_2^{\alpha}},$$

and

$$\tilde{\mho}(x,y) = \frac{m^{\alpha} n^{\alpha} h_1^{\alpha} \, h_2^{\alpha} \, I_1 - m^{\alpha} h_2^{\alpha} \, I_2 - n^{\alpha} \, h_1^{\alpha} \, I_3 + I_4}{h_1^{\alpha} \, h_2^{\alpha}}. \tag{34}$$

Integral Equation (32), after putting $x = m\,h$, becomes

$$\int_c^d \int_a^b k(|x-\zeta|,|y-\eta|)\psi^{\alpha}(\zeta,\eta)\,d\zeta d\eta = \sum_{m=-M}^{M}\sum_{n=-N}^{N} \Upsilon_{N,n;M,m}\,\psi^{\alpha}(nh_1, mh_2),$$

where

$$\Upsilon_{N,n;M,m} = \begin{cases} \mho_{n,m} + \overline{\mho}_{n,m-1} & , \quad n=-N \\ \mho_{n,m} + \hat{\mho}_{n-1,m} & , \quad m=-M \\ \mho_{n,m} + \overline{\mho}_{n,m-1} + \hat{\mho}_{n-1,m} + \tilde{\mho}_{n-1,m-1} & , \quad -N<n<N, -M<m<M \\ \overline{\mho}_{n,m-1} + \tilde{\mho}_{n-1,m-1} & , \quad m=M \\ \hat{\mho}_{n-1,m} + \tilde{\mho}_{n-1,m-1} & , \quad n=N. \end{cases} \tag{35}$$

Hence, Equation (29), will be

$$\phi(ih_1, jh_2) = \tfrac{\gamma_2(t,p)}{\gamma_1(t,p)} \sum_{m=-M}^{M}\sum_{n=-N}^{N} \Upsilon_{N,n;M,m}\,\phi^{\alpha}(nh_1, mh_2) + \tfrac{1}{\gamma_1(t,p)} g(ih_1, jh_2), \\ -N \le i \le N, -M \le j \le M. \tag{36}$$

Formula (36) represents a nonlinear system of algebraic equations, where ϕ is a matrix of $(2N+1)\times(2M+1)$ elements, while $\Upsilon_{N,n;M,m}$ elements are given by

$$\Upsilon_{N,n;M,m} = Z^{i,j}_{n,m} - V^{i,j}_{n,m} \tag{37}$$

where

$$Z^{i,j}_{n,m} = \mho_{n,m} + \overline{\mho}_{n,m-1} + \hat{\mho}_{n-1,m} + \tilde{\mho}_{n-1,m-1}\ , \qquad -N \le n \le N, -M \le m \le M, \tag{38}$$

and

$$V^{i,j}_{n,m} = \begin{cases} \overline{\mho}_{n,m-1} + \hat{\mho}_{n-1,m} + \tilde{\mho}_{n-1,m-1} & , \quad n=-N,\ m=-M \\ \hat{\mho}_{n-1,m} + \tilde{\mho}_{n-1,m-1} & , \quad n=-N,\ m\neq -M \\ \overline{\mho}_{n,m-1} + \tilde{\mho}_{n-1,m-1} & , \quad m=-M,\ n\neq -N \\ 0 & , \quad -N<n<N, -M<m<M \\ \mho_{n-1,m} + \hat{\mho}_{n-1,m-1} & , \quad m=M, \quad n\neq N \\ \mho_{n-1,m} + \overline{\mho}_{n,m-1} & , \quad n=N, \quad m\neq M \\ \mho_{n-1,m} + \overline{\mho}_{n,m-1} + \hat{\mho}_{n-1,m-1} & , \quad n=N,\ m=M, \end{cases} \tag{39}$$

here, $Z^{i,j}_{n,m}$ is the Toeplitz matrix, whereas $V^{i,j}_{n,m}$ is a zero matrix except the first and last rows and columns. Both matrices are of order $(2N+1)\times(2M+1)$.

Hence, the system (35) will be reduced to the matrices form

$$\Phi = \frac{\gamma_2(t,p)}{\gamma_1(t,p)}(Z+V)\,\Phi^{\alpha} + \frac{1}{\gamma_1(t,p)}G\,. \tag{40}$$

The nonlinear system (40) can be solved easily by Newton's method, Broyden's method, and the finite difference method.

The error term R is determined from Equation (32) by letting $\Phi(x,y)=(x.y)^2$ to get

$$\begin{aligned}R=\Bigg|&\int\limits_{mh_2}^{mh_2+h_2}\int\limits_{nh_1}^{nh_1+h_1} k(|x-\zeta|,|y-\eta|)(\zeta.\eta)^{2\alpha}\,d\zeta d\eta-\mho(x,y)(nh_1.mh_2)^{2\alpha}\\ &-\overline{\mho}(x,y)(nh_1.(m+1)h_2)^{2\alpha}-\hat{\mho}(x,y)((n+1)h_1.mh_2)^{2\alpha}\\ &-\tilde{\mho}(x,y)((n+1)h_1.(m+1)h_2)^{2\alpha}\Bigg|.\end{aligned} \tag{41}$$

10. Numerical Results

This section presents three applications that demonstrate the effects of the proposed methods on the solution of singular **NMI-FrDE** (4). We considered **NMI-FrDE** (4) with singular kernels. The algebraic system was solved numerically using the Toeplitz matrix approach. Maple18 software was used to calculate the results, accounting for the parameters $\mu_0=1,\mu_1=\frac{1}{4}$, and $\mu_2=\frac{1}{2}$. The exact solution is $\psi(x,y;t)=x^2y^2(t+0.1)^3$, $h(t)=(t+0.1)^3$, $\lambda(t)=t^2$. $n=25$ units will be used to split the position plane. Numerical solutions (Num. solution) and their corresponding errors (Error) that are represented by the absolute difference between the exact solution and the numerical solution at each point ($|\psi(x,y;t)-\text{Num.solution}|$), are shown at different points $(x,y)\in[-1,1]\times[-1,1]$ for $t=0.1$, in Tables 1–4. Figures 1–8 show the approximate solutions and the associated error behavior.

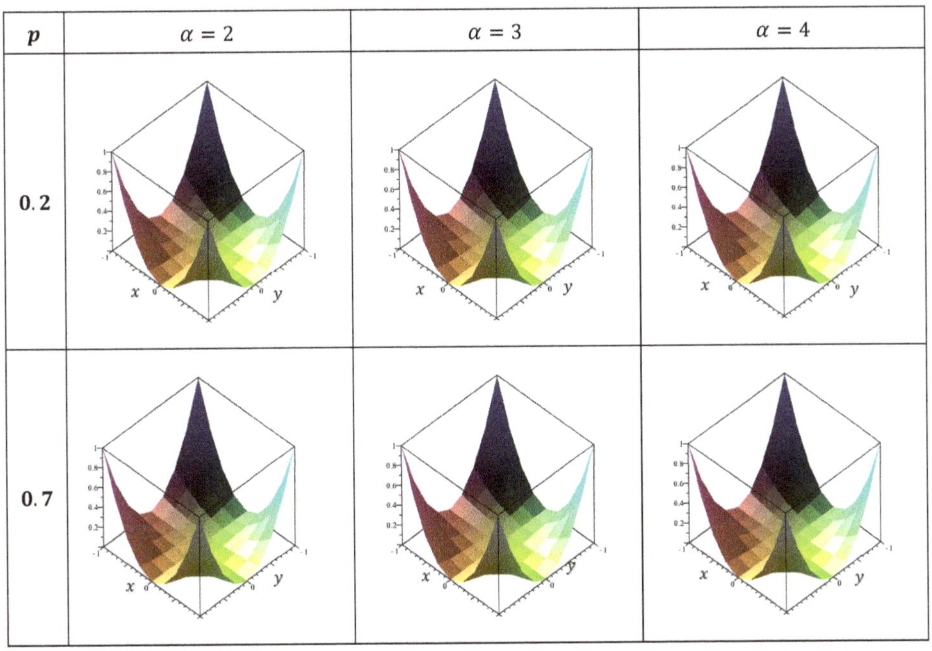

Figure 1. The numerical solution at $T=0.1$ for $\alpha=2,3,4$, according to $p=0.2,0.7$.

Table 1. The approximate solution when $p = 0.2, 0.7$ together with the associated errors.

p	(x,y)	$\alpha = 2$		$\alpha = 3$		$\alpha = 4$	
		Num. Solution	**Error**	**Num. Solution**	**Error**	**Num. Solution**	**Error**
0.2	$(\pm1, \pm1)$	1.000000522	5.220×10^{-7}	1.000000077	7.700×10^{-8}	1.000000008	8.10×10^{-9}
	$(\pm0.5, \pm1)$ $(\pm1, \pm0.5)$	0.249999061	9.394×10^{-7}	0.2499999672	3.270×10^{-8}	0.2499999986	1.40×10^{-9}
	$(0.0, 0.0)$	1.1080×10^{-7}	1.1080×10^{-7}	1.9989×10^{-9}	1.9989×10^{-9}	5.1466×10^{-11}	5.1466×10^{-11}
	$(0.0, \pm1)$ $(\pm1, 0.0)$	4.6546×10^{-7}	4.6546×10^{-7}	1.3755×10^{-8}	1.3755×10^{-8}	5.0681×10^{-10}	5.0681×10^{-10}
	$(0.0, \pm0.5)$ $(\pm0.5, 0.0)$	2.6177×10^{-7}	2.6177×10^{-7}	5.1614×10^{-9}	5.1614×10^{-9}	1.4415×10^{-10}	1.4415×10^{-10}
	$(\pm0.5, \pm0.5)$	0.062499392	6.0847×10^{-7}	0.062499867	1.328×10^{-8}	0.0624999996	4.00×10^{-10}
0.7	$(\pm1, \pm1)$	1.000000076	7.600×10^{-8}	1.000000010	1.100×10^{-8}	1.000000001	1.00×10^{-9}
	$(\pm0.5, \pm1)$ $(\pm1, \pm0.5)$	0.249999865	1.348×10^{-7}	0.249999996	4.400×10^{-9}	0.249999999	2.00×10^{-10}
	$(0.0, 0.0)$	1.5829×10^{-8}	1.5829×10^{-8}	2.7112×10^{-10}	2.7112×10^{-10}	6.6448×10^{-12}	6.6448×10^{-12}
	$(0.0, \pm1)$ $(\pm1, 0.0)$	6.6495×10^{-8}	6.6495×10^{-8}	1.8656×10^{-9}	1.8656×10^{-9}	6.5434×10^{-11}	6.5434×10^{-11}
	$(0.0, \pm0.5)$ $(\pm0.5, 0.0)$	3.7396×10^{-8}	3.7396×10^{-8}	7.0004×10^{-10}	7.0004×10^{-10}	1.8611×10^{-11}	1.8611×10^{-11}
	$(\pm0.5, \pm0.5)$	0.062499913	8.693×10^{-8}	0.062499998	1.8100×10^{-9}	0.0624999999	6.00×10^{-11}

Table 2. The numerical solutions for $p = 0.2, 0.7$, and $\beta = \gamma = 0.35$ in conjunction with the relevant errors.

p	(x,y)	$\alpha = 2$		$\alpha = 3$		$\alpha = 4$	
		Num. Sol.	**Error**	**Num. Sol.**	**Error**	**Num. Sol.**	**Error**
0.2	$(\pm1, \pm1)$	0.999992630	7.3700×10^{-6}	0.999999696	3.0450×10^{-7}	0.999999986	1.4200×10^{-8}
	$(\pm0.5, \pm1)$ $(\pm1, \pm0.5)$	0.249994314	5.6863×10^{-6}	0.2499997921	2.0540×10^{-7}	0.249999991	8.9000×10^{-9}
	$(0.0, 0.0)$	3.2027×10^{-6}	3.20267×10^{-6}	1.0853×10^{-7}	1.0853×10^{-7}	4.5129×10^{-9}	4.5129×10^{-9}
	$(0.0, \pm1)$ $(\pm1, 0.0)$	4.9111×10^{-6}	4.9111×10^{-6}	1.8476×10^{-7}	1.8476×10^{-7}	8.2953×10^{-9}	8.2953×10^{-9}
	$(0.0, \pm0.5)$ $(\pm0.5, 0.0)$	3.7338×10^{-6}	3.7338×10^{-6}	1.2219×10^{-7}	1.2219×10^{-7}	4.9895×10^{-9}	4.9895×10^{-9}
	$(\pm0.5, \pm0.5)$	0.062495648	4.3524×10^{-6}	0.062499863	1.3691×10^{-7}	0.062499994	5.5200×10^{-9}
0.7	$(\pm1, \pm1)$	0.999998947	1.0528×10^{-6}	0.999999958	4.1800×10^{-8}	0.999999998	1.900×10^{-9}
	$(\pm0.5, \pm1)$ $(\pm1, \pm0.5)$	0.249999188	8.1250×10^{-7}	0.2499999718	2.8200×10^{-8}	0.249999999	1.200×10^{-9}
	$(0.0, 0.0)$	4.5753×10^{-7}	4.5753×10^{-7}	1.4720×10^{-8}	1.4720×10^{-8}	5.8266×10^{-10}	5.8266×10^{-10}
	$(0.0, \pm1)$ $(\pm1, 0.0)$	7.0160×10^{-7}	7.0160×10^{-7}	2.5059×10^{-8}	2.5059×10^{-8}	1.0710×10^{-9}	1.0710×10^{-9}
	$(0.0, \pm0.5)$ $(\pm0.5, 0.0)$	5.3340×10^{-7}	5.3340×10^{-7}	1.6573×10^{-8}	1.6573×10^{-8}	6.4418×10^{-10}	6.4418×10^{-10}
	$(\pm0.5, \pm0.5)$	0.062499378	6.2179×10^{-7}	0.0624999813	1.8670×10^{-8}	0.06249999927	7.300×10^{-10}

Table 3. The approximate solution together with the associated errors for $p = 0.2, 0.7$, and $\alpha = 2, 3, 4$, at $T = 0.1$, related to the Carlean parameter $\beta = \gamma = 0.6$.

p	(x,y)	$\alpha = 2$		$\alpha = 3$		$\alpha = 4$	
		Num. Sol.	**Error**	**Num. Sol.**	**Error**	**Num. Sol.**	**Error**
0.2	$(\pm1, \pm1)$	0.999969268	3.07323×10^{-5}	0.999998458	1.5418×10^{-6}	0.999999914	8.5700×10^{-8}
	$(\pm0.5, \pm1)$ $(\pm1, \pm0.5)$	0.249984678	1.5322×10^{-5}	0.249999443	5.5730×10^{-7}	0.249999975	2.5200×10^{-8}
	$(0.0, 0.0)$	3.5770×10^{-6}	3.5770×10^{-6}	1.1717×10^{-7}	1.1717×10^{-7}	4.7856×10^{-9}	4.7856×10^{-9}
	$(0.0, \pm1)$ $(\pm1, 0.0)$	1.0496×10^{-5}	1.0496×10^{-5}	4.2508×10^{-7}	4.2508×10^{-7}	2.0271×10^{-8}	2.0271×10^{-8}
	$(0.0, \pm0.5)$ $(\pm0.5, 0.0)$	5.2294×10^{-6}	5.2294×10^{-6}	1.5377×10^{-7}	1.5377×10^{-7}	5.9430×10^{-9}	5.9430×10^{-9}
	$(\pm0.5, \pm0.5)$	0.062492357	7.6433×10^{-6}	0.062499798	2.0166×10^{-7}	0.062499993	7.3800×10^{-9}
0.7	$(\pm1, \pm1)$	0.999995610	4.3902×10^{-6}	0.999999791	2.0920×10^{-7}	0.999999989	1.1500×10^{-8}
	$(\pm0.5, \pm1)$ $(\pm1, \pm0.5)$	0.249997811	2.1889×10^{-6}	0.249999924	7.5700×10^{-8}	0.249999997	3.300×10^{-9}
	$(0.0, 0.0)$	5.1099×10^{-7}	5.1099×10^{-7}	1.5892×10^{-8}	1.5892×10^{-8}	6.1786×10^{-10}	6.1786×10^{-10}
	$(0.0, \pm1)$ $(\pm1, 0.0)$	1.4980×10^{-6}	1.4980×10^{-6}	5.7654×10^{-8}	5.7654×10^{-8}	2.6172×10^{-9}	2.6172×10^{-9}
	$(0.0, \pm0.5)$ $(\pm0.5, 0.0)$	7.4706×10^{-7}	7.4706×10^{-7}	2.0855×10^{-8}	2.0855×10^{-8}	7.6730×10^{-10}	7.6730×10^{-10}
	$(\pm0.5, \pm0.5)$	0.062498908	1.0919×10^{-6}	0.062499973	2.7370×10^{-8}	0.062499999	9.600×10^{-10}

Table 4. The numerical solutions and the related errors for $\alpha = 2, 3, 4$, and $p = 0.2, 0.7$ at $T = 0.1$.

p	(x,y)	$\alpha = 2$		$\alpha = 3$		$\alpha = 4$	
		Num. Sol.	**Error**	**Num. Sol.**	**Error**	**Num. Sol.**	**Error**
0.2	$(\pm1, \pm1)$	0.993913755	6.0862×10^{-3}	0.999595988	4.0401×10^{-4}	0.999972454	2.7546×10^{-5}
	$(\pm0.5, \pm1)$ $(\pm1, \pm0.5)$	0.249006059	9.9394×10^{-4}	0.249976059	2.3941×10^{-5}	0.249999207	7.9260×10^{-7}
	$(0.0, 0.0)$	4.3281×10^{-6}	4.3281×10^{-6}	1.3332×10^{-7}	1.3332×10^{-7}	5.2761×10^{-9}	5.2761×10^{-9}
	$(0.0, \pm1)$ $(\pm1, 0.0)$	1.6230×10^{-4}	1.6230×10^{-4}	7.3391×10^{-6}	7.3391×10^{-6}	3.8123×10^{-7}	3.8123×10^{-7}
	$(0.0, \pm0.5)$ $(\pm0.5, 0.0)$	2.6505×10^{-5}	2.6505×10^{-5}	4.3490×10^{-7}	4.3490×10^{-7}	1.0969×10^{-8}	1.0969×10^{-8}
	$(\pm0.5, \pm0.5)$	0.062337680	16232×10^{-4}	0.062498581	1.4187×10^{-6}	0.062499977	2.2800×10^{-8}
0.7	$(\pm1, \pm1)$	0.999130526	8.6947×10^{-4}	0.999945204	5.4796×10^{-5}	0.999996444	3.5561×10^{-6}
	$(\pm0.5, \pm1)$ $(\pm1, \pm0.5)$	0.249858006	1.4199×10^{-4}	0.249996753	3.2472×10^{-6}	0.249999898	1.0240×10^{-7}
	$(0.0, 0.0)$	6.1831×10^{-7}	6.1831×10^{-7}	1.8082×10^{-8}	1.8082×10^{-8}	6.8119×10^{-10}	6.8119×10^{-10}
	$(0.0, \pm1)$ $(\pm1, 0.0)$	2.3186×10^{-5}	2.3186×10^{-5}	9.9540×10^{-7}	9.9540×10^{-7}	4.9220×10^{-8}	4.9220×10^{-8}
	$(0.0, \pm0.5)$ $(\pm0.5, 0.0)$	3.7865×10^{-6}	3.7865×10^{-6}	5.8986×10^{-8}	5.8986×10^{-8}	1.4162×10^{-9}	1.4162×10^{-9}
	$(\pm0.5, \pm0.5)$	0.0624768109	2.3188×10^{-5}	0.062499808	1.9243×10^{-7}	0.062499997	2.9500×10^{-9}

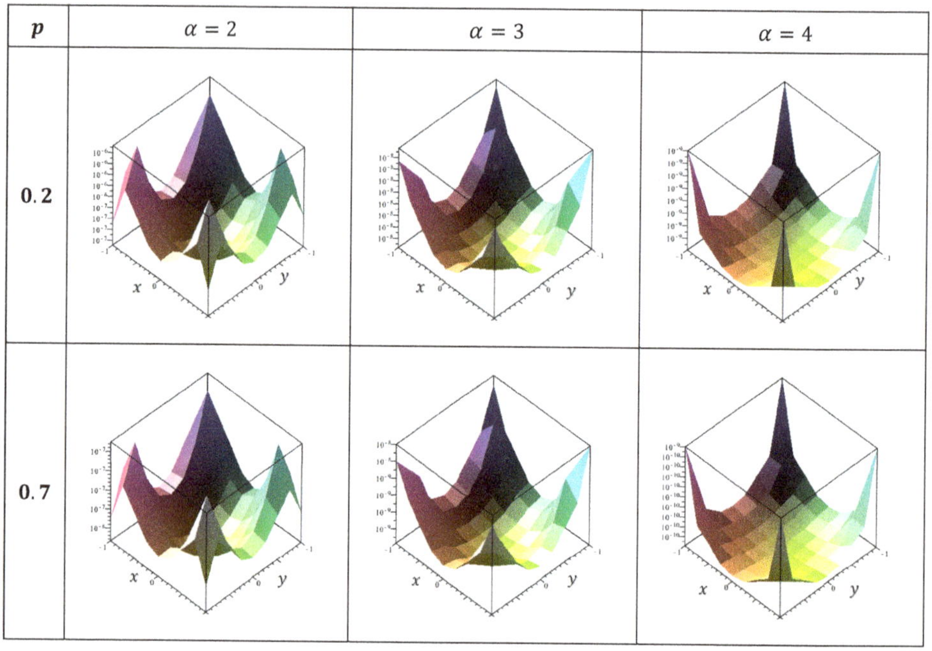

Figure 2. The errors graph at $T = 0.1$ for $p = 0.2, 0.7$, corresponding to $\alpha = 2, 3, 4$.

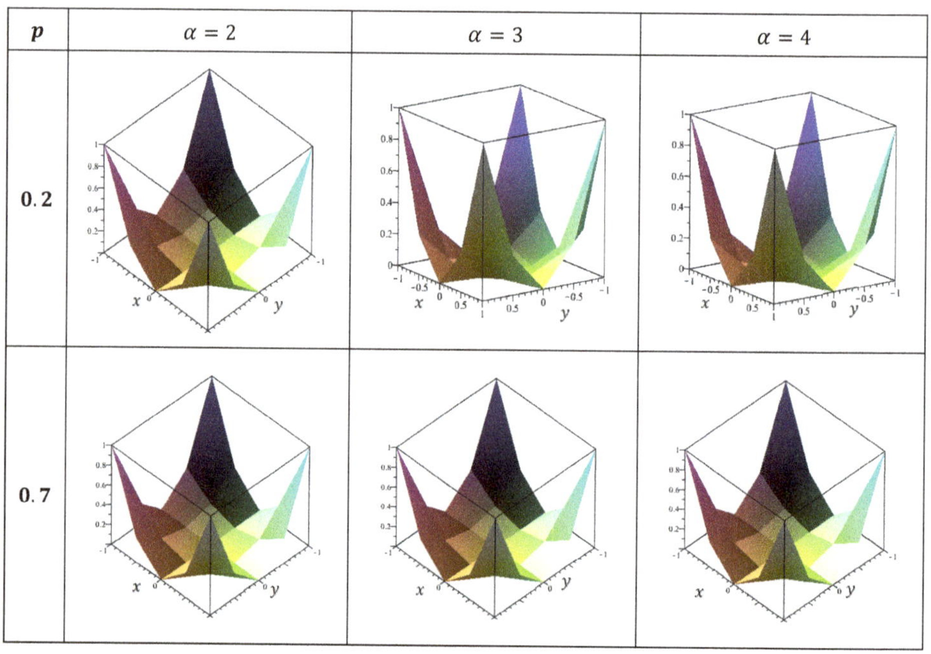

Figure 3. Using the Carlean parameter $\beta = \gamma = 0.35$, the approximate solutions at $T = 0.1$ for $p = 0.2, 0.7, \alpha = 2, 3, 4$.

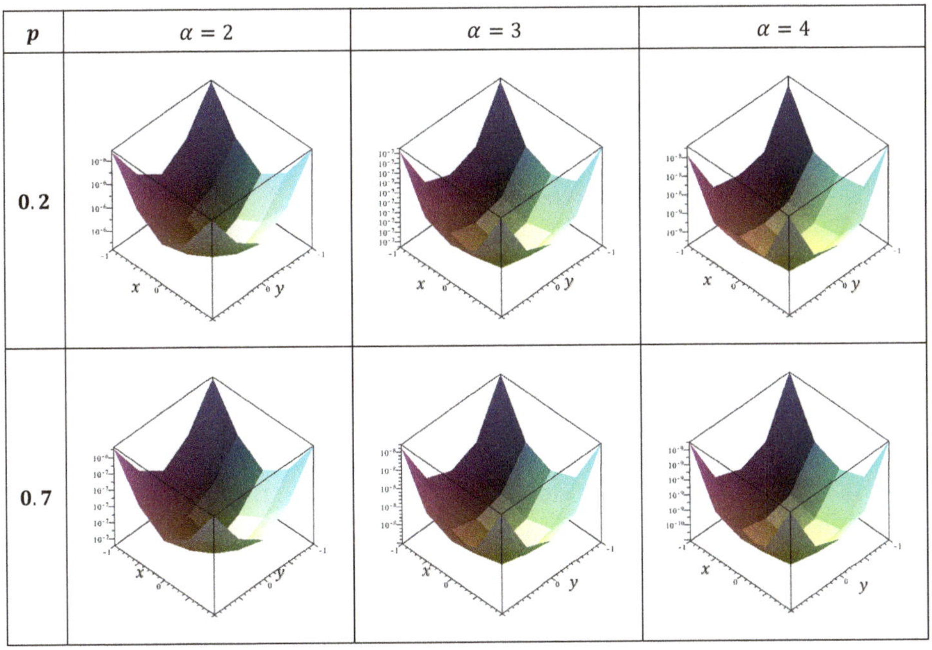

Figure 4. The absolute errors at $T = 0.1$ for $p = 0.2, 0.7$, $\alpha = 2, 3, 4$, related to the Carlean parameter $\beta = \gamma = 0.35$.

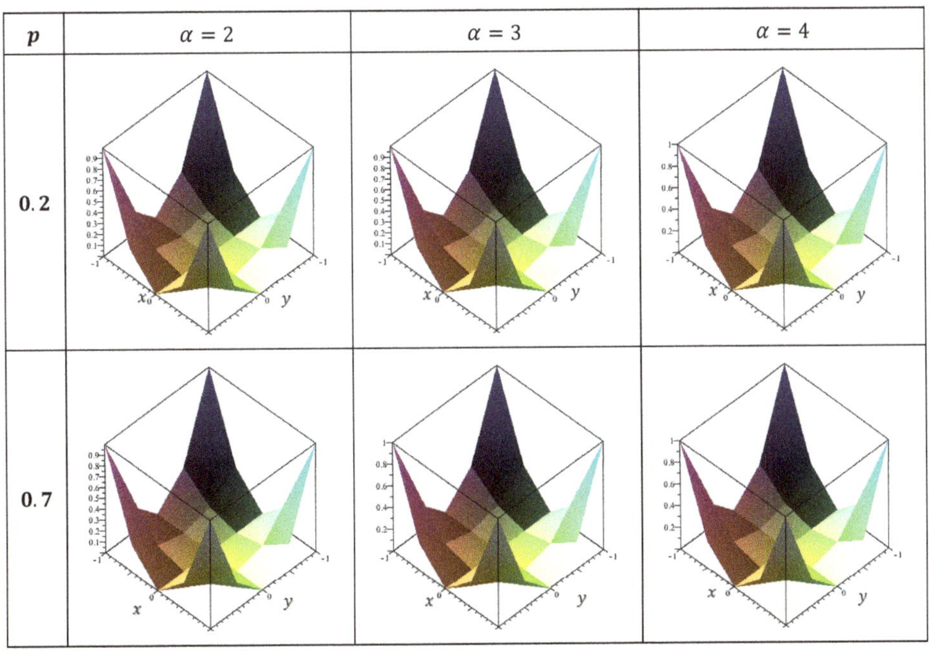

Figure 5. The numerical solution according to the Carlean parameter $\beta = \gamma = 0.6$, for $p = 0.2, 0.7$, and $\alpha = 2, 3, 4$, at $T = 0.1$.

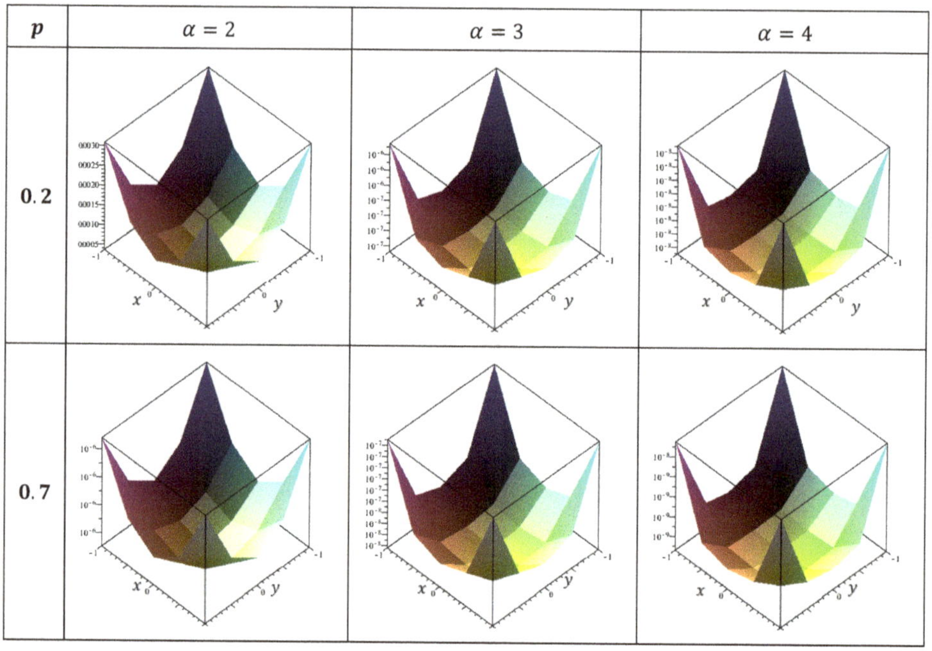

Figure 6. The absolute errors connected to the Carlean parameter $\beta = \gamma = 0.6$, at $T = 0.1$ for $p = 0.2, 0.7$, and $\alpha = 2, 3, 4$.

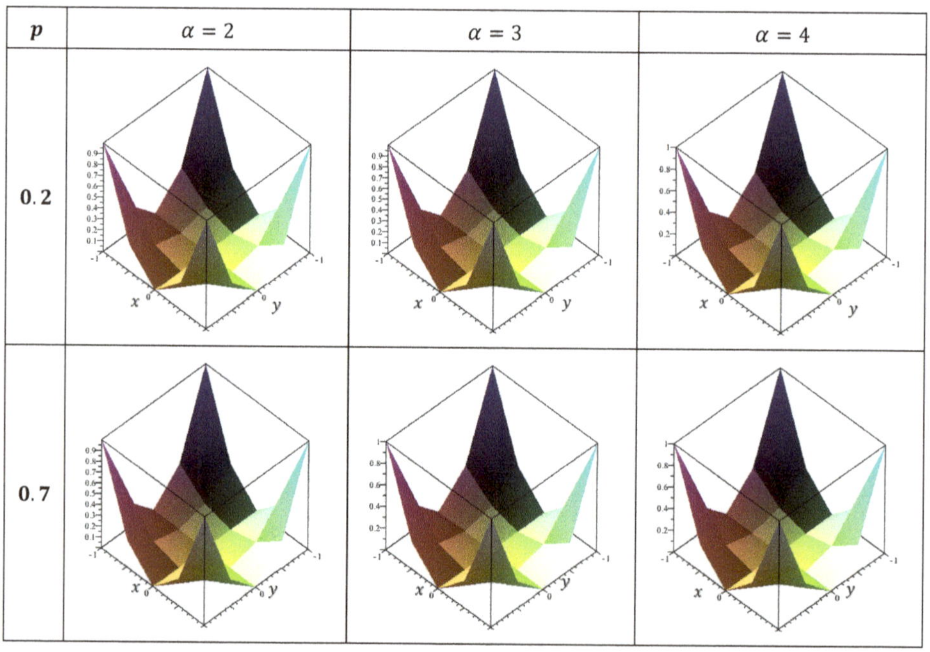

Figure 7. The computational solution provided for $\alpha = 2, 3, 4$, at $T = 0.1$ for $p = 0.2, 0.7$.

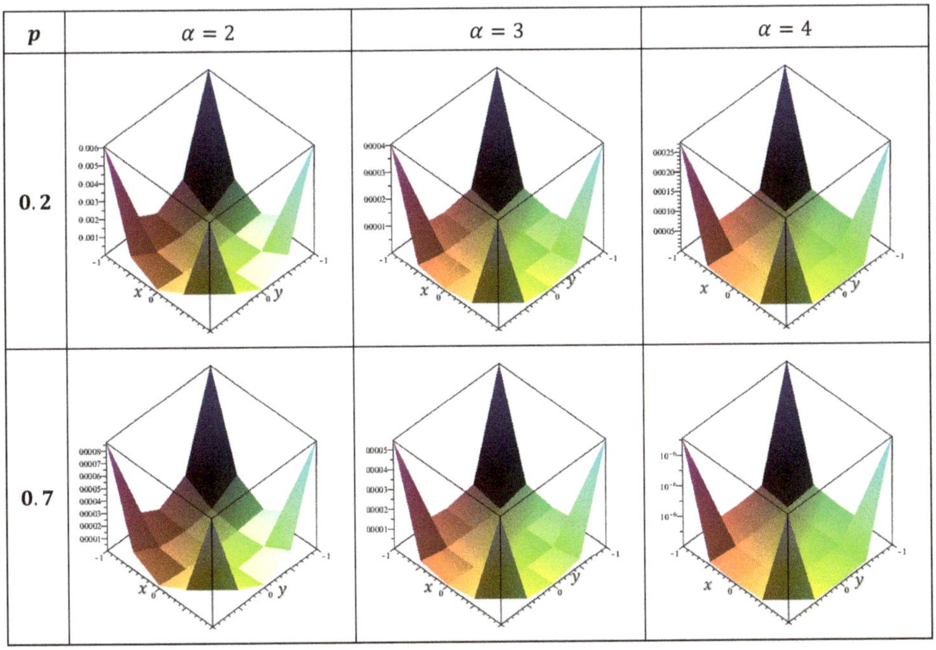

Figure 8. The absolute errors associated with $\alpha = 2,3,4$ at $T = 0.1$ for $p = 0.2, 0.7$.

Application 1: Logarithmic kernel:

Consider **NMI-FrDE** equation with logarithmic kernel

$$\begin{aligned}&\psi(x,y;t) + \tfrac{1}{4}\tfrac{\partial^p \psi(x,y;t)}{\partial t^p} + \tfrac{1}{2}\tfrac{\partial^{p+1}\psi(x,y;t)}{\partial t^{p+1}} \\ &= f(x,y;t) + t^2 \textstyle\int_{-1}^{1}\int_{-1}^{1} \ln|x-\zeta| \ln|y-\eta|\ \psi^{\alpha}(\zeta,\eta;t) d\zeta d\eta, \qquad \alpha = 2,3,4,\end{aligned} \tag{42}$$

under the conditions

$$\psi(x,y;0) = x^2y^2, \qquad \frac{\partial\psi(x,y;t)}{\partial t}\ \Big|_{t=0} = \frac{x^2y^2}{3}. \tag{43}$$

Equation (42) can be rewritten with the aid of (43) in the form of the NMIE in

$$\begin{aligned}&\tfrac{1}{2}\psi(x,y;t) + \textstyle\int_0^t \left[\tfrac{p(t-s)^p}{\Gamma(p+1)} + \tfrac{1}{4}\right]\psi(x,y;s)\ ds \\ &= \tfrac{1}{\Gamma(p+1)}\textstyle\int_0^t\ (t-s)^p\ s^2 \int_{-1}^{1}\int_{-1}^{1} \ln|x-\zeta| \ln|y-\eta|\ \psi^{\alpha}(\zeta,\eta;t)\ d\zeta d\eta\ ds + F(x,y;t),\end{aligned} \tag{44}$$

where

$$F(x,y;t) = \frac{1}{\Gamma(p+1)}\int_0^t (t-\tau)^p f(x,y;\tau)d\tau + \frac{1}{2}x^2y^2\left[1 + \frac{3\ t^p}{\Gamma(p+1)}\right]. \tag{45}$$

The integrals in relations (33) according to the logarithmic kernel type can be evaluated using the famous formula (see Gradshteyn and Ryzhik [22]).

$$\int u^n \ln(a+bu)du = \frac{1}{n+1}\left\{\left[u^{n+1} - \frac{(-a)^{n+1}}{b^{n+1}}\right]\ln(a+bu) + \sum_{k=1}^{n+1}\frac{(-1)^k u^{n-k+2}a^{k-1}}{(n-k+2)b^{k-1}}\right\}. \tag{46}$$

Application 2: Carleman kernel:

Consider **NMI-FrDE** equation with Carleman kernel

$$\begin{aligned} &\psi(x,y;t) + \tfrac{1}{4}\,\frac{\partial^p \psi(x,y;t)}{\partial t^p} + \tfrac{1}{2}\,\frac{\partial^{p+1}\psi(x,y;t)}{\partial t^{p+1}} \\ &= f(x,y;t) + t^2 \int_{-1}^{1}\int_{-1}^{1} |x-\zeta|^{-\beta}|y-\eta|^{-\gamma}\,\psi^\alpha(\zeta,\eta;t)\,d\zeta d\eta, \qquad \alpha = 2,3,4, \end{aligned} \tag{47}$$

under the conditions (43).

Equation (47) can be rewritten with the aid of (43) in the form of a **NMIE** in

$$\begin{aligned} &\tfrac{1}{2}\,\psi(x,y;t) + \int_0^t \left[\frac{p\,(t-s)^p}{\Gamma(p+1)} + \frac{1}{4}\right]\psi(x,y;s)\,ds \\ &= \frac{1}{\Gamma(p+1)}\int_0^t \left(t-s\right)^p (s)^2 \int_{-1}^{1}\int_{-1}^{1} |x-\zeta|^{-\beta}|x-\zeta|^{-\gamma}\,\psi^\alpha(\zeta,\eta;t)\,d\zeta d\eta\,ds + F(x,y;t), \end{aligned} \tag{48}$$

where $F(x,y;t)$ takes the form (45).

Integrals in (33) can be calculated for the Carleman function based on the formula

$$\int u^n|x-u|^{-\alpha}du = -\sum_{k=0}^{n}\frac{n!\,u^{n-k}|x-u|^{k+1-\alpha}}{(n-k)!(1-\alpha)(2-\alpha)\dots(k+1-\alpha)}. \tag{49}$$

Application 3: Cauchy kernel:

Consider the **NMI-FrDE** equation with the Cauchy kernel

$$\begin{aligned} &\psi(x,y;t) + \tfrac{1}{4}\,\frac{\partial^p \psi(x,y;t)}{\partial t^p} + \tfrac{1}{2}\,\frac{\partial^{p+1}\psi(x,y;t)}{\partial t^{p+1}} \\ &= f(x,y;t) + t^2 \int_{-1}^{1}\int_{-1}^{1} \frac{\psi^\alpha(\zeta,\eta;t)}{(x-\zeta)(y-\eta)}\,d\zeta d\eta, \qquad \alpha = 2,3,4 \end{aligned} \tag{50}$$

under the conditions (43).

Equation (50) can be rewritten with the aid of (43) in the form of a **NMIE** in

$$\begin{aligned} &\tfrac{1}{2}\,\psi(x,y;t) + \int_0^t \left[\frac{p\,(t-s)^p}{\Gamma(p+1)} + \frac{1}{4}\right]\psi(x,y;s)\,ds \\ &= \frac{1}{\Gamma(p+1)}\int_0^t \left(t-s\right)^p (s)^2 \int_{-1}^{1}\int_{-1}^{1} \frac{\psi^\alpha(\zeta,\eta;t)}{(x-\zeta)(y-\eta)}\,d\zeta d\eta\,ds + F(x,y;t), \end{aligned} \tag{51}$$

where $F(x,y;t)$ takes the form (45).

Integrals in (33) can be calculated for the Cauchy kernel based on the formula

$$\int \frac{u^n}{(a+bu)}du = \frac{(-a)^n}{b^{n+1}}\ln|a+bu| - \frac{1}{b}\sum_{k=1}^{n}\frac{\left(-1\right)^k u^{n-k+1}a^{k-1}}{(n-k+1)b^{k-1}}. \tag{52}$$

11. Discussion

Based on the results of previous applications, we can observe that

1. The numerical solutions were consistently extremely near to the exact solution.
2. In each case studied, the error value increases as it approaches the endpoints $x, y = \pm 1$. Additionally, it decreases as it approaches zero at the center of the position plane.
3. The smaller the error is, the greater is the value of α.
4. It is clear from comparing the corresponding results of Tables 2 and 3 that as the Carleman parameter becomes larger, the error correspondingly increases.
5. The error decreases as the p-value increases, indicating that the accuracy in nonlinear cases is greater than the accuracy in linear cases.
6. TMM is regarded as one of the greatest techniques for solving singular integral equations, where the solution can be obtained directly, and the singularity vanishes.
7. The logarithmic results in Table 1 are the most accurate.
8. The Cauchy results in Table 4 have the greatest error.

9. The techniques used in this study preserve the symmetry characteristic of the numerical results related to the plane of position.
10. The behavior of numerical solutions was described in Figures 1, 3, 5 and 7. However, the corresponding errors behavior is displayed in Figures 2, 4, 6 and 8.

12. Conclusions

From the previous study, we can deduce the following:

1. The fractional integro-differential equation is equivalent to the phase-lag integral equation.
2. Discussing the existence and uniqueness of the solution as well as the convergence and stability of the error is very important in discussing mathematical problems in general.
3. In this work, special cases were derived from the general situation of the fractional integro-differential equation, and the linear relationship of the equation was also deduced from the general equation. In addition, many and various specific types were obtained from the general kernel.
4. The investigation of the existence of a solution to the problem is classified according to the general situation of the equation to be solved and then the basic conditions for this solution: (a) Banach's fixed point theorem must be used if the integral equation that is to be solved is of the first kind. In this case, the so-called Picard method (the method of successive approximation) fails. A theorems successive approximation approach or fixed-point theorems may be used if the equation is of the second kind. Fixed point theorems are governed by the initial conditions set to solve the problem.
5. The Toeplitz matrix method is distinguished from all previous methods by the following properties: (a) The ability to formulate the kernel in general and to consider that the singular kernels such as the logarithmic kernel, the Caleman kernel, the Cauchy kernel, the Hilbert kernel, and finally the strongly singular kernel are special cases of the imposed kernel. (b) This method transforms the singular integrals into ordinary integrals that are easy to solve.

13. Future Work

The authors look forward to solving this type of equation in the future.

$$\begin{aligned} &\mu_0\psi(x,y;t) + \mu_1 \tfrac{\partial^p \psi(x,y;t)}{\partial t^p} + \mu_2 \tfrac{\partial^{p+1}\psi(x,y;t)}{\partial t^{p+1}} \\ &= f(x,y;t) + L(t)\iint_{\omega} k(|x-\zeta|,|y-\eta|)\, \psi^{\alpha}(\zeta,\eta;t)\, d\zeta d\eta,\ \ 0<p<1, \end{aligned}$$

where

$$L(t) = \int_0^t g(t,\tau)\psi(x,y;\tau)d\tau.$$

Author Contributions: Methodology, S.A.R. and M.A.A.; Software, S.A.R.; Formal analysis, M.A.A.; Investigation, M.A.A.; Writing—original draft, S.A.R.; Writing—review and editing, S.A.R. and M.A.A.; Project administration, M.A.A.; Funding acquisition, S.A.R. All authors have read and agreed to the published version of the manuscript.

Funding: This research work was funded by Umm Al-Qura University, Saudi Arabia, under grant number: 25UQU4280427GSSR01.

Data Availability Statement: The original contributions presented in this study are included in the article. Further inquiries can be directed to the corresponding author.

Acknowledgments: The authors extend their appreciation to Umm Al-Qura University, Saudi Arabia, for funding this research work through grant number: 25UQU4280427GSSR01.

Conflicts of Interest: The authors declare no conflict of interest.

Abbreviations

The following abbreviations are used in this manuscript:

NFIE	nonlinear Fredholm integral equation
V-FIE	Volterra–Fredholm integral equation
NMIE	nonlinear mixed integral equation
FrI-DEs	fractional integro-differential equations
NMI-FrDE	nonlinear mixed integro-fractional differential equation
SNFIEs	system of nonlinear Fredholm integral equations
TMM	Toeplitz matrix method
NAS	nonlinear algebraic system

References

1. Tarasov, V.E. Fractional integro-differential equations for electromagnetic waves in dielectric media. *Theor. Math. Phys.* **2009**, *158*, 355–359. [CrossRef]
2. Munusamy, K.; Ravichandran, C.; Nisar, K.S.; Ghanbari, B. Existence of solutions for some functional integrodifferential equations with nonlocal conditions. *Math. Methods Appl. Sci.* **2020**, *43*, 10319–10331. [CrossRef]
3. Verma, P.; Kumar, M. An analytical solution with existence and uniqueness conditions for fractional integro-differential equations. *Int. J. Model. Simul. Sci. Comput.* **2020**, *11*, 2050045. [CrossRef]
4. Raad, S.; Alqurashi, K. Toeplitz matrix and Nyström method for solving linear fractional integro-differential equation. *Eur. J. Pure Appl. Math.* **2022**, *15*, 796–809. [CrossRef]
5. Alhazmi, S.E. New model for solving mixed integral equation of the first kind with generalized potential kernel. *J. Math. Res.* **2017**, *9*, 18–29. [CrossRef]
6. Nemati, S.; Lima, P.M.; Ordokhani, Y. Numerical solution of a class of two dimensional nonlinear Volterra integral equations using Legendre polynomials. *J. Comput. Appl. Math.* **2013**, *242*, 53–69. [CrossRef]
7. Hafez, R.M.; Youssri, Y.H. Spectral Legendre-Chebyshev treatment of 2D linear and nonlinear mixed Volterra-Fredholm integral equation. *Math. Sci. Lett.* **2020**, *9*, 37–47.
8. El-Sayed, A.M.A.; Ahmed, R.G. Solvability of a coupled system of functional integro-differential equations with infinite point and Riemann–Stieltjes integral conditions. *Appl. Math. Comput.* **2020**, *370*, 124918. [CrossRef]
9. Huang, L.; Li, X.F.; Zhao, Y.; Duan, X.Y. Approximate solution of fractional integro-differential equations by Taylor expansion method. *Comput. Math. Appl.* **2011**, *62*, 1127–1134. [CrossRef]
10. Mojahedfar, M.; Tari Marzabad, A. Solving two-dimensional fractional integrod ifferential equations by Legendre wavelets. *Bull. Iran. Math. Soc.* **2017**, *43*, 2419–2435.
11. Li, C.; Plowman, H. Solutions of the generalized Abel's integral equations of the second kind with variable coefficients. *Axioms* **2019**, *8*, 137. [CrossRef]
12. Matoog, R.T. Modified Taylor's method and nonlinear mixed integral equation. *Univ. J. Integ. Eq.* **2016**, *4*, 21–29.
13. Abusalim, S.M.; Abdou, M.A.; Abdel-Aty, M.A.; Nili, M.E. Hybrid Functions Approach via Nonlinear Integral Equations with Symmetric and Nonsymmetrical Kernel in Two Dimensions. *Symmetry* **2023**, *15*, 1408. [CrossRef]
14. Mahdy, A.M.S.; Abdou, M.A.; Mohamed, D.S. A computational technique for computing second-type mixed integral equations with singular kernels. *J. Math. Comput. Sci.* **2024**, *32*, 137–151. [CrossRef]
15. Jan, A.R.; Abdou, M.A.; Basseem, M. A Physical Phenomenon for the Frac tional Nonlinear Mixed Integro-Differential Equation Using a Quadrature Nystrom Method. *Fractal Fract.* **2023**, *7*, 656. [CrossRef]
16. Akram, T.; Ali, Z.; Rabiei, F.; Shah, K.; Kumam, P.A. Numerical Study of Nonlinear Fractional Order Partial Integro-Differential Equation with a Weakly Singular Kernel. *Fractal Fract.* **2021**, *5*, 85. [CrossRef]
17. Abdelkawy, M.A.; Amin, A.Z.; Lopes, A.M.; Hashim, I.; Babatin, M.M. Shifted fractional-order Jacobi collocation method for solving variable-order fractional integro differential equation with weakly singular kernel. *Fractal Fract.* **2022**, *6*, 19. [CrossRef]
18. Tariboon, J.; Ntouyas, S.K.; Sudsutad, W. Some new Riemann-Liouville fractional integral inequalities. *Int. J. Math. Math. Sci.* **2014**, *2014*, 6. [CrossRef]
19. Podlubny, I.; Chechkin, A.; Skovranek, T.; Chen, Y.; Jara, B.M.V. Matrix approach to discrete fractional calculus II: Partial fractional differential equations. *J. Comput. Phys.* **2009**, *228*, 3137–3153. [CrossRef]

20. Columbu, A.; Fuentes, R.D.; Frassu, S. Uniform-in-time boundedness in a class of local and nonlocal nonlinear attraction-repulsion chemotaxis models with logistics. *arXiv* **2023**, arXiv:2311.06526. [CrossRef]
21. Raad, S.A.; Abdou, M.A. The Effect of Fractional Order of Time Phase Delay via a Mixed Integral Equation in (2+1) Dimensions with an Extended Discontinuous Kernel. *Symmetry* **2025**, *17*, 36. [CrossRef]
22. Gradshteyn, I.S.; Ryzhik, I.M. *Table of Integrals, Series and Product*; Academic Press: New York, NY, USA, 2014.

fractal and fractional

MDPI

Article

On the Laplace Residual Series Method and Its Application to Time-Fractional Fisher's Equations

Rawya Al-deiakeh [1,2], Sharifah Alhazmi [3], Shrideh Al-Omari [4,*], Mohammed Al-Smadi [4,5] and Shaher Momani [2,6]

1 Department of Mathematics, Faculty of Science, Irbid National University, Irbid 21110, Jordan; r.aldeiakeh@inu.edu.jo
2 Nonlinear Dynamics Research Center (NDRC), Ajman University, Ajman 20550, United Arab Emirates; s.momani@ju.edu.jo
3 Department of Mathematics, College of Education for Girls at Al-Qunfudah, Umm Al-Qura University, Mecca 11942, Saudi Arabia; sehazmi@uqu.edu.sa
4 Department of Mathematics, Faculty of Science, Al Balqa Applied University, Salt 19117, Jordan; malsmadi@lu.edu.qa
5 College of Commerce and Business, Lusail University, Lusail 9717, Qatar
6 Department of Mathematics, Faculty of Science, University of Jordan, Amman 11942, Jordan
* Correspondence: shridehalomari@bau.edu.jo

Abstract: In this paper, we develop an analytical approximate solution for the nonlinear time-fractional Fisher's equation using a right starting space function and a unique analytic-numeric technique referred to as the Laplace residual power series approach. The generalized Taylor's formula and the Laplace transform operator are coupled in the aforementioned method, where the coefficients, obtained through fractional expansion in the Laplace space, are determined by applying the limit concept. In order to validate and illustrate the theoretical methodology of the LRPS technique, as well as to show its effectiveness, adaptability, and superiority in solving various types of nonlinear time and space fractional differential equations, numerical experiments are generated. The obtained analytical solutions are compatible with the precise solutions and concur with those proposed by the other approaches. The outcomes show that the Laplace residual power series strategy is incredibly successful, straightforward to implement, and well suited for handling the complexity of nonlinear problems.

Keywords: Caputo fractional derivatives; Fisher's equation; time-fractional equation; residual power series; Laplace residual power series; fractional series expansion

1. Introduction

The modeling of physical phenomena requires a comprehensive understanding of both current and past events. This has led to the widespread use of fractional calculus in various fields such as fluid mechanics, chemistry, biology, and psychology [1–4]. The concept of fractional calculus has been studied since 1695 and has gained significant interest from researchers and mathematicians in different scientific disciplines [5–11]. Several definitions of fractional derivatives and integrals have been developed over time, with Caputo's formulation being widely adopted due to its practical applicability in real-world scenarios [12,13]. To accurately model a wide range of physical processes, there has been growing interest in solving fractional differential equations, particularly partial differential equations (PDEs) of the fractional order. This increasing attention stems from the ability of fractional calculus to better describe memory and hereditary properties in various scientific applications. As a result, numerous researchers have explored various methods, both analytical and numerical, to obtain approximate or close solutions for these equations. Several well-established techniques have been widely used, including the Laplace transform method [14], the Adomian decomposition method [15], the multi-step fractional differential transform method [16], the variational iteration method [17], the homotopy perturbation method [18], the reproducing kernel method [19], and the residual power series (RPS) method [20]. These techniques have shown significant effectiveness in the treatment of complex fractional differential equations in various domains [21–23].

The development and utilization of these methods highlight the ongoing research efforts aimed at effectively solving complex problems arising from the PDEs of fractional order. The RPS method is a highly effective technique for finding approximate series solutions to both fractional and non-fractional differential equations. It has been extensively tested and proven successful in solving various differential equations, including the nonlinear Kuramoto–Sivashinsky equation [20], neutron diffusion equations [24], fractional Newell–Whitehead–Segel equation [25], fractional-order coupled system of PEDs [26], and fractional logistic equation [27].

The simplicity and effectiveness of the RPS approach in determining the coefficients of the power series solution make it unique. This is especially crucial when working with nonlinear equations. The Laplace residual power series (LRPS) approach is a novel RPS method introduced by the authors in [28] in a recent paper. In this innovative technique, instead of relying on derivatives to determine coefficients, the authors utilized the concept of limits. This modification significantly enhanced both the speed and ease of determining coefficients while providing solutions in the form of converging series without resorting to linearization, perturbation, or discretization techniques. The introduction of the LRPS method opens up new possibilities for the exact and approximate series solutions to linear and nonlinear neutral fractional differential equations.

It is worth emphasizing that the LRPS expansion technique derives a solution by converting the differential equation into the Laplace domain. To obtain the solution for the original problem, the inverse Laplace transform is applied, restoring it to its original space. In this work, the nonlinear time-fractional Fisher's equation is approximated using the LRPS technique. Consider the time-fractional Fisher's equation given below:

$$Ð_t^{\gamma}\varphi = D_x^2\varphi + \lambda\varphi(1-\varphi), \ x \in R, \ t \geq 0, \tag{1}$$

equipped with the initial data

$$\varphi(x,0) = \theta_0(x), \tag{2}$$

in which λ is a constant, φ is an unknown function to be determined and $Ð_t^{\gamma}\varphi$ is a γ-th time-Caputo fractional derivative.

The organization of this document is as follows: Section 2 provides an overview of the theory of fractional calculus. Section 3 introduces the FRPS method applied to solve the nonlinear time-fractional Fisher's equation. Section 4 demonstrates the effectiveness of the LRPS technique through two illustrative examples. Finally, the conclusion is presented in the Section 5.

2. Fundamental Concepts

In this section, we provide an overview of the fundamental definitions of Laplace transform operators and fractional calculus. Additionally, we discuss the most essential characteristics of the fractional series expansion in the Laplace domain, along with Caputo operators and the Laplace transform [29–34].

Definition 1. *The Riemann–Liouville time-fractional integral operator of order $\gamma \geq 0$, denoted by J_ξ^γ, is given as*

$$J_\xi^\gamma \varphi(x,\xi) = \begin{cases} \frac{1}{\Gamma(\gamma)} \int\limits_0^\xi (\xi-\tau)^{\gamma-1}\varphi(x,\tau)d\tau, & \gamma > 0, \xi > \tau \geq 0 \\ \varphi(x,\xi), & \gamma = 0. \end{cases} \tag{3}$$

Definition 2. *For $m \in \mathbb{N}$, the time-fractional derivative $Đ_\xi^\gamma$ of $\varphi(x,\xi)$ of order $\gamma > 0$, in the meaning of Caputo is given by*

$$Đ_\xi^\gamma \varphi(x,\xi) = J_t^{m-\gamma}\partial_\xi^m \varphi(x,\xi),\ m-1 < \gamma \leq m, x \in I, \xi \geq 0. \tag{4}$$

Definition 3. *Let $\varphi(x,\xi)$ be a continuous piecewise function on $I \times [0,\infty)$, $\varphi(x,\xi)$ is of exponential order δ, then the Laplace transform $\phi(x,s)$ is given for $\varphi(x,\xi)$ as*

$$\phi(x,s) = \mathcal{L}[\varphi(x,\xi)] := \int\limits_0^\infty e^{-s\xi}\varphi(x,\xi)d\xi (s > \delta), \tag{5}$$

while the inversion formula of the Laplace transform of ϕ is derived as

$$\phi(x,\xi) = \mathcal{L}^{-1}[\varphi(x,s)] := \int\limits_{z-i\infty}^{z+i\infty} e^{s\xi}\varphi(x,s)ds, \mathrm{Re}(s) > z_0. \tag{6}$$

The following lemma discusses some useful properties of the Laplace pair of transforms.

Lemma 1. *Let φ and ω be two functions which are piecewise continuous on $I \times [0,\infty)$. Let φ and ω be of the exponential orders δ_1 and δ_2, $\delta_1 < \delta_2$, respectively, and $\mathcal{L}[\varphi(x,\xi)] = \phi(x,s)$,$\mathcal{L}[\omega(x,\xi)] = W(x,s)$, and a,b are constants. Then, for $x \in I, s > \delta_1, \xi \geq 0$, we have*

(a) $\mathcal{L}[a\varphi + b\omega] = a\phi + bW$.
(b) $\mathcal{L}^{-1}[a\phi + bW] = a\varphi + b\omega$.
(c) $\lim\limits_{s\to\infty} s\phi(x,s) = \varphi(x,0), x \in I$.
(d) $\mathcal{L}\left[Đ_\xi^\gamma \varphi(x,\xi)\right] = s^\gamma\phi(x,s) - \sum\limits_{k=0}^{m-1} s^{\gamma-k-1}\partial_\xi^k\varphi(x,0), m-1 < \gamma < m$.
(e) $\mathcal{L}\left[Đ_\xi^{n\gamma} \varphi(x,\xi)\right] = s^{n\gamma}\phi(x,s) - \sum\limits_{k=0}^{n-1} s^{(n-k)\gamma-1}D_\xi^{k\gamma}\varphi(x,0), 0 < \gamma < 1$.

Theorem 1. *Let $\varphi(x,\xi)$ have a power series expansion of fractional order around $\xi = 0$ such that*

$$\varphi(x,\xi) = \sum_{n=0}^\infty \theta_n(x)\xi^{n\gamma}, 0 \leq m-1 < \gamma \leq m, x \in I, 0 \leq \xi < R. \tag{7}$$

Let $Đ_\xi^{n\gamma}\varphi(x,\xi)$ be continuous on $I \times (0,\mathbb{R})$, $m = 0,1,2,\ldots$, then the coefficients $\theta_n(x)$ of the expansion (7) are given as $\theta_n(x) = \frac{Đ_\xi^{n\gamma}\varphi(x,0)}{\Gamma(n\gamma+1)}$, $n = 0,1,2,\ldots$, where $Đ_\xi^{n\gamma} = Đ_\xi^\gamma Đ_\xi^\gamma \ldots Đ_\xi^\gamma (n-times)$, and R is the radius of convergence of the given series.

Theorem 2. *Let the Laplace transform of the continuous function $\varphi(x,\xi)$ be given by $\phi(x,s)$. Then, $\phi(x,s)$ has the fractional series expansion*

$$\phi(x,s) = \sum_{n=0}^\infty \frac{\theta_n(x)}{s^{1+n\alpha}}, 0 < \alpha \leq 1, x \in I, s > \delta. \tag{8}$$

Theorem 3. *Let $\mathcal{L}[\varphi(x,\xi)] = \phi(x,s)$ be given by (8). If $\left|s\mathcal{L}\left[Đ_\xi^{(n+1)\gamma}\gamma(x,\xi)\right]\right| \leq M(x)$, defined on $I \times (\delta,d]$, $0 < \gamma \leq 1$, then the reminder $\Re_n(x,s)$ satisfies the following inequality:*

$$|\Re_n(x,s)| \le \frac{M(x)}{s^{1+(n+1)\gamma}}, x \in I, \delta < s \le d. \tag{9}$$

3. The LRPS Method

This section describes the techniques employed in the proposed algorithm for resolving the fractional initial value problems (IVPs) (1) and (2) in series form. The method combines the Laplace transform operator with the fractional RPS approach. By employing these techniques, we aim to solve these IVPs systematically and efficiently. The proposed method follows the procedure outlined below:

First: Let $\mathcal{L}[\varphi(x,t)] = \phi(x,s)$, and using property (e) from Lemma 1, the Laplace transform can be applied to both sides of Fisher's problem (1) to obtain

$$\phi(x,s) = \frac{\varphi(x,0)}{s} + \frac{1}{s^\gamma}D_x^2\phi(x,s) + \frac{\lambda}{s^\gamma}\phi(x,s) - \frac{\lambda}{s^\gamma}\mathcal{L}\Big\{\mathcal{L}^{-1}[\phi(x,s)]^2\Big\}. \tag{10}$$

Since $\varphi(x,0) = \theta_0(x)$. Thus, (10) can be reformulated as:

$$\phi(x,s) = \frac{\theta_0(x)}{s} + \frac{1}{s^\gamma}D_x^2\phi(x,s) + \frac{\lambda}{s^\gamma}\phi(x,s) - \frac{\lambda}{s^\gamma}\mathcal{L}\Big\{\mathcal{L}^{-1}[\phi(x,s)]^2\Big\}. \tag{11}$$

Second: According to Theorem 2, let the approximate solution of (11) have the expansion series form

$$\phi(x,s) = \sum_{m=0}^{\infty} \frac{\theta_m(x)}{s^{m\gamma+1}}, s > 0. \tag{12}$$

Subsequently, to determine the coefficients θ_m, of (12), let $\phi_i(x,s)$ be the i-th term of the series solution of (12). That is,

$$\phi_i(x,s) = \sum_{m=0}^{i} \frac{\theta_m(x)}{s^{m\gamma+1}}, s > 0. \tag{13}$$

For $i = 0$, we have $\lim_{s\to\infty} s\phi_0(x,s) = \theta_0(x)$, which yields

$$\phi_i(x,s) = \frac{\theta_0(x)}{s} + \sum_{m=0}^{i} \frac{\theta_m(x)}{s^{m\gamma+1}}, s > 0. \tag{14}$$

Third: The i-th term of the series solution (14) can be obtained after evaluating the coefficients θ_m, $m = 1,2,3,\ldots,i$, by identifying the i-th-Laplace residual function of (10) as

$$\begin{aligned}\mathcal{L}[Res\phi_i(x,s)] &= \phi_i(x,s) - \tfrac{\theta_0(x)}{s} - \tfrac{1}{s^\gamma}D_x^2\phi_i(x,s) \\ &\quad -\tfrac{\lambda}{s^\gamma}\phi_i(x,s) + \tfrac{\lambda}{s^\gamma}\mathcal{L}\Big\{\mathcal{L}^{-1}[\phi_i(x,s)]^2\Big\}.\end{aligned} \tag{15}$$

Here, the ∞-th Laplace residual function of (10) can be given by

$$\begin{aligned}\lim_{i\to\infty}\mathcal{L}[Res\phi_i(x,s)] &= \mathcal{L}[Res\phi(x,s)] \\ &= \phi(x,s) - \tfrac{\theta_0(x)}{s} - \tfrac{1}{s^\gamma}D_x^2\phi(x,s) \\ &\quad -\tfrac{\lambda}{s^\gamma}\phi(x,s) + \tfrac{\lambda}{s^\gamma}\mathcal{L}\Big\{\mathcal{L}^{-1}[\phi(x,s)]^2\Big\}.\end{aligned} \tag{16}$$

Evidently, $\mathcal{L}[Res\phi(x,s)] = 0$ and $\lim_{i\to\infty}\mathcal{L}[Res\phi_i(x,s)] = \mathcal{L}[Res\phi(x,s)]$ for each $s > 0$ and $x \in \mathbb{R}$. Furthermore, $\lim_{s\to\infty} s\mathcal{L}[Res\phi(x,s)] = 0$, which implies that $\lim_{s\to\infty} s\mathcal{L}[Res\phi_i(x,s)] = 0$.

Fourth: After substituting the i-th term of the series solution (14) into the i-th Laplace residual function, both sides of the resulting equation are multiplied by the factor $s^{i\gamma+1}$.

Fifth: To determine the coefficients $\theta_m(x)$, $m = 1,2,3,\ldots,i$, we solve $\lim_{s\to\infty} s^{i\gamma+1}\mathcal{L}[Res\phi_i(x,s)] = 0$. Subsequently, by collecting the obtained coefficients into the expansion series (14), the i-th Laplace series solution $\phi_i(x,s)$ of (11) is derived.

Sixth: The approximate solution $\varphi_i(x,t)$ of the IVPs (1) and (2) can be obtained by applying the Laplace transform inversion formula to both sides of the i-th Laplace solution $\phi_i(x,s)$.

In view of the above, to determine the first coefficient $\theta_1(x)$ in the expansion (14), we have to substitute $\phi_1(x,s) = \frac{\theta_0(x)}{s} + \frac{\theta_1(x)}{s^{\gamma+1}}$ into the first Laplace residual function as follows

$$\begin{aligned}\mathcal{L}[Res\phi_1(x,s)] &= \phi_1(x,s) - \tfrac{\theta_0(x)}{s} - \tfrac{1}{s^\gamma}D_x^2\phi_1(x,s)\\ &\quad -\tfrac{\lambda}{s^\gamma}\phi_1(x,s) + \tfrac{\lambda}{s^\gamma}\mathcal{L}\left\{\mathcal{L}^{-1}[\phi_1(x,s)]^2\right\}\\ &= \tfrac{\theta_1(x)}{s^{1+\gamma}} - \lambda\left(\tfrac{\theta_0(x)}{s^{1+\gamma}} + \tfrac{\theta_1(x)}{s^{1+2\gamma}}\right)\\ &\quad +\lambda\left(\tfrac{\theta_0^2(x)}{s^{1+\gamma}} + \tfrac{2\theta_0(x)\theta_1(x)}{s^{1+2\gamma}} + \tfrac{\Gamma(1+2\gamma)\theta_1^2(x)}{\Gamma^2(\gamma+1)s^{1+3\gamma}}\right)\\ &\quad -\left(\tfrac{\theta_0''(x)}{s^{1+\gamma}} + \tfrac{\theta_1''(x)}{s^{1+2\gamma}}\right).\end{aligned} \tag{17}$$

Now, multiplying both sides of (17) by $s^{\gamma+1}$ gives

$$\begin{aligned}s^{\gamma+1}\mathcal{L}[Res\phi_1(x,s)] &= -\lambda\theta_0(x) + \lambda\theta_0^2(x) + \theta_1(x) - \tfrac{\lambda\theta_1(x)}{s^\gamma} + \tfrac{2\lambda\theta_0(x)\theta_1(x)}{s^\gamma}\\ &\quad +\tfrac{\Gamma(1+2\gamma)\theta_1^2(x)}{\Gamma^2(\gamma+1)s^{3\gamma}} - \theta_0''(x) - \tfrac{\theta_1''(x)}{s^\gamma}.\end{aligned} \tag{18}$$

In light of the fact that $\lim_{s\to\infty} s^{\gamma+1}\mathcal{L}[Res\phi_1(x,s)] = 0$, we obtain $\theta_1(x) = \lambda(\theta_0(x) - \theta_0^2(x)) + \theta_0''(x)$. To date, the first Laplace series solution $\phi_1(x,s)$ of (11) has the form

$$\phi_1(x,s) = \frac{\theta_0(x)}{s} + \frac{\lambda(\theta_0(x) - \theta_0^2(x)) + \theta_0''(x)}{s^{\gamma+1}}.$$

For $i = 2$, the 2-nd Laplace series solution of (11) can be written as

$$\phi_2(x,s) = \frac{\theta_0(x)}{s} + \frac{\theta_1(x)}{s^{\gamma+1}} + \frac{\theta_2(x)}{s^{2\gamma+1}}. \tag{19}$$

Thus, by substituting the series expansion from (19) into (15), we obtain

$$\begin{aligned}\mathcal{L}\{Res\phi_2(x,s)\} &= -\lambda\left(\tfrac{\theta_0(x)}{s} + \tfrac{\theta_1(x)}{s^{\gamma+1}} + \tfrac{\theta_2(x)}{s^{2\gamma+1}}\right)\\ &\quad +\lambda\left(\tfrac{2\theta_0(x)\theta_1(x)}{s^{1+2\gamma}} + \tfrac{2\theta_0(x)\theta_2(x)}{s^{1+3\gamma}} + \tfrac{\Gamma(2\gamma+1)\theta_1^2(x)}{\Gamma^2(\gamma+1)s^{1+3\gamma}}\right.\\ &\quad \left.+\tfrac{2\Gamma(3\gamma+1)\theta_1(x)\theta_2(x)}{\Gamma(\gamma+1)\Gamma(2\gamma+1)s^{1+4\gamma}} + \tfrac{\Gamma(4\gamma+1)\theta_0^2(x)}{\Gamma^2(2\gamma+1)s^{1+5\gamma}} + \tfrac{\theta_0^2(x)}{s^{1+\gamma}}\right)\\ &\quad -\left(\tfrac{\theta_1''(x)}{s^{1+2\gamma}} + \tfrac{\theta_2''(x)}{s^{1+3\gamma}} + \tfrac{\theta_0''(x)}{s^{1+\gamma}}\right) + \tfrac{\theta_1(x)}{s^{1+\gamma}} + \tfrac{\theta_2(x)}{s^{1+2\gamma}}.\end{aligned} \tag{20}$$

Now, multiplying both sides of (20) by the factor $s^{1+2\gamma}$ reveals

$$\begin{aligned}s^{1+2\gamma}\mathcal{L}\{Res\phi_2(x,s)\} &= -\lambda\tfrac{\theta_2(x)}{s^\gamma} + \tfrac{2\lambda\theta_0(x)\theta_2(x)}{s^\gamma} + \tfrac{\Gamma(4\gamma+1)\theta_2^2(x)}{\Gamma^2(2\gamma+1)s^{3\gamma}}\\ &\quad +\tfrac{2\lambda\Gamma(3\gamma+1)\theta_1(x)\theta_2(x)}{\Gamma(\gamma+1)\Gamma(2\gamma+1)s^{2\gamma}} + \tfrac{\lambda\Gamma(2\gamma+1)\theta_1^2(x)}{\Gamma^2(\gamma+1)s^\gamma} - \tfrac{\theta_2''(x)}{s^\gamma} + \lambda s^\gamma\theta_0^2(x)\\ &\quad -\lambda s^\gamma\theta_0(x) - s^\gamma\theta_0''(x) + s^\gamma\theta_1(x) - \lambda\theta_1(x) + 2\lambda\theta_0(x)\theta_1(x) - \theta_1''(x) + \theta_2(x).\end{aligned} \tag{21}$$

By solving $\lim_{s\to\infty} s^{1+2\gamma}\mathcal{L}[Res\phi_2(x,s)] = 0$, we obtain $\theta_2(x) = \lambda\theta_1(x)(1-2\theta_0(x)) + \theta_1''(x)$. Hence, the second Laplace series solution can be given by $\phi_2(x,s) = \frac{\theta_0(x)}{s} + \frac{\lambda\theta_0(x)(1-\theta_0(x))+\theta_0''(x)}{s^{\gamma+1}} + \frac{\lambda\theta_1(x)(1-2\theta_0(x))+\theta_1''(x)}{s^{2\gamma+1}}$.

Once again, for $i = 3$, the 3-rd residual function of (11), $\mathcal{L}\{Res\phi_3(x,s)\}$, can be written as

$$\begin{aligned}\mathcal{L}\{Res\phi_3(x,s)\} &= \phi_3(x,s) - \frac{\theta_0(x)}{s} - \frac{1}{s^\gamma}D_x^2\phi_3(x,s)\\ &-\frac{\lambda}{s^\gamma}\phi_3(x,s) + \frac{\lambda}{s^\gamma}\mathcal{L}\left\{\mathcal{L}^{-1}[\phi_3(x,s)]^2\right\}.\end{aligned} \tag{22}$$

After substituting $\phi_3(x,s) = \frac{\theta_0(x)}{s} + \frac{\theta_1(x)}{s^{\gamma+1}} + \frac{\theta_2(x)}{s^{2\gamma+1}} + \frac{\theta_3(x)}{s^{3\gamma+1}}$ into (21), the resulting fractional equation is multiplied by $s^{3\gamma+1}$ to yield

$$\begin{aligned}s^{1+3\gamma}\mathcal{L}\{Res\phi_3(x,s)\} &= -\frac{\lambda\theta_3(x)}{s^\gamma} + \frac{2\lambda s^\gamma\theta_0(x)\theta_3(x)}{s^\gamma} + \lambda s^\gamma\theta_0^2(x) - \lambda s^\gamma\theta_0(x)\\ &+\frac{\Gamma(6\gamma+1)\theta_3^2(x)}{\Gamma^2(3\gamma+1)s^{4\gamma}} + \frac{2\lambda\Gamma(5\gamma+1)\theta_2(x)\theta_3(x)}{\Gamma(2\gamma+1)\Gamma(3\gamma+1)s^{3\gamma}} + \frac{\lambda\Gamma(4\gamma+1)\theta_2^2(x)}{\Gamma^2(2\gamma+1)s^{2\gamma}}\\ &+\frac{2\lambda\Gamma(4\gamma+1)\theta_1(x)\theta_3(x)}{\Gamma(\gamma+1)\Gamma(3\gamma+1)s^{2\gamma}} + \frac{2\lambda\Gamma(3\gamma+1)\theta_1(x)\theta_2(x)}{\Gamma(\gamma+1)\Gamma(2\gamma+1)s^\gamma} - \frac{\theta_3''(x)}{s^\gamma}\\ &-s^{2\gamma}\theta_0''(x) + s^{2\gamma}\theta_1''(x) - \lambda s^\gamma\theta_1(x) + 2\lambda s^\gamma\theta_0(x)\theta_1(x) - s^\gamma\theta_1''(x)\\ &+s^\gamma\theta_2(x) + \frac{\lambda\Gamma(2\gamma+1)\theta_1^2(x)}{\Gamma^2(\gamma+1)} - \lambda\theta_2(x) + 2\lambda\theta_0(x)\theta_2(x) - \theta_2''(x) + \theta_3(x).\end{aligned} \tag{23}$$

using the fact that $s^{1+3\gamma}\mathcal{L}\{Res\phi_3(x,s)\} = 0$ leads to $\phi_3(x,s) = \lambda\theta_2(x)(1-2\theta_0(x)) + \theta_2''(x) - \frac{\lambda\Gamma(2\gamma+1)\theta_1^2(x)}{\Gamma^2(\gamma+1)}$.

By proceeding in the same manner as above and utilizing the fact that $\lim_{s\to\infty} s^{1+i\gamma}\mathcal{L}[Res\phi_i(x,s)] = 0$ for $i = 4,5,6\cdots$, the remaining coefficients $\theta_i(x)$ can be determined. Thus, the Laplace series solution $\phi(x,s)$ can be obtained in terms of the expansion series form of (12) as

$$\begin{aligned}\phi(x,s) &= \frac{\theta_0(x)}{s} + \frac{\lambda\left(\theta_0(x)-\theta_0^2(x)\right)+\theta_0''(x)}{s^{\gamma+1}} + \frac{\lambda\theta_1(x)(1-2\theta_0(x))+\theta_1''(x)}{s^{2\gamma+1}}\\ &+\frac{\lambda\theta_2(x)(1-2\theta_0(x))+\theta_2''(x)-\frac{\lambda\Gamma(2\gamma+1)\theta_1^2(x)}{\Gamma^2(\gamma+1)}}{s^{3\gamma+1}} + \cdots\end{aligned} \tag{24}$$

Therefore, the approximate solution of the IVP's (1) and (2) will be

$$\begin{aligned}\varphi(x,t) &= \theta_0(x) + \left(\lambda\left(\theta_0(x) - \theta_0^2(x)\right) + \theta_0''(x)\right)\frac{t^\gamma}{\Gamma(\gamma+1)}\\ &+\left(\lambda\theta_1(x)(1-2\theta_0(x)) + \theta_1''(x)\right)\frac{t^{2\gamma}}{\Gamma(\gamma+1)}\\ &+\left(\lambda\theta_2(x)(1-2\theta_0(x)) + \theta_2''(x) - \frac{\lambda\Gamma(2\gamma+1)\theta_1^2(x)}{\Gamma^2(\gamma+1)}\right)\frac{t^{3\gamma}}{\Gamma(\gamma+1)}\\ &+\cdots\end{aligned} \tag{25}$$

4. Numerical Examples

This section aims to highlight the effectiveness and potential of the proposed method in addressing the time-fractional Fisher equations under well-defined initial conditions. To carry out the necessary computations, Mathematica version 12 was utilized, ensuring accurate and efficient results.

Example 1. *Considering the following IVPs*

$$\begin{cases}Ð_t^\gamma\varphi = D_x^2\varphi + \varphi(1-\varphi), x \in R, t \geq 0,\\ \qquad\varphi(x,0) = \rho,\end{cases} \tag{26}$$

where ρ represents a constant, $\gamma \in (0,1]$, and $Ð_t^\gamma\varphi$ is a γ-th time-Caputo fractional derivative. Here, $\lambda = 1$ as compared with (1). For $\gamma = 1$, the exact solution of (26) has the closed form $\varphi(x,t) = \frac{\rho e^t}{1-\rho-\rho e^t}$ [35].

As performed in the previous section, the application of the Laplace transform of (26) takes the following form

$$\phi(x,s) = \frac{\rho}{s} + \frac{1}{s^\gamma} D_x^2 \phi(x,s) + \frac{1}{s^\gamma}\phi(x,s) - \frac{\lambda}{s^\gamma}\mathcal{L}\left\{\mathcal{L}^{-1}[\phi(x,s)]^2\right\}. \tag{27}$$

According to the LRPS approach, we define the i-th Laplace residual function of (27) as follows:

$$\begin{aligned} \mathcal{L}[Res\phi_i(x,s)] &= \phi_i(x,s) - \tfrac{\rho}{s} - \tfrac{1}{s^\gamma} D_x^2 \phi_i(x,s) \\ &- \tfrac{\lambda}{s^\gamma}\phi_i(x,s) + \tfrac{1}{s^\gamma}\mathcal{L}\left\{\mathcal{L}^{-1}[\phi_i(x,s)]^2\right\}. \end{aligned} \tag{28}$$

where $\phi_i(x,s)$ represents the i-th Laplace series solution of (27) such as

$$\phi_i(x,s) = \frac{\rho}{s} + \sum_{m=0}^{i} \frac{\theta_m(x)}{s^{m\gamma+1}}, s > 0, \tag{29}$$

By substituting $\phi_i(x,s)$ as given by (29) into the Laplace residual function $\mathcal{L}[Res\phi_i(x,s)]$ of (28), and multiplying the resulting fractional equation by the factor $s^{m\gamma+1}$, we can determine the coefficients $\theta_i(x)$ for $i = 1,2,3,\ldots$, throughout solving the equation $\lim_{s\to\infty} s^{1+i\gamma}\mathcal{L}[Res\phi_i(x,s)] = 0$, for $\theta_i(x)$. This, in turn, clearly demonstrates that

$$\begin{aligned} \theta_1(x) &= \rho - \rho^2, \\ \theta_2(x) &= \rho - 3\rho^2 + 2\rho^3, \\ \theta_3(x) &= \rho - 5\rho^2 + 8\rho^3 - 4\rho^4 + \tfrac{\rho^2(2\rho-\rho^2-1)\Gamma(2\gamma+1)}{\Gamma^2(\gamma+1)}, \\ \theta_4(x) &= \rho - 7\rho^2 + 18\rho^3 - 20\rho^4 + 8\rho^5 + \tfrac{\rho^2(4\rho-5\rho^2+2\rho^3-1)\Gamma(2\gamma+1)}{\Gamma^2(\gamma+1)} \\ &+ \tfrac{\rho^2(8\rho-10\rho^2+4\rho^3-2)\Gamma(3\gamma+1)}{\Gamma(\gamma+1)\Gamma(2\gamma+1)}, \\ \theta_4(x) &= \rho - 9\rho^2 + 32\rho^3 - 56\rho^4 + 48\rho^5 - 16\rho^6 \\ &+ \tfrac{\rho^2(6\rho-13\rho^2+12\rho^3-4\rho^4-1)\Gamma(2\gamma+1)}{\Gamma^2(\gamma+1)} \\ &+ \tfrac{\rho^2(12\rho-26\rho^2+24\rho^3-8\rho^4-2)\Gamma(3\gamma+1)}{\Gamma(\gamma+1)\Gamma(2\gamma+1)} \\ &+ \tfrac{\rho^2(6\rho-13\rho^2+12\rho^3-4\rho^4-1)\Gamma(4\gamma+1)}{\Gamma^2(2\gamma+1)} \\ &+ \tfrac{\rho^2(12\rho-26\rho^2+24\rho^3-8\rho^4-2)\Gamma(4\gamma+1)}{\Gamma(\gamma+1)\Gamma(3\gamma+1)} \\ &+ \tfrac{\rho^2(2\rho-6\rho^2+6\rho^3-2\rho^4-2)\Gamma(2\gamma+1)\Gamma(4\gamma+1)}{\Gamma^3(\gamma+1)\Gamma(3\gamma+1)}. \end{aligned} \tag{30}$$

As a result, the Laplace series solution of (27) can be expressed in the following series form:

$$\begin{aligned} \phi(x,s) &= \tfrac{\rho}{s} + \tfrac{\rho-\rho^2}{s^{\gamma+1}} + \tfrac{\rho-3\rho^2+2\rho^3}{s^{2\gamma+1}} \\ &+ \left(\rho - 5\rho^2 + 8\rho^3 - 4\rho^4 + \tfrac{\rho^2(2\rho-\rho^2-1)\Gamma(2\gamma+1)}{\Gamma^2(\gamma+1)}\right)\tfrac{1}{s^{3\gamma+1}} + \ldots \end{aligned} \tag{31}$$

Consequently, the series solution for the fractional IVPs (26) can be written as

$$\begin{aligned} \varphi(x,t) &= \rho + (\rho-\rho^2)\tfrac{t^\gamma}{\Gamma(\gamma+1)} + (\rho - 3\rho^2 + 2\rho^3)\tfrac{t^{2\gamma}}{\Gamma(2\gamma+1)} \\ &+ \left(\rho - 5\rho^2 + 8\rho^3 - 4\rho^4 + \tfrac{\rho^2(2\rho-\rho^2-1)\Gamma(2\gamma+1)}{\Gamma^2(\gamma+1)}\right)\tfrac{t^{3\gamma}}{\Gamma(3\gamma+1)} \\ &+ \ldots \end{aligned} \tag{32}$$

By setting $\gamma = 1$ in the fractional expansion (32), we obtain

$$\varphi(x,t) = \rho + \left(\rho - \rho^2\right)t + \left(\rho - 3\rho^2 + 2\rho^3\right)\frac{t^2}{2!} + \left(\rho - 7\rho^2 + 12\rho^3 - 6\rho^4\right)\frac{t^3}{3!} + \ldots, \tag{33}$$

which corresponds to the given closed-form solution [35] and coincides with the Taylor series of $\frac{\rho e^t}{1-\rho-\rho e^t}$.

The results are plotted in Figure 1, for the exact solution and the approximate solution $\varphi_4(x,t)$ for different value of t. And in Table 1, the value of absolute error of exact solution and $\varphi_4(x,t)$ for various t on (0,1]. Moreover, as stated in calculations we can see the higher accuracy achieved if we found another component of the approximate solution.

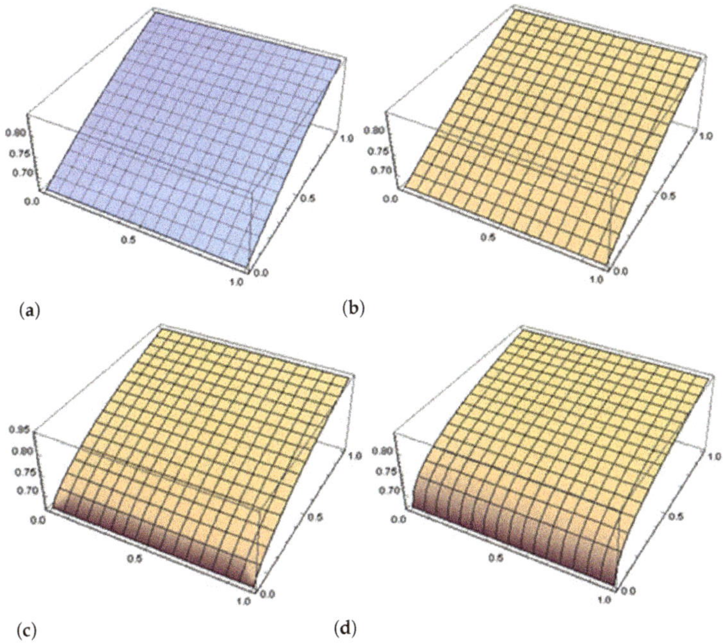

Figure 1. The surface plot of the *5th-series* approximate and exact solutions IVP (26): (**a**) exact solution $\varphi(x,t)$, (**b**) $\varphi_5(x,t)$ for $\gamma = 1$, (**c**) $\varphi_5(x,t)$ for $\gamma = 0.75$ (**d**) $\gamma_5(x,t)$ for $\gamma = 0.5$.

Table 1. Numerical results at $\gamma = 1$ with different values of t for Example 1.

t_i	$\varphi(x,t)$	$\varphi_5(x,t)$	$\lvert\varphi(x,t)-\varphi_5(x,t)\rvert$
0.15	0.0011616462485873247	0.0011616462334527696	$1.51345550675197 \times 10^{-11}$
0.30	0.0013493867127497216	0.0013493857242148680	$9.88534853583675 \times 10^{-10}$
0.45	0.0015674214008082911	0.0015674099064100775	$1.149439821362258 \times 10^{-8}$
0.60	0.0018206220327889478	0.0018205560898476433	$6.594294130451289 \times 10^{-8}$
0.75	0.0021146379659695570	0.0021143810570989283	$2.569088706286249 \times 10^{-7}$
0.90	0.0024560182992063697	0.0024552346605740850	$7.836386322845022 \times 10^{-7}$

Example 2. *Consider the following IVPs:*

$$\begin{cases} {}_t^{\gamma}\varphi = D_x^2\varphi + 6\varphi(1-\varphi), x \in R, t \geq 0, \\ \varphi(x,0) = \frac{1}{(1+e^x)^2} \end{cases} \tag{34}$$

where $\gamma \in (0,1]$, and ${}_t^{\gamma}\varphi$ is a γ-th time-Caputo fractional derivative. Here, $\lambda = 6$ as compared with (1). For $\gamma = 1$, the exact solution of (34) has the closed form $\varphi(x,t) = \frac{1}{(1+e^{x-5t})^2}$.

According to the LRPS approach and the initial data $\varphi(x,0) = \frac{1}{(1+e^x)^2}$, the Laplace transform of (34) can be expressed as

$$\phi(x,s) = \frac{1}{(1+e^x)^2 s} + \frac{1}{s^\gamma} D_x^2 \phi(x,s) + \frac{1}{s^\gamma}\phi(x,s) - \frac{\lambda}{s^\gamma}\mathcal{L}\left\{\mathcal{L}^{-1}[\phi(x,s)]^2\right\}. \quad (35)$$

The i-th Laplace series solution of (35) has the form

$$\phi_i(x,s) = \frac{1}{(1+e^x)^2 s} + \sum_{m=0}^{i} \frac{\theta_m(x)}{s^{m\gamma+1}}, s > 0. \quad (36)$$

As a preliminary step before applying the proposed method, the Laplace Equation (35) can be rewritten as

$$\phi_i(x,s) - \frac{1}{(1+e^x)^2 s} - \frac{1}{s^\gamma} D_x^2 \phi_i(x,s) - \frac{1}{s^\gamma}\phi_i(x,s) + \frac{\lambda}{s^\gamma}\mathcal{L}\left\{\mathcal{L}^{-1}[\phi_i(x,s)]^2\right\} = 0. \quad (37)$$

The substitution of $\phi_i(x,s)$ into (37) leads to the i-th Laplace residual function as follows

$$\begin{aligned}\mathcal{L}[Res\phi_i(x,s)] &= \sum_{m=1}^{i} \frac{\theta_m(x)}{s^{m\gamma+1}} - \frac{1}{s^\gamma} D_x^2\left(\frac{1}{(1+e^x)^2 s} + \sum_{m=1}^{i} \frac{\theta_m(x)}{s^{m\gamma+1}}\right) \\ &-\frac{1}{s^\gamma}\left(\frac{1}{(1+e^x)^2 s} + \sum_{m=1}^{i} \frac{\theta_m(x)}{s^{m\gamma+1}}\right) \\ &+\frac{1}{s^\gamma}\mathcal{L}\left\{\mathcal{L}^{-1}\left[\frac{1}{(1+e^x)^2 s} + \sum_{m=1}^{i} \frac{\theta_m(x)}{s^{m\gamma+1}}\right]^2\right\}.\end{aligned} \quad (38)$$

Following the same approach as the LRPS method, and based on the fact that $\lim_{s\to\infty} s^{1+i\gamma}\mathcal{L}[Res\phi_i(x,s)] = 0$, we can determine the coefficients $\theta_i(x)$ for $i = 1,2,3,\ldots,$ as follows

$$\begin{aligned}\theta_1(x) &= \frac{10e^x}{(1+e^x)^3}, \\ \theta_2(x) &= \frac{50e^x(-1+2e^x)}{(1+e^x)^4}, \\ \theta_3(x) &= \frac{1}{(1+e^x)^6\Gamma^2(\gamma+1)}(50e^x((5+e^x(-6+5e^x(-3+4e^x)))\Gamma^2(\gamma+1) - 12e^x\Gamma(2\gamma+1), \\ \theta_4(x) &= \frac{50e^x}{(1+e^x)^8}(-25+e^x(-8+e^x(170+e^x(248+25e^x(-17+8e^x)))) \\ &+\frac{1}{\Gamma(1+\gamma)}24e^x(-\frac{4^\gamma(-1+e^x(-5+11e^x))\Gamma(\frac{1}{2}+\gamma)}{\sqrt{\pi}} \\ &-\frac{5(-1+e^x+2e^{2x})\Gamma(1+3\gamma)}{\Gamma(1+2\gamma)})), \\ \theta_5(x) &= \frac{1}{(1+e^x)^{10}\Gamma^3(\gamma+1)\Gamma^2(2\gamma+1)\Gamma(3\gamma+1)}(50e^x(-24e^x(2+e^x(5 \\ &+e^x(198+e^x(-463+242e^x))))\Gamma(1+\gamma)\Gamma(1+3\gamma)+1440e^{2x}(1 \\ &+e^x)\Gamma^2(1+2\gamma)\Gamma(1+4\gamma) - 120e^x(1+e^x)\Gamma^2(1+\gamma)\Gamma(1+2\gamma)((2 \\ &+e^x(21+e^x(-69+44e^x)))\Gamma^2(1+3\gamma)+(5+e^x(-6+5e^x(-3 \\ &+4e^x)))\Gamma(1+2\gamma)\Gamma(1+4\gamma)) + \Gamma^3(1+\gamma)\Gamma(1+3\gamma)(-300e^{3x}\Gamma(1 \\ &+4\gamma)(1+\cosh(x)+3\sinh(x))^2+\Gamma^2(1+2\gamma)(125+e^x(266-705e^x \\ &-2e^{4x}(-11253+138\cosh(2x)+\cosh(x)(10062-4276\sinh(x)) \\ &+313\sinh(x)))))) \\ &\vdots\end{aligned}$$

Thus, the 5th-Laplace series solution of (35) can be expressed as

$$\begin{aligned}\phi_5(x,s) &= \left(\left(\frac{1}{(1+e^x)^2}\right)\frac{1}{s} + \left(\frac{10e^x}{(1+e^x)^3}\right)\frac{1}{s^{\gamma+1}} + \left(\frac{50e^x(-1+2e^x)}{(1+e^x)^4}\right)\frac{1}{s^{2\gamma+1}} \right.\\ &+(\frac{1}{(1+e^x)^6\Gamma^2(\gamma+1)}(50e^x((5+e^x(-6+5e^x(-3+4e^x)))\Gamma^2(\gamma \\ &\left.+1) - 12e^x\Gamma(2\gamma+1))\frac{1}{s^{3\gamma+1}} + \frac{\theta_4(x)}{s^{4\gamma+1}} + \frac{\theta_5(x)}{s^{5\gamma+1}}\right).\end{aligned} \quad (39)$$

Consequently, the 5th-series solution for the fractional IVP (34) can be obtained after operating the inversion formula of the Laplace transform of expansion (39) in the form

$$\phi_5(x,s) = \frac{1}{(1+e^x)^2} + \frac{10e^x}{(1+e^x)^3}\frac{t^\gamma}{\Gamma(\gamma+1)} + \left(\frac{50e^x(-1+2e^x)}{(1+e^x)^4}\right)\frac{t^{2\gamma}}{\Gamma(2\gamma+1)} \\ (\frac{1}{(1+e^x)^6\Gamma^2(\gamma+1)}(50\,e^x((5+e^x(-6+5e^x(-3+4e^x)))\Gamma^2(\gamma \\ +1) - 12e^x\,\Gamma(2\gamma+1))\frac{t^{3\gamma}}{\Gamma(3\gamma+1)} + \theta_4(x)\frac{t^{4\gamma}}{\Gamma(4\gamma+1)} + \theta_5(x)\frac{t^{5\gamma}}{\Gamma(5\gamma+1)}). \tag{40}$$

By inserting $\gamma = 1$, in the fractional expansion (40), the 5th-series solution for the fractional IVP (34) takes the form

$$\phi_5(x,s) = \left(\frac{1}{(1+e^x)^2}\right) + \left(\frac{10e^x}{(1+e^x)^3}\right)t + \left(\frac{50e^x(-1+2e^x)}{(1+e^x)^4}\right)\frac{t^2}{2!} \\ + \left(\frac{250e^x(1+e^x(-7+4e^x))}{(1+e^x)^5}\right)\frac{t^3}{3!} \\ + \left(\frac{1250e^x(-1+e^x(18+e^x(-33+8e^x)))}{(1+e^x)^6}\right)\frac{t^4}{4!} \\ + \left(\frac{6250e^x(1+e^x(-41+e^x(171+e^x(-131+16e^x))))}{(1+e^x)^7}\right)\frac{t^5}{5!}, \tag{41}$$

which is in good agreement with the first five terms of the Maclaurin series of the exact solution $\varphi(x,t) = \frac{1}{(1+e^{x-5t})^2}$.

The results are plotted in Figure 2, for the exact solution and $\varphi_5(x,t)$ for different value of Y and $x = 0.1$ in (a) $t = 0.15$ in (b). Also, in Table 2, the values of $\varphi_5(x,t)$ are computed for different value of Y and various value t on $(0,1]$ about $x = 0,1$. Moreover, as stated in calculations we can see the accuracy achieved for this method.

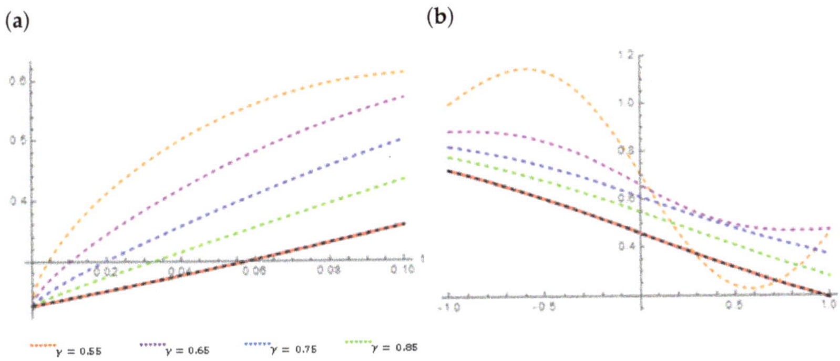

Figure 2. (**a**) Behavior of $\varphi(x,t)$, and $\varphi_5(x,t)$ solutions at various values of γ and $x = 0.1$, (**b**) Behavior of $\varphi(x,t)$, and $\varphi_5(x,t)$ solutions at various values of of γ and $t = 0.15$ for Example 2.

Table 2. Numerical results of the fifth approximate solutions for Example 2.

x_i	t_i	**γ=1**	**γ=0.95**	**γ=0.75**	**γ=0.55**
	0.2	0.533333333	0.563133166	0.666743301	0.752959158
	0.4	0.7333333333	0.730677032	0.647817002	1.729984040
0	0.6	0.6624999999	0.601221814	0.773199786	5.627232401
	0.8	0.3833333333	0.380901655	2.296503479	14.43633998
	1.0	0.4583333334	0.868175353	7.100230119	29.99511468
	0.2	0.2500655487	0.282636442	0.461938500	0.198465800
	0.4	0.5162760640	0.543258410	0.108256800	−4.62753690
1	0.6	0.4323501300	0.204044800	−3.30214140	−18.3144920
	0.8	−1.181739800	−2.27878010	−13.1558670	−44.2210390
	1.0	−6.581913800	−9.63100700	−33.7865670	−85.4023980

5. Conclusions

The objective of this paper is to extend the LRPS technique for solving the time-fractional Fisher's equation, showcasing its reliability in handling nonlinear FPDEs. The method is first applied in the Laplace space, and approximate solutions are retrieved via inverse transformation. Fisher's equation is analyzed under two different initial conditions, with accuracy evaluated through absolute error computations. The findings confirm that the LRPS technique is both efficient and precise, offering a computationally simple yet powerful approach suitable for various fractional differential models. Future research can focus on applying the LRPS method to fractional differential models in heat transfer, viscoelasticity, anomalous diffusion, and wave propagation in complex media, while also extending its application to higher-dimensional FPDEs for broader analytical insights.

Author Contributions: Conceptualization, S.A.; methodology, S.A.-O.; software, R.A.-d.; validation, R.A.-d.; investigation, M.A.-S.; resources, S.A. and S.M.; writing—original draft preparation, S.A.-O. and S.M.; writing—review and editing, S.A.; funding acquisition, M.A.-S. All authors have read and agreed to the published version of the manuscript.

Funding: This research work was funded by Umm Al-Qura University, Saudi Arabia under grant number: 25UQU4282396GSSR02.

Data Availability Statement: Data are contained within the article.

Acknowledgments: The authors extend their appreciation to Umm Al-Qura University, Saudi Arabia for funding this research work through grant number: (25UQU4282396GSSR02).

Conflicts of Interest: The authors declare no conflicts of interest.

References

1. Magin, R.L.; Ingo, C.; Colon-Perez, L.; Triplett, W.; Mareci, T.H. Characterization of anomalous diffusion in porous biological tissues using fractional order derivatives and entropy. *Microporous Mesoporous Mater.* **2013**, *178*, 39–43. [CrossRef] [PubMed]
2. Ghanbari, B.; Atangana, A. A new application of fractional Atangana-Baleanu derivatives: Designing ABC-fractional masks in image processing. *Phys. Stat. Mech. Its Appl.* **2020**, *542*, 123516. [CrossRef]
3. Zhang, S.; Zhang, H.Q. Fractional sub-equation method and its applications to nonlinear fractional PDEs. *Phys. Lett.* **2011**, *375*, 1069–1073. [CrossRef]
4. Caputo, M. Linear models of dissipation whose Q is almost frequency independent—II. *Geophys. J. Int.* **1967**, *13*, 529–539. [CrossRef]
5. Alaroud, M.; Al-Smadi, M.; Rozita Ahmad, R.; Salma Din, U.K. An Analytical Numerical Method for Solving Fuzzy Fractional Volterra Integro-Differential Equations. *Symmetry* **2019**, *11*, 205. [CrossRef]
6. Miller, K.S.; Ross, B. *An Introduction to the Fractional Calculus and Fractional Differential Equations*; Wiley: Hoboken, NJ, USA, 1993.
7. Podlubny, I. Fractional differential equations. *Math. Sci. Eng.* **1999**, *198*. Available online: https://cir.nii.ac.jp/crid/1573950399205663360 (accessed on 11 February 2025).
8. Kilbas, A.A.; Srivastava, H.M.; Trujillo, J.J. *Theory and Applications of Fractional Differential Equations*, 1st ed.; Elsevier: Amsterdam, The Netherlands, 2006; Volume 204.
9. Mainardi, F. *Fractional Calculus and Waves in Linear Viscoelasticity*; Imperial College Press: London, UK, 2010.
10. Almeida, R.; Tavares, D.; Torres, D.F. *The Variable-Order Fractional Calculus of Variations*; Springer: Cham, Switzerland, 2019.
11. Hasan, S.; Al-Smadi, M.; Freihet, A.; Momani, S. Two computational approaches for solving a fractional obstacle system in Hilbert space. *Adv. Differ. Equ.* **2019**, *2019*, 55. [CrossRef]
12. El-Ajou, A. A modification to the conformable fractional calculus with some applications. *Alex. Eng. J.* **2020**, *59*, 2239–2249. [CrossRef]
13. Gao, G.; Sun, Z.; Zhang, H. A new fractional numerical differentiation formula to approximate the Caputo fractional derivative and its applications. *J. Comput. Phys.* **2014**, *259*, 33–50. [CrossRef]
14. Kazem, S. Exact solution of some linear fractional differential equations by Laplace transforms. *Int. J. Nonlinear Sci.* **2013**, *16*, 3–11.
15. Wang, Q. Numerical solutions for fractional KdV-Burgers equation by Adomian decomposition method. *Appl. Math. Comput.* **2006**, *182*, 1048–1055. [CrossRef]
16. Alkresheh, H.A.; Ismail, A.I. Multi-step fractional differential transform method for the solution of fractional order stiff systems. *Ain Shams Eng. J.* **2021**, *12*, 4223–4231.
17. Das, S. Analytical solution of a fractional diffusion equation by variational iteration method. *Comput. Math. Appl.* **2009**, *57*, 483–487.

18. He, J.H. Approximate analytical solution for seepage flow with fractional derivatives porous media. *Comput. Methods Appl. Mech. Eng.* **1998**, *167*, 57–68.
19. Gumah, G.; Naser, M.F.M.; Al-Smadi, M.; Al-Omari, S.K.Q.; Baleanu, D. Numerical solutions of hybrid fuzzy differential equations in a Hilbert space. *Appl. Numer. Math.* **2020**, *151*, 402–412. [CrossRef]
20. Aychluh, M.; Ayalew, M. The Fractional Power Series Method for Solving the Nonlinear Kuramoto-Sivashinsky Equation. *Int. J. Appl. Comput. Math.* **2025**, *11*, 29.
21. Nikan, O.; Avazzadeh, Z.; Machado, J.T. An efficient local meshless approach for solving nonlinear time-fractional fourth-order diffusion model. *J. King Saud Univ.* **2021**, *33*, 101243.
22. Gao, X.; Jiang, X.; Chen, S. The numerical method for the moving boundary problem with space-fractional derivative in drug release devices. *Appl. Math. Model.* **2015**, *39*, 2385–2391.
23. Nikan, O.; Machado, J.T.; Golbabai, A. Numerical solution of time-fractional fourth-order reaction-diffusion model arising in composite environments. *Appl. Math. Model.* **2021**, *89*, 819–836.
24. Shqair, M.; El-Ajou, A.; Nairat, M. Analytical solution for multi-energy groups of neutron diffusion equations by a residual power series method. *Mathematics* **2019**, *7*, 633.
25. Saadeh, R.; Alaroud, M.; Al-Smadi, M.; Ahmad, R.R.; Salma Din, U.K. Application of Fractional Residual Power Series Algorithm to Solve Newell-Whitehead-Segel Equation of Fractional Order. *Symmetry* **2019**, *11*, 1431. [CrossRef]
26. Ali, A.I.; Kalim, M.; Khan, A. Solution of Fractional Partial Differential Equations Using Fractional Power Series Method. *Inter. J. Differ. Equ.* **2021**, *2021*, 6385799. [CrossRef]
27. Area, I.; Nieto, J.J. Power series solution of the fractional logistic equation. *Phys. A Stat. Mech. Its Appl.* **2021**, *573*, 125947. [CrossRef]
28. El-Ajou, A. Adapting the Laplace Transform to Create Solitary Solutions for the Nonlinear Time-Fractional Dispersive PDEs Via a New Approach. *Eur. Phys. J. Plus* **2021**, *136*, 229.
29. Karatas Akgul, E.; Akgul, A.; Baleanu, D. Laplace Transform Method for Economic Models with Constant Proportional Caputo Derivative. *Fractal Fract.* **2020**, *4*, 30. [CrossRef]
30. Baihi, A.; Kajouni, A.; Hilal, K.; Lmou, H. Laplace transform method for a coupled system of (*p*,*q*)-Caputo fractional differential equations. *J. Appl. Math. Comput.* **2025**, *71*, 511–530. [CrossRef]
31. Gomez, C.A.; Salas, A.H. Exact solutions for the generalized BBM equationwith variable coefficients. *Math. Probl. Eng.* **2010**, *4*, 394–401.
32. Estevez, P.G.; Kuru, S.; Negro, J.; Nieto, L.M. Traveling wave solutions ofthe generalized Benjamin-Bona-Mahony equation. *Chaos Sol. Fract.* **2009**, *40*, 2031–2040. [CrossRef]
33. Gomez, C.A.; Salas, A.H.; Frias, B.A. New periodic and soliton solutions for the generalized BBM and Burgers-BBM equations. *Appl. Math. Comput.* **2010**, *217*, 1430–1434.
34. Hanna, J.; Rowland, J. *Fourier Series, Transforms, and Boundary Value Problems;* John Wiley and Sons, Inc.: New York, NY, USA, 1990.
35. Al-Deiakeh, R.; Abu Arqub, O.; Al-Smadi, M.; Momani, S. Lie symmetry analysis, explicit solutions, and conservation laws of the time-fractional Fisher equation in two-dimensional space. *J. Ocean. Eng. Sci.* **2022**, *7*, 345–352.

fractal and fractional

MDPI

Article

A New L2 Type Difference Scheme for the Time-Fractional Diffusion Equation

Cheng-Yu Hu and Fu-Rong Lin *

Department of Mathematics, Shantou University, Shantou 515063, China
* Correspondence: frlin@stu.edu.cn

Abstract: In this paper, a new L2 (NL2) scheme is proposed to approximate the Caputo temporal fractional derivative, leading to a time-stepping scheme for the time-fractional diffusion equation (TFDE). Subsequently, the space derivative of the resulting system is discretized using a specific finite difference method, yielding a fully discrete system. We then establish the H^1-norm stability and convergence of the time-stepping scheme on uniform meshes for the TFDE. In particular, we prove that the proposed scheme has $(3-\alpha)$th-order accuracy, where α $(0 < \alpha < 1)$ is the order of the time-fractional derivative. Finally, numerical experiments for several test problems are carried out to validate the obtained theoretical results.

Keywords: time-fractional diffusion equation (TFDE); NL2 scheme; H^1-norm stability

MSC: 65M06; 26A33; 65M12

1. Introduction

In this paper, we consider numerical methods for the time-fractional diffusion equation with variable coefficients:

$$\begin{cases} \partial_{0t}^{\alpha}u(x,t) = \frac{\partial}{\partial x}\left(p(x)\frac{\partial u}{\partial x}\right) - q(x)u(x,t) + f(x,t), & (x,t) \in (0,l) \times (0,T], \\ u(0,t) = 0, u(l,t) = 0, & 0 \le t \le T, \\ u(x,0) = u_0(x), & x \in [0,l], \end{cases} \tag{1}$$

where $p(x) \ge C_1 > 0$ and $q(x) \ge 0$, $f(x,t)$ is the source term, and $\partial_{0t}^{\alpha}u(x,t)$ is the Caputo derivative of order α $(0 < \alpha < 1)$ with respect to t, i.e.,

$$\partial_{0t}^{\alpha}u(x,t) = \frac{1}{\Gamma(1-\alpha)}\int_0^t \frac{\partial u(x,\eta)}{\partial \eta}(t-\eta)^{-\alpha}d\eta. \tag{2}$$

Here, $\Gamma(\alpha) = \int_0^{\infty} t^{\alpha-1}e^{-t}dt$ is the Γ function.

Fractional partial differential equations (FPDEs) have extensive applications in diverse fields, as illustrated in references [1–8]. Specifically, the time-fractional diffusion equation (TFDE) overcomes the limitations of traditional integer-order calculus. It offers a general mathematical framework for depicting complex systems exhibiting non-locality, long-range correlations, and memory effects. The time-fractional diffusion equation poses a significant challenge since it is an integro-differential equation, whose analytical solution is often difficult to derive. Consequently, numerical methods are necessary for its solution. Several approaches have been developed to solve the TFDE. For example, Ahmad et al. [8] introduced Monte Carlo-based physics-informed neural networks with the cuckoo search

(PINN-CS) algorithm for addressing fractional partial differential equations. Sun and Wu [9] introduced and analyzed a finite difference scheme for the fractional diffusion wave equation. Lin and Xu [10] proposed a numerical scheme using a finite difference scheme in time and Legendre spectral methods in space. Zhang and Sun [11] presented an alternating direction implicit scheme. Sun et al. [12] devised finite difference schemes for a variable-order time fractional diffusion equation. Yan, Pal, and Ford [13] developed a $(3-\alpha)$th-order method by directly discretizing the fractional differential operator. Li and Liao [14] analyzed the well-known differential equations by applying the corresponding inverse operators.

Recently, research on numerical methods for Caputo fractional derivatives has increased significantly; see, e.g., [15–23]. Gao et al. developed a novel difference analog of the Caputo fractional derivative, known as the L1-2 formula [24]. Alikhanov used piecewise quadratic polynomial interpolation to derive the L2-1σ formula for approximating the Caputo fractional derivative at specific points [25]. The schemes proposed in [17,20,23–25] have been proven to have $3-\alpha$ order accuracy for αth-order Caputo fractional derivatives. Notably, Quan and Wu [23] established H^1-norm stability and convergence for an L2 scheme on general nonuniform meshes when applied to the subdiffusion equation. We noticed that the discrete form of these schemes at the first step $t_1 = \tau$ or the last step differs from the unified form for the rest of the steps. As an example, in [20], the approximation of the first time step is obtained by using the L1-formula on the time layer $[0, \tau]$ with step size $\tau_1 = \mathcal{O}(\tau^{\frac{3-\alpha}{2-\alpha}})$. To address this issue and preserve the order of convergence, we propose a scheme using piecewise quadratic polynomial interpolation, which computes approximate values in pairs. We call it the new L2 (NL2) discretization. We showed that the NL2 scheme's discretization matrix is a block lower triangular Toeplitz matrix with two-by-two blocks and proved its H^1-norm stability and convergence. Numerical experiments show that the NL2 scheme has better accuracy than the L2 schemes proposed in [17,20].

The rest of this paper is organized as follows: In Section 2, we propose a novel piecewise quadratic polynomial interpolation method, referred to as the new L2 scheme (NL2 for short), to approximate the Caputo fractional derivative. Subsequently, we derive the key properties of the NL2 scheme, including its consistency and the features of the discretization matrix. Section 3 presents a difference scheme based on the NL2 scheme, deriving its H^1-norm stability. In Section 4, we conduct numerical experiments to verify the theoretical findings of the proposed scheme. Finally, Section 5 offers concluding remarks.

2. A Novel L2 Scheme for the Caputo Derivative

Let $\alpha \in (0,1)$ and $v(t)$ be a function in $C^3(0,T]$. Consider approximating the Caputo fractional derivative of order α defined by (2).

2.1. A New L2 Scheme

Let M be a positive integer and $\tau = T/(2M)$. Define a uniform grid

$$t_k = k\tau,\ k = 0,1,\dots,2M.$$

Denote $v(t_i)$ by v_i and the quadratic interpolation polynomial of $v(t)$ at the points (t_{2i-2}, v_{2i-2}), (t_{2i-1}, v_{2i-1}) and (t_{2i}, v_{2i}) by $\Pi_{2,i}v(t)$. We have

$$\Pi_{2,i}v(t) = \frac{(t-t_{2i-1})(t-t_{2i})}{2\tau^2}v_{2i-2} - \frac{(t-t_{2i-2})(t-t_{2i})}{\tau^2}v_{2i-1} + \frac{(t-t_{2i-2})(t-t_{2i-1})}{2\tau^2}v_{2i}.$$

Assume $v(\cdot) \in C^3(0,T]$, then we have

$$v(t) - \Pi_{2,i}v(t) = \frac{v'''(\xi_i)}{6}(t-t_{2i-2})(t-t_{2i-1})(t-t_{2i}),$$

where $t,\ \xi_i \in [t_{2i-2}, t_{2i}]$, and ξ_i depends on t, $1 \le i \le M$. We arrive at

$$(\Pi_{2,i}v(t))' = \delta v_{2i-\frac{1}{2}} + \delta^2 v_{2i-1}(t - t_{2i-\frac{1}{2}}), \quad t \in [t_{2i-2}, t_{2i}],$$

where

$$\delta v_{2i-\frac{1}{2}} = \frac{v_{2i}-v_{2i-1}}{\tau},\ \delta^2 v_{2i-1} = \frac{\delta v_{2i-\frac{1}{2}} - \delta v_{2i-\frac{3}{2}}}{\tau} = \frac{v_{2i}-2v_{2i-1}+v_{2i-2}}{\tau^2}.$$

Now, we introduce the discretization of the Caputo derivative. It is easy to obtain

$$\begin{aligned}\left.\frac{\partial^\alpha v(t)}{\partial t^\alpha}\right|_{t=t_{2k-1}} &= \frac{1}{\Gamma(1-\alpha)}\int_0^{t_{2k-1}} \frac{\partial v(\eta)}{\partial \eta}(t_{2k-1}-\eta)^{-\alpha}d\eta \\ &= \frac{1}{\Gamma(1-\alpha)}\left[\sum_{i=1}^{k-1}\int_{t_{2i-2}}^{t_{2i}} \frac{\partial v(\eta)}{\partial \eta}(t_{2k-1}-\eta)^{-\alpha}d\eta + \int_{t_{2k-2}}^{t_{2k-1}} \frac{\partial v(\eta)}{\partial \eta}(t_{2k-1}-\eta)^{-\alpha}d\eta\right] \end{aligned} \tag{3}$$

and

$$\left.\frac{\partial^\alpha v(t)}{\partial t^\alpha}\right|_{t=t_{2k}} = \frac{1}{\Gamma(1-\alpha)}\sum_{i=1}^{k}\int_{t_{2i-2}}^{t_{2i}} \frac{\partial v(\eta)}{\partial \eta}(t_{2k}-\eta)^{-\alpha}d\eta \tag{4}$$

for $k = 1, 2, \ldots, M$.

From the above expression, we approximate $v(t)$ by making use of $\Pi_{2,i}v(t)$ on the interval $[t_{2i-2}, t_{2i}]$ $(1 \le i \le M)$. Firstly, we have

$$\int_{t_{2i-1}}^{t_{2i}} (t_j-\eta)^{-\alpha}d\eta = \frac{\tau^{1-\alpha}}{1-\alpha}a_{j-2i+1}, \quad j \ge 2i,$$

where

$$a_k = (1-\alpha)\int_0^1 (k-s)^{-\alpha}ds = k^{1-\alpha} - (k-1)^{1-\alpha}, \quad k \ge 1. \tag{5}$$

Let

$$g(r,s) = (r-s)^{-\alpha} - (r+s)^{-\alpha}, \quad r \ge \frac{1}{2},\ 0 \le s \le \frac{1}{2},$$

and let

$$\begin{aligned} b_k &= (1-\alpha)\int_0^{\frac{1}{2}} g\left(k-\frac{1}{2}, s\right)sds \\ &= \frac{1}{2-\alpha}[k^{2-\alpha} - (k-1)^{2-\alpha}] - \frac{1}{2}[k^{1-\alpha} + (k-1)^{1-\alpha}], \quad k \ge 1. \end{aligned} \tag{6}$$

Then, we have

$$\int_{t_{2i-1}}^{t_{2i}} (t_j-\eta)^{-\alpha}(\eta - t_{2i-\frac{1}{2}})d\eta = \frac{\tau^{2-\alpha}}{1-\alpha}b_{j-2i+1}, \quad j \ge 2i.$$

Based on the above discussion, we obtain

$$
\begin{aligned}
&\int_{t_{2i-2}}^{t_{2i}} (t_j-\eta)^{-\alpha}(\Pi_{2,i}v(\eta))'d\eta \\
=\;& \int_{t_{2i-2}}^{t_{2i}} (t_j-\eta)^{-\alpha}\Big[\delta v_{2i-\frac{1}{2}}+\delta^2 v_{2i-1}(\eta-t_{2i-\frac{1}{2}})\Big]d\eta \\
=\;& \Big[\int_{t_{2i-2}}^{t_{2i-1}} (t_j-\eta)^{-\alpha}d\eta+\int_{t_{2i-1}}^{t_{2i}} (t_j-\eta)^{-\alpha}d\eta\Big]\delta v_{2i-\frac{1}{2}} \\
&+\Big[\int_{t_{2i-2}}^{t_{2i-1}} (t_j-\eta)^{-\alpha}(\eta-t_{2i-\frac{1}{2}})d\eta+\int_{t_{2i-1}}^{t_{2i}} (t_j-\eta)^{-\alpha}(\eta-t_{2i-\frac{1}{2}})d\eta\Big]\delta^2 v_{2i-1} \\
=\;& \frac{\tau^{1-\alpha}}{1-\alpha}[(a_{j-2i+1}+a_{j-2i+2})\delta v_{2i-\frac{1}{2}}+\tau(b_{j-2i+1}+b_{j-2i+2}-a_{j-2i+2})\delta^2 v_{2i-1}] \\
=\;& \frac{\tau^{1-\alpha}}{1-\alpha}[(a_{j-2i+2}-b_{j-2i+1}-b_{j-2i+2})\delta v_{2i-\frac{3}{2}}+(a_{j-2i+1}+b_{j-2i+1}+b_{j-2i+2})\delta v_{2i-\frac{1}{2}}]
\end{aligned}
$$

and

$$
\int_{t_{2k-2}}^{t_{2k-1}} \frac{\partial v(\eta)}{\partial \eta}(t_{2k-1}-\eta)^{1-\alpha}d\eta=\frac{\tau^{1-\alpha}}{1-\alpha}[(a_1-b_1)\delta v_{2k-\frac{3}{2}}+b_1\delta v_{2k-\frac{1}{2}}].
$$

Finally, from (3), we obtain

$$
\begin{aligned}
&\frac{\partial^\alpha v(t)}{\partial t^\alpha}\Big|_{t=t_{2k-1}} \approx (L^\alpha v)(t_{2k-1}) \\
:=&\frac{\tau^{1-\alpha}}{\Gamma(2-\alpha)}\sum_{i=1}^{k-1}\Big[(a_{2k-2i+1}-b_{2k-2i}-b_{2k-2i+1})\delta v_{2i-\frac{3}{2}}+(a_{2k-2i}+b_{2k-2i}+b_{2k-2i+1})\delta v_{2i-\frac{1}{2}}\Big] \\
&+\frac{\tau^{1-\alpha}}{\Gamma(2-\alpha)}\Big[(a_1-b_1)\delta v_{2k-\frac{3}{2}}+b_1\delta v_{2k-\frac{1}{2}}\Big] \\
=&\frac{\tau^{1-\alpha}}{\Gamma(2-\alpha)}\Bigg[\sum_{i=1}^{k-1}c_{2k-2i+1}\delta v_{2i-\frac{3}{2}}+\sum_{i=1}^{k-1}d_{2k-2i}\delta v_{2i-\frac{1}{2}}+(a_1-b_1)\delta v_{2k-\frac{3}{2}}+b_1\delta v_{2k-\frac{1}{2}}\Bigg], \qquad (7)
\end{aligned}
$$

where

$$
c_1=a_1-b_1, \quad c_k=a_k-b_k-b_{k-1}, \quad k\geq 2
$$

and

$$
d_1=b_1, \quad d_k=a_{k-1}+b_{k-1}+b_k, \quad k\geq 2.
$$

Similarly, from (4), we obtain

$$
\frac{\partial^\alpha v(t)}{\partial t^\alpha}\Big|_{t=t_{2k}} \approx (L^\alpha v)(t_{2k}):=\frac{\tau^{1-\alpha}}{\Gamma(2-\alpha)}\sum_{i=1}^{k}(c_{2k-2i+2}\delta v_{2i-\frac{3}{2}}+d_{2k-2i+1}\delta v_{2i-\frac{1}{2}}) \qquad (8)
$$

for $k=1,2,\ldots,M$.

Let

$$
\mathbf{L}^\alpha\mathbf{v}=((L^\alpha v)(t_1),(L^\alpha v)(t_2),\ldots,(L^\alpha v)(t_{2M}))^T, \ \mathbf{v_t}=(\delta v_{\frac{1}{2}},\delta v_{\frac{3}{2}},\delta v_{\frac{5}{2}},\ldots,\delta v_{2M-\frac{1}{2}})^T,
$$

and B be a matrix defined by

$$B = \begin{bmatrix} c_1 & d_1 & 0 & 0 & 0 & 0 & \cdots & 0 & 0 \\ c_2 & d_2 & 0 & 0 & 0 & 0 & \cdots & 0 & 0 \\ c_3 & d_3 & c_1 & d_1 & 0 & 0 & \cdots & 0 & 0 \\ c_4 & d_4 & c_2 & d_2 & 0 & 0 & \cdots & 0 & 0 \\ c_5 & d_5 & c_3 & d_3 & c_1 & d_1 & \cdots & 0 & 0 \\ c_6 & d_6 & c_4 & d_4 & c_2 & d_2 & \cdots & 0 & 0 \\ \vdots & \vdots & \vdots & \vdots & \vdots & \vdots & \ddots & \vdots & \vdots \\ c_{2M-1} & d_{2M-1} & c_{2M-3} & d_{2M-3} & c_{2M-5} & d_{2M-5} & \cdots & c_1 & d_1 \\ c_{2M} & d_{2M} & c_{2M-2} & d_{2M-2} & c_{2M-4} & d_{2M-4} & \cdots & c_2 & d_2 \end{bmatrix}.$$

Then, we obtain the matrix form of the NL2 scheme for the Caputo fractional derivative

$$\mathbf{L}^{\alpha}\mathbf{v} = \mu B \mathbf{v_t},$$

where $\mu = \frac{\tau^{1-\alpha}}{\Gamma(2-\alpha)}$. It can be seen that B is a block lower triangular Toeplitz matrix with 2×2 blocks.

2.2. Basic Properties of Relevant Coefficients

In this subsection, we establish certain properties of the coefficients in the NL2 scheme, which are useful in analyzing the convergence and stability of the NL2 scheme.

We need the following results. Assuming $0 < x < 1$ and $\alpha \in (0,1)$, we have

$$(1-x)^{2-\alpha} = 1 - (2-\alpha)x + \sum_{k=2}^{\infty} g_k^{(2-\alpha)} x^k, \tag{9}$$

where $g_2^{(2-\alpha)} = \frac{(2-\alpha)(1-\alpha)}{2}$ and $0 < g_k^{(2-\alpha)} = \frac{\alpha+k-3}{k} g_{k-1}^{(2-\alpha)} < g_{k-1}^{(2-\alpha)}$ for $k \geq 3$. Moreover,

$$(1-x)^{1-\alpha} = 1 - \sum_{k=1}^{\infty} g_k^{(1-\alpha)} x^k, \tag{10}$$

where $g_1^{(1-\alpha)} = 1-\alpha$ and $0 < g_k^{(1-\alpha)} = \frac{\alpha+k-2}{k} g_{k-1}^{(1-\alpha)} < g_{k-1}^{(1-\alpha)}$ for $k \geq 2$. We obtain

$$g_k^{(2-\alpha)} = \frac{2-\alpha}{\alpha+k-2} g_k^{(1-\alpha)} \tag{11}$$

for $k \geq 2$.

Lemma 1. *(Properties of a_k, b_k, c_k and d_k). The following properties of the coefficients of the NL2 scheme in (7) and (8) hold:*

(1) $1 = a_1 > a_2 > a_3 > \ldots > a_k > 0$;
(2) $b_1 > b_2 > b_3 > \ldots > b_k > 0$;
(3) $d_2 > d_3 > d_4 > \ldots > d_k > 0$;
(4) $c_3 > c_4 > c_5 > \ldots > c_k > 0$;
(5) $c_1 = \frac{4-3\alpha}{2(2-\alpha)} > 0, c_2 = \frac{(2-3\alpha)2^{1-\alpha}}{2(2-\alpha)} \in (-\frac{1}{2}, 1), d_1 = \frac{\alpha}{2(2-\alpha)} > 0.$

Proof. (1) By (5) , the conclusion is easy to obtain from $a_k = (1-\alpha)\int_0^1 (k-1+s)^{-\alpha} ds$ for $k \geq 1$.

(2) From $g(r,s) = (r-s)^{-\alpha} - (r+s)^{-\alpha}$, we see that $g(r,s) > 0$ for $s \in (0, \frac{1}{2})$, and it follows from (6) that $b_k > 0$ for $k \geq 1$. Furthermore, we have

$$\frac{\partial g}{\partial r} = -\alpha[(r-s)^{-(\alpha+1)} - (r+s)^{-(\alpha+1)}] < 0,\ r \geq \frac{1}{2},\ 0 < s \leq \frac{1}{2}.$$

Therefore, $g(r,s)$ is a strictly monotonically decreasing function with respect to r. In particular, $g\left(k+\frac{1}{2},s\right) < g\left(k-\frac{1}{2},s\right)$ for $k \geq 1$, $s \in (0,1/2]$. By (6) again, we obtain $b_{k+1} < b_k$ for $k = 1,2,\ldots$.

(3) From (1) and (2), we obtain

$$d_k = a_{k-1} + b_{k-1} + b_k > 0$$

and

$$d_{k+1} - d_k = a_k - a_{k-1} + b_{k+1} - b_{k-1} < 0$$

for $k > 1$.

(4) For $\{c_k\}, k \geq 3$, by using (9) and (10), we have

$$\begin{aligned} c_k &= -\frac{1}{2-\alpha}[k^{2-\alpha} - (k-2)^{2-\alpha}] + \frac{3}{2}k^{1-\alpha} + \frac{1}{2}(k-2)^{1-\alpha} \\ &= -\frac{k^{2-\alpha}}{2-\alpha} + \frac{k^{2-\alpha}}{2-\alpha}(1-\frac{2}{k})^{2-\alpha} + \frac{3}{2}k^{1-\alpha} + \frac{k^{1-\alpha}}{2}(1-\frac{2}{k})^{1-\alpha} \\ &> -\frac{k^{2-\alpha}}{2-\alpha} + \frac{k^{2-\alpha}}{2-\alpha}\Big(1 - \frac{2(2-\alpha)}{k} + \frac{2(2-\alpha)(1-\alpha)}{k^2}\Big) + \frac{3k^{1-\alpha}}{2} \\ &\quad + \frac{k^{1-\alpha}}{2}\Big(1 - \frac{2(1-\alpha)}{k} - \frac{(1-\alpha)\alpha}{2}\sum_{j=2}^{\infty}(\frac{2}{k})^j\Big) \\ &= (1-\alpha)\Big(1 - \frac{\alpha}{k-2}\Big)k^{-\alpha} > 0. \end{aligned}$$

Now, we consider the monotonicity of $\{c_k\}, k \geq 3$. We have

$$\begin{aligned} c_k - c_{k-1} = &-\frac{k^{2-\alpha}}{2-\alpha} + \frac{k^{2-\alpha}}{2-\alpha}(1-\frac{1}{k})^{2-\alpha} + \frac{k^{2-\alpha}}{2-\alpha}(1-\frac{2}{k})^{2-\alpha} - \frac{k^{2-\alpha}}{2-\alpha}(1-\frac{3}{k})^{2-\alpha} \\ &+ \frac{3}{2}k^{1-\alpha} - \frac{3k^{1-\alpha}}{2}(1-\frac{1}{k})^{1-\alpha} + \frac{k^{1-\alpha}}{2}(1-\frac{2}{k})^{1-\alpha} - \frac{k^{1-\alpha}}{2}(1-\frac{3}{k})^{1-\alpha} \end{aligned}$$

for $k \geq 4$. By using (9)–(11), we have

$$\begin{aligned} c_k - c_{k-1} = &-\frac{2g_2^{(1-\alpha)}}{k^{1+\alpha}} - \frac{5g_3^{(1-\alpha)}}{k^{2+\alpha}} - \frac{8g_4^{(1-\alpha)}}{k^{3+\alpha}} - \frac{11g_5^{(1-\alpha)}}{3k^{4+\alpha}} + \sum_{j=6}^{\infty}\frac{g_j^{(1-\alpha)}k^{1-\alpha}}{j+1}\Big[(\frac{1}{k})^j + 2(\frac{2}{k})^j - 3(\frac{3}{k})^j\Big] \\ &+ \sum_{j=6}^{\infty}\frac{g_j^{(1-\alpha)}k^{1-\alpha}}{2}\Big[3(\frac{1}{k})^j - (\frac{2}{k})^j + (\frac{3}{k})^j\Big] \\ < &-\frac{2g_2^{(1-\alpha)}}{k^{1+\alpha}} + \sum_{j=6}^{\infty}\frac{g_j^{(1-\alpha)}k^{1-\alpha}}{2}\Big[3(\frac{1}{k})^j + (\frac{3}{k})^j\Big] \\ < &-\frac{\alpha(1-\alpha)}{k^{1+\alpha}} + \frac{g_6^{(1-\alpha)}k^{1-\alpha}}{2}\sum_{j=6}^{\infty}\Big[3(\frac{1}{k})^j + (\frac{3}{k})^j\Big] \\ < &-\frac{\alpha(1-\alpha)}{k^{1+\alpha}} + \frac{(1-\alpha)\alpha k^{1-\alpha}}{12}\Big[\frac{3}{k^5(k-1)} + \frac{3^6}{k^5(k-3)}\Big] \\ = &\Big[\frac{1}{4k^3(k-1)} + \frac{3^5}{4k^3(k-3)} - 1\Big]\frac{\alpha(1-\alpha)}{k^{1+\alpha}} \\ < &\Big(\frac{123}{2k^3} - 1\Big)\frac{\alpha(1-\alpha)}{k^{1+\alpha}} < 0. \end{aligned}$$

(5) Obviously, $c_1 > 0, d_1 > 0$ for $0 < \alpha < 1$, and

$$c_2 = \frac{(2-3\alpha)2^{1-\alpha}}{2(2-\alpha)} = \frac{2-3\alpha}{2^\alpha(2-\alpha)}.$$

Let $g(\alpha) = \frac{2-3\alpha}{2^\alpha(2-\alpha)}, 0 \leq \alpha \leq 1$, then

$$g'(\alpha) = \frac{-[4+(3\alpha^2-8\alpha+4)\ln 2]}{2^\alpha(2-\alpha)^2} < 0, \quad 0 \leq \alpha \leq 1.$$

Hence, the function $g(\alpha)$ is a monotonically decreasing function with respect to α, and $g(\alpha) \in [-\frac{1}{2}, 1]$. Consequently $c_2 \in (-\frac{1}{2}, 1)$ for $\alpha \in (0,1)$. □

2.3. Consistency of the NL2 Scheme

In this subsection, we prove the consistency of the NL2 scheme for the Caputo derivative, and it can achieve $(3-\alpha)$th-order accuracy.

Theorem 1. *Let $\alpha \in (0,1), k = 2M$, and $v(t) \in C^3[0,T]$, then*

$$\left|\partial_{0t}^\alpha v(t_k) - (L^\alpha v)(t_k)\right| \leq \frac{\max\limits_{0\leq t\leq T}|v'''(t)|}{6\Gamma(2-\alpha)}\left(1-\alpha+2^{1-\alpha}\alpha\right)\tau^{3-\alpha}.$$

Proof. For $k = 2M$, we have

$$\begin{aligned}
&\partial_{0t}^\alpha v(t_{2M}) - (L^\alpha v)(t_{2M})\\
=&\frac{1}{\Gamma(1-\alpha)}\sum_{i=1}^{M}\int_{t_{2i-2}}^{t_{2i}}(t_{2M}-\eta)^{-\alpha}[v(\eta)-\Pi_{2,i}v(\eta)]'d\eta\\
=&\frac{1}{\Gamma(1-\alpha)}\sum_{i=1}^{M}\int_{t_{2i-2}}^{t_{2i}}(t_{2M}-\eta)^{-\alpha}d[v(\eta)-\Pi_{2,i}v(\eta)]\\
=&\frac{-\alpha}{6\Gamma(1-\alpha)}\sum_{i=1}^{M}\int_{t_{2i-2}}^{t_{2i}}v'''(\xi_i)(\eta-t_{2i-2})(\eta-t_{2i-1})(\eta-t_{2i})(t_{2M}-\eta)^{-\alpha-1}d\eta,
\end{aligned}$$

where $\xi_i \in [t_{2i-2}, t_{2i}]$. It follows that

$$|\partial_{0t}^\alpha v(t_{2M}) - (L^\alpha v)(t_{2M})| \leq \frac{\alpha\max\limits_{0\leq t\leq T}|v'''(t)|}{6\Gamma(1-\alpha)}\sum_{i=1}^{M}\int_{t_{2i-2}}^{t_{2i}}\left|(\eta-t_{2i-2})(\eta-t_{2i-1})(\eta-t_{2i})(t_{2M}-\eta)^{-\alpha-1}\right|d\eta. \quad (12)$$

It is easy to obtain

$$\left|(\eta-t_{2i-2})(\eta-t_{2i-1})(\eta-t_{2i})\right| \leq \frac{2\sqrt{3}\tau^3}{9}, \quad \eta \in [t_{2i-2}, t_{2i}].$$

Therefore,

$$\begin{aligned}
&\sum_{i=1}^{M-1}\int_{t_{2i-2}}^{t_{2i}}\left|(\eta-t_{2i-2})(\eta-t_{2i-1})(\eta-t_{2i})(t_{2M}-\eta)^{-\alpha-1}\right|d\eta\\
\leq&\sum_{i=1}^{M-1}\frac{2\sqrt{3}\tau^3}{9}\int_{t_{2i-2}}^{t_{2i}}(t_{2M}-\eta)^{-\alpha-1}d\eta\\
=&\frac{2\sqrt{3}\tau^3}{9\alpha}\left[(2\tau)^{-\alpha}-t_{2M}^{-\alpha}\right] \leq \frac{\tau^{3-\alpha}}{\alpha}.
\end{aligned} \quad (13)$$

As for the last term of (12), we have

$$\begin{aligned}
&\int_{t_{2M-2}}^{t_{2M}} \left|(\eta - t_{2M-2})(\eta - t_{2M-1})(\eta - t_{2M})(t_{2M} - \eta)^{-\alpha-1}\right| d\eta \\
=& \int_{t_{2M-2}}^{t_{2M}} \left|[2\tau - (t_{2M} - \eta)][\tau - (t_{2M} - \eta)](t_{2M} - \eta)^{-\alpha}\right| d\eta \\
=& \int_0^{2\tau} (2\tau - s)|\tau - s| s^{-\alpha} ds \\
\leq& \frac{2^{2-\alpha}\tau^{3-\alpha}}{1-\alpha}.
\end{aligned} \tag{14}$$

Combining (12), (13), and (14), we have

$$|\partial_{0t}^{\alpha} v(t_{2M}) - (L^{\alpha} v)(t_{2M})| \leq \frac{\max\limits_{0 \leq t \leq T} |v'''(t)|}{6\Gamma(2-\alpha)} \left(1 - \alpha + 2^{2-\alpha}\alpha\right)\tau^{3-\alpha}.$$

□

3. A Difference Scheme for the TFDE Based on the NL2 Scheme

In this section, we introduce the NL2 scheme for the time-fractional diffusion equation with variable coefficients Equation (1).

Let $h = (x_R - x_L)/N$ and $\tau = T/(2M)$ be the size of spatial grid and the length of time step, respectively, where N and M are positive integers. Define the following spatial and temporal grids:

$$x_n = nh, n = 0, 1, \ldots, N; \; t_k = k\tau, k = 0, 1, \ldots, 2M.$$

In the following, we use the notations

$$u_n^k = u(x_n, t_k), \quad p_n = p(x_n), \quad q_n = q(x_n), \quad f_n^k = f(x_n, t_k).$$

Applying the new L2 scheme to discretize the temporal derivative, the TFDE (1) is written as

$$\begin{cases}
(L^{\alpha} u)(x, t_k) = \left(\frac{\partial}{\partial x}(p \frac{\partial u}{\partial x})\right)^k - qu^k + f^k, \quad x \in (0, l), \\
u_0^k = 0, u_N^k = 0, \qquad 0 \leq t_k \leq T, \\
u(x, t_0) = u^0, \quad x \in (0, l),
\end{cases} \tag{15}$$

where $p = p(x), q = q(x), u^k = u(x, t_k)$ and $f^k = f(x, t_k)$ for $k = 1, 2, \ldots, 2M$.

Lemma 2 ([25]). *Let $p(x) \in C^3[0, l]$ and $u(x) \in C^4[0, l]$, then the following equality holds true:*

$$\frac{\partial}{\partial x}\left(p(x)\frac{\partial u(x)}{\partial x}\right)\Big|_{x=x_i} = \frac{p(x_{i+1/2})u(x_{i+1}) - (p(x_{i+1/2}) + p(x_{i-1/2}))u(x_i) + p(x_{i-1/2})u(x_{i-1})}{h^2} + \mathcal{O}(h^2).$$

We use the above finite difference method in the spatial direction; then, we construct an NL2 scheme for Equation (15) with an accuracy of order $\mathcal{O}(h^2 + \tau^{3-\alpha})$.

3.1. The Positive Definiteness of $B + B^T$

In this subsection, we study the positive definiteness of the symmetric part of matrix B, equivalently, the positive definiteness of $B + B^T$.

Lemma 3 ([21]). *Given an arbitrary symmetric matrix $S \in R^{n\times n}$ with positive elements. If S satisfies the following properties:*

(P1) $\forall 1 \le j < i \le n,\ [S]_{i-1,j} \ge [S]_{i,j}$;

(P2) $\forall 1 < j \le i \le n,\ [S]_{i,j-1} < [S]_{i,j}$;

(P3) $\forall 1 < j < i \le n,\ [S]_{i-1,j-1} - [S]_{i,j-1} \le [S]_{i-1,j} - [S]_{i,j}$;

then S is positive definite.

Theorem 2. *The matrix $B + B^T$ is positive definite, and the bilinear form defined by*

$$\mathcal{B}_{2M}(u,u) := \sum_{k=0}^{2M-1} \langle (L^\alpha u)(t_{k+1}), \delta u_{k+\frac{1}{2}} \rangle$$

is positive definite.

Proof. Let

$$\beta_1 = \frac{1}{2}(c_3 + d_3 - d_5), \quad \beta_2 = c_3 + d_4 - d_5, \quad \gamma_2 = \frac{1}{2}(d_3 + d_4 - d_5).$$

We split B as $B = B_1 + B_2$, where

$$B_1 = \begin{bmatrix} \beta_1 & 0 & 0 & 0 & 0 & \cdots & 0 \\ \beta_2 & \gamma_2 & 0 & 0 & 0 & \cdots & 0 \\ c_3 & d_3 & \beta_1 & 0 & 0 & \cdots & 0 \\ c_4 & d_4 & \beta_2 & \gamma_2 & 0 & \cdots & 0 \\ \vdots & \ddots & \ddots & \ddots & \ddots & \ddots & 0 \\ c_{2M-1} & d_{2M-1} & c_{2M-3} & d_{2M-3} & \ddots & \beta_1 & 0 \\ c_{2M} & d_{2M} & c_{2M-2} & d_{2M-2} & \cdots & \beta_2 & \gamma_2 \end{bmatrix}$$

and

$$B_2 = I_M \otimes \begin{bmatrix} c_1 - \beta_1 & d_1 \\ c_2 - \beta_2 & d_2 - \gamma_2 \end{bmatrix}.$$

Here, $A \otimes B$ denotes the Kronecker tensor product of A and B: let $A = [a_{ij}]_{p\times q}$, then $A \otimes B = [a_{ij}B]_{p\times q}$. It can be easily checked that

$$2\beta_1 - \beta_2 = d_3 - d_4, \quad \beta_2 - c_3 = d_4 - d_5, \quad 2\gamma_2 - d_3 = \beta_2 - c_3,$$

and

$$2\beta_1 > \beta_2 > c_3, \quad 2\gamma_2 > d_3.$$

The positive definiteness of $B + B^T$ can be ensured if G and S are both positive definite, where $G = B_2 + B_2^T$ and $S = B_1 + B_1^T$.

We first consider the symmetric matrix $G = B_2 + B_2^T$:

$$G = I_M \otimes \begin{bmatrix} 2(c_1 - \beta_1) & c_2 - \beta_2 + d_1 \\ c_2 - \beta_2 + d_1 & 2(d_2 - \gamma_2) \end{bmatrix}.$$

Notice that

$$2(c_1 - \beta_1) = 2c_1 - c_3 - d_3 + d_5,$$

$$2(d_2 - \gamma_2) = 2d_2 - d_3 - d_4 + d_5,$$

$$c_2 - \beta_2 + d_1 = c_2 - c_3 + d_1 - d_4 + d_5.$$

For $k > 1$,

$$\begin{aligned} a_{k-1} - 2a_k + a_{k+1} =&(k+1)^{1-\alpha} - 3k^{1-\alpha} + 3(k-1)^{1-\alpha} - (k-2)^{1-\alpha} \\ =&\alpha(1-\alpha)(1+\alpha)\int_0^1\int_0^1\int_0^1 (k-2+s+s_1+s_2)^{-\alpha-2}ds_2ds_1ds > 0. \end{aligned} \tag{16}$$

From (16) and the property (3) of Lemma 1, we have

$$c_2 - \beta_2 + d_1 = (a_2 - 2a_3 + a_4) + b_5 > 0.$$

Combining with $a_1 - 2b_1 = \frac{2-2\alpha}{2-\alpha} > 0$, we have

$$2(c_1 - \beta_1) - |c_2 - \beta_2 + d_1| = (a_1 - 2a_2 + a_3) + (a_1 - 2b_1) + b_4 > 0.$$

Similarly, by using (16) and the properties of a_k, b_k in Lemma 1, we obtain

$$2(d_2 - \gamma_2) - |c_2 - \beta_2 + d_1| = (a_1 - 2a_2 + a_3) + (a_1 + b_2) + 2(b_1 - b_3) > 0.$$

Therefore, G is diagonally dominant with positive diagonal entries, and it follows that G is positive definite.

Secondly, we prove the positive definiteness of the symmetric matrix $S = B_1 + B_1^T$ by using Lemma 3.

(i) According to Lemma 1, it is easily seen that S satisfies (P1) of Lemma 3:

$$\forall 1 \le j < i \le 2M, \ \ [S]_{i-1,j} \ge [S]_{i,j}. \tag{17}$$

(ii) To prove that S satisfies (P2) of Lemma 3, we need to prove

$$c_{k+2} < d_{k+2} < c_k < d_k, \quad k \ge 3; \quad d_3 < 2\beta_1,\ d_4 < \beta_2 < 2\gamma_2.$$

For $k \ge 3$, we have

$$c_k - d_k = a_k - a_{k-1} - 2(b_k + b_{k-1}) < 0. \tag{18}$$

From (9)–(11), we obtain

$$\begin{aligned} d_{k+2} - c_k =& \frac{k^{2-\alpha}}{2-\alpha}\Big[(1+\frac{2}{k})^{2-\alpha} - (1-\frac{2}{k})^{2-\alpha}\Big] - 3k^{1-\alpha} - \frac{k^{1-\alpha}}{2}\Big[(1+\frac{2}{k})^{1-\alpha} + (1-\frac{2}{k})^{1-\alpha}\Big] \\ =& k^{1-\alpha}\sum_{j=1}^{\infty} g_{2j}^{(1-\alpha)}(\frac{2}{k})^{2j}(1-\frac{4}{2j+1}) \end{aligned}$$

Since $g_{2j}^{(1-\alpha)}(1-\frac{4}{2j+1}) < g_4^{(1-\alpha)}$ for $j \ge 3$, we have

$$\begin{aligned} d_{k+2} - c_k <& k^{1-\alpha}\Big[-\frac{4g_2^{(1-\alpha)}}{3k^2} + \frac{16g_4^{(1-\alpha)}}{5k^4} + g_4^{(1-\alpha)}\sum_{j=3}^{\infty}(\frac{2}{k})^{2j}\Big] \\ =& \frac{(1-\alpha)\alpha}{k^{1+\alpha}}\Big[-\frac{2}{3} + \frac{2(\alpha+1)(\alpha+2)}{15k^2} + \frac{8(\alpha+1)(\alpha+2)}{3K^2(k^2-4)}\Big] \\ <& \frac{(1-\alpha)\alpha}{k^{1+\alpha}}\Big[\frac{4}{5k^2} + \frac{16}{k^2(k^2-4)} - \frac{2}{3}\Big] < 0. \end{aligned} \tag{19}$$

Moreover, by (18) and (19), we obtain

$$2\beta_1 - d_3 = c_3 - d_5 > 0, \quad 2\gamma_2 - \beta_2 = d_3 - c_3 > 0, \quad \beta_2 - d_4 = c_3 - d_5 > 0.$$

Therefore, S satisfies (P2) of Lemma 3:

$$\forall 1 < j \le i \le 2M, \ [S]_{i,j-1} < [S]_{i,j}. \tag{20}$$

(iii) To prove that S satisfies (P3) of Lemma 3, we need to prove

$$d_{k+2} - d_{k+3} < c_k - c_{k+1} < d_k - d_{k+1}, \ k \ge 3.$$

For $k \ge 3$, it holds

$$\begin{aligned} & (c_k - c_{k+1}) - (d_k - d_{k+1}) \\ = & \frac{2}{2-\alpha}[(k+1)^{2-\alpha} - k^{2-\alpha} - (k-1)^{2-\alpha} + (k-2)^{2-\alpha}] \\ & -2(k+1)^{1-\alpha} + 2k^{1-\alpha} - 2k - 2^{1-\alpha} + 2(k-2)^{1-\alpha} \\ = & 2(1-\alpha)\int_0^1 \Big[\int_0^2 (k-2+s+s_1)^{-\alpha} ds_1 - (k+s)^{-\alpha} - (k-2+s)^{-\alpha}\Big] ds. \end{aligned}$$

Notice that for fixed $s \in [0,1]$ and $k \ge 3$, $g(s_1) = (k-2+s+s_1)^{-\alpha}$ is a convex function for $s_1 \ge 0$, we have

$$g(s_1) \le (1 - \frac{s_1}{2})g(0) + \frac{s_1}{2}g(2), \quad s_1 \in [0,2].$$

Hence,

$$\begin{aligned} & \int_0^2 [g(s_1) - (1-\frac{s_1}{2})g(0) - \frac{s_1}{2}g(2)] ds_1 \\ = & \int_0^2 (k-2+s+s_1)^{-\alpha} ds_1 - (k+s)^{-\alpha} - (k-2+s)^{-\alpha} \le 0. \end{aligned}$$

It follows that

$$c_k - c_{k+1} < d_k - d_{k+1}. \tag{21}$$

In the following, we prove that $c_{k-1} - c_k > d_{k+1} - d_{k+2}$ for $k \ge 4$. By using (9)–(11), we have

$$\begin{aligned} & (c_{k-1} - c_k) - (d_{k+1} - d_{k+2}) \\ = & \frac{1}{2-\alpha}[(k+2)^{2-\alpha} - (k+1)^{2-\alpha} - (k-2)^{2-\alpha} + (k-3)^{2-\alpha}] - \frac{1}{2}(k+2)^{1-\alpha} \\ & + \frac{1}{2}(k+1)^{1-\alpha} - 3k^{1-\alpha} + 3(k-1)^{1-\alpha} - \frac{1}{2}(k-2)^{1-\alpha} + \frac{1}{2}(k-3)^{1-\alpha} \\ = & k^{1-\alpha}\sum_{j=1}^{\infty} g_j^{(1-\alpha)} h(j)(\frac{1}{k})^j, \end{aligned} \tag{22}$$

where

$$\begin{aligned} h(j) & = \frac{(-2)^{j+1} - (-1)^{j+1} - 2^{j+1} + 3^{j+1}}{j+1} + \frac{(-2)^j - (-1)^j - 6 + 2^j - 3^j}{2} \\ & = \begin{cases} \dfrac{(5-j)3^j - 5j - 7}{2(j+1)}, & j \text{ odd}, \\ \dfrac{(5-j)3^j + (j-3)2^{j+1} - 7j - 5}{2(j+1)}, & j \text{ even}. \end{cases} \end{aligned}$$

We have

$$h(1) = h(2) = 0, \ h(3) = 4, \ h(4) = 8, \ h(5) = -\frac{8}{3}, \ h(6) = -28. \tag{23}$$

We now prove that

$$h(j) > -3^{j-3}j, \quad j \ge 7. \tag{24}$$

It is easy to verify that for $j \geq 7$,

$$-\frac{5j+7}{3^{j-3}} > -1, \ \frac{135-27j-1}{2j(j+1)} > -1.$$

Therefore, when j is odd and $j \geq 7$, we have

$$h(j) = \frac{135-27j-\frac{5j+7}{3^{j-3}}}{2j(j+1)}3^{j-3}j > \frac{135-27j-1}{2j(j+1)}3^{j-3}j > -3^{j-3}j.$$

It is obvious that for $j \geq 7$, $(j-3)2^{j+1} - 7j - 5 > -5j - 7$. Therefore, when j is even and $j \geq 7$, we have

$$h(j) > \frac{135-27j-\frac{5j+7}{3^{j-3}}}{2j(j+1)}3^{j-3}j > -3^{j-3}j.$$

Therefore, (24) is correct.

Since $0 < \alpha < 1$, we have $\alpha + i - 1 < i$. Therefore, for $j \geq 7$,

$$g_j^{(1-\alpha)} = \frac{(1-\alpha)\alpha(\alpha+1)...(\alpha+j-2)}{1 \times 2 \times 3 \times ... \times j} < \frac{(1-\alpha)\alpha(\alpha+1)}{2j},$$

and it follows that

$$g_j^{(1-\alpha)}h(j)\left(\frac{1}{k}\right)^j > -\frac{(1-\alpha)\alpha(\alpha+1)}{2k^3}\left(\frac{3}{k}\right)^{j-3}. \tag{25}$$

Hence, by (22), (23), and (25), we obtain

$$\begin{aligned}
&(c_{k-1} - c_k) - (d_{k+1} - d_{k+2}) \\
&>k^{1-\alpha}\left[\frac{4g_3^{(1-\alpha)}}{k^3} + \frac{8g_4^{(1-\alpha)}}{k^4} - \frac{8g_5^{(1-\alpha)}}{3k^5} - \frac{28g_6^{(1-\alpha)}}{k^6} - \frac{(1-\alpha)\alpha(1+\alpha)}{2k^3}\sum_{j=4}^{\infty}(\frac{3}{k})^j\right] \\
&=\frac{(1-\alpha)\alpha(1+\alpha)}{k^{2+\alpha}}\left[\frac{2}{3} + \frac{\alpha+2}{3k} - \frac{(\alpha+2)(\alpha+3)}{45k^2} - \frac{7(\alpha+2)(\alpha+3)(\alpha+4)}{180k^3} - \frac{81}{2k^3(k-3)}\right] \\
&>\frac{(1-\alpha)\alpha(1+\alpha)}{k^{2+\alpha}}\left[\frac{2}{3} + \frac{2}{3k} - \frac{4}{15k^2} - \frac{7}{3k^3} - \frac{81}{2k^3(k-3)}\right] > 0.
\end{aligned} \tag{26}$$

It follows from (21) and (26) that

$$\forall 1 < j < i \leq 2M, \quad [S]_{i-1,j-1} - [S]_{i,j-1} \leq [S]_{i-1,j} - [S]_{i,j}. \tag{27}$$

Finally, we obtain that S is positive definite from (17), (20), and (27).

Based on the above discussions, we see that $B + B^T$ is positive definite. According to (7) and (8), we can rewrite $\mathcal{B}_{2M}(u,u)$ in the following matrix form

$$\mathcal{B}_{2M}(u,u) = \sum_{k=0}^{2M-1}\langle (L^\alpha u)(t_{k+1}), \delta u_{k+\frac{1}{2}}\rangle = \frac{\tau^{1-\alpha}}{\Gamma(2-\alpha)}\int_0^l \mathbf{u_t}^T B \mathbf{u_t} dx.$$

It is obvious that $\mathcal{B}_{2M}(u,u)$ is positive definite. □

3.2. H^1-Stability and Convergence

Based on the consistency and H^1-stability of the NL2 scheme, we can derive the convergence results of the method. In the following discussion, we prove the H^1-norm stability of the scheme by using the positive definiteness of the bilinear form $\mathcal{B}$.

Define $\nabla u^k = \frac{\partial u(x,t_k)}{\partial x}$. $\|\cdot\|_{L^2(0,l)}$ represents the continuous L^2 norm of x on its domain. In the following, we present the proof of H^1-stability.

Theorem 3. *Assume that $f(x,t) \in L^\infty(L^2(0,l);[0,T]) \bigcap BV(L^2(0,l);[0,T])$ is a bounded variation function in time and $u^0 \in H^1(0,l)$, then the numerical solution u^k ($k = 1,2,\ldots,2M$) of the NL2 scheme (15) satisfies the following H^1-stability*

$$\|\nabla u^k\|_{L^2(0,l)} \leq C,$$

where

$$C = \sqrt{2C_0} + \frac{8lC_f}{C_1}$$

with $C_0 = \left\|\sqrt{\frac{p(x)}{C_1}}\nabla u^0\right\|^2_{L^2(0,l)} + \left\|\sqrt{\frac{q(x)}{C_1}}u^0\right\|^2_{L^2(0,l)}$, $C_1 = \min_{x\in[0,l]} p(x) > 0$, and C_f is a constant that depends on $f(x,t)$.

Proof. By multiplying (15) with $\delta u_{k-\frac{1}{2}} := \frac{u^k - u^{k-1}}{\tau}$ for $k = 1,2,\ldots,2m$, integrating over $(0,l)$, and summing up the derived equations over $2m$ terms, we obtain

$$\begin{aligned}
&\sum_{k=1}^{2m}\langle (L^\alpha u)(t_k), \delta u_{k-\frac{1}{2}}\rangle \\
= &\sum_{k=1}^{2m}\left\langle \left(\frac{\partial}{\partial x}(p\frac{\partial u}{\partial x})\right)^k, \delta u_{k-\frac{1}{2}}\right\rangle - \sum_{k=1}^{2m}\langle qu^k, \delta u_{k-\frac{1}{2}}\rangle + \sum_{k=1}^{2m}\langle f^k, \delta u_{k-\frac{1}{2}}\rangle \\
= &-\frac{1}{2\tau}\|\sqrt{p}\nabla u^{2m}\|^2_{L^2(0,l)} + \frac{1}{2\tau}\|\sqrt{p}\nabla u^0\|^2_{L^2(0,l)} - \frac{\tau}{2}\sum_{k=1}^{2m}\|\sqrt{p}\nabla(\delta u_{k-\frac{1}{2}})\|^2_{L^2(0,l)} \\
&-\frac{1}{2\tau}\|\sqrt{q}u^{2m}\|^2_{L^2(0,l)} + \frac{1}{2\tau}\|\sqrt{q}u^0\|^2_{L^2(0,l)} - \frac{\tau}{2}\sum_{k=1}^{2m}\|\sqrt{q}\delta u_{k-\frac{1}{2}}\|^2_{L^2(0,l)} \\
&+\frac{1}{\tau}\langle f^{2m}, u^{2m}\rangle - \frac{1}{\tau}\langle f^1, u^0\rangle - \sum_{k=1}^{2m-1}\langle \delta f_{k+\frac{1}{2}}, u^k\rangle,
\end{aligned} \tag{28}$$

where $p = p(x)$, $q = q(x)$, and $\delta f_{k+\frac{1}{2}} = \frac{f^{k+1} - f^k}{\tau}$. Applying the Cauchy–Schwarz inequality gives

$$\begin{aligned}
&\frac{1}{\tau}\langle f^{2m}, u^{2m}\rangle - \frac{1}{\tau}\langle f^1, u^0\rangle - \sum_{k=1}^{2m-1}\langle \delta f_{k+\frac{1}{2}}, u^k\rangle \\
\leq &\frac{1}{\tau}(2\|f\|_{L^\infty(L^2(0,l);[0,T])} + \|f\|_{BV(L^2(0,l);[0,T])})\max_{0\leq k\leq 2m}\|u^k\|_{L^2(0,l)} \\
\leq &\frac{2lC_f}{\tau}\max_{0\leq k\leq 2m}\|\nabla u^k\|_{L^2(0,l)},
\end{aligned} \tag{29}$$

where $C_f = 2\|f\|_{L^\infty(L^2(0,l);[0,T])} + \|f\|_{BV(L^2(0,l);[0,T])}$ with

$$\|f\|_{L^\infty(L^2(0,l);[0,T])} = \text{ess}\sup_{t\in[0,T]}\|f(\cdot,t)\|_{L^2(0,l)}$$

and

$$\|f\|_{BV([0,T];L^2(0,l))} := \sup\sum_{i=1}^{n}\|f(\cdot,t_i) - f(\cdot,t_{i-1})\|_{L^2(0,l)},$$

where the supremum is taken over all finite partitions $0 = t_0 < t_1 < \cdots < t_n = T$ of $[0,T]$.

Combining (28) with (29) and using the positive definiteness of the bilinear form $\mathcal{B}$ (cf. Theorem 2), we obtain

$$
\begin{aligned}
&\|\sqrt{p}\nabla u^{2m}\|^2_{L^2(0,l)} + \tau^2 \sum_{k=1}^{2m} \|\sqrt{p}\nabla(\delta u_{k-\frac{1}{2}})\|^2_{L^2(0,l)} + \|\sqrt{q}u^{2m}\|^2_{L^2(0,l)} + \tau^2 \sum_{k=1}^{2m} \|\sqrt{q}\delta u_{k-\frac{1}{2}}\|^2_{L^2(0,l)} \\
\le& \|\sqrt{p}\nabla u^0\|^2_{L^2(0,l)} + \|\sqrt{q}u^0\|^2_{L^2(0,l)} + 4lC_f \max_{0\le k\le 2m} \|\nabla u^k\|_{L^2(0,l)}.
\end{aligned} \tag{30}
$$

It follows that

$$
\begin{aligned}
C_1\|\nabla u^{2m}\|^2_{L^2(0,l)} &\le \|\sqrt{p}\nabla u^{2m}\|^2_{L^2(0,l)} \\
&\le \|\sqrt{p}\nabla u^0\|^2_{L^2(0,l)} + \|\sqrt{q}u^0\|^2_{L^2(0,l)} + 4lC_f \max_{0\le k\le 2m} \|\nabla u^k\|_{L^2(0,l)}.
\end{aligned} \tag{31}
$$

By making use of the triangle inequality of the norm:

$$
\|\nabla u^{2m-1}\|_{L^2(0,l)} \le \|\nabla u^{2m}\|_{L^2(0,l)} + \tau\|\nabla(\delta u_{2m-\frac{1}{2}})\|_{L^2(0,l)},
$$

we have

$$
\|\nabla u^{2m-1}\|^2_{L^2(0,l)} \le 2\|\nabla u^{2m}\|^2_{L^2(0,l)} + 2\tau^2\|\nabla(\delta u_{2m-\frac{1}{2}})\|^2_{L^2(0,l)}. \tag{32}
$$

From (30) and (32), we obtain

$$
C_1\|\nabla u^{2m-1}\|^2_{L^2(0,l)} \le 2\|\sqrt{p}\nabla u^0\|^2_{L^2(0,l)} + 2\|\sqrt{q}u^0\|^2_{L^2(0,l)} + 8lC_f \max_{0\le k\le 2m} \|\nabla u^k\|_{L^2(0,l)}. \tag{33}
$$

Combining (31) and (33), we obtain

$$
\max\{\|\nabla u^{2m}\|^2_{L^2(0,l)}, \|\nabla u^{2m-1}\|^2_{L^2(0,l)}\} \le 2C_0 + \frac{8lC_f}{C_1} \max_{0\le k\le 2m} \|\nabla u^k\|_{L^2(0,l)}, \tag{34}
$$

where $C_0 = \left\|\sqrt{\frac{p}{C_1}}\nabla u^0\right\|^2_{L^2(0,l)} + \left\|\sqrt{\frac{q}{C_1}}u^0\right\|^2_{L^2(0,l)}$. Obviously, u^0 satisfies inequality (34). Therefore,

$$
\max_{0\le k\le 2M} \|\nabla u^k\|^2_{L^2(0,l)} \le 2C_0 + \frac{8lC_f}{C_1} \max_{0\le k\le 2M} \|\nabla u^k\|_{L^2(0,l)},
$$

which indicates

$$
\max_{0\le k\le 2M} \|\nabla u^k\|_{L^2(0,l)} \le \frac{4lC_f}{C_1} + \sqrt{(\frac{4lC_f}{C_1})^2 + 2C_0} \le \sqrt{2C_0} + \frac{8lC_f}{C_1}.
$$

The proof is completed. □

According to the consistency and H^1-norm stability properties of the NL2 scheme, we can obtain the convergence result of the proposed method. Let $u_0 = 0$ and $u_N = 0$, and define the discrete inner product

$$
(u, v) = h \sum_{i=1}^{N-1} u_i v_i, \quad u, v \in \mathbb{R}^{N-1}
$$

and the discrete L_2-norm

$$
\|u\|_{L_2} = \sqrt{(u, u)}.
$$

Let the error in the numerical solution at $t = t_k$ be defined by $\|e^k\|_{L_2}$, and let the maximal error of all time steps be defined by $\max_{k=1,\ldots,2M} \|e^k\|_{L_2}$. The following theorem shows that the NL2 scheme has accuracy of order $3-\alpha$ in time and of order 2 in space.

Theorem 4. *Let u_i^k be the exact solution of problem (1), and U_i^k be the solution of the NL2 scheme (equation (15)). Then,*

$$\|u^k - U^k\|_{L_2} \le C_2(\tau^{3-\alpha} + h^2), \quad 1 \le k \le 2M,$$

where C_2 is a positive constant.

4. Numerical Results

In this section, we conduct numerical experiments to validate the theoretical findings discussed in previous sections. In Examples 1 and 2, we demonstrate the accuracy of the NL2 scheme for homogeneous and inhomogeneous boundary conditions, respectively. Then, in Example 3, we compare the numerical results of the NL2 scheme with the L2 schemes proposed in [17,20].

Example 1. *Consider problem (1) with $p(x) = e^x$, $q(x) = 1$, $l = 1$, $T = 1$, and the exact solution $u(x,t) = x(1-x)^2t^3$.*

Table 1 shows the numerical results for different τ's when $\tau^{3-\alpha} \approx h^2$, equivalently, $h \approx \tau^{(3-\alpha)/2}$. It can be seen that the order of the accuracy is about $3-\alpha$, which is consistent with the conclusion of Theorem 1. Table 2 shows numerical results for different τ with $h = 1/20{,}000$. We can see that the order of the accuracy is higher than $3-\alpha$. Moreover, compared to Table 1, we see that for the same τ and α, Table 2 gives more accurate results, which implies that a smaller spatial grid can generate more accurate results. Therefore, we provide results for different τ's with $h \approx \tau^{(3-\alpha)/2}/100$ in Table 3. Again, we observe that the order of the accuracy is higher than $3-\alpha$.

Table 1. The error and the temporal convergence order of the NL2 scheme in L_2 norm for different values of α's with $h \approx \tau^{(3-\alpha)/2}$ at $t = 1$ for Example 1.

τ	h	$\alpha = 0.1$	Rate	h	$\alpha = 0.5$	Rate	h	$\alpha = 0.9$	Rate
$\frac{1}{10}$	$\frac{1}{29}$	7.2124×10^{-5}	–	$\frac{1}{18}$	1.8698×10^{-4}	–	$\frac{1}{12}$	4.0492×10^{-4}	–
$\frac{1}{20}$	$\frac{1}{78}$	9.9707×10^{-6}	2.8547	$\frac{1}{43}$	3.2631×10^{-5}	2.5185	$\frac{1}{24}$	9.7403×10^{-5}	2.0556
$\frac{1}{40}$	$\frac{1}{211}$	1.3624×10^{-6}	2.8716	$\frac{1}{101}$	5.8759×10^{-6}	2.4734	$\frac{1}{49}$	2.2654×10^{-5}	2.1042
$\frac{1}{80}$	$\frac{1}{575}$	1.8344×10^{-7}	2.8927	$\frac{1}{240}$	1.0341×10^{-6}	2.5065	$\frac{1}{100}$	5.3227×10^{-6}	2.0895
$\frac{1}{160}$	$\frac{1}{1571}$	2.4575×10^{-8}	2.9000	$\frac{1}{570}$	1.8214×10^{-7}	2.5052	$\frac{1}{207}$	1.2244×10^{-6}	2.1201

Table 2. The error and the temporal convergence order of the NL2 scheme in L_2 norm for different values of α's with $h = 1/20{,}000$ at $t = 1$ for Example 1.

τ	$\alpha = 0.3$	Rate	$\alpha = 0.5$	Rate	$\alpha = 0.7$	Rate
1/10	2.8823×10^{-6}	–	7.9598×10^{-6}	–	1.6006×10^{-5}	–
1/20	4.2708×10^{-7}	2.7546	1.2356×10^{-6}	2.6876	2.2845×10^{-6}	2.8086
1/40	6.2740×10^{-8}	2.7670	1.8322×10^{-7}	2.7535	2.6335×10^{-7}	3.1168
1/80	8.8311×10^{-9}	2.8287	2.5857×10^{-8}	2.8250	1.6577×10^{-8}	3.9898

Tables 1–3 show that for the NL2 scheme, the accuracy order at the final time step may be significantly higher than $3-\alpha$. The following Table 4 shows the maximum L_2-norm errors over all time steps for different τ values with $h = 1/20{,}000$. It can be seen from Table 4 that the accuracy order of the NL2 scheme is slightly higher than $3-\alpha$.

Table 3. The error in L_2 norm and the temporal convergence order of the NL2 scheme for different values of α's with $h \approx \tau^{(3-\alpha)/2}/100$ at $t = 1$ for Example 1.

τ	$\alpha = 0.3$	Rate	$\alpha = 0.5$	Rate	$\alpha = 0.7$	Rate
$1/10$	2.8934×10^{-6}	–	7.9769×10^{-6}	–	1.6033×10^{-5}	–
$1/20$	4.2905×10^{-7}	2.7536	1.2383×10^{-6}	2.6875	2.2902×10^{-6}	2.8075
$1/40$	6.2889×10^{-8}	2.7703	1.8386×10^{-7}	2.7517	2.6406×10^{-7}	3.1165
$1/80$	8.5470×10^{-9}	2.8793	2.5477×10^{-8}	2.8513	1.6834×10^{-8}	3.9714

Table 4. The maximum L_2-norm errors over all time steps and the temporal convergence order of the NL2 scheme for different α's with $h = 1/20000$ for Example 1.

τ	$\alpha = 0.3$	Rate	$\alpha = 0.5$	Rate	$\alpha = 0.7$	Rate
$1/10$	2.8823×10^{-6}	–	7.9598×10^{-6}	–	1.7616×10^{-5}	–
$1/20$	4.2708×10^{-7}	2.7546	1.2358×10^{-6}	2.6873	3.3407×10^{-6}	2.3987
$1/40$	6.2740×10^{-8}	2.7670	2.0368×10^{-7}	2.6011	6.0243×10^{-7}	2.4713
$1/80$	9.1147×10^{-9}	2.7831	3.3265×10^{-8}	2.6142	1.0547×10^{-7}	2.5139

In the following Example 2, we investigate numerically the accuracy of the NL2 scheme for TFDE with an inhomogeneous boundary condition.

Example 2. *Consider problem (1) with $p(x) = e^x$, $q(x) = 0$ and $l = 1, T = 1$, and the exact solution is set to*

$$u(x,t) = (1-x)^4(e^{-3x}t^{3+\alpha} + x^4).$$

As clearly illustrated in Tables 5–7, the NL2 scheme is effective to the TFDE with inhomogeneous boundary conditions as well. Moreover, the accuracy order is also about $(3-\alpha)$.

Table 5. The error in L_2 norm and the temporal convergence order of the NL2 scheme for different values of α's with $h \approx \tau^{(3-\alpha)/2}$ at $t = 1$ for Example 2.

τ	h	$\alpha = 0.1$	Rate	h	$\alpha = 0.5$	Rate	h	$\alpha = 0.9$	Rate
$\frac{1}{10}$	$\frac{1}{29}$	1.1025×10^{-3}	–	$\frac{1}{18}$	2.7464×10^{-3}	–	$\frac{1}{12}$	5.7111×10^{-3}	–
$\frac{1}{20}$	$\frac{1}{78}$	1.5262×10^{-4}	2.8528	$\frac{1}{43}$	4.8277×10^{-4}	2.5081	$\frac{1}{24}$	1.4267×10^{-3}	2.0011
$\frac{1}{40}$	$\frac{1}{211}$	2.0860×10^{-5}	2.8711	$\frac{1}{101}$	8.7485×10^{-5}	2.4642	$\frac{1}{49}$	3.4056×10^{-4}	2.0667
$\frac{1}{80}$	$\frac{1}{575}$	2.8090×10^{-6}	2.8926	$\frac{1}{240}$	1.5483×10^{-5}	2.4984	$\frac{1}{100}$	8.1394×10^{-5}	2.0649
$\frac{1}{160}$	$\frac{1}{1571}$	3.7630×10^{-7}	2.9001	$\frac{1}{570}$	2.7425×10^{-6}	2.4971	$\frac{1}{207}$	1.8931×10^{-5}	2.1042

In the following Example 3, we compare the numerical results of the NL2 scheme with the L2 schemes from [17,20], denoted as L2(1) and L2(2), respectively. Notice that both coefficients p and q are time-dependent.

Example 3. *Consider problem (1) with $p(x,t) = 2 - \cos(xt)$, $q(x,t) = 1 - \sin(xt)$, $l = 1$, and $T = 1$. The source term f and the initial condition u_0 are selected such that the exact solution of the problem is $u(x,t) = \sin(\pi x)(t^{3+\alpha} + t^2 + 1)$.*

The error of the numerical solutions and the CPU time (seconds) of the three schemes for Example 3 are summarized in Tables 8 and 9, indicating that the NL2 scheme, the L2(1) scheme, and the L2(2) scheme are stable and convergent. Moreover, the L2(2) scheme often requires the minimal CPU time while the corresponding numerical solution has the largest error. Considering both accuracy and CPU time comprehensively, the NL2 scheme performs the best among the three schemes.

Notably, Table 10 shows that the maximum L_2-norm error of the numerical solution of the L2(2) scheme is significantly larger than those of other schemes; see also Figure 1. It is interesting that if we modify the first step of the L2(2) scheme, that is, replace it by that of the NL2 scheme (we call it the L2(2)* scheme), then the accuracy of the modified scheme L2(2)* is significantly higher than that of the L2(2) scheme in terms of the maximum $L2$-norm; see Figures 1 and 2. Therefore, the accuracy of the numerical solution at the first time step has a substantial impact on the accuracy of the numerical solution at subsequent time steps. It can also be observed that the numerical solutions obtained by the NL2 scheme are better than those obtained by the L2(1) scheme, the L2(2) scheme, and the $L2(2)^*$ scheme.

Table 6. The error in the L_2 norm and the temporal convergence order of the NL2 scheme for different values of α's with h = 1/20,000 at $t = 1$ for Example 2.

τ	$\alpha = 0.3$	Rate	$\alpha = 0.5$	Rate	$\alpha = 0.7$	Rate
1/10	4.3775×10^{-6}	–	1.6118×10^{-5}	–	4.3291×10^{-5}	–
1/20	6.6164×10^{-7}	2.7260	2.5993×10^{-6}	2.6325	6.8838×10^{-6}	2.6528
1/40	9.9946×10^{-8}	2.7268	4.0264×10^{-7}	2.6906	9.9279×10^{-7}	2.7936
1/80	1.6392×10^{-8}	2.6081	6.1559×10^{-8}	2.7094	1.3598×10^{-7}	2.8681

Table 7. The maximum L_2-norm errors over all time steps and the temporal convergence order of the NL2 scheme for different α's with h = 1/20,000 for Example 2.

τ	$\alpha = 0.3$	Rate	$\alpha = 0.5$	Rate	$\alpha = 0.7$	Rate
1/10	4.3775×10^{-6}	–	1.6118×10^{-5}	–	4.3291×10^{-5}	–
1/20	6.6164×10^{-7}	2.7260	2.5993×10^{-6}	2.6325	7.6302×10^{-6}	2.5043
1/40	9.9946×10^{-8}	2.7268	4.0264×10^{-7}	2.6906	1.4661×10^{-6}	2.3797
1/80	1.6392×10^{-8}	2.6081	6.1559×10^{-8}	2.7094	2.7864×10^{-7}	2.3955

Table 8. Comparison of errors and CPU times of NL2 scheme, L2(1) scheme, and scheme L2(2) with different α's for $h \approx \tau^{(3-\alpha)/2}/10$ at $t = 1$ for Example 3.

		NL2		L2(1)		L2(2)	
α	τ	Error	CPU	Error	CPU	Error	CPU
0.3	1/10	6.9936×10^{-5}	0.04	9.7721×10^{-5}	0.05	7.1219×10^{-5}	0.03
	1/20	1.0504×10^{-5}	0.05	1.5792×10^{-5}	0.06	1.0540×10^{-5}	0.05
	1/40	1.5595×10^{-6}	0.27	2.5157×10^{-6}	0.33	1.5625×10^{-6}	0.26
	1/80	2.2928×10^{-7}	2.33	3.9698×10^{-7}	3.98	2.3239×10^{-7}	3.05
	1/160	3.4675×10^{-8}	28.74	6.1642×10^{-8}	39.53	3.5997×10^{-8}	38.84
0.5	1/10	1.9262×10^{-4}	0.03	3.1207×10^{-4}	0.03	2.6041×10^{-4}	0.02
	1/20	3.0226×10^{-5}	0.04	5.7474×10^{-5}	0.04	4.5928×10^{-5}	0.04
	1/40	4.5264×10^{-6}	0.19	1.0411×10^{-5}	0.24	8.0600×10^{-6}	0.16
	1/80	6.4677×10^{-7}	1.43	1.8689×10^{-6}	2.39	1.4136×10^{-6}	1.49
	1/160	8.8360×10^{-8}	13.44	3.3283×10^{-7}	26.49	2.4905×10^{-7}	18.01
0.7	1/10	4.1540×10^{-4}	0.02	9.1721×10^{-4}	0.02	8.4960×10^{-4}	0.02
	1/20	5.7824×10^{-5}	0.03	1.9353×10^{-4}	0.04	1.7628×10^{-4}	0.03
	1/40	6.3461×10^{-6}	0.12	4.0095×10^{-5}	0.14	3.6114×10^{-5}	0.09
	1/80	3.5028×10^{-7}	0.81	8.2304×10^{-6}	0.79	7.3586×10^{-6}	0.78
	1/160	8.3050×10^{-8}	6.29	1.6812×10^{-6}	6.52	1.4960×10^{-6}	8.93

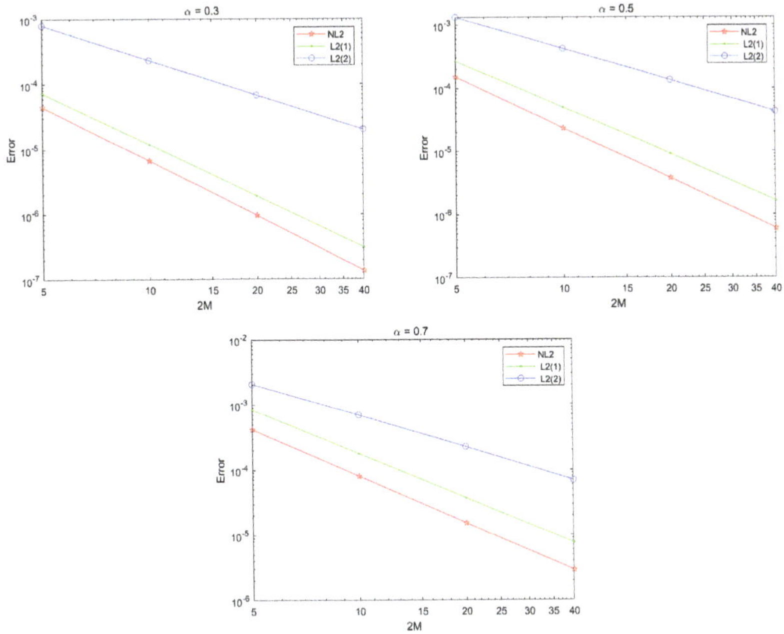

Figure 1. Maximum L_2-norm Errors of the NL2 scheme, the L2(1) scheme, and the L2(2) scheme for Example 3.

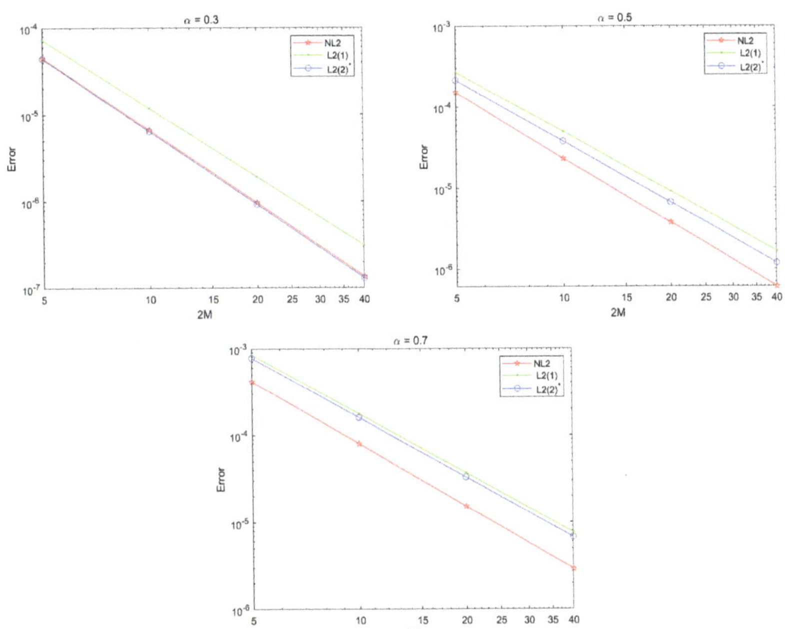

Figure 2. Maximum L_2-norm Errors of the NL2 scheme, the L2(1) scheme, and the $L2(2)^*$ scheme for Example 3.

Table 9. Comparison of errors and CPU times of the NL2 scheme, the L2(1) scheme, and the scheme L2(2) with different α's for $h = 1/20{,}000$ at $t = 1$ for Example 3.

		NL2		L2(1)		L2(2)	
α	τ	Error	CPU	Error	CPU	Error	CPU
0.3	1/10	4.5219×10^{-5}	9.31	7.3020×10^{-5}	11.35	4.6505×10^{-5}	6.79
	1/20	6.6985×10^{-6}	14.19	1.1988×10^{-5}	16.26	6.7341×10^{-6}	14.45
	1/40	9.7189×10^{-7}	33.19	1.9264×10^{-6}	31.84	9.7346×10^{-7}	30.39
	1/80	1.3681×10^{-7}	63.46	3.1677×10^{-7}	66.01	1.3761×10^{-7}	78.20
0.5	1/10	1.5383×10^{-4}	6.81	2.7330×10^{-4}	9.36	2.2165×10^{-4}	6.67
	1/20	2.3350×10^{-5}	14.20	5.0605×10^{-5}	17.38	3.9059×10^{-5}	12.86
	1/40	3.3090×10^{-6}	35.88	9.1956×10^{-6}	34.61	6.8450×10^{-6}	35.24
	1/80	4.4393×10^{-7}	67.47	1.6661×10^{-6}	80.28	1.2121×10^{-6}	71.37
0.7	1/10	3.5503×10^{-4}	7.45	8.5687×10^{-4}	9.79	7.8928×10^{-4}	6.46
	1/20	4.5470×10^{-5}	14.70	1.8119×10^{-4}	19.66	1.6396×10^{-4}	13.26
	1/40	3.8266×10^{-6}	44.72	3.7582×10^{-5}	49.59	3.3610×10^{-5}	26.25
	1/80	1.8281×10^{-7}	83.56	7.7254×10^{-6}	89.10	6.8438×10^{-6}	57.68

Table 10. Comparison of the maximum L_2-norm errors over all time steps and the temporal convergence order of the NL2, L2(1), and L2(2) schemes for different α's with $h = 1/20{,}000$ for Example 3.

		NL2		L2(1)		L2(2)	
α	τ	Error	Rate	Error	Rate	Error	Rate
0.3	1/10	4.5219×10^{-5}	–	7.2782×10^{-5}	–	8.0126×10^{-4}	–
	1/20	6.6985×10^{-6}	2.7550	1.1948×10^{-5}	2.6069	2.3188×10^{-4}	1.7889
	1/40	9.7189×10^{-7}	2.7850	1.9197×10^{-6}	2.6377	6.8228×10^{-5}	1.7649
	1/80	1.3681×10^{-7}	2.8286	3.1558×10^{-7}	2.6048	2.0150×10^{-5}	1.7596
0.5	1/10	1.5383×10^{-4}	–	2.7177×10^{-4}	–	1.3361×10^{-3}	–
	1/20	2.3350×10^{-5}	2.7198	5.0317×10^{-5}	2.4332	4.2579×10^{-4}	1.6498
	1/40	3.7704×10^{-6}	2.6306	9.1553×10^{-6}	2.4604	1.3549×10^{-4}	1.6520
	1/80	6.0767×10^{-7}	2.6334	1.6565×10^{-6}	2.4644	4.2353×10^{-5}	1.6776
0.7	1/10	4.2006×10^{-4}	–	8.4973×10^{-4}	–	2.0872×10^{-3}	–
	1/20	8.0713×10^{-5}	2.3797	1.7966×10^{-4}	2.2417	7.0047×10^{-4}	1.5752
	1/40	1.5332×10^{-5}	2.3963	3.7263×10^{-5}	2.2695	2.2659×10^{-4}	1.6283
	1/80	2.9245×10^{-6}	2.3903	7.6597×10^{-6}	2.2824	6.9574×10^{-5}	1.7034

5. Concluding Remarks

This paper proposes a new L2 (NL2) scheme for time fractional diffusion equations by combining the new L2 scheme with the finite difference method. By analyzing the positive definiteness of the symmetric part of the coefficient matrix B, we prove that the proposed NL2 scheme possesses H^1-norm stability and achieves the temporal $(3-\alpha)$th-order accuracy. Numerical experiments are presented to illustrate the accuracy and efficiency of the proposed method. The proposed scheme can be applied to a nonhomogeneous Dirichlet boundary condition directly by updating the right-hand sides of the fully discrete linear systems. On the other hand, although the NL2 scheme can be applied to other types of boundary conditions, e.g., the Neumann boundary condition, the convergence and stability properties need more research. In future work, we will consider applications of the proposed NL2 scheme to other types of boundary conditions and to non-uniform meshes.

Author Contributions: Conceptualization, C.-Y.H. and F.-R.L.; methodology, C.-Y.H. and F.-R.L.; writing—original draft preparation, C.-Y.H.; writing—review and editing, F.-R.L.; visualization, F.-R.L.; supervision, F.-R.L. All authors have read and agreed to the published version of the manuscript.

Funding: This research was supported by the National Natural Science Foundation of China (11771265) and the Guangdong Basic and Applied Basic Research Foundation, Guangdong Province of China (2023A1515030199).

Data Availability Statement: Data sharing is not applicable to this article as no datasets were generated or analyzed during the current study.

Conflicts of Interest: The authors declare no conflicts of interest.

References

1. Chukbar, K.V. Stochastic transport and fractional derivatives. *Zh. Eksp. Toer. Fiz.* **1995**, *108*, 1875–1884.
2. Podlubny, I. *Fractional Differential Equations*; Academic Press: New York, NY, USA, 1999.
3. Raberto, M.; Scalas, E.; Mainardi, F. Waiting-times and returns in high-frequency financial data: An empirical study. *Phys. A Stat. Mech. Appl.* **2022**, *314*, 749–755. [CrossRef]
4. Agrawal, O.P. A general formulation and solution scheme for fractional optimal control problems, Nonlinear Dynam. *Zh. Eksp. Toer. Fiz.* **2004**, *38*, 191–206.
5. Benson, D.A.; Wheatcraft, S.W.; Meerschaert, M.M. Application of a fractional advection-dispersion equation. *Water Resour. Res.* **2006**, *36*, 1403–1412. [CrossRef]
6. Meerschaert, M.M.; Tadjeran, C. Finite difference approximations for fractional advection-dispersion flow equations. *J. Comput. Appl. Math.* **2004**, *172*, 65–77. [CrossRef]
7. Oldham, K.B. Fractional differential equations in electrochemistry. *Adv. Eng. Softw.* **2010**, *41*, 9–12. [CrossRef]
8. Ahmad, T.; Sulaiman, M.; Bassir, D.; Alshammari, F.S.; Laouini, G. Enhanced numerical solutions for fractional PDEs using Monte Carlo PINNs coupled with cuckoo search optimization. *Fractal Fract.* **2025**, *9*, 225. [CrossRef]
9. Sun, Z.; Wu, X. A fully discrete difference scheme for a diffusion-wave system. *Appl. Numer. Math.* **2006**, *56*, 193–209. [CrossRef]
10. Lin, Y.; Xu, C. Finite difference/spectral approximations for the time-fractional diffusion equation. *J. Comput. Phys.* **2007**, *225*, 1533–1552. [CrossRef]
11. Zhang, Y.; Sun, Z. Alternating direction implicit schemes for the two-dimensional fractional sub-diffusion equation. *J. Comput. Phys.* **2011**, *230*, 8713–8728. [CrossRef]
12. Sun, H.; Chen, W.; Li, C.; Chen, Y. Finite difference schemes for variable-order time fractional diffusion equation. *Internat. J. Bifur. Chaos.* **2012**, *22*, 1250085. [CrossRef]
13. Yan, Y.; Pal, K.; Ford, N.J. Higher order numerical methods for solving fractional differential equations. *BIT Numer. Math.* **2014**, *54*, 555–584. [CrossRef]
14. Li, C.K.; Liao, W.Y. Applications of inverse operators to a fractional partial integro-differential equation and several well-known differential equations. *Fractal Fract.* **2025**, *9*, 200. [CrossRef]
15. Jiang, S.D.; Zhang, J.W.; Zhang, Q.; Zhang, Z.M. Fast evaluation of the Caputo fractional derivative and its applications to fractional diffusion equations. *Commun. Comput. Phys.* **2017**, *21*, 650–678. [CrossRef]
16. Yan, Y.G.; Sun, Z.Z.; Zhang, J.W. Fast evaluation of the Caputo fractional derivative and its applications to fractional diffusion equations: A second-order scheme. *Commun. Comput. Phys.* **2017**, *22*, 1028–1048. [CrossRef]
17. Wang, Y.M.; Ren, L. A high-order L2-compact difference method for Caputo-type time-fractional sub-diffusion equations with variable coefficients. *Appl. Math. Comput.* **2019**, *342*, 71–93. [CrossRef]
18. Mokhtari, R.; Mostajeran, F. A high order formula to approximate the Caputo fractional derivative. *Com. Appl. Math. Comput.* **2020**, *2*, 1–29. [CrossRef]
19. Shen, J.Y.; Li, C.P.; Sun, Z.Z. An H2N2 interpolation for Caputo derivative with order in (1,2) and its application to time-fractional wave equations in more than one space dimension. *J. Sci. Comput.* **2020**, *83*, 38. [CrossRef]
20. Alikhanov, A.A.; Huang, C.M. A high-order L2 type difference scheme for the time-fractional diffusion equation. *Appl. Math. Comput.* **2021**, *411*, 126545. [CrossRef]
21. Quan, C.Y.; Tang, T.; Yang, J. How to define dissipation-preserving energy for time-fractional phase-field equations. *CSIAM Trans. Appl. Math.* **2020**, *1*, 478–490. [CrossRef]
22. Fang, Z.W.; Zhang, J.L.; Sun, H.W. A fast finite volume method for spatial fractional diffusion equations on nonuniform meshes. *Comput. Math. Appl.* **2022**, *1*, 478–490. [CrossRef]

23. Quan, C.Y.; Wu, X. H^1-norm stability and convergence of an L2-type method on nonuniform meshes for subdiffusion equation. *SIAM J. Numer. Anal.* **2023**, *5*, 2106–2132. [CrossRef]
24. Gao, G.H.; Sun, Z.Z.; Zhang, H.W. A new fractional numerical differentiation formula to approximate the Caputo fractional derivative and its applications. *J. Comput. Phys.* **2014**, *259*, 33–50. [CrossRef]
25. Alikhanov, A.A. A new difference scheme for the time fractional diffusion equation. *J. Comput. Phys.* **2015**, *280*, 424–438. [CrossRef]

MDPI AG
Grosspeteranlage 5
4052 Basel
Switzerland
Tel.: +41 61 683 77 34

Fractal and Fractional Editorial Office
E-mail: fractalfract@mdpi.com
www.mdpi.com/journal/fractalfract

www.ingramcontent.com/pod-product-compliance
Lightning Source LLC
Chambersburg PA
CBHW061553220926
51850CB00005B/324

* 9 7 8 3 7 2 5 8 4 7 4 1 9 *